Privileged and Confidential

PRIVILEGED
and
CONFIDENTIAL

The Secret History of the President's Intelligence Advisory Board

Kenneth Michael Absher,
Michael C. Desch,
Roman Popadiuk,
and the 2006 Bush School Master
in Public and International Affairs'
Capstone Team

UNIVERSITY PRESS OF KENTUCKY

Scholarly publisher for the Commonwealth,
serving Bellarmine University, Berea College, Centre College of Kentucky,
Eastern Kentucky University, The Filson Historical Society, Georgetown
College, Kentucky Historical Society, Kentucky State University,
Morehead State University, Murray State University, Northern Kentucky
University, Transylvania University, University of Kentucky, University of
Louisville, and Western Kentucky University.
All rights reserved.

Editorial and Sales Offices: The University Press of Kentucky
663 South Limestone Street, Lexington, Kentucky 40508-4008
www.kentuckypress.com

16 15 14 13 12   5 4 3 2 1

Library of Congress Cataloging-in-Publication Data

Privileged and confidential : the secret history of the President's
Intelligence Advisory Board / Kenneth Michael Absher, Michael C.
Desch, Roman Popadiuk, and the 2006 Bush School Master in Public
and International Affairs' Capstone Team.
       p. cm.
   Includes bibliographical references and index.
   ISBN 978-0-8131-3608-0 (hardcover : alk. paper) —
   ISBN 978-0-8131-3609-7 (pdf) — ISBN 978-0-8131-4062-9 (epub)
   1. United States. President's Intelligence Advisory Board. 2. Intelligence
service—United States. I. Absher, Kenneth Michael. II. Desch, Michael
C. (Michael Charles), 1960- III. Popadiuk, Roman. IV. Texas A & M
University. George Bush School of Government and Public Service.
   JK468.I6P75 2012
   327.1273—dc23   2012007825

This book is printed on acid-free paper meeting the requirements of the
American National Standard for Permanence in Paper for Printed Library
Materials.

∞

Manufactured in the United States of America.

Member of the Association of
American University Presses

We dedicate this book
to Lieutenant General Brent Scowcroft,
whose service on the board, and elsewhere
in government, epitomizes the ideal of a public servant.

Contents

INTRODUCTION

The President's Intelligence Advisory Board

Learning Lessons from Its Past to Shape Its Future

Presidents could be forgiven if they did not make reconstituting the President's Intelligence Advisory Board (PIAB) their highest priority on taking office. Established in 1956 by President Dwight Eisenhower as the President's Board of Consultants on Foreign Intelligence Affairs (PB-CFIA), and known for most of its existence as the President's Foreign Intelligence Advisory Board (PFIAB), the board, which was renamed at the end of the second Bush administration, is one of the smallest and most obscure parts of the U.S. intelligence community.

This obscurity has been compounded by the fact that the board has not always, especially in recent years, distinguished itself in its mission of providing independent expert advice to presidents on the larger issues affecting the organization of the intelligence community and some of the core technologies it depends on. As a result, it has developed something of an inconsistent reputation among the intelligence cognoscenti as either a cushy "do-nothing" panel that simply offers additional slots for the "plum book" with which to reward political cronies or a highly politicized cabal that can meddle in intelligence community affairs to the annoyance of the director of central intelligence (DCI), the director of national intelligence (DNI), and even the president.

To be sure, there is much truth behind both these views of the board, particularly in recent years. But it would be a mistake for the president to ignore the fact that since its inception it has made some signal contributions to improving the organization of the U.S. intelligence community and also pushed it to remain on the cutting edge of some of the most important technological developments relevant to the acquisition, analysis, and dissemination of intelligence in the U.S. government.

It is in the president's interest, not to speak of the nation's, to make the best possible use of the PFIAB for two reasons. First, the PFIAB is now a political fact of life. Presidents have little latitude to abolish or ignore it. President Jimmy Carter tried the former and paid a political price for doing so in the 1980 election, though of course there were many other factors that contributed to his defeat. President George H. W. Bush initially ignored the Ronald Reagan board after taking office in 1989 but by 1990 found that he had to reorganize the board and involve it in at least some intelligence-related deliberations.

But, beyond such political considerations, there is a second reason for thinking hard about how the board can best assist the president in managing the intelligence community. An independent advisory panel made up of experts from a broad range of backgrounds has the potential to offer the president a unique and valuable perspective on intelligence issues. As we show in this book, the PFIAB has, with a few notable exceptions, studied almost every important intelligence issue since the Eisenhower administration. Moreover, it has made important recommendations that led to the establishment of the Defense Intelligence Agency (DIA), the CIA's Directorate of Science and Technology, and the defense attaché system and improved the operation of the National Reconnaissance Office (NRO), all of which have clearly enhanced the performance of the intelligence community. At times, its recommendations have been important factors in intelligence-related policy decisions. Thus, while the board has not consistently lived up to its potential as an intelligence advisory body for presidents in the past, its great potential is enough to warrant thinking hard about how it might be better realized in the future.

In the past few years, the U.S. government has established new positions and organizations with an eye toward enhancing the presidential coordination and oversight of intelligence. The creation of the DNI is the culmination of this trend. This position and its broad responsibilities were mandated in the Intelligence Reform and Terrorism Prevention Act passed by Congress and signed into law by President George W. Bush on December 17, 2004. This is the most far-reaching reorganization of American intelligence since the creation of the CIA in 1947. In this new environment—created largely by the 9/11 tragedy—it is particularly important to have a clear understanding of the role of the PFIAB, one of the smallest, most secretive, least well-known, but potentially most influential parts of the U.S. intelligence community.

This book undertakes such an analysis with the aim of providing a guideline for strengthening the role of the PIAB in the years to come. The aim of our analysis is to determine the strengths and weaknesses of the PFIAB in the past and to identify a productive role for the PIAB in this new environment. Given the current intelligence needs of the country, such an examination is paramount. It will help clarify the role of the PFIAB and shed light on the interrelations of various intelligence components. Most importantly, it will provide recommendations for future presidents to redefine, and possibly augment, the role of the board, thereby helping improve the performance of the U.S. intelligence community.

WHY STUDY THE PFIAB?

In the wake of 9/11, the efficiency of U.S. intelligence came under intense scrutiny, with a particular focus on the resources, methods, and coordination—or more fittingly the lack thereof—among various intelligence agencies. The outcome was threefold: the Patriot Act, with its various domestic features aimed at tightening security loopholes; the creation of the Department of Homeland Security, whose goal is to protect the nation; and the creation of the Office of Director of National Intelligence. In addition, the various intelligence agencies reorganized their own organizations and revamped procedures to be more effective in their missions.

The goal of this series of changes was to present the best intelligence possible to the president and other national security decisionmakers. This is essential because, as a former board chair, Anne Armstrong, puts it, "to a remarkable extent, high-level officials are unaware of what the intelligence community can and cannot do and of the type of guidance it needs if its work is to be as useful for policy-making as possible."[1] While these changes were still taking place, the George W. Bush administration went to war in Iraq in 2003 on the assumption that that country still possessed weapons of mass destruction and had meaningful links with al Qaeda. The discovery that neither was true raised the issue of how, why, and when intelligence has been used, or failed to be used, by those who make the ultimate decision on the use of intelligence.

The PIAB is the part of the intelligence community that is least in the thrall of preconceived ideas or captured by organizational biases and so can be of great use in thinking through these issues. Of course, there are limits to what the board can do since it can only make recommendations and has to leave implementation of them to the president and his staff.[2] Despite these shortcomings, the PIAB has a useful role and one that needs to be augmented. To this end, certain changes need to be made in order to make it even more effective as it can help the president steer the U.S. intelligence community in the right direction in the latter's exploitation of new technology, adoption of new methods of analysis, and reorganizations to deal with the new intelligence environment the United States faces.

To date, no one has conducted a detailed analysis of the PFIAB. There are only a handful of studies of the board—two by the Congressional Research Service and one by the Hale Foundation (a private association of retired intelligence professionals)—and none contain much specific information about what issues the board addressed, how it operated, and what impact it had on policy.[3] Moreover, while there is a large and generally very good literature on the rest of the U.S. intelligence community, it only contains a sketchy account of the PFIAB's role since 1956.[4] It is fair to say that the board is one of the least-known components of the U.S. intelligence community.

Why has there been so little discussion of the PFIAB in the otherwise voluminous literature on the U.S. intelligence community? One possibility is that the board has not been an important player in the major intelligence issues since its inception. For example, the Church Committee staff's comprehensive "History of the Central Intelligence Agency" devoted only a few pages to the board, remarking in passing on its "impotence."[5] We reject this explanation because, as we will show in the following pages, the board has been at the center of many of the most important intelligence decisions of the past fifty years and has on occasion, especially in its early years, made very important contributions to U.S. intelligence. As the former State Department official Howard Meyers puts it, the PFIAB was in fact "one of the two most important advisory committees to the President."[6]

Instead, we believe that the lack of discussion of the PFIAB is the result of two other factors. First, the board has historically had access to the most highly classified intelligence from the entire intelligence community and has dealt with some of the most sensitive substantive and procedural issues the community has faced. It is not surprising that very few of its deliberations and recommendations would be declassified, even after almost fifty years. Second, in addition to the sensitivity of the issues it considers, the board also falls under the purview of executive privilege, and, thus, its records are exempt from mandatory declassification, along with those of other high-level presidential advisory bodies. As Eisenhower explained the rationale for executive privilege covering the activities of such bodies to Senator Lyndon Johnson in a January 23, 1958, letter: "From time to time the President invites groups of specially qualified citizens to advise him on complex problems. These groups give the advice after intensive study, with the understanding that their advice will be kept confidential. Only by preserving the confidential nature of such advice is it possible to assemble such groups or for the President to avail himself of such advice."[7]

Thus, the historical records of the PFIAB are held by the National Archives and Records Administration (NARA), exempt from normal declassification procedures and not open to the public, despite the fact that contemporary records from other parts of the intelligence community and the National Security Council (NSC) have long since been made available to scholars. The secretary of state's Advisory Committee on Historical Diplomatic Documentation lamented the fact that as late as 2002 even official State Department historians with appropriate security clearances "still are unable to consult, cite or quote documents from the President's Foreign Intelligence Advisory Board (PFIAB) from the early 1960s."[8] In short, the PFIAB is little known, not because it has always been irrelevant, but rather because its secrets have been hidden behind two seals: secrecy and executive privilege.

Some current and former PFIAB personnel have gone to great lengths to maintain the shroud of secrecy surrounding the board. The long-term board member and chair Leo Cherne repeatedly emphasized to his fellow board members that PFIAB was special because it was the one part of the U.S. government that never leaked, and he regularly refused to cooperate with investigations of the PFIAB by other parts of the intelligence community and the congressional oversight committees.[9]

When scholars do try to conduct detailed investigations of the PFIAB, they have often encountered active opposition from some PFIAB members and staff. For example, when we approached a number of former PFIAB chairs regarding this project, one not only refused to cooperate but also actively discouraged others from participating.[10] Fortunately, this effort did not succeed, though it did make other PFIAB chairs, former members, and executive staffers hesitant about being interviewed on the record.

Given these serious obstacles, readers may wonder how we were able to proceed at all with this study beyond the very sketchy accounts available in the two Congressional Research Service reports and the

Hale Foundation pamphlet. Despite the seals on the board's archives and the cult of secrecy among board chairs, members, and staff, there is actually now a substantial amount of information available in the public domain about the board's activities. This is true not only of the period before the Reagan administration but also today. Press coverage of the PFIAB's activities has been continuous.[11] Sometimes the board has made public, or at least semipublic, important insights into its activities. For example, under President Bill Clinton, it was charged with a major study of security lapses at the nation's nuclear laboratories, and its findings were publicly released by the administration.[12] Additionally, there is a wealth of other open-source materials available that shed light on the board's activities. These include declassified PFIAB reports, PFIAB-related material in other government publications like the Department of State's historical series *Foreign Relations of the United States,* various CIA historical publications, and memoirs of presidents and other high-level government officials.

Even though the records of the PFIAB itself remain classified under the seals of secrecy and executive privilege, we have managed to amass a significant amount of primary source material from archives containing records of organizations that worked closely with the board. Research team members went to presidential archives from Eisenhower through Clinton (with the exception of the Reagan archives, which we determined had no declassified materials on the PFIAB available) and consulted records of other parts of the executive office, including the NSC, White House personnel, and White House counsel, which contain much material relevant to the PFIAB's activities. Team members have also visited other archives, including NARA (CIA's CREST online documents), the MIT Library Archives (the Thomas J. Killian Papers), the National Security Archives (George Washington University), and Boston University (the Leo Cherne Papers), and found much additional material relating to the board's activities.

Finally, former PFIAB members have not always been reticent about discussing their experiences with the board. Former PFIAB chair Warren Rudman made extensive and detailed public comments about the board in a seminar he participated in at Harvard's John F. Kennedy School of Government.[13] Other former PFIAB chairs, members, and staffers, as well as other members of the intelligence community who interacted with the board, have cooperated in our project through extensive and detailed interviews. These twenty-five interviews have made it possible to reconstruct the activities of the PFIAB in great detail, especially in recent years. For obvious reasons, most of these interviews were off the record. Without exception, all interviewees were told that this was to be an unclassified study.

Over the years, there have been a number of efforts from within the PFIAB to assess its role and improve it to better serve the president. This study should also provide an important outside perspective on the board and the issues it faces as it seeks to reorient itself to meet the challenges of the new security environment our country faces.[14] In addition to helping future presidents make the best use possible of the PFIAB, this book will, we think, accomplish two further goals: it will provide the public with both a better understanding of the history of the PFIAB and a fuller sense of the role of American intelligence in national security decisionmaking.

HOW THE PFIAB WORKS

The PFIAB has been housed in the Eisenhower Office Building on the White House grounds. It operates on a part-time basis and, traditionally, has met approximately every other month for two to three days. The current board now meets on a monthly basis. While the boards have regularly scheduled meetings, they have also set up ad hoc sessions as needed and have created subcommittees to deal with various issues. The board generally reports to the president through the NSC adviser but does meet with the president on occasion.

The board has a chair and an executive director appointed by the president and, traditionally, has had a permanent executive staff of three to four members. President George W. Bush's PIAB staff grew to eight to ten members in his second term. The staff serves as the institutional memory across administrations and has been mainly drawn from intelligence experts from various government agencies detailed to the board. These agencies absorb the salaries of those individuals since the PFIAB has only a small budget. Most of the board's direct expenses are administrative, such as travel of the members and maintenance of the board's office.

The PFIAB has been largely bipartisan, including Democrats and Republicans. Eisenhower's original board, for example, included notable Democrats such as David K. E. Bruce, the former Virginia governor and congressman Colgate Darden, and Joseph P. Kennedy. Though its members have usually shunned partisan politics while in service, there have been some clear exceptions to the general rule. For example, Clark

Clifford served as an adviser to President Lyndon Johnson's 1964 campaign and even helped draft State of the Union speeches while he was PFIAB chair. Anne Armstrong, chair during Reagan's presidency and a close associate of then vice president George H. W. Bush, served as the Texas representative of the 1988 Bush for President Campaign during her tenure on the PFIAB.

PFIAB membership has fluctuated between six and twenty-one individuals appointed by the president. Unlike staff, PFIAB members receive no salary; their compensation is limited to a per diem for the days they meet. The vetting process, however, usually involves the White House personnel office. Various members of PFIAB, mostly the chair, have made recommendations on appointments. Members of the board have been drawn from business, science, academe, the military, past practitioners in the fields of international and security affairs, and politicians. From the board's inception through the Richard Nixon presidency, there was a degree of expertise and continuity as many board members served across administrations.

Members take an oath not to divulge classified information they obtain through their service and are not allowed to discuss their deliberations on the subjects they review. Their access is unlimited: they can access the intelligence information from all sixteen agencies of the American intelligence community—including the CIA, the FBI, the DIA, and the National Security Agency. There have not been any security leaks by board members, although there were accusations that the PFIAB leaked to the media the results of the 1976 Team B outside experts' analysis of the Soviet threat. Each board has access to the resources of the government for expert advice. Boards have also consulted with nongovernment experts, some of whom have served as paid consultants. In addition, board members have traveled overseas as part of their fact-finding and investigations. PFIAB members also have the latitude to pursue their areas of expertise. Cherne, a former chair and an economist, spent extra time and effort dealing with government agencies on economic intelligence.

The functioning of the board depends not only on the president's direct interest but also on the personal relationship he has with its members, particularly the chair. Each president issues a new executive order, or adopts the existing executive order of his predecessor, authorizing the creation of the board and listing its mandate. Each of the mandates has remained basically consistent with the early orders dictated by Eisenhower and Kennedy.

In establishing the board, Eisenhower was quite explicit regarding its scope and particular function. He instructed the board to examine the gamut of foreign intelligence activities throughout the government, but with a particular focus on the CIA. The board's mandate included evaluating intelligence, personnel, research, funds, security, and the effectiveness of specific activities. Subsequent presidents usually gave a broad, generic mandate to review intelligence. President Nixon, however, added a specific charge. A few days after issuing an executive order creating his PFIAB, Nixon tasked it to provide a yearly report on the nuclear threat posed by the Soviet Union.

While the PFIAB is responsible to the president, it does have sufficient leeway to initiate studies and to respond to concerns expressed by other agencies. Nonetheless, the PFIAB faces the typical bureaucratic problem: opposition by agencies that feel their areas of jurisdiction are being infringed on. For example, in 1968, the Department of Defense (DOD) opposed a PFIAB proposal to reinstitute an NSC panel to deal with Soviet strategic capabilities. The secretary of defense at the time was Clark Clifford, a former chair of the PFIAB, underscoring the old cliché that where you sit is where you stand. The PFIAB view, however, was eventually adopted when the DOD created the Office of Net Assessment in 1973.

OBJECTIVES AND OUTLINE

Our primary objective is to determine when and how the board influenced policy and brought about change in the U.S. intelligence community. Our criteria for establishing whether the board mattered is not that it solved the key intelligence problems it addressed (surely far too demanding a standard) but rather that presidents and their advisers listened to the board and that the board's recommendations influenced subsequent policies.[15] To that end, we identify the substantive and procedural issues the board considered with an eye toward ascertaining how effectively it intervened in these matters. This will involve both identifying the many issues it addressed, either formally or informally, and looking closely at a few of the more important cases. In both cases, our objective is to determine the board's strengths and weaknesses.

Our book also explores the details of how the board worked. Since its operations varied over time, we investigated the different ways it interacted with the president, the national security adviser, the DCI, and other members of the intelligence community. We also considered the selection of chairs, members, and staff to understand how the backgrounds of the board's various personnel affected its ability to advise the president on intelligence matters. An important focus is the board's views regarding the use of science and technology in the collection, assessment, and dissemination of intelligence.

Each chapter will also compare the actual board with what we regard as the ideal PIAB. Such a board, in our view, would be small, with no more than eight to ten members. Those members would be prominent individuals, many with substantial U.S. government experience and with certain managerial or technical skills that are relevant to intelligence matters but that are not already well represented in the intelligence community. Historically, this expertise has included new technologies or modes of organization. The board and the president should have a close relationship and meet on a fairly regular basis. This is important both for the board's standing within the intelligence community and for maintaining the president's focus and interest in its activities. Finally, the PIAB should be able to take the initiative and send suggestions to the president and the NSC for the improvement of intelligence policies or activities. It also should be able to provide early warnings, serving as, in the words of one senior official we interviewed, "a canary in the coal mine" for the president and the intelligence community.

In our view, the PIAB will be at its best when it looks ahead, anticipating future technological trends or political developments. There are seven areas in which the PIAB can be helpful. It can

- help determine whether intelligence is being used properly;
- help ensure that the intelligence collection and assessment process is devoid of any bureaucratic pressures or interests;
- ascertain whether the president's tasking of the intelligence community is being carried out effectively;
- assess whether the intelligence community is properly organized;
- review past intelligence issues to learn lessons from successes and failures;
- identify potential challenges facing the United States, laying the groundwork for intelligence community planning; and
- help policymakers think about the implications for intelligence collection and analysis of new technologies and modes of organization employed outside the intelligence community.

The study concludes with recommendations for future presidents about how they can take advantage of the board's unique potential. Our findings amplify those of the Commission on the Roles and Missions of the U.S. Intelligence Community, commonly referred to as the Aspin-Brown Commission: "The commission has noted in the course of its inquiry that very little thought is given by the Intelligence Community to the future, to finding creative technical or managerial solutions to the problems of intelligence or focusing on long-term issues and trends. By virtue of its membership, the PFIAB appears uniquely positioned to serve this function by bringing to bear the experience and expertise of the private sector and respected former government officials. Presidents must ensure that persons appointed to the Board have the qualifications necessary to perform this role and adequate staff capability to support them."[16]

We believe that, in addition to helping future presidents make the best use possible of the PFIAB, this study will accomplish two further goals: (1) it will provide the public with a better understanding of the history of the PFIAB, one of the smallest, most secretive, and potentially most influential components of the intelligence community, and (2) it will provide the public with a better understanding of the role of American intelligence in national security decisionmaking. Over the years, there have been a number of efforts from within the PFIAB to assess its role and function with an eye toward better serving the president, but this study should also provide an important outside perspective on the board and the issues it faces as it seeks to reorient itself to meet the challenges of the new security environment the United States faces.[17]

Scholarly Contributions

In addition to making an important historical contribution to our understanding of the role of the board in the evolution of the U.S. intelligence community since the mid-1950s, we hope to make two further scholarly contributions. First, we are helping fill an important lacuna in the study of the U.S. presidency by exploring the underappreciated role of outside advisory boards in presidential decisionmaking.[18] Second, we see this book as furthering the efforts of scholars like Robert Jervis, Richard Betts, Ernest May, and Amy Zegart to elevate the status of the study of intelligence from a marginal to a more central topic among academics.[19] To that end, we use this study to test competing theories of when and how presidents use outside advisory boards like the PFIAB. Briefly, there are two bodies of theory relevant to this question.

First, some believe that what determines when and how such bodies are used is the personal decisionmaking style of the president.[20] Relevant elements of a president's style include comfort with cognitive complexity and previous professional experience. Willingness to utilize outside advisory boards should be associated with a president who also has a high level of cognitive complexity (and, hence, a willingness to entertain divergent and independent viewpoints) and significant previous policy experience (and, therefore, confidence in his or her own standing and judgment). Of course, continuity across administrations, or incremental change in one direction, would call into question these arguments.[21]

Second, others look to structural factors, such as the size or complexity of government, to explain changing patterns of utilization of advisory bodies such as the board over time. The problem with these structural arguments is that they tend to be inconsistent. For example, Thomas Wolanin suggests that increasing reliance on outside advisory bodies is the result of the increasing size and complexity of the U.S. government, while Joseph Kraft argues that there is an inverse relation between these two developments.[22]

It is our view that both sets of factors—style and structure—matter in explaining when and how the board has influenced intelligence policy in recent years. Of the two, the structure of government seems to have been more important, with style playing a subsidiary role. In brief, what we have found is that the actual role of the board has decreased dramatically over the years, with the period from its inception until the end of the Ford administration representing its high-water mark. Conversely, since then, the board has for the most part not lived up to its full potential. This seems roughly compatible with Kraft's suggestion that there is an inverse relation between reliance on outside boards and the size and complexity of government. Despite that general trend, we do believe that a president committed to using the board could take advantage of its unique potential, as was occasionally the case since the Carter administration.

The Rest of the Book

The following chapters will examine the board's role in the various presidential administrations from Eisenhower through George W. Bush and briefly touch on the first years of the Barack Obama administration. With the exception of the Carter administration, which chose not to reconstitute the PFIAB, the structure of each chapter will be roughly the same. Each will begin with a brief history of the decision to create, reconstitute, or, in one case, dissolve the board in that administration. Next, we will examine the operation of the board during each administration.

Specifically, we will look at the personnel of the board (who chaired it, who were the members, who were the staffers). We will also look at the recruitment process, including in some instances the decisions not to appoint certain individuals. This section will also include detailed biographies of chairs, members, and executive staff. The key objective here is to consider how changes in board and staff membership affected how the board operated and what it achieved.

As part of our investigation of the operations of the boards, we will also consider how often they met (among themselves, with the president, and with other government and intelligence community personnel), what meetings were like, and how work was organized (i.e., actions by the full board as opposed to activities of subcommittees, individual board members, or staff). We are particularly interested in the roles of the chair, individual members, and staff. We will analyze how variations in these aspects of the board's operations affected its ability to influence U.S. intelligence policy. Similarly, we will look at how the board interacted with the president, the national security adviser, the DCI, the NSC staff, and other key personnel in the U.S. intelligence community. Here, the question is whether variations in the chain of command made a difference to the PFIAB's effectiveness.

Finally, we will attempt to reconstruct in as much detail as possible what the PFIAB actually did in each administration. This will involve, first, a discussion of the major issues it addressed. We are also concerned with how the board decided to address particular issues. Did the tasking come from the president, the national security adviser, or the DCI, or did the initiative come from the board itself? If the latter was the key, did it come from the chair, subcommittees, individual members, or staff? Next, we will attempt to ascertain what recommendations the board made about these various issues. Finally, we will determine how the board's recommendations translated into policy and whether the board's interventions materially improved U.S. intelligence policy. Each chapter will conclude with a discussion of what we still do not know about the PFIAB's activities during that administration and suggested questions for future research.

In the conclusion, after briefly discussing the Obama administration's efforts to establish its own board, we will focus on two major issues. First, we offer an overall analysis of the board, highlighting the key factors that made it more or less effective in the past. Second, we suggest policy recommendations for future presidents as to how the board can be most effectively used in coming administrations. Some of these recommendations will be based on our assessment of the historical experience of the board. Others come from our interviews with many former policymakers (including board chairs, current and former members, staff, and senior officials), who regularly dealt with the PFIAB, about how the board can best serve future presidents in the post-9/11 intelligence environment.

1

Dwight D. Eisenhower

In early 1956, President Dwight D. Eisenhower issued Executive Order (EO) 10656, creating the President's Board of Consultants on Foreign Intelligence Activities (PBCFIA), the forerunner of the President's Foreign Intelligence Advisory Board (PFIAB) and today's President's Intelligence Advisory Board (PIAB). This unique consultative intelligence board was an outgrowth of a variety of external and internal factors. We identify three factors as the most important: the growing Soviet military threat, the increasing efforts by Congress to challenge the prerogatives of the president in the intelligence arena, and the precedent of using extragovernment advisory boards in the immediate post–World War II period to deal with the new challenges of the Cold War.

THE GROWING SOVIET THREAT

The first, and most straightforward, rationale for the establishment of the PBCFIA was the growing threat of Soviet power, particularly the development of nuclear weapons and strategic bombers. In 1949, the Soviets tested their first atomic bomb, and, in August 1953, they tested a hydrogen bomb. U.S. intelligence spotted a new jet-powered intercontinental bomber called the Bison in 1953. These developments caught many American policymakers by surprise and led them to fear that the Soviets were eclipsing the United States in military technology.

Linked to this was the concern that the U.S. intelligence community was not up to the task of forecasting Soviet military trends. As the Watergate-era Church Committee's history of the CIA reminds us: "The shadow of the Pearl Harbor disaster dominated policy-makers' thinking about the purpose of a central intelligence agency. They saw themselves rectifying the conditions that had allowed Pearl Harbor to happen—a fragmented military-based intelligence apparatus, which in current terminology could not distinguish 'signals' from 'noise,' let alone make its assessment available to senior officials."[1]

On taking office, Eisenhower expressed his dismay about the quality of U.S. intelligence estimates of Soviet military capabilities, particularly emphasizing the need for better aerial surveillance of the Soviet Union to monitor its military development. In particular, he was dissatisfied with U.S. reconnaissance of the Soviet Bloc, which was unable to provide Strategic Air Command with target information behind the Iron Curtain. In 1953, Eisenhower asked the Science Advisory Committee of the Office of Defense Mobilization to study the possibility of a surprise attack on the United States by the Soviet Union. The committee issued a report on March 15, 1953, recommending the establishment of a technological capabilities panel. Eisenhower approved the committee's proposal to have Massachusetts Institute of Technology (MIT) president James R. Killian Jr. form a series of task forces to investigate various aspects of the Soviet military threat. Killian assembled the Technological Capabilities Panel (TCP), composed of many of the country's leading scientists, who worked on an almost full-time basis, meeting on 307 separate occasions over the following twenty weeks. Project Three of the TCP studied the intelligence aspects of the threat and was chaired by Edwin Land of Polaroid. Other members included Land's colleague Allan Lathan Jr., James G. Baker and Edward Purcell of Harvard, Joseph Kennedy of Washington University, and John Tukey of Princeton and Bell Labs.[2] This group of scientists, who were experts in fields such as photography and jet engines, played an important role in the development of Lockheed's U-2 reconnaissance aircraft.

CONGRESSIONAL ASSERTIVENESS

The second impetus for Eisenhower's establishment of the board was increasing congressional interest in intelligence affairs. In 1947, former president Herbert Hoover headed the Commission on Organization of the Executive Branch of the Government (the Hoover Commission), a body authorized and created by the Lodge-Brown Act of 1947. The commission was tasked with examining the executive branch and making recommendations on how to improve effectiveness and efficiency. Republicans in Congress strongly supported the Lodge-Brown Act, hoping that the commission would recommend scaling back the executive branch's power, which had greatly expanded under President Franklin Roosevelt. In July 1953, Congress chartered a second Hoover Commission, which included a task force headed by Gen. Mark Clark to make recommendations on all intelligence activities of the federal government.[3]

Eisenhower was reluctant to let the Clark Task Force analyze the CIA's clandestine activities, so he directed Lt. Gen. James Doolittle to establish a group to do it instead. The final Doolittle Commission Report, "Covert Actions of the Central Intelligence Agency," was published on September 30, 1954, just as the Clark Task Force began its work. One of its recommendations was the establishment of a civilian oversight board for the CIA.[4]

Released in May 1955, the Clark report primarily addressed issues of management.[5] But it did express a larger concern about "the absence of satisfactory machinery for the surveillance of the stewardship of the Central Intelligence Agency" and called for the establishment of a "small, permanent commission" consisting of "a bipartisan group including members of both Houses of Congress and distinguished private citizens appointed by the President."[6] The Hoover Commission approved the concept of such a watchdog group but rejected the proposed framework for a hybrid private-congressional committee. It instead suggested that the president appoint a board of distinguished private citizens and recommended that Congress establish its own joint committee on intelligence.

In 1955, Montana senator Mike Mansfield proposed creating a joint congressional committee in line with the Hoover Commission report, "for the purpose of seeing that good management is maintained in the CIA and also to keep a constant check on its intelligence policies."[7] After considerable debate, Mansfield's resolution finally came to a vote in the U.S. Senate in April 1956 but was voted down fifty-nine to twenty-seven. The effort failed in part owing to the opposition by the established congressional committee system (like Senators Richard Russell and Lyndon Johnson)[8] and Director of Central Intelligence (DCI) Allen Dulles.[9] Eisenhower's creation of the PBCFIA in January 1956 was intended to head off the efforts to assert congressional oversight of the intelligence community.

THE PRECEDENT OF PREVIOUS COMMISSIONS

Finally, as Morton Halperin points out, the Truman administration established the custom of using "appointed groups of private citizens to investigate particular problems" related to national security.[10] Key examples included the Finletter, Gray, Paley, Sarnoff, Gaither, Draper, Boechenstein, and Killian commissions. From the very beginning, the intelligence community also relied on such bodies. The first was probably the board of the Office of National Estimate (ONE), which included the

"Princeton consultants," such as the retired George F. Kennan, *Foreign Affairs* editor Hamilton Fish Armstrong, and Vannever Bush, along with other "men of affairs," including Sherman Kent, Ludwell Montague, DeForrest Van Slyk, Raymond Sontag, Gen. Clarence Huebner, Maxwell Forest, and Calvin Hoover.[11] Given these precedents, a standing board of consultants to the president on intelligence affairs was not too much of an innovation.

THE ESTABLISHMENT OF THE BOARD OF CONSULTANTS

DCI Dulles acted quickly once the issue had been broached. In a November 15, 1955, letter, he wrote to Eisenhower in response to the Hoover Commission's recommendations that "the President appoint a committee of experienced private citizens . . . and that the Congress consider creating a Joint Congressional Committee on Foreign Intelligence."[12] Dulles thought it tactically unwise to come out publicly against a joint congressional committee, even though he thought that the status quo—oversight limited to the Armed Services and Appropriations committees—was extremely satisfactory.[13] Instead, he urged the president to establish the panel before Congress met the following year in order to preempt the proposal for a joint congressional committee on intelligence.

Dulles wrote to the president that he supported his proposal to have a high-level committee of civilians to meet with the CIA at the committee's discretion.[14] He suggested a committee of no more than seven members, appointed for terms of varying lengths.[15] Finally, he included a list of ten prospective members and his ideas for its framework. He wanted members with varied professional, geographic, and political backgrounds. The proposed members and their qualifications included:

> "Gen. James H. Doolittle: U.S. Air Force, Doolittle Committee chair;
> Adm. Richard L. Conolly: U.S. Navy, member of Clark Task Force;
> Gen. Omar N. Bradley or Gen. John E. Hull: U.S. Army (USA), both
>   familiar with the CIA's work during their period of military service;
> Morris Hadley: lawyer, member of the Doolittle Committee;
> William B. Franke: accountant, member of the Doolittle Committee, and serving at the time as the assistant secretary of the navy;
> Adm. Sidney W. Souers: businessman, head of the Central Intelligence Group (the predecessor of CIA), and executive director of the National Security Council (NSC) during the Truman administration;

David K. E. Bruce: former ambassador and undersecretary of state, one of Bill Donovan's chief assistants in the Office of Strategic Services (OSS);

Henry M. Wriston or Donald S. Russell: the former the ex-president of Brown University, the latter a Clark Committee member and president of the University of South Carolina."[16]

Dulles proposed three of the four Doolittle Committee members for this board.[17] A handwritten note on the letter added Killian and Land, both described as "top scientists."

The president agreed in principle with the memorandum and tasked Dulles to proceed with setting up the board, defining their duties and the nature of their reports, and indicating the security limitations on the board.[18] Early documents outlining the board's scope focused on its relationship with the CIA but were later redrafted to expand its responsibilities to include governmentwide foreign intelligence activities paralleling more closely the wording of the Hoover Commission recommendation.[19] On their way to Camp David on November 21, 1955, the president and the DCI "discussed at length . . . the creation of a board of consultants, going over draft letters and lists of possible members in detail."[20] Eisenhower indicated that the board should be organized "as formally as it could be" and suggested that Dulles consult the attorney general about whether members should be required to take an oath to protect classified information.[21] Eisenhower communicated to Dulles that the board should include more "public figures."[22] The following seems to be Eisenhower's "first cut" of prospective board members, as discussed in a November 23, 1955, conversation with Dulles:[23]

Dr. James R. Killian Jr.;

Lt. Gen. James H. Doolittle;

Gen. John E. Hull;

Adm. Richard L. Conolly or Adm. Leslie Stevens;

Morris Hadley;

David K. E. Bruce;

An industrialist (Eisenhower mentioned "Benjamin F. Fairless, Edward L. Ryerson, or Robert W. Woodruff as possibilities");

Adm. Sidney W. Souers (Dulles suggested Souers as someone "familiar with intelligence work who would give the board a bipartisan complexion").

On November 30, Dulles summarized this list, entitled "Names for CIA Board of Consultants," in a memo to Eisenhower's chief of staff, Sherman Adams.[24] Correspondence continued into the next month and resulted in a nearly complete list, save for an interesting substitution and a curious addition. In a December 7, 1955, letter to Adams, Dulles proposed inviting the following individuals to serve on the board:[25]

> "James R. Killian Jr.;
> Benjamin F. Fairless;
> Edward L. Ryerson;
> Lt. Gen. James H. Doolittle;
> Adm. Richard L. Conolly;
> David K. E. Bruce or Sidney W. Souers."

Dulles also claimed "cogent reasons" for adding to the list:[26]

> Gen. John E. Hull
> Morris Hadley (described by Dulles as an "outstanding New York lawyer and member of the Doolittle Committee");
> William B. Franke ("when available") (whom Dulles described as an "outstanding public accountant, member of the Doolittle Committee, and now assistant secretary of the navy").

We do not know why Souers, Hadley, and Franke were not ultimately invited to serve as board members. Handwritten notes on a memorandum from Staff Secretary Andrew Goodpaster to Adams suggest that Bruce may have been approached informally about serving on the board and declined.[27] Another note suggests that former secretary of defense Robert Lovett was invited in lieu of Bruce.[28]

Documents initially indicated that the board would have seven members, but Joseph P. Kennedy subsequently became the eighth member.[29] In the correspondence up to this point, his name had never been mentioned. The first documentary reference to him appears in his January 11, 1956, letter of invitation to serve as a board member.[30] Furthermore, a February 1, 1956, document stated: "After the president signed the first group of letters, one individual was added to the slate to meet a point of criticism, and new letters were prepared."[31] This individual was quite likely Joseph P. Kennedy.

Dulles played an important role in establishing the board, but he also drafted the EO and issued the press release. The final draft contained only minor changes. He also sought to strengthen the framework of the board by suggesting that both the EO and the terms of reference not be finalized until after the president's first meeting with the board so that the members would feel a "sense of participation in framing the conditions of their work."[32] Eisenhower agreed and conferred with the new members on January 23, 1956.[33]

Finally, Dulles suggested that the White House contact prospective members "in order to allay any thought that the group is under direction of CIA" and assured the president that the CIA welcomed the work of the board and would cooperate fully with it.[34]

BOARD MEMBERSHIP AND EXECUTIVE STAFF

In individual letters dated January 11, 1956, the president formally invited eight men to serve on the PBCFIA.[35] The eight original members were Dr. James R. Killian Jr., Adm. Richard L. Conolly, Lt. Gen. James H. Doolittle, Benjamin Fairless, Gen. John E. Hull, Joseph P. Kennedy, Robert A. Lovett, and Edward L. Ryerson.[36] Interestingly, the letter to Killian was initially lost in the mail, so he learned of his official appointment as chair of the board only via press reports.[37] Eisenhower included a typewritten personal note with the official invitations to Doolittle, Fairless, Hull, Lovett, and Ryan. In the notes, he lamented the "usual formidable style of . . . governmental communication," conveyed that he was "personally grateful" to them for consenting to serve, and signed off with "warm personal regard."[38] This suggests that the president had a personal and likely cordial relationship with five of the board's eight original members. Some board members had served on the Hoover Commission and the Doolittle Committee.[39] In addition to the eight charter members, three more would join the board to replace those who had resigned early.

On January 13, 1956, White House press secretary James C. Hagerty announced that the president had established "an eight-man Board of Consultants to review periodically the foreign intelligence activities of the Government."[40] The three-page press release included a list of the members, their place of residence, and, in some cases, their current occupation; the president's January 11, 1956, letter to the DCI regarding the creation of the PBCFIA (which Dulles himself drafted); and the president's official letter of invitation. Hagerty publicly released EO 10656 on February 6, 1956.[41]

Four of the original eight members of Eisenhower's board resigned before their tenure (the president's term) ended. All but Fairless were replaced, leaving the board with seven members when Eisenhower left office on January 20, 1961. There seems to have been no standardized procedure for finding replacements. The process ranged from a suggestion by the outgoing member to a lengthy set of exchanges within the administration similar to those that determined the charter members. It appears that, on their resignations, the board members were on cordial terms with the president and with their colleagues.

One possible exception is Kennedy, who resigned from the board first, less than six months after its creation. In a July 18, 1956, letter, which he wrote during a PBCFIA trip to France, he resigned, citing a growing involvement in his son's activities as a possible Democratic candidate for vice president.[42] In another July 18 letter to Adams, Kennedy again mentioned his advisory role in his son's political activities, stating: "My own conscience will not permit me to remain a member and mix in partisan politics."[43] He promised to report on his European trip at the September 22 board meeting but asked for his resignation to become effective at once.[44] A *New York Times* correspondent hints at a darker explanation for this abrupt resignation. He claims that the senior Kennedy learned that J. Edgar Hoover's FBI had amassed compromising material on his son, including details of an affair he had with a German spy during the early stages of World War II.[45]

David K. E. Bruce took Kennedy's place on the board on August 6, 1956.[46] Little archival evidence exists concerning the selection process, although an undated note by "Minnich" stated that the matter had been discussed by Adams with Bruce, Dulles, and Killian.[47] Bruce's tenure lasted only slightly longer than Kennedy's did.[48] Bruce stepped down when he was appointed ambassador to West Germany in 1957.[49]

In a May 20, 1957, letter asking for the status of the process of finding a replacement for Bruce, Killian reminded Adams: "You will recall that we both felt that someone who at some time had had a Democratic tag might be desirable."[50] A week later, Robert Gray suggested Ambassador Lewis Douglas, Robert Anderson, and Congressman James P. Richards.[51] Killian initially nominated Douglas, but he was unavailable. On June 14, Killian wrote Adams conveying the board's recommendations for a replacement in order of preference:

James P. Richards: congressman;
Frank Pace Jr.: former secretary of the army and CEO of the defense contractor General Dynamics;

George C. McGhee: former assistant secretary for Near Eastern and African Affairs, Department of State;

Cleo F. Craig: retired president and chair, AT&T;

McGeorge Bundy: dean of faculty of arts and sciences, Harvard University.[52]

By July 1957, there was still no decision on a replacement for Bruce. Killian referenced two notes from Adams suggesting "Mr. Ramspeck," "Governor Battle," and former Virginia governor Colgate Darden, then president of the University of Virginia. Darden had served as a member of the Fairless Committee on Foreign Aid, and Killian wrote that he "had a wide range of other experiences, both in politics and in public service, which makes his name look attractive."[53] In addition, Darden was a Democrat, which helped fulfill the criteria of bipartisanship noted in Killian's May 20 letter. He joined the PBCFIA on July 19, 1957.[54]

In February 1958, Killian suggested to Eisenhower that he should not continue as chair because of his duties as the president's special assistant for science and technology. Eisenhower concurred, and, on March 1, Hull replaced Killian as chair, though Killian remained as a regular member until January 1960.[55] When Killian resigned, he again cited the same time commitments as well as other assignments by the president. In an October 30, 1959, letter to Hull, he sent word of his intention to resign and suggested William O. Baker as his replacement.[56] Hull and the rest of the board members also favored Baker: "The other Board members and I feel that, because the foreign intelligence activities of our Government have scientific and technological ramifications of ever increasing significance, it is desirable to continue to include in the Board's membership an individual who, like Dr. Killian, has special qualifications of this sort. Having had the benefit of Dr. Baker's services as a consultant on such matters, we consider him to be eminently qualified in this regard."[57]

Fairless also resigned, just two days before Baker's appointment.[58] In a letter to Hull, he explained that he had essentially overextended and overcommitted himself. He was serving as president of the American Iron and Steel Institute, chair of the National Committee for the Eisenhower Presidential Library Commission, and chair of a committee to raise $25 million for the Carnegie Institute of Technology.[59] Fairless was not replaced, and, in early December 1960, the remaining PBCFIA members—Hull (chair), Baker, Conolly, Darden, Doolittle, Lovett, and

Ryerson—tendered their resignations, which became effective January 20, 1961.[60]

PBCFIA Staff

We could find very little information about the board's staff. The four names and positions that could be identified came from PBCFIA member lists—only some of which included staff—or simply from the signature line of correspondence from each of them. Staff members we can identify include Brig. Gen. John F. Cassidy (USA [Ret.], staff director),[61] Harold R. Lawrence (deputy staff director),[62] J. Patrick Coyne (staff director and, later, executive secretary),[63] and Sammie L. Newman (secretary).[64]

The PBCFIA executive secretary provided continuity in the work of the board. In between the meetings, he worked on a continuous basis, including occasionally accompanying board members on site visits of government agencies or U.S. installations overseas.[65] Only two other documents refer directly to PBCFIA staff members, and both are requests from Killian for staff salary increases. In December 1956, he suggested a salary increase for Cassidy, and, in February 1958, he urged that Lawrence be promoted. Lawrence also had served as an assistant to Killian in fulfilling the latter's duties as science adviser.[66]

Operating Procedures

In his original invitation letter to board members, Eisenhower stipulated that the board should meet "not less often than once every six months," to include sessions possibly spanning several days.[67] From its inception in February 1956 until the end of Eisenhower's term in January 1961, the PBCFIA held nineteen full meetings, covering thirty-three working days.[68] Each member also undertook specific projects.[69] In addition to the (eight) semiannual reports, the chair occasionally submitted letters directly to the president, and the chair, members, and staff also regularly relayed information and suggestions to the president's staff informally.

The board had at least six meetings with President Eisenhower that lasted approximately an hour each and were scheduled at ten- to fourteen-month intervals.[70] The known dates of, times of (if recorded), and participants in meetings with the president are as follows:

> January 1956. Eisenhower conferred with new members.[71]
> December 20, 1956, 3:00–3:49 P.M. Those present were Killian (chair), Conolly, Doolittle, Fairless, Hull, Ryerson, Cassidy, and Goodpaster.[72]

October 24, 1957, 8:30 A.M. (off the record). Those present were Killian (chair), Ryerson, Hull, Doolittle, Cutler, and Goodpaster.[73]

December 16, 1958, 9:00–10:09 A.M. (off the record). Those present were Hull (chair), Conolly, Darden, Doolittle, Lovett, and Cassidy.[74]

February 2, 1960, 11:17–12:00 P.M. Those present were Hull (chair), Baker, Doolittle, Ryerson, Coyne, and Gordon Gray.[75]

January 5, 1961, 11:10–12:09 P.M. Those present were Hull (chair), Baker, Conolly, Darden, Doolittle, Lovett, Ryerson, and Coyne.[76]

The board had substantial leeway in terms of the issues it addressed. The letters of invitation from Eisenhower to the charter members stated that their mandate would cover all the government's foreign intelligence activities and that he expected "particular detailed attention to be concentrated on the work of the Central Intelligence Agency and of those intelligence elements of key importance in other departments and agencies."[77] The president also wrote that he was "particularly anxious to obtain [the board's] views as to the over-all progress that is being made, the quality of training and personnel, security, progress in research, effectiveness of specific projects and of the handling of funds, and general competence in carrying out assigned intelligence tasks."[78] The most obvious instance of this occurred in the inaugural meeting on January 23, 1956, when the new members and the president agreed on the terms of the EO for the board.

By May 1956, the board had outlined for the president its intention as a part-time lay group to:

"• Inform itself about national intelligence and security policies and directives for purposes of appraising effectiveness and the extent to which they are being fulfilled.

• Inform itself about our intelligence agencies, their use of the means nationally available, and the quality, cost, usefulness, and security of the information they provide the President and the NSC.

• Seek ways as a continuing group of lay consultants to increase the effectiveness of our intelligence effort.

• Be available to the President for consultation and other assistance on intelligence matters requiring his attention and action.

• To report at least twice yearly to the President."[79]

Furthermore, the board emphasized that it would "neither act as an investigating body nor . . . undertake any responsibilities for operations or detailed surveillance of operations. Its function will be limited to advisory and consulting service on a part-time basis."[80] The president appreciated the thought that was "obviously reflected" in the board's consideration of its mandate in the initial months of its existence.[81] He also gave his blessing to the board to add or modify its interpretation of responsibilities as its work proceeded.[82]

On-Site Reviews and Foreign Trips

In between meetings, and accompanied by the executive secretary, individual board members often made site visits to investigate the foreign intelligence activities of the CIA, the Department of Defense (DOD), the Department of State, the Joint Chiefs of Staff (JCS), the unified and specified commands, the army, navy, and air force, the National Security Agency (NSA) and its three supporting cryptologic services (the Army Security Agency, the Naval Security Group, and the Air Force Security Service), and the Atomic Energy Commission.

Individual PFIAB members visited other sites in various countries in Europe, Asia, the Middle East, Africa, and South America. They traveled overseas to study "selected major cold war activities conducted by CIA's Clandestine Services (for example, political, psychological, propaganda, and paramilitary operations)."[83] For example, Kennedy traveled to Paris and Rome from June 1 to June 18 with Coyne.[84] Killian, Cassidy, and Edwin Land—who was then a "Special Consultant" to the board—planned to visit France, Germany, Italy, and Greece from June 27 to July 13, 1956.[85] In June 1960, Darden made a trip to the West Coast of Africa (Monrovia, Liberia).[86] On his return, he requested to speak to the president about "something he had promised to do when he was in Liberia."[87] In one instance, the board "observed selected operations both [at home] and abroad and, as a test, brought together and examined the total raw intelligence of various kinds collected and processed on a specified country for a designated period of time."[88]

Interaction with Other Groups

The PBCFIA often met with, and received formal briefings from, other government officials and advisory groups. As part of these meetings, it established a system of semiannual reports from the intelligence agencies, a mechanism that apparently proved quite useful to the agencies themselves.[89] Specifically, the board requested Dulles to "undertake certain studies" on its behalf and gave him suggestions "in regard to ways in which certain improvements and changes might be made in intelligence directives and procedures which come under his cognizance."[90]

On occasion, the president directed the board to establish specific connections with other parts of the U.S. government. After the board's December 20, 1956, report, for instance, Eisenhower said that he wanted its recommendations brought before the NSC at its next meeting. At that meeting, the president limited the number of NSC members present to control the number of people with knowledge of these intelligence-related matters.[91] In another case, he requested that the DCI consult with the U.S. Communications Intelligence Board (USCIB) and the Intelligence Advisory Committee (IAC) and furnish to the NSC the DCI's views and comments on a board recommendation.[92] Accordingly, Dulles arranged for Hull and Gen. Cutler (the special assistant to the president for national security affairs) to meet with members of the IAC and the USCIB in executive session in order to allow Hull and Cutler to discuss that recommendation.[93]

One of the board's first activities was to review "the studies of intelligence and related activities made by ad hoc groups over the past few years noting the improvements which have resulted from the adoption of many of their recommendations."[94] Not surprisingly, given the overlap between their memberships, the PBCFIA reviewed the reports of the Hoover Commission and the Doolittle Committee as one of its first tasks.[95] On occasion, the board recommended bringing in outside advisory groups. For instance, at a May 6, 1960, meeting of the DCI, the secretary of defense, the director of the Bureau of Budget, and the special assistant to the president for national security affairs, the PBCFIA recommended that an ad hoc Joint Study Group (JSG) be assembled to review certain aspects of the U.S. government's foreign intelligence effort. The terms of reference for this ad hoc group provided that the PBCFIA "would have a representative sit as an observer with the Group and that the President's Board would be given an opportunity to comment on the Group's report following its submission."[96]

ISSUES AND RECOMMENDATIONS

The PBCFIA delivered eight written and seven oral reports to Eisenhower, containing a total of forty-two recommendations on major issues in foreign intelligence, counterintelligence, and covert action. The president acted on thirty-seven of the forty-two recommendations, approving thirty-three of the thirty-seven. He did not approve the four remaining recommendations because of strong objections by the CIA and the DOD. By the time Eisenhower left office on January 20, 1961, fifteen of the thirty-three approved recommendations had been implemented by the intelligence community. Federal agencies were working to implement the remaining eighteen.[97] Eisenhower could not act on the remaining five recommendations because they were submitted at the board's last meeting with him on January 5, 1961, just days prior to his leaving office. He did, however, instruct Goodpaster to give the board's final report, which contained these five recommendations, to President Kennedy.[98]

Most of the board's agendas remain classified. Considering the number of recommendations that were made and approved and the fact that most of the PBCFIA's communications revolved around its recommendations, it seems safe to assume that a majority of the issues addressed and recommendations made were one and the same. Because the board's recommendations and the president's actions form such a sizable portion of the archival evidence regarding the PBCFIA, it is possible to offer a comprehensive summary of both the recommendations and the president's response to them.

The following recommendations are presented exactly as worded in the archival material. They are grouped together according to the PBCFIA reports in which they were originally presented. A brief summary of the actions taken by President Eisenhower follows each recommendation.

First Report—December 20, 1956

Recommendation 1. "That the DCI be encouraged to exercise a more comprehensive and positive coordinating responsibility in directing the integration, reduction of duplication, and coordination of the national intelligence effort."[99]

Eisenhower approved and referred it to Dulles for action.[100] He directed all the members of the intelligence community to cooperate completely with the DCI to achieve the objective.[101] The CIA "concurred."

Recommendation 2. "That a realistic appraisal be made of the Intelligence Community's organization and responsibilities and of its ability to guarantee proper coordination with the military in time of war."[102]

Eisenhower approved and referred it to Dulles and to the secretary of defense for action.[103] The CIA concurred. Eisenhower ordered that a progress report be submitted to him by May 1, 1957; one was submitted on April 30.[104] He acknowledged that progress would largely depend on the progress of recommendations 9, 3, and 4. He stated that the responsibility remained in the hands of the DCI and the secretary of defense.[105] The president directed the DCI to consider the policy guidance contained in paragraph 2-A, NSC 5521, with regard to the relation of the IAC to the NSC in wartime: "2. a. Under wartime conditions, the President will utilize the NSC to advise him on national security policies. The NSC will be convened by the President intermittently, on such occasions, and at such places, as he may from time to time elect."[106] The president also advised council members to consider the policy guidance in NSC Action No. 1412-c: "Noted the President's statement that future tests of the emergency relocation plan should include a number of NSC meetings, with a view to assuring that emergency relocation plans will enable the Council, under wartime conditions, to meet frequently and function effectively as the key policy advisory body to the President."[107]

Recommendation 3. "That action be expedited to bring the planning for intelligence activities in time of war to the highest feasible state of readiness and that a realistic war-gaming of them begin as soon as practicable."[108]

Eisenhower approved and referred it to Dulles and the JCS to coordinate the member agencies of the IAC.[109] The CIA responded on January 25, 1957, with an extensive clarification of the recommendation, which in summary said that primary responsibility for this matter lay with the JCS.[110] Eisenhower requested an implementation progress report by May 1, 1957,[111] a report on the progress of war-gaming during January 1958[112] (which was submitted on January 23, 1958), and further reports on July 15, 1958, and January 15, 1959.[113] Following the submission of a report on August 26, 1959, Eisenhower directed that "(a) increased emphasis be placed on efforts to achieve operational readiness of the joint planning called for in the recommendation, including the selective utilization on a priority basis of intelligence capabilities presently available in support of military plans for wartime operations; (b) continued emphasis be placed on the war-gaming of such planning; (c) no significant increase in personnel, facilities, etc., be made in connection with this directive; and (d) semi-annual progress reports continue to be submitted."[114]

Recommendation 4. "That action be taken to effect strong, centralized direction (both through the NSC and the DCI) of the Intelligence Community and its resources, in order to strengthen our national intelligence effort and to contain its costs."[115]

Eisenhower approved this recommendation and directed Dulles to act on it in consultation with the secretary of defense and the IAC.[116]

The CIA concurred and subsequently undertook changes in its own structure. With the cooperation of other IAC agencies, it established a review mechanism for making recommendations to the IAC and the NSC for reallocating concentrated resources to fulfill intelligence requirements. The centerpiece of this reorganization was the designation of a new deputy director for coordination.[117] Eisenhower also directed Dulles to submit a progress report by May 1, 1957; one was submitted on April 30.[118] After consideration, he requested a second report by September 1, 1957.[119]

Recommendation 5. "That present practices with regard to clandestine operations be regularized to insure that clandestine projects receive proper joint staffing and formalized approval, and that State and Defense are kept abreast of developments thereunder."[120]

On the board's establishment in 1956, clandestine operations became a central focus of a number of its panels. In June 1956, Joseph Kennedy and Coyne traveled to Europe and reported back to the board: "In view of the seriously adverse effects which might inure to the national security and prestige of the United States should such operation go awry, and because of the large amounts of money being expended thereon, it is recommended that appropriate steps be taken to insure that (a) projects selected for implementation in these fields are clearly consistent with U.S. national policies; (b) such projects are controlled and carried into effect by mature and experienced personnel; and (c) such implementation is carefully monitored by top level Washington personnel at frequent and regular intervals."[121] This trip clearly spurred this recommendation.

Eisenhower referred this recommendation to the representatives designated under NSC 5412/2 for study and directed them to deliver a report to him.[122] NSC Decision Directive 5412/2 of December 28, 1955, established a "special group" of representatives (at the rank of assistant secretary) for the Department of State, the DOD, and the president who were responsible for coordinating covert activities.[123] Eisenhower requested that the report be submitted as quickly as possible, before any final action was taken on this recommendation.[124] The CIA concurred, but the board, as is evident from how often it returned to this topic, was not satisfied with the response.

In a report dated December 1956, the board reported: "We do not, however, subscribe to the methods presently being employed in the implementation of these procedures."[125] In a memorandum for a January 29, 1957, meeting of the 5412/2 Group, Coyne highlighted two particular aspects of the board's concern: lack of real "jointness" in the staffing of these operations by the State and Defense departments and the absence of detailed oversight of covert actions outside the CIA.[126] The problem, Coyne told the 5412/2 Group, was that "at the present time the DD/P [deputy director (Plans)] side of CIA is operating for the most part on an autonomous and free-wheeling basis in highly critical areas involving the conduct of foreign relations, and all too frequently the Department of State knows little or nothing of what DD/P is doing. In some quarters this leads to situations which are almost unbelievable because operations being carried out by the DD/P area are sometimes in direct conflict with normal operations being carried out by the Department of State in its overt conduct of foreign affairs."[127] Coyne's briefing led the special group to add an annex to the NSC 5412/2, but the PBCFIA chair was still not satisfied that this annex resolved the "jointness" problem.[128]

Recommendation 6. "That action be initiated at once to meet the existing need for coordination of the 'unattributed' programs of USIA [U.S. Information Agency] and CIA."[129]

Concerns about USIA involvement in covert actions also arose during the Kennedy/Coyne trip to France and Italy in June 1956.[130] Eisenhower referred this action to the director of the USIA and to Dulles and directed them to deliver a report to the NSC.[131] The CIA concurred with it. Following the report of April 30, 1957, Eisenhower requested the PBFCIA to review the implementation process after six months and report back to him.[132] Unlike the larger covert action issue, the USIA problem is not referenced again in board reports and, thus, was presumably resolved to board members' satisfaction.

Recommendation 7. "That to give proper high-level direction to COMINT [communications intelligence] activities and to insure that their tremendous capabilities are exploited to the fullest, such COMINT activities should have the direct management attention of a single Assistant Secretary of Defense who should be designated for this purpose."[133]

Eisenhower referred this recommendation to the secretary of defense, as the executive agent, and Dulles, as the chair of the USCIB, under National Security Council Intelligence Directive (NSCID) No. 9 to study and report to the president.[134] He directed that the report be submitted as soon as possible, prior to taking any final action.[135] CIA concurred with it and endorsed the June 13, 1952, recommendation of the Brownell Committee to provide NSA with a "high level civilian Deputy" to the director, who was a military officer serving a tour in that billet. After considering the reports of the deputy secretary of defense on April 11,

1957, and the DCI on April 30, 1957, Eisenhower approved the DOD's recommendation that the assistant to the secretary of defense (Special Operations) provide high-level direction to fully exploit COMINT activities, providing he had sufficient time to do so. However, Eisenhower did not approve the recommendation that the assistant to the secretary of defense (Special Operations) be made a member of the IAC, for reasons Dulles explained in a subsequent letter.[136]

Recommendation 8a. "That a program be initiated at the highest level to recruit personnel to study high-level Soviet codes and communications intelligence [i.e., high-grade ciphers].[137] This program might possibly be managed by the Science Advisory Committee of the Office of Defense Mobilization or by the Weapons System Evaluation Group of the Department of Defense."[138]

Eisenhower referred this recommendation to the secretary of defense and the director, Office of Defense Mobilization, for the joint selection of a special panel of the Science Advisory Committee to develop recommendations for consideration by the Special COMINT Committee. He further directed that the secretary of state, the DCI, and the NSA director be consulted in the development of recommendations by the panel.[139] He requested that a report be submitted to him as soon as possible and prior to any final action on the recommendation.[140] The CIA responded that this was primarily in the purview of the secretary of defense, though it did endorse the DOD proposal to constitute a panel to study the problem under the leadership of William O. Baker of Bell Labs.[141] After considering the reports of the director, Office of Defense Mobilization (April 25, 1957), and the DCI (April 30, 1957), Eisenhower approved them and endorsed the idea of a panel charged with reporting to him by September 1, 1957.[142]

This recommendation resulted in the creation of the Baker Panel and the Baker Report, only recently declassified in part.[143] The panel and the report took their names from the chair, William O. Baker; the full name of the Baker Panel was "Scientific Judgments on Foreign Communications Intelligence."[144] Over a period of several months, it thoroughly examined the high-level code problem, the collection of intelligence signals (COMINT and ELINT [electronic intelligence]), the processing and analysis of communications intercept, foreign intelligence sources supplementary to Soviet high-level ciphers, and the national resources for communications intelligence, with particular emphasis on the NSA.[145] After Baker briefed the president on his panel's findings and recommendations, PBCFIA chair Killian chimed in with his views on the subject. The Baker Report's recommendations resulted in further presidential action.[146]

Recommendation 8b. "That strong support be provided to efforts now underway in Defense to develop better machines and techniques for speeding up and sifting out important items from the great mass of data accumulated daily from COMINT sources."[147]

Eisenhower approved this recommendation and referred it to the secretary of defense for action, requesting a progress report by May 1, 1957.[148] The CIA concurred. Eisenhower requested that any significant new breakthroughs in this area be reported to him.[149]

Recommendation 9. "That the NSC review its Intelligence Directives and substitute a more coherent, consolidated Directive or set of Directives for the conduct of our intelligence activities under today's conditions."[150]

Eisenhower approved this recommendation and asked Dulles to consult with the IAC to review all NSCIDs and submit recommended revisions as early as possible to the NSC through the NSC Planning Board.[151] Dulles concurred. Eisenhower also directed that the IAC submit reports to the NSC as soon as possible.[152] After considering the report of April 30, 1957, Eisenhower requested a progress report by September 1, 1957.[153]

Recommendation 10. "That, to relieve the DCI of the many management responsibilities he is called upon to discharge as Head of CIA, the DCI be provided with a Chief of Staff or Executive Director to act as his 'Executive Vice President,' thereby enabling him to direct his efforts more toward the integration, reduction of duplication, and coordination which are required within the national intelligence effort."[154]

Eisenhower requested that Dulles report back to him on the best method of accomplishing this recommendation.[155] Dulles concurred. Eisenhower also requested that Dulles submit a report as soon as possible before taking final action.[156] After considering the report of April 30, 1957, the president approved the DCI's recommendations with an understanding that the deputy director for coordination would recommend action by the DCI to coordinate all elements of the intelligence community.[157] The president also directed all members of the intelligence community to cooperate fully with the DCI in accomplishing these objectives.[158]

The Second Report—October 24, 1957

Recommendation 11. "That, as a matter of highest priority, the total resources of the Intelligence Community, under the personal direction of the DCI, be concentrated on the perfection of the communicating and processing of intelligence information related to prior warning of Soviet attack in order that the President and other members of the NSC may receive timely and accurate information necessary for action."[159]

We could find no evidence of specific presidential action on this, although Jeffrey Richelson reports that at about this time the board played a key role in advocating the CORONA reconnaissance satellite system (which returned its photos to earth in ejectable canisters) as an interim step between the increasingly vulnerable U-2 reconnaissance aircraft, the follow-on A-12 OXCART, and the next generation electro-optical SAMOS satellite.[160]

Recommendation 12. "That the policy, coordinating, and supervisory responsibilities presently being discharged separately by USCIB and IAC be vested in a single Board; that the operation of the National Indications Center be made the direct responsibility of the new Board; and that the remaining functions of USCIB and IAC be appropriately redistributed."[161]

Before taking action on this recommendation, Eisenhower requested that Dulles consult with USCIB and IAC agencies and present the DCI's views and comments by January 15, 1958.[162] On March 12, 1958, Eisenhower approved the PBCFIA proposal and requested that Dulles consult with the IAC and the USCIB and submit a draft NSCID to the NSC council within six months.[163]

Recommendation 13. "That early review be made of new developments in advanced reconnaissance systems to insure that they are given adequate consideration and receive proper handling in the light of present and future intelligence requirements."[164]

Before taking any action, Eisenhower requested that Dulles and the secretary of defense provide him with a report on the development of current reconnaissance satellite projects, along with Dulles's views and recommendations on how adaptable the system would be to the needs of the intelligence community. In addition, he also wanted to know what actions needed to be taken to support such a system. He requested this information by November 30, 1957.[165]

Recommendation 14. "That, in the light of recent Soviet accomplishments (1) primary intelligence effort be directed towards the acquisition and interpretation of information on the Soviet missile program, particularly in terms of the capabilities of propulsion-delivery systems (land and sea) and of the sizes of nuclear warheads and (2) that our intelligence on the Soviet Strategic Air Arm be re-evaluated and an all-out effort made to supplement our present knowledge with necessary, additional hard facts."[166]

We could find no evidence of specific presidential action on this recommendation.

The Third Report—October 30, 1958

Recommendation 15. "That, under the leadership of the DCI, actions be expedited to implement the new NSCIDs, and that periodic reports thereon be submitted to the NSC."[167]

Eisenhower referred this recommendation to Dulles for implementation and requested an implementation report to the NSC after six months.[168]

Recommendation 16. "That the DCI be charged with searching out areas of duplication within the Intelligence Community."[169]

Eisenhower referred this recommendation to Dulles for implementation, but we could find no evidence of any further action.[170]

Recommendation 17. "That the present mission of the Plans Group, CIA be reviewed with consideration given to relieving that Group of, and placing elsewhere in CIA, the responsibilities (1) for the review (i.e., reporting on and evaluating) of the political, psychological, and paramilitary operations of the Agency, and (2) for the formulation of the intelligence estimates and recommendations upon which the plans for such operations are based."[171]

The board's continuing concern with this issue manifested itself again in the Bruce-Lovett Panel Report detailing problems with the CIA's covert action programs, which led the board to recommend on December 16, 1958, that the agency be relieved of all responsibility for covert action.[172] The report was scathing in its critique of DD/P operations and strongly criticized the lack of accountability: "Should not someone, somewhere in an authoritative position in our government, on a continuing basis, be counting the immediate costs of disappointments [redacted] calculating the impacts on our international position, and keeping in mind the long-range wisdom of activities which have entailed our virtual abandonment of the international 'golden rule,' and which, if successful to the degree claimed for them, are responsible, in great measure, for stirring up the turmoil and raising the doubts about us that exist in many countries of the world today? What of the effects on our present alliances. Where will we be tomorrow?"[173] The board tied this recommendation explicitly to the "personal circumstances" of the current DD/P, Frank Wisner, who was suffering from increasingly severe mental illness, but it also made a more general indictment of the current structure of the directorate in which it felt that the directorate was reviewing its own activities.[174]

The board met with the president on December 16, 1958, to discuss its most recent report. After complaining that its various recommendations on this topic over the last two years "had not been fully implemented," the chair, speaking on behalf of the full board, confessed: "There is a real question in our minds as to the net long-term advantages that are being derived from many of the programs which find us involved covertly in the internal affairs of practically every country to which we have access."[175] The board attributed this to the fact that "there are no present provisions for any regular external review of Clandestine Cold War programs and no formal accounting of them."[176]

Eisenhower initially requested that Dulles provide him with his comments on this more modest recommendation by February 1, 1959.[177] After receiving the DCI's memorandum of February 16, 1959, which concurred with the board's recommendation and proposed some reorganization within the DD/P, Eisenhower requested a full report on the recommendation by June 30, 1959.[178] After reviewing the July 28, 1959, and October 17, 1959, reports from Dulles, Eisenhower then requested the PBCFIA to review the two reports and offer their assessment on the CIA's response as soon as possible.[179] The board would return again to this issue in its Sixth and Eighth reports.

Recommendation 18. "Here the Board reiterated Rec. #10, above, namely that the DCI be provided with a Chief of Staff or Executive Director and it stated: 'Action on this recommendation resulted in the designation by the DCI of a Deputy Director for Coordination. While this has served good purposes, it does not, in our view, meet the need of the DCI for the executive assistance which we still believe he should have.' A related Board recommendation called for the expansion of the authority and responsibilities of CIA's Inspector General."[180]

The president personally discussed this matter with Dulles as DCI, but we could find no evidence of any further action.[181]

Recommendation 19. "That (1) the Special Group, established pursuant to paragraph 7, NSC 5412/2, be instructed to assume responsibility for making periodic review and evaluations of significant clandestine cold war programs conducted pursuant to NSC 5412/2; (2) that a study be made of the relationship of the Special Group to the CIA; and (3) that NSC 5412/2 be re-examined in the light of these recommendations."[182]

Eisenhower requested that the special group and the DCI furnish him with their views and comments prior to any final action.[183] The special group met with the board members Hull, Conolly, and Darden on April 16, 1959, and committed itself to ensuring real joint staff for CIA covert action programs.[184]

Recommendation 20. "That a single office within the Department of Defense, and this preferably to be within the organization of the JCS, be designated as the point of contact for all official dealings between the DOD and the CIA for the planning of both Hot War and Cold War operations having military implications."[185]

Eisenhower directed the special assistant to the president for national security affairs to "follow up" on this recommendation.[186]

Recommendation 21. "That top level attention continue to be concentrated on finding the best immediate solution to the vital problem of developing a communications system which will adequately meet the need for the rapid transmission of critical intelligence (and that a system of tests of the CRITIC system be initiated)."[187] Other sources summarized this recommendation as advocating "that a series of tests be initiated with respect to critical intelligence communications."[188]

Eisenhower directed the White House staff secretary to "follow up" on this recommendation.[189]

Recommendation 22. "That in important COMINT-ELINT areas strong leadership be exercised by the NSA Director with full support by the Department of Defense and by the Military Departments (in terms of adequate facilities, proper equipment, and qualified personnel)."[190]

Eisenhower initially took "follow up" action at a meeting of the NSC.[191] After considering this recommendation once again at a special meeting on January 15, 1959, he approved it and referred it to the secretaries of state and defense and the DCI for implementation.[192]

The Fourth Report—August 12, 1959

Recommendation 23. "That (1) the existing CRITIC-COMM [critical communications] system be reviewed and reorganized to optimize its capabilities and to relate it ultimately to the sound objective of an integrated global communications network; (2) that same be accomplished under the guidance of the Sec/Def; (3) that there be searching tests of the system on a frequent basis; and (4) that there be an immediate accounting of existing practices and equipment of the present CRITIC-COMM network with a view to optimization of procedures for recognition, handling, and routing of priority messages, and for the purpose of refurbishing of any needed equipment."[193]

Eisenhower approved this recommendation, though we could not find any further evidence of specific actions taken to implement it.[194]

The Fifth Report—December 11, 1959

Recommendation 24. "That the Director of Central Intelligence complete the Strategic Warning Mechanism survey at the earliest possible date, and based on the survey, prepare expeditiously specific indicator lists to supersede the general indicator list now in use and that the facilities of the Intelligence Community's Watch Committee and its Indication Center be organized, supported and operated in such manner as to (a) maximize the Intelligence Community's efforts to effect timely receipt, processing and evaluation of available information pertaining to strategic early warning, and (b) insure the timely transmission to higher authority of significant information bearing upon the early warning problem."[195]

Dulles wrote a memorandum to Eisenhower on this issue on March 3, 1960. Eisenhower requested that the U.S. Intelligence Board (USIB) give "expeditious attention to the forthcoming report on the Warning Systems Survey and to the issuance of instructions there on as appropriate" and further requested Dulles to report to the PBCFIA on the action he took.[196]

Recommendation 25. "That a realistic appraisal of our priority national intelligence objectives be undertaken on an urgent basis; and that the Intelligence Community's emphasis on collection objectives be redirected to insure that primary emphasis and support are given by the entire Community to the fulfillment of our most critical national intelligence collection programs as distinguished from fulfillment of departmental intelligence requirements of lesser importance."[197]

Dulles submitted a memorandum on this issue to Eisenhower on March 1, 1960, in which he clarified that the key problem was "our lack of success, to date, in discovering the operational characteristics and deployment of Soviet ballistic missile unit," owing to parochialism among service intelligence units and a lack of overall direction in "national intelligence priorities." He challenged the board's diagnosis of the problem, attributing the problem instead to "the inherent difficulties" and the fact that U-2 overflights, which provided the best data, were used "only sparingly" "due to the risks involved."[198] Eisenhower then requested that Dulles report to the PBCFIA "concerning current developments related to the recommendation, including the recommendation that emphasis be redirected to insure that primary emphasis is placed on critical national intelligence collection programs," and further directed him to keep him and the board informed about the subject.[199]

Recommendation 26. "That the Office of Special Operations, in reviewing for the Secretary of Defense the development and execution of NSA's plans and programs, make periodic assessments of, and issue appropriate guidance with respect to, the many requirements which are levied on the NSA by the several agencies concerned with COMINT-ELINT activities."[200]

Before he took any action on this recommendation, Eisenhower directed both the DCI and the secretary of defense to furnish a joint report on this subject by February 26, 1960.[201] They submitted a joint memorandum on March 8, and Eisenhower then directed them to submit the memorandum to the PBCFIA and to "expedite completion of the assessments and issuance of guidance called for in the recommendation."[202] He requested another report by June 15, 1960.

Dulles and the secretary of defense submitted a second joint memorandum on July 6, 1960. Eisenhower then directed them to submit the report to the PBCFIA, directing the board to periodically review and report to the president on the status of its implementation. He also directed the secretary of defense and the DCI to report annually, on May 1, on the implementation of this recommendation.[203]

Recommendation 27. "That appropriate remedial action be taken by the Director of Central Intelligence to effect early issuance of implementing directives (DCIDs) which are essential to facilitate proper conduct and coordination of U.S. espionage and counter-intelligence activities abroad."[204]

Archival evidence indicates that the intelligence community reached an agreement about this issue among themselves, thereby preempting the need for presidential action.[205]

Recommendation 28. "That through the Director of Central Intelligence a report be submitted reflecting (a) the status of implementation of each PBCFIA recommendation, as previously approved, and (b) the status of actions which have been initiated with respect to any such recommendations which may not have been fully implemented thus far."[206]

Eisenhower requested that Dulles, together with other "interested officials," submit a report by February 29, 1960, describing "the status of the implementation of each of the board's recommendations which have been submitted in previous reports, as approved by the President," and "the status of actions which have been initiated with respect to any such recommendations which may not have been fully implemented thus far."[207]

Dulles submitted a report to the NSC executive secretary on March 5, 1960, on which Eisenhower "deferred further action thereon pending consideration by the PBCFIA of (a) the report submitted by the DCI; and (b) a further report to be made to the Board by the DCI on the current status of each of the previously approved recommendations of the Board."[208]

The Sixth Report—May 24, 1960

Recommendation 29. "That the growing evidence of unnecessary duplication of effort in the collection, analysis, interpretation, production and publication of foreign intelligence data be corrected by the exercise of a greater coordination role on the part of the DCI and by more complete implementation of the several recommendations which were previously made on matters pertaining to the integration, coordination and direction of the foreign intelligence effort."[209]

Eisenhower requested that the DCI and the secretary of defense (by July 8, 1960, and September 1960, respectively) provide their views on the matter.[210] This probably grew out of a May 6, 1960, PBCFIA recommendation to establish a National Photographic Interpretation Center (NPIC) to eliminate duplication in this area within the intelligence community.[211]

Recommendation 30. "That the administration and fusion of COMINT and ELINT be enhanced by the establishment of greater continuity in the directorship of NSA, and that this matter be reviewed by Sec/Def. to determine the feasibility of establishing broader areas of selection and great continuity in the directorship of the NSA, in lieu of the present practice of rotating the position among the three Military Services."[212]

Eisenhower initially requested that the secretary of defense provide his views on the recommendation by July 8, 1960.[213] After considering his memorandum of August 17, 1960, Eisenhower approved the recommendation of the PBCFIA while noting that the secretary of defense was already "initiating procedures" to put the recommendation into effect.[214]

Recommendation 31 (incomplete). "Status of CIA Station Chiefs Abroad—An overseas, on-the-scene review of U.S. foreign intelligence activities recently made by a member of this Board has confirmed earlier reports we have received concerning the status of CIA Station Chiefs [redacted] abroad. We believe that this problem is of sufficient importance to warrant its joint review [redacted]."[215]

President Eisenhower requested that the secretary of state and the DCI submit a joint report on their views regarding this recommendation by July 8, 1960.[216]

Recommendation 32. "That CIA's clandestine services be organized in such manner as to eliminate unnecessary duplication of effort and achieve increased effectiveness."[217]

Eisenhower requested that Dulles submit his views on this matter by July 8, 1960,[218] which he did on July 22, 1960. He directed him to forward that document to the PBCFIA "for its information and for comment or recommendation to the President" and to "continue appropriate measures to eliminate unnecessary duplication of effort and to achieve increased effectiveness." He requested a report by December 1, 1960.[219] Dulles responded on January 9, 1961, and recounted how the new DD/P, Richard Bissell, had undertaken a "complete review of the mission and organization of the Clandestine Services," which was complemented by a major review by the CIA's inspector general. As a result of these two efforts, further organizational changes were made to the DD/P, including appointment of a new DD/P for Psychological and Paramilitary Operations, the establishment of an Operational Services Group to further consolidate certain operations, and the abolition of the DD/P's Inspection and Review Staff and its responsibilities assigned to the inspector general himself.[220]

The Seventh Report—October 4, 1960

Recommendation 33. "That the Director of Central Intelligence be requested to provide the President and the Board with his views and recommendations as to: (a) the measures (legislative and/or executive) which would be required to insure strong centralized direction, co-ordination and integration of all U.S. foreign intelligence activities; (b) whether long term, national security interests will best be served by continuing to vest in one official responsibility for co-ordinating all members agencies of the Intelligence Community together with responsibility for administering an operating agency which is a component and competing element of that Community."[221]

Eisenhower requested that Dulles submit his views on this to both him and the board by November 15, 1960. Following this report, he requested that the NSC consider the subject, taking into account the board's recommendation and Dulles's views.[222]

Recommendation 34. "That you direct the Heads of the Departments and Agencies concerned to initiate immediate action to eliminate: (a) unnecessary intelligence publications; (b) undesirable duplication in the publications which are retained; and (c) unnecessary use of personnel and funds in preparing, printing, reproducing and distributing foreign intelligence publications and related issuances."[223]

Eisenhower approved this recommendation and requested that Dulles have the departments and agencies concerned implement it; he also requested an update on the implementation and action taken by January 6, 1961.[224] Dulles submitted his report on January 5, 1961.[225]

Recommendation 35. "We endorse the peripheral ELINT ferret operations of SAC [the U.S. Strategic Air Command] and we recommend their renewal and continuation under the careful safeguards which have characterized the conduct of this program over the years."[226]

Eisenhower requested that the secretary of defense provide him with his views on the matter as early as possible.[227] Following the secretary of defense's memo of December 21, 1960, Eisenhower approved the recommendation and "authorized the renewal and continuation of the peripheral ELINT ferret operations of the SAC, under the safeguards which have been directed by the JCS."[228]

Recommendation 36. "Based on review of the circumstances surrounding the employment and subsequent defection of Martin and Mitchell, and to assure more effective and more secure operations of the National Security Agency, an agency outside the Department of Defense should be brought in to investigate and report to the President on all aspects of the defection, including any which may involve espionage or other subversive activities of individuals, either in NSA or elsewhere, who may have been associated in any manner with the very serious compromise to our national security which is implicit in their defection. The FBI is the agency most eminently qualified to undertake this responsibility."[229]

Eisenhower initially requested the DOD to provide its views on this matter, and, following the submission of the deputy secretary of defense's November 21, 1960, report, it did not approve the recommendation.[230] Eisenhower also directed the attorney general to "respond promptly in the future to any related request from the Department of Defense unless there was some legal reason which militates against such cooperation" and further "instructed that the Department of Defense should feel free to call upon the FBI."[231] The FBI had declined to undertake an investigation.[232]

Recommendation 37. "Based on review of the circumstances surrounding the employment and subsequent defection of Martin and

Mitchell, and to assure more effective and more secure operation of the National Security Agency, we recommend that the Secretary of Defense be requested to submit to you his views and recommendations as to the best means of achieving the following objectives, which we deem essential to the efficient and secure conduct of NSA's functions: (a) authority to assure that no individual shall be employed or retained in employment by NSA unless it has been established by the Secretary of Defense or his designee that such employment is clearly consistent with the national security; (b) that grant of authority to the Secretary of Defense or his designee to appoint and terminate employees whenever in his discretion such actions are deemed necessary or advisable in the national interest; and (c) authority to exempt the NSA from Civil Service requirements which tend to adversely affect accomplishment of its sensitive and vital missions. It will be recalled that authority similar to that outlined above is presently provided to the Director of the Central Intelligence Agency. In the event the objectives outlined above cannot be accomplished under existing legislation, the Secretary of Defense should submit his views and recommendations on the question of seeking legislation essential to their accomplishment."[233]

Eisenhower approved this recommendation and requested that the secretary of defense provide his views and recommendations on the matter by December 1, 1960.[234] The deputy assistant to the secretary of defense (Special Operations) submitted a memorandum on December 15, 1960, and Eisenhower requested that it be referred back to the board for study.[235]

In addition to its formal recommendations, the board also offered its views on some "Major Covert Action Programs," but did so orally given their "sensitivity." It was most concerned about the CIA operation to oust Fidel Castro, which the Kennedy administration, much to its regret, would inherit. Apparently, a board panel had "extensively examined" these plans and expressed considerable reservations about them.[236]

The Eighth Report—January 5, 1961

The recommendations contained in the Eighth Report of the Board were not acted on by President Eisenhower before he left office. Instead, at his direction, the report was delivered to President Kennedy by Goodpaster. They are quoted here in full.[237]

Recommendation 38. "We believe that, in the months ahead, consideration should be given to: (1) further revising pertinent NSCIDs to reflect the increasing intelligence role of the Joint Chiefs of Staff under the Department of Defense Reorganization Act of 1958; and (2) reducing ultimately the size of the USIB membership to provide the Director of Central Intelligence with a more efficient mechanism to assist him in carrying out his mission of coordination of all foreign intelligence activities. (At present USIB is composed of 6 Defense agencies (OSO [Office of the Assistant Secretary of Defense, Special Operations], J-2 [Joint Staff Intelligence], NSA, G-2 [Army Intelligence], ONI [Office of Naval Intelligence], A-2 [Air Force Intelligence]), 2 civilian agencies (State, CIA) extensively engaged in foreign intelligence, and 2 additional civilian agencies (AEC [Atomic Energy Commission], FBI) which are engaged in the foreign intelligence effort in only a marginal way.)"

Recommendation 39. "We believe that his (Mr. Allen Dulles) effectiveness as Director of Central Intelligence is impaired somewhat by the feeling on the part of several member agencies of the Intelligence Community that he is both 'umpire and pitcher' in that he is, at the same time, the coordinator of the entire Intelligence Community and the head of an operating agency which in many quarters is looked upon as a competing element of that Community. . . . [W]e believe that the situation would be bettered substantially if the DCI would divest himself voluntarily of many of the functions he currently performs in his capacity as Head of CIA and by assigning such duties elsewhere within CIA. To accomplish this purpose we again recommend that he be provided with a Chief of Staff or Executive Director to act for him, together with the Deputy Director, in the management of the CIA, thereby relieving him to perform the even more important duty of coordinating, integrating and directing all U.S. foreign intelligence activities. After a reasonable trial period, if this course of action does not accomplish its intended goal, serious consideration should be given to complete separation of the DCI from the CIA."

Recommendation 40. "Although there has been some improvement in the fusion of COMINT and ELINT (Communications and Electronics Intelligence), we feel that it has been too slow and that much more can be done to improve their coordination by: (a) requiring positive operational and technical control of COMINT and ELINT by the Director, NSA, rather than the practice of yielding to individual service claims, and (b) actually combining COMINT and ELINT planning in USIB, rather than present handling of this in separate committees of USIB."

Recommendation 41. "We continue to have misgivings as to whether USIB's Watch Committee and its National Indications Center are organized, supported and operated in such manner as to (a) assure timely receipt, processing and evaluation of all available information pertaining to strategic warning, and (b) assure timely transmission to higher authority of significant information bearing on the early warning problem . . . we believe that there is no subject more deserving of continuing attention, if the President and the National Security Council are to place reliance on USIB's Watch Committee and its National Indications Center to supply them with timely, strategic warning of enemy attack. Accordingly, we would urge that the DCI and USIB re-examine the current organization and functions of the Watch Committee and, particularly, its National Indications Center, to assure that both are properly organized and supported in such a way as to carry out their vital mission in the most effective manner possible."

Recommendation 42. "We continue to have concern as to whether the Clandestine Services of CIA are sufficiently well organized and managed to carry out covert action programs. Further, we have been unable to conclude that, on balance, all of the covert action programs undertaken by CIA up to this time have been worth the risk or the great expenditure of manpower, money and other resources involved. In addition, we believe that CIA's concentration on political, psychological and related covert action activities have tended to detract substantially from the execution of its primary intelligence gathering mission. We suggest, accordingly, that there should be a total reassessment of our covert action policies and programs and that the Head of CIA should devote continuing attention to improving the organization and management of CIA's Clandestine Services."

The board noted that the president had approved four of its earlier recommendations regarding CIA covert action and was encouraged that the special group was exercising better oversight of them. But it expressed continuing concern about the organization and management of the CIA clandestine services and confessed: "We have been unable to conclude that, on balance, all of the covert action programs undertaken by CIA up to this time have been worth the risk or the great expenditure of manpower, money, and other resources involved."[238] Moreover, it feared that the CIA's covert action mission "tended to detract substantially from the execution of its primary intelligence gathering mission."[239]

OTHER ACTIVITIES

In addition to its own studies and recommendations, certain other panels or reports can be fully or partially attributed to the PBCFIA's efforts. One such panel was the JSG, whose primary focus was the "organizational and management aspects of the foreign intelligence effort."[240] A closer look at the JSG's framework reveals that many of the issues it was commissioned to address were similar to formal recommendations that the PBCFIA made prior to, and subsequent to, the establishment of the ad hoc study group. According to its terms of reference: "The Study Group was directed to examine requirements, which are the means by which intelligence producers or researchers request collection; the adaptation of collection assets to changing needs; the method by which the intelligence community periodically evaluates its efforts; the military intelligence coordinating machinery, particularly as related to the Department of Defense Reorganization Act of 1958; the implementation of intelligence directives, particularly as related to providing intelligence support to field commanders; and the coordination of the research and development effort of the intelligence community."[241]

The JSG began work on July 10, 1960, and published its findings on December 15, 1960, in a report commonly referred to as the Kirkpatrick Report (named for the JSG chair, Lyman Kirkpatrick, CIA inspector general, and the DCI's representative to the JSG). During that time, the JSG met ninety times, in sessions lasting two to nine hours each; received briefings or held discussions with fifty-one organizations; heard from 320 individuals who appeared before it; and visited a number of U.S. domestic and foreign installations.[242] The PBCFIA was entitled to send an observer to the meetings and to offer comments on JSG reports, though we could find no evidence that anyone from the board actually attended JSG meetings. Nor do we know the extent to which the PBCFIA's formal recommendations to the president provided the primary impetus for the JSG's establishment or whether the JSG's final report laid out recommendations parallel to those of the PBCFIA.

There was also an important synergy between the board and other bodies dealing with various aspects of intelligence. For example, the fact that board members and associates like Killian and Land were also participants in related activities like the Science Advisory Committee of the Office of Defense Mobilization and the TCP substantially increased their influence within the intelligence community and the U.S. government more generally.[243] Looking back on his activities on these various boards, Killian reminisced:

> Those individuals who served on the Technological Capabilities Panel, on the President's Board of Consultants on Foreign Intelligence Activities, and on PSAC [the President's Science

Advisory Council] provided this creative integration of which I speak. For example, the fact that William Baker, Edwin Land, and I were engaged concurrently in several groups made it possible to achieve an extraordinary synthesis of minds and ideas to aid the President in achieving his goals in shaping our defense and intelligence programs and policies. The fact that a number of us, including Baker, Land, [MIT Physicist Jerrold] Zacharias, [Science Adviser Jerome] Wiesner, [the chemical engineer David Z.] Beckler, [Harvard chemistry professor George] Kistiakowsky and many others, worked together with interdisciplinary congeniality made possible the success of such achievements as Polaris, the acceleration of our intercontinental ballistic missile program, the U-2, new techniques of undersea warfare, and spectacular advancement in our reconnaissance capabilities. Coupled with this concert of minds was the fact that the results generated could be brought directly to the President for his consideration.[244]

A declassified article from a special issue on the influence of Killian and Land in the CIA's *Studies in Intelligence* noted that their activities had "momentous impact on the U.S. Government during the next two decades."[245]

ASSESSMENT

As a part-time entity, the board was limited in what it could accomplish. The PBCFIA met as a full board only nineteen times for a total of thirty-three days, from its creation to the end of the Eisenhower administration. During that time, however, it produced forty-two separate recommendations for the president and the DCI.

Of these forty-two recommendations, twenty-two were aimed directly at trying to get the DCI to exercise more consistent and more comprehensive management of the intelligence community. One of these recommendations called for the creation of an executive director or chief of staff to run the CIA while the DCI focused on better integration and coordination of the national intelligence effort. In fact, the board made this same recommendation three separate times. It is clear that Eisenhower constantly tried to encourage Dulles to devote more time and effort to his community management role, and the board was clearly on the same track. However, Dulles never gave up his role as leader of the CIA. His collegial leadership style was well received by other intelligence chiefs but was not satisfactory to the president or the board. He did appoint the retired U.S. Army general Lucian Truscott Jr. as deputy director, but it was Truscott, rather than Dulles, who became the point man for coordinating community issues. Eisenhower accepted this "half-a-loaf" approach but continued to press Dulles for "the exercise of a more comprehensive and positive coordinating responsibility by the Director of Central Intelligence."[246] At one point, Dulles told the president that he was not the kind of administrator Eisenhower apparently wanted and that perhaps he needed another DCI. Eisenhower backed off, saying: "I'm not going to be able to change Allan [*sic*]. . . . I'd rather have Allan [*sic*] as my chief intelligence officer with his limitations than anyone else I know."[247]

Nevertheless, several improvements emerged from the president's and the board's efforts to enhance community coordination. For instance, the CIA photo exploitation office did invite other community organizations to join it, and just before Eisenhower left office the joint CIA-military NPIC was established. It remained a community endeavor until the late 1990s. While Dulles welcomed the participation of non-CIA organizations in the NPIC, he decided not to contest the air force's decision to establish a separate photo-intelligence organization under the Strategic Air Command. Dulles supported centralization and coordination of national intelligence activities, but not at the expense of divisive bureaucratic warfare or of insisting on control of entire fields of intelligence.[248]

Moreover, the second recommendation contained in the PBCFIA's second report to the president called for the separate responsibilities of the USCIB and the IAC to be unified under a single intelligence board (Recommendation 12 above).[249] Though the president told Dulles to adopt this suggestion, Dulles (who frequently met with these boards) opposed it. Dulles objected, but, at a meeting in March 1958 of the IAC, the USCIB, and the NSC, the president announced that there would nevertheless be a new unified USIB. A new NSCID No. 1 was issued in April 1958 and reissued in September 1958 creating the USIB.

Finally, Eisenhower broke new ground in codifying a stronger DCI leadership role in managing the intelligence community.[250] NSCID No. 1 also gave the DCI an explicit and formal mandate to "coordinate the foreign intelligence effort of the United States, in accordance with the principles established by the statute and pertinent National Security Council directives." This was a stronger formulation than the National Security Act of 1947, which initially created the CIA and outlined the community role of the DCI.[251]

In sum, the PBCFIA certainly fulfilled its original mission of contributing "to the task of Government" insofar as the recommendations it made were most often considered and approved by the president.[252] Moreover, there is abundant evidence that the intelligence community usually responded to the board's recommendations and that the results were generally positive in terms of improving various technological and organizational aspects of the community's activities. In our judgment, some of the board's success had to do with the personality and attitude of President Eisenhower, who cared deeply about intelligence matters and was confident enough in his professional standing to welcome outside counsel. Eisenhower's intense interest in and keen understanding of the need for all source collection and analysis of intelligence crystallized during World War II when he served as supreme commander of Operation Torch—the 1942 invasion of North Africa—and then as supreme commander of the Allied Expeditionary Forces that invaded Europe. But the fact that the U.S. government as a whole, and the intelligence community in particular, was relatively small and the national security bureaucracy not yet well established undoubtedly also allowed a unique body like the PBCFIA to have significant influence in the evolution of U.S. intelligence during its formative era.

APPENDIX A
BOARD MEMBERSHIP

Member	Appointed/Resigned
James R. Killian Jr.	
Chairman	January 13, 1956–March 1, 1958
Member	March 1, 1958–January 15, 1960
Gen. John E. Hull, USA (Ret.)	
Member	January 13, 1956–March 1, 1958
Chairman	March 1, 1958–January 20, 1961
Adm. Richard L. Conolly, USN (Ret.)	January 13, 1956–January 20, 1961
Lt. Gen. James H. Doolittle, USAF (Ret.)	January 13, 1956–January 20, 1961
Robert A. Lovett	January 13, 1956–January 20, 1961
Edward L. Ryerson	January 13, 1956–January 20, 1961
Benjamin F. Fairless	January 13, 1956–January 27, 1960
Joseph P. Kennedy	January 13, 1956–July 25, 1956
David K. E. Bruce	August 6, 1956–March 13, 1957
Colgate W. Darden Jr.	July 19, 1957–January 20, 1961
Dr. William O. Baker	January 29, 1960–January 20, 1961

Source: Coyne to President Kennedy, Tab 2: List of Members and Former Members of PBCFIA, Washington, DC, May 14, 1961, Board Briefing Material 5/61, POF, DA, PPJFK, JFKL.

2

John F. Kennedy

The new president, John F. Kennedy, did not appoint a new President's Board of Consultants on Foreign Intelligence Affairs (PBCFIA) immediately on taking office. After the resignation of Dwight Eisenhower's PBCFIA on January 7, 1961, no further meetings were held, and the board was completely inactive in the new Kennedy administration.[1] True, the PBCFIA executive secretary, J. Patrick Coyne, remained in place to report to the new president, but the presidential adviser Clark Clifford recounts that "the Board of Consultants was lying moribund and ignored, waiting for its formal termination." It was his understanding that Kennedy "originally planned to abolish it."[2] In this view, only the intelligence and covert action disaster at the Bay of Pigs provided the catalyst to bring back the PBCFIA, but under a new name: the President's Foreign Intelligence Advisory Board (PFIAB).

There are some plausible reasons for thinking that the new president was prepared to let the board wither on the vine. After all, Joseph P. Kennedy's brief experience as a member of the Eisenhower board could have affected his son's view of its usefulness.[3] Also, it was evident that President Kennedy wanted to pare down what he regarded as his predecessor's large and excessively complex national security decisionmaking apparatus.[4] In Kennedy's view, the formal advisory group members remaining from Eisenhower's tenure were "useless impediments, bureaucratic obstructions to a vigorous, activist foreign policy."[5] Kennedy himself preferred a more informal national security decisionmaking system. Instead of standing committees, he chose to task individual officials on an ad hoc basis to address his particular concerns and to engage in "spontaneous discussions" and "informal advisory meetings," usually convened in response to a specific issue.[6]

Notwithstanding the delay and the conspiracy theories that delay sparked, the archival record in fact shows that the administration was actually moving in the direction of reconstituting the board even before the Bay of Pigs debacle lent new urgency to it. One memorandum of 1963 states that, in January 1961, Kennedy "decided that there was a continuing need for a Presidential advisory board on foreign intelligence, but deferred temporarily the appointment of new members."[7] White House correspondence confirms that the administration was actively setting up a new advisory board before the Bay of Pigs. In late February 1961, the president's special assistant for national security affairs, McGeorge Bundy, wrote to James Killian, who had been the first chair of Eisenhower's PBCFIA, asking him to serve in that capacity again, noting that the president believed that there was a "clear and strong need to have the Board continue."[8] Bundy had previously spoken with Robert Lovett (of Eisenhower's PCBFIA) and "others" about the board before inviting Killian to serve as chair.[9] Killian and Bundy may have met for lunch several weeks later to discuss this plan, possibly including a meeting with President Kennedy.[10]

On April 10, one week before the Bay of Pigs invasion commenced, Bundy again wrote to Killian, this time including with his letter a draft Executive Order (EO) establishing a foreign intelligence advisory board under Killian's chairmanship. Bundy described the proposed EO as "designed to give your committee as free a hand as possible" and requested Killian to let him know "if any part of the language needs any changing from your point of view."[11] The PBCFIA was renamed.[12] Bundy's letter also mentioned prospective members of the new PFIAB, some of whom had already agreed.[13] Bundy told Killian that the president wished for the board to "have available scientific talent . . . strengthen the gathering of hard intelligence and to have a board of civilians to serve as his watchdog on the foreign intelligence activities of the government."[14] Bundy's letter concluded with an apology that he had "been slow about moving this along," yet he assured Killian: "The President has mentioned the matter to me again, and I think he would like to get it publicly announced reasonably soon."[15]

In reality, Kennedy may have used, and benefited from, his foreign intelligence advisory board more than any other president during his brief thousand days in office. The presidential adviser and PFIAB member Clark Clifford admits in his 1991 memoirs: "In the last thirty years, President Kennedy used the PFIAB the most, and got the most benefit from it."[16] In the two-and-a-half years that followed, the PFIAB became a valuable resource to Kennedy on a variety of issues.

THE BAY OF PIGS AND THE CREATION OF THE PFIAB

While the PFIAB was already in the works before the Bay of Pigs, there is no doubt that the ensuing crisis accelerated the process and increased Kennedy's commitment to using the board. On April 17, 1961, the Kennedy administration launched a covert operation to overthrow Cuba's Fidel Castro using forces trained by the CIA. This plan was formulated during the Eisenhower administration, employing a revised version of the one that the agency had used in 1954 to overthrow the leftist government of Jacobo Arbenz in Guatemala.[17] Unlike in Guatemala, the Bay of Pigs invasion ended in complete failure, leaving the new president facing a major political crisis. This debacle dramatically changed the president's views on covert action, intelligence oversight, and the role that presidential advisers should play within his administration. Kennedy told advisers: "I made a bad decision. The decision I made was faulty because it was based on the wrong advice. The advice was wrong because it was based upon incorrect facts. And the incorrect facts were due to a failure of intelligence."[18] In the aftermath of the failed invasion, the president personally called Killian seeking urgent advice on what to do with the senior CIA leaders who had planned the Bay of Pigs.[19]

The presidential adviser Arthur Schlesinger wrote that, immediately after the failed invasion, Kennedy "set quietly to work to make sure that nothing like the Bay of Pigs could happen to him again."[20] The president "now knew that he would have to broaden the range of his advice, make greater use of generalists in whom he had personal confidence."[21] Clifford confirmed that the Bay of Pigs "staggered" Kennedy's confidence in the CIA and in Director of Central Intelligence (DCI) Dulles and that he "recognized immediately that he needed a separate group of advisers on intelligence activities that reported to him."[22] Kennedy further decided that the Pentagon, not the CIA, should have the primary responsibility for future paramilitary actions and that the CIA and its unbudgeted funds needed better oversight. Ted Sorensen, special counsel to the president, agreed that, because of the need for better oversight, Kennedy "reactivated the Foreign Intelligence Advisory Board under James Killian, tightened White House review procedures under Bundy and Taylor and . . . searched for his own man to install as CIA Director."[23]

The White House moved quickly to implement these decisions. By April 27, just one week after the Bay of Pigs invasion, it sent a proposed EO establishing the PFIAB to the attorney general for review. It already had the approval of the Departments of State and Defense, the CIA, and the director of the Bureau of the Budget. The White House cover memo to the attorney general requested "that this matter be handled on an urgent basis."[24] The Department of Justice responded quickly, approving it the next day.[25] The White House, in the meantime, was busy confirming acceptances from seven prospective members of the PFIAB and drafting press releases and formal letters of appointment for the new members.[26] On May 4, 1961, President Kennedy issued EO 10938, which formally reactivated the PFIAB.[27] The language of the EO was very similar to that of Eisenhower's EO 10656. In both form and function, the PFIAB was organized much like the predecessor PBCFIA.

While the Bay of Pigs certainly provided a catalyst for bringing the PFIAB into action quickly, the board was also meant to be more than just a stopgap to contain the political fallout of the crisis. In reconstituting the board, Kennedy intended for it to act as an important advisory body to him on future intelligence matters, especially oversight of the intelligence community and covert action. The Kennedy board's work would go well beyond the Bay of Pigs postmortem. In fact, the official White House press release announcing the establishment of the PFIAB made a point of noting that the board's responsibilities were "to be distinguished from the *ad hoc* and much more limited study that is presently being made by General Maxwell Taylor" regarding the Bay of Pigs incident.[28] In the aftermath of the Bay of Pigs fiasco, Kennedy had Taylor (the White House military adviser), Allen Dulles, Bobby Kennedy, and Adm. Arleigh Burke perform a complete autopsy of the incident, which they delivered in the Taylor Report.[29]

BOARD MEMBERSHIP AND EXECUTIVE STAFF

When the White House issued EO 10938 on May 4, the new PFIAB consisted of seven members, experts in military affairs, intelligence, science, technology, politics, and foreign affairs. Each of the new members had experience with previous presidential administrations, and all were prominent figures in their respective fields. These individuals were

> Dr. James Killian, chair of the corporation, Massachusetts Institute of Technology;
> Dr. William O. Baker, vice president for research, Bell Telephone Laboratories;
> Gen. (Ret.) James H. Doolittle, chair of the board, Space Technologies Laboratories;

Dr. William L. Langer, professor of History, Harvard University;
Robert D. Murphy, president, Corning Glass International;
Dr. Edwin H. Land, president, Polaroid Corporation; and
Gen. Maxwell Taylor (Ret.), former chief of staff of the U.S. Army.

Kennedy's PFIAB appointments focused heavily on science and technology, which made sense given the central role that new technologies were playing in the Cold War conflict with the Soviet Union. Indeed, this was particularly the case in the intelligence arena. As the Church Committee's history of the CIA notes: "The most significant development for the Agency during [the 1961–1970] period was the impact of technological capabilities on intelligence production."[30] It was logical, therefore, for the PFIAB to reflect a certain expertise in this area, much as the original board had under Eisenhower.

The official press release announcing the creation of the PFIAB named just six members, omitting Land's name for some reason.[31] Most likely, Land himself did not wish to be named. His name and profession had been included in the draft press releases, but later drafts contain penciled notes from an unknown author indicating to "1) omit him from releases [and] 2) include him in letter of appointment" that each member received from President Kennedy.[32] Land's name and contact information did not appear in a subsequent draft or in the final official press release on May 4, nor did they appear in major newspaper reports on the new PFIAB.[33]

At the time of the press release establishing the board, the White House indicated that more members might be added "in the near future."[34] From these original seven members, the Kennedy PFIAB eventually grew to ten, a size it remained at for most of the administration. Two additional members, Clark Clifford and Gordon Gray, were added on May 16.[35] Clifford was a trusted confidante of President Kennedy's, and Gray had been special assistant to the president for national security affairs under Eisenhower. It is unclear why Clifford's and Gray's appointments were delayed. Finally, Frank Pace of General Dynamics was appointed to the board on July 17, 1961.[36]

MEMBER SELECTION PROCESS

The Kennedy administration's PFIAB selection process remains opaque. There is limited information available about how the original members of the PFIAB were selected in May 1961. Killian wrote in his memoirs:

"When President Kennedy appointed an advisory board on foreign intelligence under my chairmanship, he included Land at my suggestion."[37] Killian, who had nothing but praise for Land, had known him since the 1950s, when they had served together on Eisenhower's Technological Capabilities Panel task force. A second Killian memoir states that both Land and Baker were included in the PFIAB membership at his suggestion.[38] He also notes his "especial respect and affection" for Murphy and Langer.[39] But Killian offers little insight into how other members came to be named.

The April 10, 1961, letter from Bundy to Killian that discusses the creation of the PFIAB also notes that Baker, Doolittle, Murphy, and Taylor had accepted offers to serve on the board. It further mentions that the White House was "debating between Langer and [the Princeton political science professor Klaus] Knorr . . . for a scholar," indicating that some in the Kennedy White House wanted an academic on the board. Bundy also mentions that he was considering "doing without a naval officer or a business administrator," noting that, "on this last category, I continue to believe that you yourself will be able to do everything that is necessary."[40] He also asked Killian to attempt to persuade Robert Lovett (a veteran of the Eisenhower PBCFIA) to join. Bundy described Lovett's attitude toward the board as "hard headed," and Killian was apparently unable to persuade Lovett to come on board.[41]

A handwritten note from PFIAB executive secretary Coyne on April 28, 1961 (as the White House was assembling the PFIAB), provides some additional insight regarding what types of members were being sought. It indicates that the White House was waiting to hear about Murphy's decision but that "Dr. Killian suggests that if Murphy gives a negative response the matter be held in abeyance until a suitable expert in the foreign relations field can be recruited."[42] This comment suggests that the administration sought to balance the board with members from a variety of disciplines. It also illustrates, as do Killian's memoirs, that the PFIAB chair was consulted regarding potential appointments and had a major (but not the only) say in who was asked to serve on the Kennedy board.

Because of a low rate of turnover in Kennedy's PFIAB, the White House had little need to implement a member-replacement selection process. In fact, only two members of the Kennedy PFIAB left the board. On June 26, 1961, Kennedy selected Maxwell Taylor as his military representative at the White House.[43] Owing to his new role, Taylor left the PFIAB and did not return. He was subsequently named chairman of the Joint Chiefs of Staff (JCS). Pace was selected to be Taylor's replacement, and Kennedy announced his appointment on July 17, 1961.[44] Pace closely matched the profile of the generalist that Kennedy desired in PFIAB members. At the time of his appointment, he was head of General Dynamics and also had experience as secretary of the army, following a short stint as director of the Bureau of the Budget.[45]

Since Pace was named to the board relatively early in its tenure, President Kennedy essentially had a single, cohesive PFIAB during his entire administration. Indeed, Pace was the only replacement member of the PFIAB. James Killian retired from the board in April 1963 owing to health problems but was not replaced.

Clifford recounts that Kennedy "wanted the PFIAB to reflect a balance between technicians and generalists."[46] Killian, Baker, and Land were all highly experienced in science and technology issues. Killian and Land in particular had significant experience advising previous presidents on these matters and their applications to intelligence and national security issues. Generals Doolittle and Taylor were career military men whom Kennedy knew and trusted. Doolittle was undoubtedly appointed to the board not only because of his military background but also because he led a company specializing in space and technology. Gray and Langer also had strong military credentials, but as civilian defense officials. Langer and Murphy were the foreign affairs experts on the PFIAB, although the entire board was certainly well informed about national security issues. Langer, a distinguished Harvard historian, also had experience in the intelligence field as an intelligence analyst in World War II. He described himself in his autobiography as "the only strictly intelligence official" among the board's members.[47] However, Murphy was certainly knowledgeable about covert action matters, and he later chaired the PFIAB's panel on covert action.

Clifford himself was selected for several reasons. First, he was a trusted adviser to President Kennedy and a friend of the Kennedy family. President-elect Kennedy selected Clifford to head his transition team; Clifford accepted with the understanding that he would not take a position within the new administration. After the Bay of Pigs, however, Kennedy brought Clifford onto the PFIAB, which gave him an advisory role without an official, full-time position within the administration. Second, Clifford had an extensive track record serving as an adviser to several different presidents. He was an influential political figure, particularly in Democratic Party circles. Finally, he had been closely involved in the creation of the CIA, which prepared him well for PFIAB duties.

When Kennedy asked him to serve on the board, he reminded him: "You were one of the main drafters of the legislation that created the CIA, and watched it develop since its birth. I want you to join a Presidential board to oversee the operations of the intelligence community. You turned down the arms control job because of the commitment you made when you went to work on the transition, but this is not a full-time job, and I consider it important that you participate as a member of this Board."[48] Clifford immediately accepted the PFIAB appointment and, in April 1963, became chair of the board.

Finally, Gray had extensive experience as a longtime policy adviser and high-ranking official in the national security field. Like Pace, he had served as a senior civilian official in the Defense Department, including stints as secretary of the army, assistant secretary of defense, director of defense mobilization, and presidential assistant for national security affairs to President Eisenhower.[49] His extensive work as a national security policymaker gave him tremendous experience in covert action and intelligence matters and, thus, made him a natural for board membership. His appointment also added a bipartisan element to the PFIAB.

PFIAB STAFF

Little documentary evidence or biographical information exists with regard to the PFIAB staff. Coyne, who had long served in the intelligence field, continued as executive secretary, and A. Russell Ash served as a staff member in an unknown capacity.

OPERATING PROCEDURES

The new board held its inaugural meeting May 15, 1961, just days after it had been created. This initial gathering included a meeting with President Kennedy.[50] During its thirty-one months in existence, the Kennedy PFIAB held twenty-five board meetings and had nine additional meetings with President Kennedy.[51] This chapter's appendix 2 provides a complete list of PFIAB meeting dates. Collectively, these meetings spanned thirty-nine working days and were usually held in the PFIAB offices in the Old Executive Office Building. Though the PFIAB had no fixed schedule, the board tried to meet about every six weeks. On occasion, it met more frequently, but sometimes several months passed between meetings.

PFIAB Meetings

The board's regular meetings generally covered two days and generally followed a well-structured agenda. Meetings usually began with "chairman's time" (about half an hour to an hour in which the chair laid out the board's agenda and schedule). Killian occasionally designated others to serve as acting chair when he was unable to make meetings or was delayed. For example, at Killian's request, William Baker chaired the November 9, 1962, meeting while Killian was recovering from health problems.[52] On another occasion, January 25, 1963, Gordon Gray served as acting chair when Killian's arrival in Washington was delayed by weather.[53]

After chairman's time, the board then moved into executive session or panel reports and heard briefings by senior intelligence and defense officials. The PFIAB met frequently with officials from the State Department Bureau of Intelligence and Research, Defense Intelligence Agency (DIA), National Security Agency (NSA), and National Reconnaissance Office (NRO). DCIs Allen Dulles and John McCone—or another high-ranking CIA official substituting for one of them—almost always met with the PFIAB when it convened. Rather than being pro forma dog-and-pony shows, these briefings covered substantial topics and often involved detailed discussions and questioning. PFIAB members were willing and able to challenge these officials on various issues. For example, handwritten meeting notes from the director of the Bureau of Intelligence and Research, Roger Hilsman, complained that "Murphy's attitude is very belligerent."[54]

On occasion the PFIAB met with cabinet members at locations around Washington. For example, on January 25, 1963, the PFIAB met with Secretary of State Dean Rusk at the State Department. The next day, the PFIAB went to the Pentagon for three separate meetings with the director of the DIA, the chairman of the JCS (Gen. Maxwell Taylor, a former Kennedy PFIAB member), and the secretary of defense.[55] These high-level meetings occurred just as the PFIAB was finishing its "Cuban Missile Crisis" report to the president.

In addition to the meetings with these officials, the PFIAB often met with McGeorge Bundy and even on occasion with the president. Throughout its tenure, it had nine meetings with Kennedy, not including one very brief meeting to present a gift to the outgoing chair, Killian, and commission Clifford as the new chair.[56] For a list of confirmed meeting dates with the president, see this chapter's appendix 3. In addition, some

PFIAB members such as Killian and Clifford met with the president on various issues that likely pertained to the work of the board. For example, on July 3, 1961, the president met with Killian at Hyannis Port, Massachusetts.[57] This meeting took place just as the board was reporting its proposals for changes to the intelligence community.[58]

A review of the publicly available agendas and minutes from PFIAB meetings indicates that the meetings covered an extensive list of topics in some degree of detail. The group usually convened at 9:00 A.M. and adjourned after 6:00 P.M., with a forty-five-minute on-site lunch. On occasion, a board member might host the entire group at a nearby restaurant or at his home. Langer hosted a lunch at the Hay-Adams Hotel in December 1962, and Clifford hosted the PFIAB members at a Metropolitan Club lunch in honor of Killian in April 1963.[59]

Afternoon business usually included briefings by government officials or reports by the board panels. Often, there was additional time devoted to chairman's time or executive session. The final few hours of the second day were usually devoted to preparing a report for the president and discussing future business. After the day's meetings had been concluded, board members were occasionally the dinner guests of a fellow board member or a senior government official.[60] In December 1962, the board had dinner at the home of DCI John McCone and, on June 25, 1963, at Chair Clifford's home.

In other words, a PFIAB member could expect to be very busy during the entirety of the two-day meetings and to work very closely with other members of the board and senior officials within the Kennedy administration. For this service, PFIAB members received seventy-five dollars per day.[61] Eisenhower's PBCFIA had received no compensation.

At times, the Kennedy PFIAB set its own agenda, while, at others, it followed the president's lead. At the first meeting of the PFIAB on May 15, 1961, the board received a memorandum from Coyne titled "Future Undertakings of the Board."[62] This document listed the more "significant" aspects of the country's intelligence and covert activities and directed the board to "use the list as revised by the board as the basis for making review assignments to panels or task forces of the Board."[63] It also gave the board license and flexibility to move in directions it believed were necessary when it was carrying out its work. It noted: "It is suggested that the Board members (a) make such additions to or deletions from the listing as they deem appropriate."[64] The board often began work on issues as directed by the president, which ranged from the very broad to the very specific. But its work often expanded in directions that it believed were necessary. For instance, in March 1962, Chair Killian indicated that "there was a need for the Board to explore thoroughly the activities being carried out in the NSC 5412/2 (covert action) area" and further identified a need for the board to gather information on "covert action programs with respect to Cuba."[65]

Interaction with Other Groups

The PFIAB had unfettered access to the most senior levels of the national security staff of the Kennedy White House. The board, in the person of the chair or the executive secretary, worked primarily through the national security adviser. Bundy and Killian (and, presumably, Bundy and Clifford) routinely interacted with each other regarding upcoming meetings and details of the issues to be covered. Bundy met frequently with the board and usually participated in its meetings with the president. Killian also directly corresponded with other senior officials about PFIAB matters. For instance, he was in contact with Attorney General Robert Kennedy regarding the authority of the president to reorganize the CIA.[66]

Executive Secretary Coyne acted as the primary liaison between the PFIAB and Bundy or other government officials on matters of routine business. He prepared and forwarded memorandums directly to the president and even participated in some National Security Council (NSC) meetings on behalf of the board, particularly those that might overlap with its work.[67] He also undertook an on-scene review of the Middle East with Gray and may have taken other trips on PFIAB business as well.[68]

The duties of Russell Ash as a PFIAB staff member are not entirely clear. It is possible that he was primarily tasked with evaluating how PFIAB recommendations were being implemented. His name appears frequently on PFIAB agendas delivering status reports on the implementation of previous recommendations.[69] Ash also aided the board in its reviews of the CIA's covert activity. Materials for the board's meeting of January 25–26, 1962, included a memorandum "on Mr. Ash's review of Special Group records pertaining to developments in Cuba."[70] The memorandum itself consisted primarily of brief summaries of the minutes of special group meetings. But, because so many PFIAB meeting agendas and minutes remain unavailable, the full extent of Ash's contribution to the board remains unknown.

There is little in the public record about the PFIAB's relationship with Allen Dulles, who served as DCI for the first seven months of Kennedy's

PFIAB. Clifford later wrote that, since Dulles knew soon after the Bay of Pigs that he would not remain as DCI, he "did not spend much time worrying about the PFIAB."[71]

But, from the start, the PFIAB had an adversarial relationship with Dulles's successor, John McCone. Clifford states that McCone "looked with suspicion on the PFIAB," thought of meetings with the PFIAB as a "nuisance," and "continually delayed providing us information that we regarded as essential."[72] He also describes how McCone "made an early run at PFIAB, suggesting to the President that the PFIAB become *his* advisory group."[73] These are, of course, Clifford's perceptions and may not have reflected McCone's real views. Nevertheless, in May 1962, and again in June 1962, Killian discussed with Bundy the need for the PFIAB to be "fully informed" on the covert action planning of the NSC 5412/2 Group, which McCone had balked at providing to the PFIAB. Killian and McCone both finally agreed to take the dispute to the president. The matter was resolved in favor of the PFIAB through Bundy, with the president informed of its resolution.[74] Tension remained a permanent feature of PFIAB-DCI relations during the Kennedy administration, particularly after the Cuban Missile Crisis. Clifford alleges that McCone "repeatedly tried to prevent the PFIAB from obtaining material and information" during the crisis.[75]

On the positive side, McCone and the board shared a common interest in ensuring that modern science and technology were applied to intelligence collection and analysis. Two particular areas of cooperation included the creation of the CIA's new directorate of science and technology and the efforts to improve joint CIA/Department of Defense (DOD) management of the NRO. McCone also solicited the help of the board member Gray in the area of signals intelligence.[76]

April 1963: Selection of a New PFIAB Chair

James Killian had served as chair of the Kennedy PFIAB from its inception in May 1961 until April 1963, when he stepped down for health reasons. Bundy and the president selected Clifford to replace him. On March 15, 1963, Bundy wrote to the members of the PFIAB to solicit their thoughts on Clifford as the prospective chair. A memorandum from Bundy to the president notes: "Clark is clearly the preferred candidate of his colleagues on the Board."[77] Killian, Gray, Doolittle, and Langer strongly endorsed Clifford, and, as of March 25, Bundy had not heard back from the other members.[78] Indicative of his sense of the important role of the PFIAB and especially the influence of the chair, Bundy urged the president to name Clifford as chair soon, noting: "This is one place where we want a man with whom you can work in the closest personal trust, rather than a fashionable piece of window dressing which requires constant therapy."[79] The president announced Clifford's appointment on April 23.[80] In an April 29, 1963, editorial, the *New York Times* criticized his appointment on the grounds he was "essentially a politician,"[81] but Killian wrote a letter to the editor in response expressing strong support for Clifford.[82]

PFIAB Panels

The PFIAB conducted much of its work through various subcommittees, known internally as *panels*. We do not know exactly how many panels there were in the Kennedy PFIAB, but we do know about some of them. There was a board panel on covert action operations, made up of Murphy, Gray, and Langer.[83] The PFIAB also had a Cuban Panel with Murphy, Gray, Doolittle, and Baker as members.[84] Baker headed the Communications Panel.[85] Doolittle also chaired the panel on the CIA, and Clifford chaired the panel on CIA organization.[86] The "Doolittle Panel" reported on the "Organization and Operations of CIA" in noncovert action areas in June 1963. At that same meeting, the "Clifford Panel" gave a status report on "DCI's Coordination Role and on Intelligence Community Relationships with and Support of the White House," while the "Murphy Panel" reported on "State Department Intelligence Activities."[87] Although its presence is not confirmed by Kennedy-era documents, a "Panel on NRO Activities" existed as of April 1964. This panel was chaired by Baker, with Doolittle and Land as the other members.[88] Since the NRO was created in 1961 and these panel members also served on the Kennedy PFIAB, it is likely that the panel on NRO activities also operated under the Kennedy PFIAB.

These panels were a well-established part of the board. Other panels were formed to examine very specific matters. For instance, at the November 21, 1963, meeting, a panel of Clifford, Gray, and Doolittle reported on their "Review of the Dunlap Espionage Case and its Ramifications."[89]

We do not know when or how frequently the PFIAB's panels met, but the panel system does indicate that the time commitment of board members involved more than just attendance at the regular board meetings. For example, the Covert Action Operations Panel (consisting of Murphy, Gray, and Langer) consulted with CIA officials on September 6, 1963, before presenting a briefing to the full PFIAB at the September

12–13 meeting.[90] There is also some evidence that panels met at the same time as regular PFIAB meetings. For example, the board's three-member Cuba Panel spent most of the December 6, 1962, meeting at CIA headquarters before reporting to the regular PFIAB meeting at the Executive Office Building.[91] At the June 25, 1963, meeting, Chair Clifford raised the issue of the frequency of board meetings. The PFIAB discussed whether fewer full board meetings might be held by increasing the use of panels to examine specific issues.[92] The result of this discussion is unknown, but there was no real decrease in the number of full meetings in the remaining five months of the Kennedy PFIAB's existence. This discussion does indicate, however, that the panels were a vital part of the board's activities and how the board carried out its duties.

PFIAB On-the-Scene Reviews

In addition to meetings and the use of panels, the PFIAB also visited U.S. intelligence sites around the world. For example, on September 17–18, 1961, the board members took an orientation trip to the Strategic Air Command at Offutt Air Force Base in Nebraska, where they received detailed briefings.[93] No report to the president was prepared after this trip, so it appears to have been just an information-gathering exercise.

The Kennedy PFIAB prepared three large reports that were based exclusively on visits by PFIAB members to sites around the world. A report issued in January 1962 described the results of an on-the-scene review regarding "U.S. intelligence activities in Egypt, Lebanon, Iran, Turkey, Cyprus, Greece, and Israel."[94] This trip was undertaken by Gray and Executive Director Coyne.[95] Thirty different recommendations were included in this one report. The board reports of October 5 and October 19, 1962, both focused on the outcome of an on-the-scene review of U.S. intelligence activities in Southeast Asia and the Far East.[96] It is unclear which PFIAB members participated in this review.

Individual PFIAB Member Work on Intelligence Issues

In August 1962, Gray did some intelligence-related work directly for DCI McCone, assisting him with the "coordination and guidance responsibility" that the president had given to the DCI.[97] It is not clear exactly what Gray did for McCone or how long he did it.[98] McCone hoped Gray would succeed him as DCI whenever McCone chose to leave the CIA, and Gray's work for McCone may have been part of that scheme.[99]

Gray's role started debate within the PFIAB about the potential for conflict of interest. This is not a surprise, especially given that the PFIAB had spent a considerable amount of time providing recommendations to the president on the issue of coordination between various members of the U.S. intelligence community. This debate demonstrates two things. First, members of the PFIAB were experienced and knowledgeable enough about intelligence issues that senior members of the government outside the White House viewed them (individually, if perhaps not as a group) as valuable advisers. Second, the PFIAB had concerns about potential conflicts of interest.[100] The concern about Gray's work for the DCI indicates that the PFIAB took very seriously its role as an *outside* and independent advisory body to the president. In the highly competitive and political world of Washington bureaucracy, these actions by the CIA could also be seen as attempts at co-opting the PFIAB and making it an extension of the CIA or getting the PFIAB to alter its views so that they would be favorable to the CIA.

ISSUES AND RECOMMENDATIONS

At the first meeting of the PFIAB on May 15, 1961, the board received a memorandum entitled "Future Undertakings of the Board."[101] The thirty-five topics listed in the memo cover every aspect of the intelligence field. Some were fairly broad. For instance, items 4, 5, and 6 are "overt collection activities," "covert action activities," and "counterintelligence activities," respectively.[102] Other tasks were more specific, such as "capability of civilian intelligence agencies to serve the military in war time."[103] Because of the all-encompassing nature of the list, it is difficult to determine which issues were to become the highest priorities. The central message from the White House, however, comes across very clearly when reviewing this memo: Kennedy expected his PFIAB to deal with practically every aspect of the U.S. intelligence effort.

President Kennedy and the new PFIAB also received a summary of the work of the Eisenhower PBCFIA and a detailed listing of the forty-seven recommendations it had made to Eisenhower during its tenure.[104] This is a possible indication that, despite the new name, the PFIAB was intended to use the work of the predecessor board as a model. The briefing materials also gave Kennedy a clearer idea of the work of the previous PBCFIA and ideas about how to use his own board more effectively.

Summaries of Kennedy Board Recommendations

Fortunately, a complete list of the recommendations the board submitted in each of its reports is available. This list is reproduced in its entirety below, broken down by year.[105] Following the list of recommendations given in each year is a brief discussion of some of the main issues the PFIAB examined in that year as determined by the archival evidence.

Reports of 1961

The board submitted four reports in its first year: on July 2 and 18 and October 4 and 17.

The following are the recommendations of the board regarding the DCI that were submitted in 1961. The available archival evidence does not indicate which 1961 reports contained these recommendations but does make clear that the board submitted them in 1961. Most of them deal with defining the DCI's role as leader of the intelligence community and with a reorganization of the CIA.

Recommendation 1. "The Board made a series of 17 recommendations calling for (1) a redefinition of the role of the Director of Central Intelligence (DCI), and (2) a reorganization and redirection of the activities of the Central Intelligence Agency (CIA). These recommendations were submitted on the basis of a Board study requested by the President in anticipation of the appointment of a new DCI which subsequently took place on November 29, 1961. The Board recommended as follows:

"1. That the President designate the DCI as the Government's chief intelligence officer having primary responsibility for lending coordination and guidance to the total U.S. foreign intelligence effort.

"2. That the DCI consider establishing a small staff to assist him in providing coordination and guidance to the intelligence effort.

"3. That the DCI, although retaining over-all responsibility for the CIA, be directed by the President to assign to the Deputy DCI the day-to-day operational direction of the CIA.

"4. That the DCI be housed in the executive Office of the President, in order to emphasize his role as chief intelligence officer of the United States.

"5. That the DCI consider taking with him to the Executive Office those CIA personnel engaged in the preparation of national intelligence estimates and evaluations.

"6. That the DCI participate with the Bureau of the Budget in its review of the intelligence budget of the various U.S. intelligence agencies.

"7. That the DCI be responsible for (1) overseeing the preparation of national intelligence estimates by the intelligence community, (2) assuring the timely flow of information to the White House, and (3) providing intelligence briefings to the President and other White House officials as required.

"8. That the DCI serve as Chairman of the U.S. Intelligence Board (USIB) and represent the President on intelligence policy matters at the national level.

"9. That CIA (1) place increasing emphasis on the acquisition of "hard" intelligence, and (2) decrease the excessive emphasis being placed upon covert action programs.

"10. That CIA devise means for identifying and eliminating covert action programs of low potential.

"11. That CIA consider means the feasibility of transferring clandestine operations and covert operations from CIA to some other agency.

"12. That, if feasible, the headquarters administration of all clandestine activities be relocated to points outside of Washington (e.g., to New York City, and other appropriate points).

"13. That deeper cover be achieved for all clandestine activities and covert actions.

"14. That efforts be made to reduce the visibility of our foreign intelligence activities through (1) action by the DCI to reduce to a minimum the appearances of CIA officials before Congressional committees, and (2) action by officials of all intelligence agencies to refrain from public statements concerning substantive intelligence matters.

"15. That improvements be achieved in the quality of CIA personnel.

"16. That consideration be given to a possible change in the name of the CIA.

"17. That there be realignments in the organization and staffing of the CIA, with a view to increasing its effectiveness."

Recommendation 2. "That positive action on the new leadership of CIA be taken as soon as possible."

Report of July 2, 1961

The July 2 report contained twelve recommendations. Most of them dealt with reorganizing and redefining the activities of various intelligence agencies.

Recommendation 3. "That the Department of State and the CIA conduct a study of the number of CIA representatives serving overseas [redacted] with a view to an orderly reduction of such cover positions in appropriate instances."

Recommendation 4. "That the U.S. Intelligence Board create the means for assessing and reporting early warning indications of developing 'cold war' crisis situations in any part of the world (such early warning to be handled separately from 'hot war' indications dealt with in the National Indications Center of the U.S. Intelligence Board's Watch Committee)."

Recommendation 5. "That there be a strengthening of the capabilities of the National Security Agency (NSA) in the acquiring and processing of Communications Intelligence and Electronics Intelligence through the following means: (1) new legislation authorizing the Department of Defense to summarily deny or revoke the employment at NSA of any person unless such employment is found to be contingent with national security interests; (2) new legislation exempting the NSA from statutes and regulations governing employment in the U.S. civil service, as required to enable NSA to accomplish its sensitive and vital mission; (3) a requirement for full management and budgetary control of NSA by the Office of the Secretary of Defense; (4) central supervision by NSA of all collection and processing of Electronics Intelligence (ELINT) done by the military intelligence elements within the Department of Defense; (5) a realistic reexamination of the system followed by the U.S. Intelligence Board in levying intelligence collection requirements upon the NSA; and (6) support by the Defense Department to meet such vital needs of NSA as ship-borne intercept stations, and equipment for intercept coverage [redacted] and critical land areas, in order to meet national as distinct from purely military requirements."

Recommendation 6. "That the President support the Secretary of Defense in a reorganization of Defense Department intelligence activities through the establishment of a Defense Intelligence Agency."

Recommendation 7. This recommendation, on the subject of possibly changing the name of the CIA, is dealt with in the summary of Recommendation 1 (16) above.

Recommendation 8. "That the President oppose (1) the establishment of a Joint Congressional Committee on Intelligence; and (2) Congressional investigations of the CIA."

Recommendation 9. "That every effort be made to protect the President against public identification with specific U.S. projects and programs involving (1) clandestine espionage activities, and (2) covert political, propaganda, psychological, paramilitary, and related activities."

Recommendation 10. "That the President lend his influence in persuading Congress to reduce its demands for testimony by officials of the CIA."

Recommendation 11. "That the Departments of State and Defense, and the CIA, be requested to report semiannually on the status of their respective actions to implement the 43 recommendations made on December 15, 1961, by the Joint Study Group on Foreign Intelligence Activities."[106]

Recommendation 12. "That the President lend his prestige (in the period of transition involving the selection of a new DCI, and related matters) to support and enhance the morale of the intelligence community, and to restore public confidence in the CIA, by: (1) a Presidential statement commending the work of those serving in our intelligence agencies; and (2) an indication by the President of appreciation for the long, distinguished and pioneering work of Allen Dulles in the foreign intelligence field."

Report of July 18, 1961

The board's report of July 18 contained only two recommendations: dealing with the location of CIA clandestine activities and with the NSC's 5412/2 special group.

Recommendation 13. "That CIA review its plans for occupancy of the newly-completed CIA Headquarters Building at Langley, and consider the feasibility of housing at some other place the administration of CIA's clandestine activities."

Recommendation 14. "That the mechanism of the Special NSC 5412/2 Group be employed in such a manner as to ensure: (1) political control of all covert actions (including paramilitary operations whether or not assigned to the Department of Defense), with an opportunity for the Department of State to bring suggestions and judgments to bear on covert action operations in the planning and execution stages; (2) the submission for resolution by the President of matters involving disagreement by any member of the Special Group with respect to a proposed covert action operation; and (3) a current review and evaluation by the Special Group of all covert action authorizations then in effect, in order that the Department of State might be fully informed of all such situations."

Report of October 4, 1961

The board report of October 4, 1961, contained seven recommendations. They covered several areas of interest, including the ongoing push to redefine the DCI's role, reconnaissance, and improving intelligence on Soviet technical capabilities.

Recommendation 15. "That the U.S. Intelligence Board make a thorough assessment with a view to improving the collection and analysis of intelligence concerning scientific and technical capabilities of the Soviet bloc."

Recommendation 16. "That, because the need for intelligence on Soviet nuclear and missile capabilities is more urgent than the current need for geodetic and mapping information, urgent action be taken as follows: (1) the scheduling of as many additional CORONA shots as possible in the coming months, with postponement of [redacted] shots, if necessary; (2) the THOR-CORONA system to be relied upon as the photographic reconnaissance 'work horse' while other systems are in the development stage; (3) a sufficient number of CORONA systems be made available to meet basic needs, either by ordering long lead-time items beyond the present CORONA system, or by ordering additional CORONA systems until advanced systems are so improved; and (4) steps be taken to ensure launch pad availability to permit future CORONA flights for quasi-tactical objectives."

Recommendation 17. "That the Special NSC 5412/2 Group reevaluate and make recommendations to the President of the desirability and feasibility of conducting (under special security safeguards) U-2 photographic reconnaissance missions over selected areas of the China mainland."

Recommendation 18. "That the DCI, as chairman of the U.S. Intelligence Board, explore the feasibility of expediting the operational readiness date (April 1963) of the new National Photographic Interpretation Center at the Naval Weapons Plant."

Recommendation 19. "That (1) the Defense Department report on the feasibility and status of two technical projects initiated by the U.S. Air Force to eliminate delays in the transmission of Electronics Intelligence data to Strategic Air Command Headquarters; and (2) the Department of Defense comment on the adequacy of interim remedial measures which the Board had proposed as a tentative means of reducing delays in the transmission of such intelligence data to SAC headquarters."

Recommendation 20. "That preparatory to a Board review of the security of U.S. classified intelligence sources and methods, the DCI submit a detailed report on the implementation of the following: (1) Section 102-d-3 of the National Security Act of 1947 which provides that the DCI shall be responsible for protecting intelligence sources and methods from unauthorized disclosure; and (2) Section 3 of National Security Council Directive No. 1 which prescribes methods by which the DCI, in consultation with the U.S. Intelligence Board, shall ensure the development of policies and procedures for the protection of intelligence, and intelligence sources and methods, from unauthorized disclosure."

Recommendation 21. "That at the earliest possible date action be taken on the Board's previous recommendations for a redefinition of the role of the DCI and for an improved organization of CIA activities." (See Recommendation 1 above.)

Board Report of October 17, 1961

The October 17 report contained three recommendations and one report to the president. The recommendations pertained to the DCI's coordinating role, the NRO, and paramilitary activities.[107]

Recommendation 22. "The Board re-emphasized to the President its conviction as to the importance of outlining to the newly-chosen DCI the objectives of previous Board recommendations concerning the coordinating role of the DCI." (See Recommendation 1 above.)

Recommendation 23-a. "With respect to the National Reconnaissance Office (NRO), the Board proposed that it review, with the Defense Department and the CIA, the contemplated organizational structure of the NRO for purposes of clarifying its responsibilities and increasing its effectiveness in the coordinated management and operation of all satellite and overhead reconnaissance projects."

Recommendation 24. "That the Special NSC 5412/2 Group review the paramilitary operations being carried out in Laos (and elsewhere) to determine whether those operations, given their present scale, are properly assigned to the CIA."

Recommendation 25. This was not a recommendation "but a report to the president on the progress achieved by the Defense Department in performance of its share of the responsibility for the efficiency of the Critical Communications (CRITCOM) Network for the quick transmittal of vital early warning and other intelligence data from overseas posts to headquarters in Washington."

1961: Initial Undertakings of the Board

The PFIAB tackled a broad array of issues during its first year under the Kennedy administration. The following paragraphs offer a closer look into the work of the PFIAB in 1961, the main issues it examined, and its recommendations.

Organization of the Intelligence Community

The PFIAB spent a substantial amount of time reviewing how the U.S. intelligence community was organized and developing recommendations to improve it. Indeed, this topic was the primary focus of the PFIAB during its first six months. Kennedy viewed it as an important issue, and he raised concerns about how to best organize the intelligence community—especially the covert action elements of it—immediately after the Bay of Pigs. The president requested that the PFIAB examine how the "existing foreign intelligence arrangements" of the U.S. government might be modified.[108] In response to his request, the PFIAB reviewed twelve different proposals for the reorganization of intelligence activities in its first few months of existence.[109]

Two PFIAB reports were issued in July 1961, with the remaining two reports of 1961 issued in October.[110] The board paid special attention to the organization of the CIA, the role and responsibilities of the DCI, and whether a name change for the CIA and a redistribution of its functions ought to be made within the executive branch.[111] This examination of the CIA and the DCI was the primary focus of the first four reports issued by the Kennedy PFIAB, but many other intelligence organization issues were also addressed, such as the intelligence activities of the DOD.

These 1961 reports did not mark the end of the PFIAB's involvement in the organization of the intelligence community. In March 1963, the PFIAB recommended that a research and development directorate be established at the CIA to work on scientific and technological issues.[112] DCI McCone had already been active on this issue, having created a deputy director for research in 1962. This developed into the deputy director for science and technology in 1963, which became the directorate of science and technology in 1965.[113] In its last meeting on November 22, 1963, the board considered (among other issues) a series of recommendations about a "broad overhaul of the intelligence community" that the president had requested.[114]

Responsibilities of the DCI and the CIA

The board's first four reports collectively made seventeen recommendations that involved redefining the role of the DCI and the "reorganization and redirection" of the CIA's intelligence activities.[115] The board concluded that the DCI had never fully fulfilled his role as the coordinator of the nation's entire intelligence community, instead spending most of his time running the CIA.[116] To remedy this deficiency, the PFIAB believed that the DCI should be housed in the executive office of the president in order to "emphasize his role as chief intelligence officer of the United States."[117] The PFIAB further called for the DCI to designate a deputy DCI to run the day-to-day operations of the CIA, leaving the DCI to focus on the broader intelligence community and an increased emphasis on national intelligence estimates.[118]

Not surprisingly, given its origins as a response to the covert action disaster of the Bay of Pigs, the Kennedy PFIAB spent a great deal of time examining covert action issues. The board discussed covert action at twenty-one of its twenty-five meetings.[119] This issue was so important that the board formed a Covert Action Panel (chaired by Murphy, with Gray and Langer as members) to track it more closely. The PFIAB was particularly concerned about the operational aspects of the CIA, recommending not only that the clandestine service be transferred out of the CIA but also that it be relocated to a different geographic location, such as New York City. The PFIAB further sought improvement in the quality of CIA personnel, reduced visibility of foreign intelligence activities (particularly clandestine and covert activities), and a "realignment in the organization and staffing of the CIA."[120] The PFIAB reiterated its call to consider changing the name of the CIA.[121]

Reports and Recommendations on Other Aspects of Intelligence Community Organization

Having concluded this intensive look at the CIA, the PFIAB then considered how other components of the intelligence community were organized. The board's July 2 report focused on the DOD, recommending the creation of a "Defense Intelligence Agency" and "a strengthening of the capabilities of the National Security Agency."[122] The July 2 and 18 reports also offered recommendations about the U.S. Intelligence Board (USIB) and the NSC 5412/2 Group—namely, that the USIB develop a system of "early warning" of Cold War–related crises, the "Special Group" operate so as to ensure political control of covert actions, and the State Department remain aware of, and have input into, covert activities.[123]

The two October reports continued this focus on the DOD and intelligence groups such as the NSC 5412/2 Group.[124] The PFIAB appears to have undertaken an examination of intelligence efforts against the Soviet threat. In particular, it urged more analysis of the scientific and technical capabilities of the Soviet military.[125] It also engaged in an ongoing review of the National Reconnaissance Program and recommended that the DOD work with the CIA to review the NRO's organizational structure to maximize its effectiveness. Although the board first began its examination of the NRO in 1961, the reports in 1962 and 1963 dealt with that issue in greater depth. An important result of the board's efforts was additional CORONA satellite images, which provided more intelligence on Soviet missile and nuclear capabilities.[126]

The PFIAB and the Selection of a New DCI

On November 29, 1961, President Kennedy accepted the resignation of Allen Dulles as DCI.[127] Dulles's resignation was a foregone conclusion after the Bay of Pigs disaster. In fact, the PFIAB's July 2 and October 17 reports even noted that the selection of a new DCI was soon forthcoming and recommended that the president issue a public appreciation for "the long, distinguished and pioneering work of Allen Dulles in the foreign intelligence field."[128]

Killian's memoirs note that the president asked the PFIAB to identify candidates for consideration to become the new DCI. Before it could do so, the board was "disturbed" to find out that McCone had already been selected, a misstep for which Kennedy later apologized.[129] One can view this incident in two very different ways. It reflects positively on the board that Kennedy asked it to be involved in the selection process for the next DCI at all. But this incident also reflects poorly on the PFIAB because it was not told about McCone's selection or even involved in considering him as a candidate. The PFIAB's surprise with McCone's nomination may be one of the reasons why the *Washington Post* reported that Killian was "so out of sorts" with McCone's nomination that he threatened to resign as PFIAB chair. The article went on to say that Killian and Clifford did not endorse McCone for the DCI position.[130] Killian denied this claim, and his memoirs note that the PFIAB thought that the president "had been wise in his choice of McCone."[131]

Reports of 1962

The PFIAB submitted six reports in 1962, on January 11 and 20, May 16, June 26, August 1, October 19, and December 28.[132]

Report of January 11, 1962

The report of January 11 contained only one extensive recommendation, which concerned the transmission of intelligence from field offices to Washington and, later, to the president.

Recommendation 26. "Based on a review of advance intelligence concerning the Berlin Wall and Syrian Coup incidents, the Board recommended that: (1) a sense of urgency be imparted at field and headquarters levels of U.S. intelligence agencies, with a view to ensuring timely reporting, dissemination and assessment of intelligence indicating the imminence of crisis situations which are of potential significance to the foreign policy and national security interests of the United States; (2) without imposing undue delay on the transmission of raw intelligence to Washington, State Department officials at overseas posts prepare periodic appraisals of developing crisis situations, for use at the field level and for consideration at Washington in the preparation of intelligence analyses and estimates; (3) procedures of the U.S. Intelligence Board, and its subsidiaries such as the Watch Committee, ensure that intelligence appraisals reflect significant differences of view which may develop in the intelligence estimative process; and (4) in keeping with the DCI's responsibility for the timely flow of intelligence to the White House, the DCI be requested to review arrangements and procedures to ensure that (a) CIA's intelligence assessments and spot reports on developing crisis situations are made available for timely consideration by the President and other officials, and (b) copies of assessments and spot reports to the White House from other agencies are furnished to the DCI for information and for use in preparing intelligence estimates."

Report of January 20, 1962

The board's report of January 20 mainly consisted of thirty recommendations all consolidated under "Recommendation 27" in the "Summary of Recommendations" contained in the Assassination Records Review Board's archives. All the recommendations arose from the board's on-scene review of various U.S. intelligence activities overseas. Additionally, the board included three recommendations dealing with reconnaissance needs and the various issues surrounding spy satellite programs along with two recommendations concerning the DCI.

Recommendation 27. "Based on an on-the scene review (made by representatives of the Board) of U.S. intelligence activities in Egypt, Lebanon, Iran, Turkey, Cyprus, Greece, and Israel, the Board recommended as follows:

"1. That U.S. Ambassadors be given an opportunity to comment on the drafts of proposed National Intelligence Estimates prepared in Washington with due respect to foreign countries to which the Ambassadors are assigned.

"2. That Political Sections and Ambassadors at U.S. Embassies be given an opportunity to comment on all political intelligence at the time it is being sent to headquarters, except when this would unduly delay the reporting process.

"3. That U.S. Ambassadors be made aware of the capability and security of emergency clandestine radio stations installed in selected U.S. Embassies.

"4. That U.S. intelligence personnel be assigned to overseas posts where best use can be made of their language abilities.

"5. That when intelligence information is reported that later proves erroneous, appropriate corrective notification be given to recipients of the erroneous reports.

"6. That the DCI and the Chairman, Joint Chiefs of Staff, ensure the validity of intelligence collection requirements levied upon the CIA for support of the military in wartime.

"7. That the Defense Department review the Attaché Systems of the three Military Services to determine the advisability of establishing a single Military Attaché System.

"8. That the Defense Department ensure adequate foreign language training of Military Attachés prior to their assignment to overseas posts.

"9. That the Defense Department staff Military Attaché posts on the basis of specific intelligence needs and on the basis of linguistic and other specialized talents.

"10. That the Defense Department, for intelligence-related purposes, ensure efficient allocation of aircraft to Military Attachés at overseas posts.

"11. That the Defense Department equip field elements of the Critical Communications (CRITCOMM) Network with capability for rapid communication of critical messages among major and subordinate military commands in the field.

"12. That the DCI review NSC 5412/2 and related National Security Council Intelligence Directives, and recommend any necessary revisions to ensure adequate guidance to U.S. Ambassadors and CIA Station Chiefs overseas, with regard to (1) covert actions directed at targets within foreign countries, and (2) covert actions directed against third country targets.

"13. That the Signals Intelligence Panel of the President's Board, in the course of its review of National Security Agency operations, determine whether significant intelligence gathered by NSA intercept stations in the field is being furnished to U.S. intelligence agency consumers (and to field consumers) in timely fashion.

"14. That the U.S. Intelligence Board review (1) the adequacy of criteria used for the selection of a particular Military Cryptologic Service or the CIA for Communications Intelligence and Electronics Intelligence intercept operations in a given country; and (2) the grounds for selecting targets for such operations in a given foreign country.

"15. That improvements be made in the communications of the U.S. Embassy in Cairo, particularly under emergency circumstances which would not permit use of commercial communications channels.

"16. That the Defense Department consider changing the Army Attaché station in Lebanon from a 'hardship' to a 'regular' post, to permit longer tours of duty and continuity of experience.

"17. That the DCI and the Assistant Chief of Staff for Intelligence, Army, improve the coordination of clandestine espionage activities conducted by the army and the CIA in Iran (as called for in National Security Council Intelligence Directive No. 5).

"18. That the National Security Agency make an on-the-scene technical review of CIA's covert collection effort in [redacted] to ensure maximum technical use of this strategically positioned activity against Soviet [redacted].

"19. That the National Security Agency take steps in [redacted] to ensure that (1) The U.S. Embassy is furnished significant intelligence developed by the U.S. Army Security Agency intercept detachment [redacted] and (2) the National Security Agency provides to [redacted] CIA Station Chief any data developed by the Army Security Agency detachment concerning (a) communications [redacted].

"20. That the State Department and CIA review the situation in Iran with a view to: (1) improving the coordination of U.S. intelligence activities in that country; (2) agreeing on procedures for the handling by the U.S. Embassy of political intelligence developed by the CIA in Iran; and (3) maintaining an appropriate proportion between the numbers of Foreign Service Officers and CIA representatives assigned to [redacted].

"21. That the DCI ensure that (1) in [redacted] increasing emphasis is placed on covert operations particularly in the [redacted] and (2) the CIA Station Chief in [redacted] provide support to the covert actions operations of the CIA Station [redacted].

"22. That the DCI ensure that the CIA Station Chief in [redacted] keeps the U.S. Ambassador informed of the nature of a clandestine intelligence program [redacted].

"23. That the DCI ensure that the U.S. Ambassador in Athens is adequately informed about the substantive nature of the special relationship between the [redacted].

"24. That the DCI reassign CIA personnel who are in excess of the requirements of the CIA Station in [redacted].

"25. That the DCI consider furnishing the U.S. Ambassador in Tel Aviv with details of [redacted] undertakings [redacted].

"26. That the DCI consider the proposal (made to Board representatives by the [redacted].

"27. That the Air Force consider the assignment to Tel Aviv of an Air Force Attaché having jet fighter experience, because of the intelligence significance of jet aircraft operating in this area of the Middle East.

"28. That officials making up the Special NSC 5412/2 Group: (1) examine the Turkish government's request for access to operational and early warning data of the [redacted] (2) consider assigning to the U.S. Ambassador in Turkey the responsibility for negotiating the Turkish request; and (3) assure coordination of the efforts of the many U.S. elements in and out of Turkey which are working on various aspects of the strategically placed [redacted].

"29. That the National Security Agency take steps to ensure that: (1) the U.S. Army Security Agency Detachments [redacted] pass significant intelligence to the U.S. Ambassador, the Embassy Political Station, the CIA Station Chief, and to CIA headquarters in Washington; and (2) improvement is made in the communications capabilities of selected intercept sites [redacted].

"30. That the Special NSC 5412/2 Group review the desirability and feasibility of C-130 aircraft reconnaissance flights over Iran from Turkish bases, with a view to covering Soviet missile tests and related activities."

Recommendation 28. "That highest priority be placed on the acquisition of crucially-needed intelligence on the Soviet ICBM capability, with special and intensive efforts to advance the photographic reconnaissance capabilities of the [redacted] and [redacted] projects even earlier than now programmed."

Recommendation 29. "That, with regard to CORONA, [redacted] and other advanced intelligence collection projects: (1) prompt and stringent measures be taken, within the intelligence community and with outside contractors, to keep to the absolute, practicable minimum the number of persons cleared for access to information concerning such sensitive projects, and (2) there be periodic security indoctrinations of all persons cleared for access to such information, including knowledge of the special photographic capabilities involved."

Recommendation 30-a. "That there be brought to the urgent attention of the Secretary of State the intelligence aspects of the U.S. space satellite program, for consideration in connection with a United Nations requirement for the registration by member nations of all satellite launchings."

Recommendation 31. "That there be a re-examination of the status of the DCI, to determine whether his relative position and salary are in keeping with the newly-defined role and responsibility of the DCI for coordinating and guiding the U.S. foreign intelligence effort, as provided in the President's January 16, 1962 memorandum to the DCI."

Recommendation 32. "That the DCI, in consultation with the U.S. Intelligence Advisory Board, review the function of the U.S. Intelligence Board's Watch Committee and National Indications Center, to determine their effectiveness in carrying out their mission of providing early warning."

Report of May 16, 1962

The board's report of May 16, 1962, contained only one recommendation, dealing with reconnaissance satellites. It is connected to Recommendation 30-a of January 20, 1962. It is not consecutively numbered in the archival source; therefore, it appears out of order here.

Recommendation 30-b. "Subsequently, in a May 16, 1962 letter to the President, the Board: (1) pointed out the intelligence implications to the United States of international discussions of agreements to provide information on U.S. satellite launchings to the United Nations and its Committee on Peaceful Uses of Outer Space; (2) urged that U.S. control of the development of space capabilities for national defense and intelligence purposes not be foreclosed, diminished, or compromised; and (3) noted that the United States, unlike the USSR, would lose a critically needed intelligence capability if international agreements prohibiting military uses of outer space should preclude continued use of our Government's highly effective reconnaissance satellite intelligence activities. Accordingly, the Board recommended that: (1) the United States formulate a clear position on the relationship of our reconnaissance satellite intelligence programs to international discussion of peaceful uses of outer space; (2) the President review and approve the position to be taken by the United States on this subject; (3) U.S. representatives be involved in UN, Geneva, and other discussions be appropriately briefed on the sensitive U.S. intelligence collection program involved; and (4) differing points of view among U.S. Government officials on this subject be resolved as soon as possible."

Report of June 26, 1962

The board's report of June 26, 1962, contained four recommendations on a broad variety of issues, including further recommendations about reconnaissance, the U-2 program, and SIGINT (signals intelligence).

Recommendation 23-b appears out of chronological order here, as it was in the source material.

Recommendation 23-b. "With further reference to the National Reconnaissance Office, the Board noted that the NRO agreement between the Secretary of Defense and the DCI was not adequate to support an efficient NRO organization; and the Board recommended further study to achieve a better documentary basis for the NRO with particular reference to National Security Council directives possibly in conflict with the NRO plan then existing."

Recommendation 33. "That the Special NSC 5412/2 Group ensure that: (1) adequate cover stories are approved and ready for release by responsible parties, if required, with respect to the U-2, [redacted] and satellite reconnaissance programs; (2) adequate procedures are in readiness for making such releases; and (3) that U-2 and [redacted] pilots are instructed as to appropriate action to be taken in case of mission failures."

Recommendation 34. "Based on further continued studies of ways and means to strengthen the national Communications Intelligence and Electronics Intelligence effort, under authoritative control and management of the National Security Agency, the Board recommended: (1) strong control and management by NSA over these intelligence activities; (2) concentration by NSA on intelligence objectives of greatest national importance, in response to U.S. Intelligence Board guidance which must be refined; (3) NSA supervision of all Signals Intelligence collection and processing, so that national needs will be met without undue cost and effort; (4) the completion of long-pending plans for improved collection and processing of Electronics Intelligence; (5) increased Department of Defense leadership now that responsibility for NSA activities has been assigned to an Assistant Secretary of Defense; and (6) within NSA itself, the exercise of strong leadership competent to meet national intelligence needs rising beyond specific military intelligence interests."

Recommendation 35. "That the Defense Intelligence Agency and the CIA jointly (1) make an operational assessment of present and potential use of audiosurveillance as an intelligence collection technique; (2) work up a plan for developing audiosurveillance devices to meet operational clandestine intelligence requirements; (3) estimate the costs and results of a major research and development effort to produce practicable audio systems for use in clandestine collection and counterintelligence activities; and (4) on the counter-audio side, install secure rooms (electronically and acoustically shielded) in sensitive U.S. posts overseas."

Recommendation 36. "That the U.S. Intelligence Board evaluate the intelligence potential of the 'Big Dish' moon-reflector project, a [redacted] that thereafter the Secretary of Defense reach an early decision as to the future of this project."

Report of August 1, 1962

The board submitted a report on August 1, 1962, after the *New York Times* ran an article containing numerous intelligence disclosures. The board's recommendation contained suggestions on stopping leaks and improving the security of sensitive information.

Recommendation 37. "Based on a review of intelligence disclosures in a New York Times article by Hanson Baldwin, the Board recommended that: (1) the President emphasize to Government officials his concern about such disclosures and his intention in this case to identify and take action against the source of Government leaks to the newspaper writer; (2) the President take drastic action against the offender if identified by the FBI, or against the heads of offices from which the leak emanated; (3) the Departments of State and Defense and the CIA require their personnel to make memoranda of record on talks with the press, and to clear such contacts in advance with departmental Public Relations Officers; (4) those responsible for protecting intelligence data and techniques identify selected areas of sensitive data requiring special handling; (5) ways be sought to reduce the number of persons involved in preparing highly sensitive intelligence estimates; (6) the DCI and the Director of the Defense Intelligence Agency be provided with the investigative capability to run down leaks of sensitive intelligence data; (7) a confidential policy be established within the Executive Branch as to the degree of disclosure of intelligence data to be made to Congressional Committees; (8) a re-study to be made of possible proposals for legislation to protect official secrets; and (9) a review be made of Government policy and procedures with a view to declassifying non-sensitive information and thereby strengthening programs for the safeguarding of sensitive data."

Report of October 5, 1962

The board submitted its report of October 5, 1962, "based on an on-the-scene review by board representatives of U.S. foreign intelligence and related activities in Southeast Asia and the Far East."[133] The report contained five recommendations.

Recommendation 38. "That the Defense Department, the Joint

Chiefs of Staff and the Defense Intelligence Agency strengthen the intelligence elements of the Defense Intelligence Agency and the Unified Commands (drawing on resources of the military intelligence services in the process)."

Recommendation 39. "That the flow of intelligence guidance from the Defense Intelligence Agency to Unified/Specified and component commands be oriented toward a controlled integrated effort on the part of the numerous U.S. military intelligence organizations overseas (e.g., in South Vietnam, Thailand and Japan), in order to make the most effective use of their substantial resources."

Recommendation 40. "That the Defense Intelligence Agency take action regarding the military Special Security Offices (SSO) Communications System for transmitting sensitive information with a view to: (1) consolidating parallel SSO networks running between Pacific military commands and Washington civilian officials, and (2) reorienting the SSO system to make it a primary service and support to Commands in the field and command (as distinguished from Service) elements in Washington."

Recommendation 41. "That the National Security Agency accelerate [redacted] searches in [redacted] in order that the U.S. Intelligence Board may give guidance to the U.S. Ambassador in negotiating a permanent U.S. intercept site in [redacted] (which is a most favorable location for U.S. Signals Intelligence operations against targets in the Soviet bloc, North Vietnam, [redacted])."

Recommendation 42. "That the Special NSC 5412/2 Group consider authorizing selective, airborne defoliation operations against the Viet Cong in South Vietnam."

Report of October 19, 1962

The board's October 19 report was also based on the board's Southeast Asia and Far East on-site review. The report consisted of two recommendations, with ten separately numbered subrecommendations for the first and three for the second.

Recommendation 43. "Based on an on-the-scene review of U.S. intelligence activities in Southeast Asia and the Far East, the Board made the following subsidiary recommendations.

"1. That the National Security Agency review the Office of the NSA Pacific Representative with a view to clarifying its mission, and its relationship to the Pacific Command structure and to other NSA personnel deployed in the Pacific Area.

"2. That the Defense Department consider staggering the rotation schedules of U.S. Army Intelligence Advisers to the South Vietnam Government, and that such advisers be given more extensive training in the French and Vietnamese languages.

"3. That the DCI and Director of Defense Intelligence Agency emphasize efforts of U.S. civilian and military intelligence elements in South Vietnam to improve the capabilities of South Vietnamese intelligence and security matters.

"4. That the DCI and the Defense Intelligence Agency in their respective areas of responsibility ensure adequate and timely lateral exchange of intelligence reporting of operations units in South Vietnam (particularly the intelligence elements of the Military Assistance Command in South Vietnam, the U.S. Military Attachés in Saigon and the CIA Station, Saigon).

"5. That the Defense Intelligence Agency, consulting with the three U.S. Military Intelligence Services, consider the advisability of (1) extending from two to three years the tours of Service Attachés in Thailand; and (2) provide Thai language training for Military Attachés selected for future assignment to Thailand.

"6. That the Defense Intelligence Agency arrange for U.S. Air Force photo interpretation personnel on Taiwan and at Yokata, Japan, to receive all reports produced by the Chinat Air Force Photo Interpretation Center concerning U-2 and other reconnaissance flights over the China Mainland.

"7. That the Defense Intelligence Agency in consultation with Army Intelligence: (1) assess the organization, management, and effectiveness of clandestine espionage operations conducted in the Pacific area by Army's 500th Intelligence Corps Group; and (2) assure early coordination with appropriate CIA Station Chiefs of the few Army Intelligence clandestine operations not yet coordinated.

"8. That the Defense Intelligence Agency, consulting with U.S. military intelligence agencies, assure that (under guidance by the Joint Chiefs of Staff to the Unified Commands) maximum use is made of the substantial intelligence potential [redacted] deployed in foreign countries.

"9. That the Defense Intelligence Agency make maximum intelligence use of Service Attachés in foreign countries, particularly where intelligence is also being produced [redacted] and other U.S. military organizations.

"10. That the Defense Intelligence Agency, consulting with the National Security Agency and U.S. military intelligence agencies, reduces the time required for security clearances of personnel assigned to sensitive U.S. installations overseas."

Recommendation 44. "The Board also made the following additional recommendations based on its Southeast Asia and Far East review:

"1. That the State Department explore with the U.S. Intelligence Board the practicability of a mechanism to furnish U.S. Ambassadors in Southeast Asia with current, regional intelligence evaluations (of a political, economic, and military nature) concerning the Southeast Asia area—as proposed by the U.S. Ambassador to Thailand.

"2. That the State Department review the manning table of the Political Section of the U.S. Embassy at Bangkok, to determine whether an additional officer should be assigned (as recommended by the Chief of the Political Section of the Embassy).

"3. That the CIA renew efforts [redacted] (the State Department to decide whether the U.S. Ambassador should make specific overtures to Marshal Sarit in this regard)."

Recommendation 45. "That the CIA explore the feasibility of intensifying [redacted]"

Report of December 28, 1962

This report of 1962 dealt completely with a board review of the intelligence effort surrounding the Cuban Missile Crisis. This report was considered interim, created specifically to deal with the intelligence failures surrounding the crisis.

Recommendation 46. "Based on its review of intelligence coverage, assessment, and reporting by U.S. agencies with respect to the Soviet military buildup in Cuba during the months preceding October 22, 1962, the Board submitted to the President an interim report containing the following recommendations:

"1. That the U.S. Government: (1) maintain an aggressive intelligence effort to equip our policy makers with timely and adequate intelligence information to meet the possibility of continuing Soviet confrontations in Cuba; and (2) resist any tendency toward a let-down in intelligence coverage of Cuba in the wake of U.S. intelligence successes through U.S. military aircraft reconnaissance in Cuba.

"2. That the United States make intensified, hard-hitting efforts to obtain significant intelligence on Cuba through clandestine espionage operations, including efforts by U.S. intelligence agencies to lay the groundwork for 'deep cover' espionage operations in Latin American and other foreign countries [redacted].

"3. That (1) high-level and low-level reconnaissance of Cuba be continued as a means of acquiring photographic and Signals Intelligence concerning Soviet military installations, forces, weapons, and highly sophisticated communications equipment in Cuba; (2) planning be made for substitute intelligence techniques in the event that our aerial reconnaissance of Cuba is denied us by Soviet air defense systems on the island; and (3) that the United States launch a clandestine agent program to provide on-the-ground photography of intelligence targets in Cuba, as an adjunct to our aerial reconnaissance photographic coverage of Cuba.

"4. That, as an adjunct to Signals Intelligence coverage of Cuba: (1) [redacted] effort be directed toward obtaining vitally needed Signals Intelligence from [redacted].

"5. That in instances where exceptional intelligence collection techniques are suggested to meet priority U.S. intelligence objectives, but are opposed because of political or other risks involved, the issues be submitted for resolution at the Presidential level."

Recommendation 47. "That, in view of Soviet camouflage of missile installations in Cuba, the Director of the National Reconnaissance Office assign high priority to experiments to determine the effectiveness of short and long-range photography of concealed ground targets, including the use of new sensing and illuminating methods."

1962: The Board's Only Full Year

During its only full year of operation under President Kennedy, the PFIAB examined more issues than in any other year. The following paragraphs give greater details on the full extent of the PFIAB recommendations as well as the review process.

Middle East Intelligence Reviews and Intelligence Dissemination

The PFIAB submitted its first report of 1962 on January 11. It gave recommendations based on the PFIAB's review of the quality of advance intelligence the U.S. received prior to the construction of the Berlin Wall and a coup in Syria.[134] In the wake of these incidents, the PFIAB recommended improving the speed with which raw intelligence could be dispersed within the intelligence community and on to policymakers.[135] It also recommended that State Department officials overseas make appraisals of "developing crises" and that the USIB ensure that all intelligence appraisals reflected differing opinions.[136]

Soon after this report was issued, the PFIAB issued a detailed report on January 20 that presented a host of recommendations from site visits in Egypt, Lebanon, Iran, Turkey, Cyprus, Greece, and Israel.[137] The recommendations from this undertaking demonstrate a concern for making sure that senior U.S. officials overseas, such as ambassadors, were integrated into the review of intelligence estimates and were aware of covert action in their countries. The board also devoted attention to improving the coordination of military attachés and improving intelligence-related communications in the field.[138]

Reconnaissance Satellites and the NRO

On May 16, 1962, the PFIAB reported on the issue of reconnaissance satellites and the implications of current UN discussions on the peaceful uses of space.[139] There was concern that an international agreement banning military systems in space would severely limit the intelligence capability of the United States if it included prohibitions on the use of satellites for reconnaissance. The PFIAB urged the president not to disclose any information about satellite launchings to the United Nations, in the event of a future international agreement on this issue. It further recommended the formulation of a "clear position on the relationship of our reconnaissance satellite program to international discussion of peaceful uses of outer space."[140]

The PFIAB had already noted in its report of October 17, 1961, a need to review the "contemplated organizational structure of the National Reconnaissance Office (NRO)."[141] The NRO was the primary topic of the PFIAB reports of June 26, 1962, and March 8, 1963. In June 1962, the PFIAB concluded that the management of the NRO, involving both the secretary of defense and the DCI, was not an efficient arrangement—presumably, it reached this conclusion after following up on its recommendation of October 17. Instead, it urged that a new agreement between them be reached to facilitate better operation of the NRO.[142] In response to the president's 1962 memorandum and the recommendations of the PFIAB, DCI McCone and deputy secretary of defense Roswell Gilpatric agreed to place the NRO directly under the deputy secretary of defense and named the DOD as the executive agent for the NRO. The CIA would focus on developing collection devices such as cameras and ensuring program security. The DOD would concentrate on equipment such as missiles and satellites.[143] By March 1963, the PFIAB reported on a "newly-completed draft of a new NRO agreement" and urged its adoption. In addition, it offered recommendations to ensure that NRO activities dovetailed with the needs of the president, the DOD, and NSC directives.[144]

In addition to its contributions to the organizational restructuring of the NRO, the PFIAB also played a role in improving the physical infrastructure of the National Photographic Interpretation Center (NPIC). According to Jeffrey Richelson, the board and Secretary of Defense Robert McNamara paid a visit to the old NPIC office, which was located above a car dealership. They were so horrified by this facility that they recommended to the president that the NPIC be relocated to a refurbished building in the Washington Navy Yard. Kennedy approved.[145]

The Directorate of Science and Technology

Progress was made in 1962 on the long-standing board commitment, which dated back to the Eisenhower PBCFIA, to enhance the CIA's capabilities in the areas of science and technology. Killian and Land, in particular, had long advocated that the CIA recognize the importance of these areas in its mission by establishing a separate directorate of science and technology. This issue came to a head in 1959 when Richard Bissell, the head of the U-2 program, became deputy director (Plans) (DD/P). Killian and Land opposed the transfer of the U-2 and other programs to this directorate on two grounds. First, they feared that science and technology assessment would be compromised by the "dirty tricks" environment of covert operations. Second, they were concerned that, unless science and technology had its own directorate, it would not get sufficient attention. This led them to oppose Deputy Director of Intelligence (DDI) Ray Cline's later efforts to subsume science and technology in the DDI.[146]

Killian and Land felt so strongly about this issue that they raised it at McCone's first meeting with the PFIAB as DCI. In response, McCone established an ad hoc task force on the CIA's structure chaired by Lyman Kirkpatrick, the agency's inspector general, and including the PFIAB's executive secretary and a retired army general. McCone's first substantive proposal was to establish a "Deputy Director for Technical Collection" in January of 1962. In February, McCone issued a headquarters notice establishing the "Deputy Director for Research." Despite these efforts to respond to Killian and Land's recommendations, there was a general "foot-dragging attitude in many Agency quarters toward moving ahead with DCI McCone's plans to consolidate all scientific and research efforts in one directorate."[147]

Killian and Land remained dissatisfied with the deputy director for research concept, and under their leadership the board issued its

"Recommendations to the Intelligence Community by PFIAB" in March 1963 that laid out their vision for the new directorate in precise detail:

a) The creation of an organization for research and development which will couple research (basic science) done outside the intelligence community, both overt and covert, with development and engineering conducted within intelligence agencies, particularly the CIA. Institutional research, academic and industrial, must be joined to mission-oriented research.

b) The installation of an administrative arrangement in the CIA whereby the whole spectrum of modern science and technology can be brought into contact with major programs and projects of the Agency. The present fragmentation and compartmentalization of research and development in CIA severely inhibits this function.

c) The clear vesting of these broadened responsibilities in the top technical official of the CIA, operating at the level of Deputy Director. Recasting and extending the CIA's present Office of Research may accomplish this. If it does not, alternative arrangements must be devised. This technical official, as we conceive his responsibilities, should have reporting to him the following groups, each managed by a competent technical leader:
(1) Technical Requirements Group. . . .
(2) Systems Engineering Group. . . .
(3) Development Group. . . .
(4) Field Engineering Services Group. . . .
(5) Behavioral Sciences Group. . . .

d) Formation of a few special research and development groups that may be part of a natural science division, probably coordinated with the behavioral sciences group, that cross-connects various classic disciplines in ways of primary importance to intelligence missions. Thus, studies of camouflage in plant, bird, and animal systems (where it seems to be a highly developed element in survival) coupled with physical optics, radiation and spectroscopy, might reveal new methods of both disclosure and concealment. . . .

The importance of intelligence warrants a major effort to draw fully upon the most advanced science and the best scientific brains in the nation. Our scientific intelligence should be so sophisticated and advanced that it will be beyond the capabilities, if not the imagination, of our adversaries.[148]

After almost nine years of concerted effort, Killian and Land succeeded in realizing their vision of assembling "one of the nation's most productive units for employing science and technology to collect intelligence."[149] Had they not both been members of a body like the PFIAB, with its unique combination of scientific expertise and direct access to the president and the intelligence community, it is unlikely that their efforts would have met with success. Of course, the fact that McCone was also committed to this objective played a role in their success too.

Looking at Leaks

After submitting the NRO report in June, President Kennedy tasked the PFIAB to study the disclosure of sensitive intelligence in the press. Like any president, he was concerned about the issue of leaks to the media. On national security matters in particular, he had the "conviction that we must make major improvements . . . to protect our intelligence and intelligence sources and methods from unauthorized disclosures."[150]

On July 26, 1962, the *New York Times* published an article by Hanson Baldwin disclosing Soviet efforts to begin hardening their nuclear missile sites. The article contained highly sensitive intelligence concerning the U.S. and Soviet nuclear missile inventories and their capabilities.[151] This information had likely been leaked to Baldwin from a national intelligence estimate that had been prepared earlier that month.[152] The leak infuriated Kennedy, who immediately asked the FBI to investigate its source. Kennedy sought to make an example of both Baldwin and the source of the leak.[153] He also asked the PFIAB to examine the seriousness of the leak, later saying to the board: "I want to get it so it's independent . . . nonagency evaluation of the significance of this Baldwin article."[154]

In response, the board submitted a report in a meeting with the president on August 1, 1962. This meeting was also attended by Robert Kennedy and Maxwell Taylor. According to a transcript of the meeting, Killian made the following opening statement to the president: "It is the judgment of your board today that this is one of the most damaging unauthorized disclosures and leaks that we have any knowledge of in our experience."[155] He also noted that it had "been a tragically serious breach of security."[156] The PFIAB outlined a series of steps to tighten the handling of sensitive intelligence and investigate intelligence leaks, steps that are presented in full in Recommendation 37. The most controversial of the board's recommendations was that these investigations should not be conducted by the FBI but that instead "the Director of Central Intelligence [should] be encouraged to develop an expert group that would be available at all times to follow up on security leaks."[157] It also advised that the president take "drastic action against the offender if caught by the FBI."[158]

Kennedy appreciated the PFIAB's quick assessment of the damage created by the leak. On August 8, 1962, he wrote Chair Killian to express appreciation for the prompt and incisive attention given by the board to the problems created by Baldwin's article.[159] He also noted that the PFIAB's analysis was "most helpful" and that he was referring the board's recommendations to DCI McCone and others in the national security community.[160]

Laos and Vietnam

The PFIAB began inquiring about the CIA's activities in Laos and Vietnam and kept an eye on the region throughout its tenure. In its October 17, 1961, report, the PFIAB recommended that the NSC 5412/2 "Special Group" conduct a review of the "paramilitary operations being carried out in Laos (and elsewhere)" to determine whether these activities are "properly assigned to the CIA."[161] In November 1963, the CIA's William Colby, chief of the DD/P's Far East Division, briefed the PFIAB on the activities of the CIA both before and after the overthrow of Diem.[162]

However, the bulk of PFIAB efforts with regard to Vietnam and Laos occurred in 1962, culminating in two October reports to the president. An October 5 report presented the findings of the board following a visit by PFIAB members to Southeast Asia and the Far East.[163] The recommendations from this report urged the DOD to strengthen the capability of the DIA and to work for a more integrated intelligence effort in South Vietnam, Thailand, and Japan.[164] Later documentation from the Johnson administration indicates that these recommendations were approved and that the DIA, the JCS, and the DOD worked assiduously to integrate the intelligence effort not only in Southeast Asia but also throughout the world. An internal memorandum to McGeorge Bundy dated December 27, 1963, described the concrete progress the DOD had made toward fulfilling these recommendations, including establishing a DIA dissemination center and a National Military Command System Support Office and increasing DIA supervision of military intelligence operations.[165] The PFIAB specifically recommended that the Special NSC 5412/2 Group should "consider authorizing selective, airborne defoliation operations against the Viet Cong in South Vietnam."[166]

The PFIAB's report of October 19 conveyed additional board findings from the Southeast Asia tour. The bulk of this report focused on ways to improve the organization and operation of the DIA. The PFIAB recommended that the NSA clarify the mission and activities of its Pacific representative. It also gave recommendations to the State Department about improving the flow of intelligence within, and from, embassies in Southeast Asia.[167]

The Intelligence Aftermath of the Cuban Missile Crisis

About the time the second Vietnam report was submitted, the members of the PFIAB were not aware that the most intense confrontation of the Cold War was under way. On October 16, three days before the submission of their report, President Kennedy received photographic evidence of Soviet ballistic missiles in Cuba. As a result of the Cuban Missile Crisis, the PFIAB found itself focused less on Southeast Asia and, once again, more on intelligence matters concerning Cuba. Indeed, the Kennedy board focused heavily on Cuba from its inception until the president's death. Not only was the board reconstituted in the wake of an intelligence disaster involving Cuba, but Cuba would also repeatedly form the basis for other work of the PFIAB, such as studies of covert action and a review of the Cuban Missile Crisis.

The PFIAB, according to Clark Clifford, had "no role in the Cuban Missile Crises until a few hours before President Kennedy's speech to the nation on October 22, 1962."[168] Before the speech, Clifford placed telephone calls to some PFIAB members so that the board could "be prepared to fulfill their responsibilities to the President on a moment's notice."[169] It is unclear when or how Clifford learned of the crisis or why he placed the calls instead of Chair Killian. Perhaps his close relationship with the president allowed him to learn of the news first. In any event, the PFIAB already had some limited knowledge of possible Soviet missile placement in Cuba. On September 28, 1962, McCone reviewed reconnaissance photography of Cuba with the PFIAB and mentioned that he, personally (though not his intelligence officers), believed that the Soviets were preparing to install medium-range ballistic missiles.[170]

One might infer that, since the PFIAB was not consulted directly by the president during the crisis itself, Kennedy did not place a significant value on the board's advice. Otherwise, so this view would hold, he would surely have consulted with them on a matter of such importance to U.S. national security. Clifford, however, provides an alternate view: that the PFIAB had no involvement simply because its "mandate did not involve [it] in operational matters."[171] Indeed, soon after the crisis effectively ended on October 28, the PFIAB began reviewing the performance of the intelligence community in the period leading up to the crisis.[172] This supports Clifford's argument that Kennedy wanted the PFIAB to provide him with advice on matters that were of the utmost importance, especially those that pertained to potential intelligence failures.

On November 9, the PFIAB convened to begin this review, which constituted the lion's share of its activities until it issued its final report in March 1963.[173] The resulting assessment—one of four major reports on the intelligence side of the Cuban Missile Crisis (two being conducted internally by the CIA and one by the USIB)—became one of the most significant PFIAB reports to President Kennedy. Without pointing fingers at the president himself, the board found significant lapses in the intelligence community's collection and assessment of intelligence related to the Soviet military buildup in Cuba.

There are three central issues in the debate about the effectiveness of U.S. intelligence in the run-up to the crisis—the period before the discovery of the missiles after a U-2 overflight on October 14, 1962. First, on September 1, Kennedy ordered the CIA not to distribute raw intelligence information on Soviet weapons in Cuba unless it was verified through overhead reconnaissance.[174] If this order delayed discovery of the Soviet deployment of medium- and intermediate-range ballistic missiles in Cuba, it would represent a serious policy failure. Second, there is the question of whether a decision made by Bundy and Secretary of State Dean Rusk to redirect U-2 flights from interior to peripheral flights around Cuba made at a September 10 meeting at the White House delayed the discovery of the Soviet missiles in Cuba. After learning of the deployment of a surface-to-air missile (SAM) system, Bundy and Rusk restricted interior overflights out of concern about the political repercussions of a U-2 shot down over Cuba in the wake of the downing of another U-2 over China. Their fears were not unfounded as an air force U-2 was brought down by these SAMs on October 27. In its report on the crisis, the PFIAB noted that, although it was "unable to establish the existence of a policy which prevented overflying areas of Cuba where surface-to-air missile installations were present, the Central Intelligence Agency and others believed that such a restriction did in fact prevail."[175] Bundy and Rusk's opposition prevailed until DCI McCone returned to Washington and new human source intelligence was obtained that persuaded the president to resume flights over the interior. To the extent that their opposition delayed the discovery of offensive missiles being installed at sites in the interior of Cuba, the crisis should also be considered at least partially a policy failure.[176]

Finally, there is a question about whether analysts in the CIA and the rest of the intelligence community had become so convinced in their belief that the Soviets would never deploy medium- and intermediate-range missiles in Cuba that they (a) ignored other evidence pointing to the deployment and (b) showed no urgency about resuming U-2 overflights over all of Cuba. The key piece of evidence for faulting the intelligence community is the September 19, 1962, special national intelligence estimate, which dismissed the likelihood of the Soviets deploying any offensive nuclear weapons on the grounds that to do so "would be incompatible with Soviet practice to date and with Soviet policy as we presently estimate it."[177] If it was this conviction that also delayed the discovery of the missiles, then the Cuban Missile Crisis is best characterized as an intelligence failure.

It also needs to be kept in mind that there were loud voices inside and outside the intelligence community that warned early on that the Soviets were deploying offensive weapons to Cuba. Within the intelligence community, DCI McCone was almost the lone voice arguing that this was what was happening. Indeed, during the critical period of September 1962, McCone was honeymooning in France but sent numerous cables back to Washington sounding the tocsin and urging the resumption of reconnaissance flights over Cuba. Publicly, Senator Kenneth Keating of New York gave ten speeches during this period, all variations on the theme that the Soviets were deploying nuclear weapons and ballistic missiles to Cuba. Given this, there was widespread concern that U.S. intelligence had missed an important development.

At the December 6 and 7 meetings in 1962, the board met to examine materials assembled as a result of a "study conducted by the board staff of information then available concerning intelligence aspects of the Soviet military buildup of Cuba."[178] At this meeting, several board members expressed concern about whether the president did or did not receive cables from the DCI (who had then been reporting from France) on the issue of reconnaissance overflights of Cuba prior to the missile crisis.[179] Then deputy director for coordination of the State Department's Bureau of Intelligence and Research William McAfee later recalled that the DCI "kept sending back messages saying the Soviets were putting in SAMs and the SAMs were to protect strategic missiles." McAfee seemed to confirm the board members' fears when he revealed: "As a friend of mine in the Agency said, 'we didn't give wide dissemination to this view of his because we wanted to save the old man from his folly.'"[180]

On December 26, the board received a DCI report that had been prepared specifically for it, entitled "Intelligence Community Activities relating to the Cuban Arms Build-Up (14 April through 14 October 1962)."[181] Clifford bluntly referred to this report as a "snow job." In his opinion, the report understated the intelligence shortcomings of the CIA leading up to the missile crisis.[182] The PFIAB members believed that the intelligence community had erred seriously in estimating that the Soviet Union would not deploy offensive missiles in Cuba, a conclusion that foreshadowed the Stennis Report of the Senate Armed Services Committee.[183] They judged the lack of U-2 overflights of Cuba in the six weeks prior to the missiles' discovery as an intelligence failure because, according to Clifford, "the length of time it had taken to discover the missiles was dangerously and inexcusably long."[184] He attributed the CIA's negligence in reconnoitering Cuba to a "state of mind within the intelligence community . . . which rejected the possibility of offensive missiles in Cuba."[185] Clifford's version, however, omits the responsibility of Rusk and Bundy for delaying U-2 flights over Cuba during the month of September and early October.

The board devoted its December 27 and 28, 1962, meetings almost exclusively to its Cuban Arms Buildup Report, conducting additional meetings with senior intelligence officials.[186] Preparation of this report continued to bring the board in direct confrontation with DCI McCone. Clifford later characterized this as "the struggle to control the history and assessment of the Cuban Missile Crisis."[187] The PFIAB resented what it perceived as McCone's efforts to limit what materials it would have access to during its evaluation. The issue became so tense that in December the PFIAB brought the issue to the attention of Kennedy, demanding that board members must have complete access to such information or they would be unable to offer sound advice to the president. Clifford even told the board that, if McCone continued to refuse the board access to certain material, he, Clifford, would resign from the PFIAB. Apparently, the PFIAB won this turf battle—Kennedy evidently spoke with McCone, who in turn became more responsive to the PFIAB's needs.[188] Not surprisingly, tension between McCone and the board—and, indeed, the rest of the Kennedy administration—remained high for the remainder of McCone's career.[189] This deterioration was pithily summarized by the president's remark to his brother Robert Kennedy, the attorney general, on March 4, 1963: "He's a real bastard, that John McCone."[190]

Reports of 1963

The PFIAB submitted three reports and one proposal to the president during 1963. The vast majority of recommendations dealt with the ongoing review of intelligence efforts in Cuba following the Cuban Missile Crisis.

Report of January 19, 1963

The January 19 report consisted of one recommendation, aimed at preventing leaks. Though the board was concerned primarily with leaks about a specific DOD and DCI plan, information regarding the plan itself is redacted in the archival evidence.

Recommendation 48. "That, with regard to the Secretary of Defense/ DCI plan for surfacing military versions of [redacted] (1) no statements or programs should be undertaken which would result in public (and Soviet) knowledge of [redacted] or military versions thereof; (2) although leaks concerning [redacted] will eventually occur, such leaks should be avoided as long as possible in order to postpone Soviet development of countermeasures against [redacted] and (3) instead of all [redacted].

"In making these recommendations, the board confined itself to the intelligence-related aspects of the subject, noting its awareness that the problem involved military and congressional considerations (the B-70 issue, e.g.) apart from intelligence-related concerns."

Report of February 4, 1963

The February 4 report contained no recommendations but rather an assessment of the U.S. intelligence community's performance during the lead up to the Cuban Missile Crisis: "As a follow-up to the Board's interim Cuba report and recommendations of December 28, 1962, the Board forwarded to the President on February 4, 1963, the results of the Board's assessment of the performance of the U.S. intelligence community in the coverage and reporting of the Soviet military buildup in Cuba during 1962." The board concluded that there had been a series of intelligence failures in both collection—not just the delays and rerouting of the U-2 flights after September 10 but also a failure to develop adequate human intelligence sources in Cuba—and analysis, particularly faulting the assumptions of the September 19 special national intelligence estimate.[191] In terms of the restriction of raw intelligence information on Soviet weapons in Cuba, it pointed out that this restriction was originally imposed by the DCI himself in May 1962 and that, therefore, the president's September 1 reiteration of it could hardly have been decisive.[192]

The board came down squarely on the intelligence failure side, concluding: "We did not find that during this period there was within the intelligence community the focused urgency or alarm which might well have stimulated a greater effort."[193]

McCone's response to the PFIAB study was interesting given that agency analysts had discounted his own dire warnings before the crisis. On the one hand, he agreed with the board that "the estimators in preparing the September 19 estimate gave great weight to the philosophical argument concerning Soviet military intentions and thus did not weigh the many indicators."[194] On the other hand, he downplayed the importance of the September 10 restrictions on U-2 overflights on the grounds that definitive evidence of Soviet activities was not available in any case until after their resumption on October 14.[195] In its final report, the board did not endorse Clifford's categorical indictment of the CIA's failure to fully reconnoiter Cuba. Rather, it reserved its most severe criticism for the way intelligence was analyzed after being collected, concluding that the "malfunction of the analytic process by which intelligence indicators are assessed and reported . . . may well be the most serious flaw in our intelligence system, and one which, if uncorrected, could lead to the gravest consequences."[196]

Report of March 8, 1963

The board's March 8 report consisted of its final recommendations following its review of the intelligence aspects of the Cuban Missile Crisis. The archival evidence lists these recommendations as thirteen subrecommendations subsumed under "Recommendation 49." The report also contained one recommendation that advised major changes to the CIA's scientific and technological activities.

Recommendation 49. "On March 8, 1963 the Board submitted to the President its final report on Cuba (taking into account views and comments which had been received from the Director of Central Intelligence concerning intelligence aspects of the Cuba experience). The Board made a number of specific recommendations for strengthening U.S. intelligence coverage of Cuba, and for increasing the capabilities of the total foreign intelligence program of our Government, as follows:

"1. That U.S. intelligence planning include attention to possible Soviet intention to create and maintain in Cuba a Soviet base for communications surveillance and military command-and-control in the Western Hemisphere (with unprecedented opportunity to use electronic and other means to obtain intelligence on U.S. military and space capabilities).

"2. That U.S. intelligence agencies make it a major goal to discover the terms of Soviet/Cuban agreements and the programs to carry out such agreements.

"3. That intensified efforts be made for substantial improvement in U.S. clandestine espionage coverage of Cuba—because human resource espionage operations continue to be important in spite of noteworthy results obtained by the United States in using scientific and technical intelligence techniques against Cuba.

"4. That (1) there be a resumption of efforts to develop a long-focal-length camera for use in U-2 coverage of Cuba, using color and stereo photographic methods; (2) that there be a reappraisal of the decision to suspend low-level photographic reconnaissance aircraft missions over Cuba; and (3) that a vigorous clandestine agent program be instituted with a view to obtaining on-the-ground photography of intelligence targets in Cuba, as an essential supplement to aerial photographic reconnaissance of the island.

"5. That the current, intensive aerial surveillance of Cuba be accompanied by priority planning for adequate substitutes in the event that our aerial reconnaissance program is cut off by the advanced Soviet air defenses being installed in Cuba.

"6. That, as recommended earlier, a major clandestine agent effort be mounted against Cuba, with a view to intercepting emanations from sophisticated Soviet code machines through the use of intercept equipment capable of concealment on an agent's person.

"7. That, as previously proposed, the President be asked to resolve the issue when exceptional intelligence techniques are opposed at lesser levels because of the element of risk.

"8. That (1) U.S. intelligence officials be less reluctant to propose to higher authority the use of extraordinary means (such as the U-2) to acquire vital intelligence not otherwise obtainable, and (2) that there be a mechanism whereby policy officials will be informed of operational delays or other factors which call for top-level authorization of new or revised intelligence missions.

"9. That, in order to meet intelligence needs in simultaneous emergencies, pre-arranged plans be made for: (1) the rapid reassignment of personnel, equipment and other intelligence resources; (2) the designation of various processing centers for the handling of photographic intelligence; (3) the processing and communication of vital intelligence to major users in Government; and (4) planning for such related intelligence activities to meet the extra burden if two or more crises should occur concurrently.

"10. That, in the event that emergency situations should arise requiring restrictions on the normal publication and distribution of intelligence data, the U.S. intelligence community should monitor the application of such restrictions to ensure that (1) they are carried through, and (2) they are not applied in such a way as to deny critical intelligence to policy-making and command officials who need such intelligence data.

"11. That concerted efforts be made to (1) devise an effective mechanism for the integrated assessment (and cumulative periodic appraisals) of early-warning and indicator-type intelligence and prompt reporting thereof to policy-making and command officials; and (2) conduct intensified research concerning automatic data processing techniques to facilitate the review and assessment of the great volume of material dealt with in the United States intelligence community.

"12. That there be a re-examination of present methods of arriving at national intelligence estimates, with a view to ensuring that (1) all indicators and other available intelligence information are considered; (2) the views of intelligence community members are fully taken into account; (3) recognition is given to the possibility of widely-varying interpretations of a given body of evidence; (4) considerations is given to the advisability of preparing two or more estimates when evidence is susceptible of more than one interpretation—even though under current practice dissents are noted in footnotes to estimates; and (5) that every precaution be taken to avoid adherence to isolated opinions or preconceived notions.

"13. That the effectiveness of the National Reconnaissance Office be strengthened through specific measures separately summarized in Rec. 23."

Recommendation 50. "That there be a reorganization and reorientation of the CIA's scientific and technological activities in the intelligence field. Specifically, the Board recommended: (1) a research and development effort located outside the intelligence community but coupled with development and engineering conducted within CIA and other intelligence agencies; (2) an administrative arrangement in CIA to bring science and technology into contact with major intelligence programs and projects of the CIA; (3) the vesting of scientific and technological intelligence responsibilities in a top-level official of the CIA; (4) the formation in CIA of special research and development groups concerned with natural sciences and behavioral research in studies of such matters as camouflage and concealment; and (5) actions within the Defense Department to emphasize research on advanced sensing, photographic and other systems, and advanced research in the Signals Intelligence field over the next ten years."

Proposal of July 11, 1963

The board apparently did not issue a complete report on July 11 but rather proposed that the chair of the USIB take steps to strengthen American counterintelligence capabilities.

Recommendation 51. "That the Chairman of the U.S. Intelligence Board give continued attention to and report periodically on measures taken by the U.S. intelligence agencies to strengthen our Government's counterintelligence posture. Here the Board reiterated its previous endorsement of a recommendation: The Director of Central Intelligence should focus community attention of the important area of counterintelligence and the security of overseas personnel, and assign responsibility for periodic reports thereon to the United States Intelligence Board."

1963: The Final Year of the Kennedy PFIAB

The PFIAB issued an interim report on the Cuban Missile Crises to the president on December 28, 1962. The DCI responded on January 22, 1963. The PFIAB continued working on the final report during its January 25 and 26 meetings.[197] The board delivered its final report to the president on February 4 and presented its final recommendations on March 8.[198] On February 28, McCone sent a memorandum to the president presenting his comments on the PFIAB's report. While agreeing with some of the PFIAB's findings, McCone believed that his own study of the crisis reflected "a more reasonable judgment" of the intelligence community's performance.[199] He denied that any restrictions on the dissemination of information seriously affected policymakers' decisions and argued that a serious threat from Soviet antiaircraft systems created an understandable nervousness to authorize U-2 overflights.[200]

Bundy clearly understood the ramifications of this PFIAB-DCI conflict. On March 7, he sent a copy of the PFIAB's report as well as the DCI's response to the president's secretary for placement in the president's files. Bundy noted that "these are potentially explosive documents and their existence is not being widely discussed."[201] President Kennedy did discuss the report with DCI McCone. That same day, Murphy received a phone call from McCone, who noted that the president had shown him the PFIAB's critical February 4 report. McCone was evidently "quite emotional," arguing that, if the PFIAB presented the report as written, then "the top five people in the CIA, including Mr. McCone, would have to resign from the Agency."[202] There are no indications that the report was changed or that anyone resigned from the CIA.

Findings of the PFIAB's Report

Despite McCone's efforts, the PFIAB submitted a report critical of the intelligence community's performance in the six months leading up to the crisis. On March 9, the PFIAB members met with President Kennedy to formally present their findings and recommendations.[203] The board considered the post–October 14 phase of the crisis an intelligence success. It praised the intelligence community for promptly processing intelligence and providing it to the president during the crisis.[204] During the pre–October 14 phase, however, it concluded that "our foreign intelligence effort should have been more effective," with the biggest deficiencies being inadequate collection and faulty analysis.[205]

The PFIAB particularly found fault with the intelligence analysis process, noting that the president had been "ill served" by a September 19 special national intelligence estimate on the military buildup in Cuba.[206] It found the analysis process hampered by narrow thinking and an unwillingness to question assumptions. The report specifically takes the intelligence community to task for "the rigor with which the view was held that assume[s] the risks entailed in establishing nuclear striking forces on Cuban soil" and "the absence of an imaginative appraisal of intelligence indicators."[207] The intelligence community had "failed to get across to key Government officials the most accurate possible picture" of Soviet activities in Cuba before the crisis.[208] Besides the damage done by narrow-mindedness, the PFIAB attributed this failure, in part, to limitations on intelligence reporting put in place by the DCI. However, as with the restrictions on U-2 overflights after September 10, blame should probably be shared more broadly between policymakers and the intelligence community as the president himself imposed restrictions on the dissemination of intelligence regarding offensive weapons in Cuba.[209]

The Postreport Environment

The PFIAB intended its exhaustive review of U.S. intelligence prior to the Soviet arms buildup in Cuba before the Cuban Missile Crisis to provide the best advice to the president on intelligence matters despite the controversy that might result within the administration. Given the tension and high emotions surrounding the report and subsequent presentation to the president, it is somewhat surprising that records do not indicate a continuing conflict after the presentation. Despite the board's findings,

McCone remained as DCI, probably because in the months leading up to the crisis he warned repeatedly and, as it turned out, accurately about the threats posed by Soviet activities in Cuba.

Perhaps Kennedy simply accepted McCone's assessment, rather than the PFIAB's, and was satisfied that there had been no major intelligence failure. On February 2, 1963, Bundy sent a packet of papers to the president for weekend reading material.[210] This was not long after the DCI had issued his January 22 comments on the PFIAB's interim report of December 28. Bundy's cover memorandum to Kennedy notes that he was enclosing "a report from CIA on some recommendations of the Advisory Board, which is well worth reading simply because it shows some of the differences between the professionals and the advisors on the conduct of operations—on the whole I think the Agency has the better of the argument."[211] Kennedy may have shared Bundy's sentiment. Even if he did not, he might not have been willing to endure another public intelligence failure, especially one that again involved Cuba.

Protecting OXCART: Disagreements with McNamara and McCone

In the middle of the battles with the DCI over the Cuba intelligence issues, the PFIAB also presented a January 19 report dealing with an intelligence matter unrelated to the Cuban Missile Crisis.[212] The public summary of its recommendation reads that "no statements or programs should be undertaken which would result in public (and Soviet) knowledge of [redacted] or military versions thereof."[213] Documents from Bundy's files indicate that the redacted word is "OXCART," the codename given to the CIA's ultrafast reconnaissance aircraft then in development.[214] OX-CART was the predecessor of the better-known military version of the same craft, the SR-71 BLACKBIRD.

The PFIAB's recommendation not to disclose the OXCART program was at odds with Secretary of Defense McNamara's and DCI McCone's wishes. McNamara wanted to reveal the existence of the RX program, a military version of OXCART, which he was going to propose in that year's budget. He hoped that this would reduce the intense criticism he was receiving for canceling the B-70/RS-70 program. McCone supported McNamara's plan. But the PFIAB "violently criticized" this idea on the grounds that public disclosure of the RX would reveal the sensitive technology integral to OXCART.[215] The PFIAB met with McNamara, McCone, Bundy, and others to work out a compromise, and this issue was addressed at a meeting with the president on January 20, 1963.[216]

The USIB and Counterintelligence

The PFIAB issued its last report to President Kennedy on July 11, 1963. Rather than recommendations, this report presented a broad, open-ended "Board Proposal" that the chair of the USIB "give continued attention to and report periodically" on efforts to strengthen the counterintelligence capabilities of the intelligence community.[217]

The Dunlap Spy Case

In what would be its final meeting as the Kennedy PFIAB, the board convened on November 21 and 22, 1963. The DCI was invited to the meeting and briefed the board on intelligence activities in South Vietnam.[218] Chair Clifford's comments at the start of the meeting indicated that the meeting would primarily be devoted to examining a Soviet espionage case involving U.S. Army sergeant Jack E. Dunlap.[219] Dunlap had previously been assigned to work at the NSA by the Army Security Agency. Clifford noted that the PFIAB's work would be valuable because it was "the only Government entity engaged in a detailed, full-time review" of the case's ramifications.[220] Collectively, the PFIAB was "aghast" at the looseness of NSA security, and the board indicated that it planned to present its report on this case to the president in the future.[221]

That report would never be presented to President Kennedy, who was assassinated in Dallas that day. At 1:35 P.M., the PFIAB had adjourned for lunch in the White House Mess, where the members would learn of Kennedy's death. Chair Clifford immediately reconvened the board in a short session marked with "profound sorrow."[222] The board agreed that it would not present recommendations on a substantial reorganization of the intelligence effort during the transition period and further agreed to communicate to President Johnson their continuing willingness to serve on the PFIAB. Clifford requested that board members remain ready to meet on short notice, and then this final meeting of the Kennedy PFIAB was formally adjourned.[223]

Reactions to PFIAB Recommendations

During its tenure, the Kennedy PFIAB submitted a total of 170 recommendations to the president. Of these, he approved 125, disapproved 2, and deferred action on the remaining 43.[224] Of the 125 recommendations approved by Kennedy, 85 had been "substantially completed" by the time the PFIAB had its first meeting with President Johnson in

January 1964.[225] Clifford maintains that the remaining recommendations were completed under President Johnson.[226]

Owing to the tragic and sudden end of the Kennedy presidency, follow-up on many of the PFIAB's recommendations was left to President Johnson's PFIAB. This abrupt transition makes it impossible to know what Kennedy might ultimately have decided on the forty-three recommendations that were deferred. While it is unknown exactly which recommendations were approved, denied, and deferred, the numbers alone indicate that the Kennedy PFIAB had a very impressive track record of getting recommendations approved by the president.

ASSESSMENT AND FUTURE RESEARCH RECOMMENDATIONS

Three attributes of the Kennedy PFIAB demonstrate how it might have broadly influenced national security policy during the Kennedy administration. Collectively, these also show that, while Kennedy was only the second of the nine U.S. presidents to utilize a board of outside advisers on foreign intelligence issues, he may have been the one that benefited most from the advice offered by the board.

First, although efforts to revive the board were already under way, the Bay of Pigs provided a catalytic event that led Kennedy to establish his PFIAB. The fact that the PFIAB remained a relevant force throughout the Kennedy presidency and grappled with important issues indicates that it provided much more than just Bay of Pigs political cover (although it certainly was used as such). President Kennedy was serious about preventing similar future intelligence failures and wanted an independent advisory group that could assist him in doing this. The PFIAB was very diligent in fulfilling this role.

Second, the actual PFIAB membership was exactly as Kennedy envisioned it—a high-level mix of specialists and generalists with expertise in intelligence, science, technology, foreign affairs, and the military. The president got the type of board he wanted. This enabled the PFIAB to provide the type of well-rounded advice he had hoped that it would provide when he reactivated it. The PFIAB's low rate of turnover meant that Kennedy was familiar with the individuals on the board and that they each knew his preferences and expectations as well.

Third, the Kennedy PFIAB was extremely active, reviewing all aspects of the U.S. intelligence community's activities. It played a significant role in intelligence matters and operated at the highest levels of the Kennedy administration and the intelligence community. Its work placed particular emphasis on reviews of covert action, the organization of the intelligence community, and increasing the communications and cooperation among members of that community. The board was willing and able to challenge even senior administration officials, especially DCI McCone, to fulfill its mandate of providing sound and unbiased advice to the president.

In a short handwritten note to Kennedy in April 1963, Bundy told the president that the PFIAB "is the one group in all government that can keep a secret."[227] By the standards of any presidential administration, this is one of the most flattering comments that can be made, and it speaks volumes about the image of the PFIAB within the Kennedy White House.

In terms of the explanations for the effectiveness of the board during the Kennedy administration, it appears that both presidential style and structural factors played a role (as with the Eisenhower administration). On the former, Baker noted that, despite their many differences in personal style, both Eisenhower and Kennedy shared "a great sense for calling forth the resources of the country. They went to people in industry and public affairs who really knew something and paid attention to them. So there was an extraordinary coherence about Kennedy and Eisenhower."[228] On the latter, it remained the case that the Cold War organization of the American national security decisionmaking bureaucracy remained protean and inchoate enough that an unusual organization like the board could make a difference in shaping it.

APPENDIX 1
MEMBERS OF THE KENNEDY PFIAB

Member	Dates of PFIAB Membership
Dr. James R. Killian	
Member	May 4, 1961–April 23, 1963
Chair	May 4, 1961–April 23, 1963
William O. Baker	May 4, 1961–November 22, 1963
Gen. James H. Doolittle	May 4, 1961–November 22, 1963
Dr. Edwin H. Land	May 4, 1961–November 22, 1963
Dr. William L. Langer	May 4, 1961–November 22, 1963
Robert D. Murphy	May 4, 1961–November 22, 1963
Gen. Maxwell Taylor	May 4, 1961–June 26, 1961
Clark Clifford	
Member	May 16, 1961–November 22, 1963
Chair	April 23, 1963–November 22, 1963
Gordon Gray	May 16, 1961–November 22, 1963
Frank Pace, Jr.	July 17, 1961–November 22, 1963

APPENDIX 2
DATES OF TWENTY-FIVE PFIAB MEETINGS HELD DURING THE KENNEDY PRESIDENCY

1961, Seven Meetings
May 15, 1961
May 26, 1961
June 7, 1961
June 30–July 2, 1961
July 18, 1961
September 17–18, 1961 (trip to the Strategic Air Command at Offutt
   AFB, Nebraska)
October 16–17, 1961
December 9, 1961

1962, Ten Meetings
January 19–20, 1962
March 23–24, 1962
May 11–12, 1962
June 25–26, 1962
August 1, 1962
August 22, 1962
September 28, 1962
November 9, 1962*
December 6–7, 1962*
December 27–28, 1962*

1963, Eight Meetings
January 21, 1963
January 25–26, 1963*
March 8–9, 1963*
April 2–3, 1963
April 23, 1963*
June 25–26, 1963*
September 12–13, 1963*
November 21–22, 1963*

Notes: Owing to the PFIAB's reactivation in May 1961, the Board did not hold a full year's worth of meetings in 1961. Owing to President Kennedy's death in November 1963, the Board did not hold a full year's worth of meetings in 1963.

* Agendas and minutes for these meetings were obtained for this research project, although some segments are redacted. Obtaining the agendas and minutes of the meetings for the remaining dates will be an important area for further research.

APPENDIX 3
DATES OF PFIAB MEETINGS WITH PRESIDENT KENNEDY

May 15, 1961	5:30 P.M.–6:45 P.M.[a]
June 7, 1961	6:00 P.M.–time not noted. Off the record meeting.[b]
July 3, 1961	The president met with Chair Killian at Hyannis Port.[c] This meeting was held as the board was reporting its proposals for changes to the Intelligence Community.[d]
October 17, 1961	4:30 P.M.–5:30 P.M.[e]
January 20, 1962[f]	
June 26, 1962[g]	
August 1, 1962[h]	5:35–6:25 P.M. Attended by Board plus Taylor, Ash.[i]
August 22, 1962[j]	
January 21, 1963	11:00–11:50 A.M. Also attended by McNamara, Dr. Harold Brown, Dr. Scofield, McCone, and Bundy.[k] This was followed by a 20-minute private meeting (off the record) between the president and Clark Clifford.
March 9, 1963[l]	10:23–11:15 A.M.[m]
April 23, 1963[n]	5:15–5:30 P.M. Short meeting in which the president presented a gift to Killian and the Chairman's Commission to Clifford. Ash and Coyne also attended.[o]

[a] Monday, May 15, 1961 (Daily Schedule), Palm Beach, FL; AB JFK (January 21, 1961–December 31, 1961); JFKL.

[b] Wednesday, June 7, 1961 (Daily Schedule), Washington, DC; AB JFK (January 21, 1961–December 31, 1961); JFKL.

[c] Laurence Burd, "Kennedy Goes on 2D Cruise; Maps Parleys," *Chicago Daily Tribune*, July 3, 1961, Pt. 1, 3.

[d] Alvin Shuster, "CIA Circulates Account of Itself; But 20-Page Handout Tells Little New About Agency," *New York Times*, July 9, 1961, 38.

[e] Tuesday, October 17, 1961 (Daily Schedule); AB JFK (January 21, 1961–December 31, 1961); JFKL.

[f] "President Meets with Secret Board," *Washington Post*, January 21, 1962, A21.

[g] "Washington Proceedings," *New York Times*, June 27, 1962, 10.

[h] Timothy Naftali, *The Presidential Recordings: John F. Kennedy, The Great Crises, Volume One: July 30–August 1962* (New York: W. W. Norton, 2001).

[i] Wednesday, August 1, 1962 (Daily Schedule); AB JFK (January 1, 1962–December 31, 1962); JFKL.

[j] Timothy Naftali, *The Presidential Recordings: John F. Kennedy, The Great Crises, Volume One: July 30–August 1962* (New York: W. W. Norton, 2001).

[k] Monday, January 21, 1963 (Daily Schedule); AB JFK (January 1, 1963–November 21, 1963); JFKL.

[l] "Washington Proceedings," *New York Times*, March 9, 1963, 4; agenda for meetings, Washington, DC, March 8–9, 1963; PFIAB, meeting of the board, March 8–9, 1963 (The Board met with the President on March 9, 1963); PFIAB; ARRB; Record 206-10001-10012; NARA.

[m] Saturday, March 9, 1963 (Daily Schedule); AB JFK (January 21, 1963–November 21, 1963); JFKL.

[n] "Washington Proceedings," *New York Times*, April 23, 1963, 20; Agenda for the Meeting, Washington, DC, April 23, 1963; PFIAB, meeting of the board, April 23, 1963; PFIAB; ARRB; Record 206-10001-10005; NARA.

[o] Tuesday, April 23, 1963 (Daily Schedule); AB JFK (January 1, 1963–November 21, 1963); JFKL.

APPENDIX 4
DATES OF SIXTEEN KENNEDY PFIAB REPORTS

1961, Four Reports
July 2
July 18
October 4
October 17

1962, Eight Reports
January 11
January 20
May 16
June 26
August 1
October 5
October 19
December 28

1963, Four Reports
January 19
February 4
March 8
July 11

3

Lyndon B. Johnson

Lyndon B. Johnson became president after the assassination of John F. Kennedy in Dallas, Texas, on November 22, 1963. The President's Foreign Intelligence Advisory Board (PFIAB) was conducting one of its regularly scheduled meetings that same day.[1] Johnson inherited a PFIAB created by Kennedy's executive order and board members chosen by Kennedy and his administration. Nothing we could find suggests that the Johnson administration ever considered dissolving the PFIAB or making any other radical changes to it.

BOARD MEMBERSHIP AND EXECUTIVE STAFF

When Johnson unexpectedly became president in November 1963, there were eight members of the PFIAB: Clark M. Clifford (chair), William O. Baker, Gordon Gray, Edwin H. Land, William L. Langer, Robert D. Murphy, Frank Pace Jr., and Lt. Gen. James H. Doolittle (Ret.). The membership remained unchanged until August 1964, when Doolittle tendered his resignation. In a letter to the president dated August 10, 1964, Doolittle wrote: "At the request of Senator Goldwater I have agreed to accept an appointment as chair of the Citizens Group for Goldwater and Miller."[2] Doolittle, like Joseph P. Kennedy during the Eisenhower administration, resigned to work on a presidential campaign. The next change in the membership of the board came in August 1965, when Johnson appointed three new members. On August 10, 1965, a White House press release announced the appointment of Augustus C. Long, Adm. John H. Sides, USN (Ret.), and Gen. Maxwell D. Taylor to the PFIAB.[3] Long did not accept his appointment, leaving Taylor and Sides as the only appointments to the PFIAB made during the Johnson administration.[4]

The only other modification to the board came in 1968 when Clark Clifford accepted Johnson's offer to replace Robert McNamara as secretary of defense. A February 23, 1968, White House press release announced the president's intention to appoint Taylor as Clifford's successor as chair of the PFIAB. The appointment became official when Clifford took the oath of office as secretary of defense, March 1, 1968.[5]

PFIAB staff members also remained the same; J. Patrick Coyne, who previously worked as an assistant director with the FBI, remained as the executive secretary for the PFIAB, serving in the same capacity from the Eisenhower administration through the Johnson presidency. He was assisted by Russell Ash, a National Security Council (NSC) staffer assigned to support PFIAB work.

Potential Board Members

In his memoirs, Clifford reflected on the membership of the PFIAB, suggesting that his philosophy in selecting members, which he adopted in the Kennedy administration, was to strike a balance between "generalists" and "technicians." The generalists on the board, according to Clifford, were Taylor, Doolittle, Robert Murphy, Gray, Pace, and Langer.[6] Of the technicians, Clifford wrote: "To me the most valuable members of the PFIAB, though, . . . were two brilliant scientists, Edwin Land, the inventor of the Polaroid Land camera, and William Baker, the President of Bell Labs. They were to play an immensely important, and much underappreciated, role in the development of our nation's intelligence capability."[7] Having a balanced mix of technicians, people with knowledge of the intelligence field or with a military background, and accomplished civilians appears to be the general philosophy guiding the selection of PFIAB members.

An examination of how individuals were recommended for membership on the board during the Johnson administration offers some insight into the larger question of how and why certain individuals were appointed. Both former Senate colleagues and friends of Johnson wrote memos to the White House recommending individuals for appointment to the board. The responses from White House staff and the PFIAB shed light on the characteristics Johnson and his advisers considered to be prerequisites for new members. Sometime in the spring or early summer of 1965, it appears that Clifford communicated to President Johnson that it would be advisable to appoint two new members to the board. A memorandum for Director of the White House Personnel Appointments Office John W. Macy dated June 10, 1965, indicates that Clifford thought the board needed new members and provided a general description of the type of individuals he preferred: "One ex-military man and one civilian with judgment and discretion."[8] The memo indicated that Ben Shute might be a suitable candidate for the civilian position. Shute, who was nominated by Commerce Secretary John Connor, was a lawyer with the firm Cravath, Swaine, and Moore and had served in various positions within the intelligence community, particularly with the army. He was a graduate of Bowdoin College and Harvard Law School.[9] An undated handwritten note in Macy's files appears to offer a short list of all the candidates for 1965 PFIAB appointments. The document is titled "Board of Foreign Intelligence" and contains the following names: "[John] McCloy, Ben Shute, Sidney Souers, Robert Dennison, [Augustus] Gus Long, Crawford Greenwalt."[10] Of those named on the list, only Long received an appointment to the PFIAB. The other two appointees from 1965—Taylor and Sides—were recommended to the president by close advisers or friends.

Sides was apparently chosen because of his connection to Admiral Raborn, an old friend of President Johnson and the director of central intelligence (DCI). In a July 12, 1965, memorandum to the U.S. Civil Service Commission, Macy wrote that Sides "was recommended to the President by Admiral Raborn for membership on the Foreign Intelligence Advisory Board."[11] On July 21, Macy wrote a memorandum to President Johnson recommending, with the consent of Clifford, Long and Sides for appointment to the PFIAB. Almost as an aside, Macy broached the possibility of appointing Taylor to the PFIAB to retain his services in an advisory role. At the bottom of the memo, there were spaces where Johnson could approve the Sides and Long nominations, but there was no space for Taylor. Johnson approved the nominations of both Sides and Long and added this handwritten note: "also Taylor all 3 go ahead at once."[12] It appears that the board, or at least Chair Clifford, was consulted when appointments to the PFIAB were under consideration, although it is not clear how much weight was given to the other members' views.

The facts surrounding Augustus Long's rejection of his appointment to the PFIAB add some intrigue to the story. On September 16, 1965, approximately a month after Johnson announced Long's appointment to the PFIAB, Clifford notified the president that he had just received a letter from Long declining his appointment to the board. Clifford appeared perturbed by this development and wrote: "I am at a loss to understand his attitude because he said nothing to me about his not accepting the appointment."[13] In his letter to Clifford, dated September 15, 1965, Long wrote that he did not believe he was qualified to serve in an advisory capacity in foreign intelligence because his background was in operations and administration.[14] In a September 17 memo to the president, National Security Adviser Bundy conceded that the administration had not consulted with Long before announcing his appointment.[15] Although Long denied that this had anything to do with his decision, the administration wanted to minimize the embarrassment for Johnson of having a presidential appointee reject an appointment. Bundy wrote a letter to Long on October 30 laying out a plan that would allow the president to save face, proposing that an announcement be made indicating that the president was accepting Long's resignation from the PFIAB because his personal commitments prevented him from carrying out his duties. Bundy wrote: "Both Mr. Clifford and I felt that there would be less question of any embarrassment to the President if this announcement could be a little bit delayed."[16] Bundy suggested that sometime within the next few weeks they ask Johnson aide Bill Moyers to release a routine announcement that Long had asked to be relieved from service on the board.[17] A November 6 memo from Bundy to Moyers indicates that Long agreed to the plan and asks Moyers to release a statement to the effect that Johnson had accepted Long's resignation to allow Long to focus on personal commitments.[18] Despite all the damage control done by his staff, a handwritten note on a November 11 memo indicates that Johnson decided against making any announcements.[19] Instead, he allowed the issue to fade away.

After the 1965 appointments, the Johnson administration continued to receive letters, usually from senators, recommending someone for a position on the PFIAB should one open up. In February 1966, Senator Everett Dirksen, an Illinois Republican, wrote to the White House to recommend retired Navy Reserve captain John M. Shaheen for a position on the PFIAB. In response, the White House asked PFIAB chair Clark Clifford whether Shaheen's appointment was advisable. In a March 2, 1966, memo, PFIAB executive secretary Coyne indicated that Clifford believed the board to be at full strength and did not want any new members. Coyne advised the White House to say that the board had no vacancies, even though there was no limit to how many members could serve at the same time.[20] This memo also provides a glimpse into what the PFIAB may have sought in a potential member's background. Regarding Shaheen's experience in intelligence, Coyne wrote: "We have not yet determined the extent and nature of his experience with the OSS [Office of Strategic Services]. Accordingly, we do not know at this time how well equipped he may be for service with the President's Board."[21] The White House decided to respond to Senator Dirksen by advising him that there were no vacancies on the PFIAB at the time, an excuse that it would regularly offer in the future.[22] Coyne's effort to verify Shaheen's intelligence bonafides suggests that at least some on the PFIAB thought that this was an important qualification.

Clifford's nomination to become the secretary of defense in February 1968 occasioned more letters to the Johnson administration from various senators recommending replacements. On February 16, Senator Michael Monroney, a Democrat from Oklahoma, wrote the White House to recommend Tom Finney Jr. to fill the expected vacancy. Finney was a former administrative assistant to Senator Monroney, a member of Clifford's law firm, and apparently had also spent a few years working for the CIA.[23] Finney's nomination, not surprisingly, received a favorable response from Clifford, who indicated that he would support such a nomination.[24] Unfortunately for Finney, Johnson did not make any more nominations to the PFIAB during his last year in office. Another recommendation from a senator made in February 1968 elicited a less favorable response from the White House staff. Senator Clinton Anderson, a Democrat from New Mexico, wrote the White House to propose Clint Murchison Jr., a Texas oil baron and the founder of the Dallas Cowboys football team, for the newly vacant position at the PFIAB.[25] The White House responded to the senator indicating the matter would be considered. It is unclear whether further interventions were made on behalf of Murchison, but an October 1968 memo notes Macy's decision: "I will not recommend him. He is absolutely unqualified. This is not a board to play around with."[26]

Macy's statement, along with Coyne's memo, suggests that a potential member's qualifications, particularly a background in intelligence, were important to the Johnson administration when considering potential board members. Johnson's actual appointments during his presidency, however, do not reflect this concern. Long, the former president of Texaco, had no intelligence background. Admiral Sides's naval career involved ordnance and guided missiles, not intelligence. Taylor was the only appointee who had experience in the intelligence field, having served as a military attaché in China and on Eisenhower's staff during the Second World War. In sum, personal and political connections, along with substantive professional expertise, were the primary criteria for appointment to the Johnson board.

OPERATING PROCEDURES

PFIAB Board Meetings

Detailed information about PFIAB meetings is not available for most of the Johnson presidency. There are, however, complete agendas and minutes from several PFIAB meetings. These documents offer a fairly comprehensive picture of how PFIAB meetings were conducted, what issues were discussed, and who attended. There is also general information available regarding the number and frequency of meetings during Johnson's administration.

According to a November 1968 memo from PFIAB chair Taylor to Johnson, the PFIAB held two-day meetings on alternate months. Taylor notes that during the Johnson administration the PFIAB met for a total of fifty-two days, which means they held roughly twenty-six meetings of the full board. During these meetings the board "(a) received extensive briefings from representatives of the intelligence community on significant current intelligence developments and problems; (b) reviewed and acted upon reports of the Board's Panels and reports of on-the-scene reviews made by representatives of the Board; (c) held discussions on matters of mutual interest with the Director of Central Intelligence . . . ; (d) met with high level consumers of the intelligence community's products . . . ; (e) reviewed implementation by the intelligence community of earlier Board recommendations; and (f) prepared reports to the President."[27] Clifford notes that Johnson attended fewer meetings than Kennedy, who met with the board at least twelve times during his presidency. Johnson, however, "relied as much on individual members, sending us on special missions to various parts of the world."[28] The available meeting agendas provide a more detailed picture of who attended the meetings and what they discussed.

The PFIAB met for the first time during the Johnson administration on January 30, 1964. On the agenda was a meeting with Johnson scheduled for 4:00 P.M. Clifford briefed the president on the history and accomplishments of the PFIAB up to that point. The rest of the agenda included a briefing from Deputy DCI Lt. Gen. Marshall Carter, filling in for DCI McCone, who was out of the country, a briefing from the director of the National Reconnaissance Office (NRO), and time to meet in executive session to discuss future board business.[29]

The written report of the meeting indicates that all board members were present as well as Coyne and Ash. Carter briefed the board on the subjects it had indicated were of interest through a memo sent to the DCI. These included the status of clandestine collection efforts in Cuba, analysis of the current regime in South Vietnam, the crisis in Panama, the feasibility of separating the office of the DCI and the CIA, and the U.S. counterintelligence posture.[30] On the topic of Cuba, Carter conceded that all sabotage efforts had ceased and that policymakers were scheduled to meet to consider new options. In response to a question from Doolittle, Carter stated that clandestine collection operations remained ongoing. At one point, Desmond FitzGerald, a CIA officer accompanying Carter, produced a chart illustrating the deployment of agents in Cuba.[31] Deputy Director (Plans) (DD/P) Richard Helms, who was also in attendance at this meeting, complained about the ineffectiveness of sabotage operations in Cuba. Carter went on to discuss recent riots in Panama, which the agency believed were instigated by Communist elements. Carter then turned to the recent coup in Vietnam, where Gen. Nguyen Khanh had replaced Gen. Duong Van Minh. In response to questions from the board, Carter discussed the lack of progress since the last coup had removed Diem.[32] Pages 11–24 of the report are completely redacted. The board set April 2 and 3 as the dates for the next meeting. Unfortunately, no documents are available for that meeting.

The next available agenda is for the June 4, 1964, meeting. The agenda items include an update on the National Reconnaissance Program (NRP), several different briefings on audio penetrations of the U.S. embassy in Moscow and discussion of the potential damage caused by these penetrations, current intelligence briefings on Chinese activities in Southeast Asia, the situations in South Vietnam and Cuba, a report of an on-the-scene review of the U.S. embassy in Moscow, an update on the implementation of prior board recommendations, and the regular discussion with the DCI.[33] The "memorandum for the file" indicates that the meeting was scheduled to last two days but was squeezed into one day so that a board panel meeting could be held on June 5. The entire board was present with the exception of Doolittle, who was not able to attend owing to transportation troubles. Coyne and Ash were also present.[34]

In this meeting, the PFIAB devoted considerable attention to discussing the Soviet audio penetration of the U.S. embassy in Moscow and its possible ramifications. Clifford noted that, when some of the audio cables were discovered, he requested that the State Department not cut them immediately. The response he received is revealing in that it illustrates the tensions that sometimes emerged between PFIAB and the State Department. The report reads: "Mr. Coyne said that this [keeping cables in place] was urged on the State Department but certain State Department officials thought the Board was getting into operations, and a cable went to Ambassador [Foy] Kohler instructing him to proceed and to lodge a protest with the Soviet government."[35] After discussing the Moscow penetration among themselves, the board members were joined by Robert Bannerman, the chair of the U.S. Intelligence Board (USIB) Security Committee, Louis Tordella, deputy director of the NSA, and Marvin Gentile, director of the Office of Security at the State Department. The board asked these individuals to go into detail about the technical aspects of the audio penetration of the embassy.[36] Then McCone, along with Lyman Kirkpatrick, FitzGerald, and Cord Meyers from the CIA, joined the board for the scheduled briefing. The first topic broached was Cuba, and FitzGerald again outlined the state of clandestine collections on the island. McCone made observations about Cuba and the audio penetration in Moscow.[37] He then turned to the deteriorating situation in Vietnam and concluded by complaining about the damage to the CIA that would result from the journalists David Ross and Thomas B. Wise's book *The Invisible Government,* which was soon to be released by Random House.[38]

During the meeting, Peter Jessup discussed the operating procedures for the NSC 5412 group, which considered and approved proposals for covert action operations. According to Jessup, the group approved twenty-three of thirty-nine covert action proposals that year.[39] Following Jessup's presentation, Helms updated the board on the status of covert action in Cuba and Southeast Asia. He conceded the difficulty in infiltrating North Vietnam and pointed out that the Military Advisory Command–Vietnam was now responsible for sabotage operations against the North. The board questioned Alexis Johnson of the State Department on the handling of the audio penetration in Moscow and on the 5412 group's procedures for reviewing previously approved recommendations.[40]

The next meeting for which documentation is available is that of August 6 and 7, 1964. This meeting was unusual because the first day involved a visit to the U.S. Strategic Air Command (SAC) at Offutt Air Force Base in Omaha, Nebraska. Board members flew to Offutt the night before, on military aircraft. Only Baker and Murphy could not participate in the SAC visit.[41] The agenda for the August 6 meeting indicates that the board received briefs from SAC personnel on intelligence warning, intelligence war planning, and the Soviet strategic threat. The board members left Offutt that evening and returned to Washington, DC, through Andrews Air Force Base.[42] Though a large portion of the agenda for the August 7 meeting is redacted, we know from the declassified sections that the board was scheduled to receive a current intelligence update from Ray Cline, the deputy director of intelligence (DDI), covering North and South Vietnam, Laos, Cambodia, Communist China, Cyprus, the Congo, and Cuba. The agenda also indicates that the board had requested further presentations pertaining to the audio penetration of the Moscow embassy and an update by Lt. Gen. Joseph Carroll on the Defense Intelligence Agency (DIA). DCI McCone delivered his usual brief to the board near the end of the second day of meetings.[43] The written report of the August meetings is heavily redacted; only portions of the first and twelfth pages are declassified.

Meeting agendas and minutes for an October 1 and 2, 1964, meeting are also available. The agenda for October 1 begins with a presentation by Ash on the status of major board recommendations. The board then spent the majority of the morning discussing audio surveillance collection and countermeasures, in particular focusing on the USIB's final assessment of audio penetrations of the Moscow embassy. After lunch, the board received presentations on the Gulf of Tonkin incident of September 18. It showed particular interest in intelligence community capabilities during crisis situations. It heard briefings from the director of DIA, the director of the State Department's Bureau of Intelligence and Research, and a senior official from the CIA's current intelligence staff concerning early warning and crisis situation capabilities.[44] The agenda for the second day began with an intelligence briefing covering Vietnam and Southeast Asia, Indonesia, Cyprus, the Congo, and Cuba. Other agenda topics are redacted except the end-of-the-day discussion with McCone.[45]

The written report of the meetings indicates that all the members were present except for Murphy, who was in Brazil (whether he went on PFIAB business is unclear). Doolittle was not present because he had resigned his position after the August meetings.[46] Clifford began the meeting by informing the members that time was set aside on the agenda so that they could raise issues that were of personal interest or concern. Clifford also provided insight about what the president thought about the usefulness of the PFIAB. According to the report of the meeting: "Mr. Clifford pointed out to the Board that, unlike President Kennedy who had reconstituted the Board in 1961 and was thoroughly familiar with its functioning, President Johnson has not been as intimately associated with the Board, primarily for the reason that no intelligence-related incidents have thus far arisen in President Johnson's term to evidence his special need for the Board's assistance."[47] Clifford noted that he mentioned the board and its functions to Johnson whenever he had the opportunity. Regarding the president's views about how the PFIAB should operate, the report continues: "For the time being the President prefers a quiet, unostentatious operation of the Board. It is the President's desire to try to avoid any explosions in the intelligence field, and any resignations in heat by any members of the intelligence community."[48]

During meetings with Helms and State Department officials, possible short-term solutions to the audio surveillance problem in Moscow were discussed. In response, Baker and Land informed these officials that there were particular paints and plasters available that could serve as barriers to electronic surveillance and, thus, should be considered for use. Board members also asked whether anyone in the bureaucracy had considered requesting permission from the Soviet government to build a new embassy under U.S. supervision. Helms indicated that the USIB was considering this but that there was a bureaucratic disagreement over which agency should lead this effort.[49] DCI McCone discussed the Gulf of Tonkin incident with board members. He was particularly concerned with channels for reporting incidents not being properly utilized. He noted that some raw traffic regarding the Tonkin incident was not immediately relayed to the appropriate CIA office for analysis, adding that he had already instituted measures to correct this. He also complained that policymakers had improperly based decisions on raw intelligence before the information could be analyzed and placed in context.[50] Continuing the discussion of the routing and analysis of raw intelligence during the Tonkin incident, the written report highlights the broad responsibilities of the PFIAB's executive secretary. Following up on the board's discussion, it indicates that "Mr. Coyne thereupon spent two days at NSA observing the work of NSA officials in reviewing and summarizing the messages which had come in from NSA field collection points, and the operational U.S. Navy messages to the extent that they had been made available to NSA."[51]

At the September 23–24, 1965, meeting, the PFIAB planned to hear briefings from DDI Cline on intelligence situations in Vietnam, India and Pakistan, Indonesia, Malaysia and Singapore, Cuba, and the Dominican Republic. DD/P FitzGerald was scheduled for a presentation, but his topic is redacted. Dr. Albert Wheelon, a representative from the newly created deputy directorate of science and technology, gave a presentation on the implementation of board recommendations for strengthening scientific and technical capabilities at the CIA. The board closed its meeting on September 24 with a discussion of a recurrent concern: the role of the DCI.[52]

An agenda is available for a meeting on November 22, 1965, that focused on Southeast Asia. Clifford delivered the highlights of a Southeast Asia review, and Taylor delivered the findings of various panel studies with respect to Vietnam and Southeast Asia issues. High-ranking representatives from the DIA, the White House, the NSA, the State Department's Bureau of Intelligence and Research, the Joint Chiefs of Staff (JCS), and the State Department also addressed this subject. DCI Raborn gave the CIA's assessment and recommendations concerning "Chicom—Vietnam—Southeast Asia Problems."[53]

Although there are no available declassified agendas for PFIAB meetings in 1966, there are many references to PFIAB meetings scattered in declassified CIA documents. On January 25, 1966, the DCI was scheduled to discuss major problems affecting the coordination of the U.S. foreign intelligence effort, including audio surveillance measures and resource management.[54] He also discussed the issue of China and the need for a specialist at the CIA to coordinate the intelligence effort on that country.[55] On May 27, 1966, CIA representatives were scheduled to brief the board in response to public revelations of the CIA's collaboration with Michigan State and other universities for intelligence purposes, along with new proposals for the safeguarding of intelligence sources and methods.[56] The DCI met with the board on July 29, 1966, to discuss the procedures for producing the national intelligence estimates.[57] On September 29, 1966, the DCI discussed with the PFIAB gaps in the coverage of intelligence related to State Department and Department of Defense (DOD) areas of interest, possible revisions of NSC intelligence directives relating to intelligence budgets, the possibility of a new letter of authority from the president to the DCI, and the DCI's objections to providing regular briefings to a subcommittee of the Senate Committee on Foreign Relations (the DCI had no issues with briefing the whole committee occasionally).[58]

A December 5, 1966, memo indicates that the president approved a request from Clifford to meet with the board on February 3, 1967. The board apparently was scheduled to meet on February 2 and 3, 1967. The memo described the president's possible role in the meeting as follows: "Clark envisaged brief (3-minute) presentations of five or six key subjects, with you having an opportunity to question, probe, and comment."[59] A very brief summary of the proposed topics for discussion included intelligence gaps and deficiencies, intelligence efforts in Vietnam and China, the NRP, improving the processing of intelligence, and counterespionage.[60] At this meeting, the board also requested DCI Helms to speak on lessons learned from the Czechoslovakian crisis and how it reflected on the effectiveness of the USIB's watch committee in assuring "the earliest possible intelligence warning of, and a continuing judgment on, Sino-Soviet intentions to engage in aggressive action by regular or irregular armed forces."[61] The board also wanted to hear about intelligence contingency plans for South Vietnam and the impact of "arms limitations agreements on the safeguarding of advanced U.S. intelligence systems."[62]

CIA records contain a proposed agenda for the board's February 15–16, 1968, meeting. On February 15, the board planned to examine developments related to Vietnam, Cambodia, Korea, and the disposition of the OXCART reconnaissance plane. On February 16, the board examined China and the Soviet presence in the Middle East with presentations from the State Department, DOD, and the DIA.[63] A February 23, 1968, memo mentions this meeting as well and also the fact that the board discussed intelligence failures "at the time of the attack on the South Vietnamese cities."[64] The board did eventually examine intelligence issues surrounding the Tet Offensive in January 1968 and produced a full report with recommendations on the issue.

In March 1968, the PFIAB received an NSA briefing on communications intelligence (COMINT) tracking Vietcong personnel and supplies infiltrating South Vietnam. The board also heard NSA representatives' thoughts as to how to improve COMINT.[65]

CIA archives also contain notes summarizing the DCI's April 12, 1968, meeting with the board, in which he discussed the difficulty of finding enough reconnaissance aircraft for operations in Vietnam, the reduction of overseas intelligence personnel, information handling, OXCART, and CIA recruiting. The board concluded that information-handling projects were progressing well in all agencies but the State Department.[66] CIA records also contain notes on the August 9, 1968, DCI meeting with the board, which included an overview and introduction to the National Intelligence Resources Board (which was designed to advise the director on expensive and important elements of intelligence programs), intelligence support for the Paris peace negotiations, the methods of disseminating CIA reports and raw intelligence (particularly the difference between appraisals and situation reports), an Appropriations Committee report on the DIA, and surveillance of North Vietnam (which was found to be severely lacking).[67]

One April 1968 memo mentions that the board planned to review the activities of the 303 Committee (the committee that replaced the NSC 5412/2 "Special Group" in overseeing covert operations) at the board meeting of June 6–7, 1968. This review apparently took place, as the PFIAB's final report to Johnson included recommendations on the 303 Committee.[68]

The Johnson Presidential Library archives contain several documents making reference to PFIAB meetings in 1968. For example, an October 8, 1968, letter from PFIAB chair Taylor to Secretary of Defense Clifford mentions a PFIAB meeting that occurred on October 3–4, 1968, at which the board discussed a proposal to establish "an interagency mechanism for the preparation of comparative evaluations of the strategic military offensive and defensive capabilities of the United States and the USSR."[69]

Panels and On-Site Reviews

Like the Kennedy PFIAB, the Johnson board used panels composed of board members, outside consultants, and the executive secretary to examine a wide variety of issues. There were panels devoted to scientific or technical issues in intelligence, the organization and management of the intelligence community, counterintelligence concerns within the government, and various regions of the world. Documents from the June 4, 1964, board meeting illustrate how panels were used within the board. In a memorandum from Coyne to the members of the PFIAB regarding audio penetration of the embassy in Moscow, Coyne mentions the Baker Panel, which examined the technical aspects of the Moscow penetration. This panel included several distinguished members: William Baker; Edward E. David and J. R. Pierce from Bell Telephone Laboratories; Andrew M. Gleason, Department of Mathematics, Harvard University; and John W. Tukey, Department of Mathematics, Princeton University.[70] It is possible that this particular panel was an ad hoc grouping formed to study a specific issue, inasmuch as Baker was the only PFIAB member on it. The board also had a related Communications Panel, though its members are unknown.[71] The Covert Action/Special Group Panel consisted of Robert Gray and Langer. It held a meeting on June 5, 1964, attended by the panel members as well as Doolittle, Coyne, Ash, Jessup from the NSC 5412 Group, Helms and Meyer of the CIA, and Alexis Johnson of the State Department.[72]

The Johnson PFIAB also had panels for inter-American affairs (Murphy and Sides), Near Eastern and South Asian affairs (Langer and Taylor), African affairs (Langer and Gray), East Asian and Pacific affairs (Taylor and Baker), and European affairs (Langer and Land).[73] The panels were apparently chosen to coincide with the geographic bureaus of the State Department and five interdepartmental working groups.[74] The CIA (and, presumably, other intelligence agencies) prepared reports and presentations specifically for the various area panels, as evidenced by an October 28, 1966, memorandum for the record on CIA presentations.[75]

Taylor highlighted the importance of on-the-scene reviews, a practice common to both the Kennedy and the Johnson boards. Individual board members, accompanied by the executive secretary, traveled to U.S. intelligence posts around the world to conduct interviews and gauge the effectiveness of particular intelligence operations. While overseas, board members often met with the U.S. ambassador, the heads of the political and economic sections, CIA station chiefs, defense attachés, and other officials. During the Johnson administration, overseas reviews were conducted in Southeast Asia, the Far East, Western Europe, the Middle East, and Latin America.[76] For instance, in October 1965, Clifford and Coyne visited Japan, Taiwan, Hong Kong, and Vietnam to review "significant foreign intelligence and related activities."[77] Clifford indicated that they intended to primarily review activities directed at North Vietnam, the Vietcong, and Communist China.

Meetings with the President

There are only a few confirmed instances of Johnson meeting with the full board. PFIAB members' interactions with the president, however, were not restricted to official meetings. For instance, Clifford frequently met with him on an individual basis to discuss matters related to intelligence and other domestic issues. In January 1966, for example, after a meeting with DDI Cline, Clifford conveyed to the president the message that DCI Raborn was undermining morale at the CIA. This intervention reportedly led directly to Raborn's "resignation" later that spring.[78]

Interaction with Other Groups

The Johnson PFIAB usually submitted official reports and communications through the special assistant to the president for national security affairs (commonly referred to as the national security adviser). Both Bundy and Walt Rostow served as intermediaries between the board and the bureaucracy. Generally, if the president approved the board's recommendations, the national security adviser sent out action memos to the relevant agencies. This, however, was not always the case. For instance, Clifford submitted the PFIAB report on the September 18, 1964, Gulf of Tonkin incident as a memorandum to President Johnson.[79] Clifford's role as a personal adviser to the president on a wide range of issues allowed him to broach topics directly with Johnson.

Since members served on a part-time basis, Executive Secretary Coyne worked full-time on PFIAB agenda items and was the primary liaison with the rest of the bureaucracy and the White House. All evidence suggests that he had substantial responsibility for the board's activities.

The PFIAB also maintained a close relationship with key officials of the intelligence community, primarily through its meetings. The DCI and high-level officials from the NSA, the DIA, the State Department, and the CIA were frequent participants in them.

The CIA's Annual Reports to the Board

To fulfill its mission, the PFIAB depended on receiving accurate and complete information from intelligence agencies. In addition to presentations by the DCI and other representatives at the regular meetings, the CIA submitted reports to the board every year to which each department and directorate contributed. These included information on the progress of various research and other types of projects, identified deficiencies and problems, and in general gave the board a comprehensive status report on the activities of the organization.

ISSUES AND RECOMMENDATIONS

Chair Taylor's 1968 report to President Johnson highlighting the achievements of the PFIAB since its reestablishment in 1961 provides a fairly complete list of the subjects the PFIAB examined on behalf of the president. These issues ranged from broad topics such as the proper role for the DCI as leader of the intelligence community to more narrow and focused analyses of intelligence community responses to specific crisis situations.

Taylor mentioned that the PFIAB studied the performance of the intelligence community during the 1964 Gulf of Tonkin incident, investigated the June 1967 Israeli attack on the USS *Liberty* and the North Korean capture of the USS *Pueblo* in January 1968, assessed the quality of intelligence leading up to the Tet Offensive in January 1968, weighed measures to prevent U.S. combat aircraft operating in North Vietnam from straying into Chinese airspace, tested the quality of intelligence of the August 1968 Soviet invasion of Czechoslovakia, and assessed intelligence programs tracking Soviet and Chinese developments in science and technology.[80]

Taylor drew attention to board recommendations that had been acted on by the president and resulted in improved operation of the intelligence community. As an example of these positive steps, he cited the creation of the directorate of science and technology within the CIA and the establishment of the defense attaché system in 1964.

Referring to intelligence-information-handling procedures, Taylor wrote: "In response to a series of reports and recommendations by the Board, combined action has been initiated by the member agencies of the intelligence community toward the planning, development and ultimate establishment of a computer-assisted, community-wide system for the management, storage and retrieval of the vast quantity of intelligence information which is collected, processed, analyzed and reported by these agencies on a continuing basis."[81] In addition to Taylor's 1968 report, documents from the Johnson Presidential Library provide windows into many of the issues the PFIAB considered and the recommendations that resulted from its studies. Only a few of the actual reports submitted to the president have been declassified, although a review of declassified memos and correspondence reveals many of the other issues and recommendations the PFIAB discussed.

Counterintelligence and the Dunlap Spy Case

Although Kennedy's board was asked to examine the Dunlap case, the PFIAB and the intelligence community continued to consider the matter after the president's death. A February 8, 1964, memo to the secretaries of state and defense, the attorney general, and the chair of the USIB covering the Kennedy PFIAB's final report states: "The enclosed report of November 22, 1963 contains findings and recommendations of the President's Foreign Intelligence Advisory Board based on the detailed review which the board had completed, at President Kennedy's request, concerning the Soviet espionage penetration of the National Security Agency involving Army Sergeant Jack E. Dunlap."[82] The board's twenty-one recommendations were assigned to the agencies they affected for study and implementation.

We could find only a partial list of these recommendations.[83]

Recommendation 4. "That, within each sensitive agency where the practice is not now being followed: (a) strict personnel security standards, including standards of personal conduct, be applied to all personnel having access to sensitive information or sensitive operations; (b) that these standards be applied equally to civilian and military personnel regardless of rank; and (c) that serious questions of doubt concerning personnel having such access be resolved in favor of the national security."

Recommendation 6. "That, as a means of achieving major counter-intelligence objectives, actions be taken within the sensitive agencies, as required, to assure the conduct of periodic, comprehensive, inspections concerning the adequacy of compliance with approved policies relating to personnel security investigations and clearances, security suspension of employees, physical security, document control, and the like."

Recommendation 8. "That arrangements be made within each sensitive agency, as required, to assure that security counterintelligence-oriented personnel participate in the timely review at the Headquarters level of all questionable security cases which develop within that agency."

Recommendation 9. "That, in the continuing effort to instill an enhanced sense of security responsibility on the part of all personnel in the sensitive agencies, the Dunlap case be used in the security indoctrination processes of those agencies as a striking example of a most serious espionage penetration and of the failure to inculcate the degree of security consciousness which should obtain among the personnel of all sensitive agencies."

Recommendation 10. "That investigative and security-review personnel associated with sensitive activities be provided with more sophisticated and professional information and guidance concerning the nature and potential security implications of abnormal sexual activities, such as homosexuality and perversion, which they encounter in the course of their inquiries and interviews."

Recommendation 11. "That consideration be given by the several agencies concerned to the establishment of an interdepartmental counterintelligence mechanism for the purpose of assuring (a) the promulgation of adequate counterintelligence policy and guidance to all agencies concerned; (b) timely and carefully controlled exchange of all counterintelligence-related information (other than that of a strictly operational nature), including information on approaches made by hostile intelligence services to U.S. personnel; and (c) effective coordination of our counterintelligence effort, including the allocation and use of our counterintelligence and investigative resources."

Recommendation 12. "That, apart from any action taken on the preceding recommendation concerning the establishment of a counter-intelligence mechanism, immediate action be taken to assure that any agency having action responsibility in a personnel-security type case is promptly furnished all pertinent information possessed by other departments and agencies."

Recommendation 13. "That the National Security Agency, and other sensitive agencies as appropriate, take steps to assure that the 'need-to-know' principle is applied rigorously in the granting of access to sensitive information."

Recommendation 16. "That our Government take steps so that the Soviet Government is not finally allowed to proceed with the establishment of a new embassy in the Washington area until our Government satisfies itself that we will be allowed to proceed with the establishment of generally comparable embassy facilities in the Moscow area."

Recommendation 17. "That wherever feasible, a policy of reciprocal arrangements be pursued by our Government in an effort to correct the serious imbalance in the numbers of official U.S. Government personnel permitted to be assigned in Soviet bloc countries, and the numbers of Soviet bloc official personnel authorized to be associated with bloc diplomatic establishments in the United States."

Recommendation 21. "The White House be informed promptly of developing situations indicating the existence of a serious penetration of any sensitive activity of our Government."

The impact of these recommendations can be gauged from a March 10, 1964, response from the deputy secretary of defense, the deputy secretary of state, and the acting DCI. The DOD, which was tasked with responding to Recommendations 1, 2, 3, and 5, reported that it had already adopted Recommendation 1: "That the National Security Agency be given the complete personnel security responsibility for all personnel employed by and assigned to it."[84] Recommendation 2 advised that all efforts be made to pass House Resolution 950, designed to give the NSA maximum personnel security.[85] The memo does not report the substance of Recommendation 3, but Recommendation 5 advised reinvestigating all previously cleared personnel, especially "questionable" security cases.[86] Deputy Secretary of Defense Cyrus Vance also reported successful implementation of Resolutions 2 and 5 and noted that the department concurred with Resolution 3 but had yet to complete the measures it prescribed. On April 24, Bundy sent another memo that consolidated the responses of the agencies to the board's twenty-one recommendations.[87]

The State Department concurred with Recommendations 4, 6, 8, 9, 10, 12, and 21. It did not concur with Recommendations 16 and 17. Acting Secretary of State Ball's memorandum also contained some cryptic discussions of the redacted Recommendations 14 and 15 that indicate that they dealt with the relationship between the CIA station and the U.S. ambassador in the context of covert operations overseas.[88] Carter responded the next day in his capacity as acting DCI and acting chair of the USIB and on behalf of both the CIA and the State Department. In those capacities, he concurred with Recommendations 4, 6, 8, 9, 10, 12, 13, and 21. He provided an "interim response" to Recommendation 11, observing that the CIA "firmly believes that existing organs of counterintelligence and security coordination, and the utilization of bilateral channels for case work are adequate and are achieving the purposes outlined in the Recommendation," but noting disagreement among other parts of the intelligence community and the fact that the FBI had not yet weighed in. He deferred to the State Department position on Recommendations 16 and 17.[89]

The board also considered counterintelligence issues in agencies beyond the NSA. In 1965, the CIA Office of Security implemented two PFIAB recommendations, specifically "the establishment of a uniform glossary of terms as applicable in personnel security matters concerning homosexuality and perversion; and procedures for exchanging pertinent security cases for use in security indoctrination."[90] A January 31, 1967, memorandum from Coyne to Rostow mentions that the board received annual reports on "U.S. intelligence agencies' efforts to enhance the Government's counterintelligence posture."[91] The USIB's Security Committee, a group made up of CIA, State Department, DIA, military intelligence organizations', and NSA representatives, prepared these reports. Coyne's memorandum approved of the integrated approach to counterintelligence that the agencies were employing. He also attached a suggested memorandum for Rostow to sign and send to the DCI that would signal Rostow's "continuing interest in their (the agencies) efforts."[92]

The National Signals Intelligence Program

In January 1964, the PFIAB examined the National Signals Intelligence Program and submitted five recommendations.[93] The president approved four of them.[94] Although the report and the corresponding recommendations are unavailable, an unsigned memorandum from the office of the deputy secretary of defense indicated that the board's recommendations could be boiled down to three basic elements: "to make more efficient and responsive the ongoing efforts in the signals intelligence and security field, to make certain we provide the fully adequate management and development of capabilities to handle future problems . . . and to remedy some deficiencies noted by the Board and by other authoritative advisory groups in the past."[95] These recommendations closely coincided with the recommendations given in the waning days of the Kennedy administration. The unsigned memo consisted primarily of the DOD's comment on the recommendations of the board and describes the DOD's efforts to evaluate and improve its signals intelligence programs. The memo was submitted in response to Bundy's request that both the secretary of defense and the chair of the USIB submit their views on the PFIAB's report and recommendations.

Secure Rooms at Overseas Installations and the Moscow Embassy Bugging

The PFIAB first recommended installing secure rooms in embassies and other overseas installations to prevent audio surveillance in 1962.[96] It continued to revisit this issue throughout the Johnson administration. Several memoranda in the archives reference semiregular reports on the progress made by the CIA and the Department of State on installing these facilities. Between July 10, 1965, and December 28, 1966, for instance, the CIA and the State Department submitted four reports on the matter to the PFIAB.[97] The DOD also submitted reports and memorandums on the issue. By December 1965, the DCI was reporting that secure rooms of two types (acoustically shielded conference rooms and electronically shielded communications rooms) had been installed in several posts, indicating that the PFIAB's efforts were paying off.[98]

Though the PFIAB had recommended installing secure rooms in 1962, the bugging of the Moscow embassy underscored the urgency of having secure communications in embassies. In the spring of 1964, State Department security officers found thirty-six microphones in the walls of the Moscow embassy, covering key offices such as that of the ambassador, the deputy chief of mission, army communications and code centers, embassy conference rooms, defense attachés' offices, and political and economic offices. Bugs were also discovered in residences, and one hundred pairs of wires were found running from the embassy toward apartment blocks. Coaxial cables exiting the embassy indicated that the Soviets had installed more sophisticated listening devices as well.[99] The PFIAB was so concerned by the Moscow embassy bugging that it "assembled a panel of scientific experts who are looking into all technical aspects of this development, including implications for the security of our coded communications."[100] Additionally, the board intended to review the issue and submit a full report to the assistant for national security affairs.[101]

Although the report itself is unavailable in archival sources, we found some evidence about what aspects of the bugging the PFIAB studied. In addition to the scientific panel, the board sought a damage assessment from the Department of State that included information on sweeping procedures for the embassy, the sort of detection equipment used in such sweeps, the results of previous sweeping operations, the types of encryption systems the embassy used, the possibility that coded messages or encryption systems were compromised, and the effect of the penetration of positive intelligence collections.[102] In the wake of this incident, the entire intelligence community gave higher priority to developing audio surveillance countermeasures.

The NRP

The PFIAB undertook a major study of the nation's reconnaissance capabilities, which the board members believed were in need of improvement. The study was, according to a subsequent report, carried out by a special panel of the PFIAB with the assistance of the executive secretary. The May 2, 1964, report concluded: "Basically, the problem is one of inadequacies in the present organizational structure and support of the national reconnaissance effort."[103] In the board's view, the NRP was plagued by an unclear division of responsibility for oversight among the participating elements of the intelligence community. The board recommended that primary responsibility for oversight of the NRP should rest with the new NRO, part of the DOD. However, it also encouraged the CIA to invest $10 million in a new post-CORONA satellite imaging system with wider area and greater resolution capabilities.[104]

In addition, the board recommended that the president issue a directive to provide guidelines for the centralized direction of the NRP. It suggested the following guidelines:[105]

- That the NRP be defined as a single program for the "collection of intelligence, mapping, and geodetic information through over-flights."
- That the secretary of defense be designated as "executive agent" of the NRP.

- That the NRO be established within the DOD with its own director responsible to the secretary of defense.
- That the DCI, as chair of the USIB, be assigned to sharpen and expedite the USIB with respect to establishing "realistic intelligence collection requirements to guide the national reconnaissance effort," "ensuring prompt processing, analysis, and reporting" to users of reconnaissance information, and guaranteeing "the fullest utilization of such intelligence in the preparation of national intelligence estimates."
- That there be a coordinated and comprehensive budget for the NRP, with the secretary of defense, the DCI, and the director of the budget jointly reviewing the matter.
- That the heads of the DOD, CIA, and other agencies use the resources of various agencies to conduct research projects designed to develop improved reconnaissance technology.
- That the CIA provide the executive agent of the NRP with policy guidance for a uniform security system procedure.
- That, instead of the "monitor and review" system then in place for the program, the executive agent report to the special assistant for national security affairs and the PFIAB on the program periodically.
- That the director of the NRO establish a Scientific Advisory Board to provide advice related to reconnaissance objectives.

The board further added the following additional recommendations in the event the president approved the previous recommendations:

- Collaboration between the secretary of defense and the DCI to evaluate reconnaissance programs and systems and ensure that resources were properly used to meet reconnaissance needs.
- "Continued designation of the Under Secretary of the Air Force as Director of the National Reconnaissance Office."
- That the DOD and the CIA contribute personnel to staff the NRO and perform required functions.
- That the secretary of defense have the authority to issue directives to the DOD and to make requests of the CIA and other agencies to enable the operations of the NRP.
- That the DOD (Air Force) assume responsibility for "management, over-all systems engineering, procurement, and operation of all satellite reconnaissance systems."

- "Elimination of the interagency Configuration Control Board as a decision making entity within the satellite reconnaissance program."
- That the CIA continue to maintain responsibility for the OXCART program, and that the NSC 5412/2 Group oversee the operational use of advanced aircraft following the developmental stage.
- That the A-11, R-12, and TAGBOARD projects continue under the current management arrangements.

The PFIAB's May 2, 1964, report on the NRP elicited differing responses from members of the intelligence community. Indeed, several recommendations ignited a bureaucratic battle over the NRP, particularly the assignment of satellite systems to the air force. This recommendation caused the DCI to protest the diminished research-and-development role of the CIA in future reconnaissance programs. The DCI's lengthy response to the PFIAB's report claimed: "If these proposals are adopted, I do not believe that it will be possible to discharge the responsibilities which the report itself envisages for the Director of Central Intelligence or that the Central Intelligence Agency can perform the mission which the report apparently contemplates for the Agency."[106] In contrast to the board's vision, the DCI supported an organizational structure that emphasized the joint responsibilities of the CIA and the DOD in the NRP. Not surprisingly, the DOD agreed with the recommendations put forth in the PFIAB study.[107]

The bureaucratic battle to settle the issues presented in the PFIAB report continued for more than a year. The CIA had powerful allies on the NSC, including Spurgeon Keeny, who held a joint appointment on the NSC and as the technical assistant to the president's science adviser. Keeny supported the DCI position because he believed it would be harmful to place so much authority and responsibility in the hands of the air force.[108] Peter Jessup, an NSC staffer who served on the Special Group 5412, also wrote a memo to Bundy opposing those aspects of the PFIAB's recommendations that weakened the CIA. Final agreement on the NRO came in August 1965. As Jeffrey Richelson notes: "The agreement assigned responsibilities to the Secretary of Defense, DCI, and NRO, as well as formally establishing a National Reconnaissance Program Executive Committee."[109] The August 13, 1965, agreement conceded more authority to the DCI than the PFIAB recommended. As a result of the compromise, the NRO director lost a considerable amount of independence.[110]

Vietnam

As might be expected, the board regularly examined intelligence issues relating to Vietnam during Johnson's administration. Some incidents and issues related to Vietnam merited their own reports, but the board examined general issues relating to Vietnam and the war as well.

The September 18, 1964, Gulf of Tonkin Incident

Following an incident in the Gulf of Tonkin on September 18, 1964 (similar to the incident of August 4, in which U.S. destroyers fired on targets detected by radar), the PFIAB conducted a review of the intelligence aspects of the incident. It drafted a special study of the incident for President Johnson, submitting a brief report, in the form of a memorandum, that has been released in full. Bundy, the national security affairs adviser, forwarded the report to the DCI as chair of the USIB and to the secretary of defense for their consideration. The board identified a "need for re-examination of the doctrine and procedures which presently govern the intelligence coverage, reporting, and evaluations of crisis developments involving actual or threatened engagements of U.S. military forces in limited, tactical-warfare situations."[111] The report noted that policymakers (including the president) did not receive "collective evaluations" of intelligence obtained from North Vietnamese intercepts and that they were, thus, forced to rely on "unilateral and, at times, conflicting judgments" of individual analysts and other officials.[112] Finally, the PFIAB mentioned that important encoded North Vietnamese messages were not immediately transmitted to NSA headquarters, which delayed "prompt and accurate" decoding.[113]

The PFIAB submitted two recommendations in connection with this report.

> 1. The Director of Central Intelligence, as Chairman of the United States Intelligence Board: (a) conduct a study of the intelligence related responsibilities and functioning of U.S. agencies in the Gulf of Tonkin incident, and (b) submit to the President a report and recommendations on the desirability of establishing within the intelligence community a central evaluation mechanism having the specific responsibility of furnishing the President and other top officials with timely, interagency evaluations of current intelligence with respect to developing crisis situations such as the Gulf of Tonkin incident (perhaps using

the intelligence community's Watch Committee and National Security Indications Center for this purpose); and that

2. The Director of the National Security Agency: (a) conduct a review of the signals intelligence collection and reporting aspects of the Tonkin Gulf Incident, and (b) furnish the President a report and recommendations designed to insure timely transmission to National Security Agency Headquarters of the complete encoded text of intercepted messages which on preliminary analysis in the field appear to contain indications of possible hostile actions having a significant bearing on the national defense and security of the United States.[114]

Vietnam Site Review and General Vietnamese Issues

Clifford traveled to Vietnam in October 1965 in his capacity as PFIAB chair to explore several intelligence-related issues. He wrote to President Johnson on November 1, 1965, informing him that he had just returned from his twelve-day trip. In the letter, he noted that the president needed improved intelligence reporting on the Vietcong, the Hanoi leadership, and Chinese intentions. He also indicated that, after he reported his findings to the entire board, it would submit a report with recommendations for presidential approval.[115]

A January 4, 1966, memo from Bundy to the secretary of state, the secretary of defense, and the DCI references a report submitted by the PFIAB to the president in December 1965 and based on an on-the-scene review of the intelligence situation in Vietnam. This report is most likely the result of Clifford's October trip to Vietnam. According to the memo: "The President has approved the Board's recommendations and asks that priority actions be taken to implement them."[116] The memo indicates that the PFIAB's report contained sixteen recommendations. Bundy assigned action responsibility for the recommendations to the agency he believed was best suited to take appropriate action to facilitate implementation. For example, the DCI was assigned responsibility for undertaking Recommendations 3, 4, 5, 8, and 14. Bundy also requested that each agency submit a status report to his office and the PFIAB by February 15, 1966.[117] A March 2, 1967, memorandum from Coyne to Rostow indicates that the agencies involved submitted several status reports regarding these recommendations, with the CIA, the State Department, and the DOD submitting additional reports in February 1967.[118]

While the original PFIAB report and its recommendations are not available, these documents note that a report was submitted, that the recommendations were approved by the president, and that the intelligence community was tasked with implementing the recommendations and reporting the status of its efforts. In his memoir, Clifford makes reference to this mission but laments that his recommendations did not have much effect.[119] It would seem that Clifford was encroaching on the operational authorities and responsibilities of the secretary of state, the secretary of defense, and the DCI during his trip to Vietnam, and this might explain why his recommendations ultimately had little effect.

The on-site review did not constitute Clifford's only engagement with Vietnam-related issues. In November 1967, Clifford responded to an unavailable November 1, 1967, memorandum about Vietnam. Rostow submitted Clifford's response to the president on November 7, 1967.[120] In his memo, Clifford disagreed with the recommendations presented in the original November 1 memorandum. He expressed his conviction that the North Vietnamese continued to resist in a war they had "no chance of winning" because they were "depending upon a weakening of the will of the United States."[121] He strongly objected to a recommendation to stop bombing in North Vietnam and considered it a show of weakness.[122] He further objected to any attempts to "stabilize" the U.S. military presence in the South by announcing that the United States would not increase forces, call up reserves, expand action in North Vietnam, and engage in restricted war.[123] He concluded his memo by calling for a renewed commitment and show of resolve to win the war in Vietnam.

Clifford's site review of the intelligence situation in Vietnam did not constitute the board's only examination of intelligence issues in that country and the rest of Southeast Asia and the Far East. As might be expected, the PFIAB spent a significant amount of time examining issues related to Vietnam and the broader region throughout the Johnson administration. Several memoranda and other correspondence indicate its interest in the region. For example, a September 28, 1966, memo from Rostow to the secretary of state, the secretary of defense, and the DCI directed the various agencies to submit status reports regarding the implementation of various recommendations the board made about intelligence-related activities in Southeast Asia and the Far East.[124] These recommendations, which are unavailable, came from Clifford's October 1965 on-site review. A memorandum of June 9, 1966, indicates that the board submitted its report on December 9, 1965, and that the president approved the recommendations.[125]

1966 Chinese MIG 17 Incident

In 1966, Johnson requested that Clifford, as chair of the PFIAB, submit a report on a claim that U.S. aircraft operating in the Vietnam theater downed a Chinese MIG 17 fighter in Chinese airspace. In response, Clifford undertook a special study of the issue. In a May 20, 1966, memo, submitted on PFIAB letterhead, he reported that he had reviewed the intelligence and operational messages concerning the incident and that there was not enough information available to reach a definitive conclusion, but he recommended that the JCS send an investigative team to the area to conduct interviews and collect more information. He noted that he would submit another report after he reviewed the information obtained by the investigative team.[126]

The report itself, which Clifford forwarded to the president on June 3, 1966, reached a number of conclusions. It confirmed that Chinese MIG 17s attacked a U.S. air mission consisting of an RB 66 and three F-4C aircraft. The RB 66 was engaged in a reconnaissance mission involving "electronics countermeasures and electronics intelligence" over North Vietnam, and the F-4Cs provided protection for the mission.[127] Clifford concluded that the American aircraft had, indeed, penetrated Chinese airspace (a penetration of less than twenty-five nautical miles) and that the unplanned penetration arose as a result of navigational errors and a failure of "border warning" systems.[128] When the Chinese MIGs attacked the mission, an F-4C shot down one of the MIGs. Clifford reported that most likely the MIG fell on the North Vietnamese side of the border, although he did not establish this fact definitively.

The report also dealt with the conflicting information that came out in the days following the incident. Clifford stated that the situation arose as a result of "the absence of adequate operational data which should have been at hand" and "the tendency on the part of some evaluators in Washington to place undue dependence on the statements of U.S. operational personnel, while discounting unduly signals intelligence data derived from Chicom/NVN [Chinese Communist/North Vietnamese] tracking of the aircraft involved in the event."[129]

To reduce the likelihood of such an event occurring again, Clifford submitted two recommendations with his report. These recommendations apparently were submitted simultaneously with those of the JCS investigative team. Clifford recommended that

1. The Department of Defense establish an effective system for positive flight-following of U.S. aircraft operation over NVN

and the Tonkin Gulf, in order to (a) minimize the possibility of navigational errors, and (b) reduce significantly the probability of border violence. In achieving an effective system the Department of Defense should consider the remedial actions recommended by the JCS investigative team.

2. Following establishment of such a system, the Defense Intelligence Agency and the National Military Command Center should jointly review and report periodically to the Joint Chiefs of Staff on the effectiveness of the means established for the purpose of providing timely information and evaluations to policy levels concerning military intelligence/combat operations of the type involved in the May 12 incident.[130]

A June 7, 1966, cover memo from Rostow to Johnson indicated that Clifford's final report on the MIG incident was submitted with the memo. Rostow noted: "Clifford's exhaustive review of the incident has been of real value and already has resulted in tightening up existing procedures."[131] Interestingly, Rostow mentioned that Clifford felt strongly that he should not be named as the source of the report or its recommendations. In a June 11, 1966, memo to Secretary of Defense McNamara, Rostow forwarded Clifford's report but identified the author only as "a White House Staff member."[132] It is not clear what prompted Clifford to make this request. One possibility is that, given the negative reaction to his Vietnam report, he was concerned that the secretaries of state and defense and the DCI would tend to discount the report if he was associated with it.

Evaluation of U.S. Intelligence during the Tet Offensive

Following the Tet Offensive in January 1968, the PFIAB undertook a review of the alleged "intelligence failure" surrounding the major coordinated attacks on South Vietnamese cities during the Vietnamese holiday period. The resulting report would be one of the PFIAB's "special studies." By its own report, the board sought to determine "whether adequate intelligence indicators had been available to serve as warnings," "whether these warnings reached the proper officials in time," and "what lessons bearing on intelligence might be learned from the experience."[133] In the course of preparing this report, the board received briefings from various agencies and departments involved in Vietnam intelligence. The requests that it made for additional information led to the formation of a working group composed of representatives from the

CIA, the Department of State, the DIA, and the JCS. This group visited South Vietnam, where, among other things, it met with General Westmoreland, Ambassador Bunker, U.S. military and intelligence officials, and South Vietnamese intelligence, police, and military officials. The working group conducted a postmortem of U.S. intelligence activities leading up to the Tet Offensive that aided the PFIAB in crafting its final report and recommendations.[134]

In a memorandum to the president, the PFIAB found that, although the "intelligence apparatus was filled with indications that the enemy was preparing for a series of coordinated and simultaneous attacks on a larger scale than ever before attempted" (including some reports that suggested attacks during the Tet holidays), most reports "indicated that the offensive would occur just prior to or immediately following the holiday period."[135] None of the reports, however, accurately predicted "the extent of the attacks . . . or the degree of simultaneity achieved."[136] The report also found that, though pre-Tet intelligence mentioned some of the cities and towns actually targeted as possible targets, the reports forecasted "harassment" by rockets and mortars, rather than the large-scale ground attacks that actually occurred.[137] However, despite these intelligence failings, the board also found "no case in which United States forces appeared to have suffered defeat in this period because of a lack of timely intelligence."[138]

The board did criticize the lack of urgency that accompanied intelligence reporting from Vietnam to Washington. It found that, although the intelligence reports created a sense of urgency in Saigon and Vietnam, "finished intelligence disseminated in Washington did not contain the atmosphere of crisis."[139] It reached this conclusion on the basis of its postmortem, but it disagreed with the study's conclusion that little could have been done as "atmosphere is not readily passed over a teletype circuit."[140] Rather, the board concluded, several avoidable factors influenced this "difference of tone": "the appearance of intelligence indicators against a background clutter of conflicting or confusing reports which dulled to some extent the sharpness of the warnings," the "difficulty of framing synthesized reports accurately portraying a distant situation," the "effect of the reworking of reports in intermediate intelligence agencies between the field and the senior Washington officials," and the "difficulty at the Washington level of sorting out and properly emphasizing the important in the mass of intelligence flowing to Washington from the field."[141] The report further found fault with how long the intelligence community took to release processed intelligence.

Finally, the board concluded that the intelligence assessments prior to the offensive highlighted the difficulty in "expecting the unusual" as officials had never before experienced North Vietnamese attacks during the Tet holidays or such well-coordinated, simultaneous attacks.[142] Ultimately, the report concluded, intelligence did contribute to decisions to cancel the Tet truce and place U.S. command on full alert, which contributed to U.S. success in fending off attacks, so there were no grounds to "support the charge of a major intelligence failure."[143] Instead, the board concluded, the main failure was not conveying a timely sense of urgency to Washington through intelligence products. Accordingly, the report contained the following recommendation: "Your Board is increasingly concerned that the normal intelligence process in critical circumstances is neither timely nor adequate. Further, there is a concern that the reliance upon sources other than that process will continually weaken its effectiveness. Therefore your Board recommends a careful study by the Director of Central Intelligence, in consultation with the heads of the several intelligence agencies, to determine whether the normal process can be improved to remedy the defects noted in this report. If not, alternate means should be sought and made a part of the institutional process."[144] Johnson did approve this recommendation, directing the DCI to conduct such a study and submit it to him by September 15, 1968.[145] The DCI's study on this topic is not currently available.

Communications and Signals Intelligence for Vietnam

Several pieces of correspondence indicate that in the spring of 1968 the PFIAB assessed the quality of signals intelligence (SIGINT) and communications intelligence (COMINT) collection in South Vietnam. A memorandum from Lieutenant General Carter of the NSA to Taylor mentioned that the PFIAB heard briefings from NSA representatives on March 27 regarding COMINT, focusing on North Vietnamese and Vietcong infiltration of South Vietnam, and heard proposed requirements for further collection.[146] In particular, this memorandum described the various aircraft required by the NSA to improve COMINT collection. On April 19, Taylor submitted a memorandum to Rostow suggesting two "quick fixes" to supply the NSA with aircraft needed to fly surveillance equipment just outside Vietnamese airspace.

The first involved diverting electronic warfare aircraft already stationed in Vietnam; the other involved diverting reconnaissance aircraft under JCS control from other areas such as Germany.[147] On June 10, Taylor submitted another memorandum to Rostow on COMINT, noting with displeasure that the "quick fix" solutions the board proposed were not addressed in a June 5 status report to the board entitled "Status Report on Increased Intelligence Collection in Southeast Asia."[148] Taylor went on to underscore the board's belief that increasing the SIGINT and COMINT collection capability with additional collection aircraft should be a high priority. In response to these criticisms, Rostow forwarded the board's memo to Secretary of Defense Clifford, mentioning that Taylor remained "quite exercised on the question of allocating aircraft to obtain critically important data on infiltration."[149] Rostow further mentioned that diverting aircraft was a "hideously entangled bureaucratic affair" but that there were "few things more important for all of us than to have the best possible fix on the rate of infiltration."[150] We do not know what, if any, action Clifford took in response to Rostow's memorandum.

Lull in Enemy Activities in Vietnam

On July 30, 1968, President Johnson tasked Taylor, in his capacity as chair of the PFIAB, to evaluate recent intelligence information about a "lull" in enemy activity in South Vietnam.[151] Taylor submitted a brief report to the president on August 2 in the form of a three-page memorandum. He found that there had been a significant lull in enemy activity in South Vietnam since mid-June but that it was the result, not of any lessening of the will to fight, but of military necessity. It was certainly not a signal of North Vietnam's or the Vietcong's desire to facilitate peace talks in Paris. The main evidence for this conclusion was that political activity increased during the lull, as did North Vietnamese/Vietcong efforts to replace lost forces.[152] Taylor mentioned that, owing to time constraints, he had not consulted other members of the board in the preparation of the memo, but he promised that the board would prepare another report with recommendations. This report is unavailable.[153]

Intelligence-Information-Handling Procedures

The PFIAB's report to President Johnson on intelligence-information-handling procedures is also declassified. A July 20, 1967, memo to Johnson indicates that this is the second report the PFIAB had submitted on this subject. The board first submitted a report on information handling in June 1965, and it states that the president approved the board's two recommendations:

- "The establishment of specialized training programs for personnel of the intelligence agencies.

- "The establishment of an experimental interagency system utilizing computers for the storage of intelligence information accessible to user agencies at remote locations over secure communications circuits."[154]

Over the subsequent two years, the board followed the implementation of these recommendations. Although some progress was made, the board believed that "much more must be done."[155] It also recommended a "broad study of the information handling problem" in its first report, to be conducted by a panel of experts under the sponsorship of the PFIAB and the director of the Office of Science and Technology.[156] The board submitted a report based on the study on July 20, 1967. One of its several conclusions was that "the U.S. intelligence community has not yet exploited modern methods and technologies for information-handling, including automation techniques, as promptly or as widely as could be done to meet the problem, except for some significant steps taken by individual U.S. agencies."[157] On the basis of its conclusions, the board suggested that Johnson issue a presidential directive creating a central office, under the DCI, to manage the effort to improve information-handling procedures. The board's second report advanced three primary recommendations:

- "That the DCI undertake as a high priority the design and management of a scientifically advanced unified information handling system." The PFIAB also identified a need to establish an "Office of a Deputy to the Director" to aid him in this effort and advised that a phased plan be submitted in time for the fiscal year 1969 budget. The board further recommended that the DCI submit semiannual reports to the president on the subject.
- "That the Director of the Bureau of the Budget, the Special Assistant for National Security Affairs and the Special Assistant for Science and Technology review and assist the DCI in his attempts to create a unified information handling system."
- "That the member agencies of the U.S. Intelligence Communities develop systems that meet the requirements of the DCI's system, once developed. The Board also advised that the DCI, the Secretary of State, and the Secretary of Defense establish central 'focal points' that managed and reviewed internal intelligence handling systems and that worked with the Deputy Director of Central Intelligence to achieve a community wide system."

In addition to the above recommendations, the board submitted eight supplemental recommendations:

- That a pilot system be created to handle the intelligence that made up biographical files of "elite" Soviet personalities, using tasking and funding of the experimental COINS project to create this system.
- That an "experimental program" to provide automated support to the National Indications Center be established.
- That each U.S. intelligence agency establish a "staff function to be concerned with operations research and systems analysis directed toward the formulation of new and improved information handling methods and procedures."
- That the DCI lead communitywide studies to determine how "automated data storage and recall and improved information handling procedures might assist other elements of the community."
- That the DCI provide policy guidance to other U.S. intelligence agencies "with respect to the establishment and conduct of experimental research facilities for the development of improved information handling techniques."
- That U.S. intelligence agencies "under the leadership" of the DCI develop an "automation-supported system providing increased efficiency and economy in the control, dissemination and accountability of classified documents."
- That the DCI develop new communitywide "physical security regulations, procedures, and guidelines" to provide protection for intelligence-handling systems using automatic data processing.
- That the position of "Deputy Director of Central Intelligence" should be created so that an individual could "act as an interface between intelligence agencies and the scientific and technical community" to ensure that improved information-handling techniques are applied when possible.[158]

The DCI and Coordination of the Foreign Intelligence Effort

The Johnson PFIAB, like its predecessors, continued to take an intense interest in the DCI's role as the coordinator of the entire U.S. foreign intelligence effort. The board remained concerned that the DCI placed too much emphasis on his role as the director of the CIA, neglecting his responsibilities to manage the rest of the intelligence community. Evidence of the PFIAB's concern appears in a September 8, 1965, memo to the secretary of state. In the memo, Bundy states: "For some time Clark Clifford has been recommending a new, general letter of instructions from the President to the Director of Central Intelligence on the coordination of our foreign intelligence effort."[159] To his memo Bundy attached a draft of the proposed letter and sought to make sure that none of the language undercut the secretary of state's role as the president's primary foreign policy adviser.[160]

Johnson eventually did issue a new letter of direction to the DCI on September 24, 1965. The letter requested that the DCI "pursue as a primary responsibility the task of coordinating and guiding the total U.S. foreign intelligence effort."[161] Johnson further directed the DCI to work with the heads of the various agencies engaged in foreign intelligence activities. The PFIAB inspired the president to draft this new letter of direction. This effort by no means constituted the only work on this topic by the PFIAB. The board received briefings, reports, and updates throughout the Johnson administration on the effectiveness of the DCI as coordinator of the entire foreign intelligence effort. It continually pushed the DCI to fulfill this role and always sought ways to aid him to do so.

Gordon Gray Unknown Site Review

Between July 5 and 10, 1966, Gray traveled overseas to unknown locations to conduct an on-the-scene review for the PFIAB. As a result of his trip, he submitted a report, which is partially declassified, with several recommendations. The board approved the report and conclusions and submitted them to Rostow on August 3, 1966.[162] Although the exact locations he visited are redacted, unclassified portions reveal that he reviewed activities in Europe, and one recommendation deals with Sweden in particular.

The board wished to bring one recommendation in the report to the president's attention. Though substantially redacted, it indicated the board's continuing interest in counterintelligence: "That the Director of Central Intelligence, in consultation with the Director, Defense Intelligence Agency, review the question of whether U.S. counterintelligence and counterespionage efforts targeted against the personnel of Soviet bloc installations overseas are adequately oriented, financed and staffed to achieve maximum success in exploiting the vulnerabilities of such personnel."[163]

The report contained four recommendations that the board did not believe needed consideration by the president. In the declassified version of the report, all but one of these recommendations is redacted, although it is apparent that the USIB, the DIA, and the Department of State each were the focus of one of these recommendations. The final recommendation advises that a PFIAB panel review the CIA inspector general's office: "That an appropriate Panel of the Board review the policies and procedures of the Inspector General's (I.G.) Office at CIA Headquarters with a view to determining their adequacy and orientation."[164]

Although the recommendation that the PFIAB sent to the U.S. Intelligence Advisory Board remains unknown, two memoranda written by Rostow, which are available at the Johnson Presidential Library, reveal the substance of the recommendations in the report regarding the DIA and the Department of State. The board recommended that the director of the DIA:

(a) Determine whether in exceptional cases some flexibility can be introduced into the Defense Attaché System with a view to retaining, as long as possible, the services of experienced Attachés who contribute substantially and in some cases, perhaps uniquely, to our intelligence effort and who tend to be lost to that effort by virtue of automatic rotation and mandatory retirement practices.

(b) Explore with the Director, Bureau of Intelligence and Research, State Department, the question of whether it would be desirable for the European Office of Aero-Space research to clear with U.S. Embassies concerned any scientific, technical, engineering, and related projects which that Office proposes to undertake in European countries in order to assure that such projects (which are normally unclassified) do not inadvertently encroach upon or lead to the disclosure of sensitive, intelligence-associated activities being carried out in those countries by elements of the U.S. intelligence community.

(c) Seek an early decision within the Department of Defense as to the type of equipments which should be acquired to meet the needs of the BACK YARD program in [redacted].[165]

Rostow forwarded the following PFIAB recommendation in a separate memo to the secretary of state: "That the Department of State, in consultation with the appropriate officials of the USIA and Central Intelligence Agency, consider the advisability of undertaking more extensive programs in Sweden with a view to: (a) offsetting the massive propaganda programs which the Soviet have targeted against Sweden; (b) placing that propaganda effort in better perspective; and (c) achieving in Sweden improved understanding of and attitudes toward significant policies being pursued by the United States in international fields."[166]

William Langer Site Review of Greece, Cyprus, Turkey, and Iran

According to an August 4, 1966, memorandum from Rostow to the secretary of state, the board member William Langer conducted a similar overseas site review of intelligence activities from June 2 to June 16, 1966.[167] Although the locations of this site review are redacted in the release report and Rostow's memo, other memoranda and documents reveal that Langer traveled to Greece, Cyprus, Turkey, and Iran. An itinerary for Langer and Ash for the dates June 2–16 (though without the year) reveals that they visited all the above except Cyprus, staying for three days in Athens, two days in Ankara, and two in Teheran (the other days were devoted to travel). A note on the itinerary also indicates that the two were to receive mail at the American embassy in each of those countries.[168] For further confirmation, a November 18, 1966, memorandum from Rostow referencing his redacted August 4 memorandum mentions in its subject line "Foreign Intelligence and Related Activities in Greece, Cyprus, Turkey, and Iran."[169]

The PFIAB report submitted as a result of Langer's review is similar in format to the report submitted as a result of Gray's review that same year. It found that the U.S. intelligence effort in the countries Langer visited was "proceeding satisfactorily" and that U.S. ambassadors were well informed as to the nature and extent of intelligence collection and covert action.[170] The PFIAB submitted one recommendation, which is heavily redacted, that it believed required presidential consideration:

> The President's Foreign Intelligence Advisory Board recommends that appropriate steps be taken to assure that the Senior Interdepartmental Group (SIG) and the Interdepartmental Regional Groups (IRGs) are appropriately utilized to ensure that U.S. foreign intelligence needs (e.g., the concession of base rights for vital U.S. signals intelligence collection operations against Soviet missile, nuclear, and air defense activities) are taken into account in the formation of policies involving the supplying of U.S. military and economic aid to foreign countries.
>
> [A paragraph here is completely redacted.]
>
> The Board holds no brief for the selection of any particular

integration mechanism to meet the objectives of this recommendation. However, we feel that the authority and responsibilities of the SIG and IRG's, as set forth in the President's National Security Action Memorandum 341, make these interagency bodies logical forums for ensuring that U.S. formulations of foreign policy toward a particular country take into account those grants and concessions which may appropriately be sought for use by U.S. intelligence agencies in meeting critical national intelligence needs.[171]

The report contained three recommendations that the board wanted forwarded directly to relevant department and agency heads. Two of those recommendations were for the DCI, and one was for the DOD. These recommendations are completely redacted in the report. Rostow's November 18 memorandum, however, states that the report called attention to "the reported desire of the U.S. Ambassador, Nicosia, that situation reports on local crisis development be prepared and forwarded to Washington in consolidated form."[172]

Net Evaluations

In an August 9, 1968, memorandum to the president, Chair Taylor recommended that an office similar to the disbanded Net Evaluation Subcommittee (NES) of the NSC be created. The board was concerned with the quality of analysis of Soviet strategic capabilities and cited this as its rationale for recommending that "the Secretary of Defense be directed to prepare proposed terms of reference whereby he would undertake the net evaluation studies in collaboration with the appropriate other government agencies."[173] A September 3, 1968, telegram from Rostow to Johnson conveyed Clifford's response to Taylor's recommendation that an office similar to the former NES be reestablished. Rostow wrote: "Sec. Clifford and General Wheeler believe that present staff work within the Department of Defense fully covers the work formerly done by the Net Evaluation Subcommittee and, therefore, they do not believe a new study is required."[174] Rostow himself was much more sympathetic to Taylor's recommendation on the grounds that nuclear parity and the likelihood of strategic arms control negotiations made such a body useful.[175]

On September 20, Clifford wrote directly to Taylor, apparently in response to another memo that Taylor was drafting to send to Johnson. Here, Clifford reiterated his view that the DOD's current capabilities were sufficient to provide the type of strategic analysis that Taylor and the PFIAB believed were necessary. He attached a lengthy description of the many functions within the DOD that fill the gap left by the dismantling of the former NES and offered to brief the PFIAB on these efforts.[176] Taylor responded to Clifford's letter with a short reply on September 24, thanking him for providing the board with information on the DOD's current efforts and for offering to brief the PFIAB on this issue.[177] Taylor again wrote to Clifford on October 8 to update him on the PFIAB's meeting of October 3 and 4. He notified Clifford that the PFIAB decided that, "rather than pursue this subject in the form of a further recommendation to the President at this time," the board would instead categorize this as an issue for future consideration.[178] Net assessment pitted the current and former chair of the PFIAB against each other, with Clifford's argument prevailing in the short run. However, the DOD eventually established the Office of Net Assessment in 1973.

OXCART

Though no relevant reports or recommendations are available, it is apparent that the PFIAB continued to take an interest in OXCART, the CIA's high-speed, high-altitude reconnaissance aircraft program. A January 1968 memorandum recounts CIA officer John A. Bross's discussions with "Mr. Nitze and Dr. Flax," outside consultants for the PFIAB, about whether the SR-71 should replace OXCART and whether the CIA should even fly manned reconnaissance missions.[179] Four options were on the table for the future of this program: (1) transferring the whole program to the SAC; (2) do option 1, but store eight SAC SR-71s; (3) close the OXCART program, but have the CIA manage the SR-71 program; or (4) keep OXCART going under the control of the CIA.[180] The debate regarding these options was tied directly to the larger issue of the CIA's role in the manned reconnaissance program, a lingering bureaucratic battle left over from the NRP fight. The CIA's manned reconnaissance programs were eventually terminated, and the OXCART assets common to the SR-71 program were transferred to the air force.[181] The CIA submitted a final overview of the OXCART program and the missions it flew to the PFIAB on June 30, 1968.[182]

Special Studies

The Johnson PFIAB conducted numerous "special studies" at the request of the president. In the board's final report to the president, which summarized the work of the PFIAB over the course of Johnson's entire administration, Taylor submitted a list of these studies on "intelligence-related matters of particular national security interest."[183] Some of the reports on these special studies are at least partially classified and have been discussed in greater detail above, while other reports remain classified. The board conducted the first three special studies for Kennedy, and all the rest were completed under Johnson:

(a) The performance of U.S. intelligence agencies in providing advance information on the erection of the Berlin Wall in August 1961.

(b) The intelligence community's performance regarding the introduction of Soviet strategic missiles in Cuba in 1962.

(c) The Soviet penetration in the 1961–63 period of highly sensitive elements of the NSA, prompting improved counterintelligence measures relating to personnel security investigations, clearances, and to the safeguarding of sensitive intelligence data.

(d) The intelligence coverage of the Gulf of Tonkin incident involving U.S. Naval Forces in September 1964.

(e) The quality, timeliness, and handling of intelligence bearing on the enemy military offensive in South Vietnam during the TET holidays in January 1968.

(f) The intelligence aspects of the Israeli attack on the USS Liberty in June 1967, and the North Korean capture of the U.S. Signals Intelligence vessel, Pueblo, in January 1968.

(g) The system for the control of military intelligence/combat aircraft operating over North Vietnam and the Tonkin Gulf, with a view to minimizing navigational errors and unintentional intrusions over the Chicom border.

(h) The intelligence community's coverage of the Soviet Invasion of Czechoslovakia in August 1968.

(i) Measures to strengthen the intelligence community's capability for providing the President and other top officials with timely, interagency evaluations on developing crisis situations.

(j) The scope and effectiveness of the intelligence community's special programs to keep abreast of Soviet and Chinese Communist scientific and technological developments, particularly in the strategic weapons field.[184]

These studies were conducted in addition to the regular reviews that the PFIAB conducted of broader, longer-term intelligence issues.

Using the declassified special reports as a guide, the PFIAB would have released its findings in a special report directed either to the assistant for national security affairs or to the president himself, usually in the form of a memorandum. These reports contained the PFIAB's findings and a few recommendations based on their investigative work. In addition to conducting its own investigation, the PFIAB made use of reports and studies conducted by outside bodies. A good example is the role of the JCS's investigative team in the formation of Clark Clifford's report on the Chinese MIG incident.

Long-Term Intelligence Issues and the Final Report to Johnson

The board identified problems of particular long-term significance in its final report to President Johnson, indicating that it spent a significant amount of time examining these issues during its term. These were general issues that dealt with virtually every aspect of the intelligence community. They were much broader than the specific recommendations and issues the board examined in its special studies. Most likely, the board would have submitted its analysis and recommendations about these issues and problems in its regular reports to the president, which for the most part remain classified. The PFIAB's final report to the president, which summarizes much of the board's work over the course of the Johnson administration, offers a window into these issues and some broad recommendations.

Current Intelligence Support to the President

The board identified serious problems in the intelligence community's attempts to provide the president with up-to-date intelligence reporting. It specifically recognized the difficulty the DCI faced in keeping abreast of the rapidly changing needs of the president and responding to them in a timely fashion. As a possible solution, it proposed assigning a senior intelligence officer to work with the special assistant for national security affairs in the White House with the explicit task of anticipating presidential intelligence needs and meeting them expeditiously.[185]

Early Warning Capabilities

The board advised that the improvement of early warning procedures should merit priority attention every year, admitting: "We shall probably never be satisfied with our early warning capabilities for crisis situations."[186]

Comparative Evaluations of Military Capabilities

The PFIAB recommended that the intelligence community, through an interagency process bringing together civilian and military departments and agencies, make regular comparative evaluations of offensive and defensive capabilities of the United States and the Soviet Union. It recommended that the executive branch be given access to these comparative evaluations.[187] This is the first mention of such an exercise that would be revisited by subsequent boards and, ultimately, implemented with the "Team B" study during the Ford administration.

Science and Technology

The board followed up on its successful effort to get the CIA to establish a separate directorate of science and technology by continuing to insist on the critical role of science and technology to the intelligence effort, stating that "the substantial and innovative resources of the nation's scientific and technologic community" needed to be "brought to bear upon critical intelligence problems."[188] A key example was the board's interest, owing primarily to the efforts of the board members Baker and Land, in keeping abreast of developments in electro-optical technology that would eventually make real-time satellite imaging possible.[189] The board, however, was never satisfied with the progress on this score. In one report, its executive director complained: "The DCI's current progress report reads quite a bit like the progress report . . . a year ago, with more detail included, and with further advances in certain areas still in the future tense."[190]

Signals Intelligence

The board identified a need to more effectively manage and conduct signals intelligence programs, with an emphasis on national intelligence needs.[191] Documents from earlier in the Johnson administration indicate that this was an issue with which the board had been concerned from the beginning. A 1964 memo from Deputy Secretary of Defense Vance to Bundy indicated that the PFIAB had recommended improvements to the National SIGINT Intelligence Program in the areas of product evaluation, the systems analysis and operations group, research and development, and scientific and technical foresight. The correspondence outlines the steps being taken to rectify perceived deficiencies and implement PFIAB recommendations and highlights the need for continuing PFIAB communication and review of improvement to SIGINT programs.[192]

Communication of Signals Intelligence

Though this recommendation is heavily redacted, unclassified portions reveal that the board recommended continued NSA administration of facilities that communicated signals intelligence.[193]

NSA Direction

The PFIAB was concerned that the military directors of the NSA rotated too frequently and that this had a detrimental effect on the quality of the NSA's work. It recommended a longer term for NSA directors and even suggested that the president consider whether a civilian or military director would better serve the NSA.[194]

Information Handling

Important enough to merit a separate, full report from the PFIAB earlier during the Johnson administration, intelligence handling procedures continually occupied the board's attention. In its final report, the board recommended that the "highest Governmental levels" needed to stimulate the intelligence community to take advantage of automated procedures, machines, and computers to more efficiently handle intelligence information.[195]

Espionage

In the portion of this recommendation not redacted, the board found U.S. espionage efforts "inadequate" and recommended that the community intensify its efforts to gather information through clandestine operations.[196]

Counterespionage

The PFIAB noted the "unrelenting efforts to subvert military and civilian personnel of our government." In response, it recommended that clandestine operations attempt to collect intelligence "both home and abroad" on possible foreign espionage operations.[197] Moreover, it identified a gap in intelligence owing to "an absence of policy authorization for the use of audio surveillance devices against the espionage activities of foreign agents operating within the U.S."[198]

Validation of Intelligence Requirements

The PFIAB identified a need for the intelligence community to screen its own intelligence collection requirements to ensure that they aligned with broader national security needs and priorities. In its final report to the president, it stated that by implementing more effective screening methods the intelligence community could substantially reduce the workload and resources dedicated to unnecessary intelligence collection efforts.[199]

Covert Operations

The board recommended that the 303 Committee should more often review covert programs to "evaluate progress being made, and in appropriate instances, cancel unproductive projects."[200]

The DIA

The board had earlier endorsed the establishment of the fledgling DIA under the Kennedy administration. It took a great interest in the DIA's continued growth and development and recommended that it "receive the real and continuing cooperation of each of the military departments, and be provided as soon as possible with all necessary means in the way of proper space, advanced equipment and qualified personnel."[201]

Increased Policy Guidance by the NSC

In its final report, the PFIAB argued: "A number of the major problems confronting the intelligence community stem from inadequacies in the policy guidance and coordination which is provided to the intelligence community."[202] It recommended that the NSC strengthen and improve its policy guidance and directives to the various intelligence agencies. It specifically recommended "an early review, and up-dating where appropriate, of the National Security Council Intelligence Directives and related directives which govern the responsibilities and activities of the Central Intelligence Agency and the conduct of the total U.S. foreign intelligence and covert action effort."[203] It also called for the president and the NSC to provide greater support and guidance for the DCI in his role as coordinator of the U.S. intelligence effort.

Retention of Overseas Intelligence Facilities

As the final recommendation of this report, the Johnson PFIAB advised that policymakers carefully consider intelligence requirements and needs before making decisions to close down bases or installations overseas. It pointed out that closing some installations would also eliminate the intelligence work carried out through those installations, as it could not be performed elsewhere.[204]

ASSESSMENT AND FUTURE RESEARCH RECOMMENDATIONS

The PFIAB during the Johnson administration significantly influenced intelligence policy and debate. The list of achievements that can be traced at least partially to its recommendations is impressive. The board had a free hand to study the quantity and quality of U.S. intelligence concerning all the major international events that occurred during the Johnson administration. These included the Dunlap case, the Soviet audio penetration of the American embassy in Moscow, the 1964 Gulf of Tonkin incident, the June 1967 Israeli attack on the USS *Liberty,* the North Korean capture of the USS *Pueblo* in January 1968, the Tet Offensive in January 1968, and the August 1968 Soviet invasion of Czechoslovakia.

On the basis of its studies, the board made some recommendations that changed the organization and operation of the U.S. intelligence community. These changes included the creation of the directorate of science and technology in the CIA (originally submitted to President Kennedy); the creation of the defense attaché system in 1964 (originally submitted to President Kennedy); the planning and subsequent establishment of a computer-based system for the storage and retrieval of intelligence information; the August 13, 1965, agreement assigning responsibilities for running the NRP to the secretary of defense, the DCI, and the NRO; recommendations to improve intelligence reporting on the Vietcong, the North Vietnamese leadership, and the intentions of China in the aftermath of the Tet Offensive; and steps to improve the U.S. counterintelligence posture.

The strong relationship between the president and Clifford may provide part of the explanation for the PFIAB's success during Johnson's administration. The bureaucracies of the intelligence community, aware of the influence Clifford had with Johnson, would hesitate to ignore PFIAB recommendations approved by the president. Nevertheless, Johnson met with the full board on only a handful of occasions, and there is evidence that PFIAB recommendations did not always win the day (e.g., the NRO debates) or have the desired effect (e.g., Clifford's Vietnam recommendations). The success of the PFIAB seems also to have depended on the issues it was dealing with. The many significant military and intelligence issues that arose during the Johnson presidency forced the administration to turn to the board for analysis and advice. But, when the board sought to challenge large, complex, and well-established bureaucracies, it had less success. Conversely, when it addressed areas in which it did not meet such bureaucratic resistance, it had far more success in having its recommendations implemented.

4

Richard M. Nixon

President Richard Nixon established his President's Foreign Intelligence Advisory Board (PFIAB) with Executive Order (EO) 11460 on March 20, 1969. The process of thinking about the PFIAB began even before the new president's inauguration with a January 7, 1969, memorandum from the CIA to Nixon's national security adviser designate, Dr. Henry Kissinger, describing the board's functions: "The President's Foreign Intelligence Advisory Board (PFIAB), now chaired by General Maxwell Taylor, is comprised of former high ranking government officials and prominent businessmen who agree to monitor on the President's behalf the caliber of the intelligence community's performance. PFIAB meets regularly or at the call of its Chairman for the purpose of assessing the intelligence 'record' during a crisis (the Tet Offensive in 1968, for example), to receive briefings on emergent crises. It assures the Chief Executive of an impartial, outside evaluation of the intelligence he receives."[1]

The drafting of the new EO was initially handled by the Nixon transition lawyer, and eventual board member, Franklin Lincoln and Chair Maxwell Taylor.[2] The Lincoln/Taylor draft was apparently controversial as it raised objections from both Secretary of Defense Melvin Laird and Director of Central Intelligence (DCI) Richard Helms. Attorney General John Mitchell and Kissinger discussed two major concerns in a series of phone conversations on February 11 and 12, 1969. The first was the proposal to rename the board the "Foreign Intelligence Board," which Laird and Helms thought downplayed its advisory function. The second was the proposal to upgrade the title of the board's executive secretary to "executive director," a change that apparently J. Patrick Coyne had been pushing for some time, but which Laird and Helms thought inappropriately "up-grade[d]" the position. Kissinger told Mitchell that neither he nor the president had "any views" on these changes, so Laird's and Helms' objections carried the day, at least in terms of the board's name.[3]

The final version of the new EO charged the PFIAB with three general tasks and gave little more in the way of specific guidelines:

1. Advise the President concerning the objectives, conduct, management, and coordination of the various activities making up the overall intelligence effort.

2. Conduct a continuing review and assessment of foreign intelligence and related activities in which the Central Intelligence Agency and other U.S. Government departments and agencies are engaged.

3. Report to the President concerning the Board's findings and appraisals, and make appropriate recommendations for actions to achieve increased effectiveness of the U.S. foreign intelligence effort in meeting national intelligence needs.[4]

Four days after issuing EO 11460, Nixon also requested that the board provide a "yearly, independent assessment of the nuclear threat, supplementing regular intelligence assessments made thereon by the intelligence community."[5] There is no correspondence indicating why the president waited to issue this additional tasking until after releasing his EO. EO 11460 also directed all relevant department heads and the DCI to cooperate with the board and to provide all necessary information.

The order outlined general guidelines for the selection of PFIAB members and discussed the board's staff, which included an executive director. Section 5 of the order indicated that the board's costs would be paid from the "Special Projects" section in the Executive Appropriations Act of 1969. Finally, the order revoked EO 10938 of May 4, 1961, with which President Kennedy had created his PFIAB.[6] President Nixon held contradictory attitudes toward the PFIAB and lacked a clear sense of its function in his administration. On the one hand, in a January 7, 1969, letter to Chief of Staff H. R. "Bob" Haldeman and White House Counsel John Erlichmann, he indicated a desire to stock the board with his political supporters and to remove some of the older members.[7] On the other hand, he ultimately decided to reappoint six members of President Johnson's board. Because Johnson kept the board he inherited from President Kennedy, this meant that Nixon retained many board members appointed by his past political rivals. In a subsequent EO of March 8, 1972, he recognized the PFIAB as one of eleven bodies in the executive department that could classify material, indicating that he regarded its products as sensitive and important.[8]

At the outset of his administration, Nixon seemed to value the board and its work. According to Wheaton Byers, the executive secretary of the PFIAB from 1973 to 1977, however, the president's attitude toward the board changed during his time in office. As the Watergate scandal spun out of control and his administration shifted into crisis mode, Nixon had less time for, and interest in, the PFIAB and its activities. During this tumultuous time, the activities of independent advisory boards were, not surprisingly, the least of the administration's concerns.[9]

Toward the end of Nixon's second term, White House staff attempted to collect as many files as possible from the various executive agencies, boards, and committees to pass on to the National Archives for eventual transfer to a Nixon presidential library. Byers, however, refused to relinquish the PFIAB files for reasons of confidentiality. As a result, the Nixon materials in the National Archives contain few board recommendations or records of subsequent efforts to implement them. Information on these topics has, therefore, been gleaned largely from letters, memoranda, and other secondary sources within the administration or other parts of the government such as the intelligence community.

BOARD MEMBERSHIP AND EXECUTIVE STAFF

Members of the Board

When President Nixon reconstituted the PFIAB, he appointed a ten-person board. Six members were carryovers from Johnson's board: General Taylor, the former chairman of the Joint Chiefs of Staff and ambassador to South Vietnam, remained as chair; Robert Murphy, the chair of the board at Corning Glass; Gordon Gray, a former national security adviser to President Eisenhower; William O. Baker, a vice president of research at Bell Laboratories; Edwin H. Land, the president of Polaroid; and Franklin Pace Jr., the president of the International Executive Service Corps.[10] Adm. John Sides and William L. Langer both submitted their resignations on January 20, 1969.[11] The other two Johnson PFIAB members who did not remain on the board—Clark Clifford and James H. Doolittle—had resigned during the Johnson administration. President Nixon also chose to retain Coyne as executive secretary. New members appointed by Nixon on March 20, 1969, included Nelson Rockefeller, Adm. George Anderson, Franklin Murphy, and Lincoln.

The PFIAB's membership remained stable until April 9, 1970, when Chair Taylor resigned.[12] President Nixon quickly named Anderson as the

board's new chair on May 1, 1970. To fill the open seat, Nixon turned
to his longtime adviser and the former Texas governor John Bowden
Connally.[13]

The most significant changes to Nixon's PFIAB took place in the
fall of 1972. With Connally's reappointment to the board on August 3,
1972, after a brief stint as secretary of the treasury, the board's membership stood at eleven.[14] Nixon apparently did not feel constrained by
the fact that it had contained only ten individuals under every previous
administration. In Byers's view, this type of disregard for operational
tradition illustrated the president's lack of clarity on the purpose of the
board. Putting people on the board without consideration of their potential contribution to its mission inevitably weakened it in comparison
with other groups like the National Security Council (NSC).[15]

On August 26, 1970, Executive Secretary Coyne left his position to
become special assistant to the director of the National Security Agency
(NSA), a position previously held by Gerard Burke.[16] Burke replaced
Coyne as executive secretary of the PFIAB. It appears that the two simply switched positions. This arrangement makes sense given that staff
positions on the board were usually filled by personnel from various
parts of the intelligence community.

The biggest shake-up of the PFIAB under Nixon occurred when
Franklin Pace, Lincoln, Robert Murphy, Franklin Murphy, and Executive Secretary Burke submitted their resignations on November 9, 1972.
Though the Nixon archives provide no definitive evidence as to why these
five individuals decided to depart at the same time, Byers did provide us
with some hints. He told us that Burke and Admiral Anderson agreed
together that Burke should resign for personal, health-related reasons.[17]
Byers also mentioned that Franklin Murphy had personal reasons for
stepping down. Murphy had been very active in persuading the *Los Angeles Times* not to publish a story on Project Jennifer and the *Glomar
Explorer* while the actual attempt to recover the Soviet submarine was
under way, and Byers believed that Murphy might not have wanted
to be again put in the position of having to exert this sort of influence
outside the intelligence community.[18] Byers had no idea why Lincoln
chose to resign. Finally, he pointed out to us that Robert Murphy left
the board to head the Commission on the Organization of the Government for the Conduct of Foreign Policy. The Murphy Commission, as it
was known, conducted an extensive review of the government's foreign
policy apparatus and organization, including an extensive examination
of the intelligence community. It completed its study in 1975 after Nixon

had resigned from office, and its findings had major implications for the entire intelligence community, including the PFIAB. In sum, Byers argued that these members and staff did not all resign at the same time for the same reasons. In his view, there was "no hidden agenda," and the resignations were not in any way connected to the Watergate affair.[19]

Regardless of the reasons behind the exodus, the departure of four PFIAB members and the executive secretary left a significant void in the board that was not filled until June 1973, when President Nixon selected Clare Booth Luce, Robert Galvin, John S. Foster, and Leo Cherne to fill the vacated seats and named Byers the board's new executive secretary. Lionel Olmer, a commander in the U.S. Navy, also joined the PFIAB to fill the vacant staff position left by Byers's promotion.

Individuals Considered for Membership

Many other prominent Americans were considered or recommended for positions on the PFIAB but never nominated, including conservative political activist Phyllis Schlafly, the West Coast newspaper magnate James Copely, the oilman John Shaheen, former U.S. senator William F. Knowland, and the University of Pennsylvania political science professor William Kitner. None of them appeared to garner much significant interest inside the administration. Documents also indicate that in 1969 President Nixon and his staff considered appointing Gen. Mark W. Clark, a retired U.S. Army officer who had served in the European theater during World War II and as the commander of UN forces in Korea.[20] Clark's candidacy made its way to the highest levels of government before being rejected.[21] There is evidence, however, that Kissinger, Nixon's influential national security adviser, desired a smaller board and may have dissuaded Nixon from adding more than ten members.[22]

PFIAB Staff

In keeping with established practice, the PFIAB had a small staff assigned to assist the board with its day-to-day functions and administrative issues. The board depended on the staff to do much of the work involved in gathering information on various issues, and it relied on them to liaise with other agencies. The staff was headed by an executive secretary, who was borrowed from another agency and remained on that agency's payroll. Coyne remained as executive secretary until 1970, when he was replaced by Burke. Burke had served for only three years when Byers took his place. Little biographical information is available for Burke, aside from the fact that he served as special assistant to the director of the NSA prior to his appointment as PFIAB executive secretary.

Outside Consultants

In the course of its activities, the PFIAB relied not only on the experience and knowledge of its members and staff but also occasionally brought in outside consultants. These professionals provided expertise in law, the military, and specific technical areas that were essential to the PFIAB. These individuals, like the members of the board, were paid only for the time they actually worked and were not considered full-time employees. Known outside consultants include Gen. William F. Cassidy of the U.S. Army Corps of Engineers, Dr. Lloyd A. Free, the Harvard mathematician Dr. Andrew Gleason, the former NSC and PFIAB executive secretary Col. James S. Lay, the Harvard mathematician Anthony Oettinger, the retired FBI special agent Sam Papich, the computer expert Dr. Oliver Selfridge, and the Princeton statistician John Tukey.

OPERATING PROCEDURES

PFIAB Meetings

Under previous administrations, the PFIAB met on the first Thursday and Friday of alternate months. Nixon's board followed these same general guidelines and met thirty-five times during his presidency. Its inaugural meeting was held on April 17 and 18, 1969, and included a one-hour session with Nixon himself.[23] The president and National Security Adviser Kissinger expressed interest in attending regular PFIAB meetings in letters and memoranda, but scheduling conflicts often prohibited this from happening. Sometimes, the board could go several months without meeting with Kissinger.[24] Nevertheless, there are frequent references to board meetings with Nixon and Kissinger scattered throughout archival sources. According to a Congressional Research Service report, the president met with the board eight times while in office.[25] Archival evidence confirms that the PFIAB met with Nixon more than once each year, at meetings that were far more than simple photo opportunities and handshake sessions.

For instance, Nixon met with the PFIAB on October 4 and 5, 1973, at which time the board discussed how best to communicate its findings and recommendations to the president (the president advised that they should communicate through Kissinger or, if Kissinger was unavailable, Brent Scowcroft, who was the military assistant to the president). At the same meeting, the board recommended that DCI Colby be named vice chair of the NSC Intelligence Committee in view of Kissinger's busy schedule. The president immediately assented, waving his hand, saying that "it was done."[26] Personal communication with Nixon aided the PFIAB and increased its stature and influence. One former PFIAB staffer maintains that the Nixon board had more regular procedures and met more often with the president than previous boards. Accordingly, it "may have been more effective."[27]

Because such information is not included in the CRS report or is unavailable in the Nixon archives, it is unclear how many times Kissinger met with the board. Byers, however, indicates that Kissinger met with the board as often as possible. He also conceded that some board members attended PFIAB meetings more consistently than others. Land, for example, preferred to attend only meetings that were relevant to his area of expertise: imaging. Another former PFIAB staffer lamented that "members lived busy lives and some had a poor attendance record" and that "sometimes you could pull your hair out" trying to get them all to attend.[28] Because of the broad mandate of the PFIAB and the narrow focus of many of its members, assembling the entire board at once was a challenge throughout Nixon's presidency.[29]

Unfortunately, meeting agendas are unavailable for Nixon's board. It is clear, however, that the PFIAB continued its tradition of having briefs from high-ranking intelligence officials—particularly the DCI—on issues of interest. For instance, a 1971 internal memorandum for the DCI contains a list of topics the board expected him to speak about during the December 6 meeting. These topics included COINS (an automated data-processing system for the intelligence community), the management of the National Reconnaissance Program, the U.S. oil shortage, the Soviet Union's meddling in the Arab world, and economic intelligence.[30] Another memorandum for the record indicates that the DCI briefed the board on a variety of topics, including the CIA's role in Laos, the proliferation of Soviet intelligence operatives in the West, the situation in India and Pakistan, and guerrilla activity in Mexico.[31] Available evidence indicates that the DCI discussed multiple issues at his regular meetings with the board, although, given time constraints, not all were examined in equal depth.

Operating Procedures and Interaction with Other Groups

While the PFIAB was designed to be an independent advisory board free from the various restrictions constraining other components of the intelligence community, it still needed standard operating procedures to convey its recommendations and assessments. Documents in the Nixon archives indicate that the majority of the board's correspondence and memoranda went to Kissinger, who then passed them on to Nixon; this is confirmed by a memorandum of October 11, 1973. At the time, however, the president also authorized the board to communicate through Deputy National Security Adviser Scowcroft or DCI Colby if Kissinger was not available.[32]

There is some evidence that the board and Kissinger had a complex and at times acrimonious relationship. For instance, in August 1974, Robert Galvin complained to George Anderson of Kissinger's "open distrust of intelligence."[33] There were several instances in which General Taylor and Admiral Anderson bypassed Kissinger and wrote directly to the president. Byers said that in such instances the PFIAB tried to work directly through the president's secretary but that Kissinger often interjected himself into the correspondence.[34]

Because the board covered topics ranging from broad security policy to specific technical issues affecting the intelligence community, it took care to establish an efficient division of labor. Like previous boards, Nixon's PFIAB chose to continue operating through panels composed of members with special knowledge or experience in a particular field. Members often served on more than one panel. At times, the board also formed ad hoc working panels designed to address specific tasks or issues that it did not plan to revisit over the course of an administration. The panel arrangement also helped keep members engaged in the many different topics the board discussed.[35] These panels focused on particular topics of interest and served as a vital link with the other less-knowledgeable board members.

For instance, Baker chaired the Information Handling Panel, a topic his work at Bell Labs made him uniquely qualified to address. Admiral Anderson chaired the Naval Panel, which also included Gray, Galvin, and Executive Secretary Byers as members. This panel had the task of advising the president on how to achieve his goal of keeping the U.S. Navy "second to none."[36] The Technical Panel, composed of Baker, Foster, Land, and Edward Teller, addressed topics such as nuclear arms control and intelligence collection.

The PFIAB's ability to fulfill its taskings depended on its relationship with the intelligence community. According to minutes taken by a CIA officer during a 1973 meeting, Admiral Anderson was confident that the board had a strong relationship with the intelligence community.

The board's chair requested various briefings for each meeting.[37] The DCI or the deputy DCI attended virtually every meeting and provided the board with requested briefings or reports. For instance, the DCI appeared at the PFIAB's October 5–6, 1972, meeting to give the members eight "area situation briefings" (on the Middle East, the Soviet Union, China and the Far East, Southeast Asia, Latin America, Western Europe, Africa, and South Asia). The DCI or the deputy DCI usually prepared a "PFIAB briefing book," which was used as a reference during meetings, and would occasionally bring along other colleagues when the board required more in-depth briefings on a specific theme.

The PFIAB also gathered information from annual reports submitted by the CIA and other agencies. Perhaps indicative of the board's importance, the CIA began working on its report months in advance.[38] Such reports were organized into three sections: changes in the CIA's mission or in the operating environment; a summary of the CIA's major successes and failures in the past twelve months; and an outline of the CIA's plans for the future. Agency memoranda indicate that this report was intended to be not an exhaustive catalog of every minute detail of operations but merely an efficient summary of the past year's events. The CIA took the report quite seriously and required virtually all departments and directorates to contribute. Little information is available about the individual reports other agencies such as the FBI, the Defense Intelligence Agency, and the NSA submitted. The board stopped requesting these individual reports in 1974, instead requesting a single integrated report on foreign intelligence activities from the DCI, perhaps to encourage the DCI to assume a greater degree of community management.[39] The DCI suggested, however, that the FBI continue to provide its own report because of the fundamental difference between the missions of foreign intelligence agencies and the domestic role of the FBI.

The board's relationship with the national security adviser was more complicated. A former staffer states that, between PFIAB and the national security adviser, "almost 100% of the time cordiality and politeness were the order of the day. . . . They knew how to comport themselves while slipping a knife into your ribs. . . . [I]n the presence of the Board butter wouldn't melt."[40] The same staffer described the board's relationship with the NSC as "superficial."[41]

Financially, the PFIAB was an unusual organization. According to EO 11460, it was funded by the "Special Projects" section of the Executive Appropriations Act of 1969. Correspondence indicates that there was discussion as early as 1969 of transferring the costs associated with the PFIAB to another agency.[42] While Nixon took no action at that time, records indicate that the CIA absorbed the board's expenses in 1973.[43] Since the board operated on a budget of approximately $164,000 in 1973, this would not have been an onerous expense. Because its members were not full-time employees, the board's costs stayed very low—members were paid only $100 for each day they met, though they were reimbursed for associated travel expenses.[44] Furthermore, the executive secretary position was funded by the home agency of its incumbent. As a result, much of the PFIAB funding went to travel expenses, administrative staff, and other incidental expenditures. The board's 1973 request for redecoration and security improvements was denied owing to lack of funds.

Since its members met only two days a month, the board required only modest office space in the Old Executive Office Building. The space included a conference room, offices for the chair and the executive secretary, and a vault for maintaining records.

Because most PFIAB members were either considered experts in fields related to intelligence and technology or were highly connected political appointees, their dealings with foreign policy, defense issues, and the Nixon administration were by no means confined exclusively to the PFIAB. In some cases it is difficult to determine which actions involved the board members in their capacity as PFIAB members and which actions were unconnected to the board. Often there may have been significant overlap—for instance, Nelson Rockefeller's visit to Latin America and the Caribbean, which is discussed more fully below.

An excellent example of the extent to which PFIAB members maintained a personal relationship with the administration is a May 1970 letter from Clare Booth Luce to Kissinger that can be described only as a bouquet thrown to Kissinger and Nixon. Written before her appointment to the board, Luce commends Kissinger for the difficult decision to resume bombing and send troops into Cambodia.[45] After her appointment, Luce continued to offer her advice and support. For instance, on July 31, 1973, she told the president's assistant, Rose Mary Woods, that the president should "hang in there tough" and "don't hand over the tapes."[46]

Another example includes Foster's remarks on receipt of the Forrestal Award from the National Security Industrial Association, in which he called particular attention to the gap between the United States and the Soviet Union in terms of funding for research and development—a gap that favored the Soviet Union. The text and a summary of Foster's remarks and suggestions were circulated at the highest levels of government and even reached Kissinger himself.[47] Though the issues Foster raised were similar to those examined within the context of the PFIAB, he was not speaking as a PFIAB member. In another case, Lincoln requested a personal meeting with Kissinger in November 1970 to discuss the "Palestinian problem" and "unspecified PFIAB administrative matters."[48]

Robert Murphy met with the Pakistani ambassador to Washington and discussed Chinese-backed support for East Pakistan (Bangladesh). Murphy did not hesitate to write Kissinger a letter directly to report the details of this meeting. In sum, PFIAB members did not hesitate to contact high-ranking administration officials, on occasion, to share their views on national security issues with the broader public.

ISSUES AND RECOMMENDATIONS

Even though the majority of the substantive reports and recommendations issued by the PFIAB during President Nixon's term of office are either still classified or kept by the board itself, a combination of open source material and declassified documents from elsewhere in the intelligence community sheds light on many of the topics addressed. In a confidential interview, a former PFIAB staff member suggested that Nixon submitted to the board only topics that interested a majority of the members, although it is unclear what process the president or his staff took to gauge such interest.[49] The PFIAB made a total of seventy recommendations during Nixon's presidency, but only a fraction of these are available to the public.

The Quality of the Intelligence Community's Analysis

Nixon came into office with great skepticism about whether the intelligence community, and particularly the CIA, was capable of providing him with useful and unbiased intelligence. At a June 18, 1969, NSC meeting, the president complained: "People have been showing a tendency to use intelligence to *support* conclusions, rather than to *arrive* at conclusions. I don't mean to say that they are lying about intelligence or distorting it, but I want you fellows to be very careful to separate facts from opinions in your briefings."[50] A recurrent theme in Nixon's tirades against the CIA is the overrepresentation of Ivy League and Georgetown graduates, whom the president identified as being opposed to his policies, particularly in Vietnam.

At a July 17, 1970, meeting with the board, Nixon stated that he deplored the "tendency in CIA to a 'muted kind of thinking'": "He said that he simply cannot put up with people lying to the President of the United States about intelligence. If the intelligence is inadequate or if the intelligence depicts a bad situation, he wants to know it and he will not stand being served warped evaluations."[51] The focus of discussion in that meeting was a series of trips to Southeast Asia taken by the PFIAB members Anderson, Gray, Franklin Murphy, and Lincoln. The five board members were disappointed with the overall quality of the U.S. intelligence effort in the region and particularly faulted CIA analyses that had initially minimized the importance of the Cambodian port of Sihanoukville as a transit point for supplies for the Vietcong.[52] "The President wondered," meeting minutes indicate, "if such mistakes could be made on a fairly straightforward issue such as this one, how should we judge CIA's assessments of more important developments."[53] "The time may be coming," the president told the board members, "when he would have to read the riot act to the entire Intelligence Community. He said perhaps the most important function for the PFIAB would be to help eradicate subjective judgments from intelligence reports."[54]

At the president's request, the board conducted an in-depth study of the Sihanoukville intelligence failure. Kissinger forwarded that report to Nixon on January 21, 1971, along with a note saying that he had demanded that DCI Helms make some high-level personnel changes at the agency. Nixon wrote on the margin: "Give me a report on these changes—I want a real shake up at C.I.A., not just symbolism."[55] At a July 23, 1971, budget meeting, the president was even more scathing: "The CIA tells me nothing I don't read three days earlier in *The New York Times*. Intelligence is a sacred cow. We've done nothing since we've been here about it. The CIA isn't worth a damn. We have to get out of the symbolism; so a 25 percent cut across-the-board, get rid of the disloyal types."[56] Nixon returned to this theme again in a May 1972 memorandum to Haldeman in which he again complained of the presence of too many liberal Ivy League types at the CIA, demanded a housecleaning, and urged his aide to push for more diversity in the recruitment of agency personnel from Midwestern, Southern, and Western (save for Berkeley and Stanford) colleges.[57] Nixon's response to his perception of political bias in the intelligence community was to try to counter it both from the inside, by purging the community, and from the outside, by bringing other political perspectives to bear on the assessment process.

Soviet Nuclear Capabilities/Strategic Threat

One particular issue that concerned the president from the beginning of his administration was the CIA's estimates of the Soviet nuclear posture. Speaking at a June 19, 1969, NSC meeting, Nixon complained: "The intelligence projections for 1965, 1966, 1967, and 1968—I've seen them all—have been up to 50 percent off in what the Russians were going to have—and on the low side."[58] The focus of debate about Soviet nuclear forces in the later 1960s and early 1970s revolved around a new intercontinental ballistic missile (ICBM) system the Soviets were deploying: the SS-9. The primary question was whether this new system would carry more than one warhead in a system called multiple independent reentry vehicles (MIRVs). If the SS-9 did have this capability, the concern was that it might give the Soviet Union a first-strike capability against the U.S. Minuteman ICBM force. This issue, in turn, was inextricably linked to the debate about whether the United States should deploy the Safeguard antiballistic missile system.[59]

In response, the president gave the PFIAB a special task—to annually assess the nuclear threat to the United States.[60] While the actual reports are not available, it is likely that the board directed its efforts to gauging the accuracy of American intelligence on Soviet nuclear capabilities. Similarly, it studied the adequacy of American weapons systems as compared to their Russian counterparts, a process referred to as *net assessment*.[61] Some archival evidence does indicate specific conclusions reached by the PFIAB. For instance, in May 1974, DCI Colby submitted his comments on an April 30, 1974, PFIAB strategic threat assessment, which concluded that by 1974 the Soviets perceived "themselves as approaching the threshold of overall superiority in strategic power."[62] Colby also shared the PFIAB's concern "over the need to improve the substantive intelligence requirement to support U.S. policy objectives, especially in areas of significant Soviet R&D effort or potential." In addition, he reported that the board had identified three crucial areas—"accuracies of Soviet missiles, prospects for detection of U.S. missile submarines and the strategic implications of Soviet laser developments."[63] The board also recommended that the CIA participate in the preparation of the "Red Integrated Strategic Operations Plan . . . used in war-gaming the SIOP [Single Integrated Operations Plan]" and advised that intelligence estimates required the "keenest possible technical evaluations."[64]

The Soviet threat preoccupied every part of the U.S. government concerned with foreign policy. The PFIAB's examination of Soviet capabilities did not end with an assessment of its nuclear arsenal. For instance, PFIAB chair Admiral Anderson took a great interest in Soviet naval capabilities. A letter of February 8, 1974, from the senior CIA official George Carver stated: "For some weeks, if not months, Anderson has apparently been busily contacting US Naval officers around the world, soliciting their views and assessments of Soviet Naval capabilities and intentions." Anderson also expressed great interest in the CIA's assessments of the Soviet navy.[65] On a related matter, the PFIAB in 1974 requested from the DCI an intelligence assessment of the benefits the Soviet Union obtained from détente.[66] Teller, in particular, took a keen interest in the SALT I treaty and verification process. He personally visited CIA headquarters to let the agency know of his concern that the Soviets might do things "permissible under the wording of the SALT agreement but not within the SALT spirit."[67] In 1974, Teller wrote a memorandum on the possibility of the Soviets testing nuclear weapons in the atmosphere, which DCI Colby took quite seriously.[68]

National Intelligence Estimates

The PFIAB explored the national intelligence officer concept, a community system organized and led by senior regional and functional analysts. It also expressed concern that strategic assessments of the Soviet Union that looked ten years into the future were of questionable utility. It believed that such a time frame was unrealistic considering the pace of technological developments and the political shifts that could occur over the course of a decade.

But the major concern of the board throughout the Nixon administration was that national intelligence estimates (NIEs) of Soviet strategic forces did not adequately consider the full range of explanations for Soviet strategic behavior. As Kissinger told the president in November 1969: "This estimate [NIE 11-8-69, "Soviet Attack Forces"] illustrates what I believe are serious limitations in the process by which estimates are made. The process is an inadequate means for providing basic analysis of Soviet Strategic developments and prospects for the future." The president wrote "Agreed" on the memo.[69]

In response to the Nixon administration's unhappiness with the intelligence community's assessment of the Soviet threat, the PFIAB became deeply engaged in the national intelligence estimative process, an effort championed by a new member of the board. After he stepped down as deputy director of defense research and engineering in the Department of Defense (DOD) and joined the board in 1973, John Foster pushed very hard on this issue. As he recounted: "It soon became clear to me that in a number of cases the NIE overstated the situation. They stated as facts things for which they didn't have the sources to defend the statement. After I bitched for about a year, Chairman Anderson said, 'why don't you [John S. Foster], Teller [Edward Teller] and Galvin [Robert Galvin], form a committee on NIE Evaluation?'"[70]

While there was general agreement that there was a problem with the NIE system, it took some time for a solution to become evident. Eventually, consensus crystallized around "competitive analysis" as the best means to improve the estimate process. In a speech to military reserve officers at the CIA in September 1969, Col. Alexander Haig, Kissinger's senior military adviser, told the audience: "The President . . . feels 'the intelligence community is best served by a certain degree of competition.'"[71] A major 1971 review of the structure of the intelligence community undertaken by George Schultz, the director of the Office of Management and Budget (OMB), and Kissinger raised the possibility of "whether new review board should be created, especially to evaluate the analytical and estimating activities of the community."[72]

This was a sentiment that the board's chair shared. Admiral Anderson stressed the need to have outside observers provide a "check and balance" before releasing the final estimate. In his view, these observers should consist of three or four senior people from outside government that would be responsible only to the DCI.[73] This philosophy would lead the board to endorse a competitive national estimating experiment—referred to as Team B—under President Gerald Ford.

Information Handling

Intelligence handling had been a continuing concern of the PFIAB since the Johnson administration. Under its previous chair, Clifford, the board had advocated centralizing the "design and management" of intelligence community information systems under the DCI.[74] Not satisfied with the modest reform in securing classified documents, it made information handling a priority concern in the fall of 1969.[75] According to Byers, multiple suspected intelligence penetrations of the DOD may have been responsible for the board's interest in safeguarding classified information.[76] In January 1970, Kissinger informed Nixon of the board's continuing concern with this issue.

To better educate senior managers in the intelligence community about this issue, the board's Information Handling Panel organized a seminar on protecting sensitive information on January 8, 1970, and invited representatives of the State Department, the DOD, the Bureau of the Budget, the CIA, the NSA, and the DIA to attend.[77] The seminar was conducted by the board member Baker and featured presentations from various board consultants. A report on the seminar from an NSC consultant was skeptical that the seminar accomplished the board's objective of pushing a greater effort on this issue. He told Kissinger that the presentations were too technical, did not adequately address budget constraints, and ignored what the intelligence community was already doing in this area with the COINS (Community On-Line Information System) program, a system that already allowed analysts in different parts of the community to access select data files. The difficulty of understanding the ins and outs of this issue was evident from Haig's response to this discussion: "Memo is tough to grapple with." Not surprisingly, no decision was made on the board's recommendation at that time.[78]

Nevertheless, the PFIAB continued to examine the issue of information handling and the safeguarding of classified information well into 1970. On March 31, the board again revisited the DCI's role and responsibility in safeguarding intelligence community information.[79] It once again recommended that President Nixon issue a directive that the federal government consolidate its information handling under the DCI.[80] While the letter from Kissinger to Nixon on this topic contains no date, this recommendation probably originated around 1970. Kissinger's letter also includes reference to similar PFIAB recommendations in 1967 that apparently spurred no meaningful action. Evidently, the DCI was against such action, although it is unclear why. Finally, with the PFIAB's request for Nixon's intervention, the DCI responded in 1970 that a presidential directive was unnecessary because the intelligence community was already engaged in the process of centralizing information handling as the board had urged. The PFIAB also examined technical questions surrounding information handling and processing. According to a CIA report from July 1970, the PFIAB served as the driving force behind "Project ASPIN" (Automated Systems for the Production of Intelligence). According to the report, the board noted that the "Agency's information activities had not taken advantage of new information technology to support intelligence information handling and the production of intelligence."[81] Throughout the Nixon administration, the PFIAB examined COINS. The board had advised the intelligence community to implement such a system in 1965 under President Johnson. COINS seemed to have been a major focus of the board's Communication Panel, whose members, at times, became upset at the lack of progress in the system's implementation.[82] Little progress was made on COINS until the fall of 1972, when a test of the system using biographical files (as recommended by PFIAB) proved of limited value.[83] In 1972, however, an internal intelligence community panel reviewed the project and recommended pursuing it with renewed vigor.[84]

The CIA and DCI supplied the PFIAB with a steady stream of reports and updates on the progress of COINS development. The DCI presented the findings of the internal panel's study to the board in 1973. The board concluded that, even though technological progress had been made on the system, it remained under an "ad hoc management structure" and suffered from "insufficient program visibility and support" and "reluctant participation from some agencies."[85] The board recommended that COINS should be given "immediate high level attention," which would "delineate the specific objectives which a community system should achieve," "develop an agreed upon community plan to implement these objectives," and, finally, "identify the management structure best suited to implement the plan."[86] The PFIAB further advised that the DCI himself should provide direct guidance to the project. The board's interest in COINS and its implementation continued, and it received regular reports and briefings on it from the DCI.

Economic Intelligence

Though several members of the PFIAB believed that accurate economic intelligence was critical to the nation's overall intelligence effort, the key proponent of pushing to upgrade the intelligence community's coverage of this topic was Leo Cherne, an economist. The board was particularly concerned about the availability and accuracy of economic intelligence. This issue had been a staple of the PFIAB's agenda since at least 1970. In June of that year, the board heard briefings on the Soviet economy from the CIA's director of economic research.[87] In December 1971, it produced a report that the CIA described as "the first major survey of the U.S. economic intelligence effort since at least 1960."[88] It found that "responsibility for fiscal, monetary and trade matters was fragmented among Government agencies and that the supporting intelligence effort had suffered disproportionately over the years." It recommended that economic intelligence be "considered an essential element in national security policy" and urged the "DCI to take the lead in formulating a broad concept of economic intelligence and resources devoted to it."[89] More specific recommendations and findings of the report are for the most part unavailable, but it is apparent that the PFIAB found fault with the Department of State's efforts in providing accurate economic intelligence.[90]

Spurred by the board member Connally's prescient predictions of the oil embargo and the wheat shortage, the PFIAB issued an update to the 1971 report in December 1973. The report concluded that, while the oil embargo of 1973 had an economic dimension, it was clearly also a political weapon against the United States. Therefore, U.S. dependence on foreign oil was a source of great concern to the board.

In addition, the board cited currency crises in various countries, the sale of American grain to the Soviet Union, and technology transfers to the Soviets as examples of economic issues that needed to be examined by the intelligence community.[91] The board recognized that the U.S. Foreign Service was the primary source of raw economic intelligence and, thus, placed the burden for increased collection on the State Department.[92] However, it also suggested that the CIA dedicate more resources to the collection of economic intelligence.[93] The update observed that too much economic intelligence was "over-classified," called for the CIA to resolve its own diverging views on economic matters, and urged a greater use of SIGINT (signals intelligence) as a source for economic intelligence.[94] The CIA apparently agreed with the report's conclusions. Byers believed that the agency may have shifted its focus to draw on more open sources of economic intelligence, such as the business community, Wall Street, and the oil and banking industries.[95]

Intelligence Community Organization

There were two major efforts at intelligence community reorganization during the Nixon administration. First, in the summer of 1970, a blue-ribbon panel led by Gilbert Fitzhugh looked into the problem of disorganization in the intelligence effort at the DOD.[96] Second, in the spring of 1971, Director of the OMB Schultz and Kissinger initiated a more general effort to reorganize the intelligence community that Haig predicted to Kissinger would "be the most controversial gunfight in recent bureaucratic experience."[97] Given that the organization of the intelligence community was of long-standing concern to the PFIAB, it is no surprise that it would be deeply involved in both of these efforts.

Since the bulk of the intelligence community, whether measured in budget or personnel, falls under the purview of the DOD, reorganization of the defense intelligence effort is a huge task. The Fitzhugh Panel considered a variety of reorganization schemes but finally settled on one that "would put all authority for defense intelligence under an

Assistant Secretary of Defense for Intelligence, who would represent DOD on the USIB and have as his principal subordinates 'Defense Security Command' with functions now performed by service collection agencies and NSA and NRO [National Reconnaissance Office] and a 'Defense Production Agency' which would have charge of all intelligence production to combatant forces."[98] The board's executive secretary, Gerard Burke, who attended an October 20, 1970, meeting on the Fitzhugh Panel recommendations, concluded that all of them were "at best unrealistic," and the board recommended that decisions about the reorganization of defense intelligence be made by the NSC because of their communitywide implications.[99]

Indeed, the general inclination within the Nixon administration by the end of 1970 was to pursue a more ambitious intelligence community reorganization agenda. Senior aides like Haig thought that the board had an important role to play in this larger effort. "One of the most valuable services the President's Foreign Intelligence Advisory Board could perform," Haig wrote to Kissinger in preparation for a meeting with the board on December 3, 1970, "would be to take a hard look at the entire intelligence community to see what we can do to make sure the President and the National Security Council get the best possible intelligence support."[100] He reminded Kissinger of the context of the president's concerns about intelligence reorganization, which included the Sihanoukville, Soviet strategic force development, Middle East ceasefire violations, and Chilean political trends intelligence failures. Finally, he agreed with the board's earlier assessment that military intelligence reorganization ought to be folded into a larger reorganization of the entire community.[101]

The Nixon administration's larger effort at intelligence community reorganization was spurred by three interrelated problems: (1) there was a lack of leadership in the community, a point the board had emphasized since its inception under Eisenhower; (2) the defense intelligence functions, which constituted the lion's share of the community effort, were disorganized internally and not well integrated into the intelligence community; and (3) the divisions of functional responsibility within the community were unclear and often duplicative.[102] The result, in the view of Kissinger and Schultz's staff study "A Review of the Intelligence Community," was that "the operations of the intelligence community have produced two disturbing phenomena. The first is an impressive rise in their size and cost. The second is an apparent inability to achieve a commensurate improvement in its scope and overall quality of intelligence products."[103] Their solution, which reflected arguments the board had long made, was greater community leadership under the DCI. Without such outside leadership, the study explained, "internally generated values predominate in the community's institutions. These values favor increasingly sophisticated and expensive collection technologies at the expense of analytical capabilities."[104]

Despite the fact that the board was in general agreement with the thrust of the Nixon administration's efforts, support for the Schultz/Kissinger schema was, in Deputy OMB Director (and later DCI) James Schlesinger's view, "less clear as each member [of the PFIAB] has somewhat different views."[105] The depth of the board's reservations can be gauged from the fact that Chair Anderson requested a meeting directly with the president during its regular meeting in June 1971.[106]

The board submitted a major report directly to the president on this issue in June 1971.[107] This report to the president was prompted by a joint NSC/OMB paper called the "Schultz Report," which examined the issue of intelligence organization and the need for improved intelligence.[108] The gist of the board's concerns about the NSC/OMB proposal were (1) that it overstated the problems in the community and ignored the real strengths of the current arrangement and (2) that the proposal for reorganization was so sweeping that it would require new congressional legislation, which the board thought imprudent.[109] The board felt that the central problem—the lack of intelligence community leadership—could be solved by the reconstitution of the U.S. Intelligence Board (USIB) by the appointment of "consumers" of intelligence, rather than "producers," so as to better serve as a tool of community management by the DCI.[110] The board's reasoning for the former suggestion was that a USIB made up of intelligence consumers rather than producers would better serve the needs of policymakers.[111] The board also recommended that the USIB create two new committees—an Intelligence Evaluation Committee and an Intelligence Resource Committee—to facilitate its larger role in community management. It also weighed in on a number of related issues, including endorsing the idea of establishing an assistant secretary of defense for intelligence to better centralize the community efforts in the Pentagon, opposing any change in the status of the DIA in the defense intelligence scheme, removing the cartographic mission from the community's budget, and seeking authorization for the PFIAB chair to attend USIB meetings. At its root, the fundamental difference between the NSC/OMB and the PFIAB schemas, Haig reported to Kissinger in September 1971, was the former's preference for centralization of the community under a single individual as opposed to the latter's desire to accomplish this objective through a reformed USIB and associated committee system.[112]

By the fall of 1971, the momentum within the Nixon administration appeared to be moving in favor of the more limited PFIAB reorganization proposal.[113] In a September 24, 1971, memo to Kissinger, Haig found only a handful of minor PFIAB recommendations "unacceptable," and, when the president issued his own memorandum on November 5, 1971, announcing the final version of the reorganization plan, he adopted almost all the major board recommendations and also charged the board with "coordinating" the new NSC intelligence directives (NSCIDs) to implement it.[114] The PFIAB's victory came at a slight cost. Senior senators—Stuart Symington (D-MO) and J. William Fulbright (D-AK)—complained bitterly to Kissinger about this major effort being undertaken without coordination with their committees. In an effort to smooth ruffled feathers, Kissinger called each to apologize but in the process laid the blame for this lack of coordination on the OMB and the PFIAB.[115]

In its discussions of intelligence reorganization, the board also touched on a number of related issues. Byers indicated that the board discussed such drastic measures as relocating the CIA's operations division outside Washington, DC, and even making it a separate agency. In the PFIAB's view, this change would allow more independence of action and facilitate recruiting. However, the board decided that such suggestions were too radical to approve and made no formal recommendation.[116]

The PFIAB recommended that the head of the NSA should be a four-star military officer or a civilian of similar rank. It also discussed the lack of cooperation between the CIA and the FBI in covering the overlap between domestic and foreign intelligence and the need to improve the rapport between the agencies. The board and the president were particularly concerned about the lack of FBI wiretaps directed at foreign diplomatic facilities in the United States.[117]

Human Intelligence

In May 1972, President Nixon tasked the board with conducting a study of how U.S. human intelligence capabilities could be improved. In his memorandum to Admiral Anderson, the president advised: "Because of the special sensitivity of this method of collection, the study is to be conducted exclusively by the Board with assistance from appropriate consultants as deemed necessary by the Board." Once it was completed, Nixon directed, the "report, with its recommendations, should be transmitted to [him] alone, through [his] Assistant for National Security Affairs."[118]

In response, the PFIAB conducted an exhaustive study of human source intelligence, which Admiral Anderson believed to be the first of its kind, releasing the study in March 1973.[119] The board recommended that the intelligence community centralize the process under the DCI as community leader, arguing that "systematizing, amalgamating, and optimizing these efforts is a national problem and not a problem to be solved individually by several agencies."[120] It also suggested that the CIA should recruit operations officers with more linguistic and ethnic diversity and leave them in locations longer than the standard two-year assignment. Additional findings included a recognition that the Foreign Service could theoretically make a much larger contribution to the human intelligence effort, that the defense attaché system "needed better career development and training," that the FBI's legal attachés were not sufficiently used, and that human intelligence needed better national "overall-direction and planning."[121]

The study annoyed the DCI, who feared not only the possible compromise of methods and sources but also the interference of an outside advisory board in an activity long considered the exclusive purview of the CIA.[122] Despite his opposition, the board continued to investigate human intelligence as late as August 1974.[123]

Technical Intelligence Collection

The Nixon PFIAB continued the board's long-standing engagement with the technical aspects of intelligence collection. Under the leadership of Land, the PFIAB made important contributions to the improvement of the U.S. satellite reconnaissance systems. The key debate within the community was whether the United States should continue to rely on imaging systems using film canisters that had to be retrieved by aircraft over the Pacific Ocean after they reentered the earth's atmosphere or whether a new generation of spy satellites using a real-time, electro-optical camera system should be developed. The NRO took a cautious approach and advocated staying with the tried-and-true film canister system the United States had employed since the later 1950s. Conversely, the CIA pushed the radical new electro-optical approach. As DCI Helms argued in a memorandum to the incoming president-elect in January 1969: "Obviously the development of such a [real-time satellite surveillance] capability would be expensive and may burden the facilities presently available to exploit and interpret photography. Nevertheless, I believe that we should acquire this new system and am assured by technical experts, including Dr. Edwin Land of the Polaroid Corporation, that it is technically feasible."[124]

Land's long-standing interest in overhead imagining technology had led him to conclude that by the early 1970s the electro-optical technology was then ripe, so he supported the CIA's position. Land convinced his colleagues on the board, who in turn convinced the president to side with the CIA. Nixon himself reportedly was present at a board meeting dedicated to this issue. After the discussion concluded, the president asked Land, then one of the foremost photography experts in the world, his opinion. Land responded that Nixon should choose the new electro-optical system proposed by the CIA. Nixon agreed, and the DOD's proposal never moved forward.[125] Richelson rightly concludes that the development of a new satellite imaging system was "'a direct consequence'" of the PFIAB's intervention into this debate.[126]

Energy

Though the board's interest in energy issues initially arose in conjunction with its broader interest in economic intelligence, eventually energy would become a discrete focus of the board in its own right. In 1972, the board urged the administration to take the possibility of an energy crisis seriously and to publicize a classified State Department report on the issue to inform the American public of the gravity of the energy problem and its possible effects on the economy and national security. On February 8, 1973, Kissinger also requested that the board prepare a report on how to best spend federal research-and-development funds for energy. It delivered this report to him at their October 4, 1973, meeting, though it was not submitted to Nixon until December 7.[127] Foster and Teller took the lead in preparing this report, which noted that the ever-increasing demands for energy would slowly begin to overwhelm the available supply, particularly regarding oil.[128] Among the board's recommendations were the following:

- "That the senior staff of an energy research and design agency be recruited as a team."
- "That many should come from private industry."
- "That the greatest priority should be placed on short-range programs designed to provide benefits before 1980."
- "That recruitment of technical manpower for government laboratories should receive early attention."[129]

The board advised focusing on projects that would reduce consumption, improve efficiency, recover and save more fossil fuels, and improve nuclear energy technology.[130] The report examined many technical issues and identified areas where investment would produce short-term payoffs. It also included a proposed 1975 energy research-and-development budget.

Other Issues

The PFIAB examined several issues that, unfortunately, have little archival documentation.

Nixon Doctrine

According to one former PFIAB staffer, several staff members examined the issue of how to implement the administration's new policy, the Nixon Doctrine, in Vietnam; the policy expected American allies to provide for their own military defense, with the United States continuing to provide logistic support and training to help them do so. Connally, Lincoln, and Pace examined this issue in depth and submitted a report to the president.[131]

China

In 1970, board members conducted extensive discussions with the CIA's China Intelligence Activities Coordinator that covered a variety of topics. Taylor, Lincoln, and the PFIAB's China Panel were particularly interested in the prospects for Chinese acquisition of advanced weapons.[132]

Sino-Soviet Relations

Admiral Anderson requested, and received, a report from the CIA in February 1971 on "Sino-Soviet Relations and the Question of Hostilities." Although we know little about the report or any subsequent PFIAB actions or recommendations arising from it, the paper did discuss the Soviet view of the Chinese threat, particularly in light of the latter's nuclear weapons and ballistic missile programs.[133]

The Pentagon Papers

In 1971, the board formed a special panel to conduct an assessment of the damage to U.S. intelligence caused by the release of the Pentagon Papers to the press. Lincoln chaired the panel, and Baker and possibly Pace served as members. The only piece of archival evidence for this is an internal CIA memorandum for the general counsel directing him to prepare a briefing for the PFIAB panel. No report or recommendations resulting from the board's examination of the Pentagon Papers affair are available.[134]

Narcotics Intelligence

In keeping with the Nixon administration's declaration of a "War on Drugs," the PFIAB examined intelligence issues surrounding the narcotics industry. The White House believed that overseas intelligence coverage of the drug trade was inadequate owing to bureaucratic parochialism, the absence of central responsibility for the production of drug intelligence, the inability of Customs and Bureau of Narcotics and Dangerous Drug operators to work effectively in foreign environments, and the general disinterest at the CIA in the issue of narcotics trafficking. The president hoped to get the PFIAB to participate in a comprehensive review of overseas narcotics intelligence efforts, and the board received a briefing on and tasks to perform related to the issue.[135] No additional information about actions taken or specific findings and recommendations issued is available.

Intelligence Legislation

The PFIAB dealt extensively with the issue of an increasingly assertive Congress demanding more access to information about the intelligence community's operating procedures and products. Its recommendations concerning intelligence-related legislation were made initially within the context of intelligence community reorganization, as we discussed above, but it also examined the issue of congressional intelligence legislation explicitly. In 1972, Anderson informed Nixon of the board's opposition to proposed legislation—aimed at amending the National Security Act of 1947—that would keep Congress "better informed on matters relating to foreign policy and national security by providing it with intelligence information obtained by the Central Intelligence Agency and with analysis of such information."[136] The board also advised the president to continue to oppose a 1972 bill that would have required the executive branch and the intelligence community to keep Congress better informed of intelligence matters, on the grounds that it would politicize the intelligence analysis and would compromise sensitive information.[137]

American Prisoners of War

In a letter to National Security Adviser Kissinger on October 11, 1972, Anderson urged the administration, on behalf of the board, to inform the American public about a special DOD program to help assist American prisoners of war reintegrate into society following their release. The board also advised cautioning the American public that the North Vietnamese often released small numbers of prisoners of war for propaganda purposes and not as an expression of good faith.[138]

Naval Affairs

The PFIAB established a Naval Panel in response to Nixon's desire to help ensure that the U.S. Navy remained competitive with the Soviet Union at sea. Although very little information about the panel's work is available, it apparently did meet frequently following Nixon's tasking on October 4, 1973. By November 20, 1973, the Navy Panel had already had three meetings. At the November 20 meeting, it examined the naval command and control procedures of both the U.S. and the Soviet navies. The board also revisited the persistent issue of whether the intelligence community was producing accurate assessments of Soviet forces. Senior U.S. Navy officers believed that Soviet naval forces were consistently underestimated.[139]

Educating the Public on Intelligence

In 1973, the board considered advising the president to release an unclassified statement on the importance of intelligence to the United States. The proposal was submitted by Nelson Rockefeller, who wrote a paper explaining the rationale for such a public declaration. The board eventually reached a consensus that it would be a good idea to submit the recommendation to the president, and Cherne and the staff drew up a proposal. It is unclear how this proposal was received by the administration.[140]

Chile

At the behest of Kissinger, the PFIAB made an inquiry into the election of Salvador Allende in Chile. However, this inquiry was eventually aborted when the board's request for meeting minutes of the NSC and Forty Committee was rejected.[141]

On-Site Reviews, Individual Travel, and Area Examinations

Nixon's PFIAB continued the tradition of sending individuals or small groups of board members and staffers abroad to investigate intelligence issues or perform related tasks on behalf of the president.

Latin America

New York governor Nelson Rockefeller traveled to Latin America in 1969 on behalf of the president at least once. He made an extensive tour of Central and South America and the Caribbean, returning with a laundry list of observations and controversial recommendations designed to improve U.S. policy in the region. It is unclear, however, whether Rockefeller made this trip as a member of the PFIAB or in another capacity.

Some of Rockefeller's suggestions and recommendations strayed far from the PFIAB's usual domain—for instance, advising that Pan American should build a hotel without a casino in Guatemala and recommending that the United States assist Trinidad in building ships for interisland passenger and freight traffic.[142] Other advice did have direct relevance to intelligence and security affairs—for instance, that the United States extend aid to El Salvador's Radio Nacional and that it explore the possibility of "sharing the cost of Che Guevara['s] campaign of approx. $6 million."[143] Finally, some of his recommendations strayed far into the realm of foreign policy making: he advised that the U.S. support Panama's Gen. Omar Torrijos, encourage possible candidates to run for president in El Salvador, and extend financial assistance to Salvadoran political parties.[144] The evidence thus appears to indicate that his trip was at most only partly dedicated to PFIAB matters.

Kissinger dutifully referred several of Rockefeller's suggestions to his advisers for further study. He was skeptical of Rockefeller's foreign policy advice, so the latter's suggestions were not taken seriously. Nevertheless, General Torrijos enjoyed meeting with Rockefeller so much that he expressed interest in dealing exclusively with him as a U.S. envoy. But Nixon, acting on Kissinger's advice, instructed Rockefeller to inform the general that he should continue to communicate with the U.S. government through the U.S. ambassador in Panama City.[145]

Southeast Asia

In 1970, four members of the PFIAB (Gray, Anderson, Franklin Murphy, and Lincoln) made a fact-finding trip to Southeast Asia and met with Nixon on their return.[146] As discussed previously, their primary mission was to investigate U.S. intelligence operations in the region. As a result of his trip, Admiral Anderson informed the Saigon CIA station that he believed the United States needed better intelligence about North Vietnamese intentions.[147] In response, the DCI instructed a subordinate to review "all materials published during the past five years on what we have said about North Vietnamese intentions and to prepare a paper on where we have been right and wrong." The DCI discussed this paper and the CIA's performance in Vietnam over the years with the PFIAB.[148] There are many other documentary references to the

PFIAB receiving briefings or requesting information on the situation in Vietnam. For instance, in June 1974, the DCI requested estimates on "the short term prospect for Cambodia" and "the likelihood of a major North Vietnamese Offensive against South Vietnam before June 30, 1974" for his PFIAB briefing book.[149] In addition to investigating U.S. intelligence operations in the region, the board recommended that the president increase publicity for a program to assist American prisoners of war who had escaped or were missing in action.[150]

The Eastern Mediterranean, the Yom Kippur War, and the Middle East

In 1970, the board received an extensive briefing on the Middle East situation from the deputy DCI. It covered such diverse topics as the Soviet Union's activities in the region, the effect of Nasser's death on Egypt's foreign policy, and the interplay between the United States, the Soviet Union, the Arab states, and Israel.[151]

According to a former PFIAB staffer, Nixon asked the board to evaluate the naval balance in the eastern Mediterranean following the October 1973 Yom Kippur War. The president was concerned about the possibility that U.S. allies might waver in the area if they thought that the United States was overmatched by the Soviet Union. Olmer and Chair Anderson did most of the research, traveling around the world to gather information for the report.[152] The PFIAB examined the issue and submitted a report about the views of the English, German, Italian, Japanese, and other allies and U.S. capabilities in the eastern Mediterranean.

The PFIAB by no means restricted its examinations of the Middle East to these two occasions. Archival sources indicate that it was a frequent topic at meetings and briefings. The most significant report the board issued dealing with the Middle East was its postmortem of the intelligence failure in the run-up to the October 1973 Yom Kippur War, though, as the State Department intelligence analyst David E. Mark observed, the report "left things unclear."[153]

Taiwan

Robert Murphy traveled to Taiwan on behalf of the president in 1971 to carry a "personal message" to Generalissimo Chiang Kai-shek. It is unclear whether he undertook this mission as a member of the PFIAB or simply in his capacity as an influential and highly connected private citizen. He conveyed the message that, despite warmer relations between the United States and the People's Republic of China (PRC), the United States remained committed to the defense of Taiwan. Murphy was also instructed to discuss the PRC's nonrepresentation in the United Nations and work with Chiang to resolve the issue in a manner acceptable to the PRC and to Taiwan.[154]

West Germany

In 1971, Anderson made a trip to West Germany on behalf of the PFIAB and held discussions with U.S. commanders in the area. Although he reported that U.S. intelligence capabilities in West Germany were good, he concluded that they still needed to improve to keep pace with Soviet military modernization in Europe. Anderson also urged the director of the NSA to work with U.S. commanders in Europe to increase SIGINT coverage of Soviet forces in Europe.[155]

Iberian Peninsula

Anderson visited both Portugal and Spain in the summer of 1973 on behalf of the PFIAB and met with both civilian and military officials and U.S. citizens residing there. On his return, he urged that an ambassador to Portugal be named as soon as possible as the Portuguese were dismayed that no U.S. ambassador had been posted throughout 1973. He also commended the conduct and work of the U.S. ambassador to Spain, Admiral Rivero, who was doing his job "with no fanfare" and was "liked and respected by his own people in the Embassy, by the American community here, by Spaniards and by the Foreign Diplomatic Corps."[156]

Saudi Arabia

In December 1972, both Connally and Lincoln visited Saudi Arabia. Connally was the guest of King Faisal. Both trips appear to have been personal in nature, and it is unclear whether either of them was connected with any PFIAB business.[157]

ASSESSMENT AND FUTURE RESEARCH AND RECOMMENDATIONS

The members of President Nixon's PFIAB came from a wide variety of backgrounds, including government, academe, science, and business. All brought unique skills and experiences with them to serve on the board. Turnover was commonplace during Nixon's presidency. Between 1969 and 1974, the PFIAB lost six members and added eight. The staff also fluctuated greatly, with three different executive directors supporting the board's activities. Despite personnel changes and the loss of influence in the administration over time, the board managed to address numerous topics of considerable interest to the U.S. intelligence community and national security. Despite an initial impulse to use a board appointment as compensation for friends and political allies, Nixon retained some of Johnson's most qualified appointees and made good use of the board at times during his administration.

The PFIAB received decreasing attention from the White House over the course of the Nixon administration. Fresh from his 1968 election victory, Nixon began his administration engaged and interested in the topics the board addressed and receptive to its recommendations. As his presidency became mired in the Watergate scandal and managing the crisis became all-consuming, the president paid less attention to the PFIAB. Another problem the board faced was that, although it often found allies and support inside the intelligence community, the relationship could be tense. For instance, the DCI and the rest of the community offered substantial resistance to the board's efforts to investigate human source intelligence and sometimes resented PFIAB criticisms of NIEs.

Even before the Watergate crisis erupted, the Nixon administration's view of the board was mixed. As we saw above, the board was involved in many of the most important intelligence-related policy decisions and often had a significant impact on their outcome. Some of the most important of these include intelligence community reorganization and reform of the NIE process. The board's focus on economic intelligence led to a new emphasis on the subject within the intelligence community.

On the other hand, there were hints from early in the Nixon administration of a cavalier and at times dismissive attitude toward the board. In a December 3, 1970, memo prior to a lunch meeting with the board, Haig advised Kissinger to brief the board on certain topics on which it had shown "inquisitiveness" and about which it "would benefit greatly from receiving from you the party-line . . . [t]o divert [its] activities from these sensitive issues."[158] At a meeting the next day with Helms, the board discovered to its surprise that the Nixon administration had excluded the DCI from discussions of policy, a move it regarded as unwise.[159] In discussion of the OMB/NSC intelligence reorganization proposals in the spring of 1971, Assistant Director of OMB Schlesinger suggested involving the PFIAB in the deliberations because it "may be essential for cosmetic reasons."[160] But nothing better illustrates Nixon's ambivalent view of the board than a December 27, 1972, memorandum to Haldeman in which he admitted that the PFIAB was "a prestigious group" but complained that, instead of being an independent advisory group, "it really represents various segments of the status quo in the intelligence community."[161]

If the board had received the authority (or even just some encouragement) from the White House, it could have investigated a number of the most important intelligence and national security issues, such as the impact of the prolonged U.S. air campaign against economic and military targets in North Vietnam and the likelihood of the durability of the Paris Peace Accords of 1973. However, we can find no indication that it did. It is possible that Nixon did not ask it to examine these issues because of his suspicion of the CIA, which he regarded as at best inept and at worst as populated with disloyal liberals who would not hesitate to collude with the Democrats against him, as he suspected Dulles had with Kennedy in the 1960 election.[162]

What explains the Nixon board's mixed success? There is a great temptation to fall back on presidential style and personality explanations in this case, particularly given Nixon's extreme negative scores on each of those things. But the fact that, despite Nixon's centralizing style and paranoid personality, the board did in some cases still play an important role suggests that we need to look instead at other explanations. In this case, the best explanation seems to be that the increasing size and scope of government—what the historian Arthur Schlesinger would famously call the *imperial presidency*—provides a better account for the board's role during the Nixon years.[163] In brief, the board began losing influence during the Nixon administration at precisely that period in the political development of the American presidency in which such independent, outside advisory boards became not only irrelevant, given the increasing institutionalization of the presidency, but also a downright nuisance.[164]

5

Gerald R. Ford/Jimmy Carter

When President Richard Nixon resigned from office on August 9, 1974, a tumultuous time loomed on the horizon for the CIA and the intelligence community as a whole—1975 would be "*the* year of intelligence."[1] President Gerald Ford was not a novice when it came to intelligence matters; he had seen firsthand the role of intelligence during his service in the U.S. Navy and in Congress and as vice president. But as Christopher Andrew observes: "Ford had concentrated on the nuts and bolts of administration rather than the great issues of national and international policy."[2] To aid him in navigating the murky waters of intelligence, Ford turned to the President's Foreign Intelligence Advisory Board (PFIAB) assembled by former President Nixon.

The role of the PFIAB in the mid- and late 1970s must be seen in the context of its history and the new concern with intelligence oversight and reform during the Ford administration as Congress charged into a comprehensive review of the American intelligence apparatus. Loch Johnson described this process as taking place in terms of a transition between two "eras of intelligence oversight"—an "era of trust" and an "era of uneasy partnership"—where there has been an "ebb and flow in the attitude of lawmakers toward oversight."[3] This changing institutional structure of oversight is important in understanding the changing role of the PFIAB in the mid-1970s.

Era of Trust

Oversight during the period after World War II until the early 1970s was virtually nonexistent. What minimal oversight that existed involved a large element of trust. The leadership of the House and Senate Armed Services committees, which was charged with oversight of the CIA, tended to be lax about policing the intelligence community owing to its trust in the CIA and unquestioning support of its Cold War mission of protecting the United States against the Soviet threat. Despite intelligence failures such as the loss of Francis Gary Powers's U-2 over the Soviet Union in 1960, the Bay of Pigs invasion in 1961, covert meddling in democratic Chile between 1963 and 1973, and the Watergate scandal of 1972, Congress showed little concern about the state of the intelligence community.[4] According to Marvin Ott: "Oversight hardly existed, and what there was occurred outside the purview of most of Congress and the public."[5] This situation changed dramatically in the 1970s.

Era of Uneasy Partnership

Domestic developments in the United States ended the "era of trust" in congressional oversight. Allegations about illegal domestic intelligence operations such as the CIA's domestic surveillance program, Operation CHAOS, and questionable foreign covert action in Chile surfaced in the *New York Times* in a series of articles written by Seymour Hersh in late 1974. These allegations drove members of Congress into a fury over the misdeeds of the intelligence community. On December 31, 1974, Congress passed its first significant legislation to assert control over the CIA, the Hughes-Ryan Act, which required a finding—written presidential authorization—to authorize covert action and mandated that Congress be given timely reports on all the presidential findings that were approved.[6] From 1975 to 1976, the Church Committee in the Senate and the Pike Committee in the House conducted the largest investigation into U.S. intelligence operations in American history and left no stone unturned in their reviews. Revelations of improprieties such as assassination plots targeting foreign leaders, illegal wiretaps, smear campaigns against Vietnam War protesters, the maintenance of files on American citizens, drug experiments, and covert action plans became staples of the Church and Pike Committee hearings.[7] The intelligence oversight institutional structure was dramatically altered with the establishment of the Senate Select Committee on Intelligence in May 1976 and the House Permanent Select Committee on Intelligence in July 1977 under the Carter administration.[8] These permanent committees were given the power to oversee the intelligence community and were bolstered, according to Johnson, "with sizable professional staffs, subpoena powers, and the rights to conduct hearings and establish budget authorizations."[9]

As a direct result of these reforms, President Ford now faced the task of coordinating intelligence policy with both the executive and the legislative branches of government. The PFIAB also faced a challenge: either strengthen and improve its own oversight capabilities, or appear to be redundant with the establishment of permanent legislative oversight bodies. One unique asset the board had during this era of reform was its direct relationship to the president.

REFORM

Starting in 1975, and continuing through 1976, the Ford administration and Congress conducted four separate investigations concerning the propriety of intelligence operations and the adequacy of intelligence organizations and procedures.[10] Each had specific recommendations concerning the role of the PFIAB.[11] The Senate Church Committee Report, the House Pike Committee Report, and the Rockefeller Commission (which was investigating CIA activities within the United States and headed by Vice President Nelson Rockefeller, a former PFIAB member) all had a major role in addressing oversight of the intelligence community and shaping the future of the PFIAB.[12] In addition, a fourth report written by the Murphy Commission (headed by the former [and future] PFIAB member Ambassador Robert D. Murphy) entitled *Organization of the Government for the Conduct of Foreign Policy* focused on larger America foreign policy issues but also provided recommendations for intelligence reform.[13]

Since the Rockefeller Commission's chair was also the vice president, it was likely the Ford administration would follow that commission's recommendations for the board.[14] In its June 6, 1975, report, the commission recommended an increased role for the PFIAB as part of its larger effort to improve the oversight of the intelligence community.[15] In chapter 7 of the Rockefeller Report, Recommendation 5 outlined an expanded role for the PFIAB. This included direct oversight of the CIA on issues of statutory authority and the quality of intelligence collection procedures and products. The report further recommended that the PFIAB have access to all the information within the CIA and that the CIA inspector general be granted authority to report directly to the board.[16] The scope and authority of the PFIAB would have been substantial if the Rockefeller Commission recommendations had been implemented.

The Murphy Commission, which reported three weeks after the Rockefeller Commission, also recommended strengthening the PFIAB's oversight of the CIA.[17] "In view of the special importance and sensitivity of intelligence," the report noted, "the Commission believes the President should have sources of advice independent of the . . . [director of central intelligence (DCI)]. The PFIAB should become the principal such source. In the past, PFIAB has played an important role in the development of technical collection systems, in conducting useful analysis of apparent intelligence failures, and in directing attention to new issues for intelligence concern."[18]

In response to the Rockefeller and Murphy commissions' reports, President Ford did consider expanding the mission of the PFIAB. A draft executive order (EO) in August 1975 stated that the board would "receive, investigate, consider, and make appropriate recommendations with respect to allegations of improprieties involving agencies within the Foreign Intelligence Community made by employees of such agencies."[19]

DCI Colby raised concerns about this proposed expanded role for the board, however, arguing:

> PFIAB, as it is proposed in the draft Executive Order, would act as a civilian review board, much like the organizations created in the late 1960s to oversee metropolitan police forces. As a civilian review board, it is susceptible to many of the vices attached to such organizations. Now, PFIAB plays an important role in the major questions relating to foreign intelligence. It is questionable whether the same talented people would be interested or sufficiently free to handle the continuous "watch dog" assignment. Thus I recommend that PFIAB continue its present role as independent advisor to the President on major intelligence problems but not be brought into detailed management review for which its part-time membership is not well suited.[20]

Despite the DCI's objections, the president continued to consider expanding the PFIAB's role. A White House memorandum of September 30, 1975, stated: "The President has approved expanding the responsibilities of PFIAB to include oversight of intelligence matters. He has also approved renaming the board to clearly indicate its new responsibilities."[21] Again, DCI Colby returned the draft order with alterations to the text emphasizing the PFIAB's advisory capacity.[22] On October 16, 1975, John Marsh, counsel to the president, circulated yet another revised EO that expanded the PFIAB's role to management and oversight and renamed it the President's Advisory Board on the Foreign Intelligence Community. This draft EO would also have banned current intelligence professionals serving on the new board's staff.[23] A draft response by the DCI noted that his previous proposed alterations to the proposed EO had apparently not been incorporated, and he voiced his strong objection to a ban on intelligence community professionals serving on the staff of the new board.[24] Whether this objection was forwarded to Marsh is unknown, but the idea of substantially altering the PFIAB's mission and scope was eventually abandoned.

Instead, the combined recommendations of the Murphy and Rockefeller commissions and the effect of the Church and Pike Committee hearings pushed the Ford administration to issue EO 11905 on February 18, 1976. This new EO redefined intelligence operations, banned political assassinations, and increased oversight activities with structural changes to the government. It also left in place the guidance contained in EO 11460, issued on March 20, 1969, which continued to define the duties and role of the PFIAB under President Ford.[25] The failure of the effort to extend the board's mandate is, in retrospect, not surprising inasmuch as the institutional framework for intelligence oversight—in both the executive and the legislative branches—had by the mid-1970s become quite dense, leaving little room for an organization like the PFIAB to play a greater role.

On September 24, 1975, five months before the release of EO 11905, the PFIAB chair, Adm. George W. Anderson Jr., wrote to President Ford to reiterate his vision of the PFIAB's role in the intelligence community. He stressed the uniqueness of the PFIAB as a "presidentially-appointed Board independent of the bureaucracy, responsible to the President, with membership which provides continuity." He continued: "We believe we can assist you in the restoration of confidence in the effectiveness and propriety of the nation's foreign intelligence activities."[26] Anderson advocated strengthening the PFIAB in order to improve relationships between "agency and departmental heads and Inspectors General thereof and the Board."[27] He further argued that the president needed to have a significant role and interest in intelligence matters because it is the "most compelling and inspiring influence not only on his own staff, but the intelligence community."[28] He went on to identify what he judged to be the three foundations of a successful PFIAB:

- "It should publicly be represented as a group of private American citizens with direct regular access to the President; his cabinet officers, and intelligence community officials; it should have continuous access to the central aspects of the nation's foreign, economic, and military policies, and to all necessary information concerning the national security, in order to ensure that effective intelligence contributes to the strengthening of these policies and the nation's security."

- "It is a group of experienced citizens representative of various professional disciplines in American life whose understanding of world affairs and national interest, of scientific achievement and its applications, transcends partisanship: a group whose stature and reputation enable it to develop insights into the current and future intelligence requirements of the President and other senior policy-makers."
- "It is a group which understands the need for an intelligence community meriting special trust consistent with the need for public reassurance that this trust will be faithfully guarded."[29]

Even with these foundations, the PFIAB had inherent limitations as it was a part-time board, completely dependent on its relationship with the president to establish its authority among various components of the intelligence community.

The issuance of EO 11905 supplemented the National Security Act of 1947 concerning the conduct of intelligence community oversight, improvement of the quality of intelligence produced, and assurance of compliance with the laws of the United States. President Ford also challenged Congress to create a Joint Foreign Intelligence Oversight Committee to supplement the PFIAB.[30] While the PFIAB retained its original scope and responsibilities under EO 11460, Ford created the Intelligence Oversight Board (IOB) with EO 11905.[31] The IOB was designed to work in conjunction with the National Security Council (NSC) and the Committee on Foreign Intelligence (CFI) to monitor the performance of U.S. intelligence operations.[32] Overall responsibility for oversight of the U.S. intelligence community would still reside with the president, to whom all three oversight components reported.[33]

The new IOB membership was composed of three individuals from the private sector who did not have ties to the intelligence community, although they could also serve as members of the PFIAB.[34] The IOB was given three functions:

- "Receive and consider reports by Inspectors General and General Counsels of the intelligence community concerning activities that raise questions of legality and propriety."
- "Review periodically the practices and procedures of the intelligence community Inspectors General and General Counsels designed to assist the Oversight Board."
- "Report periodically and in a timely manner, as appropriate, to

the Attorney General and the President on any activities that raise serious questions about legality. It shall report to the President on activities that raise questions of propriety of intelligence community activities."[35]

In a memorandum for the White House press secretary, Wheaton Byers, the executive secretary of the PFIAB, reiterated that the IOB was "an independent body and not a subcommittee of the PFIAB" and that it was to be free of influence from both the intelligence community and the White House.[36] Byers also noted that "the members of the Oversight Board also serve on the PFIAB [which] provides them with additional access to the activities of the intelligence community at the highest level."[37]

When the Church Committee released its final report in April 1976, EO 11905 had been in effect for two months. This report recommended against making the PFIAB the oversight body for the intelligence community, in contrast to the Rockefeller and Murphy Commission reports. President Ford and Senator Church were in agreement that the scope of the PFIAB should remain the same as it had been under President Nixon. EO 11905 therefore did not designate the board as an oversight body. The Church Committee's final report summarized the debate about the role of the PFIAB in the oversight of the intelligence community:

> Whether PFIAB should adopt this oversight or "watchdog" function, or whether Congress should be involved in the activities of the Board is open to question. President Ford, in his Executive Order [for the intelligence community], decided against transforming the Board into a CIA watchdog. Instead, he created a new three-member Intelligence Oversight Board to monitor the activities of the intelligence community.
>
> The Board has not been an executive "watchdog" of the CIA. To make it so would be to place the Board in an untenable position: advisor to the President on the quality and effectiveness of intelligence on the one hand and "policeman" of the intelligence community on the other. These roles conflict and should be performed separately.[38]

While the Church Committee was not overly kind to the entire intelligence community, especially the CIA, the PFIAB earned wide respect on Capitol Hill for its role as an independent advisory body to the president. The Church Committee agreed that "Board reports and recommendations have contributed to the increased effectiveness and efficiency of our foreign intelligence effort."[39] It attributed the PFIAB's effectiveness to the fact that it has only one customer, the president, and strongly recommended that "this executive relationship should be maintained."[40] It noted the board's successes since its inception in 1956: "For example, the Board played a significant role in the development of our overhead reconnaissance program. It has made recommendations on coordinating American intelligence activities; reorganizing Defense intelligence; applying science and technology to the National Security Agency, and rewriting the National Security Council Intelligence Directives (NSCIDs). The Board has conducted post-mortems on alleged intelligence failures and, since 1969, made a yearly, independent assessment of the Soviet strategic threat, thereby supplementing regular community intelligence assessments. Most recently, it has reported to the President on economic and human clandestine intelligence programs."[41]

But, as Loch Johnson notes, the board did not significantly advance presidential initiatives to strengthen intelligence oversight: "Executive branch oversight of intelligence agencies in the United States has been anaemic. None of the major intelligence abuses during the 1960s and 1970s were uncovered by institutions of accountability inside the executive branch, but rather by media and legislative investigators. In 1975, the Ford Administration strengthened the President's Foreign Intelligence Advisory Board (PFIAB) and created an Intelligence Oversight Board (IOB), both arms of the Executive Office of the Presidency; yet, with an occasional exception, neither of these panels has been engaged in a continuous and robust review of intelligence operations."[42] In sum, the PFIAB was useful for providing presidents with advice about intelligence matters, but it was limited in its oversight capacity because it was part-time and had limited resources.

BOARD MEMBERSHIP AND EXECUTIVE STAFF

A June 20, 1977, letter from Chair Leo Cherne to former president Ford states that the members "appointed to the Board were people whose experience was substantial in the fields of science, military affairs, weapons technology, law, communications, international economics, and foreign policy."[43] Cherne added: "Their participation was, in the richest sense of the word, nonpartisan. Their stature was such as to assure the most informed critical capability and total detachment from any bureaucratic involvements. And their character assured the president the certainty of independent judgment."[44] Cherne's view represents the ideal of what the board membership should be.

Although its membership overlapped with the Nixon board, the Ford PFIAB experienced a lot of turnover. Its members, along with the dates they served, include:

Adm. George W. Anderson: March 20, 1969–May 5, 1977 (chair, May 1, 1970–March 11, 1976);

Leo Cherne, economist: June 28, 1973–May 4, 1977 (chair, March 11, 1976–May 4, 1977);

Stephen Ailes, lawyer and former secretary of the army: March 11, 1976–May 4, 1977;

Leslie C. Arends, former Illinois congressman: March 11, 1976–May 4, 1977;

William O. Baker, Bell Labs director: December 24, 1959–January 20, 1961, May 4, 1961–May 4, 1977;

William Casey, lawyer and former Office of Strategic Services (OSS) member: March 3, 1976–May 4, 1977;

John B. Connally, former Texas governor and secretary of the treasury: December 1, 1970–February 11, 1971, June 12, 1972–January 19, 1975, March 11, 1976–May 4, 1977;[45]

John Foster, former Department of Defense (DOD) official: June 28, 1973–May 4, 1977;

Robert Galvin, Motorola founder: June 28, 1973–May 4, 1977;

Gordon Gray, former Eisenhower NSC aide: May 16, 1971–May 4, 1977;

Edwin H. Land, Polaroid president: May 4, 1961–May 4, 1977;

Gen. Lyman L. Lemnizter, former chairman of the Joint Chiefs of Staff: March 11, 1976–May 4, 1977;

Clare Boothe Luce, author and congresswoman: June 28, 1973–May 4, 1977;

Robert B. Murphy, diplomat: May 1961–June 1973, March 11, 1976–May 4, 1977;

Nelson D. Rockefeller, former New York governor: March 20, 1969–December 19, 1974;[46]

George P. Schultz, former director of the Office of Management and Budget, June 5, 1973–March 1976;

Edward Teller, physicist: July 22, 1971–May 4, 1977;

Edward Bennett Williams, Washington, DC, attorney: March 11, 1976–May 4, 1977.

IOB Members during the Ford Administration
Robert B. Murphy, chair of the IOB, member of the PFIAB;
Leo Cherne, chair of the PFIAB;
Stephen Ailes, member of the PFIAB.

PFIAB Recruiting and Selection under Ford

Byers, the former PFIAB executive secretary, and another former government official both confirmed that the recruitment and selection process for the PFIAB was conducted within the executive office of the White House. Nevertheless, a memorandum from PFIAB chair Adm. George Anderson to Chief of Staff Donald Rumsfeld dated November 5, 1974, suggested possible candidates for PFIAB membership, along with their areas of expertise.[47] Anderson also advised that the ideal board "should be composed of no more than 12 members selected on a politically nonpartisan basis; it should be allowed to develop considerable membership continuity."[48] He believed that the ideal board should draw on a broad range of backgrounds: "a retired senior officer; a former senior Foreign Service Officer; a retired Cabinet-level official; a distinguished jurist; a journalist; a scientist; university professor; an economist; a former Congressman; or prominent businessman."[49] This diversity of backgrounds reflects the range of issues faced by the PFIAB. Unfortunately, actual board appointments have often been viewed as compensation for a political favor or a reward for a close friend.[50]

Records of votes concerning new PFIAB appointments and the selection process for chair provide us with an additional window into how and why Ford chose certain individuals to serve. During the Ford administration, the secretary of defense, the special assistant to the president for national security affairs, the White House counsel, and the vice president were polled about potential appointments.[51] However, the final decision about PFIAB and IOB appointments rested with the president, and his decision was conveyed through the White House chief of staff. A former NSC official under President Ford explained that the president ultimately resolved all questions of PFIAB membership because the members served him exclusively.[52]

President Ford significantly expanded the PFIAB in March 1976 when he announced the appointments of Ailes, Arends, Casey, Connally, Lemnitzer, Murphy, and Williams and also appointed Cherne to chair the board in place of Anderson. This occurred in the larger context of the release of EO 11905 and as a result of Ford's eagerness to demonstrate the administration's commitment to oversight and management of intelligence activities. Internal correspondence indicates that Ford and his advisers spent a great deal of time putting together the expanded board. Between 1975 and 1976, the president and his staff made a number of "final decisions" regarding PFIAB membership that were later reversed. Individuals selected to be members of the PFIAB but never appointed include the former Strategic Air Command (SAC) commander Gen. John C. Meyer (who died in 1975 before his appointment), the Continental Airlines founder Robert Six, Michigan State University president Clifton P. Wharton Jr., the civil rights attorney Mitchell Rogovin, the former Wisconsin congressman Melvin Laird (who did not accept his appointment), the former Johnson DOD official Harold Brown, the former Treasury secretary C. Douglas Dillon, and the American Federation of Labor and Congress of Industrial Organizations official J. Lane Kirkland.[53] What follows is a composite list of possible candidates with specific subject categories for potential PFIAB members and annotations in the nine categories senior military officers, diplomacy, science, economics, government, industry, legal, academe, and media:

Joseph Alsop, media
Frank Barnett
William Gordon Bowen, academe
William Buckley, media
Erwin Canham, media
Archibald Cox
Peter Frelinghuysen, government
General Andrew Goodpaster, senior military officer
Rita Hauser
Leon Jaworski
George Kennan, diplomacy
William Kintner
Foy Kohler, diplomacy
Jewel S. Lafontant
Melvin Laird, government
John McCone, industry
David Packard, industry
John Richardson
Eugene Rostow, legal
William D. Ruckelshaus
Dean Rusk, diplomacy
Dr. Jonas Salk

William Scranton, government
Paul Seabury, academe
Marshall Shulman, academe
Robert Six, industry
Margaret Chase Smith
George Woods, economics[54]

Like those PFIAB members who were selected but never appointed, Ford made several successive selections for board chair, changing his mind each time. These included Dr. John S. Foster Jr. on September 16, 1975, the former OSS operative and defense contractor Itek founder Franklin A. Lindsay on July 16, 1975, C. Douglas Dillon (n.d.), and William J. Casey on October 20, 1975.[55]

PFIAB Executive Staff

In addition to the PFIAB members, there was a small staff to assist in the board's operations. A level V executive series officer oversaw the staff as executive secretary. Byers, a career intelligence officer, served in that capacity from July 28, 1973, until February 28, 1977.[56] The staff also maintained a special assistant to the executive secretary, whose grade varied. Under Ford, Commander Lionel Olmer, a specialist in cryptology and tactical intelligence with the navy, served as Byers's deputy from June 1973 until March 1977, when he took over as the executive secretary.[57] The PFIAB also had four other secretaries on staff, one at the FSS-3 level, two at the GS-10 level, and one at the GS-8 level. All staff positions were normally filled with personnel on loan from other government agencies (the DOD, the CIA, or the military), and staff members' home agencies normally continued to pay their salaries.

OPERATING PROCEDURES

PFIAB Meetings

Ford's PFIAB met on the first Thursday and Friday of even-numbered months (February, April, June, August, October, and December).[58] For each meeting, the chair and the executive secretary set the agenda, and each session examined questions raised by the president, the national security adviser, and individual board members. At the meetings, the PFIAB received briefings and updates from intelligence community principals, cabinet officers, government officials, and experts. Various PFIAB panels also regularly gave updates on their particular projects. The board had few opportunities to meet with the president, and quite often those meetings were restricted to photo opportunities and brief discussions. There are some records of formal meetings with the president—in December 1974 and December 1976 the PFIAB delivered a yearly report, and in August 1975 it met regarding its evaluations of the national intelligence estimate (NIE) process. There was also an unconfirmed meeting with Ford regarding a competitive analysis update in October 1975.[59] At times, individual members arranged meetings with the president, and there was no barrier preventing the chair or a member from contacting Ford directly. Routine communications to the president, however, normally were channeled through the national security adviser.

PFIAB members varied in their levels of participation and attendance at meetings. Because of travel considerations, those based in Washington, DC, and the surrounding area generally had better attendance records than those who had to travel from across the country or from overseas. Most had extensive professional and private commitments, and at times attendance was based on the individuals' personal interest in the projects and topics on a meeting's agenda. Occasionally, the PFIAB staff would travel to individual members to present information or projects that might spur greater interest.[60] Land attended only intermittently but played a vital role in projects he had a special interest in, such as the review of Project Jennifer and the satellite technology assessment for the DOD and the CIA. Cherne strongly advocated economic intelligence and devoted additional time to work with various departments and agencies in that field. Foster believed strongly in the competitive analysis of NIEs and worked hard to garner support for the Team A/Team B exercise. Williams had intense interest in expanded wiretapping operations for national security purposes and worked together with the attorney general regarding their authorization and the drafting of EOs related to these operations. Teller was interested in alternative intelligence assessments and technological intelligence issues.

Operating Procedures and Interaction with Other Groups

The PFIAB did not have routine or scheduled meetings with the national security adviser or any other White House staff or cabinet officers. When meetings did occur, they tended to be on an ad hoc basis. The national security adviser, the secretary of defense, and the DCI, however, did attend PFIAB meetings with some regularity.

When the PFIAB was not meeting, its staff kept the members abreast of important issues via correspondence or telephone calls. They did not send members classified information owing to storage and security concerns, and members had to travel to secure installations, such as a military base or a federal installation, to read or see classified material. The staff forwarded meeting agendas and special topics to members on a regular basis, and the chair made a great effort to keep in contact with the other board members.

PFIAB members received $100 per day for attending PFIAB meetings. When members traveled for PFIAB-related research or went on fact-finding missions overseas in relation to their PFIAB duties, they received standard government compensation for travel and a per diem for their expenses. The PFIAB received a modest budget each year: $105,013 ($93,744 for compensation and $10,769 for travel) in 1975 and $155,473 ($140,086 for compensation and $14,477 for travel) in 1976.[61] It kept its permanent offices in Room 340 of the Old Executive Building, a location viewed as essential owing to its proximity to the president.[62] The board's authority in the intelligence community was enhanced as a result of this location, which also facilitated its efforts to coordinate with the White House.[63]

Byers reports that the PFIAB determined which topics and issues it would examine through a variety of mechanisms. The president could task it to examine particular issues or perform a certain study. These projects normally had participation from the majority of the board members. The board could also raise its own issues for study. Normally, it would reach a consensus that a particular topic merited examination, and the various panels within the PFIAB would then be tasked with the project through the PFIAB staff. Alternatively, an individual member might choose to examine an item of special interest. The member typically studied and researched the issue alone and then prepared a presentation to the entire board.[64]

The board received several regular publications from the Directorate for Intelligence, including the *National Intelligence Bulletin*, the *National Intelligence Daily*, the *Current Intelligence Weekly Review*, *Current Intelligence Special Reports*, the *Economic Intelligence Weekly*, *International Oil Developments*, and the *Strategic Research Monthly Review*.[65] The board members apparently used these publications to keep abreast of current issues facing the intelligence community and to aid them in selecting topics for study.

According to a former senior government official, the PFIAB was never able to look at all the issues on the table, simply because of the small size of the board and the vast array of issues that deserved attention.

Staff and personnel restrictions also limited what it could examine. Nevertheless, the board was able to offer nonpolitical assessments of the quality of intelligence and make recommendations for improving it, which the House and Senate committees could not offer because of their more partisan orientations.[66]

Meeting Agendas

Agendas, memos, and other documents provide some insight into the structure of PFIAB meetings and the issues discussed. The agendas that are available are often redacted and limited in number, meaning that only a fraction of the topics discussed are known.

The complete agenda for the October 3–4, 1974, meeting is available. It offers an excellent overview of how PFIAB meetings were structured during the Ford administration. In general, the board began its meetings at 9:00 A.M. with thirty minutes of "reading time." Presumably, the board read various background materials relating to briefings they would hear later on. Following reading time, the chair had thirty minutes of "chairman's time," a practice long in place for the PFIAB. The board would then hear briefings for the next two hours on topics of interest and would then adjourn for lunch at a nearby restaurant, club, or government building. Often, guests from the senior or cabinet levels of government service joined the board for lunch. The board would then return for briefings, presentations, and discussions from 2:00 to 5:00 P.M. The second day of meetings generally ran from 9:00 A.M. to noon or 1:00 P.M., during which time the board heard briefings and received updates on earlier work. The board tried to fit in a meeting with the DCI during meetings, although his level of participation varied.

On October 3, 1974, the board began with reading time at 9:00 A.M. From 9:30 to 10:30 A.M., instead of chairman's time, Cherne discussed a meeting with the economic summit conference. From 10:30 to 11:30 A.M., the board heard a briefing from the undersecretary of state for political affairs on the Middle East. The undersecretary of the navy then briefed the board on special projects from 11:30 A.M. to 12:30 P.M. The board adjourned for lunch at the Pentagon and returned at 2:30 P.M. to hear a brief on the Single Integrated Operations Plan and on NICKEL-PLATE, a command and control exercise. Finally, the board members closed their day by touring the National Military Command Center and National Military Intelligence Center.[67]

On October 4, 1976, the board reconvened at 9:00 A.M. for reading time. From 9:30 to 10:30 A.M., it received a briefing on Soviet antisubmarine warfare, and, from 10:30 A.M. to 12:30 P.M., it met with Gen. Vernon Walters, who "discussed Cyprus intelligence postmortem, the facts on Chile, and other covert activities, and Portugal." Finally, it had lunch at the Blair House with Rumsfeld.[68]

A November 1974 memorandum for the DCI, submitted by PFIAB executive secretary Byers, contains a proposed agenda for the December 1974 meeting. The scheduled meeting examined primarily intelligence issues in the Middle East. Reading time was set aside for 9:00–9:30 A.M. on December 5, followed by thirty minutes of chairman's time. The PFIAB dedicated 10:00 A.M.–12:00 noon to an examination of the current situation in the Middle East and Persian Gulf, including:

"Military capabilities of Arab, Iranian, Israeli and Soviet forces"
"Political realities and intentions"
"Economic factors"[69]

At least part of the briefing contained information on the oil policies of Middle Eastern nations, specifically their desire to maximize profits and their ability to use oil as a weapon in the event of a war in the region.[70]

From 12:45 to 1:15 P.M., the board planned to meet at the Metropolitan Club/FDIC for lunch, with Rumsfeld and Secretary of Defense James Schlesinger joining as guests. From 2:00 to 4:00 P.M., it again turned its attention to the Middle East with the following agenda:

"Review of the intelligence requirements"
"Intelligence significance of foreign bases"
"Allied intelligence contributions"
"Intelligence deficiencies: for meeting current requirements; for meeting requirements anticipated in the event of hostilities (strategic/tactical)."[71]

The board closed its day of meetings on December 5 with a presentation from Treasury secretary William Simon from 4:00 to 5:00 P.M. The proposed agenda noted: "Following his reading of the transcript of Mr. Cherne's remarks on economic intelligence at the October meeting, Secy Simon requested an opportunity to meet with the full board prior to any meeting the Board might have with the President. Secy Simon does not agree with some aspects of the report and is anxious to discuss his reservations."[72]

On December 6, the board reconvened. It again dedicated thirty minutes starting at 9:00 A.M. to reading time and then heard updates on special projects from 9:30 to 10:30 A.M. The DCI met with the board from 11:15 A.M. to 12:30 P.M., and at 12:45 P.M. the board closed the December meetings with lunch at the State Department, hosted by Secretary Kissinger.[73] The board also met with President Ford on December 6, although details of this meeting are unknown.[74]

A January 1975 memorandum for the DCI lays out a rough sketch of the board's agenda for the February 6–7 meeting. On February 6, it included a presentation from the DCI from 10:00 A.M. to noon on the impact of the Rockefeller Commission and the Senate Select Committee on Intelligence Activities. The memorandum also indicated that the board wished to hear about any problems the DCI faced as a result of the Freedom of Information Act and the Hughes-Ryan Amendment to the Foreign Assistance Act, which limited CIA overseas spending to necessary intelligence collection, unless the president determined another activity to be in the national security interest and described the activities to congressional oversight committees.[75] If time permitted, the board hoped to hear about the "vulnerability of satellites" and other items that have been redacted.[76] A proposed agenda indicates that, following the DCI's report, the board planned to hear a briefing (originally planned for the previous meeting) from 2:00 to 4:00 P.M. on the Persian Gulf. On February 7, the board intended to hear an update on "the strategic threat" from 9:30 to 11:30 A.M.[77] Finally, it closed its meeting with an update on the political and military situation in Southeast Asia from 11:30 A.M. to 12:30 P.M. The agenda does not indicate who was to give the briefings, except for the DCI, though it is probable that intelligence community members versed in the issues performed the task.[78]

A proposed agenda is also available for the DCI's meeting with the board on June 5, 1975. The agenda covers only the portion of the meetings involving the DCI, not the entire two-day schedule. The DCI was scheduled to meet with the board at 2:15 P.M. to discuss the following:

- "Possible scenarios for Arab–Israeli Conflict (responding to Adm. Anderson's request for a 'what if we are wrong' analysis)"
- [redacted]
- "Actions taken in response to PFIAB's HUMINT [human intelligence] report"
- "The Mayaguez Operations"
- "Intelligence losses in Southeast Asia and Options for recovery of adequate coverage"

- [redacted]
- "Your commitment under the 'no surprises letter.'"
- "Meeting of the Economic Intelligence Committee, NSIC"
- [redacted][79]

The "no surprises letter" was sent from DCI Colby to Admiral Anderson on April 23, 1975. In it, Colby committed to a "positive obligation" to raise with the board and Anderson any matters of "possible interest to you in fulfilling your obligation to the President to review the overall national foreign intelligence effort." He further affirmed that he would report regularly on current activities that might constitute a "bombshell or surprise." The letter apparently was written in order to demonstrate the DCI's commitment to aiding the board in expanding its oversight activities.

A similar agenda is available for the DCI for a December 4, 1975, board meeting. The DCI was scheduled to meet with the board from 3:30 to 5:45 P.M. and proposed to speak about the following:

"PFIAB comments on the NIE 11-3/8 process"
"The Taylor Report"
"The new PFIAB executive order"
"The ICG 'Ogilvie Group' Study"
"Legislative needs"
"The satellite vulnerability problem"[80]

On April 2, 1976, the DCI and the deputy secretary of defense met with the PFIAB. Little is known about this meeting save for the topics the DCI discussed. In keeping with the overall political climate, the PFIAB heard about legislative issues affecting intelligence:

- "The effect on Intelligence Community Organization and operations of Executive Order 11905";
- "The Attorney General's procedures and guidelines issued pursuant thereto";
- "Prospective legislation restricting intelligence activities."[81]

The DCI met again with the PFIAB on June 3, 1976, to follow up on these legislative issues, particularly to discuss the DCI's new responsibility to report to the Senate Select Committee on Intelligence.[82]

An agenda and the chair's guide to the October 7 and 8, 1976,

PFIAB meeting describes in detail the board's discussions on intelligence for the future (discussed in detail below). As usual, the first day of meetings began with chairman's time, at which Cherne outlined the green book affair (discussed in greater detail below) and ran through the details of the upcoming day's events. From 9:30 A.M. to 12:30 P.M., the board held a panel discussion on future intelligence needs with DCI Bush, Director of Defense Research and Engineering Malcolm Currie, Deputy Secretary of Defense Robert Ellsworth, and Deputy Assistant for National Security Affairs William Hyland. Following lunch with the vice president at the Blair House, the board reconvened at 2:45 P.M. for board member presentations. Casey discussed technology transfer, and Foster discussed deception. From 4:00 to 5:00 P.M., the board had a discussion with former secretary of defense James Schlesinger on an unknown topic.[83]

The board reconvened the next day at 9:00 A.M. Following chairman's time, Galvin, Teller, and Land briefed the board on net assessments, an unknown theme, and a memorandum regarding intelligence needs for the future. From 11:45 A.M. to 12:30 P.M., Dr. Fred Ikle, the director of the Arms Control and Disarmament Agency, spoke on intelligence and the role it could play in the arms control process. After another lunch at the Blair House, the board heard from General Andrew Goodpaster about intelligence requirements for national security in the coming decade. It closed by making plans for the December 1976 meeting.[84]

A draft agenda for the December 2–3, 1976, meeting is also available in Cherne's papers at the Ford Library. From 9:00 to 9:30 A.M. on December 2, Chair Cherne spoke on transition, while, from 9:30 to 11:30 a.m., the agenda simply states "telephone," with no further explanation. From 11:10 A.M. to noon, the board heard from Sam Hoskinson on the "status of the intelligence community," and, from noon to 12:30 P.M., it reviewed the activities of the IOB. After a lunch at the Blair House with Secretary of Defense Rumsfeld and Secretary of the Treasury Simon, the board reconvened to discuss NIEs from 2:15 to 5:00 P.M. It closed December 2 with a cocktail party.[85]

On December 3, the board met at 9:00 A.M. to prepare for a meeting with the president. The assembled board reviewed the past nine months of activity and the intelligence for the future report. The meeting adjourned at 12:15 P.M., and the board had another lunch at Blair House, with Kissinger and Brent Scowcroft.[86]

The available agendas and correspondence concerning PFIAB meetings provide a valuable glimpse into the board's official operations. They reveal a board that had regular access to high-level administration figures and experts in various fields related to intelligence. They further demonstrate the dependence of the PFIAB on information furnished by the intelligence community itself. The board could not perform its work without relying on a forthcoming and cooperative DCI (and other intelligence community figures). Finally, the available agendas shed light on some of the issues the PFIAB examined and discussed. Scant documentary evidence exists outside the available agendas on the specifics of the issues, save for a few passing references in various correspondence.

On-Site Reviews

Board members continued their tradition of conducting on-site reviews of various overseas intelligence installations during the Ford administration, although scant documentary evidence exists about the trips. A March 7, 1975, memorandum mentions that the White House had received a confirmation of Cherne's travel plans for Paris, Munich, Rome, Brussels, Geneva, London, and Ottawa for March 15–27, 1975.[87] This memorandum also requested Cherne to add Bonn and Vienna to his itinerary, owing to Germany's economic importance and the fact that Vienna was the headquarters of OPEC.[88] Board correspondence indicates that Cherne visited Europe to investigate economic intelligence issues.[89] This overseas visit occasioned the loss of Olmer's "green book" and the subsequent media exposé of the issue, which we will discuss below. White House files also indicate that Teller visited Southeast Asia (Manila, Kuala Lumpur, and Bangkok) in February 1975 and Israel in March and June 1975.[90] Nothing else is known about these trips or the specific reasons for examining intelligence activities in these areas.

Panels and Organization

Admiral George Anderson and Cherne served as PFIAB chairs under President Ford. The chairs set the tone and the path for the board and guided the various board members in their tasks. Byers states that effective communication skills were vital for the chair as he was the board member who conveyed data and intelligence to the president and relayed issues of concern to various members of the intelligence community.[91]

The large Ford board further subdivided itself into various panels, each tasked with examining specific intelligence concerns. As Cherne recounted: "Individual members of the Board, in the fields of their special competence, devoted a substantial portion of their time to the particular areas of intelligence they were best equipped to assess for the board so that it might discharge its responsibilities [as a presidential advisory body]."[92] Under President Ford, the PFIAB board maintained five panels. Baker, Land, and Teller sat on the Science Panel; Gray, Cherne, Boothe Luce, and Galvin constituted the Human Intelligence Panel; Anderson, Rockefeller, and Connally made up the Estimates Panel; Anderson, Gray, and Connally constituted the Executive Committee; and Cherne alone sat on the Economic Intelligence Panel.[93] Ford's expanded PFIAB was simply too large and examined too many issues for the entire board to tackle everything at once. All evidence indicates that much of the board's work was conducted through panels and individual study.

ISSUES AND RECOMMENDATIONS

Under previous presidents, the PFIAB focused primarily on technology issues. However, under Ford, the focus shifted away from technology toward achieving a better understanding of the intentions of other nations. Not surprisingly, the analysis and discussions it produced for the president changed.[94] Concerns about the quality and perspective of NIEs, rising debates about the role of economic intelligence, the increasing importance of HUMINT in gauging other states' intentions, the surge of terrorism around the world, and the use of telecommunications for intelligence purposes, postmortem investigations, and forecasts of technology needs all filled the docket for the PFIAB during the Ford administration.

Alternate Assessments and Faulty NIEs

The board spent a substantial amount of time examining NIEs and offering criticism and advice about the entire NIE process. Indeed, this was arguably the single most important issue the board addressed during the Ford administration, both substantively and because of the impact the board's intervention had on subsequent presidents' views of the board.

As we documented in previous chapters, the PFIAB had long been concerned about the quality of the process and the product of the NIEs. The board's complaints did have some impact on the intelligence community. In response to them, DCI Colby disbanded the CIA's Board of National Estimates and established the national intelligence officer system in an effort to make the NIE process more of a community undertaking.[95] This organizational change did not satisfy the board's concerns about the substance of the NIEs. The board had come to the conclusion that the mind-set of the analysts in the CIA's directorate of intelligence and other parts of the community was so narrow that only by bringing in outsiders with a very different ideological worldview could a truly comprehensive assessment of Soviet capabilities and intentions be produced.

In June 1975, the board member Teller submitted an "alternative" NIE designed to address the perceived shortcomings of official estimates. Teller believed that current NIEs did not address the worst-case scenarios of conflict with the Soviet Union. Among the propositions he submitted in the alterative NIE were that the Soviet missiles were more accurate than estimated and would continue to improve, that American nuclear ballistic missile submarine invulnerability was becoming doubtful given Soviet breakthroughs in antisubmarine warfare, and that American bombers might be destroyed before reaching the Soviet Union.[96]

The report itself stated that, although the NIE predicted stability for ten years, a usable NIE needed to allow for a range of possibilities. Among the questions Teller believed the NIE should have addressed were the possibility that Soviet leaders might attempt to eliminate American influence outside the Western Hemisphere before the end of 1975, to eliminate American influence outside the Western Hemisphere before the end of 1977, to restrict American leadership to the English-speaking part of North America by 1980, or to destroy the United States in 1985.[97]

Teller argued that none of these scenarios could be regarded as impossible and proceeded to outline arguments in favor of taking such propositions seriously in future NIEs. He admitted that none of his nightmare scenarios could be answered with a single war plan but that increased military preparation could diminish the danger of any one of the scenarios outlined. He further argued that, as the United States moved closer to 1985, the Soviets would continue to improve their civil defense and military capabilities to increase the probability that they could launch a first strike and survive any retaliatory strike the United States could deliver. Teller believed that NIEs should examine all possible contingencies, not just the most probable ones, which the intelligence community had focused on in past NIEs.[98]

On August 8, 1975, Chair Anderson submitted a scathing PFIAB assessment of NIE 11-3/8-74, "Soviet Forces for Intercontinental Conflict through 1985." The board alleged that the NIE was "misleading" in several judgments, most importantly, that the Soviets would be very unlikely to conclude that they could launch an attack within the next ten years that would prevent a "devastating U.S. retaliation."[99] Anderson's memo further charged that "the evidence . . . is conflicting, often flimsy, and in certain cases does not exist."[100]

The PFIAB found a number of specific areas in NIE 11-3/8-74 to be deficient. It submitted that the United States had no accurate, indisputable data about the accuracy of Soviet intercontinental ballistic missiles (ICBMs) and the likelihood that U.S. Minuteman missiles could survive an attack. Further, it questioned the assumption of the NIE that U.S. ballistic missile submarines would remain invulnerable until 1985, especially in light of the new Soviet experiments in antisubmarine tactics. The memo also alleged that the NIE did not take seriously the level of uncertainty about Soviet low-altitude air defense capabilities, the danger that U.S. bombers could be intercepted before reaching their targets, and the vulnerability of SAC bases to Soviet submarine-based missiles.[101]

Not only did the PFIAB critique the actual NIE; it also found fault with the NIE process itself. The memo stated that, because of the natural uncertainty involved with forecasting ten years into the future, especially considering the limited factual evidence available, intelligence "holes" were filled by "judgments."[102] The board stressed the danger that these judgments could become accepted at a level "approaching fact," which would lead the intelligence community to form a monolithic view and reject any alternatives.[103]

Not content merely to offer criticism, the PFIAB also offered a plan of action to help remedy the situation. It argued that critical intelligence needed to be subject to separate and competitive analysis and then submitted to decisionmakers. It also wanted decisionmakers to become more involved in the process and asked the intelligence community to marshal evidence to support two competing alternatives: the existence of a serious problem and the absence of a serious problem. The PFIAB saw this recommendation as vital because it would allow all parties involved to understand the limitations of the information and spur the intelligence community to offer a more complete product. Finally, the board recommended that the NIE abandon its attempt to offer a net assessment of U.S. capabilities in the face of the Soviet threat. Instead, the intelligence community should first produce an NIE as a "purely intelligence document." Second, the NSC should produce a net assessment, based on the first NIE, taking into account the views of the intelligence community and other interested agencies. Finally, an entity independent of the assessment process should offer a critique of the NSC product. The PFIAB believed that taking these steps would ensure objectivity and allow for competing viewpoints in the NIE process.[104]

The PFIAB's recommendations were widely circulated. On August 15, 1975, a national security decision memorandum dealing with NIEs was sent to the secretary of defense, the deputy secretary of state, and the DCI. It directed that the board's suggestions be implemented on a trial basis. There were four components to the process. First, the DCI was directed to establish an experimental competitive analysis group, made up of professionals from both the intelligence community and the private sector, that would work alongside the established process. Second, the NSC intelligence committee was directed to submit a list of the most critical intelligence issues to the national security adviser, who would then assign three of those issues to the DCI for the competitive analysis group to examine. Third, the Interdepartmental Political-Military Group would establish an ad hoc net assessment group chaired by the secretary of defense and select issues from the pared-down national security adviser's list for assessment. It would then perform a net assessment of the selected issues and forward its product to the chair of the Undersecretaries Committee. Finally, the Undersecretaries Committee would provide an independent critique of each net assessment and forward both the assessments and its critiques to the president.[105]

The various components of the intelligence community and the NSC debated these directives over the next year. In a September 1975 NSC memorandum for Kissinger, the staffers Jan Lodal and Richard Ober characterized the increased effort that would be devoted to the alternative NIE "of dubious value" and went on to say that it would "hopelessly tie up major analytical assets with minimal prospects for producing a coherent final document in any timely fashion."[106] Colby gave his opinion in a November 1975 letter to President Ford, dismissing the alternative assessment process: "It is hard for me to envisage how an ad hoc 'independent' group of government and non-government analysts could prepare a more thorough, comprehensive assessment of Soviet strategic capabilities . . . than the Intelligence community can prepare."[107] In early May 1976, the CIA official George Carver wrote a blistering internal assessment of the alternative assessment process for the incoming deputy director and his staff:

> What the Board wants is a national estimate which will set forth all the things—especially the unpleasant things—which the Soviets could or might do, without any estimative judgments of the relative probability of the Soviets achieving these various goals or pursuing these alternative lines of behavior. The real reason (I think) why some members of the Board are pushing for "the competitive estimate" by a group composed of at least some persons outside the Intelligence Community is that they want to

be sure that the total package includes all the worst case possibilities that can be thought of. Under the approach the board is recommending, the President and his senior policy advisors will simply have this range of possibilities laid before them, hence powerful arguments could be advanced that the only responsible course to follow to protect the nation's interests would be to hedge against the worst case threats, and NIEs developed through the recommended procedure would serve as ammunition supporting such a pitch. If our nation's resources were infinite, this might be an intellectually defensible thesis. They are not, however, and hence, it isn't. This procedure would leave the decision makers at the mercy of technical shamans with no basis for ascertaining which of these shamans' analyses or predictions were more credible than their competitors.[108]

During the midst of this debate, Colby was replaced as DCI by George H. W. Bush on January 30, 1976. A Texas businessman and former member of Congress, Bush had served as ambassador to the United Nations and envoy to China, but his appointment as DCI was considered a political reward for his service as chair of the Republican National Committee in 1973. In Tim Weiner's view, Bush was happy to appease the right wing of the Republican Party by endorsing the Team B exercise "with a cheery scribble: 'Let her fly!! OK G. B.'" on the letter proposing it from the board member Robert Galvin, whose NIE Evaluation Panel had proposed an "NIE Track Record" study since the previous December.[109] In truth, Bush's view of the alternative assessment was far more ambivalent. In Anne Hessing Cahn's account, the new DCI was "not enamored" of the idea and had to be persuaded to cooperate with the Team B study by Deputy National Security Advisory William Hyland.[110]

Another issue that arose during these discussions was what should be the specific focus of the alternative assessment experiment. Initially, the three panels were to cover Soviet ICBM accuracy, air defense capabilities, and antisubmarine warfare developments. According to Cahn, when Director of Naval Intelligence Bobby Inman learned of the third panel, he thought that he detected an end run by the CIA to encroach on some of the navy's most sensitive secrets and opposed including this topic in the exercise.[111] In its place, the board substituted a panel on Soviet strategic objectives that would subsequently become the most controversial part of the Team B study. Despite much controversy about the whole project within the U.S. government, by June 1976 there was

grudging agreement that the exercise should be run in the context of
NIE 11-3/8-76, with Team A (the intelligence community) and Team B
(an outside group) looking at identical intelligence and producing separate but competitive analyses of Soviet ICBM accuracy, low-altitude air
defense capabilities, and strategic goals.[112]

Team A/Team B: Exercise in Competitive Analysis

The PFIAB's concern about the NIE process and the president's subsequent direction to implement the PFIAB recommendations on a trial basis
led to the now famous Team A/Team B exercise in competitive analysis.
Indeed, Cahn argues that the board was the "primary impetus behind
alternative threat assessments."[113] At the time, President Ford was under heavy attack from the right wing of his own party for his support
of détente and SALT and needed to bolster support for his reelection
campaign.[114] Although he considered beginning the competitive analysis experiment in 1975, the NIE was already in the draft stage, so the
experiment was delayed until 1976.[115] Robert Gates told us that at the
time many on the Right had the impression that the CIA was being soft
on the Soviets' strategic threats and had underestimated their military
capabilities and mischaracterized their leadership's malign intentions.[116]
However, another former senior U.S. government official believed that
the Team B experiment was not political in nature, and he supported
the competitive analysis program as a way to improve the picture for
the vast number of consumers of intelligence.[117]

The PFIAB had produced a scathing review of NIE 11-3/8-76. Foster, Teller, Baker, Land, Galvin, Casey, and Olmer were the board members and staff most concerned with the proposed competitive analysis
experiment, and the new DCI, George H. W. Bush, signed off on the
experiment on May 26, 1976.[118] The PFIAB and the DCI agreed that
three specific topics would be evaluated by CIA analysts (Team A) and
also by outside experts (Team B): Soviet ICBM accuracy, low-altitude
air defense capabilities, and strategic policy and objectives.[119] Professor Richard Pipes, Professor William Van Cleave, Lt. Gen. Daniel Gra-
ham, Dr. Thomas Wolfe, Gen. John Vogt, Ambassador Foy Kohler, Paul
Nitze, Ambassador Seymour Weiss, Maj. Gen. Jasper Welch, and Dr.
Paul Wolfowitz constituted Team B, which was subdivided into three
groups—one for each analysis topic.

The Team A/Team B exercise did not turn out as well as the members
of the PFIAB had hoped. The problem was not with the entire exercise.
Indeed, the ICBM accuracy and air defense teams worked well together.

But the strategic objectives teams had a very different experience. Unlike the other two issues, which were highly technical in nature and about which there was relatively hard intelligence data, the third was more subjective and, not surprisingly, quite contentious. But the controversy over that third issue cast a pall over the whole exercise. Worse, from the standpoint of the intelligence community, the proceedings were leaked to the *Boston Globe,* which published a major article on the Team B Strategic Objectives report in its October 20, 1976, issue. Although initially he acquiesced in the exercise, DCI Bush complained at the January 13, 1977, NSC meeting: "The competitive analysis ideas seemed good at the time and I certainly did not think it would go public. But now I feel I have been had."[120] DCI Bush reportedly "storm[ed] into" PFIAB Chair Leo Cherne's office in the Old Executive Office Building and accused the board itself of leaking the results. Cherne, in turn, blamed the members of Team B.[121] Either way, Bush responded coldly to Cherne's suggestion early in 1977 to repeat the exercise again: "The recommendation that adversarial procedures similar to the Team B experiment be continued, perhaps every year, is one I oppose." He explained: "When one sets out to establish an adversarial Team B, one sets in motion a process that lends itself to manipulation for purposes other than estimative accuracy."[122]

Although the process did result in some valuable information, a public disclosure of the intelligence assessment had deleterious effects on the administration and the intelligence community. Indeed, the perception of the PFIAB as being a political body very quickly took hold in popular discourse (as well as inside the intelligence community), with many commentators tracing a direct line from the board through Team B and the Committee on the Present Danger to the Reagan administration.[123] The political Right used the Team B report to bolster support for defense spending increases and reinforce the image of the Soviet Union as an aggressive power bent on expansion. Though the Team B report itself remained classified for sixteen years, the major conclusions of the panel became public knowledge during the first year of the Carter administration. The report accused the CIA of "constantly underestimating the 'intensity, scope, and implicit threat' posed by the Soviet Union by relying on technical or 'hard' data rather than 'contemplating' Soviet strategic objectives in terms of the Soviet conception of 'strategy' as well as in light of Soviet history, the structure of Soviet society, and the pronouncements of Soviet leaders."[124]

Ultimately, the Team A/Team B experiment did not lead to permanent changes in the NIE production process. The two teams that evaluated ICBM and air defense did find common ground and produced effective reports. However, the third team, which evaluated Soviet strategic policy and objectives, caused long-term problems that would outlive the experiment in competitive analysis.[125] In the wake of the Team B experiment, the Senate Select Committee on Intelligence conducted a review concerning the competitive NIEs on Soviet strategic capabilities to find the truth about the events that had transpired and what could be learned from the process.[126] The primary result of the whole process was to delegitimize the PFIAB in the eyes of subsequent administrations.[127] Carter would abolish the board altogether, but subsequent presidents would either politicize it (Ronald Reagan and Bill Clinton) or ignore it (George H. W. Bush and George W. Bush, the latter at least in his first term).

Terrorism

The PFIAB also looked at the growth of terrorism around the world and its possible impact on American foreign and military policy through its effect on the health of the U.S. economy and U.S. access to strategic materials and its ability to cause social disruption. In a letter addressed to Cherne, Michael Deutch complained that the Council on Foreign Relations was drifting toward two inconsistent positions, both extreme: "(a) We must draw up our sleeves and stop terrorism for good, if necessary by bombing the protectors of the terrorist or their people at home. . . . (b) There is nothing we can do to stop terrorism. We just have to learn to live with it, even if it grows, provided it does not result in mass destruction."[128] The solution the PFIAB proposed was somewhere in the middle of these two positions, though specifics of what the board proposed are unknown.

The board also examined trends in international terrorism and transnational terrorism and their impact on U.S. foreign policy. In a 1976 executive study for the board, the CIA distinguished between international and transnational terrorism. The summary found that transnational (nonstate actor) terrorism had increased substantially and that terrorist groups were cooperating among themselves to become more bold and dramatic in their actions. Further, American targets were becoming more popular. Moreover, developments in technology facilitated terrorist mobility, provided them with new weapons, and presented them with a broader range of media outlets for publicity campaigns. The summary also reported that the growth of regional and global ties fed a reactive nationalist/ethnic upsurge around the globe and that second-tier

nations, rogue Communist states, and developing nations were supporting terrorist groups with arms, training, documentation, and aid. The
summary contended that a global economy with large populations of
émigré workers provided terrorist groups with recruits, cover, and operational support.[129] It concluded that international (state-supported)
terror had not seen a parallel upsurge and that, despite tensions in the
Middle East, the threat had remained relatively unchanged since 1968.
Legal and practical constraints combined to make states employing terrorism as a tactic the exception rather than the rule.[130]

The summary further explored the implications of terrorism for policymakers. Among its nightmare scenarios were the seizure of a nuclear
weapon or facility and the possibility that terrorists might somehow
acquire chemical, biological, or radiological weapons. The report concluded that terrorism would affect U.S. interests abroad and increase
government action concerning terrorism on U.S. soil by foreign groups
and that it would affect international relations, energy resources, arms
sales, and technology transfers. It saw a need for a counterterrorism
policy that had "timely intelligence and sound multidisciplinary analytic support, flexibility, and extensive coordination (both intra and
inter-state)" while at the same time minimally affecting the social, economic, and political cost to the United States.[131] According to Byers,
the PFIAB held numerous discussions centered on the vulnerability to
terrorist attacks of the U.S. water infrastructure, communication links,
and nuclear facilities.[132]

Economic Intelligence

Ford's PFIAB, led by Cherne, took an intense interest in the quality of
American economic intelligence. The board moved rapidly to look at
economic intelligence problems after the "October Yom Kippur War
in the Middle East, coupled with the shock in the United States over
the Arab oil embargo," pushed economic concerns to the forefront.[133]
In a November 7, 1974, letter to W. D. Eberle, the executive director
of the Council on International Economic Policy, Cherne stated: "[The
PFIAB] has had a long-standing concern for the responsiveness of the
U.S. Intelligence Community to the needs of economic policy makers.
The Board has been an influential element in shaping the organization
and priorities of the Intelligence Community to reflect the realities of a
growing interdependent world wherein economic issues are at the forefront in formulating national strategies."[134]

Cherne led efforts for better economic intelligence and submitted an influential report charting the course for future improvements in the arenas of "economic intelligence collection, analysis, reporting." "Equally important," according to Andrew Smith, "[the report] drew the attention of senior government policymakers to the enormous significance of economic intelligence and the array of resources that could be directed to answering their needs."[135] In September 1974, Cherne delivered an extensive oral report to the PFIAB outlining the critical nature of economic intelligence, assessing the quality of collection in the intelligence community, and offering a broad overview of economic issues that could have an effect on national security.[136]

Cherne also pushed for better communication between economic policy makers and the intelligence community. On June 4, 1976, he wrote to Treasury Secretary Simon and recommended that the principals of the Economic Policy Board occasionally invite the DCI and other senior intelligence officials to its meetings.[137] A series of letters between Secretary Simon and DCI Bush indicate that Cherne's proposal was adopted and that the DCI and other officials began attending certain meetings of the Economic Policy Board.[138]

Though Cherne led the crusade for improving economic intelligence, he was not the only board member to take an interest in the issue. For instance, John Connally pushed for improved economic forecasting as a requirement for intelligence to provide data to policymakers. He foresaw the oil embargo and the grain and beef shortages of the 1970s as well as the negative impact these developments would have on the U.S. economy.[139]

According to Byers, the PFIAB also examined the role of foreign trade, strategic materials, energy supplies, investment by foreign governments in the United States, and commodities trading. It maintained that economic policy was just as important as military and political intelligence. Accordingly, it recommended increasing the role of the national intelligence officer for economic affairs in guiding economic intelligence assessment and collection. It further insisted that policymakers initiate NIEs focused on forecasting the future economic outlook, including reports on Arab oil, OPEC, and petro dollars. It also argued that the intelligence community, the Department of the Treasury, and the Department of Commerce needed to coordinate their efforts in economic intelligence analysis and collection.[140] Finally, it recommended that the president needed a program to retain senior analysts from within the U.S. government and the CIA for economic analysis positions.[141] Byers states that the PFIAB's interest in economic affairs benefited the intelligence community by fostering improved CIA contacts with the American private sector.[142]

Counterintelligence

The PFIAB also examined issues surrounding counterintelligence. In May 1975, it released an unclassified paper about the counterintelligence problem in the United States. Although Admiral Anderson used the paper as his submission to the Rockefeller Commission, the entire board commented on its content and scope. The paper concluded that the lack of a coherent counterintelligence program was allowing Soviet espionage to undermine the security of the United States. Further, it alleged that the espionage threat from the Soviet Union continued to grow and that the American public and policymakers were steadily becoming more aware of how the policy of détente had encouraged the United States to lower its guard against Soviet spies and subversives. It further supported current investigations of the intelligence community by the executive and legislative branches, which the board believed offered an opportunity to reform and improve counterintelligence efforts.[143]

The counterintelligence problem remained on the board's agenda throughout the Ford administration. On April 7, 1976, the PFIAB submitted a memorandum on counterintelligence. Though the complete text remains classified, the report came to the conclusion that, "within the Intelligence Community, policy level coordination of counterintelligence activities is inadequate [sic]" and that "at the national policy level there is insufficient counterintelligence guidance."[144] The board offered two "principal recommendations":

- "The establishment at a senior level of a counter-intelligence coordinating mechanism (individual—possibly assisted by a small committee) responsible to the DCI and the Attorney General."
- "The development by the Attorney General, in consultation with the DCI, of a national counterintelligence policy directive."[145]

Information about specific follow-up action on these recommendations is not available, but the CIA did support the creation of an "NSC-level National Counterintelligence Policy Committee."[146] A proposed EO creating the National Counterintelligence Policy Committee and a National Counterintelligence Policy Board was prepared, but the order was never issued.[147]

Intelligence for the Future/Technology

A board meeting on October 1–8, 1976, laid a foundation for the end-of-year report to the president, which considered intelligence for the future and for technology. President Ford had requested this information from the PFIAB, and Cherne prepared a memorandum with the board's reply on December 3, 1976.[148] The board hoped to answer several key questions through member presentations as well as briefings by intelligence officials and private citizens.

The first task the PFIAB tackled was to devise a list of "the principal intelligence requirements of senior policymakers during the period 1977–1985." It identified the need to forecast intelligence requirements in the vital fields of "political, economic, and military affairs, strategic weapons, scientific and technical intelligence, combat support, counterintelligence, and terrorism." It also hoped to identify what the intelligence community would need to fulfill the requirements of the policymakers. Accordingly, it examined how the intelligence community should be structured, where the likely stresses and constraints on the system might originate, and how to alleviate those problems. Finally, it hoped to identify the major innovations (conceptual and technological) that might emerge, or that should be pursued, and, thus, affect the intelligence community and policymakers' requirements. To achieve this goal, the board wanted to consider what sorts of research-and-development efforts the United States should pursue in the coming years. Specifically, it hoped to encourage innovative approaches to intelligence collection, analysis, and dissemination.[149]

In response to these questions, Teller replied with a memorandum entitled "Prospects for the Next Decade," which analyzed potential sources of instability and conflict around the globe, including Russia, China, India, Western Europe, and Africa. In the memo, Teller painted an image of a technologically driven Russian brand of Marxism that had enabled the Soviet Union to catch up to, and would, eventually, allow it to surpass, the United States technologically. In particular, he cited progress in lasers, in atmospheric sciences, and in naval capacity as evidence of the Soviet Union's increasing technological sophistication.[150] He also noted that the United States needed to expand its methods of intelligence collection. He highlighted the need for visual satellite platforms (using the space shuttle as a launching vehicle), greater exploitation of open source and Department of State assets, and cultivation of scientific and academic relations with nations with which the United States had minimal contact (including the Soviet Union). He believed that covert collection in these countries would become increasingly unreliable and insufficient in years to come.[151]

William Casey also submitted a memorandum on future needs in the field of economic intelligence. In that memorandum of October 6, 1976, he identified the requirements for more precise intelligence and estimates on the following:

- "The level of the Soviet military effort"
- "The stability and vulnerability of the Soviet economy"
- "The significance of the technological, financial and organizational impacts provided by the West to the growth of the Soviet economy"
- "The economic vulnerabilities of Europe, Japan, and other countries and how adversaries might exploit them"
- "The progress of efforts to coordinate economic policies among advanced free-market economies"
- "The consequences of international agreements to establish commodity reserves and maintain prices"
- "What initiatives other countries are taking to secure energy and other critical resources"
- "What steps U.S. adversaries and competitors are taking to make other countries dependent on them"
- "What is the net cost of trade in technology to the United States"
- "To what degree U.S. adversaries 'stack' the terms of trade in order to take advantage of other countries"
- "What technological breakthroughs could seriously impact U.S. trade position"[152]

Casey's lengthy memorandum also concedes the difficulties of collecting economic intelligence and highlights the importance of having accurate information on other states' economies.

In addition to Teller and Casey (who presented their memoranda), the PFIAB members Cherne, Galvin, Foster, Baker, and Land gave presentations at the meeting on future intelligence needs. From the government, DCI Bush, Deputy National Security Adviser William Hyland, Deputy Secretary of Defense Robert Ellsworth, and the director of the Arms Control and Disarmament Agency, Fred Ikle, all presented as well. Other presenters included Schlesinger, Schultz, and Goodpaster.[153]

The PFIAB received an enthusiastic reception for this product inside the CIA. E. H. Knoche, the deputy DCI, wrote Cherne on January 3, 1977, to express his "personal admiration for PFIAB's report to the president on 'Intelligence for the Future.'"[154] He characterized the report as "very constructive and helpful," a useful focus "around which the Community can plan a good deal of its future."[155] William Wells, the deputy director for operations, further described the report as one of the most thoughtful and perceptive papers to be produced on the intelligence community and intelligence activities.[156] He also reported: "This Directorate joins the Directorate for Intelligence and the Directorate for Science and Technology in strongly endorsing most of the Board's recommendations."[157] However, in his comments on the report, the DCI noted that the intelligence community staff believed that the PFIAB made several recommendations "without recognizing that, in many cases, efforts are underway already to satisfy them," which indicates that at least the board and the community were moving in the same direction.[158]

Wiretapping and Surveillance

On July 21, 1976, President Ford solicited the PFIAB's advice "on whether or not he should invoke Executive Privilege with respect to the AT&T documents relating to wiretaps and services tendered to the FBI and NSA."[159] According to the former NSC staffer Morton Halperin, AT&T had been providing telephone taps for the FBI without any legal backing: "AT&T went to the Ford Administration and said, you know, that we cannot continue to conduct this surveillance just on the word of an FBI official. We're going to have to have some more routine system. The Ford administration feared that the phone company would stop providing the cooperation that they needed, unless there was a legal system established by Congress."[160] The board members Cherne, Casey, Land, Murphy, and Williams attended the meeting, in which Williams came out in favor of expanding wiretapping for national security purposes.[161] Apparently, his opinion greatly influenced the PFIAB's response to President Ford.[162] The president, in turn, did eventually invoke executive privilege.[163]

This debate within the administration occurred in conjunction with a 1976 effort under way in Congress to investigate Operation Shamrock, in which the NSA had received access to microfilms of all international telegraphs through Western Union. The exposure of this operation led to the passage of the Foreign Intelligence Surveillance Act, which created a system of warrants and judicial review for intelligence surveillance within the United States.

Review of Project Jennifer

Ford's PFIAB also conducted a review of a project to recover a Soviet ballistic missile submarine that had sunk in seventeen thousand feet of water in the Pacific Ocean approximately 750 miles northwest of Hawaii. Codenamed Project Jennifer, the attempt to salvage the Golf II–class submarine was conducted by Howard Hughes's ship *Glomar Explorer*.[164] Hughes used a deep-sea mining project as a cover for building the *Glomar Explorer*, which was, in fact, intended solely for the top-secret salvage attempt. The hull of the submarine broke apart during the operation, and several missiles and the Soviet codebooks were lost.[165] Land conducted an after-action review of this project for the PFIAB, the results of which remain classified, though the project was exposed in the national media and discontinued because the publicity compromised it.[166]

Mayaguez Incident

Between May 12 and May 15, 1975, the Khmer Rouge in Cambodia seized the American cargo ship *Mayaguez* in international waters and detained its crew. In a large-scale rescue attempt involving U.S. Marines and the navy, American forces sustained several casualties. Unbeknownst to the United States, the Khmer Rouge had already released the ship's crew. The incident was portrayed as a disaster in the press. We found a PFIAB file on the *Mayaguez* incident in 1975, so we know that the board examined intelligence issues surrounding the incident, but we know little about what conclusions it reached or what recommendations, if any, it made.[167]

Postmortem of Nikolai Shadrin (also known as Nikolai Artamonov)

The PFIAB reviewed the mysterious disappearance of the Soviet defector and later FBI and CIA agent Nikolai Shadrin in Vienna during December 1975.[168] President Ford assigned this case to the PFIAB to determine what happened to Shadrin after inquiries with the Soviets, not surprisingly, produced little information about his whereabouts.[169]

HUMINT Improvement

Byers states that, during Ford's tenure, the board examined methods of improving U.S. HUMINT collection capabilities. Among the options explored included a consolidation of all HUMINT capabilities into one intelligence organization based outside the Washington, DC, area. The PFIAB also noted the need for increased language ability, cultural experience, and ethnic diversity within the clandestine service as a way to improve intelligence about adversaries' intentions. It also recommended replacing the agency's current rotational personnel system with the permanent basing of clandestine officers overseas, which would, it believed, bolster officers' experience and contacts. While it recognized that technological intelligence had been improved significantly, the lack of confidence in the HUMINT process was already emerging as a new problem. Though the PFIAB took issues of HUMINT seriously, reform of these programs ultimately proved too difficult for it to achieve.[170] There are several more scattered references in CIA archives to PFIAB requests for materials on HUMINT and submissions by the CIA to the board, but we could glean little of a concrete nature.

The Green Book Affair

Although the green book affair was not actually an issue examined by PFIAB, it nevertheless deserves mention because it resulted in extensive and unfavorable media coverage of the board and of Cherne in particular. Following Cherne and Olmer's trip to Western Europe, Olmer discovered that his notebook (the "green book"), which contained extensive notes from meetings with American and foreign officials, was missing. Cherne and Olmer attempted to locate it through the airline and reported its loss to the CIA and Chair Anderson. The CIA determined that the loss of the notebook constituted a loss of classified information.[171]

In late July 1975, Michael Casey, a self-described free-lance journalist who had been convicted of writing forged checks, called Cherne to say he had the book. At the time, Casey was assisting Vietnamese refugees and worked for the International Rescue Committee (headed by Cherne), though Cherne was not aware of that fact. Cherne notified the FBI, which requested that he play along to attempt to recover the book. Casey claimed that he had received the book from a man aboard an Air Vietnam flight between Saigon and Hong Kong in April of 1975.[172]

Casey mailed the book to Cherne on August 28, 1975, and then was dismissed from the International Rescue Committee. He also surrendered copies of the book to U.S. attorneys. He subsequently told reporters that he had copies of the book and offered to show it to them. One reporter was Robert Dietrich of the *San Diego Evening Tribune.* On April 14, 1976, he wrote a story alleging that his paper had warned the FBI about the existence of the notebook, which he claimed contained names of CIA officers working abroad (including the CIA officer Robert Welch, who was recently murdered in Greece), but his warnings went unheeded.[173] Dietrich claimed that he had attempted to discuss the issue with Cherne, asking him to review copies Casey made of the papers given to the U.S. attorneys. He alleged that Cherne made veiled threats and that an armed interrogator and two FBI agents came to his house in response to a "request" from Cherne.[174] In a statement to the IOB regarding the matter, Cherne denied ever using the FBI to intimidate Dietrich and stated that the copies given to Dietrich were not copies of his notebook.[175]

PFIAB Recommendations and Implementation

Despite the ample archival material available regarding the issues the Ford PFIAB studied, no specific and formal PFIAB recommendations are currently available aside from the two on counterintelligence gleaned from CIA documents. The PFIAB's final reports on these topics remain classified, as do its implementation plans and recommendation reviews.

ASSESSMENT

In a dinner speech in 1976 to the members of the PFIAB and invited guests, Cherne stated:

> It is clear that there have been a number of crises which have not been adequately foreseen or in sufficient time to alert our government and others with whom we are associated. Do we have failures in collection? Or in analysis? Or in estimation? Or in communications? Does desired political policy or personal necessity have too great an effect on those who are expected to present objective evaluation and assessment? It is clear that no intelligence mechanism will anticipate all crises. It may also be that post-mortems have more the effect of catharsis than guiding us toward substantial change. If this Board can narrow the gap between critical events and an advance understanding of them—if we can narrow that gap slightly, this Board will have made a major contribution indeed.[176]

This description of the role of the PFIAB suggests that it ought to focus not on current problems but on future trends. Cherne continued: "I do not perceive our function as that of another National Security Council or shadow Cabinet. It is very easy for us to slip into that unrequested function. If we do, we will neglect the role we must play—to understand the problems and policies sufficiently for the purpose of seeing the President is provided with intelligence adequate to the Executive's need."[177] In addition, he raised the idea of partnering the PFIAB with nongovernment research groups, such as the National Strategy Information Center, to provide additional resources for analysis and assessment of national security interests. He believed that collaboration with substantive experts outside government would allow the board to better analyze the performance of the intelligence community with critical detachment and objectivity.[178]

Finally, the secrecy, confidentiality, and low public profile of the PFIAB greatly aided it in its mission to provide useful advice to the president. As Cherne stated: "The content of [our] advice and the discussions which precede that advice have always been and must continue to be totally sheltered."[179] Nevertheless, he recognized that "the cost of such secrecy is that the PFIAB can and will be misrepresented in the public press and thus be subject to misimpressions of our work by members of government and the public."[180] In June 1977, he stated: "It has always been clear that if the PFIAB were to usefully serve the President in the areas of the greatest sensitivity, the task would be made more difficult if it were to attract attention to itself."[181] However, extreme secrecy led to a lack of "any public understanding of the role of the Board or the contributions it made, and only those intimately familiar with the intelligence community were able to perceive the significance of the close and completely confidential nature of the relationship between the Board and the President."[182]

So how should we gauge the effectiveness of the Ford PFIAB? On the one hand, DCI Bush expressed appreciation for its work and endorsed its continuation in a letter he wrote to Cherne dated January 17, 1977: "I believe that 1976 was a good year for the U.S. foreign intelligence community—a year in which we were able to restore confidence in the integrity of our foreign intelligence mission at the highest levels of the Government, a year marked by innovations in the development of our most important intelligence products; 1976 was also a year in which we wrestled with new problems and new threats to our ability to fulfill our mission. The Board's contribution to these activities, through its advice to me and its recommendations to the President, has been significant."[183] This was a fitting compliment to the board, which had persevered during the harsh political climate of the mid-1970s that was characterized by the trials and tribulations of the myriad of investigations and committees examining the performance of the intelligence community.

On the other hand, the erosion of the seriousness with which the board was treated under the Nixon administration accelerated under Ford. In a brutally candid assessment, the NSC staffer Jan Lodal confessed to Cahn that he and his colleagues "ignored PFIAB." His rationale was that the members were all "hard core right-wing": "Teller was kept at bay through PFIAB. They were shown secrets in the hopes of keeping them (the PFIAB members, not the secrets) quiet."[184] Of course, this effort to keep the Right quiet failed spectacularly with the Team B leaks, which, if anything, added further fuel to the fire of criticism of the intelligence community. It also obscured the many good things the board accomplished during this time and soured its image among future presidents.

CARTER DISBANDS THE PFIAB

After five months of intense speculation about the fate of the PFIAB, the newly elected president, Jimmy Carter, released EO 11984 on May 4, 1977, abolishing it. Carter publicly explained that the PFIAB duties could be handled by the overhauled NSC and the reformed intelligence community, assisted by the newly formed Senate and House Intelligence committees.[185] This sudden decision to terminate the board came as a rude shock to PFIAB chair Cherne, who was not directly notified by the president but learned about it from a news report.[186] While there is some reason to think that the delayed reconstitution of the PFIAB under President Kennedy indicated that he was thinking about abolishing it (and reconstituted it only after the Bay of Pigs fiasco), it was the Carter administration that made an explicit decision not to retain this group of independent advisers to the president. Although Carter dismissed the PFIAB, he did retain the IOB, albeit with new members. On May 5, 1977, he thanked Ambassador Robert Murphy, Cherne, and Ailes for their services and simultaneously announced the appointment of the new members of the IOB: Thomas Farmer, a lawyer and political associate of Kennedy and Johnson; William Scranton, a former governor of Pennsylvania and the U.S. ambassador to the United Nations; and Senator Albert Gore Sr., the chair of Island Creek Coal Company and a former senator from Tennessee.[187]

The Decision to Disband the PFIAB

The December 23, 1976, White House Study Project Report No. 2, the "Analyses of the Current Executive Office of the President," contains the first mention of disbanding the PFIAB. This report considered alternative structures for the executive branch. It evaluated all components of the executive office of the president (in 1976) as part of the transition process for the new Carter administration. In all the proposed iterations and organizational configurations explored in the report, the PFIAB was eliminated and the IOB retained. According to the report: "The Board would be abolished and its functions merged with the National Security Council."[188] It further noted: "The more realistic appraisals of the PFIAB suggest that it can be eliminated with little, if any, loss. If at a later time, the President decides he needs such an intelligence advisory board, it could be reactivated quickly, as President Kennedy did after the Bay of Pigs."[189] Conversely, it suggested: "[The IOB] would be retained and its responsibilities broadened. Its membership would be replaced and consideration given to enlarging its staff."[190] It concluded: "The idea of a citizen's 'watchdog' committee to oversee intelligence agency abuse is a good one, although the individuals appointed to such a committee should be different from those appointed by President Ford."[191] It also stated that both the PFIAB and the IOB could be altered or eliminated without congressional action via executive order.[192]

On February 8, 1977, Adm. Stansfield Turner first met with Carter to discuss the possibility of Turner becoming the DCI. Theodore Sorensen, Carter's first choice, withdrew after comments he made during the Vietnam War were construed as "unduly critical, perhaps unpatriotic."[193] In his 2005 book, Turner takes credit for the elimination of the PFIAB. When asked his opinion about what to do with the board, he told Carter that it was "loaded with right-wing ideologues" and that "we would have wanted to change the membership substantially to give it more balance."[194] He rationalized that "Congress had just formed two committees for oversight of intelligence and that those would serve most of the purposes of the PFIAB."[195] This indicates that Turner did not understand the role of the board, which was intended from the beginning to serve as an advisory body to the president and not as an oversight body for the intelligence community. Douglas Garthoff argues that the talk of eliminating the PFIAB just underscored "[Carter's] confidence in his new DCI (as well as in his own ability to oversee intelligence without a stable of private advisors)."[196]

Former DCI Gates explained that Carter was eager for a complete break with the past and that disbanding the Ford PFIAB was part and parcel of that process. Carter also believed that the PFIAB under Ford had become nothing more than a group of political hacks.[197] In the opinion of Byers, the disbandment of the PFIAB was a political move meant to remove any trace of Republican influence from the White House.[198] It reflected the Carter administration's larger goal to downsize the executive branch and to rely on the DCI and the congressional intelligence committees to oversee the intelligence community.

On April 14, 1977, a joint memorandum from Vice President Mondale and DCI Turner reiterated the opinion that the PFIAB could be eliminated as the responsibilities of the board "can be adequately performed within the NSC system and by the intelligence community itself."[199] Additionally, Mondale and Turner argued for the retention of the IOB and the appointment of Thomas Farmer as its chair. Secretary of State Cyrus Vance and Attorney General Griffin Bell concurred.[200] On April 25, 1977, in a memorandum from Vice President Mondale to President Carter regarding the status of the new candidate IOB members, Carter himself wrote, "Let's abolish PFIAB at the same time," thus signifying that he had made the final decision to announce the new IOB members and disband the PFIAB simultaneously.[201] On April 29, 1977, the White House counsel Robert Lipshutz wrote a memo to Robert Linder requesting him to prepare "as quickly as possible an appropriate amendment to Executive Order 11905, undated, which would abolish PFIAB."[202] By May 2, 1977, a proposed EO had been prepared and was being circulated for approval.[203]

In a letter to PFIAB members dated February 18, 1977, Cherne wrote: "There have been a number of developments within the last two weeks which suggest that the matter of the PFIAB may be approaching resolution in the near future. It is my present conviction that the Board as an entity will be continued."[204] He seemed optimistic that the PFIAB would survive but expected that its functions would change and that there would be substantial turnover of its current membership.[205] Still unaware of Carter's decision to abolish the board, Cherne wrote Senator Claiborne Pell of Rhode Island on May 3, 1977, and informed him of the three new members appointed to the IOB. Cherne also noted: "I believe he [President Carter] has not yet made up his mind on a variety of questions regarding the President's Foreign Intelligence Advisory Board. There is, I am told, a substantial debate in the Executive Branch involving the question whether the Board should be eliminated altogether."[206]

Carter abolished the board on May 4, 1977, only one day after Cherne's letter. In his letter to Cherne announcing the decision, Carter stated: "I have taken this action because the National Security Council system and the intelligence community themselves, as structured in this administration, can now effectively review and assess foreign intelligence activities."[207] Carter's decision to disband the board resulted from a pervasive view within his administration of the PFIAB as "an institution which for many years served a very useful purpose but whose function can be more effectively performed by new organizations within the intelligence community itself, through the National Security Council system and by the Congressional oversight process."[208] Cherne conceded: "It is not difficult to understand why people who do not relish having someone look over their shoulder might advance such a recommendation [PFIAB elimination]. In fact, unless the President actively understands that Board and from time to time turns to it, the Board's functions are minimal and its friends are few."[209] Byers commented that the power of the PFIAB is derived from the status the president gives it. Without the support of the president, the PFIAB would be ineffective.[210]

Second Thoughts

On November 4, 1979, militant students stormed the U.S. embassy in Tehran, Iran, and took approximately seventy American diplomats captive. This action triggered the most serious foreign policy crisis of the Carter administration and began a personal ordeal for Carter and the rest of the country that lasted 444 days.[211] Some evidence suggests that the so-called hostage crisis may have led the Carter administration to consider reconstituting the PFIAB to review the disastrous chain of events that eventually compromised U.S. interests and damaged its prestige in the Middle East. On March 5, 1980, Donald Gregg (a NSC staff member on loan from the CIA) sent a letter to National Security Adviser Zbigniew Brzezinski to convey his personal opinion that reconstituting the PFIAB would be in the administration's best interests. He suggested that the board could provide "an external viewpoint on the quality and efficacy of intelligence which we do not have today." He continued: "I believe that a well-selected, experienced and prestigious PFIAB could help considerably in stabilizing the intelligence function."[212] Brzezinski responded in a handwritten note at the bottom of the page that Gregg should quietly pursue further this option of reconstituting the PFIAB.[213]

In April 1980, Brzezinski approached Cherne about the possibility of reconstituting the PFIAB. There seemed to be a growing realization within the Carter administration that the PFIAB's return could deflect "congressional initiatives that might get out of hand" and that it "ha[d] a precedent in the post-Bay of Pigs evaluation."[214] A specific reference to Operation Eagle Claw, the failed attempt to rescue fifty-three American hostages in Tehran with a special operations rescue team, seems to have been a catalyst for discussion of reconsidering the board.[215] Ambassador David M. Abshire referenced the aborted Iran rescue mission in an opinion piece in the *New York Times* on May 3, 1980, in which he called for the Carter administration to consider establishing a "blue-ribbon advisory board—call it, say, the President's National Security Advisory Board—broadened to include intelligence, defense and foreign-policy jurisdiction."[216]

After this article appeared, the NSC began discussing the issue further, and, on May 15, 1980, Gregg sent a memorandum to Brzezinski summarizing the need for a new PFIAB "to observe the intelligence community externally."[217] Additionally, Gregg advised Brzezinski: "[It] might be a good time to call Leo Cherne in, and discuss with him the pros and cons of a new board. Such a body could focus on the Iran post-mortem, if you favor that, or could turn to the question of getting better and timelier analysis out of the intelligence community."[218] In *Rescuing the World: The Life and Times of Leo Cherne,* Andrew Smith writes: "Cherne disagreed with many of Carter's foreign policy positions and decisions. When Carter offered to recreate PFIAB with Cherne serving as chair, Cherne declined."[219] Smith provides no date for when Brzezinski supposedly invited Cherne to restart the PFIAB. The invitation may never have been officially extended. Brzezinski annotated the May 15, 1980, Gregg memorandum with the statement "better hold for after elections," thus pushing any reconstitution of the PFIAB beyond 1981.[220]

CONCLUSIONS ON A DISBANDED PFIAB

Because of political concerns and a fundamentally different vision of how to oversee the intelligence community, President Carter and his advisers moved quickly to eliminate the PFIAB after they took office. The retention of the IOB did not provoke much debate because it was more in tune with the Carter administration and Congress's view of how to exercise oversight of the intelligence community. The IOB aided Carter in his pursuit of oversight rather than advice on intelligence matters. Even so, it floundered during this period, in Gregg's colorful allusion, like "Pirandello characters in search of a role."[221]

Nevertheless, by the end of his term, events forced Carter and his foreign policy team to reassess the performance of the intelligence community. Given the situation in the late 1970s, the elimination of the board seemed to have been a rash decision that limited the president's ability to get independent advice and support on intelligence matters. Had Carter won reelection in 1980, he likely would have reconstituted the PFIAB. The administration's reluctance to admit a mistake and reverse course on the eve of the 1980 election postponed the return of the PFIAB until after Ronald Reagan's inauguration in January 1981.

As in the case of the Nixon administration, it seems that the best explanation for the declining effectiveness of the board has more to do with structural factors—both the increasing institutionalization of executive branch national security management within the NSC and the emergence of new legislative institutions of intelligence oversight—than with presidential personality and style. While Ford and Carter had very different styles and personalities, the general trend under both was to not take the board seriously as an independent source of advice on intelligence matters. Ford allowed the board to become thoroughly politicized in the Team B exercise, and Carter, largely in response to that, abolished the board altogether. What both administrations were more interested in was control of the intelligence community, rather than independent advice about it. Given that, it is hardly surprising that the board withered under Ford and then was abolished under Carter.

APPENDIX A
TABLE OF FORD ADMINISTRATION PFIAB MEMBERS AND STAFF

Member	Start	End	Eisenhower 1953–1961	Break	Kennedy 1961–1963	Johnson 1963–1969	Nixon 1969–1974	Ford 1974–1977	Carter 1977
Stephen Ailes	3/11/76	5/4/77							
George W. Anderson	3/20/69	5/4/77					Chair	Chair	
Leslie C. Arends	3/11/76	5/4/77							
Willam O. Baker	12/24/59; 5/4/61	1/20/61; 5/4/77							
Wheaton Byers	6/23/73	2/28/77					Asst. exec. sec.	Exec. sec.	Exec. sec.
William J. Casey	3/11/76	5/4/77							
Leo Cherne	6/28/73; 1981	5/4/77; 1990						Chair	Chair
John B. Connally	12/1/70; 6/12/72; 3/11/76	2/11/71; 1/19/75; 5/4/77							
John S. Foster	6/28/73; 1981	5/4/77; 1983							
Robert W. Galvin	6/28/73	5/4/77							
Gordon Gray	5/16/61	5/4/77							
Edwin H. Land	5/4/61	5/4/77							
Lyman L. Lemnitzer	3/11/76	5/4/77							
Clare Boothe Luce	6/28/73; 1981	5/4/77; 1983							
Robert D. Murphy	5/61; 3/11/76	6/73; 5/4/77						IOB chair	IOB chair
Lionel Olmer	6/1973	1977					Asst. exec. sec.	Asst. exec. sec.	Exec. sec.
George P. Schultz	6/5/74	3/76							
Edward Teller	7/22/71	5/4/77							
Edward Bennett Williams	3/11/76; 1981	5/4/77; 1983							

APPENDIX B
PFIAB MEMBER ASSESSMENTS BY LEO CHERNE

Name	Appointed	Political Party	Specialized Field	Problems
Arends	1976	Republican	Congress	Gone but powerful
Ailes	1976	Democrat	Law and Defense Department	
Anderson	1970	Republican	Military counterintelligence	Gone
Baker	1959	Republican	Electronic intercepts	Bell Labs
Casey	1976	Republican	Economic intelligence	ITT
Cherne	1973	Democrat	Economics, future intelligence, and law	
Connally	1976	Republican	Economics	Intermittent and blatantly political
Foster	1973	Independent	Weapons, science, and estimates	TRW
Galvin	1973	Republican	Management and estimates	Motorola
Lemnitzer	1976	Unknown	Military intelligence	Alive, niche not clear yet
Luce	1973	Republican		Gone
Land	1961	Democrat	Photography, creativity, Kennan, diplomacy	Intermittent
Murphy	1976	Democrat*		None
Gray	1961	Democrat	Counterintelligence and NSC expert	Very willing and experienced
Teller	1971	Republican*	Science and nuclear	Apple in Nelson's eye
Williams	1976	Democrat	Law, attorney general guidelines	Very hawkish

Sources: Chart of PFIAB Members Biographical and Assessment Data, Tab D—
Possible Candidates for Membership, n.d., PFIAB—Membership Expansion (New
Board), PFIAB, SF, LCP, Box 6, GRFL; Samuel A. Schulhof to President Ford, Tab
A—Roster of Current PFIAB Membership, Washington, DC, October 24, 1974,
PFIAB 1974, Staff Secretary Connor, 1974–77, GRFL.

* Uncertain.

6

Ronald W. Reagan

President Ronald Reagan reestablished the President's Foreign Intelligence Advisory Board (PFIAB) on October 20, 1981, through Executive Order (EO) 12331.[1] Four years earlier, President Jimmy Carter had disbanded the board on the grounds that it was irrelevant given the institutional developments in both the executive and the legislative branches in terms of intelligence oversight and also because he felt that it had become deeply politicized in the 1970s. Several weeks after his election, Reagan told *Newsweek* that he would reconstitute the board.[2]

The decision to bring the PFIAB back was the result of several factors. First, Reagan had promised during his campaign to reconstitute the board, in part in response to intelligence failures during the Carter administration. Second, the idea had support from Richard Allen (who would become Reagan's first national security adviser) and William Casey (Reagan's campaign manager and a former PFIAB member, who would later be named director of central intelligence [DCI]).[3] The Hale Foundation, an influential group of former intelligence officers, also lobbied for the board's revival. In a 1981 report, it said: "PFIAB can serve as an antidote to an occupational weakness of all highly specialized fields, including intelligence—loss of ability to see the forest for the trees."[4] The report also stated: "There can be little doubt that its [PFIAB's] revival will contribute materially to the national security through improved intelligence."[5] Adopting a resolution at its 1980 convention, the Association of Former Intelligence Officers agreed: "The President [should] reestablish the PFIAB to perform the functions in which it was formerly engaged and other such functions as the President finds appropriate."[6] In a letter dated April 21, 1981, Allen wrote Leo Cherne that he had "no doubt that our commitment to having a functioning Board will be implemented soon."[7] Despite these high hopes, it is also apparent that, at least at the beginning of his presidency, Reagan saw the board as an excellent place to put political and personal friends who did not qualify for higher appointments. According to one former member, the PFIAB is a particularly attractive place for political appointees because it is an extremely prestigious board that does not demand too much from its members.[8]

EO 12331, which gave the PFIAB new life, instructed the board to "assess the quality, quantity, and adequacy of intelligence collection, of analysis and estimates, of counterintelligence, and other intelligence activities" and gave it authorization to review all U.S. intelligence organizations. Section 3 required the board to report at least twice annually on its findings, while section 4 delineated the agencies and persons who could request its input, including the CIA and the DCI. Section 5 outlined the security clearances for board members and required them to sign a promise not to reveal classified information to unauthorized persons. Finally, while board members were not compensated for their time, they were guaranteed transportation, expenses, and per diem allowances while on PFIAB business.[9]

Among the many advisory boards, councils, and committees, the PFIAB seems to have enjoyed a special relationship with the White House. In fact, a 1983 letter by the staff member Randall Fort indicated that the board was the only advisory body that had access to the White House mess and to White House transportation as well as the only one whose members received White House security badges. Fort also reported that, with the exception of the Intelligence Oversight Board (IOB), the "PFIAB is the best endowed and most privileged board in the entire United States Government."[10]

BOARD MEMBERSHIP AND EXECUTIVE STAFF

President Reagan's reconstituted PFIAB began with nineteen members, far more than the usual ten to twelve of previous administrations. The original members came from different backgrounds and brought with them a variety of experience—some relevant to intelligence and some not. From its reconstitution, it was clear that Reagan's PFIAB would be more political than previous bodies, although many members did have significant experience in intelligence and national security matters. Respected former PFIAB members under Presidents Nixon and Ford, including former ambassador Clare Boothe Luce, William O. Baker of Bell Laboratories, Dr. John S. Foster of TRW, the former secretary of the Treasury and governor of Texas John Connally, and the renowned criminal attorney Edward Bennett Williams, formed the core of the new board along with Chair Anne Armstrong and Vice Chair Cherne. Others with strong qualifications included the Center for Strategic and International Studies founder, Dr. David Abshire, former ambassador Seymour Weiss, former chairman of the Joint Chiefs of Staff (JCS) Thomas H. Moorer, and the Watergate special prosecutor, Leon Jaworski. Some members were accomplished in fields related to intelligence or government, such as the Berkeley professor Paul Seabury, the former astronaut Frank Borman, the Electronic Data Systems founder H. Ross Perot, and the Hoover Institution director W. Glenn Campbell. Some members, however, found their way onto the board despite their lack of intelligence-related experience. The Diner's Club founder, Alfred Bloomingdale, Republican National Committee finance chair Joe M. Rodgers, Continental Airlines chair Robert F. Six, and the Dallas banker Peter O'Donnell seem to have been purely political appointees.

Although the decision to reconstitute the PFIAB was probably made before Reagan's election, disagreement over who would chair the board delayed its rebirth. James Baker, who would become Reagan's first chief of staff, and Vice President George Bush championed Anne Armstrong, a Texas Republican and the first woman ever to hold a cabinet-level post in the U.S. government.[11] Casey, however, wanted Cherne, the noted economist and chair of the board during its final days during the Ford administration.[12] Casey and Cherne were longtime friends and colleagues dating back to the 1940s when Casey joined the staff of Cherne's Research Institute of America. Armstrong's supporters won—more evidence of the primacy of politics over expertise on the Reagan board—and the admitted intelligence novice assumed the chairmanship of the PFIAB from 1981 to 1990 with Cherne serving as vice chair.

To fill the spaces left by the departures of Borman, Bloomingdale, Jaworski, and Connally, who resigned on January 18, 1983, Reagan added Martin Anderson, Alan Greenspan, and Eugene Rostow. It is likely that Connally, never a favorite of Reagan, was unhappy with his appointment to what he regarded as a less prestigious post than his previous cabinet position. Anderson left his position as a domestic policy adviser to President Reagan in late 1981 and joined PFIAB in January 1982 after the board had met only one time, while the economist Greenspan and the former government official Rostow joined the PFIAB shortly afterward.

After the addition of Rostow, the board's membership stood briefly at eighteen. Soon after, however, David Abshire left to become the U.S. ambassador to NATO. The Reagan administration decided to replace

Abshire with two new members: the former astronaut Harrison Schmitt and the first director of science and technology at the CIA, Albert D. Wheelon.

The first quarter of 1984 saw two more new members join the board, bringing the total number of Reagan's PFIAB to twenty-one. General Robert H. Barrow, a former commandant of the Marine Corps, and Henry Kissinger, a former national security adviser and secretary of state, joined the board on January 6 and March 2, respectively. Kissinger requested the appointment in compensation for chairing a major bipartisan task force on U.S. security interests in Central America.[13]

Two more members joined the board during the first half of 1984, while two departed for different reasons. Howard Baker, a former senator from Tennessee, and William French Smith, a longtime Reagan confidante who had just resigned as attorney general, came aboard in January and April, respectively. Smith, like Kissinger, asked President Reagan to appoint him to the PFIAB after planning to resign as attorney general following Reagan's reelection in 1985.[14] Their addition, combined with the exit of Perot in March and Rodgers in July, ensured that the board's membership remained at twenty-one, a fact that would precipitate the most drastic reorganization in the history of PFIAB later in the year. The Halloween Massacre of 1984 (discussed below) led to the removal of eleven members—Anderson, Barrow, Greenspan, Moorer, O'Donnell, Rostow, Schmitt, Seabury, Six, Weiss, and Williams—and the appointment of four new ones. Those added included former U.S. ambassador to the United Nations Jeane Kirkpatrick, the noted nuclear arms expert Albert Wohlstetter, the Harvard professor James Q. Wilson, and Air Force general Bernard Schriever. This high rate of turnover is further evidence that the Reagan board would be very different from previous boards, which had little turnover, even between administrations.

The membership and staff of President Reagan's second-term PFIAB were substantially more stable than those of his first term. The first change did not take place until March 1987, when Howard Baker, known as a Reagan supporter during his time in the U.S. Senate, left to become the new presidential chief of staff after the departure of Donald Regan. Many on Capitol Hill and elsewhere were surprised that Baker, who had his own presidential aspirations, would join the Reagan administration in the latter half of a second term. The next loss occurred on October 9, 1987, when Clare Boothe Luce died of a brain tumor. The former ambassador had served three presidents on the PFIAB and, despite her lack of intelligence experience, brought a unique perspective to the board that would be difficult to replace. Baker's departure and Luce's death left PFIAB membership at only twelve. To get the board back to strength, President Reagan appointed former senator John Tower of Texas. In February 1988, board membership again reached fourteen with the addition of Caspar Weinberger, who had just resigned as secretary of defense. With an eye to the future, President Reagan in January 1988 issued EO 12624 expanding the membership of PFIAB to sixteen.[15] This step enabled him to appoint Gordon Luce and Zbigniew Brzezinski in March 1988.

The next modification to the PFIAB member roll came on July 1, 1988, when Albert Wheelon resigned. Wheelon also left Hughes Aircraft at the same time. Coincidentally, Howard Baker stepped down as chief of staff that same month and was reappointed to the board.[16] The board's membership remained stable at sixteen throughout the rest of the Reagan administration. In general, Reagan's appointees to the PFIAB were successful, patriotic individuals from a wide variety of fields. Nevertheless, a significant number lacked the expertise of many of the previous board members. In particular, Gordon Luce, Peter O'Donnell, Robert F. Six, and Joe M. Rodgers seemed less qualified than their colleagues and appear to have received their appointments through their political or personal connections to the Reagan White House.

Vice Chair Cherne offered a unique window into the board's internal workings through the chart he kept of the various members' contributions graded 1 (lowest) through 10 (the highest) on various categories such as attendance, substantive contributions, uniqueness of contribution, participation on task forces, and balance and objectivity. He gave the highest overall score of 49 to Bud Wheelon, a longtime technical intelligence specialist, both in government and the private sector, and the lowest score of 10 to General Robert H. Barrow, a former commandant of the U.S. Marine Corps.

After the board's re-creation by President Reagan, many proponents fought to keep its membership small. Anne Armstrong tried to use her influence as chair to discourage political appointments, while nearly every person who joined the board during Reagan's first term complained about its size. In a 1984 letter, Armstrong sought members' answers to several operational questions, such as, "What should be the Board's proper size?" and "Should we maintain our present task force system?" Numerous members indicated that the board would operate most efficiently with anywhere from ten to eighteen members rather than the twenty-one it had at the time. Not surprisingly, none

Table 1. Board Members

	Attendance at Board Meetings	Substantive Contribution at Board Meetings	Uniqueness of Contribution to PFIAB	Participation in Task Forces or Individual Study Efforts	Any Negative Factors	Balance and Objectivity
M. Anderson	9	6	5	5		4
W. O. Baker	9	2	10	7		8
R. H. Barrow	7	1	1	1		
W. G. Campbell	9	1	1	1		1
J. S. Foster Jr.	10	9	9	9		9
A. Greenspan	6	6	8	4		9
H. A. Kissinger	3	8	9	3		7
C. B. Luce	9	5	7	5		4
T. H. Moorer	8	2	2	3		2
P. O'Donnell	8	5	3	2		8
H. R. Perot	7	4	3	1		2
J. M. Rodgers	8	2	2	1		3
E. Rostow	5	5	5	2		8
H. H. Schmitt	9	8	8	7		8
P. Seabury	10	7	7	10		9
R. F. Six	10	0	0	1		
S. Weiss	10	8	7	10		7
A. D. Wheelon	10	10	10	10		9
E. B. Williams	8	8	10	3		7

Source: Reproduced from Member Ratings Chart, 1984, Loose Documents, LCP, Box 72, DSC HGARC.

Table 2. The Halloween Massacre II

Members as of 11/1/85	Purged	New Membership
Martin Anderson	Martin Anderson	Anne Armstrong
Anne Armstrong	Robert Barrow	Howard H. Baker
Howard H. Baker	Alan Greenspan	William O. Baker
William O. Baker	Thomas H. Moorer	Clare Boothe Luce
Robert H. Barrow	Peter O'Donnell	W. Glenn Campbell
Edward Bennett Williams	Eugene Rostow	Leo Cherne
W. Glenn Campbell	Harrison Schmitt	John S. Foster
Leo Cherne	Paul Seabury	Jeane Kirkpatrick
John S. Foster	Robert F. Six	Henry Kissinger
Alan Greenspan	Seymour Weiss	Bernard Schriever
Henry Kissinger	Edward Bennett Williams	William French Smith
Clare Boothe Luce		Albert D. Wheelon
Thomas H. Moorer		James Q. Wilson
Peter O'Donnell		Albert Wohlstetter
Eugene Rostow		
Harrison Schmitt		
Paul Seabury		
Robert F. Six		
William French Smith		
Seymour Weiss		
Albert D. Wheelon		

Note: The moniker "the Halloween Massacre II" was coined by William Safire in "ESSAY; In Flagrante Defecto," *New York Times*, November 7, 1985, A35.

volunteered to excuse themselves from the PFIAB to improve the quality of its activities.[17]

Even though all the members rarely, if ever, attended a meeting together, the board's excessive size posed several problems. First, it made in-depth discussion of issues difficult. Many PFIAB members were considered experts in their fields and were passionate about their membership on the prestigious board. As a result, few were satisfied with the limited time they had to speak on the wide range of topics the PFIAB addressed. Second, many members and outside observers believed that the board's size could be worrisome to intelligence community officials who came to brief the PFIAB or to answer questions on very sensitive or highly technical matters that they did not want widely known.

Despite the members' reluctance to volunteer to give up their position to downsize the board, there was a move afoot to accomplish that goal, although there are conflicting reports about exactly what happened. According to Martin Anderson, Armstrong expressed displeasure with the board's size to National Security Adviser Robert McFarlane, who then assigned the National Security Council (NSC) intelligence staffer Ken de Graffenreid the task of fixing the problem. Though Anderson does not say who did it, someone concocted the story that the PFIAB was full of tension and discord. When Reagan found out about the planned reduction, he asked Chief of Staff Regan for justification. Regan, in turn, called in Armstrong and Cherne to explain to the president the difficulties posed by such a large PFIAB. Anderson's account begins with the premise that DCI Casey wanted to weaken the board by reducing its membership. A declawed board would be less able to investigate the Iran-Contra Affair and would be less problematic for Casey, who resented the board's (or anyone else's) oversight.[18] Evan Thomas, in his biography of Edward Bennett Williams, supports Anderson's thesis and adds that Armstrong purged all the "tough questioners," perhaps in an effort to make the PFIAB friendlier toward the intelligence community.[19] Thomas also includes a conversation between DCI Casey and the *New York Times* columnist William Safire:

> At a dinner party, Safire accosted Casey for cleaning out the PFIAB. The director adamantly denied that he had played any role in the purge. "They even threw off Ed Williams [a close friend of Casey]." Surely Casey wouldn't purge his own friend and ally EBW. "That's a cover," Safire shot back. Casey couldn't suppress a smile. "Is it that transparent?" Safire's suspicions were

confirmed when Williams was back on the Board less than a month later [as general counsel].[20]

Other descriptions of events, however, do not support Anderson's story. Both a former board member and Executive Director Gary Schmitt contradicted Anderson's thesis that covering up the Iran-Contra debacle was the motive for PFIAB cuts. One former board member claims that resignations were requested at the end of the first Reagan administration, as had become common practice with previous boards. Concerns about the board's size, which had already been expressed to National Security Adviser McFarlane, were then shared with the president. Since Reagan did not have strong feelings about the number of people on the board, he was receptive to these concerns and authorized major cuts to achieve what many agreed would be a more effective body.[21] Furthermore, Schmitt stressed that the PFIAB knew nothing of Iran-Contra at that time and that Casey played no part in encouraging or discouraging the changes. According to Schmitt, an unwieldy PFIAB was in Casey's best interests.[22] At least one part of Anderson's account may be correct, however. In a *New York Times* article, a senior Reagan administration official described the PFIAB as "strife-ridden and contentious" and said that "there were many people who disagreed so much it became useless."[23] This reasoning was not cited during interviews with various PFIAB-affiliated individuals, so it is possible that the administration planted this story to justify cutting a board that had become bloated with political appointees. Contrary to Martin Anderson's view, Robert Gates told us that Casey was not antagonistic toward the PFIAB—Casey had friends on the board and was a former member. Casey did have a "mind your own business" attitude from time to time, but that was his view of everyone who tried to interfere with him as the DCI.[24]

The climax of the Halloween Massacre II came on November 1, 1985, when eleven members of the PFIAB received their letters of termination. Those purged fell into three categories. The most capable included some members who had made important contributions to the board, such as Edward Bennett Williams (who would soon return as counsel to the PFIAB), Weiss, and Seabury. Some were qualified individuals who had been useful but whose expertise was either not in intelligence or shared with another member. Schmitt, Greenspan, Rostow, and Anderson fall into this category. Finally, a few of the roster reductions never contributed much to the PFIAB at all. Barrow, Moorer, Six, and O'Donnell played a minimal role on the board during their tenure.[25]

These changes brought the membership of the PFIAB down to only ten, the smallest it had been under Reagan. Two weeks later, however, four more individuals joined the board: Kirkpatrick, Wohlstetter, Wilson, and Schriever. In addition to the reduction in size of the board, the other major change resulting from the purge was that all future appointments were made for two years, which essentially gave the president a painless method of firing PFIAB members should they prove unsatisfactory.[26] EO 12537 fixed the new and improved PFIAB's membership at fourteen.[27]

The PFIAB became a more effective body after the purge. Not only did fewer members make it possible to have more in-depth discussions, but the reduced membership also encouraged intelligence officials to be more open and forthright with the board. Finally, Reagan himself became more involved with the PFIAB after November 1985.[28] Although one cannot say that the board entirely lost its political complexion, it did drop several intelligence neophytes who may have detracted from its effectiveness. The new members were clearly more qualified than some earlier appointments. The second-term Reagan PFIAB was, overall, a leaner, more efficient body, better able to operate within the Washington bureaucracy and to interact with the intelligence community.

Staff and Consultants

Unlike the membership, the staff at the PFIAB was typically composed of professionals working in some area of intelligence prior to their appointment to the board. Typically, the PFIAB staff consisted of an executive director, a deputy executive director, and three to four other individuals who came from all over the government.

Col. C. Norman Wood, an air force intelligence officer, served as executive director from 1981 to 1983. Fred Demech served as deputy executive director from 1981 to 1983 and as executive director from 1983 to 1984. Gary Schmitt served as executive director from 1984 to 1988.

In 1988, the staff of the PFIAB changed yet again. Schmitt, who had been executive director for nearly four years, resigned, and Captain Demech returned from Scotland to direct the PFIAB staff once more until Reagan left office. Now working under him were Ryan Malarely; Nina Stewart, as deputy executive secretary; and Randy Deitering, as assistant executive secretary. The latter two would later go on to serve as executive secretary for the George H. W. Bush and Bill Clinton PFIABs, respectively.[29]

In addition to members and staff, the PFIAB also utilized a number of outside consultants. Some received compensation for their time, but most were unpaid. For fiscal year 1985, the paid consultants were Dr. Anthony Oettinger (a Harvard University professor), Roy Godson (a Georgetown University professor), and Lawrence Sternfield (a former CIA operations officer). The unpaid consultants were Adm. Bobby Inman (who would later serve as the acting chair under President Clinton), Dr. Lew Allen, Joseph Amato, Dr. Alexander Flax, Judy Harbaugh, Dr. Roland Herbst, Dr. Eberhard Rechtin, and Warren Meeker.[30] Demech showed, during his stints as executive director, a greater preference for using outside consultants than did other executive directors.[31]

OPERATING PROCEDURES

Board Meetings

Under President Reagan, the PFIAB met every other month for two days. Meetings were typically held on Wednesdays and Thursdays in PFIAB offices in Washington, DC, but occasionally the board convened at other locations. In one instance, it spent an entire day at the Strategic Air Command in Omaha, Nebraska. Board members toured the facilities and heard briefings on the Soviet threat, control and warning, and intelligence.[32] On another occasion, the PFIAB traveled to California to hold its bimonthly meetings at the Hoover Institution, though documentation does not indicate why the change of venue was necessary. Records do indicate, however, that secrecy was paramount, particularly regarding the Hoover trip. Memos instructed members not to mention PFIAB when making travel arrangements or on arrival in California. It is possible that the trip included visits to several Bay Area companies that were contractors to the intelligence community.[33] Armstrong hinted at the purpose of traveling to California by writing in a memo that it would put the PFIAB "within reach of several fascinating facilities."[34]

Meetings normally followed a standard format. Time was allotted to the chair and to individual members to report on topics the PFIAB had chosen to address. Sometimes the agenda included a short period for discussion as a group, but, because of the infrequency of meetings and the number of outside speakers and guests, this was not common. Meetings also routinely included a briefing by the DCI or his deputy. The DCI's presentation would usually occupy about an hour highlighting important developments in the intelligence community. During his tenure as DCI, William Casey often confounded the PFIAB with his evasiveness and indistinct speaking voice to the point that the board staff had to place a microphone in front of him to make him audible.[35]

In addition to the DCI, other prominent officials from the intelligence community regularly spoke at PFIAB meetings. The director of the National Security Agency (NSA) appeared, as did high-ranking officials of the FBI and staffers from the NSC. Secretary of Defense Caspar Weinberger and Secretary of State George Shultz were two of the more frequent visitors from the administration. Furthermore, representatives from the private sector, such as Cray Supercomputers, appeared before PFIAB to answer questions specifically related to their products or expertise.[36] After the formal meetings concluded, board members often had social gatherings with prominent government officials and distinguished guests such as Donald Rumsfeld and Brzezinski (before he joined the PFIAB).

During Reagan's first term, the entire PFIAB generally met for two days. However, in a January 1985 letter, Chair Armstrong told members that the meetings would be one day with the entire board and one day with task forces meeting independently.[37]

President Reagan never attended a full meeting of the PFIAB, but the full board met with Reagan about once a year. Similarly, while individual members did not enjoy great access to Reagan, Armstrong did in her capacity as chair.[38] Perhaps owing to its decreased size, the president became more involved with the PFIAB after the 1985 purge.[39] In addition, on numerous occasions, board members visited the White House and spoke with Reagan briefly about the subjects of their inquiries or their conclusions. Records kept by Vice Chair Cherne indicate that, during Reagan's first term, the president met perhaps more frequently with the PFIAB but for shorter periods than did some of his predecessors. Records show that the vice president attended at least one meeting in 1984.[40]

Another common area of concern for PFIAB members was the number of briefings the board heard. Some thought that it was excessive and that the board would better utilize its time by exploring fewer issues in greater depth. One member went so far as to say that, if he were retired, the briefings would be fascinating but that, because he was not a pensioner, they were just a waste of time.[41] Various members thought that the board's docket was too full, and one former staffer described its approach as like a "moth to a flame" assessing various issues.[42] Members believed that a superficial review of many topics was less beneficial to the government and the intelligence community than a more focused approach to a few pressing problems. There is no evidence, however, that the PFIAB followed this advice.

Operating Procedures and Interaction with Other Groups

Although there was a spider web of relationships and uncertain chains of command in the White House, the PFIAB generally operated through the NSC. The board delivered reports and recommendations to the senior intelligence staffer on the NSC, who then disseminated them to the rest of the members, including the national security adviser. The PFIAB conducted 95 percent of its work in formal, written form, and all of it was seen by President Reagan.[43]

While the method of communication through the NSC senior intelligence staffer put the PFIAB's work in the hands of relevant officials, it did not ensure follow-through. The PFIAB had no formal mechanism to find out what had become of its reports or to assess what impact its recommendations may have had. One former staffer characterizes this inability to generate feedback as the PFIAB's biggest shortcoming.[44] Occasionally, the board would hear that its advice had encouraged changes in policy or action through a briefing from an official in the intelligence community, but, frequently, members discovered the effect of their efforts only through media reports and other open sources.

The PFIAB received its taskings from a variety of sources. Requests sometimes came directly from the president—as in the case of the board's Moscow embassy security investigation. Open PFIAB records indicate that this was not especially common, though perhaps it became more so during Reagan's second term as a result of his increased interest in the board. The PFIAB could also receive requests from the NSC. This too, however, was rare. The DCI or other intelligence officials could ask the PFIAB to investigate certain topics. According to both Schmitt and a former staffer, Casey regularly consulted with the board to determine topics for it to investigate.[45] Finally, the members themselves were never shy about suggesting issues for discussion or examination. This is not surprising as the board membership included experts in a wide array of disciplines, with the result that there was never a shortage of ideas. In general, the PFIAB gravitated toward the burning issues of the day.[46]

The PFIAB's internal method of organization changed over time. During the first Reagan administration, the board split into semipermanent task forces to address the wide variety of issues that filled its agendas. Each task force had a chair who was an expert in its area of responsibility, but other members were not necessarily specialists in that

Table 3. Task Forces during the First Reagan Administration

Analytical and Political	Economic	Legal	Scientific and Technological
Abshire	Bloomingdale	Jaworski	Baker
Campbell	Cherne	Moorer	Borman
Cherne	Connally	Weiss	Foster
Seabury	O'Donnell	Williams	Perot
Weiss	Perot		
	Six		
Communications	**Future**	**Military**	**Strategic**
Baker	Abshire	Borman	Abshire
Borman	Baker	Connally	Borman
Six	Campbell	Foster	Campbell
Williams	Cherne	Moorer	Foster
	Seabury		Moorer
Counterintelligence	**Human and Covert**	**Resources**	
Campbell	Bloomingdale	Abshire	
Jaworski	Luce	Connally	
Luce	Perot	O'Donnell	
Seabury	Weiss	Six	
Williams			

Source: Reproduced from LCP, Box 72, PFIAB, July 1981.

area. Members could participate in multiple task forces—such as the Military, Economic, Legal, and Counterintelligence panels. The task forces submitted reports to the full board and sometimes met for a day before the full PFIAB gathering. At meetings, the smaller groups often heard briefings by experts in their field. Despite the logic of the task force setup, many were dissatisfied with the quality of work the groups delivered. Schmitt, for instance, recognized the need to divide the sizable membership into more manageable units but lamented the questionable utility of those units' efforts.[47]

After Reagan's reelection, the PFIAB adopted a different method of organization. Instead of standing task forces, it shifted to using ad hoc committees to address issues as they arose.[48] Members could more easily change assignments to match the board's varying needs.

Financially, the PFIAB was a complicated organization. During the Reagan administration, it had a line item on the NSC budget. PFIAB members themselves, as specified in EOs since the board's inception, received no compensation for their services. Travel and other expenses were covered, but Martin Anderson complained that members had to pay four hundred dollars a year for meals and other meeting expenses.[49] The executive secretary was paid through the U.S. Navy by the precedent established during the Ford administration. Since other staff members received their salaries from their home agencies, the Reagan board was constrained in terms of staffing and other organizational resources.

ISSUES AND RECOMMENDATIONS

The board addressed a variety of issues and made many recommendations during Reagan's eight years in office. Though most of its records
remain classified, interviews and other sources provide an outline of
some of the major issues that it tackled.

Moscow Embassy Security

Perhaps the most important topic the board addressed was embassy security. In 1969, President Nixon and Soviet premier Leonid Brezhnev
signed an exchange of sites agreement for new embassies in both capitals.
After years of negotiations about construction details, the two superpowers finally agreed that the host country would supply all materials
and perform the basic assembly functions while the owner would be
responsible for all other construction details using host-country labor.[50]
This agreement would prove disadvantageous for the United States.

The cornerstone of the new U.S. embassy in Moscow was laid in
1979, and construction proceeded for many years without incident. In
August 1985, however, U.S. officials discovered that the chancery was
filled with listening devices installed by Soviet construction workers.
Despite the fact that other nations had found listening devices in their
Moscow embassies, much of the building had been constructed using
prefabricated modules developed and assembled at a site that was closed
to Americans.[51] As a result, the floors, walls, and ceilings of what was
supposed to be the most important American diplomatic installation
in the world were completely inundated with advanced eavesdropping
devices.[52] The Soviets had also inserted devices in a number of embassy
typewriters that transmitted keystrokes to receiving stations, effectively
opening America's mail to them.[53] While the State Department dithered
over how to respond, Reagan asked the PFIAB to investigate the matter
and offer recommendations on how the United States should respond to
the bugging as well as how it could increase embassy security worldwide.
At the same time, Reagan appointed a separate panel headed by former
secretary of defense James Schlesinger to examine the issue concurrently.

In its 1987 report, the PFIAB recommended spending $79 million to
use advanced technology to purge the new embassy of listening devices,
though, according to the *New York Times,* this idea won little support
from government officials. It also recommended that responsibility for
the security of America's embassies shift from the Department of State
to a new agency reporting directly to the secretary of state. Schlesinger's

panel disagreed, saying that the United States should destroy and rebuild the top three levels of the chancery and then construct a new six-story building to house the most sensitive embassy operations.[54] A 1988 State Department study performed by BDM Corporation and MK-Ferguson challenged both recommendations. It concluded that salvaging the existing building would be extremely costly. "The building experts are saying that a partial deconstruction isn't feasible, because it is very difficult to take a portion of the building and build on the existing structure," then assistant secretary of state for diplomatic security Robert E. Lamb told the press in 1988. "Just from the efficiency of construction, you're better off taking the whole thing down."[55] As a result, the State Department advocated the complete demolition of the new building and the construction of a new chancery. It is unclear why the PFIAB and the Schlesinger's panel concluded that the United States could salvage the existing building because the reports are still classified.

The Reagan administration was in no hurry to resolve the construction issue as the new building was never occupied. But a senior Reagan White House official asserted that the administration did take follow-up action to locate Soviet listening posts. While they waited for recommendations from the PFIAB and Schlesinger's panel, senior officials also authorized a refurbishment budget of $32.5 million for the old embassy, which had housed America's diplomatic corps in the Soviet Union since the 1950s. The purpose of the upgrades was to improve security and to increase safety since the building had been neglected for years in anticipation of the new embassy. Essentially deciding not to decide, the Reagan administration continued to prohibit the Soviets from occupying their new embassy in Washington, DC, and to run American operations from the old compound in Moscow. In 1986, the United States ordered the Soviet Union to reduce its diplomatic presence in Washington, and the Russians responded by ordering their nationals out of the American embassy in Moscow, effectively ending the security risk posed by foreign nationals. The PFIAB issued its report before the discovery that marine security guards stationed in Moscow had allowed Soviet nationals access to restricted areas and did not specifically address the marines as a security risk.[56]

It was not until President Bill Clinton took office that the United States government finally made a decision on the disposition of the Moscow embassy. The Democrats decided to follow the spirit of the Schlesinger panel's recommendation by destroying the bugged portion of the building and rebuilding the necessary floors. They awarded the contract for the new secure chancery facilities (SCF) to Hellmuth, Obata, and Kassebaum. To create a new SCF, the firm destroyed the top two floors of the existing eight-story building and rebuilt four new floors and a penthouse, including a transition on the fifth floor to the secure facilities above. Zachry, Parsons, Sundt won the contract to partially reconstruct the new office building. Embassy personnel finally occupied the new facilities in May 2000, thirty-one years after Nixon and Brezhnev signed the exchange of sites agreement.[57]

The PFIAB also addressed the issue of embassy security as a whole in 1984 when it investigated the risk of penetration by hostile intelligence services. At that time, the board had concluded that American installations were at risk because they often employed large numbers of foreign nationals. The American embassy in Moscow, for example, had over two hundred Soviet nationals on the payroll despite information indicating that at least fifty worked for the KGB. "KGB agents worked in the U.S. embassy," said the PFIAB member Rostow. "We thought that was crazy. The State Department liked it because they could get theater tickets."[58] Known KGB employees worked in the embassy carpool, where they had access to diplomatic vehicles as mechanics and drivers, in the convenience store, where they could observe the purchasing habits of embassy employees, and inside the embassy itself as telephone operators, where they could monitor who called and possibly even the calls themselves.[59] The State Department resisted the idea of replacing Soviet workers with American employees on economic grounds, which prompted the PFIAB member Perot to offer his own money to help increase security.[60]

Defectors and Counterespionage

In 1985—"the Year of the Spy"—nine U.S. citizens were arrested for committing espionage against the United States. Six of these had been espionage agents for the Soviet Union, one had spied for Communist China, one had been a spy for Israel, and the ninth had provided information to the Ghanaian government in Africa. Four of the six persons arrested for spying for the Soviet Union were part of a single espionage ring. In May 1985, a former U.S. Navy chief warrant officer, John Anthony Walker Jr., was arrested for providing cryptographic and other sensitive information to the Soviets since 1968—a period of almost seventeen years. He had recruited as accomplices his son Michael Lance Walker, who also served in the U.S. Navy, his brother Arthur Walker, and his friend Jerry Alfred Whitworth, who served in the U.S. Navy from

1956 to 1983. The senior KGB officer Vitaly Yurchenko told the FBI after he defected in July 1985 that he had received a briefing in Moscow about the Walker-Whitworth case. Yurchenko said he learned that the KGB regarded the work of this spy ring as "the most important operation in the KGB's history."[61]

Yurchenko also provided information that led to the arrest in November 1985 of Ronald Pelton, who had become a Soviet espionage agent after he resigned from the NSA in 1979. Yurchenko also provided information that the former CIA officer Edward Lee Howard had been working for the KGB. Howard escaped FBI surveillance and resurfaced in Moscow.[62] In July 1985, a young CIA operations support assistant, Sharon Scranage, was arrested for providing information to a boyfriend who worked for the Ghanaian government. Four months later, Jonathan Pollard, a civilian analyst with the U.S. Navy, was arrested for spying for Israel. Also in November 1985, the longtime CIA officer Larry Wu-tai Chin was arrested as a spy for Communist China. That same month, Yurchenko redefected to the Soviet Union, culminating a year of embarrassment for Casey and the CIA.[63]

The escape of Edward Lee Howard, after Yurchenko's disclosure that Howard was a KGB spy, brought into question several CIA practices.[64] Howard had been a CIA trainee for a number of months before failing a routine polygraph and being dismissed in October 1983. Angry at his dismissal, he then traveled to Vienna, the center of European espionage, and passed American secrets to the KGB for "an undisclosed amount of money." After Yurchenko named him as a Soviet agent, the FBI put him under surveillance at his New Mexico home. But, because they did not have authorization to arrest him, the agents maintained their distance from the home, allowing him to slip away undetected. He later evaded his FBI pursuers by using tactics he learned during his training at the CIA.[65] After his defection to the Soviet Union, at least one Soviet agent working for the CIA disappeared, presumably imprisoned or killed for his betrayal of the Soviet Union. By late 1986, it became clear to U.S. intelligence that Howard's treason could not be responsible for the number of failed operations behind the Iron Curtain.[66] While his knowledge of the CIA's tactics and, more importantly, agents was limited, he still proved extremely harmful to American national security.

DCI Casey was particularly embarrassed and angered by the CIA handling of the Howard case, and he commissioned an investigation of the case by the agency's inspector general. He was, however, dissatisfied with the inspector general's report because of its failure to discuss "specific responsibility for the appalling confusion and inattention to detail" in the Directorate of Operations' handling of the case. The PFI-AB conducted its own investigation of the Howard case and concluded that a major part of the problem had been the unwillingness of the CIA's SOVA division to "think the unthinkable" about the possibility of a foreign penetration.[67] Six months later, after reading the PFIAB investigation of the Howard case, Casey's anger boiled over. On June 4, 1986, he wrote a personal memo to Clair George, the head of the Directorate of Operations, in which he blasted George for deficiencies that led to "this catastrophe." The DCI said that he was "appalled at the DO's handling of the Howard case as described in the recent PFIAB report" and held George personally responsible for correcting it. Robert Gates wrote in his memoirs that he worked closely with Casey for five and a half years but that he had never seen Casey write a memo that strong to any other CIA officer.[68]

The PFIAB also examined the defection of Vitaly Yurchenko, a twenty-five-year KGB veteran. Yurchenko, the chief of the Fifth Department of Directorate K under the First Chief Directorate—the unit responsible for investigating KGB officers to prevent defections and double agents—defected in Rome on August 1, 1985.[69] During the subsequent CIA interrogation, he revealed several KGB spies in the U.S. intelligence community, including Howard and the former NSA communications specialist Ronald William Pelton. In a strange turn of events back in the United States, Yurchenko slipped through a window at Au Pied du Cochon, a French restaurant in Washington, DC, and walked to the Soviet embassy on November 2, 1985. Two days later, he participated in a press conference at the Soviet embassy at which he claimed that the CIA had kidnapped him and injected him with psychotropic drugs.[70] His short-lived defection confounded many in the American government and prompted questions about how the CIA and the FBI handled Soviet defectors.

Much to DCI Casey's chagrin, the PFIAB attempted to determine whether Yurchenko was a legitimate defector or a double agent sent by the KGB and to offer recommendations on how to improve the American handling of defectors.[71] FBI director William Webster apparently remained convinced of Yurchenko's bona fides, but the PFIAB counterintelligence task force under James Q. Wilson did not share his confidence.[72] It doubted the Soviet spy's legitimacy, though it never issued a formal report to that effect to the president. Former executive secretary Gary Schmitt said that the impact of the Yurchenko debacle increased as time passed and additional problems, such as embassy security, arose in Moscow.[73]

The fact that he was not executed on his return to the Soviet Union seemed to indicate that Yurchenko was not a legitimate defector. Instead, he was welcomed back with open arms and even appeared to have resumed his previous KGB duties.[74] While Yurchenko did expose Howard and Pelton as traitors, he did not divulge the identity of the KGB's most prized agent, the CIA officer Aldrich Ames, who began to work for the KGB in May 1985. As a CIA Soviet operations and counterintelligence officer, Ames provided information that resulted in the deaths of nine or more Soviet agents recruited by the CIA prior to his arrest in 1994.[75]

But it is also conceivable that Yurchenko was a legitimate defector who had become infuriated by his treatment at the hands of the CIA and FBI. It would not have been the first time the American intelligence services alienated a defector. Nicolae Horodinca, a Romanian who escaped to the United States in 1980, said: "The CIA makes zombies of defectors. It destroys their self-esteem and sense of security." He nearly returned to his home country after Romanian officials told him the stiffest penalty he would face was a twenty-year prison sentence, but a well-timed phone call to his mother in Bucharest convinced him to stay in the United States.[76] In its 1987 report to the president, the PFIAB was critical of how the CIA handled the defection. Though specifics are still classified, the board undoubtedly concurred with Yurchenko, who, in a news conference after his return to Russia, faulted the CIA for using low-level agents who did not speak Russian to handle his case. To improve the management of defectors, the PFIAB recommended using the U.S. Marshals Service because its expertise and experience in witness relocation programs made it better suited to assisting defectors in search of a new country and a new identity.[77]

The PFIAB also investigated the CIA's personnel security practices and made several recommendations. It first examined the screening process for potential CIA officers. While the agency used a battery of personality tests to attempt to predict future behavior, the PFIAB pointed out that factors like drug and alcohol abuse should also influence hiring decisions. A former PFIAB staffer explained that the CIA accepted the board's proposals, and today the CIA screens potential employees for a history of drug or alcohol abuse in addition to requiring applicants to take a polygraph test.[78]

The PFIAB also examined how the CIA dismissed employees who

had access to sensitive information. Wilson was an expert in the field of personnel management and likely influenced the board's discussion. While we do not know all the details of its recommendations in this area, it appears that the board encouraged the CIA (and other parts of the intelligence community) to transfer such employees to nonsensitive areas for a while before taking them off the payroll completely. In this way, it hoped that any classified information the employees possessed would be out of date and, therefore, useless should they decide to betray their country.[79]

Leaks and Personnel Security

DCI Casey requested that the board look into a series of leaks during Reagan's first term that caused great concern in the White House. In 1983, news of American plans to respond militarily to attacks on American personnel in Lebanon undercut Deputy National Security Adviser Robert McFarlane's attempt to negotiate a cease-fire there.[80] Casey was also incensed that the American media had discovered that the CIA had mined Nicaraguan harbors, which he blamed on opponents of Reagan's policies in the U.S. government. When he approached the PFIAB, Casey's old friend Edward Bennett Williams replied: "You declare a war, mine the harbors, and then say the worry is leaks. You were caught with a smoking gun and you yell robbery!"[81] Casey also deplored reports that a former CIA analyst left the agency after the DCI allegedly ordered him to alter a report on Mexico to match administration policy, which proved embarrassing for the Reagan White House.[82]

The PFIAB's investigation into the Nicaragua harbor incident may have touched on another controversial topic in Washington: the polygraph. President Reagan had first approved use of the polygraph in leak investigations in early 1983. The original proposal for its extensive use provoked open dissent in the Reagan administration, with Secretary of State George Shultz saying he would resign if forced to take a polygraph. Reagan subsequently removed the specific references to using polygraphs, but investigators understood that they still had the authority to use them.[83] Two years later, however, Reagan responded to unspecified leaks and the increased threat of espionage by again threatening to make polygraph examinations more common throughout government by signing National Security Decision Directive 196. Shultz again threatened to resign, and the president diluted the directive.[84] The PFIAB's precise role regarding leaks and use of the polygraph is still classified.

Human Intelligence

During the 1980s, U.S. intelligence discovered through unknown sources that all the Cuban agents recruited over the years were, in fact, double agents working for the Castro regime. Policymakers were incredulous that the situation went undiscovered for so long. The PFIAB's investigation of this human intelligence failure also tied in with its work on the utility of the polygraph because the supposedly legitimate Cuban agents had all been screened using that device.[85]

Economic Intelligence

Reagan's PFIAB evinced a great deal of interest in economic intelligence, largely at the prodding of Vice Chair Cherne. Available records point to strategic resources—such as oil, metals (such as manganese, cobalt, chromium, platinum, and titanium), and other critical products that the U.S. imported—as the primary focus of the board's attention. In 1983, the PFIAB initiated "a study on the adequacy of intelligence as related to U.S. strategic and critical materials policy."[86] In a letter to the members of the PFIAB task force on economic intelligence, Cherne outlined four areas of interest:

- "Though our dependence on these materials has long been recognized, what we know about the dependence, our present and future needs, the sources of supply, and the threats which may interrupt that supply, may not be current."
- "There have been changing doctrines concerning the nature of war in which the U.S. may find itself engaged. Those changing concepts may or may not be matched by the adequacy of our stockpiles of those materials, or the knowledge which is required to make sure that supply will match possible need."
- "In the absence of war, as in the case of oil, economic warfare conducted by us or against us may find us vulnerable in relation to some of these commodities."
- "The increasing importance of high technology to our national eminence and the urgency of high technology to national security intensifies our dependence on certain imported minerals and materials increasingly vital to high technology manufacture."[87]

Cherne noted that, of the thirty-six minerals prevalent in American manufacturing, twenty-two came from outside the United States. Some countries that provided chromium, manganese, and cobalt were

American allies, but others frequently opposed U.S. policy. Because many believed that the Soviets had stockpiled significant amounts of critical minerals, the United States could conceivably find itself at a disadvantage should demand grow or supply fall. Cherne challenged the widely held assumption that nuclear weapons had made protracted war an anachronism, arguing that protracted conventional conflict was still possible. The vice chair also addressed the related question of whether the United States depended excessively on Japan for high-technology products vital to the command and control of U.S. forces.[88] While the PFIAB reports and recommendations regarding economic intelligence and strategic materials are still classified, a 1983 letter from Cherne to the new board member Alan Greenspan provides one clue as to their findings. On the basis of the preliminary investigation by the board staffer Randall Fort, Cherne's letter conceded that there was "a more substantial state of 'readiness' than either the Chairman or I had assumed."[89]

A related area of economic intelligence that the PFIAB addressed was the debt crisis. Vice Chair Cherne expressed concern about three aspects of the problem in an April 19, 1983, letter to Secretary of the Treasury Regan. First, the board believed that American intelligence should not overlook "the social and political repercussions within the debtor nations" resulting from excessive debt in less-developed countries. Second, it worried about the effects of the developing world's debt on the U.S. economy. Third, Cherne wondered whether U.S. intelligence resources were sufficiently engaged in monitoring the long-term debt repayment schedules. The vice chair made it clear in his letter that he was not criticizing the intelligence community or the Department of the Treasury but merely passing along the board's concerns. Cherne also promised that he would try again to convince the PFIAB to recommend to the president that the secretary of the Treasury join the NSC. Although his previous attempt under President Ford proved fruitless, Cherne believed that changing conditions during the Reagan administration might make a second effort successful.[90] There is no evidence, however, that the secretary of the Treasury ever joined the NSC during the Reagan administration.

Soviet Union and Arms Control

Not surprisingly, given the reintensification of the Cold War in the early 1980s, the PFIAB spent much of its time studying the Soviet Union. It investigated the state of U.S. intelligence about the strength of the Soviet economy. Because economic data on the Soviet Union were so difficult to obtain, it worried that the assessments of the U.S. intelligence community were flawed.[91] The board also examined the military balance between the United States and the Soviet Union.[92] While a decrease in tension between the two superpowers and more openness on the part of the Soviets were positive steps, there remained substantial skepticism in the U.S. government about whether glasnost and perestroika were genuine and whether they would have short- and long-term implications for American economic, military, and intelligence industries.[93] The PFIAB thus tried to ascertain the depth and extent of Mikhail Gorbachev's reforms.

Finally, the PFIAB played an influential role in assessing the proposed Strategic Arms Reduction Treaty (START), a controversial subject that preoccupied large portions of the U.S. government during the 1980s.[94] START originated in 1982 with Reagan's proposal of a two-part plan to reduce significantly the superpowers' nuclear arsenals. The first phase would place limits on strategic ballistic missile inventories and deployments while also reducing the destructiveness of warheads. The second phase envisioned similar restrictions on bombers and other delivery vehicles. The negotiations faltered several times after the Soviet Union balked at the U.S. Strategic Defense Initiative (SDI) and NATO's deployment of nuclear missiles in Western Europe. After discussions began again in 1985, the two sides exchanged proposals and counterproposals for years.[95] As part of its work, the PFIAB solicited assessments from the JCS on acceptable maximum arsenal reductions and also tried to gauge the Soviets' response to START. Cognizant of the Soviet Union's history of deceitfulness and the importance of nuclear arms reduction, many on the board expressed doubts about the ability of the U.S. intelligence community to confirm Soviet compliance with an agreement. The board apparently made enough noise about verification to disturb Vice President George Bush, who later considered disbanding the advisory board in part because of its outspokenness on START, which no doubt brought back memories of the Team B fiasco during his tenure as DCI.[96]

Able Archer

The Able Archer exercise and the heightened tensions between the Soviet Union and the United States early in the Reagan administration also attracted PFIAB interest. In 1983, NATO forces conducted a major command-post exercise simulating the transition from conventional to nuclear war. These actions coincided with a significant jump in cable traffic between the United States and Great Britain following the invasion of

Grenada, a Commonwealth member. The Soviets, interpreting the spike in communications as indicating possible preparations for a nuclear first strike, became uneasy. The increased security at American military installations in the wake of the bombing of marine barracks in Lebanon also made the Soviets wary. Finally, and most ominously from the Soviet vantage point, President Reagan, Vice President Bush, and the JCS coincidently disappeared from public view simultaneously. The Soviets interpreted this combination of factors to mean that the United States and its allies were planning a first strike under the guise of a military exercise. The United States did not appreciate the gravity of the situation until years later when the double agent Oleg Gordievsky told DCI Casey how close the superpowers had come to nuclear war.[97]

Then executive director Gary Schmitt suggested that the PFIAB revisit the issue in order to help American policymakers understand how the Soviets could find exercises such as Able Archer so threatening. Despite opposition from some board members to the investigation, Kissinger took the lead in analyzing the near crisis.[98] Although the results of the effort are unavailable, the former CIA analyst Melvin Goodman told CNN that the Able Archer period was the turning point that convinced Reagan to restrict military exercises and engage the Soviets diplomatically.[99]

SDI and Space Technology

The PFIAB looked into President Reagan's SDI ("Star Wars"), the U.S. effort to create a ballistic missile shield using kinetic and directed energy in space-based systems. Deployed high above the earth's atmosphere, these systems would theoretically destroy incoming missiles in midflight. Little is known about the PFIAB's role in the SDI project, but it seems to have centered on intelligence issues such as satellite architecture and denial and deception programs.[100] Because of their unrivaled expertise in satellites and space-based weapons, Wheelon and Foster probably took the lead in PFIAB discussions of Star Wars.

The PFIAB also investigated possible military applications of the space shuttle, a request that may have come from the Department of Defense or from other PFIAB members. Foster and Wheelon concluded that, despite its great utility for certain scientific and exploration missions, the shuttle had very little potential for military applications.[101] As the latter told a meeting of the Association of Former Intelligence Officers in 1985: "I think that the decision which was made during the Carter years to compel the Air Force to rely exclusively on the shuttle was a tragic mistake. That mistake has now been corrected in large part at the urging and intervention of the PFIAB. . . . The Air Force is once again buying Titan Rockets so as to have supplementary launch capability."[102]

Finally, board members once again played the role of umpire in settling a dispute between the CIA and the National Reconnaissance Office (NRO) about new satellite programs. In 1985, the particular issue at stake was whether to replace the ORION signals intelligence satellite with a much larger system, as the NRO's Program A advocated, or a more modest upgrade of ORION, as the CIA's Program B suggested. DCI Casey asked the PFIAB to weigh the merits of each proposal, and Wheelon "concluded that [the] extensive improvements suggested by program A were not necessary—that its staff had missed two key technical points—and that the CIA proposal to stay with the same basic system and the same contractor (TRW) make the most sense." Wheelon's support for Program B helped carry the day.[103]

Communications Security

The PFIAB assessed the security of American government communications in Washington, DC. William O. Baker, a long-term PFIAB board member, was concerned about the vulnerability of radio and microwave transmissions in the nation's capital. PFIAB members were acutely aware of hostile nations' penchant for placing surveillance equipment on top of their embassies in the hopes of intercepting valuable information. The new Soviet embassy was particularly well suited for this mission by virtue of its location in the Mt. Alto neighborhood of northwest Washington. To prove its point that communications were susceptible to eavesdropping, the PFIAB used Bearcat scanners—available at commercial electronics stores like Radio Shack—at various locations around the Washington metro area and found that they could intercept transmissions from many government officials. Deputy Chief of Staff Michael Deaver was overheard on U.S. government car phones many times. One former staffer believes that the PFIAB efforts did persuade the administration to reroute some of its communications to protect them better from prying ears, although no documentation is available on the actual recommendations.[104]

Operation LANDBRIDGE

In 1983, the board investigated another secure information issue known as Operation LANDBRIDGE. LANDBRIDGE was an operation run by Bulgarian intelligence that used large trucks filled with eavesdropping equipment to attempt to spy on Western diplomatic and military installations. The trucks would simply drive past American, British, and especially French embassies and pick up whatever stray communications emanated from the buildings. A September 19, 1985, letter from Seymour Weiss to Armstrong and Cherne indicated that the PFIAB had made very little progress on the issue over the span of several years and, in Weiss's words, had "dropped the ball on this one."[105]

Assassination Attempt on John Paul II

On May 13, 1981, the Turkish extremist Mehmet Ali Agca shot Pope John Paul II as he traveled in an open-top car through St. Peter's Square in Rome. The holy father sustained serious injuries to his abdomen, left arm, and right hand but survived because none of the bullets struck a vital organ. Agca gave conflicting reasons for his actions, which led some to speculate that he had not acted alone. The PFIAB decided to investigate whether the Soviets were behind the attempt on the pope's life, although it is unclear who prompted this inquiry. After hearing a CIA briefing on the subject, some members were adamant that the Soviet Union was to blame. Edward Bennett Williams, never known for being shy, said: "There is no doubt in my mind that the KGB did it. I don't know why we don't use this for propaganda purposes."[106] In May 1985, the CIA conducted a major study of the assassination attempt entitled "Agca's Attempt to Kill the Pope—the Case for Soviet Involvement." Robert Gates, who was then in charge of analysis at CIA as the deputy director for intelligence, said that this was "a compelling study" but that there were "gaps in information" that prevented definitive conclusions. PFIAB chair Armstrong received this CIA study and, in June 1985, sent DCI Casey a memo critical of the CIA's overall "handling" of the "Papal Plot." No additional evidence came to light about Soviet involvement in the assassination attempt, even after the collapse of the Soviet Union.[107]

Camouflage, Concealment, and Deception

The PFIAB also made an important contribution to American intelligence in the area of camouflage, concealment, and deception (CC&D).[108] CC&D involves attempts to hide equipment and personnel from enemy eyes, but it can also refer to attempts to obscure attacking aircraft and vehicles—such as stealth bombers and fighters. Within the last twenty years, CC&D has become more important as precision weaponry has rendered static defenses, such as fortifications, obsolete. This topic appeared on at least one PFIAB agenda in 1983 when the board received a briefing from Maj. Gen. John Marks, the commander of the Electronic

Security Command and director of the Joint Electronic Warfare Center.[109] Perhaps the PFIAB took an interest in assessing the viability of CC&D tactics in protecting nuclear facilities or in enabling a new type of offensive aircraft. More likely, it was concerned with America's ability to detect and counter Soviet CC&D.

Information-Sharing Technology

Baker was particularly alarmed about America's diminishing edge in technology and lobbied the PFIAB to investigate the state of U.S. supercomputers.[110] While available board records provide few details, the topic of supercomputers appears on one meeting agenda.[111] In addition, representatives from the Cray Supercomputer manufacturer attended at least one board meeting. This interest in supercomputing dovetailed nicely with the board's desire to improve the dissemination of intelligence throughout the government. In the early 1980s, a pervasive anti-computer culture impeded the intelligence community's ability to get the right information to the right person at the right time.[112] Considering the PFIAB's long-standing enthusiasm for introducing emerging technologies into the intelligence community, it likely advocated the increased usage of computers or other equipment that would make the business of intelligence collection and dissemination more efficient and effective.

Central America and Caribbean

In the aftermath of the invasion of Grenada, the U.S. military complained about the inability of the intelligence community to provide tactically useful information in a timely fashion. The disconnect between national intelligence and frontline military units in combat had bedeviled policy-makers for years. This would not be the last time the PFIAB addressed the problem as it was a central board concern again after the First Gulf War.[113] General Vessey, the JCS chair, complained to DCI Casey about the lack of tactical intelligence. But, in reality, Adm. Wesley McDonald, commander in chief, Atlantic, who had been put in overall command of the Grenada operation, was fully briefed by Duane Clarridge, the chief of the CIA Latin American Division, about the Clandestine Service officer who was on the island and available to be tasked. Despite this briefing, McDonald never once provided any tactical intelligence requirements to the senior CIA Clandestine Service officer whom Clarridge had assigned to his headquarters. Finally, General Vessey complained to the CIA that the U.S. military had to use tourist maps when it went into Grenada. But it was the Defense Mapping Agency, not the CIA, that was supposed to produce maps of foreign countries for use by the U.S. military. Vessey never asked for maps from his own Defense Mapping Agency. In this case, the military's complaint was overdrawn.[114]

The board also worked on Panama, and Schmitt and Wilson took a trip there on its behalf. Unfortunately, Schmitt does not recall the specific purpose of the trip, and available records offer few clues.[115] The board also worked on narcotics issues in the region, most of which related to Mexico, but one former PFIAB staffer felt that the board "tip-toed" around the issue.[116]

A Few Hints of Other Topics

Despite the extensive list of topics already covered, members also found time to tackle other issues for which only a passing reference exists in PFIAB records. These include West German defenses, Lebanon, Grenada, Panama, permanent "red team" collaboration with the U.S. intelligence community, and covert action.[117] The PFIAB even received a briefing on the conspiracy theorist and perpetual presidential candidate Lyndon Larouche.[118]

Topics the PFIAB Avoided

For all the issues investigated by President Reagan's PFIAB, several are glaringly absent. The board did not do much with terrorism because Vice President Bush led a separate task force to deal with that issue.[119] The PFIAB also did not discuss immigration, even though the long-time member Luce thought that it had potentially grave implications for U.S. intelligence.[120] But one issue stands out for its absence from Reagan PFIAB agendas: the Iran-Contra Affair.

For obvious reasons, the Reagan administration was undoubtedly wary of any investigation of a scandal that implicated several high-level officials. According to former executive director Gary Schmitt, however, he steered the PFIAB away from the topic because he believed the board had no "comparative advantage" in the highly politicized foreign affairs issues in Central America.[121] Reagan's IOB, on the other hand, became deeply entrenched in the Iran-Contra Affair. On October 18, 1984, the White House announced that the president had asked the IOB to "investigate allegations concerning the possibility of improper conduct on the part of employees of the Central Intelligence Agency in regard to the publication of a manual for Nicaraguan democratic resistance forces." Given the confidential relationship between the IOB and the president, "no further comments [could] be made."[122]

Around that time, Lt. Col. Oliver North approached the IOB seeking legal advice on NSC involvement in Contra resupply efforts—since Congress had officially cut off such funding on October 3, 1984. The IOB, "at some point" within the next year, prepared a "classified legal memo discussing the NSC's relationship to the congressional ban." The IOB argued that, since the NSC was not designated as a member of the intelligence community in the EO that created it and since the congressionally prescribed role of the NSC was coordination, rather than implementation, of covert action, the NSC was "not covered by the prohibition."[123]

The Tower Commission investigated the entire Iran-Contra Affair and concluded that the IOB was an "odd source" of legal justification. By offering North and the NSC legal advice, it ceased to serve as a legal watchdog. Former IOB members believe that the confluence of a new mandate and a new member caused the board to fail in its primary mission of giving the president objective advice. According to former IOB chair Thomas Farmer: "What the president did, in effect, was rip out the smoke-alarm system, and then, when a fire broke out and he didn't hear any bells go off, he acted surprised."[124] Though the subject was only briefly mentioned by the Tower Commission, it seems that the IOB played a significant role in the Iran-Contra Affair. In the mind of one former PFIAB staffer, if North had approached the PFIAB, rather than the IOB, with questions regarding the legality of the NSC resupplying the Contras after the congressional ban, "this whole thing would never have happened."[125] The extent of the PFIAB's contribution to the Iran-Contra investigation was the delivery of relevant documents to Congress, the first such transfer in its history.[126] Otherwise, as far as we know, the board made no investigation, issued no report, and made no recommendation on the matter.

ASSESSMENT

After four years in limbo, no one knew what to expect from the reconstituted PFIAB. Initially, the new board consisted of several members better known for their political connections than for their expertise in the fields of intelligence or national security. The heavy-handed role of the White House Personnel Office yielded a board that was too large to be productive during the first term of the Reagan administration. Although accounts of the details differ significantly, the Halloween Massacre II trimmed the membership by half and resulted in a more manageable body for the chair and a more effective board for the president and the intelligence community. Even the addition of four new members shortly afterward put membership at only fourteen, a far cry from the board's peak of twenty-two.

To be effective, an independent advisory board must have competent members to credibly advise the president. Reagan's willingness to appoint political friends, in addition to members with experience in intelligence affairs, to the PFIAB was a marked departure from previous administrations, which had generally appointed mostly seasoned professionals of a bipartisan character to serve on the board. By initially augmenting his PFIAB with many political appointees, Reagan established an unfortunate precedent of using the board as a repository of political patronage, a legacy that has plagued the PFIAB ever since.

The PFIAB addressed a wide array of topics during the seven years it served President Reagan. Though embassy security, the Soviet Union, and defections and counterespionage failures dominated agendas at times, subjects as diverse as the attempted assassination of the pope and the consequences of long-term debt in developing nations also occupied members' attentions. Responding to a questionnaire from the chair, many members lamented the board's lack of focus. One member wrote: "We are into entirely too many things." Another said: "It all goes down to fewer subjects, more oomph, more follow-through."[127] Nevertheless, the Reagan PFIAB seems to have made an impact on CIA hiring practices, embassy security, and the negotiations surrounding the controversial START treaty.

The track record of the Reagan board cannot be attributed to the president's personal style. Presidential style arguments predict variation across administrations but consistency within them. Reagan, however, shifted gears in terms of how he used the PFIAB during his term in office without really changing elements of his personal style. Thus, the Reagan case seems far more in line with a structural argument that would focus on the expansion of oversight institutions as an explanation for the Reagan board's experience. Given the post-1970s development of oversight institutions in both branches of the U.S. government, which made an independent presidential advisory board like the PFIAB seem like an irrelevant anachronism, it is not at all surprising that the board would have only mixed success in this case.

7

George H. W. Bush

President George H. W. Bush seemed ambivalent about the President's Foreign Intelligence Advisory Board (PFIAB) at the beginning of his term. His experience with the board during the Team B exercise of the 1970s reportedly colored his views, as did the board's outspokenness about the difficulties of verifying the START treaty.[1] As a result, he made no changes to the Reagan PFIAB and issued no executive orders (EOs) concerning the board, and it lay dormant for the first eighteen months of his presidency. The members of Reagan's board remained on the official roster, and the staff continued to work on projects initiated during the Reagan administration. There is, however, no evidence that the board held meetings or received new tasks from the Bush White House.

Other high-ranking members of the administration also had doubts about the utility of the board. Secretary of State James Baker reportedly supported abolishing the PFIAB because he disliked its access to the president and its potential as an alternative source of advice.[2] Further, he regarded those appointed to the PFIAB as merely receiving a reward for political favors. He could not name one example of the board doing something that improved U.S. intelligence. One former cabinet member told us that Baker believed that there were already too many overlapping organizations in American intelligence.[3] Thus, there was little pressure on the president from his most senior advisers to make use of the board.

Moreover, during the first year of President Bush's tenure, the PFIAB found itself in the center of media and congressional controversy—an unusual position for the normally low-profile and secretive advisory body. The controversy centered around the divisive figure of Henry Kissinger, a Reagan appointee who remained on the official PFIAB roster. In April 1989, the *New York Times* released a special report describing the possible conflicts of interest between Kissinger's membership on the board and the activities of his consulting firm, Kissinger Associates.[4] The article concerned Kissinger, but it also called into question the activities of Scowcroft, the new national security adviser, and Deputy Secretary of State Lawrence Eagleburger, who both were consultants for Kissinger Associates. The report alleged that Kissinger regularly examined arms control issues with the PFIAB while at the same time advising clients who built or maintained missile systems for the U.S. military.[5] Finally, an unnamed PFIAB member also charged that Kissinger took classified documents from board meetings in violation of security regulations.[6]

Despite Kissinger's long association with the Grand Old Party, conservative Republicans in Congress took the lead in calling for an investigation of his activities.[7] During Senate Foreign Relations Committee hearings on the matter in May 1989, Senator Jesse Helms said of Kissinger: "He's up to his armpits in deals with foreign countries. . . . He's not the king; he doesn't have to serve on this board."[8] In September 1989, both the House and the Senate Intelligence committees submitted reports on the fiscal year 1990 Intelligence Authorization Bill that directed the president to issue regulations on the use of classified information by the PFIAB.[9] Congress also began to consider bills that would make PFIAB members' financial statements public. Although board members had always been required to file financial disclosure statements when they joined the board, the reports had previously been kept confidential.

In December 1989, Kissinger found himself in the media spotlight again, this time over Bush's decision to send a diplomatic delegation to Beijing in the wake of the Tiananmen Square massacre. Regardless of the true extent of Kissinger's involvement in this controversial decision to engage the Communist regime despite its atrocious human rights record, some critics thought they detected his influence behind it. In the wake of this controversy, Congress resumed debate on the bills requiring public financial disclosure for all PFIAB members, bills that Bush had earlier threatened to veto.[10] Although Kissinger vehemently denied ever advising his clients on issues related to arms control and disputed the claim that his service on the board and his business activities caused any conflict of interest, congressional and media scrutiny continued to build. As a result, in January 1990, he submitted his resignation from the PFIAB on the grounds that he was too busy to serve. He did mention, however, that he would be pleased to continue to offer informal advice to the president.[11]

Following Kissinger's resignation, President Bush ultimately decided to retain the board but to streamline it and reduce the scope of its work. It is unclear why he ultimately decided to keep the PFIAB. One former executive director during the Bush administration believes that it was the result of political pressure.[12] A former board member told us that David L. Boren, the chair of the Senate Select Committee on Intelligence (SSCI), strongly believed in the value of the PFIAB. The former member recalls that Boren informed Bush that the SSCI would push for legislation requiring a PFIAB if Bush did not appoint one himself.[13]

When Bush announced his decision to keep the board, administration officials reported to the *New York Times* that Anne Armstrong and National Security Adviser Scowcroft had helped persuade him not to abolish it.[14] Former DCI Robert Gates recalls that Bush was urged by his advisers to reconstitute the board along the 1950s model, which meant a smaller PFIAB of only four to five members consisting primarily of scientists and other technical experts.[15] On June 16, 1990, Bush followed this advice by scrapping the large Reagan PFIAB and replacing it with a six-member panel of respected science, intelligence, and foreign policy experts.

Although previous presidents issued a new EO to establish the responsibilities and duties of the PFIAB, President Bush did not. Instead, there was an understanding within his administration that, unless a new order was issued, the existing Reagan EOs remained in force.[16] While the Bush PFIAB had the same Reagan-era mandate, experts outside the government expected the new board to move in a very different direction and focus on the changes U.S. intelligence agencies needed to make in order to address new security concerns in the post–Cold War era.[17]

BOARD MEMBERSHIP AND EXECUTIVE STAFF

Bush inherited a fifteen-member board from Reagan. After Kissinger's resignation in February 1990, thirteen of the remaining members submitted their letters of resignation on July 16, 1990, when Bush announced his plans to restructure the board. Only John Tower, appointed by President Reagan in 1987, remained after the restructuring.

While Reagan's original PFIAB was loaded with political cronies and friends, President Bush appointed members with nonpartisan backgrounds and significant experience with intelligence, technology, and defense-related matters. John Tower was the only former politician on the board. John M. Deutch of MIT, the former National Security Agency (NSA) director and physicist Lew Allen, and the Technologies Strategies and Alliances founder, William Perry, brought strong science backgrounds to the PFIAB. William Hyland, the editor of *Foreign Affairs,* and Adm. Bobby Ray Inman, a former Deputy DCI and NSA director, provided the board with expertise in intelligence and international affairs. Both Perry and Deutch would later serve in key high-ranking positions for President Bill Clinton. Inman would be Clinton's nominee for secretary of defense in 1994 after Les Aspin stepped down from the position in 1993. Vocal opposition from the Right subsequently led Inman to withdraw his name from consideration, but Bush's choices for the board were a testament to the board's nonpartisan, expert makeup.[18]

Bush turned to Tower to replace Armstrong as the chair. The former Republican senator from Texas had cast himself as a defense specialist during his time in the Senate and remained involved with defense and international affairs following his retirement from office in 1985. Under President Reagan, he acted as the U.S. chief negotiator at the START talks in Geneva, chaired the Tower Commission investigation into the Iran-Contra scandal, and advised defense firms and contractors through the consulting firm of Tower, Eggers, and Green.

Originally Bush intended for Tower, a longtime Texas Republican, to serve as secretary of defense in his administration, but the Senate refused to confirm his appointment. Although during his years in the Senate he had significant experience with matters of intelligence and defense, including a stint as chair of the Senate Armed Services Committee from 1981 to 1984, the confirmation hearings elicited extensive testimony alleging that he was unsuited for the job. In addition, committee members questioned his actions as a consultant to defense firms, with Senator Sam Nunn suggesting he had advised firms on the possible implications of arms reduction talks while serving as chief negotiator at the same talks.[19]

Following the failed nomination for secretary of defense, Bush announced that Tower would chair the PFIAB on July 16, 1990. Some close to the administration viewed the appointment as a consolation prize following the bitter confirmation hearings and subsequent rejection. Speaking before Tower's appointment as chair, the White House chief of personnel, Charles G. Untermeyer, said: "The President has always been a great personal friend and admirer of John Tower and wants him to have a meaningful role somewhere in his administration."[20] Tower chaired the PFIAB until his death on April 5, 1991, in the Atlantic Southeast Airlines Flight 2311 crash. President Bush did not name another member to the PFIAB to bring the board back up to six members. Instead, he tapped Admiral Inman as acting chair. In our interview on April 12, 2006, Gates explained that President Bush simply never got around to appointing a permanent PFIAB chair during his presidency.[21]

Proposed Members

Although Bush appointed no other members to his PFIAB, he received numerous nominations and requests for appointments from lawmakers and businessmen, who nominated colleagues, subordinates, and themselves as potential members. A few of the more prominent individuals mentioned included the businessman James Thompson, the entrepreneur John Sheehan, and the congressional aide Vaughn Forrest.

James Thompson, who requested appointment to the PFIAB, served in the marines from 1950 to 1951 and received his bachelor's degree from Yale University in 1954 and his law degree from the University of Louisville eight years later.[22] After graduating from Yale, Thompson became a sales trainee at Glenmore Distilleries, working for five years before becoming president of the Old South Life Insurance Company in 1959. Fifteen years later, he moved back to Glenmore as CEO, but otherwise he had no real expertise relevant to the board.[23]

Senator Arlen Specter recommended his fellow Pennsylvanian Sheehan for membership on the PFIAB in April 1990. Sheehan received his bachelor's degree in engineering from the U.S. Naval Academy in 1952. After graduation, he attended flight school and flew fighter planes until leaving the navy to obtain his MBA from Harvard in 1958.[24] The résumé enclosed with Senator Specter's letter indicates that Sheehan served as an officer for three Fortune 500 companies (though the firms are not named).[25] In addition, he served as a member of the Board of Governors of the Federal Reserve System from 1971 to 1975. After leaving the Federal Reserve, he founded and chaired eight companies in Pennsylvania and New York.[26] It is clear from Specter's letter that Sheehan was a successful businessman, but his total lack of intelligence experience would have made him an unsuitable addition to Bush's small, expert PFIAB.

Finally, in March 1990, the Florida Republican representative William McCollum wrote to the president to recommend his longtime administrative assistant Vaughn S. Forrest to a "senior level position with the administration and on your Foreign Intelligence Advisory Board."[27] While the letter includes little biographical information, it does indicate that Forrest had spent time in Central America, South Asia, Southeast Asia, and Afghanistan. Furthermore, McCollum pointed out that Forrest was a Knight of the Order of Malta, which gave him "ready access to those in leadership in countries with a dominant Catholic presence."[28] The letter closes with an appeal to keep Forrest in government, citing his probable departure to the business sector should an appropriate position prove unavailable.[29] Little is known about Forrest's background, but he worked closely with McCollum on intelligence and defense-related issues. McCollum founded the U.S. House Task Force on Terrorism and Unconventional Warfare and served as chair of the House Subcommittee on Intelligence during his time as representative.[30] While serving as McCollum's chief of staff, Forrest coauthored several reports for the Republican Task Force on Terrorism and Unconventional Warfare together with Youssef Bodansky. Despite this background, he did not seem to have the professional stature or technical expertise of the members of Bush's PFIAB.

Other recommendations included Bo Callaway, Thomas Farmer, Trammell Crow, and Robert Nesen, but none of them generated serious interest among senior administration officials.

PFIAB Executive Staff

The staff of the PFIAB during the Bush administration changed very little. Nina Stewart, who was the assistant executive secretary under Fred Demech during the latter years of the Reagan presidency, took over as executive director under President Bush. Randy Deitering was the assistant director from 1988 to 1991 and deputy executive director from 1991 on. Following Nina Stewart's resignation in October 1991, the president waited until October 14, 1992, to announce Eugene F. Yeates's appointment as executive director.[31]

Bush's PFIAB operated as a single unit and did not employ any outside consultants, perhaps because of its small size and the extensive intelligence experience of most of its members. The PFIAB consisted of the staff and the board members. Aside from the executive director and the assistant executive director, little is known about the rest of the small PFIAB staff.

OPERATING PROCEDURES

Board Meetings

Because the board under President Bush contained fewer members, it was possible to hold meetings frequently, although available records do not include an exact tally of the meetings held. The board met bimonthly until the announcement of restructuring in March 1990, after which it met more often.[32] Meetings were less formal than during the Reagan administration; the board usually met with National Security Adviser

Scowcroft but rarely with the president, though the chair could have had a meeting with him if he wanted one.[33]

Operational Procedures and Interactions with Other Groups

The Bush board operated under the same EO as Reagan's larger board, so its financial and management principles remained unchanged. The members received no pay, only a per diem and transportation allowances. The staff remained in their old offices. Additionally, the small board met as a whole rather than dividing into subcommittees, which had been the norm under Reagan.[34]

The operations of the PFIAB under Bush can be clearly delineated into two periods—before and after the restructuring in July 1990. The pre-restructured board finished working on some projects from the previous administration, and the staff met from January 1989 until July 1990.[35] Apparently, the board sat nearly idle for those eighteen months while Bush vacillated over whether to keep a PFIAB.[36] The *New York Times* columnist William Safire wryly noted during this period of inactivity that the board had been reduced to "technological kibitzing."[37]

Even after the 1990 restructuring, available records indicate that, while the PFIAB may have met more often than before, it remained relatively inactive as compared with previous boards. A significant amount of its time was consumed by briefings and reports designed to familiarize members with their roles, which might partially explain why it had relatively little to do under President Bush.[38]

The new Bush PFIAB worked with the NSC staff as "equals and colleagues." The PFIAB staff did not communicate often with the individual members of the board but were in frequent contact with the chair.[39] The board did not have much direct access to President Bush. Instead, requests and directions were relayed primarily through Scowcroft, who had the most interaction with the board.[40] Robert Gates observed that under President Bush the PFIAB was "fairly inactive," which he at least partially attributes to the death of Chair John Tower. He reports that Scowcroft had never really been a "big fan" of the PFIAB and that he did not seek out projects for the board to work on. He believes that national security advisers were never "terribly enamored" with the PFIAB and viewed them as "kibitzers" in foreign policy.[41]

Because Bush's board consisted primarily of scientists and intelligence specialists, it did not have as much political clout as the Reagan board. Although one former member acknowledges that it did have some "informal" contact with Congress, he believes that the PFIAB was most effective in its formal role as an advisory body reporting to the president.[42]

ISSUES AND RECOMMENDATIONS

Virtually all the Bush board's papers and products remain classified, and most members and staff are unwilling to discuss their work in any great detail. It is fair to say that, in keeping with the new board's technical orientation, it spent far more time than other boards examining technical issues and current events and less time on retrospectives. But information about specific issues the board addressed is extremely limited and gleaned primarily from secondary sources and interviews. Therefore, the issues discussed below probably do not represent the full scope of the PFIAB's work under President Bush.

Gulf War Postmortem

The most significant project undertaken by the Bush PFIAB was a postmortem of the 1990 Iraqi invasion of Kuwait and the Desert Shield and Desert Storm operations that followed. Although the Gulf War was a resounding victory for the United States and its coalition partners, the war also revealed substantial problems with U.S. intelligence collection and dissemination. Early CIA analysis of the buildup of Iraqi troops concluded that Saddam Hussein was merely bluffing in an attempt to convince OPEC to increase prices and cut production. The invasion caught important administration officials by surprise at inopportune times: the American ambassador to Iraq was on vacation in London, Scowcroft was at home, and Defense Secretary Cheney was preparing to travel with Bush to Aspen.[43] As late as July 31, 1990, the CIA was calling an Iraqi invasion of Kuwait "unlikely," and it was not until twenty hours before the invasion that the CIA warned the president of an imminent attack.[44] Problems with intelligence surfaced during the war as well. For instance, the CIA and General Schwarzkopf argued extensively over the issue of battle-damage assessments (BDA), with the CIA charging Schwarzkopf and his CENTCOM staff of exaggerating the damage done to Iraqi forces.[45]

The media and the Congress took notice of the intelligence problems soon after the end of the war. As early as July 7, 1991, William Safire was calling for a review of the intelligence failures in Iraq, to find out "why our expensive machinery was wrong about Iraq's buildup, wrong in so many damage assessments during the war, wrong about when to stop."[46] Further, he took the intelligence services to task for advising President Bush that Saddam Hussein was likely to be overthrown by mutinous generals, leading the president to prematurely end the war and allow the escape of seven hundred modern and over twenty-seven hundred older Iraqi tanks that were later used against Kurds and Shiites.[47] Safire also castigated the intelligence community for failing to discover and destroy all of Iraq's nuclear facilities. In March, the Senate Select Committee on Intelligence announced its plans to investigate the intelligence shortfalls of the Iraq War.[48]

As the SSCI began its investigation, Scowcroft conveyed to the PFIAB President Bush's desire for a detailed "lessons learned report" examining the entire war. One former member told us that the board proposed to conduct an examination of just the intelligence issues, but Bush felt that the PFIAB had the competence and the ability to complete a report on the entire war effort.[49] The board worked on this project for months without hearing anything else about it from the president. Another Bush cabinet official we talked to said that he could not recall ever receiving a post–Gulf War report from the PFIAB.[50] Scowcroft reportedly thought that the board's effort was useful, but Secretary of Defense Cheney resented its criticisms of the Department of Defense.[51]

A former staffer recalls that the report was a substantial product, providing in-depth analysis on a wide range of topics.[52] It discussed the importance of transitioning from the strategic to the tactical use of intelligence, the status of nuclear weapons programs in Iraq, and overall intelligence support during the Gulf War. One of the key "lessons learned" in the report dealt with the difficulty of transmitting timely information from the intelligence agencies to the frontline troops. According to former DCI Robert Gates, signals intelligence (SIGINT) flowed smoothly from NSA headquarters to units in the field, but imagery intelligence (IMINT) went to Riyadh, Saudi Arabia, and was not sent to field units that needed it on the battlefield. SIGINT flowed more smoothly than IMINT in part because the NSA had an established structure for disseminating it but also because intercepts were easier to disseminate to various parts of the military than imagery.[53] Conversely, IMINT was constrained in part because CENTCOM did not have sufficient bandwidth in its computer systems to handle the transfer of this sort of intelligence.[54]

The PFIAB addressed the bureaucratic and technological aspects of the IMINT problem, both during the initial Iraqi invasion and then during the American-led coalition response. It recommended standardizing the methods used to distribute IMINT, although specific details are unavailable about how it expected intelligence agencies to accomplish this standardization. It may have had something to do with the increased support for the National Imaging and Mapping Agency (NIMA). This was a particularly controversial recommendation because the CIA was reluctant to give away a task that traditionally fell within its sphere of operations. Furthermore, Gen. Colin Powell and Secretary of Defense Cheney opposed the idea. Gates says that, despite these objections, he began the process of streamlining IMINT dissemination methods during his tenure as DCI. He proposed creating the NIMA in 1992 along the model of the NSA. The Defense Mapping Agency would also be folded into the NIMA. Gates said that Congress supported his idea, but only a half step of creating a Central Imagery Office was accomplished at the time. The NIMA was not finally established until 1996.[55]

The board also discovered that during the war there were major problems with the collection of tactical imagery. General Schwarzkopf did not use satellite imaging platform resources to collect IMINT for battle damage assessments but rather diverted the imagery to create maps. The air force complained that there was a lack of BDA. A new version of the U-2 was used in the Gulf, but it did not have the capability for real-time transmission of its images to troops in the field.[56] As we noted in previous chapters, the board played a major role in the development of optical satellites with real-time imaging capability, so it was no doubt acutely sensitive to this problem in its Iraq postmortem report.[57]

Another problem that the board's Gulf War study uncovered was that air force planning and navy planning were incompatible and did not have interoperable communications. The navy had to use airplanes to transport airstrike plans to its pilots on its carriers.[58] The PFIAB also found that the navy had a very limited satellite feed and broadband access on board. The navy had one carrier battle group in the Persian Gulf and another in the Red Sea. While the Red Sea group would launch planes to carry out strikes, the Persian Gulf group sat on the sidelines, unable to carry out the required strikes.

Middle East Intelligence and Strategy Pre–Gulf War

In addition to the postmortem report, the board may have examined intelligence and strategy related to the Gulf War before the hostilities began. Chair Tower made a public statement regarding the allies' relative air superiority against Iraq on December 4, 1990, at a conference on the future of Iraq. In his statement, he described Hussein's 240,000 troops as "sitting ducks" in the event the bulk of the Iraqi force amassed inside Kuwait's territory.[59] These comments, made publicly by the PFIAB chair, seem to indicate that the PFIAB might have taken a close look at the Gulf situation before the outbreak of war, though no official documents are currently available on this matter.

Other Issues

The PFIAB examined embassy security, considered the issues surrounding German reunification, and tracked the progress of the Soviet Union's collapse—from the coup attempt against Gorbachev in August 1991 to Boris Yeltsin's takeover and dismantling of the Soviet Union—but its specific findings and recommendations on these topics are still classified.[60] The board also wanted to examine the quality of the clandestine service, but it encountered significant resistance from the CIA's Directorate of Operations when it attempted to address this issue. After the board "finally" got a deputy director for operations to speak with it candidly, it filed several reports about clandestine collection sources and the quality of the intelligence, which at least one former member thinks had an impact.[61] One former member reports that the revelation in 1987 of the fact that many of the U.S. Cuban human intelligence (HUMINT) sources were in fact double agents piqued the board's interest in HUMINT.[62] The Cuban double-agent program was more fully examined by the Reagan and Clinton boards.

As individuals, some board members also affected intelligence policy. For example, while serving on the board, Admiral Inman became one of the most vocal advocates for Robert Gates during the latter's contentious confirmation hearings for DCI, submitting an editorial column in his support that appeared nationwide.[63]

It is unclear what, if any, other topics the PFIAB addressed under President Bush. Overall, both the fifteen-member PFIAB inherited from the Reagan administration and the restructured PFIAB seem to have had a limited amount of work during Bush's term in office.

Issues Not Addressed

In August 1989, a report written by four former national security advisers and a former undersecretary of state for the Center for Security Policy recommended that the PFIAB investigate the alleged espionage carried out by Felix Bloch for the Soviet Union to avoid a "possible cover-up."[64] Bloch was a senior American diplomat dealing with European affairs at the time. The NSA reportedly intercepted conversations between Bloch and a KGB agent in which they arranged a meeting in

Paris. Bloch was photographed meeting with the agent in Paris, and he left the meeting with a different bag than the one he had brought. The resulting investigation never conclusively proved that he passed information to the Soviets, but he was fired and lost his pension. The spy scandal and investigation were covered extensively in the media, and Bloch was tailed for months by reporters. Despite this recommendation, there is no evidence to suggest that the board actually carried out an investigation.

But perhaps the most telling indicator of the board's low status and minimal operations under President Bush is the issues it did not examine. During Gates's tenure as deputy national security adviser and then DCI, the PFIAB was conspicuously absent from such major issues as the reform of the CIA and the intelligence community. Instead, President Bush chose to rely on the NSC and the DCI to guide these projects, which in previous administrations had involved the PFIAB.

Gates drafted National Security Review (NSR) 29 while on staff at the NSC.[65] It was a response to the collapse of the Soviet Union and the realization that "these developments urgently require a top to bottom examination of the mission, role, and priorities of the intelligence communities."[66] The goal of NSR 29 was to identify the intelligence capabilities required from 1992 to 2005. Departments and agencies were directed to identify the sorts of "political, economic, and military" intelligence needed for a post-Soviet international environment in addition to possible new fields of intelligence requirements, such as the examination of environmental issues. The findings were to be submitted to the Deputies Committee, which would then submit an integrated report to the NSC by February 1992.[67] After the departments and agencies submitted their findings, the DCI was to submit to the NSC a report detailing the possible structural, organizational, legislative, and budget adjustments and changes needed to address the new intelligence requirements identified in the Deputies Committee report.[68]

After becoming DCI on November 6, 1991, Gates acted to implement NSR 29, establishing a "blitz" of task forces, initially ten, followed by fourteen others after March 14, 1992.[69] Once the final NSR 29 reports were submitted to the NSC, Bush signed National Security Directive (NSD) 67. The new directive endorsed several changes recommended by the DCI, including "changes in the intelligence process and initiatives for improving human intelligence collection," along with a "comprehensive restructuring of the intelligence community."[70] Among the specific recommendations included under this restructuring were the "replacement of the IC staff with a new Community Management Staff

(CMS), measures to strengthen the NIC [National Intelligence Council] and community management of resources and requirements, improved coordination and management of the four major collection disciplines, the reorganization of the NRO [National Reconnaissance Office], and initiatives to improve intelligence support to the needs of the military."[71] NSD 67 further states that "these measures, together, represent the most dramatic reconfiguration of the Intelligence Community in decades" and that they "must be implemented without delay.[72]

The PFIAB was conspicuous in its absence from the NSR 29 review process and the subsequent drafting of NSD 67. Under previous administrations, the PFIAB was regularly utilized to examine and advise the president on the organization of the intelligence community and collection priorities. President Reagan's EO creating the PFIAB (which remained in effect throughout President Bush's term in office) authorized it to review and advise the president on some of the same issues examined during the NSR 29 review process. Though the PFIAB had made recommendations regarding intelligence support for the military in its postmortem report on Iraq, there is no evidence that it examined in depth any of the other topics included in NSR 29. Rather than requesting advisory recommendations and reports from the PFIAB, the president relied on the DCI and professional intelligence specialists to complete the NSR and make subsequent recommendations for the NSD.

The PFIAB again was pushed aside when Gates ordered the new CMS to undertake a communitywide management review in the fall of 1992. He hoped to address issues such as the division of labor, integrated activities, and realignments to achieve better cooperation within the entire intelligence community. Although issues such as these had been addressed by previous PFIABs, Gates instead chose to appoint senior officers within the intelligence community to undertake the review.[73]

President Bush's handling of the Intelligence Oversight Board (IOB) further illustrates the PFIAB's reduced role in his administration. EO 12334, issued on December 4, 1981, stipulated that the president would appoint the chair of the IOB from among the members of the PFIAB.[74] On February 14, 1990, President Bush amended the order, removing the requirement that the IOB chair come from among PFIAB members.[75] He then proceeded to appoint James R. Thompson, then the governor of Illinois, as chair of the IOB. Gen. Amos Jordan and Michael W. McConnell rounded out the board. These appointments broke with the precedent set by Ford and Reagan because the new IOB did not count among its members anyone from the PFIAB.[76] This arrangement also meant that no PFIAB member had the opportunity to assess the appropriateness of U.S. intelligence collection activities. It remains unclear why the president chose to separate the IOB from the PFIAB, but perhaps it was so that all PFIAB members could concentrate exclusively on technical intelligence issues, in keeping with the makeup of the board. The IOB remained a completely separate entity until President Clinton transformed it into a permanent standing committee of the PFIAB.

It is telling that the major reviews and examinations of the intelligence community conducted during President Bush's term in office did not involve the PFIAB. In keeping with the pattern of the increasing institutional power of the presidency, Bush felt confident that full-time government employees could handle the requirements. The PFIAB simply was not a major player in his administration. Aside from the Iraq postmortem report, there is little evidence that the board conducted major reviews or evaluations of the quality of intelligence or made any major recommendations on how to improve it. Instead, it appears to have submitted narrow, focused reports on limited, technical topics.

ASSESSMENT

President Bush entered office unsure about the future of the PFIAB. He inherited a large PFIAB from his predecessor that was filled with foreign policy heavyweights and statesmen but seemed content to allow it to drift during the first eighteen months of his administration, especially as its most highly visible member became embroiled in controversy.

When Bush did choose to act with regard to the PFIAB, he acted swiftly, trimming it down drastically, and staffing it with scientists and intelligence experts. He asked for the resignations of all but one of the Reagan PFIAB holdovers and appointed their five successors on the same day—July 16, 1990.

Despite its new look and narrower focus on technical issues, the downsized PFIAB failed to play a major role within the Bush administration. A number of factors combined to limit its activities. Bush and Scowcroft chose to use intelligence professionals to conduct the major intelligence community shake-ups of the time, and Bush consciously chose to select a technically oriented board that would have a narrower set of interests compared to previous boards. To complicate matters, Chair John Tower died less than a year into his tenure, and briefings and familiarization activities occupied much of the board's time. Bush also let the PFIAB sit idle for the first eighteen months of his single term in office, leaving it relatively little time to examine issues and work on projects.

Nevertheless, the PFIAB did play a useful, albeit limited, role. It issued a comprehensive postmortem on intelligence issues that arose during the first Gulf War. Some of the recommendations within the report produced important changes in the methods the intelligence community used to collect and disseminate critical imagery intelligence. The PFIAB also examined issues surrounding HUMINT, clandestine operations, and the dramatically changing political environment in Eastern Europe and the Soviet Union.

The board's limited role in the first Bush administration was not a result of presidential style and personality. Indeed, George H. W. Bush was more inclined to use an independent body like the PFIAB than were many of his immediate predecessors. Rather, two other factors play a much larger role in his minimal use of the board. First, his experience with the board as DCI during the Team B exercise, in which a politicized board produced a public relations disaster for the CIA, and the Reagan period, in which the board was reduced to another entry in the "plum book" for political appointees, undoubtedly made him wary and skeptical of its usefulness. Second, the Bush administration was also part of the larger trend since the mid-1970s in which presidential power was centralized in the formal institutions of the executive branch, which made an extrainstitutional body like the board increasingly irrelevant. The parallel development of congressional intelligence oversight committees reinforced this trend by further reducing the space within which an independent advisory body like the PFIAB could operate.

8

William J. Clinton

President William J. Clinton established his President's Foreign Intelligence Advisory Board (PFIAB) when he signed Executive Order (EO) 12863 on September 13, 1993. This EO revoked both EO 12334, signed on December 4, 1981, and EO 12537, signed on October 28, 1985, which governed the PFIAB under President Ronald Reagan. According to EO 12863, the membership of President Clinton's board was not expected to exceed sixteen. Clinton also established the specific terms of the board's service to the president, appointed each member, and set the protocol to govern future appointments. The appointment of members to Clinton's PFIAB was unique because, to the extent possible, the president wanted to impose a two-year term limit.

In addition, in the new EO President Clinton designated the Intelligence Oversight Board (IOB) as a standing committee of the PFIAB. The IOB was limited to four members selected from the PFIAB. Clinton specified that the IOB chair would be selected by the PFIAB chair, could conceivably serve as chair of both the PFIAB and the IOB, and would have the same resources as the PFIAB chair. As with previous boards, membership on Clinton's PFIAB came without financial compensation beyond those transportation and per diem expenses allowable under federal law. Staff and consultants to the PFIAB, however, were to receive payment commensurate with work performed and authorized by President Clinton.[1]

In 1993, the first media coverage concluded that, aside from an expansion from eight to twelve members, Clinton's PFIAB did not significantly differ from its predecessors. Starting with the PFIAB chairmanship, Clinton returned to the Reagan pattern of using PFIAB appointments as a way to repay political supporters.[2] For example, his appointment for board chair was the former chairman of the Joint Chiefs of Staff (JCS) Adm. William Crowe, who had been one of Clinton's most prominent military supporters during the campaign.

In a nod toward bipartisanship, and to gain support on Capitol Hill, President Clinton named former Democratic representative Les Aspin as board chair and former Republican senator Warren B. Rudman as vice chair in 1994 after Crowe stepped down to become Clinton's ambassador to the Court of St. James.[3] Like Aspin, who was the recently ousted secretary of defense, other appointments—such as Zoë Baird (Clinton's failed nominee for attorney general), Vernon Jordan (the chair of Clinton's transition team who did not get a permanent job in the Clinton White House), and Thomas F. Eagleton (the 1972 Democratic vice presidential candidate abruptly removed from the ticket owing to allegations of mental illness)—could be seen as compensation for a past political misfortune.

A spot on President Clinton's PFIAB was a highly sought-after appointment in Washington. Demand for placement also came from Democratic financial donors. According to former PFIAB chair Warren Rudman, many individuals who sought appointment to the board were rich political benefactors who were not qualified for the job. He characterized Clinton's PFIAB as having "three or four heavy-hitting political types" and eight or nine individuals who had the requisite knowledge and experience for this appointment.[4]

BOARD MEMBERSHIP AND EXECUTIVE STAFF

Membership

By the end of Clinton's second term, twenty-one people had held appointments on his PFIAB, although the board typically consisted of thirteen members at any given time.[5] The board membership reflected an emphasis on technological expertise and intelligence community experience. Chairs of Clinton's PFIAB included

Adm. William Crowe;
Les Aspin, a former secretary of defense;
Thomas Foley, a lawyer and former congressman; and
Warren Rudman, a former senator.

Other members with extensive government experience included

Ann Caracristi, a former deputy director of the National Security Agency (NSA);

Anthony Harrington, a lawyer;
Gen. Lew Allen, a former Bush PFIAB member;
Dr. Robert Hermann, a former director of the National Reconnaissance Office;
Dr. Sidney Drell, a former deputy director of the Stanford Linear Accelerator Center;
Zoë Baird, a former associate general counsel to President Carter;
Cresencio Arcos, a former deputy assistant secretary of state for international narcotics and crime;
James Hamilton, a former U.S. appellate court justice;
Thomas Eagleton, a former Missouri senator; and
Elmo Zumwalt, a former chief of naval operations.

A number of individuals without government service also served on President Clinton's PFIAB, including

Stanley Shuman, an investment banker;
Harold Pote, a private investment and retail financial services specialist;
Maurice Sonnenberg, a foreign trade and international investment adviser;
Stephen Friedman, a global business manager;
Lois Rice, an education consultant;
John Shelby Bryan, a communications entrepreneur; and
Richard Bloch, a tax and finance entrepreneur.

Clinton also used appointment to his PFIAB to repay political favors and reward longtime Democratic Party supporters such as John Shelby Bryan and Richard Bloch. However, some turned down this reward, such as Vernon E. Jordan, the prominent civil rights activist, a distinguished DC-area attorney, the chair of the Clinton presidential transition team in 1992, and a close, personal friend to President Clinton.[6]

Overall, the composition of Clinton's PFIAB followed the outline he sketched in EO 12863—an eight- to twelve-person board with a few political appointees but mostly populated with highly experienced individuals. Clinton's desire to refocus his board toward technical intelligence matters was manifest by the appointments of Hermann and Drell. Clinton also limited his PFIAB members to short terms (two years)—presumably to be able to appoint large numbers of people to this prestigious position.

PFIAB Executive Staff

Although the PFIAB members themselves were, in accordance with EO 12863, not full-time employees, staff members were full-time, which allowed them to maintain continuity on PFIAB projects between board meetings. PFIAB staffs typically do not consist of a large number of individuals. According to former PFIAB chair Warren Rudman, the staff for President Clinton's board was small but able to support and meet any request made by any board member at any time. Rudman was confident that the PFIAB staff could pick up the phone and contact counterparts in any intelligence agency in the U.S. government to complete a task assigned by the chair or a board member.[7]

Eugene F. Yeates remained as director until 1995, when he was replaced by Randy Deitering. Serving under Deitering as assistant directors of the PFIAB were Brendan G. Melley and Mark F. Moynihan.[8] Melley (assistant director 1998–2001) graduated from Providence College and completed the postgraduate intelligence program at the Defense Intelligence Agency (DIA). After several years of active duty in the U.S. Army, ultimately serving as a collection manager for combatant commands at the DIA, he spent the mid-1990s working for the director of the DIA, as a professional staffer for the Commission on the Roles and Capabilities of the U.S. Intelligence Community, and as a senior consultant for Booz Allen Hamilton. In 2001, he served under Senators George Mitchell and Rudman on the Sharm el-Sheikh Fact Finding Committee that produced the "Mitchell Plan."[9] From late 2001 until 2005, he was the director for counterproliferation, proliferation strategy, and homeland defense and director for intelligence programs for the National Security Council (NSC). After leaving public service, he became an associate vice president at the Cohen Group, a global business consulting firm.[10]

Like Melley, Moynihan had an extensive intelligence background that made him a perfect fit for Clinton's PFIAB staff. He was also a proponent of further collaboration between scientific and intelligence communities, and, in 2001, he authored an article in *Physics Today* arguing that academic scientists should, and will, continue to play an essential role in helping the intelligence community exploit technology for national security. At the end of the Clinton administration, he returned to the CIA.[11]

Other staffers included the assistant director and chief counsel, Frank W. Fountain, the administrative officer, Roosevelt A. Roy, and the research and administrative officer, Jane E. Baker.[12] One former senior administration official praised the quality of the PFIAB staff but thought that the board probably needed a larger one. In fact, he found the staff more useful than the board itself.[13]

OPERATING PROCEDURES

Board Meetings

The first official meeting of President Clinton's PFIAB was held on April 18, 1993. It was purely for organizational purposes, and no official business was conducted as several of the board members were still waiting for the appropriate security clearances.[14] According to former PFIAB chair Rudman, between 1993 and 2001, the entire board met approximately every six weeks.[15] As with previous boards, Clinton's PFIAB was housed in a suite of offices in the Old Executive Office Building. Continuing the board's historical trend, Clinton's PFIAB members completed much of their work outside formal board meetings. A former senior official states that the board met with the national security adviser only twice a year and "never" with the president.[16]

Operating Procedures and Interaction with Other Groups

Given Clinton's four different PFIAB chairs, the organization and operating procedures of the board varied dramatically over the course of his two terms. Clinton did introduce one significant change to the board: the IOB, previously a separate body, was turned into a standing committee of the PFIAB. Little else is known about how the board organized itself internally. Also unclear are the channels and procedures the board used to communicate with the president and other administration officials. One former senior administration official told us that issues for the board's examination originated in the Oval Office, in the national security adviser's office, and within the board itself.[17]

One constant factor was that the president himself did not seem interested in engaging the issues of the intelligence community—let alone the workings of his own PFIAB. Clinton's "largely indifferent [attitude] to bureaucratic reform" and his "passing interest" in the intelligence community complicated the operating procedure of the PFIAB.[18] The board's first chair, Admiral Crowe, recounted that, when asked where he would like to serve in the administration, he told the president "PFIAB," to which Clinton responded "What's PFIAB?"[19] The board member Sonnenberg confirmed that "Clinton didn't listen to the PFIAB."[20]

Given that the PFIAB consisted of individuals selected by the president for advice on intelligence matters—and the measure of legal oversight inherent to the IOB—it is curious that Clinton did not make more use of it. Indeed, in former chair Rudman's view, Clinton's biggest mistake was his disinterest in intelligence matters and his penchant for delegating such issues to subordinates.[21] A former senior official concurred that the PFIAB has never actually fulfilled its potential. In his eyes, it should have functioned like a "canary in the coal mine," warning the administration about future problems and crises.[22] But it never did, despite warnings from both Congress and the intelligence community that the latter was underresourced for its post–Cold War mission.[23]

A former senior official in the Clinton administration confirmed Clinton's lack of interest in intelligence. The PFIAB was simply not a top priority for his administration. The criteria for membership on his PFIAB was not so much intelligence or foreign policy expertise as political connections.

Despite the president's disinterest in intelligence issues, Rudman nonetheless insisted that he had a good relationship with Clinton, National Security Adviser Sandy Berger, and the entire NSC staff. Rudman also claimed that he had complete access to both the president and Berger. According to Rudman, all he had to do was contact Berger or Clinton's presidential secretary, Betty Curry, and, if the president or the national security adviser was in the country, he could request as much time as he needed—anywhere from five to forty-five minutes. Thus, the PFIAB theoretically had direct and immediate access to its principal customer. In an attempt to reconcile the disconnect between perceptions of Clinton's lack of interest in intelligence matters and his willingness to meet with the PFIAB chair, former chair Rudman acknowledges that the key to gaining and maintaining Clinton's attention was to keep any correspondence focused on pressing national security issues.[24]

The members of Clinton's PFIAB had to balance the board's position in the larger intelligence oversight bureaucracy and its extragovernment advisory role with the president's disinterest in its very purpose. Since only the board chair—and, specifically, Rudman—had unfettered access to Clinton and Berger, he was often an ex officio member of any inner-PFIAB working group, committee, or task force. For project management, Rudman favored assigning studies to small task forces of two or three members and necessary staff members. This structure allowed him to oversee project development, and it built in a measure of compartmentalization. He thought it inappropriate to burden board members with information not pertinent to their particular workload; therefore, "not everyone [in the PFIAB] knew everything."[25] For instance, he did appoint a special investigative panel to examine the issue of security at U.S. research laboratories, indicating that the board retained the tradition of using special panels to examine issues in depth.

Despite Clinton's disinterest in intelligence issues, the PFIAB produced eighty-five reports at the behest of Clinton or National Security Adviser Berger between 1993 and 2001. In Rudman's view, his was a "very effective PFIAB that did a lot of good things. Fifty years from now, they can open up the archives and see what we did."[26] But, without knowing what the eighty-five reports were about or their impact on intelligence policy, it is impossible to conclude that Clinton's PFIAB was effective.

ISSUES AND RECOMMENDATIONS

Of the eighty-five reports produced by Clinton's PFIAB, only two are declassified. Information about other reports and issues examined has been gleaned from secondary sources and interviews with former administration officials. While not as an official PFIAB undertaking, several prominent board members also served on the Commission on the Roles and Capabilities of the United States Intelligence Community—more popularly known as the Aspin-Brown Commission—which analyzed the function of the U.S. intelligence community in the post–Cold War world. In 1996, the PFIAB/IOB completed a review of CIA management of human intelligence (HUMINT) sources in Guatemala. Just before the turn of the new millennium, the PFIAB conducted a thorough evaluation of security and counterintelligence mechanisms across the system of U.S. national laboratories. In addition to these two unclassified studies, Clinton's PFIAB handled smaller, more immediate matters like studying the intelligence failure in Somalia in the fall of 1993, reviewing the internal intelligence community's handling of the computer security violations of former director of central intelligence (DCI) John Deutch, and recommending the release of long-withheld classified PFIAB documents of possible relevance to the investigation of the assassination of President Kennedy.

The Somalia Intelligence Failure

One of the Clinton PFIAB's first major undertakings was to study the intelligence failure associated with the botched Ranger/Delta Force raid in the Bakara marketplace in the fall of 1993 to try to capture aides to the warlord Mohamed Farrah Aidid, which instead resulted in the deaths of eighteen and the wounding of almost one hundred U.S. troops. According to Admiral Crowe, the board concluded that much of the blame for the intelligence failure lay with Clinton's NSC staff, who, owing to their inexperience, "expected intelligence to make their decisions for them," with the result that there "was considerable confusion at the top as to what was going on in Somalia." Ultimately, Crowe blamed the president's lack of interest in intelligence for this situation.[27]

The Aspin Brown Commission

The Commission on the Roles and Capabilities of the United States Intelligence Community was not a formal undertaking of President Clinton's PFIAB. It did, however, have many connections to the board. In early fall 1994, Clinton asked his PFIAB to undertake a "roles and missions" study on the current state of the U.S. intelligence community in a post–Cold War world.[28] Senator John Warner (R-VA) was not satisfied with a PFIAB study of this topic, concerned that it would whitewash some recent intelligence failures such as the Aldrich Ames spy case, and threatened to sponsor legislation to establish a congressionally appointed commission.[29] As a compromise, the Aspin-Brown Commission was created on September 20, 1994, by the U.S. Congress in the Intelligence Authorization Act for fiscal year 1995 (Public Law 103-359) and signed into being by President Clinton on October 14, 1994. PFIAB chair Les Aspin was named head of the commission, and the review was given a March 1, 1996, deadline for publication of its findings. In addition to Aspin, other members of Clinton's PFIAB who served on the commission included Rudman, Allen, Baird, Caracristi, Friedman, Harrington, and Hermann.[30] To supplement the PFIAB members named to the commission, the following commission members were chosen by the leadership of the 103rd Congress: Ambassador Paul Wolfowitz, Tony Coelho, David Dewhurst, Representative Norm Dicks, Senator James Exon, former senator Wyche Fowler, Representative Porter Goss, Gen. Robert Pursley, and Senator John Warner.[31] After Aspin's untimely death in 1995, former defense secretary Harold Brown was named head of the commission (hence, the commission is often referred to as the Aspin-Brown Commission).[32]

There is some debate as to why the commission was convened. Loch Johnson, the only academic on the commission staff, argues that the catalyzing event was the Somalia intelligence failure.[33] L. Britt Snider, the staff director of the Aspin-Brown Commission, counters that, while the incident in Somalia might have piqued the interest of former secretary of defense (and then PFIAB chair) Aspin, the primary motivation for Congress to create the commission was the arrest of the CIA officer Aldrich Ames in February 1994 on charges of having been a Soviet agent since 1985.[34]

Johnson also recounts that a dispute between Senator Warner and Aspin over control of the review commission almost led to separate congressional and PFIAB commissions. He suggests that it was not until after Aspin offered Warner a seat on the commission, or at least a spot for Warner's choice of staff director, that the senator capitulated.[35] Snider, however, maintains that it was not until Warner had proposed his own plan for a review commission that Clinton's PFIAB finally decided to take the lead on this issue.[36] After months of political wrangling between the White House, the intelligence community, and Congress over who would conduct the review, a joint presidential-congressional commission was assembled as a compromise.

In its final report, "Preparing for the 21st Century: An Appraisal of U.S. Intelligence," released on March 1, 1996, the commission addressed the need to maintain a strong U.S. intelligence capability, the role of U.S. intelligence, the need for policy guidance, the imperative for a coordinated response to global crime, the optimal organizational structure of the U.S. intelligence community, improving intelligence analysis, "rightsizing" and rebuilding the intelligence community, space reconnaissance and technical collection management, international cooperation, the cost of intelligence, and accountability and oversight.[37] The report offered three major recommendations: (1) increase integration of intelligence into the policy community it serves by enhancing responsiveness and relationships between intelligence producers and consumers; (2) increase cooperation between intelligence agencies so that they act as a collective "community" to produce the best possible intelligence and analysis; and (3) increase the level of efficiency throughout the intelligence community (from modern management practices to more streamlined analysis procedures) to restore public confidence in the it.[38]

The Aspin-Brown Commission's report was well received by both the president and Congress. Less than two months after the report was submitted, President Clinton authorized several changes within the intelligence community. First, in an effort to promote openness, he "authorized Congress to make public the total appropriation (the bottom-line amount) figures for intelligence at the time the appropriations bill is approved." Second, he authorized "a cabinet-level Committee on Foreign Intelligence to establish priorities on long-term intelligence needs." Third, "he endorsed the addition of two presidentially appointed deputy director positions," requiring Senate confirmation, in addition to the (then) current position of deputy DCI. One of the two new positions would run the CIA, and the other would oversee the Community Management Staff. Finally, Clinton "endorsed the DCI's proposed personnel reforms to allow the intelligence community to realign its resources" to address future intelligence challenges while meeting its downsizing goals.[39] While it is true that "the intelligence community was unaffected in any large way by the Aspin-Brown inquiry," it did lay the groundwork for the subsequent efforts of George W. Bush's PFIAB and the 2004 Keane Commission to establish stronger leadership to ensure a more cohesive intelligence community.[40] In so doing, the Aspin-Brown Commission was echoing something that had been called for by every PFIAB since Eisenhower's.

Disappearance of U.S. Citizens and CIA Activities in Guatemala

The PFIAB's next major undertaking during the Clinton administration also focused on reform in intelligence community activities, though at a more specific level. One former senior Clinton administration official describes the IOB's *Report on the Guatemala Review* as "the only time when they [the Clinton administration] felt the need for PFIAB."[41]

On March 30, 1995, the president directed the IOB to review the actions of the CIA in Guatemala in the 1980s and early 1990s. Specifically, it was "to conduct a governmentwide review of the 1990 death of the U.S. citizen Michael DeVine, the 1992 disappearance of the Guatemalan guerrilla leader Efrain Bamaca Velasquez, and other related matters." The terms of reference, issued in an April 7, 1995, memorandum from National Security Adviser Anthony Lake to IOB chair Anthony S. Harrington, outlined the scope of the report to include "existing intelligence on all U.S. citizens who were tortured, disappeared, or died in Guatemala since 1984." They specifically cited the cases of Dianna Ortiz, Griffith Davis, Nicholas Blake, Peter Wolfe, Janey Skinner, Jennifer Roitman, Meredith Larson, June Weinstock, and Daniel Callahan. Extensive reviews and commentary were offered for each of these cases except the Dianna Ortiz case, which, at that time, was still the subject of an open Department of Justice investigation.[42] This report required the highest level of independence and integrity, which is why Clinton specifically chose the IOB, with its record of thorough and fair review of intelligence oversight issues.[43]

At the time the review was assigned, the IOB consisted of Chair Harrington and the PFIAB members Gen. Lew Allen Jr., Ann Z. Caracristi, and Harold W. Pote. The IOB's broad charter was to review and report to the president about all intelligence activities believed to be unlawful or contrary to an EO or a presidential directive.[44] In reviewing the cases of the missing U.S. citizens in Guatemala, the terms of reference from the White House mandated reporting on direct or indirect involvement by U.S. government personnel; levels of intelligence asset validation; information gathering by the U.S. government before, during, and after the incident; the amount of information provided to and withheld from victims' families; and any Department of Justice regulations, procedures, or directives that were violated. The IOB was also asked to look into the timeliness and accuracy of intelligence and policy coordination between different elements within the intelligence community. Possible improvements to inter- and intraagency protocol, the adequacy of communication between the field and headquarters, and cooperation between the intelligence community and the Department of Justice in Guatemala were specific points of concern. To clarify the bilateral relationship, the IOB was to report on the state of the intelligence relationship between the U.S. government and the government of Guatemala. Additionally, it was asked to review, critique, and offer suggestions on the intelligence asset validation system, especially vetting assets against possible human rights abuses.[45]

The independent review of the IOB was to be augmented by the inspectors general of the various members of the intelligence community, but only if needed, and then only to ensure that the president's questions were being fully answered. If necessary, the IOB could independently choose to validate the facts and conclusions offered by the inspectors general pursuant to the full review of President Clinton's tasking. The IOB was given no deadline for the report but rather had the discretion to set its own schedule to more adequately address the breadth of questions. It dealt directly with the national security adviser, who in turn kept President Clinton apprised of the IOB's progress. The Guatemala review was structured to allow the IOB to report lessons learned during the course of the review and to make recommendations about any existing policies, regulations, or directives governing the U.S. intelligence community.[46]

On its completion, the Guatemala review received an unprecedented level of publicity for a PFIAB report. Throughout the inquiry, IOB members received significant help from the inspectors general and liaisons for all the appropriate elements inside the CIA, the DIA, the Department of Defense (DOD), the Department of State, the Drug Enforcement Agency, the FBI, and the NSA. The IOB conducted interviews with hundreds of American and Guatemalan witnesses and read thousands of documents pertaining to its mandate. It also requested that the inspector general of the CIA conduct a "review of all clandestine assets in Guatemala since 1984 for allegations of human rights abuses." The rare openness exhibited by the White House resulted in increased media interest in the officially released version of the Guatemala review.[47]

The *Report on Guatemala Review,* in line with the IOB's mandate, concentrated on nine main elements: "the context of U.S. relations with Guatemala, U.S. intelligence objectives in Guatemala, possible U.S. intelligence asset involvement in human rights violations, assessment of the asset validation system in general, the interaction between the U.S. intelligence and policy communities, congressional oversight, a potential crimes report to the Department of Justice, human rights reporting, and any intelligence bearing on the cases of U.S. citizens who were violent crime victims in Guatemala." The policy objectives identified by the IOB also supported Guatemala's transition "to civilian democratic government, furthering human rights and the rule of law, supporting economic growth, in combating illegal narcotics trafficking and Communist insurgencies, and advancing the (then) current peace process between the government and the rebelling guerrillas."[48]

The IOB found that U.S. national security interests in Guatemala justified dealing with individuals and institutions with questionable backgrounds. In the world of intelligence, it concluded, the expected value of dealing with "unsavory" characters "must outweigh the costs of such unseemly" and risky relationships. To that end, it found two specific areas in which it deemed the CIA's performance unacceptable. The first was the insufficient attention paid to the allegations of human rights abuses against assets and liaison contacts through the end of 1994. The second was the failure to provide adequate information regarding these human rights abuse allegations to policymakers and bring them to the attention of proper congressional oversight committees. The allegations of human rights abuses leveled against several CIA assets and liaison contacts were found to be credible, including their ordering, planning, or participating in "assassination, extrajudicial execution, torture, and kidnapping." According to the IOB, some assets actively participated in such activities before their involvement with the CIA, some became involved once their CIA involvement was terminated, and others were involved in covering up human rights abuses.[49] During its inquiry, however, the IOB found that none of the assets involved in human rights abuses had any type of relationship with the CIA or any element of the U.S. intelligence community at the time of the abuses. As of early 1995, the CIA had terminated its relationships with the few remaining Guatemalan assets allegedly involved in human rights abuses.

Despite claims from some in Washington, DC, the IOB found no evidence that the CIA station in Guatemala was "'a rogue' operating independently" of CIA headquarters. The station conducted its business within the ad hoc—and ambiguous—instructions of the Directorate of Operations of the 1980s and 1990s to avoid assets with human rights abuses. The difficult task of balancing human rights abuse allegations against potential intelligence contributions was carried out primarily by the chief of station. The IOB found this practice problematic because many chiefs of station gave less weight to human rights abuse allegations owing to the need to increase the number of assets.[50] The problem was a lack of an appropriate calculus for middle-level managers to perform the associated cost/benefit analysis, and the IOB concluded that this allowed U.S. intelligence activities in Guatemala to become tainted by allegations of human rights abuses.

This was compounded by the lack of a clear mechanism for sharing intelligence information with Department of State officials in-country or policymakers in Washington, DC. The problem was the result of a significant level of mistrust that had built up between the intelligence and the diplomatic communities. The IOB faulted the CIA for not immediately notifying the appropriate outside authorities (including the NSC, the State Department, and the Department of Justice) when the human rights abuse allegations initially surfaced. It asserted that "the system for collecting and disseminating intelligence information can function properly" only if the executive and legislative branches are accountable for compromising or improperly handling classified information—a consistent cause of mistrust between the intelligence community and the diplomatic corps. As a remedy, the IOB recommended that the 1977 State Department–CIA agreement—obligating "the CIA to reveal to ambassadors the identities of those assets with whom embassy officers are in contact"—be revised to include information on "all intelligence activities with significant policy implications," including allegations of human rights abuses and asset involvement in the attack or death of U.S. citizens.[51]

In addition to the CIA's lack of communication with State Department counterparts, the IOB found that the agency violated its duty to keep Congress "fully and currently informed" of activities in Guatemala. In committing this violation, the IOB ascertained, the CIA did not intentionally mislead Congress but rather inadvertently withheld information under the auspices of protecting sources. The IOB also noted that the lack of a systematic notification process hindered information sharing with congressional oversight committees. Also, semiannual reviews of efforts made to improve Guatemalan respect for human rights prepared by the CIA for Congress misled members by focusing on the positive developments without mentioning the alleged human rights abuses of CIA liaison contacts. Whereas the IOB did not find sufficient evidence for a criminal referral of CIA officers to the attorney general, it did notify the Department of Justice that the CIA seemed to have been in violation of Title 50 of the U.S. Code. The IOB noted that, despite the violation, no criminal action had taken place and that, given the remedial action already undertaken by the CIA, there was no danger of continuing violation of the U.S. Code.[52]

The IOB found many of the allegations about attacks on U.S. citizens untrue. A clear "preponderance of evidence" cleared Guatemalan Col. Julio Alpirez from allegations that he had killed the U.S. citizen Michael DeVine. The IOB thought that the most likely scenario was that DeVine was tortured during interrogation and died as a result. But Alpirez and several other CIA assets and liaison contacts were found to be involved in the massive "cover-up" of Guatemalan military involvement in DeVine's death. The CIA was not found to be complicit in DeVine's death, and there was no evidence that agency assets or liaison contacts had prior knowledge or were involved in the planning of DeVine's death. The IOB also found evidence that directly contradicted allegations that Colonel Alpirez killed the Guatemalan guerrilla leader Efrain Bamaca Velasquez—though it did conclude that Alpirez was most likely involved in Bamaca's interrogation. The IOB believed the Bamaca was tortured and killed approximately a year after his capture and found that "no CIA official was involved in or was aware of Bamaca's torture or death." Like the DeVine case, the IOB believed, CIA assets and liaison contacts were involved, but the CIA had no indication of their active relationship with these assets and contacts.[53]

During the course of its review, the IOB also discovered evidence that cleared the U.S. intelligence community from several other charges. For example, it concluded that the CIA did not increase funds to compensate for reduced overt financial aid to Guatemala mandated by Congress. It also "found no evidence" to support the March 1995 allegations that the NSA and the U.S. Army altered reports on Guatemala to prevent oversight investigations. While it concluded that allegations of impropriety concerning U.S. intelligence community activity in Guatemala were unfounded, it did criticize some of its behavior in the United States. For example, the IOB found that, in the case of the death of Nicholas Blake, the NSA originally told the Blake family it had "no relevant documents." Only after an appeal by the family did NSA find six relevant documents. Following IOB prodding, sixteen more documents were discovered. The IOB concluded that, whenever possible, the intelligence community should provide families and victims with more information regarding their cases.[54]

The IOB *Report on the Guatemala Review* offered fourteen specific conclusions and recommendations to improve the intelligence community's performance in the future. First, the IOB determined that the intelligence community had to undertake activities in Guatemala "in support of U.S. policy objectives," establishing "a liaison relationship with Guatemalan security services widely known for reprehensible human rights records" and, with the knowledge of the NSC, the State Department, and congressional oversight committees, continuing "covert aid after the cutoff of overt aid in 1990." Second, the IOB recommended that the intelligence community "establish clear guidance in the recruitment and retention of assets with human rights or criminal allegations" against them and explicitly consider the balance between such allegations and potential U.S. national security interests. It pointed to general guidance already promulgated within the intelligence community for dealing with liaison services with serious violations against them. It agreed that such relationships should be avoided unless senior officials authorized them on the grounds of national security concerns. Third, the IOB recommended that CIA notification to ambassadors and other policymakers "should, at a minimum, include reasonably credible allegations of asset or liaison participation in assassination, kidnapping, or torture"—especially if a U.S. citizen was involved. It found that the CIA circulated a guidance memo in October 1995 clarifying the 1977 State Department–CIA agreement but, ultimately, concluded that the agreement itself needed to be rewritten.[55]

The IOB's fourth recommendation was for the State Department to "implement a program to ensure that . . . appropriate intelligence-based information" is shared with U.S. citizens, both families of those abducted, killed, or tortured and the victims themselves. The IOB recognized the importance of protecting "sources and methods" but also suggested that the Freedom of Information Act be amended to permit consolidation of DOD and intelligence community reports to help dilute attributions to specific sources and methods. As the IOB's report was being published, an interagency group was studying mechanisms by which to "improve the provision of information to U.S. citizens in human rights cases." Fifth, the IOB advocated increased accountability for those who "compromise or improperly handled classified information," including members of the NSC, the executive branch, and congressional oversight committees. Sixth, the IOB found "no indication" that U.S. government officials were involved in or knew of the disappearance, torture, or death of U.S. or Guatemalan citizens.[56] Seventh, communications between field stations and CIA headquarters, and specifically within the Directorate of Operations, were consistent, and the flow of information generally kept headquarters well informed of developments involving CIA assets.[57]

In contrast to its intracommunity communications, the IOB's eighth recommendation was for both the CIA and the DOD "to implement a systematic process" to notify Congress in a timely fashion about intelligence operations. The IOB believed that the system recently put in place by the CIA, the DIA, and the NSA to determine what briefings and written memos Congress had received increased "performance and accountability." Ninth, and with regard to the intelligence community's referral of the Alpirez allegation case to the Department of Justice, the IOB stated that "new internal and interagency" cooperation was necessary "to ensure that significant criminal referrals receive attention." It applauded the Justice Department's completion of a new system to track criminal reports and new memoranda of understanding from the intelligence community to ensure that the documents all received sufficient attention—effectively correcting the problems that emerged in the breakdown in reporting about the DeVine case. Tenth, the IOB recommended that the asset validation system mechanism consider both counterintelligence and derogatory (specifically human rights allegations) information associated with government and nongovernment sources. It concluded that the CIA expanded its asset validation system to include "derogatory allegations" in response to IOB recommendations.

The eleventh IOB conclusion was that the allegations that Alpirez murdered Michael DeVine were unfounded. The IOB was convinced, however, that Alpirez participated in the interrogation and torture of Bamaca—probably with the involvement and knowledge of CIA assets prior to their relationship with the CIA. Twelfth, the IOB found no evidence that the NSA destroyed classified documents. Thirteenth, it recommended an immediate and prompt review by both the CIA and the State Department of the "shortcomings in their systems" for retrieving, storing, and sharing intelligence information. In response, the CIA's Directorate of Operations improved its record-tracking system to better facilitate intelligence collection and dissemination. The final recommendation was to task inspectors general from each government agency to evaluate the report, implement its recommendations, and report to the IOB each year.[58]

The IOB's mandate to investigate the U.S. intelligence community activity involving human rights abuses against U.S. citizens in Guatemala was an "unprecedented" undertaking.[59] The specific questions posed by the White House were intended as a rough guide and not meant to restrict the investigation in any way. The IOB was given free rein—backed by the authority of the Oval Office—to conduct its own investigation of facts and reach its own conclusions. It was unrelenting in uncovering all the relevant facts and clearly demarcated when it thought allegations were false or true. The timing and scope of its report were commensurate with law enforcement requirements, which is further proof that it conducted a thorough, lawful, and beneficial review.[60] The *Report on the Guatemala Review* established higher, more prominent standards for the protection of human rights "in the conduct of our intelligence relationships."[61]

Security at U.S. National Laboratories

Three years later, Clinton's PFIAB would again have the opportunity to conduct a major investigation involving the U.S. intelligence community. It began when Wen Ho Lee, a Taiwanese-American scientist who worked for Los Alamos National Laboratory (LANL), was suspected of stealing secrets concerning the U.S. nuclear arsenal in March 1999. Lee was accused of being a Chinese spy on the basis of information received from an intelligence agent in China indicating that the Chinese had detailed, classified information regarding the W88 nuclear warhead—a closely held U.S. weapons secret. In the end, Lee pleaded guilty to a lesser charge of illegally downloading information from LANL computers, but the involvement of the FBI and the U.S. national laboratories, and the accusations of Chinese racial profiling, brought the case to national prominence.

In early 1999, after the case burst into the mainstream media and a federal judge publicly excoriated and embarrassed the FBI, President

Clinton asked his PFIAB to investigate what happened and make recommendations to avoid similar debacles.[62] To demonstrate his administration's commitment to fixing intelligence failures and cracking down on civil liberties violations, Clinton made this investigation the only public PFIAB report in forty-eight years.[63] For the first time in its existence, the board was assigned to prepare an *unclassified* report for release to the general public.

On March 18, 1999, Clinton tasked his PFIAB to investigate and report on "the security threat at the Department of Energy's weapons labs and the adequacy of the measures that have been taken to address it." Under this broad mandate, the board was to focus on "the nature of the present counterintelligence security threat," the evolution of the counterintelligence threat over the previous twenty years, and any prior measures taken to combat the counterintelligence threat and to provide recommendations on additional measures to be taken at the national laboratories. Ultimately, it was to deliver a completed report to Congress and the president and release an unclassified version for the general public.[64]

PFIAB chair Rudman, in line with his general approach of using small working groups, appointed only three board members in addition to himself to the special investigative panel: Ann Z. Caracristi, Dr. Sidney Drell, and Friedman. Rudman also made extensive use of the PFIAB staffers Deitering, Moynihan, Roy, Fountain, Melley, and Baker in completion of this report. In addition to the various intelligence community personnel detailed from the CIA, the DOD, the Department of Energy (DOE), and the FBI, Rudman's project adjunct staff consisted of Roy B. (DIA), Karen DeSpiegelaere (FBI), Jerry L. (CIA), Christine V. (CIA), David W. Swindle (DOD/Naval Criminal Investigative Service), and Joseph S. O'Keefe (DOD/Office of the Secretary of Defense).[65]

Over the three months of the investigation, the PFIAB panel interviewed more than one hundred witnesses, reviewed more than seven hundred classified and unclassified documents, and conducted investigations at Lawrence Livermore National Laboratory, LANL, Oak Ridge National Laboratory, Sandia National Laboratory, and the Pantex nuclear weapon assembly and disassembly plant. The investigation concentrated on the twenty-year history of security and counterintelligence issues at the DOE national laboratories—especially those primarily responsible for weapons-related research. From the outset, the president restricted the PFIAB's mandate to "analysis of structural and management problems" in DOE's security and counterintelligence operations and infrastructure.[66]

The overall conclusion reached by this special investigative PFIAB panel was that the DOE failed in security and counterintelligence operations, especially at weapons-related national laboratories.[67] The DOE and the national laboratories have produced "brilliant scientific breakthroughs" over the years, but they have also had "troubling records" of security shortcomings, with the PFIAB panel finding that many of the security problems had persisted for twenty years.[68] On the basis of this long-standing inability to maintain security, the panel concluded that the DOE was incapable of reforming itself.[69] It discovered that "the inherent tension between security concerns and scientific freedom" directly affected the institutional DOE culture. The DOE was permeated with "cynicism, an arrogant disregard for authority, and a staggering pattern of denial."[70] The panel also found that the DOE and the national laboratories were dismissive of—if not downright hostile toward—security concerns. PFIAB members emphasized that melding the cultures of nuclear technology and scientific research with the appropriate levels of security and control was essential.[71] The panel's final suggestion was to place U.S. nuclear weapons research and stockpile management under "a new semiautonomous agency within the DOE." This agency would have "a clear mission, a streamlined bureaucracy, and . . . simplified mechanisms for authority and accountability."[72]

Based on more than a quarter of a century of previous findings, the PFIAB's investigation identified a multitude of causes for the chronic security and counterintelligence problems at the national laboratories. The panel believed that "the organizational disarray, managerial neglect, and culture of arrogance" at the DOE national laboratories were "an espionage scandal waiting to happen."[73] In past inquiries into DOE security deficiencies, both the executive branch and Congress fell victim to oversimplification and "hyperbole" when describing security problems.[74] The panel found that, within the DOE, changes in "institutional culture" and "ingrained attitudes" were as important as changes to the organizational structure.[75] This tension between ingrained attitudes and security precautions was most pronounced at U.S. nuclear weapons laboratories.[76] Within the national laboratories, nuclear scientists often think—and are often correct—that they are smarter than most other Americans. It is understandable, then, that nuclear scientists would balk at the thought of constraints, security driven or not, imposed on their work by bureaucrats who do not understand the complexity of what they do on a daily basis.[77] The result of this cavalier attitude about security concerns among nuclear scientists was that nuclear material and plans have likely been lost or stolen over the years.[78]

The DOE's Office of Intelligence has also been an "impediment to," rather than a catalyst for, coordination and cooperation between the national laboratories and the intelligence community. The PFIAB panel found it to be outdated and not commensurate with the needs of the DOE or the national laboratories.[79] Security and counterintelligence efforts were further hindered by the diffusion of—and continual changes to—control of and accountability for the U.S. nuclear arsenal, as the organizational structure of the government bureaucracy in charge of energy issues has diminished.[80] The DOE's expanding and increasingly difficult challenge of being the "guarantor of the safety, security, and reliability of the nuclear weapons program," in addition to its many other operational priorities, further exacerbated security problems at the national laboratories.[81]

The PFIAB panel also concluded that, in addition to the its structural obstacle to effective security and counterintelligence initiatives, the DOE was very effective in avoiding organizational reform. Any time a series of security or counterintelligence reforms was suggested, it tended to stall and wait for the item to be dropped from the agenda rather than addressing it. This situation persisted because the DOE went through nine secretaries of energy in the first twenty-two years of its existence. The lack of accountability trickled down to field offices from the DOE headquarters.[82] In the selection of previous secretaries of energy, the PFIAB panel found no consistent protocol or the required balance of energy, national security, intelligence, and management experience.[83] Part of this inconsistency stems from the confusing origin of the DOE, which began as an amalgamation of over forty "government agencies and organizations."[84] The ad hoc manner in which the DOE was formed necessitated "major departmental shake-ups" and reorganization every two or three years, which often also meant that security and counterintelligence problems were not addressed consistently.[85]

Perhaps the biggest obstacle to effective security and counterintelligence measures at the national laboratories was the source of their greatest measure of vibrancy: the ability to attract leading scientists from all over the world. The PFIAB panel concluded that the national laboratories did not recognize the fact that such scientific exchange programs made the laboratories major targets for friendly and hostile foreign intelligence services.[86] It never suggested that the national laboratories eliminate the

Foreign Visitors and Assignment Program, but it did argue that "losing national security secrets should never be accepted as an inevitable cost of obtaining scientific discovery."[87] At the time of the investigation, the level of international cooperation with the DOE national laboratories was high and, as of 1990, boasted 157 bilateral research-and-development agreements with countries that included Russia, several other former Soviet states, and China.[88]

From 1977 until the convening of the PFIAB panel in 1999, the gap between DOE security programs and the extent of counterintelligence threats grew especially "pronounced." While U.S. reliance on foreign brainpower grew (in 1988, the national laboratories hosted thirty-eight hundred foreign scientists, with five hundred from sensitive countries; by the mid-1990s, the numbers were fifty-nine and sixteen hundred, respectively), DOE spending on security decreased by one-third.[89] Citing a classified appendix not yet released, the panel uncovered evidence that pointed to "sporadic penetrations of the labs by foreign intelligence services." Despite the small number of penetrations, "volumes of sensitive or classified information may have been lost" owing to lax security measures.[90] Measures like the 1992 Visitor Assignment Management System were supposed to provide increased monitoring of foreign scientists. They often failed because individual laboratories did not catalog visitor information, the system did not link the various laboratories electronically, and each laboratory developed its own independent computer system.[91] The national laboratories seemed further vulnerable to an insider threat because it was standard procedure for the DOE to grant clearances to all employees, regardless of whether they actually required access to classified information or not.[92] The panel also found numerous instances where classified information was "vulnerable to theft or duplication."[93]

The PFIAB panel concluded that the focus on the physical protection of the national laboratories exacerbated the insider threat. To seize nuclear secrets from the U.S. weapons laboratories prior to the PFIAB panel, it would have been easier for a foreign agent to "apply for an access pass, walk in the front door, and strike up a conversation" than to try to shoot his or her way past the guards. Historically, the national laboratories have not had to worry about a physical breach in their more than formidable system of "guns, guards, and gates."[94] Even so, by the early 1990s, the management of physical security was dismal. During this time, the security budget had been reduced by 50 percent, forcing a reliance on local law enforcement for protection.[95] The DOE did not seem to understand the magnitude of the security risk, nor did it seem interested in cooperating with other U.S. government agencies in the security and counterintelligence realms. For example, it did not have a formal relationship with the FBI until 1992, nor was it officially named part of the National Counterintelligence Policy Board, established in 1994 by Presidential Decision Directive (PDD)–24, until 1997.[96] In its report, the panel predicted that, given the poor security track record of the DOE and the national laboratories, a cyber attack would be the next threat that the DOE would be unable to meet.[97]

In its final assessment, the PFIAB panel concluded that previous administrations and Department of Energy leaders and managers shared some responsibility for the sorry state of security at the national laboratories. It limited its conclusions and final comments since its purview did not give it the authority to make specific appraisals of whether espionage had occurred indiscriminately or whether there was leadership malfeasance.[98]

The PFIAB panel recommended that, to rectify the shortcomings of past leadership, the DOE in the next administration needed to pay very close attention to these issues. Sooner rather than later, the DOE and the national laboratory leadership would have to accept the severity of the security situation.[99] Even in the course of the PFIAB investigation, the panel found that the national laboratories were "still resisting" security reforms.[100] This resistance led the PFIAB to conclude that mismanagement of security and counterintelligence was routine at the national laboratories. Therefore, it recommended deep and lasting structural changes—above and beyond those offered by PDD-61 and the 1999 panel the CIA assembled under the leadership of former JCS vice chief Adm. David Jeremiah—to make the national laboratories more accountable to give the nation's nuclear weapons research adequate security.[101]

PDD-61, signed on February 11, 1998, was an attempt to increase DOE security and counterintelligence measures. The directive divided counterintelligence and foreign intelligence issues within the DOE into two separate offices that both reported directly to the secretary of energy. The director of the Office of Counterintelligence was also to be a senior executive from the FBI with direct access to the secretary, the director of central intelligence, and the FBI director. DOE contracts were modified to include counterintelligence program goals and expectations, assign counterintelligence personnel, and provide implementation compliance mechanisms. Within ninety days of PDD-61, the Office of Counterintelligence was to complete and produce a report for the secretary of energy on short- and long-term counterintelligence strategic plans. Within four months, the secretary of energy was to brief the national security adviser on these strategic plans and immediate actions to be taken.[102]

Despite the findings of the April 1999 intelligence community damage assessment led by Adm. David Jeremiah detailing the efforts of China to steal nuclear secrets, the DOE shocked the PFIAB panel with its continuous "foot-dragging" and resistance to security-based change. The panel was especially concerned with the slow implementation of recommended changes, deeming the four-month time frame between PDD-61 and recommendations given to the national security adviser as "unacceptable."[103] Even after the Jeremiah Commission and PDD-61, the PFIAB panel was still worried by the "recalcitrance" of the DOE and the national laboratories. Almost a year had elapsed since PDD-61 before the energy secretary's plan was implemented—a troubling delay that illustrated to the PFIAB panel that the DOE was still not convinced of the need to increase security and counterintelligence efforts at the national laboratories.[104] As of the completion of the panel's report in June 1999, all the PDD-61 requirements had been met, and some progress had been made to address security and counterintelligence. But the panel concluded there was still more to do.[105]

The PFIAB ultimately found that a complete reorganization of the DOE was necessary since the department fell under "no less than eighteen congressional committees and funded federal and contractor jobs in more than fifty congressional districts."[106] Such a "convoluted and bloated management" and oversight system resulted in "confusing and often contradictory mandates."[107] The PFIAB also faulted the inconsistency in DOE leadership, as energy secretaries averaged only two and half years in office, deputy energy secretaries two years, and assistant energy secretaries one and a half years.[108] Until the PFIAB investigation, the DOE leadership rarely considered security and counterintelligence an important issue. For this reason, the PFIAB panel urged the creation of a new agency that was "more mission focused, more bureaucratically streamlined, and devoted principally to nuclear weapons and security matters."[109] Such a new agency, however, could come about only through an act of Congress.[110]

In its final report, the PFIAB panel made specific recommendations about how the new agency could effectively address DOE security and counterintelligence problems. The new agency should be semiautonomous, focused on nuclear stewardship, and have a director who reports directly to the secretary of energy. The new agency should streamline its management of nuclear weapons and the national laboratories by abolishing the previous DOE system of regional and field offices. The director of the new agency should be appointed by the president and then confirmed by the Senate. Appointees ought to have a balance of science, national security, and management experience. The new agency should create a coherent security and counterintelligence strategy for U.S. weapons laboratories. The DOE's Office of Energy Intelligence should be abolished and replaced with a smaller intelligence liaison office similar to the Office of Intelligence Support in the Treasury Department. The new agency should also make efforts to shift its analytic capabilities toward the DCI's Nonproliferation Center (now the Center for Weapons Intelligence, Nonproliferation, and Arms Control) to bolster the intelligence community's technical ability.[111] The PFIAB panel also suggested that "the CIA and the FBI should expand the 'National Security Partnership' to include the new agency and the weapons labs."[112] Along with the new agency, the panel recommended complete reform in the personnel security program and "a total revamping of the Q clearance" process.[113]

On completion of the PFIAB panel's report, Clinton praised the board's efforts and reiterated his commitment to instituting the best possible safeguards for the security of the DOE facilities.[114] In addition to the praise received from the White House, the panel's report also met with acclaim from Republicans, who cited it as validation of their own proposed DOE reforms offered in the Kyl-Domenici-Murkowski Amendment of 1999. During the fiscal year 2000 Defense Authorization Bill deliberations, Republican senators John Kyl, Pete Domenici, and Frank Murkowski offered amendments affecting the DOE that were similar to the proposed changes in the PFIAB panel report. A Democratic filibuster and veto threat, however, forced the Republicans to withdraw the amendment. But, once the panel published its findings, which were consistent with the original Republican amendment, Senators Kyl, Domenici, and Murkowski obtained unanimous consent for their amendment as part of the deliberation for the fiscal year 2000 Intelligence Authorization Bill.[115]

The Kyl, Domenici, and Murkowski Amendment (Amendment 446) passed the Senate on July 21, 1999, by a vote of 96 to 1. This amendment, calling for a semiautonomous agency to coordinate and control the U.S. nuclear weapons programs, was rolled into the fiscal year 2000

National Defense Authorization Act. The act was approved by the House of Representatives on September 15, 1999, by a vote of 375 to 45 and by the Senate on September 22, 1999, by a vote of 93 to 5. On October 5, 1999, President Clinton signed the fiscal year 2000 National Defense Authorization Act into law and created the National Nuclear Security Administration (NNSA).[116] The NNSA is the semiautonomous agency tasked with responsibility for overseeing U.S. nuclear weapons research and production.[117] It was expected to help change the hidebound bureaucratic culture that permeated the DOE and the national laboratories that the PFIAB panel report blamed for the serious lapses in security.[118] NNSA administrators worked directly for the secretary of energy. The administration's director would be a DOE undersecretary "charged with executing the U.S. nuclear weapons program."[119] The weapons laboratories and production facilities were to report directly to the NNSA director—a step that provided "unambiguous lines of authority, responsibility, communication, and . . . accountability."[120] A reformed security and counterintelligence strategy was to be directly implemented by the director of the NNSA.[121]

The mission of the NNSA consists of six components:

(1) to enhance U.S. national security through military application of nuclear technology; (2) to maintain and enhance the safety, reliability, and performance of the U.S. nuclear weapons stockpile, including the ability to design, produce, and test, in order to meet national security requirements; (3) to provide the U.S. Navy with safe, militarily effective nuclear propulsion plants and to ensure the safe and reliable operation of those plants; (4) to promote international nuclear safety and nonproliferation; (5) to reduce global danger from weapons of mass destruction; and (6) to support U.S. leadership in science and technology. The NNSA administrator has authority over, and is responsible for, all programs and activities (except for the functions of the deputy administrator for naval reactors under EO 12344) of the NNSA: strategic management; policy development and guidance; budget formulation, guidance, execution, and other financial matters; resource requirements determination and allocation; program management and direction; safeguards and security; emergency management; integrated safety and management; environment, safety, and health operations; administration of contracts, including the management and operations of

the nuclear weapons production facilities and the national security laboratories; intelligence; counterintelligence; personnel,
including the selection, appointment, distribution, supervision,
establishing of compensation, and separation of personnel in
accordance with Subtitle C of Title XXXII; legal matters; legislative matters; public affairs; and liaison with other elements
of the DOE and with other federal agencies, state, tribal, and
local governments and the public.[122]

A former commander in chief of the U.S. Strategic Command, Richard
Mies (the military command responsible for all U.S. strategic nuclear
forces supporting the national security objective of strategic deterrence),
was asked to perform an independent review of the NNSA five years after it was established.[123] His commission acknowledged that the NNSA
was a good step toward resolving many of the security issues at DOE
weapons laboratories, but it still recommended a number of additional
mechanisms to ensure the security and safeguarding of the U.S. nuclear
program.[124]

John Deutch Security Violations

In the spring of 2000, the PFIAB was asked to review the internal CIA
handling of former DCI John Deutch's home computer security violations. After Deutch was accused of "storing highly classified intelligence
reports on unsecure home computers," the results of the PFIAB investigation were requested by Senators Richard C. Shelby (R-AL) and Richard
H. Bryan (D-NV). The White House, the NSC, the Justice Department,
and Congress all sought a swift investigation of this matter. There was
particular concern to distance the Deutch incident from the Wen Ho
Lee case, in which the Los Alamos scientist was indicted on fifty-nine
counts of downloading nuclear secrets to unsecure computers. In the
conclusion to its investigation, the PFIAB criticized the CIA's internal
investigation into the Deutch case, complaining that then DCI George
Tenet and other high-ranking officials failed to aggressively pursue the
case. PFIAB chair Rudman made little further comment on the PFIAB's
findings except to say that investigations and conclusions had been "exhaustive, thorough, and tough."[125]

Release of PFIAB Files Relating to Kennedy Assassination

On January 19, 2001, President Clinton overruled his PFIAB and released
"hundreds of pages of PFIAB records loosely related to the assassination

of President Kennedy" to the National Archives. In a December 10, 1998, meeting of the Department of State's Advisory Committee on Historical Diplomatic Documentation (ACHDD), the Assassination Records Review Board (ARRB) declared a number of PFIAB documents related to Cuba and the Moscow embassy relevant to the JFK assassination. It identified excerpts of seventeen PFIAB documents between 1961 and 1963 as "assassination records" subject to the 1992 law requiring their release. PFIAB chair Rudman "challenged the ARRB's authority to designate PFIAB records as assassination records or dictate their release."[126]

Each of the documents in question was reviewed and cleared by the CIA and the State Department, but the PFIAB dissented, saying that its records were exempt from declassification on the grounds of executive privilege, the board being a nongovernment advisory body to the president. The ARRB overruled the PFIAB's objection. The PFIAB then appealed to Clinton just as the ARRB disbanded—a strategic move planned to ensure that the ARRB would not be able to challenge the appeal. PFIAB chair Rudman argued that the records were the property of the board, which offers "private" advice to the president and is, thus, not subject to most information access requests. ACHDD chair Warren Kimball countered that several documents concerning the intelligence establishment had already been cleared by the CIA (their "owner") and only awaited PFIAB review. Similarly, the PFIAB claim of ownership undermined "the State Department's legal obligation to publish a thorough, accurate, and complete record of U.S. foreign policy."[127] ACHDD executive secretary William Slany noted that Rudman's objection was based on his view that no PFIAB documents should ever be released. Prior to this incident, some PFIAB documents had been released under the Freedom of Information Act, but the PFIAB staff was apparently unaware of this.

The records in question dealt with "U.S. and Cuban exile operations against Cuba between the Bay of Pigs and the Cuban Missile Crisis." According to the American University professor Anna Nelson, these records would provide "new insight into this period." The National Archives specialist Steven Tilley, who reviewed all the ARRB-requested documents, said that the documents were unique because they offered the PFIAB's "take on the world and how they presented it to the President." With his rejection of his PFIAB's appeal to withhold these records, President Clinton may have set a precedent, making historical PFIAB records easier to request and have released.[128]

Cuban Double Agents

In 1987 the CIA received a cable at Langley from the Cuban Direccion General de Intelligencia (DGI) stating that the DGI was determined to counter any "attempts to thwart our international solidarity, against every machination aimed at destroying our socialist revolution."[129] The cable was signed MATEO, the code name for one of the CIA's most important sources in Cuba. The CIA interpreted the cable as a sign that "MATEO actually worked for the DGI." A few weeks later, the Cuban DGI station chief in Prague, Florentino Aspillaga Lombard, walked into the American embassy in Vienna to defect. He informed CIA officers in Vienna that he used to work for DGI counterintelligence and that the DGI had successfully recruited every CIA asset in Cuba since 1961.[130] Aspillaga stated that virtually everything the CIA's assets in Cuba provided was disinformation disseminated by the DGI itself. Aspillaga's story was true, and the Cubans' successful deception of the CIA through the use of double agents represented a tremendous failure of intelligence. The Cuban double agent program had provided the DGI, and, by extension, the KGB, valuable insight on American intelligence procedures and technology. In return, the CIA received only disinformation from the DGI.[131]

Although it examined this issue to some extent during the Reagan administration, the board tried and failed to get more involved in HUMINT issues such as the Cuban double agent disaster under President Bush.[132] A former senior administration official reports that the board revisited this issue of HUMINT and the Cuban double agent disaster under Clinton but offered no information with regard to specific conclusions or recommendations.[133]

Nuclear Arms Proliferation and Other Issues

During a seminar at Harvard University, former PFIAB chair Rudman intimated that he and his colleagues on the board embarked on a five-, ten-, and fifteen-year look at nuclear arms proliferation.[134] No other unclassified information on this project is available.

In this same talk, Rudman also took credit, along with his colleague Dr. Sidney Drell, for the board in the creation of the DCI's Advanced Technology Panel.[135] The Advanced Technology Panel is a group of "industry representatives providing expert advice, consultation, and analysis on scientific, technical, and engineering matters to the DCI (now both the director of the CIA and the director of national intelligence) and other senior intelligence community leadership on scientific, technical, and engineering matters."[136] This effort would subsequently give rise to the CIA's Intelligence Technology Innovation Center, which was the umbrella under which a number of innovative efforts, including the CIA's nonprofit technology venture capital firm In-Q-Tel, sheltered.[137]

ASSESSMENT

Clinton's PFIAB handled many sensitive issues and completed several major investigative projects. The Guatemala review changed the intelligence community's asset validation system and how the CIA handled assets or liaison services with suspected human rights abuses. The PFIAB's DOE report completely restructured the national nuclear strategy, safeguard protocol, nonproliferation prevention, and research-and-development efforts. Nevertheless, Clinton's PFIAB seems to have been a minor player in the intelligence community, in contrast to earlier, more influential boards.

One former senior administration official who had significant interaction with the PFIAB was quite candid with us in his assessment of the strengths and weaknesses of the board during the Clinton administration. He admitted to the inherent weakness that exists with any part-time organization and conceded that the temptation to use the board as a reward for political friends was almost irresistible for most presidents.[138] He also candidly acknowledged that "push-back" from the board would have been unwelcome in the intelligence community, but he nonetheless maintained that it would have been helpful. In his view, the optimal role for the board was to act, as he colorfully put it, as a "knowledgeable pain in the ass" to press the national security advisers and presidents to establish proper intelligence priorities.[139]

The same official offered a few suggestions that he believed would have aided the board in performing its stated mission. For example, he argued that the board needed a larger staff and fewer members with more experts among them. A former member concurs, stating that the board would have been better off with a mix of people with relevant knowledge (especially technical knowledge) and smaller numbers of members.[140] This former official also recommended that successive boards should incorporate two or three "fresh" people with a new perspective, but he also suggested that an effective board needs holdovers from previous administrations. This individual also felt that, even as a part-time body, the board should have held meetings more often, including with the president and his national security adviser.[141] Above all, however, he stressed the need to avoid playing politics with the board because it needs to be a nonpartisan group.[142]

Clinton used his PFIAB in the most public manner in the board's history. Though this is, in some respects, a boon to researchers, it leads us to wonder how seriously he regarded it as a source of advice on critical intelligence issues. There is a temptation to attribute his cavalier attitude toward the board to his personality and his generally lax presidential style vis-à-vis intelligence matters. While those factors no doubt explain part of his use of the board during his two terms, we should not ignore the very important institutional changes in the executive branch—particularly with regard to the management of intelligence—that made it much easier for any president to treat the board less as a source of unique confidential advice about intelligence matters and more as just another set of entries in the "plum book" to be doled out to political cronies.

9

George W. Bush

Unlike most of his predecessors, President George W. Bush did not issue a new executive order (EO) to establish his President's Foreign Intelligence Advisory Board (PFIAB). Instead, he allowed Clinton's EO 12863 to carry over through much of his administration. This initial laissez-faire attitude toward the PFIAB left many of Clinton's appointees in place during the opening year of his administration. Warren Rudman stayed on as chair until late in the autumn of 2001, but there is debate about whether other members remained as well. In April 2006, White House spokesperson Dana Perrino stated that members of Clinton's PFIAB stayed until Bush named his first set of PFIAB members in October 2001.[1] Other sources say that members of Clinton's PFIAB offered their resignations soon after the elections, never meeting again, and that Bush's PFIAB was full of vacancies during the first years of his administration.[2]

Regardless of whether Bush had a fully staffed board, a fully staffed PFIAB that was not meeting, or a ghost PFIAB, all directives were delayed until after new board members were selected. Even in the immediate aftermath of the 9/11 attacks—the largest intelligence failure in U.S. history—the president did not task the PFIAB to investigate it. Similarly, he did not staff the Intelligence Oversight Board (IOB) until March 17, 2003, well after much of the intelligence oversight work on the 9/11 attack had taken place. Rudman supported this decision because he believed that all members of the intelligence community needed more time before the postmortems began.[3] He also hoped that, since the country was in the process of responding to 9/11, President Bush would appoint intelligence experts and not political friends to his PFIAB.[4]

Unfortunately, Bush continued with the practice of using PFIAB membership as a political reward and filled his board with those to whom he owed political favors and large campaign donors. Though this selection practice was commonplace among recent presidents, Bush seems to have taken it to an extreme by placing more financial donors on the PFIAB than ever before.[5] When naming the second set of PFIAB members in 2005, he appointed nine campaign donors—including three longtime fund-raisers—to fill his sixteen-member board. His early steps with the PFIAB seem to validate the commonly held view that his administration favored cronyism and loyalty to the president over independent expertise.[6]

To be sure, previous PFIABs have included political appointees, but the majority of those appointed to the board in the early years possessed significant scientific, intelligence, or national security experience. Bush's PFIAB, according to the director of the Federation of American Scientists' Project on Government Secrecy, Steven Aftergood, is the first one to favor friends and supporters over those who have genuine competence in areas relevant to intelligence.[7]

On May 14, 2003, two years into his first term, Bush finally signed EO 13301, which further amended Clinton's EO 12863 by expanding the maximum number of members of the IOB from four to five.[8] His only other amendments to the legal mandate of the PFIAB occurred when he signed EO 13376 on April 15, 2005. The first amendment replaced the phrase "Director of Central Intelligence (DCI)" with "Director of National Intelligence (DNI)" (the change reflected the newly created post). The second amendment added a concluding section (Section 3.4) to EO 12863 that reads: "This order is intended only to improve the internal management of the executive branch of the Federal Government, and is not intended to, and does not, create any right or benefit, substantive or procedural, enforceable at law or in equity, against the United States, its departments, agencies, or other entities, its officers or employees, or any other person."[9] Other than these small amendments, President Bush did not promote or codify any significant changes to the basic structure of the PFIAB until the last year of his presidency.

In an EO issued on February 29, 2008, President Bush reorganized the PFIAB to reflect the new realities of the restructured intelligence community and the amorphous nature of the post-9/11 intelligence issues with which it grappled. His order renamed the PFIAB as the President's Intelligence Advisory Board (PIAB). This name change reflected the fact that intelligence no longer starts or ends at the border. To meet terrorist threats and thwart industrial espionage, the line between foreign and domestic intelligence activities has become blurred.

The board was mandated to report its findings to the president at least twice a year. The order also directed the board to report its findings to the DNI and relevant department heads if it was deemed appropriate.

The order, furthermore, directed the DNI and the department heads to provide, as permitted by law, any information and assistance necessary for the board to carry out its functions. It held the departments responsible for carrying out the board's recommendations and, if they failed to do so, mandated them to report the reason through the DNI.

This new order also placed an upper limit of sixteen members on the board. It further stipulated that members cannot be employed by the federal government and will receive no compensation other than their per diem and travel expenses in the exercise of their duties. The EO indicated that the president names the executive director of the PIAB, who, if the president so desires, can serve the IOB in the same capacity. It is the executive director's responsibility to supervise the professional and administrative staff.

The new EO retained the IOB as a standing committee of the PFIAB, but its other modifications to that board proved quite controversial. The new EO lessened the board's authority to refer matters to the Department of Justice for investigation. It also severed the links between the IOB and the inspectors general of the various agencies of the intelligence community. Many observers saw this as part of the Bush administration's efforts to roll back the 1970s-era intelligence frameworks. These changes formally emasculated a board that had in any case been quite inactive in previous years.[10]

BOARD MEMBERSHIP AND EXECUTIVE STAFF

Through his two terms in office, President Bush had appointed a total of twenty-nine people to serve on his PFIAB. Aside from a few individual appointments in 2002 (Johns Hopkins University president Dr. William Brody) and 2006 (the banker Denis Bovin and the former economic adviser to President Reagan Dr. Martin Feldstein), he made two distinct rounds of PFIAB appointments. In October 2001, under the chairmanship of Lt. Gen. Brent Scowcroft (Ret.), the former national security adviser to President George H. W. Bush, President George W. Bush appointed the following individuals to serve on the PFIAB:

> Cresencio Arcos, a former deputy assistant secretary of state for international narcotics and crime;
> James Barksdale, a former president and CEO of Netscape Communications Group;
> Robert Day, the founder and CEO of Trust Company of the West;

Stephen Friedman, a global business manager;

Alfred Lerner, the Cleveland Browns co-owner;

Ray Hunt, the president and CEO of Hunt Consolidated;

Rita Hauser, a former U.S. Department of Justice lawyer;

Adm. David Jeremiah, a former chairman of the Joint Chiefs of Staff;

Arnold Kanter, a former undersecretary of state for political affairs;

James Langdon, a senior executive partner of Akim, Gump, Strauss, Hauer and Feld;

Dr. Marie Paté-Cornell, a Stanford University management and engineering professor;

John Streicker, a New York real estate mogul;

Peter Wilson, a former California governor and senator; and

Dr. Philip Zelikow, a Harvard professor of government and public policy.

After the 2004 elections, the entire board submitted resignations. In December 2004, Scowcroft was removed from the chairmanship after publicly dissenting from the administration's handling of the Iraq situation.[11]

In February 2005, Bush appointed James Langdon, a Washington, DC, lawyer, to replace Scowcroft. His stint in the position ended in December of that same year in large part owing to a political flap surrounding Langdon's dual role as PFIAB chair and energy lawyer for Akin, Gump, Strauss, Hauer and Feld. This controversy once again focused attention on the potential conflicts of interest when members of advisory boards are granted access to high-level, sensitive information that had first been raised during Henry Kissinger's brief service on the board during the first Bush administration.[12]

On October 27, 2005, Bush appointed another core group of PFIAB members to serve two-year terms beginning in late December 2005. Only four members of his first-term PFIAB were reappointed: James L. Barksdale, Ray L. Hunt, Marie E. Paté-Cornell, and Adm. David E. Jeremiah. Stephen Friedman, who served as a PFIAB member under both Bill Clinton and George H. W. Bush, was named chair of both the PFIAB and the IOB on December 20, 2005.[13] New members included the chair of O'Melveny and Myers, Arthur Culvahouse; the St. Louis Cardinals owner, William DeWitt; a former Commander of the U.S. Strategic Command, Adm. James Ellis; a former U.S. secretary of commerce, Donald Evans; a former director of the National Reconnaissance Office (NRO), Martin Faga; a former House of Representatives member, Lee Hamilton; and the Pillsbury International Group president, John Morrison. One day prior to the December 20, 2005, start date for Bush's second-term PFIAB, the White House announced the addition of the George Mason University professor and former Virginia Senator Charles S. Robb to the board.[14]

In the fall of 2006, President Bush announced the addition of two new members—Denis Bovin and Martin Feldstein—to his second-term PFIAB.[15] These additions did not seem to result from any specific international event or domestic political development. Rather, they apparently reflected the president's desire to have a full complement of sixteen board members.

Although Bush's first- and second-term PFIABs were, in fact, similar in makeup, it was his second-term board that really came under fire for cronyism. Each PFIAB had a small number of intelligence, military, foreign policy, or national security professionals with the requisite experience and skill to handle the complex intelligence issues facing the White House. Both also had a slightly larger number of members with only modest levels of experience in national security–related fields. More blatantly than those of previous administrations, the Bush boards were populated with a greater percentage of political supporters and campaign fund-raisers.[16]

PFIAB Executive Staff

A former PFIAB member also stated that the board's staff budget was cut at some point during Bush's administration. Staffers were on unreimbursed details from other agencies, and the PFIAB began having trouble filling its allotted staff slots—especially when Donald Rumsfeld cut off all Department of Defense (DOD) staffers.[17] He also reported that, after the cuts, the PFIAB staff consisted of an executive secretary, a counselor, and one other staffer. The executive staff included Joan Avalyn Dempsey (2003–2005) and Stefanie Osburn (2005–) as executive directors. Other staffers included the administrative officer Carol Blair and the counsel to the board Homer Pointer.[18]

OPERATING PROCEDURES

The Bush administration did not release information about how often the PFIAB met, the total number of board staff, or the board's operating budget. Likewise, the White House did not reveal much about the organization or operating procedures for either of Bush's PFIABs. Such secrecy is not a surprise given the second Bush administration's very assertive view of executive privilege and the president's closely held leadership style.

Board Meetings

Little information is available regarding the PFIAB's meeting schedules and procedures. One member of the board did tell us that during the second term it met every month rather than every other month. He also said that the chair briefed the president personally every month on its activities.[19] Another member revealed that—in a radical break with former practice—the board had no standing subcommittees.[20] Most reports went directly to the president or the national security adviser for consideration and that sometimes the full board or just the chair submitted the report and recommendations.[21]

In 2004, the board's offices were moved from their longtime headquarters in the Old Executive Office Building to much smaller quarters across the street in the New Executive Office Building. One unnamed source inside the PFIAB called the move "very dispiriting."[22] Ostensibly done "as a precaution against car bombs" (the old offices faced the street), the move nevertheless sparked rumors of "retribution" for Scowcroft's criticism of the Iraq War. The general sense is that it signaled a downgrade in the prestige of the PFIAB.

Operating Procedures and Interaction with Other Groups

A former senior intelligence official told us that both Condoleezza Rice (a former national security adviser) and Stephen Hadley (her successor) often came to the board to discuss issues that were weighing on their minds.[23] A former senior administration official mentioned that the DNI also met fairly regularly with the board, both formally and informally.[24] He also told us that the board virtually always came to the DNI with issues to examine or learn more about, not the other way around.[25]

As with earlier boards, the PFIAB under George W. Bush received most of its information about intelligence issues through briefings from personnel from the various intelligence agencies. One former PFIAB member complained, however, that the briefings were of questionable quality. Intelligence community personnel assigned to brief the PFIAB were often not enthusiastic about sharing information with the board. Though he never claimed that different agencies were "blowing off" the board, he and his colleagues had the distinct feeling that some people were not "excited" to be in front of the board. He was quick to admit, however, that at times the PFIAB did not communicate clearly what it wanted from intelligence community briefers.[26]

Finally, we also learned through interviews with a member of the Bush board that the staff had established a system for keeping track of the status of the implementation of board recommendations by setting up a "dashboard" display on which they tracked their progress using a system of red, yellow, and green indicators.[27]

ISSUES AND RECOMMENDATIONS

Because the PFIAB deals with highly sensitive, classified information, little official documentation is available yet regarding its activities during the Bush administration. Unlike President Clinton, Bush did not use the board in a public fashion. Therefore, the only information available regarding the board comes from open sources, press releases, media coverage, and our interviews with board members and other senior administration and intelligence community officials. Despite the Bush administration's efforts to clamp down on information regarding its inner workings, the PFIAB was nevertheless covered frequently in the media. Another former member assured us that Bush's PFIAB examined several major issues and produced a large number of reports and recommendations for the president.[28] Unfortunately, all remain classified, so our assessment of the board's activities is perforce provisional.

Middle East Peace Process

In April 2001, then PFIAB chair Rudman participated in the Sharm el-Sheikh Fact-Finding Committee on the Mitchell Plan for resolution of the Israeli and Palestinian conflict. The Mitchell Committee, as it has become commonly known, recommended that both the government of Israel and the Palestinian Authority recommit themselves to the Sharm el-Sheikh spirit of building trust and propagating peace by "ending the violence, rebuilding confidence, and resuming negotiations."[29] It is unclear whether Rudman involved any other PFIAB members in the course of his duties on the fact-finding committee.

Comprehensive Review of U.S. Intelligence

A former senior official told us that the PFIAB was "primarily, if not exclusively, interested in intelligence reform."[30] In May 2001, Bush issued National Security Presidential Directive-5, which called for a comprehensive review of U.S. intelligence by an internal and an external panel.[31] Members of the external panel—whose report was scheduled to be completed by September 2001—included the future Bush PFIAB members General Scowcroft and Adm. David Jeremiah. Both panels were directed to concentrate their efforts on four specific areas: "twenty-first-century intelligence threats and priorities, current capabilities, new and 'highly advanced' technologies for intelligence collection and analysis, and possible reorganization of the community."[32]

The panel was scheduled to release its findings to the president in November 2001. One of its major recommendations involved intelligence community reorganization. Specifically, it proposed the transfer of the NRO, the National Security Agency, and National Imagery and Mapping Agency to the direct control of the DCI.[33] Of course, this had long been a concern of the board—because 80 percent of the intelligence community's budget was under the control of the DOD, the DCI was always quite constrained in his exercise of community leadership. According to press accounts and discussions with a current board member, this effort was spearheaded by Scowcroft under the auspices of the PFIAB when he was named chair. Unfortunately, as in the past, this effort sparked opposition from Secretary of Defense Rumsfeld. Rumsfeld admitted that steps needed to be taken to better integrate the intelligence community, but he fought hard and successfully, with Vice President Dick Cheney's support, for this to be done not under the DNI but rather under a new post in the Office of the Secretary of Defense designated the undersecretary for intelligence.[34]

In 2002, Scowcroft's special PFIAB task force on intelligence urged the president to create a cabinet-level DNI to lead the intelligence community.[35] Five years later, the PFIAB launched a review of the fledgling Office of the DNI (ODNI). Though details of the board's findings are not likely to be made public soon, the board member Lee Hamilton described the ODNI as "a work in progress . . . clearly doing a better job of sharing information than . . . [it did] prior to 9/11, but [it is] trying to change cultures."[36] This PFIAB review of the ODNI, as recounted to us by a former DNI official, is another and more successful part of the board's continuing look at the overall organization of the intelligence community. Finally, as part of this larger reorganization effort, Scowcroft reportedly also pushed for the creation of a "Terrorist Threat Integrated Center."[37]

Iraq Intelligence and Weapons of Mass Destruction

A 2003 *New York Times* editorial entitled "Reviewing the Intelligence on Iraq" put Bush's PFIAB in the public eye by urging the president to assign his board the task of assessing the extent to which the intelligence community had been "manipulated" to justify the spring 2003 Iraq invasion.[38] A former member states unequivocally that that editorial played a major role in pushing Bush to allow the PFIAB to examine the Iraq weapons of mass destruction failure.[39] In December 2003, the PFIAB concluded that the White House had made, at best, a "questionable claim" in the 2001 State of the Union address regarding Iraqi efforts to acquire nuclear materials. It also reportedly concluded that the dubious assertion had been made out of desperation to show that Saddam Hussein was actively pursuing a nuclear weapons program in order to justify launching a preemptive war. The board concluded that the administration's claim that Iraq was attempting to procure uranium from Africa was "not [a] deliberate effort to fabricate" a story but instead the result of trying to "grab onto something affirmative" for the State of the Union speech. The PFIAB also found that the infamous sentence in the 2003 State of the Union address was included because "there was no organized system at the White House to vet intelligence."[40] As a result, all intelligence items to be included in subsequent presidential speeches were to be explicitly approved by a CIA officer.[41] According to a former senior intelligence community official, President Bush felt "betrayed" by the intelligence community's performance in its assessment of Iraq's weapons of mass destruction program, and it is likely that he therefore had mixed views of the PFIAB's report and recommendations that seemed to focus more on the White House.[42]

Implementing 9/11 Commission Recommendations

A former senior intelligence official told us that in the spring of 2004 a window of opportunity opened for the then-dormant PFIAB to advise the president on how best to implement its recommendations in intelligence areas.[43] He explained that the Intelligence Reform and Terror Prevention Act of 2004 and the Silberman-Robb Commission Report (formally known as the Commission on the Intelligence Capabilities of the United States Regarding Weapons of Mass Destruction) revitalized the board and gave it, under Chair Friedman, a "mission . . . [to] provide a framework of the issues that are important to the President."[44] Another former senior official concurred, observing that the PFIAB looked at issues of human intelligence (HUMINT), integrated collection activities, analysis, the National Counterintelligence Executive, and FBI HUMINT transformation. Neither source could offer specific information other than to state that the board worked on a variety of aspects of the implementation of 9/11 Commission recommendations.[45]

Privacy and Civil Rights

In late 2005, the PFIAB's oversight arm, the IOB, was in the news again, this time in connection with a charge by the public interest group the Electronic Privacy Information Center (EPIC) that multiple allegations of FBI violations of the privacy of U.S. citizens were not being properly investigated. EPIC indicated that case numbers relating to FBI allegations referred to the IOB suggested over 150 instances of such FBI misconduct in 2003.[46] It found that, between 2001 and 2005, the IOB did not once ask the Justice Department to investigate allegations of violations of intelligence-gathering laws.

Former Clinton IOB chair Anthony Harrington remarked that it was "apparent that the IOB was not actively employed in the early part of the [George W. Bush] administration . . . a crucial period when its counsel would seem to have been needed the most." Harrington complained: "[The] White House counsel's office and the attorney general should have known and been concerned if they did not detect an active and effective IOB."[47] This lack of activity was undoubtedly the result of the fact that the IOB was not staffed until March 2003, well after the administration had begun an aggressive expansion in the domestic operations of part of the intelligence community. President Bush's failure to appoint members to the oversight arm of the PFIAB lent weight to the charge that his administration established a pattern of resisting outside scrutiny and possible dissent from his policies.[48]

Porter Goss's Resignation as Director of the Central Intelligence Agency

In the spring of 2006, the PFIAB reportedly played a key role in the resignation of Porter Goss as the director of the CIA. Goss's problems began with a criminal investigation of his executive director, Dusty Foggo. Foggo was eventually indicted on fraud, conspiracy, and money-laundering charges as a result of his improper connections with an agency contractor. This issue piqued the board's concern, and subsequent discussions with CIA officials left the PFIAB "very alarmed" about Goss's tenure as CIA head. A consensus among the members quickly emerged that Goss had to step down, and the board reportedly provided the final push for his removal.[49] Neither the White House nor Goss offered a satisfactory public explanation for his ultimate resignation (Goss called it "one of those mysteries"). The PFIAB's assessment of Goss's tenure was said to be devastating.[50] His replacement at the CIA, Gen. Michael Hayden, reported that the board's report contained sharp criticisms of his resistance to the transformation of the intelligence community, including reducing the CIA's traditional role as the center for intelligence analysis.[51] A former senior intelligence community official remarked to us that, though the ouster of Goss was not a "formal PFIAB thing," nevertheless the board played a key role in forcing his resignation. He says that "in fact [Commerce Secretary Don] Evans and PFIAB brought down Goss."[52]

Iraq Study Group

Though the PFIAB did not have a formal role in this bipartisan, blue-ribbon initiative, several of its members participated in the influential 2006 Iraq Study Group (ISG), which produced the Baker-Hamilton Report. The board member Lee Hamilton served as the cochair, and Charles Robb was a member. The ISG was intended to be a "forward-looking, independent assessment of the current and prospective U.S. situation in Iraq" and its effects on other U.S. interests.[53] Despite the lack of a formal PFIAB role in the ISG, the board undoubtedly influenced its findings and recommendations.

Other Issues

A former senior intelligence official reported to us that the PFIAB examined the intelligence community's system of competitive alternative analysis, this time focusing on its use of "Red Cell" teams to attempt to identify weaknesses in the regular analytic process. He said that the PFIAB completed a report with seventeen recommendations on this issue and presented it to the president. He also mentioned that the DNI worked closely with the PFIAB on the issue but only "in draft" so as not to "taint" any final conclusions.[54]

Another former senior official reports that the board under Scowcroft's direction compiled a prospective report on the DNI and terrorism that he described as "great, but no one listened."[55] The PFIAB also apparently examined the issue of security clearances, together with the DNI, and advocated completely revamping the whole clearance procedure.[56]

A former senior intelligence official observed that, by the second Bush term, the PFIAB had a "full plate" with intelligence community reform issues. He pointed specifically to the board's examination of HUMINT capabilities, again a perennial board concern, as well as its assessment of the state of the integration of overhead imagery and signals intelligence.[57] Another former senior official told us that Bush's board was also especially concerned with covert action and reforming its implementation and management.[58]

Finally, as of May 2007, the PFIAB was preparing a report on the FBI's intelligence performance, which one former senior intelligence official confided to us would "not be glowing." The board has apparently gone into field offices and found major problems with intelligence collection.[59]

ASSESSMENT

The full impact of Bush's PFIAB, and the extent that its members influenced intelligence decisionmaking in the aftermath of 9/11, is only beginning to be understood. It is unclear how seriously the board was regarded by policymakers during the Bush administration. Given the obvious distrust of the board by his father and the public rift with his first PFIAB chair, Scowcroft, it is not surprising that President George W. Bush's use of it would be mixed at best.

Because so much of the board's work is classified and deals with issues currently relevant to national security, many sources were reluctant to go into detail about specific reports or recommendations the board made or even to discuss specific issues it examined. When all the records become declassified, we anticipate that a majority of the PFIAB assignments will have revolved around the post-9/11 intelligence reorganization, Iraq, and the growing potential nuclear problem in Iran.

Despite the secrecy, our sources were nonetheless willing to share their general impressions and evaluations of the board and its performance. Among the most common themes administration insiders discussed was the somewhat tempestuous relationship between Scowcroft and the president. The rift was so obvious that it received widespread media coverage, a new development considering the board's intentionally low profile in years past.

Toward the end of Bush's first term, the PFIAB made media headlines more for what it did not do than for what it did accomplish. Even before the public Iraq debate, Scowcroft's effort to shift intelligence assets from the DOD to the DCI raised hackles elsewhere in the Bush administration. White House officials reportedly were concerned about the board's independence under Scowcroft and did not give the PFIAB any additional critical tasks for analysis.[60] Scowcroft's estrangement from the Bush administration increased after he became an open critic of the Iraq War. This, of course, further limited the activities of the PFIAB. Though the board continued to meet, it was not assigned any new tasks.[61]

One former senior intelligence official remarked to us that Scowcroft's board had more fundamental problems than just mere disagreement with the president and his closest advisers. In his view, the problem was that Scowcroft was unable to distinguish between his views on foreign policy as a whole and the advice he was expected to provide on intelligence specifically. He complained that, under Scowcroft, there was never a PFIAB meeting that did not turn into a "global overview" of "ten thousand" different issues.[62] In his view, the problem was that Scowcroft had some difficulty adjusting to his role as an adviser in a very limited sphere, as opposed to the broad range of influence he had on foreign policy as a national security adviser.

In December 2004, the members of Bush's first-term PFIAB submitted their resignations.[63] Even after Scowcroft's resignation, another former senior official observed that the board remained dormant during Langdon's brief tenure as chair.[64] Another former board member told us that, under Langdon, the PFIAB "looked at a lot of issues and wrote a lot of reports."[65] But a former PFIAB member who served on the boards chaired by both Scowcroft and Langdon states that there was "no reason to think that President Bush thought that PFIAB was important."[66]

By his second term, it was clear that the president wanted to make the board a more activist body. Several interviewees commented on the board's renewed vigor under Chair Stephen Friedman. A former senior intelligence official described the board under him as "one of the best PFIABs" and reports that the "hard charging" Friedman had "good access to the national security adviser."[67] A former senior administration official confirms that the board was more active under Friedman than it had been under Langdon or Scowcroft, something that he attributes in part to Friedman enjoying the "personal confidence of the president."[68]

Nonetheless, some of our sources were critical of the makeup and operating procedures of Bush's board. For example, one former senior intelligence official believed that the board should have nine to twelve, rather than sixteen, members and only "a few lawyers." The Bush PFIAB had more lawyers on it than previous boards.[69] A former senior official concurred, saying that "small is better," and he also believed that the board needed a larger staff so that it would be able to conduct its own research. Moreover, this official lamented that Bush's PFIAB was often driven too much by "impressions."[70] Another former senior official agreed that the board needed a larger staff and fewer members, ideally six to eight. He also complained that its "amateur" status prevented it from being used effectively. If it was serious, in his view, the members could address at most only two or three major issues a year.[71] Ideally, one of these tasks should be to deliver to the president a report on the state of U.S. intelligence every year and discuss it with the entire National Security Council. Finally, this official, anticipating the 2008 EO, argued that the word *foreign* in PFIAB limited the board's scope, especially in an era where the lines between foreign and domestic intelligence have grown ever more blurry.[72]

Overall, a common theme emerged from our discussion of the George W. Bush PFIAB with individuals familiar with its work. First, there was a widely shared impression that Bush did not take the board very seriously from the start, as demonstrated by his appointment of a large board stacked with political appointees. Second, loyalty made a difference in terms of the PFIAB's effectiveness. This theme has been sounded repeatedly regarding all facets of Bush's administration. When Scowcroft broke from the administration's consensus regarding the Iraq War, the PFIAB suffered for his defiance. When Friedman, a more consistent Bush supporter, replaced him, however, more work filtered to the board, and, apparently, it made its voice heard. Finally, virtually all the officials felt that the PFIAB needed greater resources and fewer members if it was to be effective as an independent source of advice on intelligence affairs for the president.

An EO of February 29, 2008, changed the name of the PFIAB to the PIAB—the first name change since the Kennedy administration. The mere fact that an EO relating to the PFIAB was issued indicated that the White House finally came to view it as a useful part of the intelligence community—an attitude not consistently manifested earlier in Bush's presidency. The actual content of the order, especially the directions to federal agencies to supply the board with assistance and to implement its recommendations, seemed intended to reestablish the board's influence and provide it with the resources necessary to make substantial changes in the intelligence community. It remains to be seen whether the new order fundamentally altered the way the newly christened PIAB did business or to what use Bush's successor, Barack Obama, will put the board. For now, the new order can serve only as an indication that the Bush administration came around to thinking about how to make the board more effective in its last days in office.

The Bush administration is in many respects a most likely case for arguments that explain the changing role of the board on the basis of presidential personality and style. For example, the board's lack of relevance, particularly early in the first term, seems easily explained by Bush's penchant for centralization of presidential power and authority. The problem with such an explanation is that it cannot account for the fact that, toward the end of the second Bush term, the board seemed to enjoy something of a renaissance. Unless we think that Bush's personality and style changed dramatically, an implausible hypothesis, it seems more likely that institutional factors explain the changing fortunes of the board. Specifically, the 9/11 and Iraq intelligence failures demonstrated the weaknesses of the old institutional arrangements overseeing the intelligence community, so the board's revitalization was a function of some opening of institutional space in which an independent advisory board could once again operate in the context of major institutional reform.

Conclusion

On January 19, 2009, President Bush's President's Intelligence Advisory Board (PIAB) members submitted their resignations to incoming President Barack Obama, as is customary during a change in administrations. The Obama administration did not reach out to the PIAB during the transition phase or after it came into office. It did, however, set in motion the process for constituting its own board. Well into its first year in office, the Obama administration did not appear to be moving expeditiously to create its own board. In this manner, it paralleled many other new administrations that did not act on the board quickly.

President Obama finally announced the creation of his PIAB on October 29, 2009, by issuing an amendment to George W. Bush's Executive Order (EO) 13462. The most notable difference from President Bush's order was the authority that was granted back to the Intelligence Oversight Board (IOB) to inform the attorney general concerning "intelligence activities that involve possible violations of Federal criminal laws or otherwise implicate the authority of the Attorney General."[1] Critics of President Bush's move had feared that his action had emasculated the IOB's oversight activities and, thus, took away an independent voice charged with examining possible violations of laws related to intelligence matters.

The IOB is charged with reviewing violations of laws related to clandestine operations. However, under President Bush's EO of February 29, 2008, the board's authority was diminished. The order ended its authority to oversee the inspectors general and general counsels of the intelligence agencies. It also stopped the quarterly reports each inspector general needed to provide to the IOB and abrogated the IOB's right to call to the Justice Department's attention matters of a criminal nature. The order reserved the right for the IOB to bring possible violations of law to the president's attention only if it is clear that other officials are not adequately addressing the violations. President Obama's order abolished Bush's restrictions.

President Obama's order calls for the board to be composed of a maximum of sixteen members and provides for a chair or—for the first time in board history—cochairs. Indeed, Obama did name cochairs, former senators David Boren (D-OK) and Chuck Hagel (R-NE). This step was likely taken to highlight his commitment to bring transparency and nonpartisanship to Washington, DC. The cochairs bring a great deal of intelligence experience to their tasks. Boren had served as chair of the Senate Select Committee on Intelligence. He was also behind the legislation that established the position of a statutory inspector general at the CIA, a position that must be approved by and report to the U.S. Senate. Hagel, in turn, had served on the Intelligence Committee as well as on the Senate Foreign Relations Committee.

In making his announcement, the president said: "They will report to me, they will have my full support and they will have the full co-operation of my National Security Council staff and the organizations represented here [the intelligence community agencies]."[2] He therefore made a formal commitment to provide the cochairs access to him and assured his full support for their activities. In making his announcement before the press, Obama broke the tradition of just sending out a press release. This move, he stated, was to underscore his administration's commitment to transparency. In his announcement, he did not, however, name additional members of the board.

According to a well-placed adviser to the Obama campaign, the administration had great interest in the PIAB. It viewed the board as important for both political and policy reasons. It saw the board as providing cover against any difficult political issues such as detainment of terrorist suspects. It also viewed it as a possible vehicle for helping move the American intelligence community into the future. In this regard, the White House was interested in nominees with economic, intelligence, and technology backgrounds. In particular, the Obama administration realized the importance of global issues, such as economics and technology, and wanted a board that would be able to address the intelligence challenges these issues raise. In this regard, the Obama board returned to one of the board's original mandates when it was first established in 1956, and that was to examine the impact of new technologies on intelligence collection, analysis, and dissemination.

The administration's interest in the board was underscored by the fact that an initial list of approximately two hundred names was drawn up for consideration to be appointed to it. In late July or early August 2009, the list was whittled down to sixteen potential nominees and was forwarded to the president. Both the White House personnel office and policy people were involved in the vetting process.

According to the former Obama campaign adviser, the administration decided to create a real working board that would be directly responsible to the president, charged with advising him on contentious intelligence issues, and act as a venue for thinking about long-term efforts, such as further adjusting the structure for managing the U.S. intelligence community. Indeed, in December 2009, President Obama asked his new PIAB to look at the structure of the Office of the Director of National Intelligence (ODNI).[3] According to press reports, the board delivered its report, "Study of the Mission, Size, and Function of the Office of the Director of National Intelligence," to the President in May 2010, finding that the director of national intelligence (DNI) Adm. Dennis Blair's office was "distracted from its core missions" and, therefore, not serving as the leader of the U.S. intelligence community.[4] It concluded that, while changing the original statute that established the board would be too difficult, a number of other changes were in order.[5] The changes reportedly involved both structure and personnel. On the former, the board concluded that the ODNI was not effective because it was too large, making it "bureaucratic and resource heavy."[6] It therefore recommended that four parts of the ODNI—an office for coordinating interagency information, the National Intelligence University, a center dedicated to protecting sources and methods overseas, and the office that produces *Intelligence Today*—be moved elsewhere. On the latter, the board was reportedly "sharply critical" of Admiral Blair himself, and this was a factor in the president's decision to ask for his resignation.[7] In addition to this major assessment of the ODNI in the wake of the "Christmas Bombing" attempt, the Obama administration also tasked the board with reviewing information security in the intelligence community in the wake of the WikiLeaks scandal, in which a U.S. Army intelligence analyst reportedly downloaded thousands of U.S. intelligence items that were then subsequently posted to the Internet.[8]

On the one hand, this report indicated that the Obama administration was serious about using the board for one of its historic functions—assessing the structure of the U.S. intelligence community. On the other hand, at the same time as Obama was using the board in this fashion, members of his administration were reportedly offering membership on the board through former President Bill Clinton to Representative Joe Sestak of Pennsylvania to encourage him not to challenge Senator Arlen Specter in the Democratic primary.[9] If true, this sort of appointment unfortunately also continued the recent tradition of using the board as a political dumping ground as well. When the White

House Press spokesman, Joe Gibbs, denied that Clinton offered Sestak a seat on the board, one senior intelligence official was quoted as saying: "Thank goodness. We hoped POTUS [the president of the United States] thought more of the PIAB than that."[10]

The purpose of this chapter is to summarize the lessons from the historical experiences of previous boards and to offer policy recommendations for how future presidents can best use this unique part of the intelligence community. These recommendations derive from our assessments of the historical cases and from the thoughts of senior policymakers, high-level intelligence officials, and former chairs, members, and staff of various boards—who, in our interviews with them, reflected on their experiences with the board and thought prospectively about the optimal role of the board in the emerging intelligence environment.

This chapter discusses the role of the board historically, focusing particularly on what we should learn from these cases. It then assesses various explanations for why the effectiveness of the board has varied over the course of its history. Finally, it applies these lessons to future boards with an eye toward answering the following questions: Do we still need a board? If so, how should it be used, and how should it be configured to best advise future presidents about America's intelligence needs?

There is vigorous debate about the utility of the board among intelligence experts. Its defenders hold that it has played and can continue to play a useful role both for the president and for the overall intelligence community. The PFIAB is uniquely positioned: it has access to all the top secrets of the government, on the one hand, and direct access, without any filters, to the president (the ultimate decisionmaker), on the other hand. Thus, it can serve as an amalgam of whistleblower, conceptual thinker, adviser, sounding board, and any other role the president envisages for it. These roles are enhanced by the fact that it is unfettered by any bureaucratic vested interests, oversight from other agencies, and limits as to its agenda. Properly configured, the board has expertise unavailable within the rest of the intelligence community. In short, it is positioned to be a powerful and effective tool that supports the president's leadership of the policies, organization, and operations of American intelligence.

Critics maintain that the board is duplicative, often populated by individuals lacking real expertise, highly politicized, lacking the time and resources to consider issues in depth, and critically dependent on the president's commitment to use it. At best, in this view, the PFIAB appears to function merely as a conduit for the intelligence community to voice its concerns and to move its own agendas—whether operational or organizational. Several National Security Council (NSC) advisers we interviewed could not remember any substantive achievement of the PFIAB, nor did they have any significant recollection of their interaction with the board. One NSC adviser referred to PFIAB meetings as a "necessary duty." In this view, the board's recommendations are rubber stamps of intelligence community policies, rather than the result of the board's own initiative.

It should also be noted that, over the years, while various commissions have praised the PFIAB, they have also recommended numerous steps to help augment its role. Ironically, these recommendations actually raise questions about whether the board is actually fulfilling its mission and living up to its potential, about whether it is an institution looking for a clearer role.

The key challenge we face is assessing accurately whether the board has successfully fulfilled its mandate. Presidential statements about and evaluations of the PFIAB serve as one indicator of success. However, presidents usually do not make such evaluations, at least publicly. Evaluations from other senior officials such as the director of central intelligence (DCI), national security advisers, and secretaries of state and defense are also helpful.

Another method of measuring success is to examine the nature and breadth of issues and problems studied by a particular board, its recommendations to the president, and the extent to which these recommendations have been implemented. Much of the information about issues studied is available in unclassified form, but specific recommendations and their subsequent implementation often are not. Nonetheless, enough unclassified information is available through a variety of open sources to enable us to make a general evaluation as to whether the PFIAB of a specific president was successful.

Using those criteria and evidence, we are able to conclude that each PFIAB since the Eisenhower administration has been generally successful in fulfilling its mandate, though the general trajectory since then has been downward. We illustrate this conclusion in the following discussions of each president's PFIAB. Of course, it is impossible to speculate what would have happened had there been no PFIABs. Each president could have used existing agencies or appointed ad hoc outside advisory bodies to provide studies and recommendations, but there is no way of knowing if such studies would have produced recommendations as thorough, objective, and nonpartisan as those generally provided by the PFIAB.

We have enough evidence to conclude that the PFIAB has often provided valuable advice and recommendations on sensitive issues—including intelligence failures—to each president, except for President Carter. Many of these recommendations have been implemented by the presidents.

Historical Overview of the PFIAB

The history of the PFIAB can be divided into two phases, with the Carter years serving as a dividing point. The early boards fit the mold of a disciplined professional advisory body. This period included the Eisenhower, Kennedy, Johnson, Nixon, and Ford administrations.

The Eisenhower and Kennedy years were instrumental in the development of the PFIAB. During this time, much of the groundwork was laid for the future functioning of the board. It was involved in numerous studies, most notably the aftermath of the Bay of Pigs fiasco and the Cuban Missile Crisis. These two studies established the precedent for using the PFIAB as an investigative body to ascertain the causes of past intelligence and policy failures, thus moving it away from any future policymaking role.

The Reagan administration revived the PFIAB following its disestablishment under the Carter administration, thus ushering in the second historical phase of the board. Indeed, the Reagan team made Carter's failure to reconstitute the PFIAB a campaign theme, holding it up as emblematic of the intelligence and foreign policy failures of the Carter presidency. This, however, turned out to be more of a political ploy, aimed at questioning Carter's ability to conduct foreign policy, and not necessarily an indication of Reagan's support of the PFIAB. In fact, Reagan did not establish his own board until October 1981, almost a year into his first term; and, once he did, he appointed as members a large number of individuals with little intelligence-related experience. This action set a precedent for future presidents. Indeed, after Reagan, subsequent presidents would either reduce their use of the board (George H. W. Bush and George W. Bush, during his first term) or further politicize it (Clinton).

WHAT EXPLAINS THE VARIATION IN THE BOARD'S EFFECTIVENESS THROUGH THE YEARS?

As we suggested at the beginning of this book, the most attractive explanation for the changing effectiveness of the board is some variation of the well-known presidential-style-of-decisionmaking theories.[11] Such an argument would begin with the reasonable assumption that the effectiveness of a presidential advisory board would depend very heavily on the willingness of the particular president to avail himself of it. Style would explain whether, when, and how different presidents would use the board. Those open to outside advice and willing to listen to it from outside the formal bureaucratic structures of government would, so this argument goes, be more likely to use the board and use it effectively than those who have a more closed and formal decisionmaking style. The central observable implication of presidential style explanations is that there should be a strong association between a particular presidential style and the effective use of the board.

There are, however, two serious limitations with the presidential style/personality approach. First, there is great variation in the coding of the particular styles of each president among various proponents of this theory. There are two elements of this limitation: the categories that scholars use are often different (Eisenhower, e.g., is designated "formalistic," "good guy," and "passive negative"); and, more troubling, these different categories are not applied consistently to the same president (Alexander George and Eric Stein designate Eisenhower as "formalistic," and James Barber types him "passive negative," but George and Stein characterize Ford as "formalistic," and Barber calls him "active positive").[12]

Second, if you try to connect the effectiveness of the board since its inception—which we have investigated in this book—with the particular style of each president, you find that there is, in fact, little consistent association between a particular style and what we conclude to be its effective use. As figure 1 makes clear, the relationship between presidential style and effective or ineffective use of the PFIAB is essentially random using James David Barber's typologies.

Figure 1. The relation between presidential style and PFIAB effectiveness, with boldface indicating PFIAB effectiveness

Passive/Negative — **Eisenhower**	Active/Positive — **Kennedy,** Ford, Carter, Bush
Passive/Positive — Reagan	Active/Negative — **Johnson,** Nixon

For example, we judged that the PFIAB was effective under both the Eisenhower and the Kennedy administrations. Indeed, the early years of the board were in most respects its golden age in terms of influence and sustained positive contributions to the organization of the intelligence community and the creative application of new technologies to the acquisition, analysis, and dissemination of intelligence. But, in terms of style and personality, the two presidents could not have been more different. Given that, relying exclusively on presidential style or personality to explain how presidents have used (or not used) their PFIABs is unwise in our opinion.

All this leads us to suggest an alternative explanation for the pattern of the changing effectiveness of the board over the years. This explanation looks to the process of the institutionalization of the presidency as the best, though certainly not the only, explanation of the board's effectiveness over time. Following Lyn Ragsdale and John Theis, we conceive of the increasing institutionalization of the presidency as involving four components: its increasing autonomy, adaptability, complexity, and coherence.[13] Therefore, it would not be surprising that, as the American presidency became more institutionalized, presidents would have less incentive to look outside the normal bureaucratic channels to find guidance in sensitive areas like intelligence. As I. M. Destler concludes: "The size and complexity of modern government have sharply limited the advisory influence of outsiders compared to 'the trained intellectual bureaucrat' who is there, inside government, to push his objective hour by hour, day by day."[14] In Ragsdale and Theis's judgment, the process of the institutionalization of the American presidency reached its apex in the mid-1970s.[15] We measure this process in the national security realm by looking at the size of the NSC staff, the key White House office dealing with intelligence matters. As figure 2 illustrates, the size of the NSC staff took off in the early 1970s. Conversely, it was precisely at this point that the effectiveness of the board reached its nadir. This is not at all surprising from an institutional perspective given that many of the intelligence oversight functions that the board once conducted had, by the 1970s, become duplicative of what the NSC staff was now doing.

It is not our argument that there is no room for presidential leadership in the management of the board. Rather, we argue that, as the presidency becomes more institutionalized, it is more challenging for presidents to overcome the resultant institutional inertia. As Ragsdale and Theis said: "The greater the institutionalization, the more resources individuals require and the larger the environmental shock needed to effect change."[16] Today, an American president faces something of a bad news/good news situation. On the one hand, the institutionalization of the NSC staff and the intelligence community means that there will be powerful bureaucratic obstacles to allowing an extrabureaucratic entity

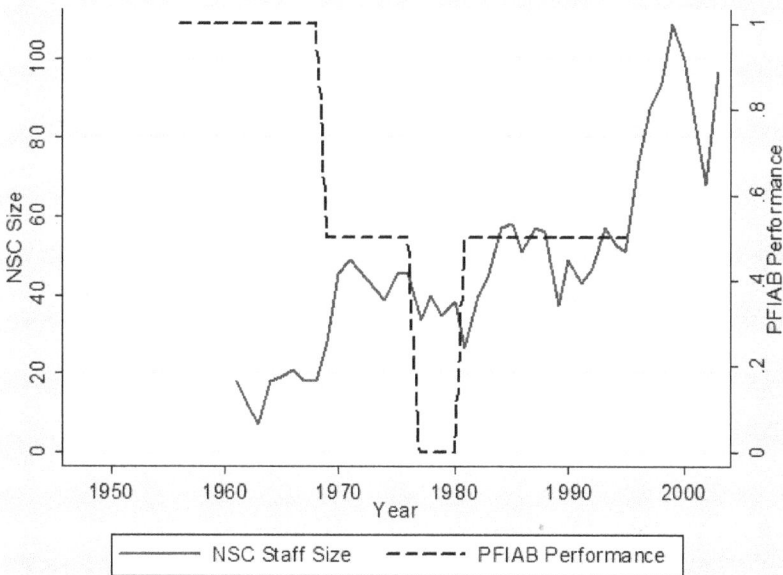

Figure 2. The growth of the NSC staff and the decline of the board's effectiveness.

like the board to have much real influence on intelligence policy. On the other hand, in the wake of the 9/11 intelligence failures, the weaknesses of the current institutional arrangements became readily apparent, which in turn has opened space for outside bodies to play a significant role.

Nothing could better illustrate this than the very different roles played by the PFIAB during the first and second terms of the George W. Bush administration. In the first term, the board was largely ineffective, in part because of political differences between the board's chair, Brent Scowcroft, and the president over the Iraq War, but also because of the successful bureaucratic resistance of the Department of Defense (DOD) to Scowcroft's effort to finally unify all the intelligence community's resources under the DCI by removing the National Security Agency and the National Reconnaissance Office from the DOD. Conversely, as pressure mounted in the post-9/11 environment to engage in a significant reorganization of the U.S. intelligence community, the board during Bush's second term became much more active and more influential in shaping that process. This leads us to a qualified optimism that, with committed leadership by President Obama and his successors, which includes a willingness to appoint people with real expertise and then listen to them, the board can once again play an important role in shaping the further evolution of the intelligence community.

Recommendations

In our judgment, the PFIAB's strengths far outweigh its weaknesses. The weaknesses themselves, moreover, can be rectified to produce a more effective board. The PFIAB is a unique presidential asset that, if properly utilized, could help identify and meet the intelligence challenges that future presidents will invariably encounter. Presidents need to have a body that they can rely on to provide advice and guidance on intelligence issues, aside from the intelligence community or the congressional oversight committees.

Only the PFIAB can get the attention of the president, has good access to him, can leverage his authority against the rest of the federal bureaucracy, can operate in a confidential manner outside the glare of public scrutiny, and does not have any institutional interests to protect.

The fact that each president since Eisenhower, save Carter, has created a PFIAB underscores the value, at least in principle, that most administrations ascribe to such an independent intelligence advisory body. Even Carter belatedly realized the need for such an organization at the end of his administration. Various studies, beginning with the 1975 Commission on the Organization of the Government for the Conduct of Foreign Policy (the Murphy Commission), have also highlighted the value of the PFIAB and its important role as an independent source of advice for the president on intelligence issues. The boards have provided useful reports and analyses on topics ranging from the Cuban Missile Crisis to the security leaks at Los Alamos that have helped identify weak procedures or methods in the intelligence community.

The PFIAB has served not only as an in-house think tank but also as a kitchen cabinet. In this role, it serves to lay the groundwork for serious discussion of various issues. For example, in 1976, the board examined the problem of international terrorism. The topics it examined—nonstate and state actors, the possible theft of nuclear weapons, chemical and biological weapons, and the threat of terrorism to U.S. interests—foreshadowed many of the issues that burst onto the national agenda in the wake of 9/11. In our view, the PFIAB has been least effective when it was involved in resource issues or in ongoing day-to-day operational or crisis issues, such as the first bombing of the World Trade Center.

Future administrations can take a number of steps to strengthen the

PFIAB. Our specific recommendations derive from two sources: the views expressed by those officials, past and present, who were involved with the PFIAB and our own analysis of the historical record of the board's contributions. Our recommendations are offered with an eye toward strengthening the role of intelligence and helping future presidents use the board more effectively.

These specific recommendations are divided into three categories: the internal organization of the PFIAB, the ways in which it should interact with the rest of the intelligence community, and, finally, the role of the president and White House in helping the PFIAB carry out its intended role.

ORGANIZATIONAL

Members

The president needs to resist the temptation to make appointments to the board simply as a payoff to political supporters. Historically, the most successful boards have contained scientists and other technical specialists (Edwin Land and William O. Baker), general foreign affairs specialists (William Hyland and Henry Kissinger), experts from outside government in business and academia (Stephen Friedman and William Langer), and distinguished political figures (Clare Booth Luce and Anne Armstrong). Members of the board should have a wide range or mix of backgrounds, but there must be several with extensive in-depth knowledge of the American intelligence community. Other members should have extensive technical and scientific, academic, foreign policy, or military backgrounds. Two to three should be career intelligence officers (Adm. Bobby Inman and Gen. Lew Allen).

A particularly important position on the board is the chair. The president needs to select a chair that has his confidence and trust. An executive secretary should be appointed who understands intelligence and can work well with the intelligence community. Ideally, the chair should live in the Washington, DC, metropolitan area to provide ready access to the president and the intelligence community. Not only should the chair be an expert in intelligence matters, but he or she should also have a flexible enough schedule to participate in the regular bimonthly meetings of the full board. The PFIAB can be most effective only if it has an activist chair—someone who organizes effectively, demonstrates leadership ability, knows how to run a meeting, commands respect, and speaks with authority.

Five specific recommendations should be considered:

- Two-year term limits should be maintained with no reappointments. The term limit is to ensure a rotation of members, thus guaranteeing that the board will always have a fresh outlook or approach.
- The president should consider giving the members of the Senate Intelligence Committee courtesy notification of prospective appointments to the board. Knowing that Congress is watching more closely may help prevent the PFIAB from becoming a political dumping ground for the president's friends and political supporters who have no other qualifications. Such a step ensures that candidates have the requisite qualifications for service and can pass the scrutiny of the Senate and public. The Senate notification process will also raise the visibility and importance of the PFIAB in the eyes of the administration, the intelligence community, and the public. Senate notifications can be arranged in a manner that would not undermine presidential prerogatives or executive privilege.
- A procedure needs to be established that defines criteria for selection to protect the selection process as much as possible from political needs and cronyism. Certain standards should always be adhered to: the board should be bipartisan and reflect certain expertise, and members should be appointed in six areas—technology, defense, national security, intelligence, management, and economics—and should be drawn from the private sector and the ranks of past practitioners. This diversity will guarantee a good cross section of bipartisan experts.
- Membership should be fixed. In the first years of its existence, the PFIAB appears to have operated efficiently with eight members. Board membership has ranged from a low of six in George H. W. Bush's administration to a high of twenty-one under Ronald Reagan. The board should not exceed ten members. Ten is large enough to ensure broad expertise on the board but small enough to keep it manageable. A larger board becomes unwieldy, preventing careful examination of issues. A smaller one facilitates a certain comfort level among the members that can aid in the board's functioning.
- The president should avoid appointing members who also concurrently have other management or staff jobs in the present

administration. Appointing individuals who have concurrent jobs inside the government has led the PFIAB to become involved in ongoing day-to-day operational or crisis issues and situations. Avoiding such involvement was a recommendation made to us by virtually every former official that we interviewed. If board members concurrently serve in other government positions, there is a risk that they would view intelligence issues through the lens of the political interests of the administration. They might also be led to represent the bureaucratic interests of some department or agency and, thereby, tarnish the public's image of the board as an independent advisory body.

These five points should be institutionalized in President Obama's PIAB, thus establishing a precedent to which future presidents will be expected to adhere.

Organization

Part of the problem the PFIAB faces is that its membership is part-time and cannot devote its full attention to issues. Currently, it meets for two days every month. While it is important to have highly qualified, expert members, this criterion carries some risks. Highly qualified members usually lead active and busy public lives, a fact that, along with the limited number of board meetings, further truncates the amount of time that they can devote to board business. It may be advisable, therefore, to create an executive committee consisting of the chair and two other members that can assemble quickly if necessary.

In extraordinary circumstances, the board must have the ability to shift into a full-time mode, if only with a few board members, staffers, and consultants working on a panel devoted to studying a critical and timely intelligence issue. In addition, at the discretion of the president, the chair or members should be included in NSC meetings—not to assume an operational role in crisis management, but rather to help the board better understand the nature and dynamics of such crises. In this manner, the PFIAB will have direct knowledge of a situation, and the advisory role of the board and the chair, in particular, can be more effective and timely.

Finally, the board should continue to use small panels to focus on specific issues. These panels could be composed of members, staff, or outside consultants depending on the issue being studied or reviewed. This organization will allow the board to stay current with pressing issues. In particular, the PFIAB should create a permanent science committee that can focus on the application of science and technology to intelligence needs. Such a body could provide guidance to efforts like the CIA-backed not-for-profit firm In-Q-Tel that invests in companies that provide future technologies of use to the intelligence community. This proposed science committee should have experts assigned to it from various government agencies who can meet on a regular basis to monitor technological changes potentially relevant to both the collection and the analysis of intelligence. It should also issue a report regarding the progress of science in the field of intelligence, which would be shared with the intelligence community. Technology is an important part of intelligence, but the current approach to integrating new technologies is too often ad hoc and prevents a detailed long-range examination.

Staff

The board's staff has been insufficient. An executive director and two or three staffers do not give the PIAB the resources to stay current with events and to adequately monitor implementation of its recommendations. The George W. Bush administration's PIAB staff of eight to ten was a step in the right direction. While the PIAB can draw on the personnel and resources of other agencies, this is not a substitute for a permanent staff that can enhance institutional memory and independence from bureaucratic influences. The board needs to have a core of employees hired by and working solely for it. It also needs to have an independent budget. About half the PIAB's staff should be career intelligence, homeland security, or law enforcement officers. But we agree with one former chair's recommendation that these staffers ought to leave their home agencies and *not* return after PIAB assignment. Additionally, outside consultants remain an important talent pool to draw on to provide needed expertise for specific studies or reviews.

Orientation Training

Even if new members have substantial intelligence expertise, they still need some form of systematic orientation. Newly appointed members already receive briefings about the intelligence community and the role of the PIAB. These briefings are conducted by the board staff and representatives of the various intelligence agencies. Still, a more formal introduction may be necessary because the board is a truly unique part of the intelligence community. This introduction should include briefings regarding legal issues, activities of past boards, and site visits. A broader introduction to the intelligence community, as well as formal functional and geographic briefings on world issues, would also help new members become more productive members of the president's team.

The IOB

President Obama's restoration of the IOB was welcomed by observers who had viewed Bush's measure as undermining the investigation of possible intelligence wrongdoing and, thus, condoning the administration's secretive and possibly illegal approaches to intelligence matters in the War on Terror.

In reality, neither Bush's nor Obama's steps bring much value in either direction. First, the IOB is composed of members of the PIAB; thus, nothing would prevent the PIAB from taking steps it saw as warranting administration attention. Indeed, even in George W. Bush's last EO, the IOB could bring to the president's attention issues it believed had not been brought to his attention by other officials. Indeed, the close personal relationship that often exists between some members of the PIAB and the president allows for a line of communication that no formal structure or barrier can impede. Second, as a part-time advisory body that meets infrequently and has few budgetary or personnel resources, the IOB (and the PIAB) would be hard-pressed to conduct serious investigations of criminal malfeasance. Finally, the statutory inspectors general of the various intelligence agencies and the House and Senate Intelligence committees have both the responsibility and the resources to conduct such investigations of the intelligence community. It is for these various reasons that we have recommended that the IOB be abolished. Given the oversight roles of the statutory inspector general and the House and Senate Intelligence committees, the IOB is duplicative. Moreover, since IOB members have been members of the PIAB, there is a temptation to draw the board into backward-looking assessments and operational matters. Ironically, eliminating the IOB will help strengthen the PIAB.

FUNCTIONAL

Feedback

The board's work can be facilitated by establishing a more formal follow-up procedure to monitor its recommendations. The PIAB has demonstrated that it can produce helpful studies and recommendations. A shortcoming in this process is the lack of consistent feedback. The board has no regular way of gauging the impact of its reports. A mechanism needs to be put in place whereby members or the president can be briefed regarding the impact of any report the board issues. This can be done either by a regular interagency review process or through an individual report by the agency in question.

Annual Report

The PIAB should issue its own annual report on intelligence. The report would examine the strengths and weaknesses of the intelligence community and suggest future goals. The board is in a good position to play this critical role. It has no institutional or bureaucratic turf to protect. It thus provides an excellent forum for an effective review of intelligence-related legislation, proposed intelligence directives, and other new initiatives in the intelligence community. In particular, this annual report ought to look ahead to identify key trends in technology or new modes of organization that might affect intelligence collection and analysis in the years to come.

Community Use

The board can also serve as a sounding board for estimating the usefulness of potential initiatives by individual intelligence agencies. It should take the pulse of the intelligence community in order to warn the White House of impending problems or looming issues. It may be beneficial for these agencies to submit their plans to the board for an impartial review before implementation. To fulfill that role, the PIAB must maintain extensive informal contact with the components of the intelligence community, such as the CIA and the Defense Intelligence Agency.

ROLE OF THE PRESIDENT AND THE WHITE HOUSE

Timing

The president should name a board early, possibly even during the transition phase of a new administration, to underscore for the intelligence community the importance the administration attaches to the board. It will also put in place a functioning body that can help frame and assess the president's policy options. It may be beneficial for the president-elect to meet with the PIAB to learn about the intelligence issues that he will be facing. The chair of the PIAB should have regular contact with the president-elect's transition team, just as regular foreign policy bureaucracies do. The chair may be retained in an advisory or ex officio position for a few months to help a new board adjust.

The President

The attitude of the president toward the PIAB and intelligence is critical, particularly now that the institutional growth of the national security and intelligence bureaucracy tends to squeeze the space available for such a part-time presidential advisory board. The extent to which the president really understands and is interested in national intelligence is an important factor in the success of the board. One former executive director emphasized that, unless the president appreciates intelligence and the role that the board can play in it, the board will not be effective. Indeed, the administration that needs the PIAB the most is often the one least likely to want it.

On the other hand, even a president who is not very interested in intelligence can be forced by international crises or domestic politics to use the board. As for the former, the Bay of Pigs led John F. Kennedy to move quickly to reconstitute the board, and 9/11 persuaded George W. Bush to listen to his board. As for the latter, it was, after all, the threat of congressional action that prompted Eisenhower to create the board in the first place, and it took Senator David Boren's prompting to get George H. W. Bush to reconstitute his board.

The fact that the PIAB's authority flows from the president makes it important for the board to have access to him. As another former executive director reminded us: "Other government officials believe you have power based upon your relationship with the president." To telegraph his support, the president should meet with the board early in the administration, even if only ceremonially. The chair of the PIAB should meet with the president every month for updates and feedback. The next president might even consider institutionalizing meetings with the board in the enabling EO to guarantee that attention be given to the PIAB at the highest levels, thereby reinforcing the board's authority and effectiveness within the intelligence community.

The NSC Adviser

The PIAB's relationship with national security advisers has not always been satisfactory. The meetings were, according to one former national security adviser, a "necessary duty" that occasionally degenerated into some individual members lecturing on what U.S. foreign policy should be—an issue outside the board's domain. There is also an inherent conflict between the board and the NSC because the board does not deal with operations; its role is analytic, focusing on examining what may have gone wrong, or prescriptive, suggesting how something in the intelligence community can be strengthened. The NSC staff is action driven: there is a need to deal with crises immediately. Accordingly, most national security advisers did not attach much importance to dealing with the board. A president and his national security adviser constantly face issues that warrant immediate policy attention and deal with agencies that can exercise direct influence and/or support.

In this environment, the PIAB appears irrelevant because it is not geared toward real-time action. It could, therefore, be dismissed as a useless drain on the time and resources of the White House staff. Thus, it behooves future administrations to establish a more formal link between the PIAB and the NSC so that the national security adviser can benefit from the members' views regarding developing initiatives. While these meetings occur now, we believe that there should be regular monthly meetings between the PIAB and the NSC Intelligence Directorate.

The president may also consider having the PIAB chair attend relevant NSC, cabinet, and White House meetings with members of Congress. As an outside observer, the chair can bring a unique perspective to these proceedings. According to a former national security adviser, simply having to meet regularly with the PIAB and its staff kept the NSC staff sharp and alert. Care needs to be taken, however, that any such meetings be limited to conceptual discussions to keep the PIAB separated from policy and operations.

Finally, the board must also be able to initiate the study or review of issues itself. It is important that the board, including its staff, have good working relationships with the NSC and its staff, but, in the end, the PIAB must retain its independence as a presidential advisory board.

Commission

To help institutionalize these recommendations, future presidents should consider setting up an independent panel to study the effectiveness of the PIAB and to make recommended changes. Admittedly, such changes might fit that particular president's view of intelligence and the role of the PIAB but not necessarily those of his successors. The recommendations of the panel, if accepted, can then be formalized in an EO. The prestige of the panel and the EO should then serve as a template for future presidents in structuring their own PIABs. A uniform structure regarding membership, selection, and meetings can be put in place that will guide all future PIABs.

Intelligence Studies

One of the ironies of the various scholarly and government assessments of the U.S. intelligence community over the years is that no in-depth study of the role of the PIAB has been undertaken. The board has historically resisted and even thwarted such efforts, defending, wrongly in our view, an overly broad and expansive definition of *executive privilege* that isolates the board from other executive branch agencies. This mind-set contributes to the inability of the intelligence community to fully realize the potentially valuable contribution that the PIAB can make. Future studies of the intelligence community need to include an analysis of the PIAB. Such classified in-house studies can help identify what the rest of the intelligence community seeks from the it. But, for this to happen, the board will have to fully cooperate in such efforts.

Conclusion

One of the board's strengths—but also a potential weakness—is that it is subject to the whims of each president. Previous presidents have used the board well, ignored it, politicized it, and even disbanded it. The value-added of the PIAB is that it can function outside the political, managerial, and bureaucratic world of government and the intelligence community. If properly staffed and focused on certain types of issues (such as the impact of new technologies or different modes of organization on the collection, analysis, and dissemination of intelligence), it can bring expertise not available in the community. Such a fresh perspective has been, and will continue to be, in our view, invaluable to presidents as they formulate and implement effective intelligence policies.

Acknowledgments and Disclaimer

This was a group project, with many different people involved at different stages in the research and drafting of various chapters. We thank, particularly, the members of the Bush School Spring 2006 PFIAB Capstone Team, including Eric Vela, Will Eyres, and other members who asked to remain anonymous, who researched and wrote early drafts of the historical cases. Adam Williams, Griffin Rozell, and Brandon Krueger of the Bush School of Government and Public Service, who also wrote drafts, and Melissa Curvino and Maria Petnuch of the University of Notre Dame served ably as research assistants. Ms. Rose Williams typed multiple drafts and Ms. Sally Dee Wade and Ms. Carol Arnette helped turn our tortured scribblings into prose.

We also wish to thank our outside experts—Loch K. Johnson of the University of Georgia and James Wirtz of the Naval Post-Graduate School—for their review of an earlier draft of the manuscript. Peri Arnold of the University of Notre Dame and the late Henry Y. K. Tom, formerly of the Johns Hopkins University Press, generously commented on a later draft of the manuscript.

We wish to thank the Richard Lounsbery Foundation for its generous financial support in underwriting this book. We are grateful to all who assisted with this challenging project.

Portions of this book were previously published as "The President's Intelligence Advisory Board," in *The Oxford Handbook of National Security Intelligence,* ed. Loch K. Johnson (New York: Oxford University Press, 2009), 172–88; and "Getting on Board: How an Obscure Panel Could Fix the U.S. Intelligence Community," Foreign Affairs.com, September 19, 2009. Both are reprinted here with permission.

Finally, we need to include the following standard disclaimer: "All statements of fact, opinion, or analysis expressed are those of the authors and do not reflect the official positions or views of the Central Intelligence Agency (CIA) or any other U.S. government agency. Nothing in the contents should be construed as asserting or implying U.S. government authentication of information or CIA endorsement of the authors' views. This material has been reviewed by the CIA to prevent the disclosure of classified information." In other words, any errors, factual or analytic, are our own.

Biographical Sketches of PFIAB Members

David Manker Abshire—Member 1981–1983

David Manker Abshire was born in Chattanooga, Tennessee, on April 11, 1926. He attended the University of Chattanooga briefly before joining the U.S. Army in 1945. During his time in the military, Abshire graduated with a bachelor's degree from the U.S. Military Academy in 1951 and was awarded a Bronze Star for service as a company commander and division assistant intelligence officer in the Korean War. After leaving the army in 1956, Abshire obtained his doctorate in history from Georgetown University in 1959. Abshire was the director of the American Enterprise Institute until 1962, when he cofounded the Center for Strategic and International Studies, a Washington, DC–based think tank and policy research institute then affiliated with Georgetown. In addition to working in the field of policy research, Abshire had extensive government experience. He served as assistant secretary of state for congressional affairs under President Richard Nixon. He also served on the Murphy Commission from 1973 until 1975, headed the U.S. Board for International Broadcasting during President Gerald Ford's tenure in office, and was on the Naval War College board. After Ronald Reagan's victory in 1980, Abshire headed the national security group transition office. He left the PFIAB in 1983 to become the U.S. ambassador to NATO.[1] Given this government experience, Abshire was a strong candidate for appointment to the board.

Stephen Ailes—Member 1976–1977

Stephen Ailes was born in Romney, West Virginia, on March 25, 1912. In 1933, he graduated from Princeton University before earning a law degree from West Virginia University in 1936. After law school, Ailes joined the District of Columbia and West Virginia bars. In addition to practicing law, Ailes was an assistant professor of law at West Virginia University from 1937 to 1940. In 1942, Ailes began his public service career on the legal staff of the Office of Price Administration, where he was promoted to assistant general counsel in 1946. The following year, Ailes became the counsel for the American Economic Mission in Greece. In 1961, President

John F. Kennedy appointed Ailes as undersecretary of the army. President Lyndon Johnson made Ailes secretary of the army in January 1964, a position he held until July 1965. On January 1, 1970, Ailes was appointed as the president and chief executive officer of the Association of American Railroads. In addition to the American Bar Association, he was a member of the National Institute of Social Sciences, the National Defense Transportation Association, the Washington Institute of Foreign Affairs, and the American Law Institute.[2] Given his national security experience, Ailes was a solid candidate for the board.

Gen. Lew Allen Jr.—Member 1990–1999

Lew Allen Jr. was born in Miami, Florida, on September 30, 1925. He graduated from the U.S. Military Academy and received his commission as a second lieutenant in the U.S. Air Force on June 4, 1946.[3] Serving as a pilot at Carswell Air Force Base in Fort Worth, Texas, Allen later became one of the air force's first qualified nuclear weaponeers. He enrolled at the University of Illinois for graduate study, earning his master's and doctorate in physics in 1952 and 1954. After graduation, Allen was transferred to Los Alamos National Laboratory, where he took part in nuclear tests in Nevada and Bikini Atoll.[4] Allen later served as the science adviser at Kirkland Air Force Base from 1957 to 1961 and in the Office of Special Technology at the Department of Defense from 1961 to 1965. He spent eight years in the office of the secretary of the air force, first as a deputy director for advanced plans, then as deputy director and director of space plans. During that time he was involved with the Dyna-Soar, Manned Orbital Laboratory, and Blue Gemini programs. After leaving the office of the secretary of the air force, Allen worked as director of the National Security Agency (NSA) at Fort Meade, MD, from 1973 until 1977. He was the first NSA director ever to testify before Congress. In 1977, he briefly worked as the commander of the Air Force Systems Command. Before being named chief of staff of the air force in 1978, Allen spent a few months as vice chief of staff. He remained chief of staff until July 1, 1982, when he retired from the air force and accepted positions as director of the Jet Propulsion Laboratory and vice president of the California Institute of Technology. His extensive background in physics and in space and technology with the Jet Propulsion Laboratory was a perfect fit for George H. W. Bush's more technically focused PFIAB.

George Whelan Anderson—Member 1969–1970; Chair 1970–1977

George Whelan Anderson was born in Brooklyn, New York, on December 15, 1906, and graduated from the U.S. Naval Academy in 1927. He served in the navy for thirty-six years, commanding several aircraft carriers and

Task Force 77 in the Taiwan Strait. He also commanded Carrier Division 6 and the Sixth Fleet. He became chief of naval operations under President Kennedy. Despite Admiral Anderson's successful management of the naval blockade of Cuba during the Cuban Missile Crisis, disagreements with Secretary of Defense Robert McNamara led to his retirement in 1963. President Kennedy appointed Anderson ambassador to Portugal from October 1963 until June 1966.[5] After leaving the navy, Anderson became chair of the Lamar Corporation, an outdoor advertising company, and served on several boards of directors. Anderson died on March 20, 1992. Given his naval background, Anderson was a strong candidate for board membership.

Martin Anderson—Member 1982–1985

Martin Anderson was born in Lowell, Massachusetts, on August 5, 1936. He attended Dartmouth College, where he received his bachelor's degree in 1957 and went on to earn his master's degree in engineering and business administration one year later. After receiving his Ph.D. in 1962, Anderson taught at Columbia University until 1968, when he became the director of research for Nixon's successful 1968 presidential campaign. He served in the Nixon administration as a special assistant until 1971, when he became the public interest director of the Federal Home Loan Bank in San Francisco. During his time in California, Anderson worked as an adviser to Ronald Reagan during both his 1976 and his 1980 presidential campaigns. He was also a member of the Commission on Crucial Choices for Americans, the Defense Manpower Commission, and the Committee on the Present Danger. After Reagan took office in 1981, he appointed Anderson as special assistant for policy development, though he dismissed him a year later. At the same time he was appointed to the PFIAB, Anderson also joined the Economic Policy Advisory Board.[6] While Anderson was a talented economist, he had little or no experience with intelligence, and his appointment seems to have been a consolation prize after his dismissal from the White House after only a year of service. Anderson was purged from the PFIAB during the 1985 Halloween Massacre.

Cresencio S. Arcos Jr.—Member 1999–2003

Cresencio S. Arcos Jr. was born in San Antonio, Texas, on November 10, 1943. He completed his B.A. at the University of Texas in 1966 and then attended the School of Advanced International Studies at the Johns Hopkins University, where he completed his M.A. in 1973.[7] Arcos served as a graduate research fellow at the University of Oregon's Institute of International Studies and then as a postgraduate student at the Institute of Sino-Soviet Studies at George Washington University. Arcos was appointed a Foreign Service officer and served in various public and cultural affairs positions at U.S. embassies in Leningrad, Sao Paulo, and Lisbon. In 1988, he was named the deputy assistant secretary of state for inter-American affairs. Arcos was appointed ambassador to Honduras from 1989 until 1993. In 1993, Arcos also served on the State Department's Task Force on the North American Free Trade Agreement. He served as the senior deputy assistant secretary of state for international narcotics and crime, until he retired from the Foreign Service in 1995. After briefly leaving government, Arcos returned to government service in 2003 as the director of international affairs for the newly formed Department of Homeland Security. In 2005, Arcos was promoted to be Homeland Security's assistant secretary for international affairs. In October 2006, Arcos retired from the Department of Homeland Security and joined the international law firm Kirkpatrick and Lockhart Preston Gates Ellis.[8] Arcos was a solid appointment to the board given his foreign affairs experience.

Leslie Cornelius Arends—Member 1976–1977

Leslie Cornelius Arends was born in Melvin, Illinois, on September 27, 1895. He was a student at Oberlin College in Ohio from 1912 to 1913 and received an LL.D. from Illinois Wesleyan University. After graduation, Arends served in the navy from 1918 to 1919.[9] In 1935, Arends was elected to Congress, and he served until 1974. He became the longest-serving whip in U.S. House of Representatives history, alternately serving as majority whip and minority whip for House Republicans from 1943 to 1974. Arends rose to become the minority ranking member of the House Armed Services Committee during the height of the Vietnam War. He died on July 16, 1985. Given his congressional experience, Arends was a reasonable appointment to the board.

Anne Legendre Armstrong—Chair 1981–1990

Anne Legendre Armstrong was born in New Orleans, Louisiana, on December 27, 1927.[10] In 1929, she graduated with a B.A. in English from Vassar College in Poughkeepsie, New York. While at Vassar, Armstrong worked on Harry Truman's reelection campaign. After his reelection in 1972, Nixon appointed her counselor to the president, which made her the first woman in American history to hold cabinet-level rank. After Nixon's departure, Armstrong served as the first female U.S. ambassador to the United Kingdom under President Ford.[11] In 1980, she returned to Washington to serve as cochair of the Reagan-Bush campaign before being appointed chair of the PFIAB in October 1981. She died on July 30, 2008. While Armstrong had a strong record of service for the Republican Party and extensive experience in domestic politics, her limited experience with intelligence issues suggests that President Reagan chose her—at least in part—for political reasons. Other senior officials, including National Security Adviser Richard V. Allen, opposed Armstrong's nomination to the PFIAB.[12] Anderson claimed that

Vice Chair Leo Cherne rolled his eyes whenever Armstrong spoke, while Edward Bennett Williams's biographer Evan Thomas wrote: "Many of the PFIAB members, including Williams, were disdainful of Armstrong behind her back."[13] Even some outside the PFIAB disagreed with Armstrong's appointment as chair. Then deputy director of operations at the CIA John McMahon said: "[Casey] didn't enjoy dealing with Anne Armstrong."[14] Despite these concerns, Armstrong remained as chair throughout both Reagan administrations. The support of Vice President Bush and Chief of Staff James Baker helped her overcome this opposition.[15] Another former senior official at the time also gave Armstrong high marks. He said that she "was outstanding and could be very persuasive."[16]

Leslie "Les" Aspin—Chair 1994–1995

Leslie "Les" Aspin was born in Milwaukee, Wisconsin, on July 21, 1938. He graduated from Yale in 1960. After earning his M.A. in economics, politics, and philosophy at Oxford in 1962, Aspin completed a Ph.D. in economics at the Massachusetts Institute of Technology. Aspin served as a captain in the U.S. Army from 1966 to 1968 and was assigned to the Pentagon undersecretary of defense McNamara. He left the military in 1968 and spent the next three years teaching economics at Marquette University and dabbling in Wisconsin politics. Aspin's election in 1971 as the representative for Wisconsin's First Congressional District to the U.S. House of Representatives marked the beginning of a twenty-two-year term that ended in 1993. Specializing in national security affairs in the House, Aspin quickly gained a reputation as a military expert. Aspin was appointed chair of the House Committee on Armed Services in 1985, where he supported the MX missile program and providing aid to Nicaraguan Contras. In 1991, Aspin broke with the Democratic Party when he authored a paper supporting President George H. W. Bush's decision to use military force to remove Iraq from Kuwait. During the 1992 presidential campaign, Aspin served as Bill Clinton's adviser on defense and national security issues.[17] Aspin was named as Clinton's first secretary of defense on January 21, 1993. Aspin stepped down as secretary of defense on February 3, 1994, after the disastrous U.S. military intervention in Somalia on October 3, 1993. In March of that same year, Aspin was approved as the head of the Commission on Roles and Capabilities of the United States Intelligence Community, a blue-ribbon panel tasked with investigating how to adapt the intelligence community to a changing post–Cold War world. Two months later, President Clinton named Aspin the chair of the PFIAB. Aspin suffered a stroke and died on May 21, 1995.[18] Given his academic training, his congressional focus on national security issues, and his service as secretary of defense, Aspin was a strong candidate for board membership.

Zoë Baird—Member 1993–2001

Zoë Baird was born in Brooklyn, New York, on June 20, 1952. After completing her B.A. at the University of California, Berkeley, in 1974, Baird stayed in California to complete her J.D. three years later. After law school, Baird spent two years as a law clerk for the Honorable Albert Wollenberg of San Francisco. In 1979, Baird became an attorney and adviser in the Office of Legal Counsel with the U.S. Department of Justice. In 1980, Baird became an associate legal counsel in the White House. After Ronald Reagan's election, Baird left government and joined the law firm O'Melveny and Myers as an associate in 1981 and within five years had become a partner. In 1986, Baird became legal counsel and a staff executive for General Electric in Fairfield, Connecticut. Four years later, Baird was named vice president and general counsel for Aetna Life and Casualty insurance company in Hartford and was promoted to senior vice president and general counsel in 1993.[19] At the beginning of his first term in the White House, President Clinton nominated Baird to be the first female attorney general in U.S. history. During the course of congressional testimony, Baird chose to withdraw her nomination after revelations that she employed two undocumented Peruvians in her home from 1990 to 1992.[20] Shortly thereafter, Baird was named to President Clinton's PFIAB as well as to the International Competition Policy Advisory Committee to the Attorney General, likely in compensation for the failed effort to make her attorney general.[21]

Howard Henry Baker Jr.—Member 1985–1990

Howard Henry Baker Jr. was born in Huntsville, Tennessee, on November 15, 1925. After graduating from high school, he joined the navy and studied engineering at the Naval Academy before receiving his commission in the summer of 1945. Baker received his law degree in 1949 from the University of Tennessee, where he served as student body president.[22] In 1964, Baker ran for the U.S. Senate from Tennessee as a Republican and was soundly defeated in the Johnson landslide that propelled many Democrats into office. Two years later, he was victorious and served three terms in the Senate. During the Carter administration, Baker helped secure passage of the Panama Canal Treaty.[23] Ronald Reagan considered Baker for the position of director of central intelligence but instead appointed him to the board in 1985.[24] He left the PFIAB in 1987 to become President Reagan's chief of staff. On leaving that position in 1988, Baker returned to the board and stayed for the remainder of the administration. Baker was largely, but not exclusively, a political appointment to the board.

William Oliver Baker—Member 1957–1977, 1981–1990

William Oliver Baker was born in Chestertown, Maryland, on July 15, 1915. In 1935, he received a B.S. in physical chemistry from Washington College, Maryland. In 1938, he completed a Ph.D. in physical chemistry from Princeton, researching in the field of solid-state physics. From 1937 to 1938, he was a member of the Harvard University Society of Fellows and then earned a Procter Fellowship at Princeton from 1938 to 1939. In May 1939, Baker joined Bell Labs, eventually becoming head of Bell Telephone Laboratories' Polymer Research and Development Department in 1948, vice president of research in 1955, president from 1973 to 1979, and then chair of the board until retiring in 1980. Baker first became involved with national security affairs during the Eisenhower administration. In 1958, his "Baker Report" outlined the role that technology would play in intelligence-gathering efforts. Baker was particularly influential in promoting the increased use of computers and reconnaissance satellites. Following the issuance of the Baker Report, Eisenhower tasked Baker with drafting a plan for the creation of the Defense Communications Agency. This plan would be implemented during the Kennedy administration. In addition to serving on the PFIAB from 1957 to 1977 and from 1981 to 1990, Baker also served on the President's Science Advisory Committee. He died on October 31, 2005.[25] Given his scientific background and his work in the defense-related private sector and for the U.S. government, Baker was one of the strongest candidates for board membership in its history.

James Love Barksdale—Member 2001–2009

James Love Barksdale was born in Jackson, Mississippi, on January 24, 1943. He graduated from the University of Mississippi in 1965 with a bachelor's degree in business administration. Barksdale spent most of his professional life in the private sector, serving as the chief information officer of Federal Express, president and chief operating officer of McCaw Cellular Communications, and president and CEO of Netscape Communications, holding the latter position until Netscape was acquired by America Online in 1999.[26] In April 1999, he founded the Barksdale Group—a private investment management company for Internet-centric companies.[27] Barksdale also served as a special adviser for the General Atlantic Partners and currently serves as the cochair of the Markle Foundation Task Force on National Security in the Information Age.[28] Barksdale appears to have been a political appointee to the board in view of his lack of intelligence-related experience.

Robert Hilliard Barrow—Member 1984–1985

Robert Hilliard Barrow was born in Baton Rouge, Louisiana, on February 12, 1922. He attended Louisiana State University briefly before joining the

U.S. Marines in 1943. Commissioned as a second lieutenant, Barrow led an American unit paired with Chinese guerrillas in Japanese-occupied China during World War II.[29] He also served in the Korean War as a rifle company commander, and from 1952 to 1953 he led a covert operations team off the coast of China.[30] After graduating from the National War College, Barrow commanded the Ninth Marines regiment in Vietnam during 1968–69. He subsequently commanded three Marine Corps bases and the Fleet Marine Force in the Atlantic before being promoted to assistant commandant of the Marine Corps in 1978 and then commandant in 1979, a position he held until his retirement in 1983.[31] Though one of the less well-known members of President Reagan's PFIAB, General Barrow did have extensive military experience and direct experience with covert operations. Barrow attended board meetings regularly but, in Vice Chair Cherne's view, did not contribute much to the board's activities.[32] He died on October 30, 2008.

Richard L. Bloch—Member 1996–1998

Richard L. Bloch was born in Pontiac, Michigan, on June 12, 1929. He earned his B.S. from the University of Chicago in 1949 and did postgraduate work at the University of Arizona from 1950 to 1952. From 1951 to 1953, Bloch served in the U.S. Army, leaving service with the rank of first lieutenant. Bloch set up his own real estate development company in Arizona and California in 1957. Bloch went on to have a successful business career, becoming the president and controlling partner of the Phoenix Suns in 1968, serving as director of Filmways in 1969, and eventually becoming CEO of that company. He subsequently purchased an NBC affiliate station in Tucson in 1973.[33] In addition to his business career, Bloch was active in politics, even being invited to the White House for coffee with other financial supporters of the Democratic National Committee.[34] Bloch's regular contributions of large sums of money—anywhere from $500 to $25,000—to individual Democratic candidates and donations of up to $100,000 to the Democratic national convention appear to have been his primary qualifications for membership on President Clinton's PFIAB.[35]

Alfred S. Bloomingdale—Member 1981–1982

Alfred S. Bloomingdale, the grandson of the founder of Bloomingdale's department store, was born in New York, New York, on April 15, 1916. He graduated from Brown University in 1938 and joined the family's business as an assistant merchandise manager. Bloomingdale then made the move to show business, producing first on Broadway and then in Hollywood.[36] After moving to California in 1950, Bloomingdale set up a credit card called Dine and Sign, which later merged with Diner's Club. Bloomingdale became vice president and president and eventually served as chair of the board of Diner's Club.[37] Bloomingdale, who first met Ronald and Nancy Reagan during the 1964 Republican national convention, donated $10,000 to Reagan's campaign in 1980.[38] His close personal and political ties to the Reagans, rather than government and intelligence experience, appear to have been the main rationale for President Reagan's appointment of him to the PFIAB. Bloomingdale died on August 20, 1982, after less than a year on the board.

David Boren—Cochair, 2009–Present

David Boren was born in Washington, DC, on April 21, 1941. He graduated from Yale University in 1963. He was named a Rhodes Scholar and earned a master's degree in politics, philosophy, and economics from Oxford University in 1965. In 1968, he received a law degree from the University of Oklahoma College of Law. He taught for four years in the Department of Political Science at Oklahoma Baptist University, serving as chair of the Division of Social Sciences. He was governor of Oklahoma from 1974 through 1978. He was elected to the U.S. Senate in 1979, served on the Senate Finance and Agriculture Committees, and was the longest-serving chair of the Senate Select Committee on Intelligence. He was also the author of the National Security Education Act in 1992, which provides scholarships for study abroad and for learning additional languages. He is currently the thirteenth president of the University of Oklahoma, having assumed the position in November 1994. Given his experience in Congress with national security and intelligence issues, Boren was a strong candidate for board membership.[39]

Frank Borman—Member 1981–1982

Frank Borman was born in Gary, Indiana, on March 14, 1928. Borman graduated from the U.S. Military Academy in 1950 and was commissioned as a second lieutenant in the air force. He served in a number of assignments before becoming an instructor in thermodynamics and fluid dynamics at the U.S. Military Academy in 1957. He then served as an instructor at the Aerospace Research Pilots School until 1962.[40] In the mid-1960s, Borman made the move to NASA as an astronaut, serving as the command pilot on Gemini 7 in 1965, which successfully rendezvoused with Gemini 6 in space. He also piloted Apollo 8, the first lunar orbital mission. After he retired from space travel and flying in 1970, Borman became a vice president at Eastern Airlines and later served as CEO and chair of the board.[41] Despite these impressive professional achievements, Borman had little or no intelligence experience and was probably selected for appointment to the board more as a result of his national prominence than for the specific contribution he could make to the PFIAB. However, Borman did have a unique understanding of aeronautics and space that may have been useful on matters involving space and intelligence. Borman resigned from the board in 1982 in the wake of the financial crisis that engulfed Eastern Airlines that year.

Denis Alan Bovin—Member 2006–2010

Denis Alan Bovin was born in New York, New York, on November 4, 1947. After completing a B.S. degree at the Massachusetts Institute of Technology in 1969, Bovin completed his M.B.A. at Harvard University in 1971. Bovin has worked in finance in the private sector, most recently as director of the BISYS Group and vice chair for investment banking and senior managing director of Bear Stearns. Bovin is a member of the Council of Foreign Relations and has served as a consultant to both the Defense Science Board and the Defense Business Board—which advise the secretary of defense, the chairman of the Joint Chiefs of Staff, and other senior defense executives.[42] In light of his service on two defense-related advisory boards, Bovin was a reasonable candidate for appointment to the board.

William Ralph Brody—Member 2002–2005

William Ralph Brody was born in Stockton, California, on January 4, 1944. Brody received B.S. and M.S. degrees in electrical engineering from the Massachusetts Institute of Technology in 1965 and 1966. In 1970, Brody earned his M.D. and in 1975 completed a Ph.D. in electrical engineering—both at Stanford University. Brody subsequently worked in the medical, electrical engineering, and biomedical engineering fields in both academe and the public sector. In 1987, he became the chief radiologist at Johns Hopkins Hospital and worked in a variety of faculty and staff positions at the university. Brody took a short hiatus from Johns Hopkins between 1994 and 1996 when he served as provost for the University of Minnesota Academy Health Center. In 1996, Brody was named the thirteenth president of Johns Hopkins University.[43] While he lacked government experience, Brody's scientific and academic background nonetheless made him a solid appointment to the board.

David Kirkpatrick Este Bruce—Member 1956–1957

The son of U.S. senator William Cabell Bruce, David Kirkpatrick Este Bruce was born in Baltimore, Maryland, on February 12, 1898. He attended Princeton, the University of Virginia, and law school at the University of Maryland. Bruce served in the state House of Delegates for Maryland (1924–26) and Virginia (1939–42). He was an Office of Strategic Services (the precursor to the CIA) officer between 1941 and 1945. However, he spent much of his professional career as a U.S. diplomat, holding the post of ambassador to France (1949–52), Germany (1957–59), the United Kingdom (1961–69), and China (1973–74). Bruce was an active member of the Democratic Party, and, thus, his appointment by President Eisenhower to the PBCFIA was clearly an effort to make the board truly bipartisan, but Bruce also had solid credentials in intelligence and diplomacy. He died on December 5, 1977.[44]

John Shelby Bryan—Member 1999–2001

John Shelby Bryan was born in Houston, Texas, on March 21, 1946.[45] He received his B.A. and J.D. from the University of Texas and his M.B.A. from Harvard University. Bryan was a pioneer in experimental cellular frequencies and personal communication service frequency provision and created Millicom—one of the largest cellular companies in the world.[46] Throughout the 1990s, Bryan was one of the top fund-raisers for Clinton's presidential campaigns, including raising $1.5 million for Democratic congressional candidates in 1997, before Clinton appointed him to the PFIAB in 1999—making him a likely political appointment given his lack of any relevant intelligence credentials.[47]

Zbigniew Brzezinski—Member 1988–1989

Zbigniew Brzezinski, the son of a Polish diplomat, was born in Warsaw, Poland, on March 28, 1928. He lived in France and Germany as a child before moving to Canada, where he graduated from McGill University with his bachelor's degree in 1949 and his master's degree in 1950. He received his doctorate from Harvard in 1953 and became a U.S. citizen five years later. Brzezinski then worked as a research fellow at the Russian Research Center at Harvard University until 1956, when he became an assistant professor of government. After being denied tenure at Harvard, he moved to Columbia University in 1960 as an associate professor of public law and government.[48] After leaving the faculty of Columbia University in 1962, Brzezinski became the director of the Institute for International Change and an adviser to the Kennedy and Johnson administrations. Brzezinski was subsequently the presidential candidate Hubert Humphrey's foreign policy adviser. In 1973, he became the director of the Trilateral Commission, a group of Western European, Japanese, and American businesspeople, academics, and political leaders dedicated to strengthening trans-Atlantic and trans-Pacific ties. Jimmy Carter made Brzezinski his national security adviser in 1977. After leaving government in 1981, Brzezinski returned to Columbia University as a full professor and became a counselor at the Center for Strategic and International Studies.[49] Even though the Carter administration did not reconstitute the PFIAB, Brzezinski was a proponent of the board, attending at least one PFIAB meeting before he was formally appointed to the board by Reagan. He left the board when George H. W. Bush reorganized it in 1990.

W. Glenn Campbell—Member 1981–1990; Intelligence Oversight Board Chair 1981–1990

W. Glenn Campbell was born in Ontario, Canada, on April 29, 1924. He attended college at the University of Western Ontario and received his doctorate in economics from Harvard in 1948. He remained at Harvard as a teaching fellow and later a professor.[50] In 1960, Campbell became the director of the Hoover Institution at Stanford University on the recommendation of the former president and Ray Moley, an adviser to President Franklin Delano Roosevelt. Campbell came to know Ronald Reagan during the latter's campaign for governor of California and became a member of Reagan's informal group of advisers known as the "Kitchen Cabinet." Campbell later worked as an adviser for Senator Barry Goldwater's 1964 presidential campaign. In 1968, Reagan appointed Campbell to a sixteen-year term as a regent of the University of California. During the Nixon and Ford administrations, Campbell served on the President's Commission on White House Fellows and the National Science Board.[51] Despite scoring poorly on Vice Chair Leo Cherne's grade sheet, he remained on the board throughout the Reagan administrations owing to his long friendship with Reagan.[52] Campbell died on November 24, 2001.

Roel C. Campos—Member 2009–Present

Roel Campos was born in Harlingen, Texas, in 1949. He received an appointment to the U.S. Air Force Academy and then went on to earn an M.B.A. from the University of California, Los Angeles, and a J.D. from Harvard Law School. He served in the U.S. Air Force as a procurement officer. On discharge from the air force, Campos was named a federal prosecutor in the U.S. Attorney's Office in Los Angeles. Campos left government service for a time to found the Houston-based El Dorado Communications broadcasting company. From 2002 to 2007, Campos served on the Securities and Exchange Commission. He is currently partner in charge of the Washington, DC, office of the law firm Cooley Godward Kronish. Given his lack of experience with intelligence affairs, Campos appears to be primarily a political appointee to the board.[53]

Ann Z. Caracristi—Member 1993–2001

Ann Z. Caracristi was born in Bronxville, New York, on February 1, 1921. In 1942, she graduated with a B.A. from Russell Sage College in Troy, New York.[54] Caracristi pursued advanced graduate work at the Federal Executive Institute.[55] She joined the Army Signal Intelligence Service in 1942 as a cryptanalyst, marking the beginning of a long career in signals intelligence. Little information is available about her early career at the National Security Agency (NSA), but in 1975 she become the first woman in NSA history to reach the rank of GS-18, and in 1980 she became the first woman to be named NSA deputy director.[56] After her retirement from the NSA in 1982, Caracristi served as a member of the Chief of Naval Operations Executive Panel from October 1982 to September 1991. In addition to her service on the board, Caracristi also served for a short time under PFIAB chair Aspin on the Commission on the Roles and Capabilities of the U.S. Intelligence

Community, which later became known as the Aspin-Brown Commission when former secretary of defense Harold Brown took over its chairmanship after Aspin's death on May 21, 1995.[57] Given her long career in the intelligence community, Caracristi was a strong candidate for board membership.

William Joseph Casey—Member 1976–1977

William Joseph Casey was born in Queens, New York, on March 13, 1913. He graduated from Fordham University with a B.S. in 1934 and St. John's University with a LL.B. in 1937. After law school, Casey was commissioned into the U.S. Naval Reserve in 1943 and served in the Office of Strategic Services, becoming the chief of the Special Intelligence Branch in the European Theater of Operations between 1944 and 1945. After the war, Casey served as counsel to the law firm Rogers and Wells. He remained active with the U.S. government as chair of the Securities and Exchange Commission from 1971 to 1973, undersecretary of state for economic affairs from 1973 to 1974, and president and chair of the Export-Import Bank of the United States from 1974 to 1976. Casey served as the former chair of the Board of Editors of his friend Leo Cherne's Research Institute of America; he was a past member of the General Advisory Committee for Arms Control, the President's Task Force for International Development, and the Commission on the Organization of the Government for the Conduct of Foreign Policy (the Murphy Commission). Casey died on May 6, 1987, while serving as the director of central intelligence during the Reagan administration.[58] Casey obviously had strong credentials for board membership.

Leo Cherne—Member 1973–1977, Vice Chair 1981–1990

Leo Cherne was born in New York, New York, on September 8, 1912. In 1931, he graduated from New York University before earning an LL.B. from New York Law School in 1934. In 1936, Cherne founded the Research Institute of America and served as its executive director. Cherne was also a practicing attorney and held numerous leadership positions: chair of the Executive Committee of Freedom House from 1946 to 1976, chair of the International Rescue Committee since 1951, and chair of the Lawyers' Cooperative Publishing Company. He was on the faculty of the Georgetown School of Foreign Service, the New School for Social Research, and the Industrial College of the Armed Forces. In addition to Cherne's private-sector and academic career, he also served six presidents in multiple capacities. He served as an army and navy industrial war planner, an economic adviser to General MacArthur in Japan, a public member of President Johnson's Select Committee on Western Hemisphere Immigration, and a member of President Nixon's U.S. Advisory Commission on International Education and Cultural Affairs (which he chaired until 1976) and was a member of the Board of Advisers at the National Defense University. Cherne famously challenged Senator Joseph McCarthy in a televised debate in which he defended Secretary of Defense General George Marshall against charges of treason.[59] Cherne is regarded justifiably as one of the strongest nontechnical members of the board during its entire history.

Clark McAdams Clifford—Member 1961–1963, Chair 1963–1968

Clark McAdams Clifford was born in Fort Scott, Kansas, on December 25, 1906. He received an LL.B. from Washington University in St. Louis in 1928. After graduation, Clifford began working at the law firm Holland, Lashley, and Donnell in St. Louis, where he became partner in 1938. Interrupting his law career in 1944, Clifford served as a captain in the U.S. Naval Reserve. From 1946 to 1950, Clifford served as special counsel to the president before returning as a senior partner to his law firm, Clifford and Miller. From 1968 to 1969, Clifford served as President Johnson's secretary of defense before returning as a senior partner to his law firm, where he worked until his retirement in 1991. Clifford was awarded the Presidential Medal of Freedom in 1969 and died on October 10, 1998.[60] Despite Clifford's extensive government service, his appointment began the period of the board's overt politicization.

John Bowden Connally—Member 1970–1977

One of eight children, John Bowden Connally was born in Floresville, Texas, on February 27, 1917. After receiving both his bachelor's and his law degrees from the University of Texas, Connally joined the U.S. Navy as a flight director aboard aircraft carriers. After leaving the navy, Connally worked as campaign manager for Lyndon Johnson during his successful bid for the U.S. Senate. Connally also managed Johnson's failed campaign for the Democratic presidential nomination in 1960 and his successful presidential run in 1964. In 1961, he served as President Kennedy's secretary of the navy before stepping down to run for governor of Texas in 1962. Though he started his political career as a Democrat, Connally was close to President Nixon, serving as his secretary of the Treasury from 1971 through 1972. He sought the Republican presidential nomination in 1980 but was defeated by Ronald Reagan. Connally died on June 15, 1993.[61] Connally clearly represented a political appointment to the board.

Richard L. Conolly—Member 1956–1961

Richard L. Conolly was born in Waukegan, Illinois, on April 26, 1892. Conolly studied at Lake Forest Academy from 1906 to 1909 and received his B.S. from the U.S. Naval Academy in 1914 and his M.S. from Columbia University in 1922. He attended the U.S. Naval War College and received his LL.D. from Muhlenberg College and Villanova University. Conolly was a highly decorated admiral who served on destroyers during World War I and II. He commanded a destroyer squadron at the time of the Japanese attack on Pearl Harbor and commanded the task force that took back Guam from the Japanese in July 1944. He attended the Paris Peace Conference in 1946 and served as commander in chief, U.S. Naval Forces, East Atlantic, and Mediterranean, until 1950. Conolly served on the staffs of the U.S. Naval Academy and the Naval War College, becoming president of the latter from 1950 to 1953, before becoming president of Long Island University in 1953. Conolly was also a member of the Clark Task Force. He died on March 1, 1962.[62] Conolly was a reasonable candidate for the board given his military background.

Admiral William J. Crowe—Chair 1993–1994

William J. Crowe was born in La Grange, Kentucky, on January 2, 1925. He graduated from the U.S. Naval Academy at Annapolis in 1946—in the same class as future president Jimmy Carter and future director of central intelligence Stansfield Turner. Crowe subsequently earned an M.A. in education from Stanford in 1956 and a Ph.D. in politics from Princeton in 1965. Crowe spent most of his navy career serving in Washington, DC. In the mid-1950s, he served as the assistant naval aide to President Eisenhower's White House. Crowe spent five years at sea serving as the executive officer of the USS *Wahoo* from 1957 to 1959 and from 1960 to 1962 commanding the USS *Trout*.[63] Crowe joined the staff of the chief of naval operations in the Pentagon in 1965 but then served as the senior adviser to the Vietnamese navy riverine force in the Mekong Delta. After his tour in Vietnam, Crowe returned to the Department of Defense, where he was director of the East Asia and Pacific Region element of the Office of the Secretary of Defense until 1976. From 1976 to 1977, Crowe was based in Bahrain as the commander of U.S. naval forces in the Middle East. After being promoted to vice admiral and serving as the deputy chief of naval operations for plans, policy, and operations, Crowe was appointed as the commander in chief of NATO forces in Southern Europe in Naples in 1980. In 1983, Crowe was designated the commander in chief of U.S. Pacific naval forces. Crowe became the eleventh chairman of the Joint Chiefs of Staff in 1985.[64] After two terms as chair, Crowe retired from the navy in 1989. Crowe spent the next five years as a professor of geopolitics at the University of Oklahoma and as a counselor and scholar at the Center for Strategic and International Studies. Crowe chaired Clinton's PFIAB from its inception in 1993 until 1994, when he was named U.S. ambassador to the United Kingdom and Northern Ireland, a post he held until 1997.[65] Crowe died on October 18, 2007. In view of his long and distinguished military career, Crowe was a very strong candidate for board membership.

Arthur Boggess Culvahouse—Member 2005–2010

Arthur Boggess Culvahouse was born in Athens, Tennessee, on July 4, 1948. After graduating from the University of Tennessee in 1970 with a B.S., Culvahouse was a Root-Tilden Scholar at New York University's School of Law, where he earned his J.D. in 1973. From 1973 to 1976, Culvahouse was the chief legislative assistant and counsel to U.S. Senator Howard H. Baker Jr. In 1987, Culvahouse was named counsel to President Ronald Reagan, whom he advised on a range of issues, including the Iran-Contra investigations, the legal aspects of the Intermediate-Range Nuclear Forces Treaty, and the Supreme Court nominations of Robert Bork and Anthony Kennedy. Culvahouse also chaired the Committee on War Powers and the President's Committee for Federal Judicial Nominations. In 1989, Culvahouse returned to private practice with his former firm, O'Melveny and Myers, and in 2000 became the chair and CEO. Culvahouse also served as a member of the Federal Advisory Committee on Nuclear Failsafe and Risk Reduction, the Supreme Court Fellows Commission, and the Counterintelligence Advisory Panel to the U.S. Senate Select Committee on Intelligence.[66] Given his White House experience related to national security affairs, Culvahouse was a plausible candidate for board membership.

Colgate Whitehead Darden Jr.—Member 1957–1961

Colgate Whitehead Darden was born in Southampton County, Virginia, on February 11, 1897. He earned a B.A. from the University of Virginia, an M.A. and an LL.B. from Columbia University, and a Carnegie Fellowship at Oxford University. He served with the French army (1916–1917) during World War I and later as a lieutenant in the U.S. Marine Corps Air Service. As a Democrat, Darden first served as a U.S. representative before becoming governor of Virginia in 1942, a post that he held until 1946. He was president of the University of Virginia for over a decade (1947–1959). Darden was also a U.S. delegate to the Tenth General Assembly of the United Nations (1955), a member of the President's Board of Consultants on Mutual Security, and a presidential appointee to the Commission on National Goals (1960). He died on June 9, 1981, in Norfolk, Virginia.[67] Given his military and political experience, Darden was a strong candidate for board membership.

Robert Addison Day Jr.—Member 2001–2005

Robert Addison Day Jr. was born in Los Angeles, California, in 1943. Day graduated from Claremont McKenna College in 1965 with a B.S. in economics. He began his career with White Weld and Company in New York but branched off in 1971 and founded the Trust Company of the West, where he served as chair of the board of trustees and CEO. Day has also been a trustee of the Brookings Institute, a member of the Council on Foreign Relations, and a member of the Center for Strategic and International Studies.[68] Day was a long-time supporter and fund-raiser for George W. Bush, and in both the 2000 and the 2004 presidential campaigns he was named a "Bush Pioneer" for having raised $100,000 for each campaign.[69] This political support appears to have been Day's only qualification for the board.

John M. Deutch—Member 1990–1993

John M. Deutch was born in Brussels, Belgium, on July 27, 1938. He became a U.S. citizen in 1946 and received his bachelor's degree from Amherst College in 1961. He attended the Massachusetts Institute of Technology (MIT), earning a doctorate in physical chemistry in 1965. During graduate school, Deutch worked as a systems analyst with the Office of the Secretary of Defense.[70] After finishing his doctorate, Deutch received a fellowship with the National Academy of Sciences from 1966 to 1967 before joining the faculty at Princeton University. Deutch stayed at Princeton only three years before returning in 1970 to teach at MIT, where he was a Guggenheim Fellow in 1974 and became the chair of the Chemistry Department in 1976. In 1977, he returned to Washington as the director of the Office of Energy Research, and, in 1979, he became the acting assistant secretary of energy for technology. Later that year, Deutch became undersecretary of energy, a post he held until his return to MIT in 1980. He served as the dean of science at MIT until 1985, when he was named provost.[71] In 1974, he chaired the advisory panel on chemistry at the National Science Foundation. He also served as a member of the President's Nuclear Safety Oversight Committee, the Defense Science Policy Board, the Army Science Advisory Panel, the White House Science Council, and the President's Commission on Strategic Forces.[72] Deutch stayed on the PFIAB throughout the George H. W. Bush presidency. Under President Clinton, he served as undersecretary of defense for acquisitions and technology (1993–1994), as deputy secretary of defense (1994–1995), and finally as the director of central intelligence (1995–1996).[73] Given his scientific credentials and significant government experience, Deutch was a very strong candidate for board membership.

William O. DeWitt—Member 2005–2010

William O. DeWitt was born in St. Louis, Missouri, on August 31, 1941. DeWitt completed a B.A. in economics at Yale University in 1963 and an M.B.A. two years later at Harvard University. DeWitt founded Reynolds, DeWitt and Company and currently serves as its president.[74] During the 1990s, DeWitt joined George W. Bush in several large oil and professional baseball ownership ventures and became the principal owner of the St. Louis Cardinals major league baseball team in 1996. DeWitt was also a consistent and successful fund-raiser for President Bush and raised $100,000 for the

2000 campaign and $200,000 for the 2004 reelection campaign.[75] This, combined with his lack of relevant professional experience, makes it likely he was a political appointment to the board.

James Harold Doolittle—Member 1956–1963

James Harold "Jimmy" Doolittle was born in California on December 14, 1896. He received an A.B. from the University of California in 1922. He earned an M.S. in 1924 and a Sc.D. in aeronautical engineering from the Massachusetts Institute of Technology (MIT) in 1925. Doolittle served as an army aviator from 1917 to 1930 and taught aerospace engineering at MIT in 1925. From 1930 to 1940, he was the manager of the Aviation Department of Shell Petroleum. In 1934, Doolittle was appointed to the Baker Board, officially known as the Army Investigation Committee. In 1940, Doolittle returned to the Army Air Force, rising to the rank of major general by 1942 and lieutenant general in 1944. He is most famous for leading the famous "Doolittle Raid" to bomb Japan, for which he received the Congressional Medal of Honor. Doolittle subsequently commanded the Twelfth Air Force in North Africa, the Strategic Air Force, the Fifteenth Air Force, and the Eighth Air Force before going on inactive duty in 1946. He served as vice president of Shell Oil from 1946 to 1958 before serving as chair of the board for Space Technology Labs from 1959 to 1962. In 1954, he headed the Doolittle Commission that investigated the covert action activities of the CIA. His other service included adviser to the Commission on National Security Organization, chair of the President's Airport Commission (1952), and membership on the Stassen Disarmament Commission (1955), the Air Force Science Advisory Board (1955–58), the Defense Science Board (1957–58), the President's Science Advisory Committee (1957–58), and the National Aerospace and Space Council (1958). Doolittle died on September 27, 1993.[76] Given his military and high-level government experience, Doolittle was a strong candidate for board appointment.

Dr. Sidney D. Drell—Member 1993–2001

Sidney D. Drell was born in Atlantic City, New Jersey, on September 13, 1926.[77] He received his B.S. from Princeton University in 1946 and completed his M.S. and Ph.D. at the University of Illinois in 1947 and 1949, respectively. He was an assistant professor at the Massachusetts Institute of Technology from 1953 to 1956. Drell was named the Stanford Linear Accelerator Center's deputy director in 1969—a position he retained until his retirement in 1998—and also was the executive head of Stanford's theoretical physics program. He was named codirector of Stanford University's Center for International Security and Arms Control in 1983, a post he held until 1989.[78] Drell served as a consultant for the Office of Science and Technology in the Executive Office of the President in 1963. In 1966,

Drell joined the President's Scientific Advisory Committee. He also served as a technical consultant to the U.S. Arms Control and Disarmament Agency and the National Security Council from 1969 to 1981 and from 1973 to 1981. From 1974 to 1976, Drell served as a technical expert member of the U.S. Defense Science Board Task Force. Beginning in 1974, Drell was a member of the High Energy Physics Advisory Panel (HEPAP) at the U.S. Department of Energy, which he chaired from 1974 to 1982. Drell was also chair of the HEPAP subpanel on superconducting super collider physics in 1990 and the subpanel on the vision of the future of high energy physics in 1994. From 1975 to 1991 Drell served as a consultant to the Office of Technology Assessment in the U.S. Congress and from 1977 to 1982 served as a consultant for the Office of Science and Technology Policy. In 1978, Drell became a member of the Energy Research Advisory Board for the U.S. Department of Energy and consultant to the U.S. Senate Select Committee on Intelligence, positions he held until 1980 and 1982, respectively. From 1990 to 1991, Drell was the chair of the House Armed Services Committee Panel on Nuclear Weapons Safety. He also served as a member of the Director's Advisory Committee at Lawrence Livermore National Laboratory until 1993. Beginning in 1990, Drell served for three years as the chair of the Technology Review Panel for the Senate Select Committee on Intelligence. Drell then followed a one-year term as the chair for the JASON Study for the Department of Energy (DOE) on science-based stockpile stewardship in 1994 with a one-year commitment as the chair of the JASON Study on Nuclear Testing for the DOE in 1995.[79] In 1998, Drell was a member of the Commission on Maintaining U.S. Nuclear Weapons Expertise and from 1992 until 2001 served as a member of the Nonproliferation Advisory Panel. In 2001, Drell was named both the chair of the Senior Review Board for the Intelligence Technology Innovation Center and a member of the Advisory Committee to the fledgling National Nuclear Security Administration of the DOE.[80] In view of his unique combination of outstanding academic credentials and high-level government service, Drell was an ideal candidate for the board.

Thomas F. Eagleton—Member 1992–2000

Thomas F. Eagleton was born in St. Louis, Missouri, on September 4, 1929. He enlisted in the U.S. Navy and served on active duty from 1948 to 1949. After his discharge, Eagleton graduated with a B.A. from Amherst College in 1950 and an LL.B. from Harvard in 1953. After moving back to Missouri, Eagleton became a partner in the law firm Eagleton and Eagleton.[81] In 1956, he was elected circuit attorney for St. Louis. Four years later, Eagleton became attorney general of Missouri, a post he held until being elected the state's lieutenant governor in 1964. Eagleton won a U.S. Senate seat in 1968 but was appointed earlier owing to the sudden resignation of

Missouri senator Edward V. Long. In 1972, Eagleton became the vice presidential candidate on the unsuccessful Democratic ticket with Senator George McGovern. Eagleton remained in the Senate until 1987.[82] On retirement, Eagleton became a professor of public affairs at Washington University and remained on the faculty until his resignation in 1999. Eagleton also served on the board of the Chicago Mercantile Exchange. Some regarded Eagleton's PFIAB appointment by Clinton as political consolation for his unsuccessful bid for the vice presidency, which failed after reports of his frequent hospitalization for depression and electroshock therapy were made public. Eagleton died on March 4, 2007.[83]

Admiral James O. Ellis Jr.—Member 2005–2009

James O. Ellis Jr. was born in Spartanburg, South Carolina, on July 20, 1947.[84] He earned his B.S. degree from the U.S. Naval Academy in Annapolis in 1969. Ellis graduated with two M.S. degrees in aerospace engineering from the Georgia Institute of Technology and in aeronautical systems from the University of West Florida. Ellis completed the U.S. Navy's nuclear power training program, test pilot school, fighter weapons school (commonly referred to as "Top Gun"), and the Senior Officer Program in National Security Strategy at Harvard University in 1989.[85] Ellis served in a variety of operational posts as a fighter pilot, executive officer, and commanding officer. In 1998 he began service as commander in chief of the U.S. Naval Forces, Europe and Allied Forces, Southern Europe, and in 2001 was named commander of the U.S. Strategic Command, where he stayed until retirement in 2004. After Ellis left military service in 2005, he became the CEO of the Institute of Nuclear Power Operations—an independent company promoting the highest levels of nuclear safety and reliability that was part of the Lockheed Martin Corporation.[86] Given his military career and postmilitary defense industry experience, Ellis was a solid candidate for board membership.

Donald L. Evans—Member 2005–2009

Donald L. Evans was born in Houston, Texas, on July 27, 1946. He completed his B.S. degree in mechanical engineering in 1969 and earned his M.B.A. in 1973, both from the University of Texas. On graduation, Evans worked his way up through the ranks of Tom Brown, Inc., an independent energy company in Midland, Texas, and eventually became its CEO. From 2001 to 2004, Evans served as secretary of the U.S. Department of Commerce in the George W. Bush administration. In 2005, Evans was named CEO of the Financial Services Forum.[87] Evans worked on George W. Bush's 1994 and 1998 gubernatorial campaigns, served as the chair of the Bush/Cheney 2000 presidential campaign, and was named a "Minor Bush Pioneer" for the 2000 campaign for his fund-raising efforts; hence, he should be regarded as a political appointment to the board.[88]

Martin C. Faga—Member 2005–2009

Martin C. Faga was born in Bethlehem, Pennsylvania, on June 11, 1941.[89] He received both B.S. and M.S. degrees in electrical engineering from Lehigh University in 1963 and 1964, respectively. Following his graduation, he entered into public service, serving in a variety of intelligence- and reconnaissance-related positions, most notably as the assistant secretary of the air force for space and the director of the National Reconnaissance Office (NRO) from 1989 to 1993.[90] After leaving government, Faga joined the MITRE Corporation as a senior vice president and manager of MITRE's Center for Integrated Intelligence Systems. Faga was later promoted to executive vice president and in May 2000 was named MITRE's president and CEO, a position he held until he retired on June 30, 2006. Faga's experience with the intelligence community and his technical background made him a regular participant on such government panels as the Commission for the Protection and Reduction of Government Secrecy, the Jeremiah Panel to review the mission and organization of the NRO, and the Defense Science Board Task Force.[91] Given these credentials, Faga was a strong candidate for board membership.

Benjamin F. Fairless—Member 1956–1959

Benjamin F. Fairless was born in Pigeon Run, Ohio, on May 3, 1890. He attended Wooster College and graduated with a civil engineering degree from Ohio Northern University in 1913. Beginning as a worker for Central Steel, he worked his way up the ranks and became a vice president only seven years later. Fairless became president of United Alloy Steel, where he worked until 1930. He also served in the highest positions at Republic Steel (1930–35), Carnegie-Illinois Steel (1935–37), and U.S. Steel (1938–53). Known also for his leadership of the industry as president of the American Iron and Steel Institute, Fairless participated in charitable and civic activities such as chair of both the National Committee for the Eisenhower Presidential Library Commission and a committee to raise $25 million for the Carnegie Institute of Technology. Fairless also served as chair of Eisenhower's Committee of Citizen Advisers on foreign aid policy. He died January 1, 1962.[92] Fairless appears to have been largely a political appointment to the board.

Martin Stuart Feldstein—Member 2006–2009

Martin Stuart Feldstein was born in New York, New York, on November 25, 1939. Feldstein graduated with an A.B. summa cum laude from Harvard University in 1961 and completed an M.A. and a Ph.D. at Oxford

University in 1964 and 1967, respectively. Feldstein spent much of his professional career in academe, and in 1984 he was named the George F. Baker professor of economics at Harvard University and president of the National Bureau of Economic Research.[93] Feldstein also served for two years in the White House as the chair of the Council of Economic Advisers from 1982 to 1984. He is a member of the board of the Council on Foreign Relations and is a board member of the Belfer Center for Science and International Affairs at Harvard University's Kennedy School of Government.[94] Feldstein was a reasonable appointment to the board, particularly in the area of the interface between economics and intelligence, given his academic credentials and significant government service.

Thomas S. Foley—Chair 1996–1997

Thomas S. Foley was born in Spokane, Washington, on March 6, 1929. He graduated from the University of Washington with a B.A. in 1951 and an LL.B. in 1957. After two years in private practice, Foley served as deputy prosecuting attorney for Spokane County from 1958 to 1960. In 1960, Foley became the assistant attorney general for the state of Washington. Foley left Washington State to serve as the special counsel to the Interior and Insular Affairs Committee of the U.S. Senate from 1961 to 1964. Foley then won election to the Fifth Washington District seat in the House of Representatives and began a thirty-year career in the U.S. Congress.[95] While in the House, Foley served as a member of the Committee on the Standards of Official Conduct, the House Permanent Select Committee on Intelligence, the Committee on the Budget, and the Committee on Interior and Insular Affairs and also as chair of the Committee on Agriculture from 1975 to 1980. From 1981 to 1986 Foley was the Democratic majority whip, then majority leader from 1987 to 1989, and the Speaker of the House from 1989 to 1994.[96] After stepping down as Speaker of the House in 1995, Foley returned to private practice at a firm in Washington, DC, but remained involved in government by accepting Clinton's appointment as chair of the PFIAB. As PFIAB chair, Foley oversaw the completion of the Aspin-Brown Commission Report (officially known as the Commission on Roles and Capabilities of the United States Intelligence Community) and the Guatemala review conducted by the Intelligence Oversight Board, both in 1996. In 1997, Foley was appointed U.S. ambassador to Japan.[97] Given his congressional experience, Foley was a reasonable candidate for board membership.

John Stuart Foster Jr.—Member 1973–1977

John Stuart Foster Jr. was born in New Haven, Connecticut, on September 18, 1922, and attended McGill University in Montreal, Canada, before receiving his Ph.D. in physics from the University of California, Berkeley.

Beginning as the associate director of Berkeley Laboratory, Foster served as the director of Lawrence Livermore Laboratory in 1952. On leaving Lawrence Livermore in 1965, Foster became the director of defense research and engineering at the Department of Defense, a post he occupied until 1973. Before being nominated to the PFIAB, he served as vice president of energy research at TRW, a government weapons and satellite contractor. Foster served as a member of both the Army and the Air Force Scientific Advisory Boards. Given his academic background and government experience, Foster was a strong candidate for appointment to the board.

Stephen Friedman—Member 1999–2010, Chair 2005–2009

Stephen Friedman was born on December 21, 1937. He earned his B.A. degree from Cornell University in 1959 and his J.D. from Columbia University three years later. Friedman joined Goldman Sachs in 1966 and worked for that company for nearly thirty years. In 1973, Friedman was named partner, and from 1990 to 1992 he served as the company's cochair in New York City. His final two years with Goldman Sachs were spent as a senior partner and company chair until his retirement in 1994. From 1998 to 2002, Friedman was a senior principal for Marsh and McLennan Capital—the private equity business of Marsh and McLennan. From 2002 to 2004 Friedman served simultaneously as assistant to the president for economic policy and as director of the National Economic Council.[98] Friedman also served as a member on the influential Roles and Capabilities of the U.S. Intelligence Community (better known as the Aspen-Brown Commission) and on the Jeremiah Panel that studied the National Reconnaissance Office.[99] Given his White House and intelligence advisory panel service, Friedman was a solid candidate for board membership.

Robert W. Galvin—Member 1973–1977

Robert W. Galvin was born in Marshfield, Wisconsin, on October 9, 1922, and attended the University of Notre Dame and the University of Chicago.[100] Galvin achieved enormous success at Motorola, the company his father founded, when sales skyrocketed from just a few million to over $10 billion. He also worked as the director of the Harris Trust and Savings Bank and as the director and president of the Electronics Industry Association. In addition to success in the private sector, Galvin had substantial government experience by the time he was appointed to the PFIAB in 1973 as a member of the President's Commission on International Trade and Investment and the President's Advisory Council on Private Sector Initiatives and was the recipient of numerous public service awards, including the National Technology Medal and the World Trade Award.[101] He died on October 10, 2011. Galvin was a strong appointment to the board given his background in the defense and intelligence-related business sector.

Gordon Gray—Member 1961–1977

Gordon Gray was born in Baltimore, Maryland, on May 30, 1909. He received an A.B. from the University of North Carolina in 1930 and an LL.B. from Yale University in 1933. Gray practiced law and was the president of a publishing company before serving in the army from 1942 to 1945, eventually rising to the rank of captain. In 1947, Gray was appointed assistant secretary of the army. He served as undersecretary of the army for less than a month in 1949 before being named secretary of the army from 1949 to 1950. He also served in a short stint as a foreign economic policy adviser to the president from April to November 1950. Gray then left government service to become the president of the University of North Carolina from 1950 to 1955. In 1955, he returned to government, working as the assistant secretary of defense for international security affairs until 1957. In 1957, Gray became the director of the Office of Defense Mobilization. In 1958, he became the special assistant to the president for national security affairs under Eisenhower. On retirement in 1961, he received the Presidential Medal of Freedom. Gray died on November 26, 1982.[102] Given his military and White House service, Gray was a strong candidate for board membership.

Alan Greenspan—Member 1982–1985

Alan Greenspan was born in New York, New York, on March 6, 1926. He received his bachelor's degree (summa cum laude) from New York University (NYU) in 1948 along with his master's in economics in 1950.[103] Twenty-seven years later, NYU awarded him a doctorate despite the fact that he never wrote a dissertation.[104] From 1948 until 1953, Greenspan was a research associate at the National Industrial Conference Board, a business-oriented think tank. In 1954, he began work for his own economic consulting firm called Townsend Greenspan, where he was president and chair. In 1974, he joined the Ford administration as chair of the Council of Economic Advisers. When President Carter took office, Greenspan served as a consultant to the Congressional Budget Office and returned to his New York City–based firm. President Reagan appointed Greenspan to the President's Economic Policy Advisers Board and made him chair of the National Commission on Social Security Reform in 1981. In addition, Greenspan was a member of the board of economists at *Time* magazine and on the board of trustees at the Rand Corporation. He also served on the board of overseers at the Hoover Institution at Stanford University on War, Revolution, and Peace and on the boards of numerous private corporations.[105] Given his academic background and extensive government service (albeit not in national security or intelligence affairs), Greenspan was a solid candidate for the board.

Chuck Hagel—Cochair, 2009–Present

Chuck Hagel was born in Platte, Nebraska, on October 4, 1946. He graduated from the University of Nebraska at Omaha and served in Vietnam with the U.S. Army from 1967 through 1968. Hagel spent the years after his discharge from the military in the private sector before being named deputy administrator of the Veterans Administration in 1981. Prior to his election to the U.S. Senate, Hagel was president of McCarthy and Company, an investment banking firm in Omaha, Nebraska. Hagel served two terms in the U.S. Senate (1997–2009). He was a senior member of the Senate Foreign Relations, Banking, Housing and Urban Affairs, and Intelligence Committees. He chaired the Foreign Relations International Economic Policy, Export and Trade Promotion Subcommittee and the Banking Committee's International Trade and Finance and Securities Subcommittees. Hagel also served as the chair of the Congressional-Executive Commission on China and the Senate Climate Change Observer Group. He is currently a distinguished professor at Georgetown University and the University of Nebraska at Omaha. He chairs the Atlantic Council and is a member of the Secretary of Defense's Policy Board and Secretary of Energy's Blue Ribbon Commission on America's Nuclear Future. He serves on many other corporate boards. Hagel recently wrote a book, *America: Our Next Chapter*.[106] Given his service on the Senate Foreign Relations and Intelligence Committees, Hagel was a strong candidate for board membership.

James Hamilton—Member 1995–1997

James Hamilton was born in Chester, South Carolina, on December 4, 1938. In 1960, he completed his A.B. at Davidson College. Hamilton then received his LL.B. in 1963 from Yale University and his LL.M. in 1966 from the University of London. In 1977, he clerked on the Seventh Circuit of the U.S. Court of Appeals and a year later clerked on the U.S. Supreme Court. Beginning in 1980, Hamilton was assigned to the U.S. Temporary Emergency Court of Appeals. After transferring to the U.S. Court of Claims in 1981, Hamilton spent the next seven years in the U.S. Court of Appeals system with the Fourth Circuit (1983), the Eleventh Circuit (1985), and the Second Circuit (1987). From 1966 to 1973, he was an associate with the firm Covington and Burling in Washington, DC. After leaving it, Hamilton served as the assistant chief counsel for the Senate Select Committee on Presidential Campaign Activities, the ad hoc group better known as the Watergate Commission. Hamilton returned to private practice until 1992, when he served as the Clinton-Gore transition counsel for confirmations and nominations as well as the adviser for Supreme Court nominations. In 2000 and 2004, Hamilton was in charge of vetting vice presidential candidates for Al Gore and John Kerry, respectively. Most recently, Hamilton has worked for the

Washington, DC–based firm Bingham McCutchen, which represents a variety of corporate and government officials, political personages, and other attorneys.[107] Despite his previous government service and legal credentials, Hamilton appears to have been largely a political appointee.

Lee H. Hamilton—Member 2005–Present

Lee H. Hamilton was born in Daytona Beach, Florida, on April 20, 1931. In 1952, Hamilton completed his B.A. at DePauw University and spent the next year as a scholar at Germany's Goethe University. Hamilton completed his J.D. at Indiana University's Law School in 1956.[108] Hamilton was in private practice before starting a political career, serving for sixteen consecutive sessions as a Democratic representative of Indiana's Ninth Congressional District. During his tenure in Congress, Hamilton served as chair of the House Permanent Select Committee on Intelligence, as a member of the Select Committee to Investigate Covert Arms Transactions with Iran, the Joint Economic Committee, and the Committee on Foreign Affairs. Hamilton also served on the Joint Committee on the Organization of Congress and the House Standards of Official Conduct Committee, where he drafted several key House ethics reforms.[109] After retiring from the House of Representatives, Hamilton became the president and director of the Woodrow Wilson International Center for Scholars as well as the director of the Center on Congress at Indiana University. Hamilton also participated in numerous high-level government advisory and review panels, including the President's Homeland Security Advisory Council, the FBI Director's Advisory Board, the CIA Director's Economic Intelligence Advisory Panel, the Secretary of Defense's National Security Study Group, and the U.S. Department of Homeland Security Task Force on Preventing the Entry of Weapons of Mass Destruction on American Soil. Most recently, Hamilton was a vice chair for the National Commission on Terrorist Attacks upon the United States (better known as the 9/11 Commission), a cochair of the 9/11 Public Discourse Project established to oversee implementation of the 9/11 Commission's recommendations, and cochair of the 2006 Iraq Study Group.[110] Given this background, Hamilton was a very strong candidate for appointment to the board.

Anthony S. Harrington—Member 1993–2000, Vice Chair 1997–2000, Intelligence Oversight Board Chair 1994–2000

Anthony S. Harrington was born in Taylorsville, North Carolina, on March 9, 1941. As an undergraduate at the University of North Carolina, Harrington earned the prestigious designation of Morehead Scholar. After completing his B.A. in 1963, Harrington earned his LL.B. at Duke University's Law School in 1966. Harrington stayed at Duke, serving as assistant dean until 1968.[111] Harrington left Duke University Law School in 1968 to join the Washington, DC, law firm Hogan and Hartson as a corporate lawyer. Three decades later, Harrington retired from Hogan and Hartson in 1999 to pursue other professional ventures. In 2000, President Clinton nominated Harrington to be the U.S. ambassador to Brazil.[112] Harrington appears to have been largely a political appointee to the board.

Rita E. Hauser—Member 2001–2004, 2009–present

Rita E. Hauser was born in New York, New York, on July 12, 1943. She graduated magna cum laude from the City University of New York's Hunter College in 1954. Hauser then earned her Ph.D. in political economy, with highest honors, from the University of Strasbourg in France in 1955. Hauser spent a year studying at Harvard in 1956 but returned to France to earn a *Licence en droit* from the University of Paris in 1958. After two years with the Department of Justice beginning in 1959, Hauser worked with the New York firms Moldover, Hauser, Strauss and Volin and Stroock and Stroock and Levin. In 1992, she returned to academe as a lecturer on law, international law, and constitutional law at a number of institutions. Hauser also served on the U.S. Department of State's advanced panel on international law, the UN Commission on Human Rights, the Brookings Institute Middle East Study Group, the board of the Rand Corporation, the Advisory Panel for the International Parliamentary Group for Human Rights in the Soviet Union (chair), the U.S. Department of State's Special Refugee Advisory Panel, the board of directors for the Council on Foreign Relations, and the board of directors for the International Institute for Strategic Studies. Given her background in international affairs, Hauser was a solid appointment to the board.

Robert Jay Hermann—Member 1993–2001

Robert Jay Hermann was born in Sheldahl, Iowa, on April 6, 1933. He received his B.S., M.S., and Ph.D. in electrical engineering from Iowa State University in 1954, 1959, and 1963, respectively. After spending twenty years rising through the ranks of the National Security Agency, Hermann was named the deputy assistant secretary of defense for communications, command, control, and intelligence in 1977. In 1979, Hermann was named assistant secretary of the air force for research, development, and logistics. That same year, Hermann was named director of the National Reconnaissance Office, the element of the U.S. government responsible for overhead imagery intelligence collection.[113] In 1981, Hermann was assigned as a special assistant for intelligence to the secretary of the air force. Hermann left government service in 1982 to pursue a second career with United Technologies, as the president of systems technology. Just after his promotion to senior vice president, President Clinton asked Hermann to be a member of his PFIAB.[114] In light of his long career on the technical side of the intelligence community, Hermann was a very strong candidate for board membership.

John Edwin Hull—Member 1956–1958, Chair 1958–1961

John Edwin Hull was born in Greenfield, Ohio, on May 26, 1895. He obtained his B.A. in 1917 from Miami University in Ohio. In 1953, he attained a doctorate in military science from Pennsylvania Military College and was awarded an honorary LL.D. in 1954. Hull was commissioned as a second lieutenant on August 15, 1917, and became a highly decorated army general. Hull served as chief of Theater Group (1944–46) and assistant chief of staff (1944–46) of the Operations Division of the General Staff. He was commanding general of U.S. Army Forces Pacific, Hawaiian Department (1946–48), and of U.S. Army Pacific (1948–49). His posts in Washington included director of the Weapons Systems Evaluation Group of the Office of the Secretary of Defense (1949–51), deputy chief of staff for Operations–Administration (1951), and vice chief of staff (1951–53). In the last years of his military career, Hull served as commander in chief of UN Forces, Far East, and commander in chief, Far East Command. Finally, he was governor of the Kyuku Islands from 1953 to 1955. After retiring from the army in 1955, Hull was elected president of the Manufacturing Chemists Association. He died on June 10, 1975.[115] Hull was a solid candidate for the board in view of his military experience.

Ray Lee Hunt—Member 2001–2009

Ray Lee Hunt was born in New York, New York, on April 6, 1943, and is the son of the influential Texas oilman H. L. Hunt.[116] Hunt graduated with a B.A. from Southern Methodist University in 1965. He spent most of his professional career at his father's Hunt Oil Company. He is chair, president, and CEO of Hunt Consolidated and served on the board of directors of Halliburton and on the board of trustees for the Center for Strategic and International Studies.[117] Hunt was a long-time Bush supporter and reportedly made campaign contributions of at least $100,000 in 2000, probably his only claim on a political appointment to the board.[118]

William G. Hyland—Member 1990–1993

William G. Hyland was born in Kansas City, Missouri, on January 18, 1929. He graduated with a bachelor's degree from Washington University in St. Louis in 1946 at the age of seventeen and graduated from the University of Missouri with his master's degree in 1952.[119] After graduate school, Hyland worked for the federal government for twenty-three years. He spent time with the CIA, the National Security Council, and the State Department as director of the Bureau of Intelligence and Research.[120] During the Ford administration, Hyland served as deputy assistant for national security affairs. On leaving the public sector, Hyland accepted a position as a professor at Georgetown University in 1977 and in 1984 became the editor of *Foreign Affairs,* a well-known journal of international relations published by the Council of Foreign Relations. Hyland died on March 28, 2008. In view of his combination of government service and academic experience, Hyland was an ideal candidate for the board.

Bobby Ray Inman—Vice Chair 1990–1991, Acting Chair 1991–1993

Bobby Ray Inman was born in Rhonesboro, Texas, on April 4, 1931. He received his bachelor's degree from the University of Texas in 1950 and was commissioned as an ensign in the U.S. Navy in 1952.[121] He served in a variety of posts during his career, including assistant naval attaché in Stockholm, Sweden, from 1965 to 1967, senior aide to the vice chief of naval operations from 1972 to 1973, the director of the Naval Intelligence Department from 1974 to 1976, and vice director of the Defense Intelligence Agency. In 1972, he graduated from the National War College. While on active duty, Inman also occupied high-ranking positions in the intelligence community, serving as director of the National Security Agency from 1977 to 1981 and then deputy director of the CIA from 1981 to 1982. He was promoted to the rank of admiral shortly before his retirement in 1982.[122] After leaving the military, Inman became involved in several technology firms in Austin, Texas. In 1990, before his appointment to the PFIAB, he served on a panel that conducted a counterintelligence policy review for Senators David Boren and William Cohen, the chair and vice chair of the Senate Committee on Intelligence.[123] Inman was an ideal candidate for board membership.

Leon Jaworski—Member 1981–1982

Leon Jaworski was born in Waco, Texas, on September 19, 1905. The son of Polish and Austrian immigrants, Jaworski received his bachelor's degree from Baylor University in 1925 and graduated with an LL.M. degree from George Washington University in 1926.[124] After obtaining his law degree, he joined the Houston law firm Fulbright, Crooker, Freeman, and Bate. Jaworski also served in the judge advocate general's office of the U.S. Army as chief of the trial section during the war crimes proceedings following the defeat of Nazi Germany. He represented Lyndon B. Johnson in 1960 when the latter was attempting to run for both the U.S. Senate and vice president. When Johnson joined Kennedy in the White House in 1961, he appointed Jaworski to several important government positions, including the Permanent International Court of Arbitration. Jaworski also served as special counsel in the investigation into President Kennedy's assassination.[125]

Despite these close ties to Johnson and the Democratic Party, Jaworski supported Nixon for the presidency in 1969. Jaworski is best known for his role as special prosecutor during the Watergate investigation in 1973 and 1974. When Archibald Cox was dismissed after the Saturday Night Massacre, Jaworski took up the constitutional battle against the White House for possession of the disputed audiotapes. Though he resigned in 1974, Congress soon called Jaworski back to Washington in 1977 to head the House Panel on the Standards of Official Conduct.[126] "Koreagate" was a scandal involving cash gifts to U.S. politicians who might have had influence on U.S. decisions to aid South Korea. The investigation and cases developed by Jaworski resulted in disciplinary action against six members of Congress and two private citizens. Jaworski's service to the PFIAB ended with his death on December 9, 1982. Despite his distinguished career of government service, his lack of national security or intelligence experience made Jaworski mostly a political appointee.

Admiral David E. Jeremiah—Member 2001–2010

David E. Jeremiah was born in Portland, Oregon, on February 25, 1934. In 1955, Jeremiah completed a bachelor of business administration degree at the University of Oregon and earned an M.S. in financial management from George Washington University in 1968. In 1971, Jeremiah graduated from both the Armed Forces Staff College and Harvard University's Program for Management Development.[127] Jeremiah received his commission as an ensign in the U.S. Navy in 1956 and rose through the ranks while serving in a number of operational and planning posts. He was promoted to admiral in 1987 and served for four years as commander in chief of the Pacific Fleet. During the George H. W. Bush administration, he served as vice chairman of the Joint Chiefs of Staff.[128] After retiring, Jeremiah became director of Man Tech—a contractor for national security programs for various parts of the federal government.[129] Jeremiah also served on a number of intelligence-related bodies, including the National Reconnaissance Office Technical Advisory Group, the National Defense Panel, the Commission to Assess U.S. National Security Space Management and Organization, and the Defense Science Board Task Force on Human Resources. He chaired a high-level panel that recommended changes on the structure of the National Reconnaissance Office (commonly referred to as the Jeremiah Panel) and another key panel that recommended changes to the intelligence community after the late-1990s Indian nuclear tests.[130] In view of his long and distinguished military career and extensive experience in the intelligence community, Jeremiah was a very strong candidate for board membership.

Paul G. Kaminski—Member 2009–present

Paul Kaminski was born in Cleveland, Ohio, on September 16, 1942. He was appointed to the Air Force Academy, from which he received a B.S. degree. He then earned dual M.S. degrees in aeronautics and astronautics and in electrical engineering from the Massachusetts Institute of Technology (MIT) and a Ph.D. in aeronautics and astronautics from Stanford University. He served in the U.S. Air Force for twenty years, including as director for low observables technology, a position in which he was responsible for the "development and deployment of stealth technology." After a stint in the private sector, he served as the undersecretary of defense for acquisition and technology from 1994 to 1997. He chairs the Defense Science Board and consults for the Office of the Secretary of Defense. He has served as a consultant and adviser to many other government agencies, including the Senate Select Committee on Intelligence Technical Advisory Board, the FBI Director's Advisory Board, the Air Force Studies Board of the National Research Council, and the Atlantic Council. He is also a trustee of the Johns Hopkins Applied Physics Lab and the MIT Lincoln Laboratory. Kaminski chairs the board of the Rand Corporation, HRL (the former Hughes Research Labs), and Exostar. He is a director of General Dynamics, Bay Microsystem, CoVant, and the U.S. Air Force Academy Endowment. Currently, Kaminski is chair and CEO of Technovation, a consulting company. Given his military service, academic credentials, and extensive experience in defense technology–related positions in government and the private sector, Kaminski was a very strong candidate for board appointment.[131]

Arnold Lee Kanter—Member 2001–2005

Arnold Lee Kanter was born in Chicago on February 27, 1945. In 1966, Kanter completed a B.A. degree at the University of Michigan and earned a master's and a Ph.D. in political science from Yale University in 1969 and 1975, respectively. While working toward his Ph.D., Kanter was a research fellow and assistant at the Brookings Institute. After he earned his Ph.D., Kanter taught political science at Ohio State University and the University of Michigan.[132] In 1977, Kanter left academe for the Department of State, rising to the level of principal deputy assistant secretary of state in 1984. Kanter left the State Department in 1985 to become the program director for international security and defense policy at the Rand Corporation, where he also served as the program director for national security studies from 1986 to 1987 and as a member of the senior research staff until 1989.[133] President George H. W. Bush brought Kanter back into public service when he appointed him special assistant to the president for national security affairs.[134] In late 1991, Kanter was appointed undersecretary of state for political affairs, the third highest official in the Department of State. He retired from federal service in 1993 and joined Brent Scowcroft to cofound the Scowcroft Group.[135] He died April 10, 2010. Kantor's academic background, combined with his extensive government experience in the national security realm, made him a strong candidate for appointment to the board.

Joseph Patrick Kennedy Sr.—Member 1956

Joseph Patrick Kennedy was born in Boston on September 6, 1888. He received his B.A. in music appreciation from Harvard University and several honorary degrees. Kennedy was appointed by Franklin D. Roosevelt in 1934 to serve as the first chair of the Securities and Exchange Commission and later, in 1936, to serve as chair of the Federal Maritime Commission. From 1937 to 1940, he served as U.S. ambassador to Great Britain, the first Irish Catholic ever to hold the post. Appointed by the Senate, Kennedy served on both the First and the Second Hoover Commissions. He was the father of eight children, including President John F. Kennedy and Senators Robert and Ted Kennedy. He died on November 8, 1969.[136] Despite his ambassadorship and service on the Hoover Commissions, Kennedy appears to have been largely a political appointee to the board.

James R. Killian—Chair 1956–1957, Member 1958–1960, Chair 1961–1963

James Rhyne Killian Jr. was born in Blacksburg, South Carolina, on July 24, 1904. Killian completed his B.S. at the Massachusetts Institute of Technology (MIT) in 1926 after transferring from Trinity College, which became Duke University. Killian's career began in technology publishing, as assistant managing editor for *Technology Review* in 1926. He later became a managing editor and then the editor from 1930 to 1939. From *Technology Review*, Killian returned to his alma mater, MIT, in 1939 as the executive assistant to the MIT president. From 1943 to 1945, he served as MIT's executive vice president and as vice president from 1945 to 1948. In 1948, Killian became president of MIT, holding that title until 1959, when he became chair of the MIT Corporation, where he served until 1971. During his career, Killian also served on the boards of Polaroid, IBM, General Motors, AT&T, the Cabot Corporation, and Ingersoll-Rand. Killian had a long history of service to a number of presidents, serving on the President's Communication Policy Board (1950–51), Committee on Management (1950–52), and Science Advisory Committee (1951–57), chairing it from 1957 to 1959. Killian also chaired several other boards, including the Army Science Advisory Panel (1951–56), the President's Science Advancement Commission (1957–59), and the PBCFIA from 1956 to 1957. Killian served as special assistant to the president for science and technology under Eisenhower from 1957 to 1959. After serving as chair of the Kennedy PFIAB from 1961 to 1963, Killian later served on the advisory board of the U.S.

Arms Control and Disarmament Agency (1969–74). Killian also received numerous honorary degrees. He died on January 29, 1988.[137] Killian was an ideal candidate for board membership given his academic credentials and high-level government service in the areas of science and technology.

Jeane Duane Jordan Kirkpatrick—Member 1985–1990

Jeane Duane Jordan Kirkpatrick was born in Duncan, Oklahoma, on November 19, 1926. She received a bachelor's degree from Barnard College before pursuing her graduate education at Columbia University, where in 1968 she received both a master's and a doctorate in comparative politics. Kirkpatrick joined the faculty at Georgetown in 1967 as an associate professor before making full professor in 1973. In 1977, she joined the American Enterprise Institute for Public Policy Research as a senior fellow. She entered the Reagan administration with her appointment to the cabinet-level position of permanent representative to the United Nations in 1981, a post she held for four years as the first woman to occupy that office.[138] She died on December 7, 2006. Kirkpatrick was a reasonable appointment to the board given her academic credentials and government experience, but she lacked much in-depth experience in the intelligence field.

Henry Kissinger—Member 1984–1990

Henry Kissinger was born in Fuerth, Germany, on May 27, 1923. He and his family fled Nazi persecution of the Jews by immigrating to the United States in 1938. He became a naturalized citizen in 1943 and was promptly drafted to serve as an interpreter for the U.S. Army Counter Intelligence Corps. From 1946 until 1949, he was a captain in the Military Intelligence Reserve. After leaving the military at the end of the war, Kissinger attended Harvard University and received three degrees, including his doctorate in 1954.[139] After graduation, Kissinger joined the faculty of Harvard as a professor and member of the Center for International Affairs. He was also the executive director of the Harvard International Seminar and the director of the defense studies program. From 1955 to 1956 Kissinger was the study group director for Nuclear Weapons and Foreign Policy at the Council of Foreign Relations and from 1956 to 1958 the director of the Special Studies Project for the Rockefeller Brothers Fund. Kissinger was also a consultant to the National Security Council, the Department of State, the Arms Control and Disarmament Agency, and the Joint Chiefs of Staff. In 1969, President Nixon appointed Kissinger to serve as his national security adviser, a post he held until 1975. Under Nixon, Kissinger also served as the secretary of state, starting in 1973 and continuing under President Ford. After leaving government, he founded Kissinger and Associates, an international consulting firm.[140] Kissinger remained on the PFIAB until new financial disclosure regulations prompted him to resign early in the first Bush administration.[141]

Kissinger was a strong candidate for board membership given his academic credentials and government experience, but political factors also undoubtedly influenced his appointment.

Ellen Laipson—Member 2009–Present

Ellen Laipson was born on February 22, 1952, in Worcester, Massachusetts. She attended college at Cornell University and earned a master's degree from the Johns Hopkins School of Advanced International Studies in Washington, DC. She was a specialist in Middle East affairs in the Foreign Affairs and National Defense Division of the Congressional Research Service before joining the Policy Planning Staff at the Department of State in 1986. From 1990 through 1993, she served as national intelligence officer for Near and South Asia on the National Intelligence Council (NIC). She was named director for Near Eastern and South Asia Affairs on the National Security Council in 1993 and then special assistant to the U.S. permanent representative to the United Nations in 1995. She returned to the NIC in 1997 as the vice chair. In 2002, she was named president and CEO of the Stimson Center, "a nonprofit, nonpartisan institution devoted to enhancing international peace and security." Laipson is a member of the Council on Foreign Relations and serves on the boards of the Asia Foundation and the Education and Employment Foundation.[142] Given her twenty-five-year career in the U.S. government, much of it spent in intelligence-related positions, Laipson was a very strong candidate for board membership.

Edwin Herbert Land—Member 1961–1977

Edwin Herbert Land was born in Bridgeport, Connecticut, on May 7, 1909. He was educated at Norwich Academy and Harvard but left Harvard to pursue a career in science. Land founded Polaroid in 1937, serving as president from 1937 to 1975 and as chair of the board from 1937 to 1982. Land's contributions to aerial reconnaissance and photography were extensive. He was also the founder of the Rowland Institute for Science, serving simultaneously as president, scientist, and director of the institute's research. Land was also a visiting lecturer in psychology (1966–67) and physics (1974) at Harvard and a visiting professor at the Massachusetts Institute of Technology from 1956 to 1991. In 1954, Land served on a task force studying ways to prevent a surprise attack against the United States, and he contributed to the U-2 program and its cameras. From 1957 to 1959 he was a member of the President's Science Advisory Committee (PSAC) and served as a counselor-at-large to the PSAC from 1960 to 1973. Land served on Eisenhower's Technological Capabilities Panel and was a member of the President's Committee on the National Medal of Science (1969–72) as well as the National Commission on Technology, Automation, and Economic Progress (1964–66). Among many other notable awards and honorary degrees, Land received the Presidential Medal of Freedom in 1963 and the National Medal of Technology in 1988. He died on March 1, 1991.[143] Given this background, Land was an ideal candidate for board service.

James Calhoun Langdon Jr.—Member 2001–2005, Chair 2005

James Calhoun Langdon Jr. was born in Los Angeles on September 20, 1945. Langdon received his bachelor's in business administration in 1967 and his J.D. in 1970 from the University of Texas. Langdon worked in an administrative role in the Federal Energy Office, the Federal Energy Administration, and the Department of Treasury before joining the Washington, DC, international law firm Akin, Gump, Strauss, Hauer and Feld in 1975, where he is now a senior executive partner on energy-related issues and a member of the management committee.[144] Langdon was a "Bush Pioneer"—donating at least $100,000—for both of President George W. Bush's campaigns (2000 and 2004), likely the main reason for his appointment to the board.[145]

William L. Langer—Member 1961–1969

William Leonard Langer was born in Boston on March 16, 1896. He graduated from Harvard with his bachelor's in 1915, an M.A. in 1920, and a Ph.D. in 1923. He would later earn an LL.D. from Harvard in 1945. His academic career began as an instructor in modern languages at Worcester Academy (1915–17). He became an assistant professor of history (1923–25) and an associate professor (1925–27) at Clark University. He then returned to Harvard as an assistant professor of history (1927–31) and an associate professor (1931–36). Langer spent the bulk of his Harvard career as the Coolidge Professor of History (1936–64) and professor emeritus (1964–77). During this time, he was the director of the Russian Research Center and Center for Middle Eastern Studies (1954–59). Langer also had extensive experience in the intelligence field, beginning as a member of the board of analysts in the Office of Coordinator of Information from 1941 to 1942. From 1942 to 1945, Langer served as chief of the research and analysis branch of the Office of Strategic Services. In 1946, he worked as a special assistant to the secretary of state. From 1950–51, Langer was the assistant director for national estimates within the CIA. Langer died on December 26, 1977.[146] Given his combination of academic credentials and intelligence community experience, Langer was an ideal candidate for the board.

Gen. Lyman L. Lemnitzer, USA (Ret.)—Member 1976–1977

Lyman L. Lemnitzer was born in Honesdale, Pennsylvania, on August 29, 1899. He graduated from the U.S. Military Academy at West Point in 1920, the Command and General Staff College at Fort Leavenworth in 1936, and the Army War College in 1940. In 1947, he became deputy commandant at the National War College before becoming director of the Office of Military Assistance within the Office of the Secretary of Defense from 1949 to 1950. On July 1, 1959, Lemnitzer became U.S. Army chief of staff before becoming chairman of the Joint Chiefs of Staff from 1960 to 1962. From 1962 to 1969, Lemnitzer served as commander in chief of the U.S. European Command and, beginning in 1963, held a concurrent position as supreme allied commander Europe until his retirement in 1969. He also served as a member on the Rockefeller Commission that investigated the domestic activities of the CIA in 1975. After retirement, Lemnitzer served as president of the Washington Institute of Foreign Affairs, a member of the board of directors of the Atlantic Council of the United States, and a member of the Council on Foreign Relations. He died on November 12, 1988.[147] Given his military and high-level international affairs experience, Lemnitzer was a very strong candidate for board membership.

Alfred Lerner—Member 2001–2002

Alfred Lerner was born to Russian immigrant parents in Brooklyn, New York, on May 8, 1933. Lerner earned a B.A. degree from Columbia University in 1955. He served for two years in the Marine Reserves and then embarked on a successful career in the business world, becoming chair and CEO of MBNA in 1991 and chair and CEO of Town and Country Trust in 1993. In 1998, he became the coowner and chair of the Cleveland Browns football team.[148] Lerner died on October 23, 2002. Lerner appears to have been largely a political appointee to the board.

Franklin B. Lincoln—Member 1969–1972

Franklin B. Lincoln was born in Brooklyn, New York, on January 18, 1908. He attended Colgate University before receiving his law degree from Columbia University in 1934. He practiced law for many years in New York City, although he did work briefly as the civilian counsel to the fiscal director of the Department of the Navy. He also served as assistant secretary of defense from 1959 to 1961.[149] Lincoln died on November 2, 1993. Lincoln's appointment to the PFIAB was undoubtedly the result of his personal and professional connections with Nixon's attorney general, John Mitchell, a political reward for a close friend of the president.[150]

Robert Abercrombie Lovett—Member 1956–1961

Robert A. Lovett was born in Huntsville, Texas, on September 14, 1895. He received a B.A. from Yale in 1918 and took postgraduate courses in law and business administration at Harvard (1919–21). He served in the U.S. Navy, where he was highly decorated and reached the rank of lieutenant commander. Lovett began his career as a businessman and became a prominent member of the New York business community. Always greatly interested in aeronautics, Lovett became assistant secretary of war for air in 1941. Returning only briefly to serve again as partner at Brown Brothers Harriman, Lovett was soon back in Washington, this time as undersecretary of state. After yet another short stint in business, he eventually returned to serve as secretary of defense from 1951 to 1953. When Lovett left office on January 20, 1953, at the end of the Truman administration, he returned for the last time to Brown Brothers Harriman, where he remained active as a general partner for a number of years. He died on May 7, 1986, in New York.[151] Lovett was a strong candidate for board membership given his combination of government and business experience.

Clare Boothe Luce—Member 1973–1977

Clare Boothe Luce was born in New York, New York, on March 10, 1903.[152] While she never graduated from college, she briefly attended a theater school in New York. In 1929, she joined the staff of *Vogue* as an editorial assistant before rising quickly to become an associate editor in 1931 and managing editor in 1933. Later on, Luce traveled extensively during World War II writing for *Life,* visiting China, Burma, Italy, and many other countries. Luce's political career began in 1942 when she was elected to the U.S. House of Representatives. After serving two terms in the House, Luce was appointed U.S. ambassador to Italy in 1952, a post she held until 1956. Before her retirement in 1964, Luce was also a member of White House Preservation Committee, the Academy of Political Science, and the American Institute for Foreign Trade.[153] Luce died on October 9, 1987. Luce was a unique combination of a political and a substantive appointee to the board.

Gordon Coppard Luce—Member 1988–1989

Gordon Coppard Luce was born in San Diego, California, on November 21, 1925, and served in the U.S. Army from 1944 to 1946, earning a Bronze Star. Luce received his bachelor's degree from Stanford University in 1950 and an M.B.A. two years later. He enjoyed a successful career in banking, including serving as vice president of marketing and administration at the Home Federal Savings and Loan Association, president and CEO of the Great American Bank, and later chair and director of the Great American First Savings Bank. In addition to a flourishing business career, Luce also occupied several government posts at both the state and the federal level. From 1967 to 1969, he worked as Governor Ronald Reagan's secretary of the Business and Transportation Agency in California. Later, Reagan named him a member of the President's Commission on Housing and made him an alternate delegate to the UN general assembly in 1982.[154] He remained on PFIAB until June 16, 1990. Luce died on August 21, 2006. Luce seems to have been largely a political appointment.

Lester L. Lyles—2009–present

Lester Lyles was born April 20, 1946, in Washington, DC. He earned his bachelor's in mechanical engineering from Howard University and a master's in mechanical/nuclear engineering from New Mexico State University. He also attended the Defense Systems Management College, the Armed Forces Staff College, the National War College, and the National and International Security Management Course at Harvard University and was awarded honorary degrees from New Mexico State University and Urbana University. He served as an officer in the air force for thirty-five years, retiring as a general officer in 2003. His major assignments included vice commander of Ogden Air Logistics Center at Hill Air Force Base in Utah from 1993 to 1994, the commander of the Space and Missile Systems Center at Los Angeles Air Force Base from 1994 to 1996, the director of the Ballistic Missile Defense Organization from 1996 to 1999, and then vice chief of staff at the Air Force Headquarters in 1999. In 2000, Lyles was named the commander of the Air Force Material Command at Wright-Patterson Air Force Base in Ohio. On his retirement from the U.S. Air Force in 2003, Lyles was appointed the vice chair of the Defense Science Board. In addition, he serves as a member of the NASA Advisory Council and on the National Academies of Science and Engineering Committee on the Rationale and Goals of the U.S. Civil Space Program.[155] Given his academic credentials and long experience with military and space technology, Lyles was a very strong candidate for appointment to the board.

Jami Miscik—Member 2009–present

Jami Miscik was born in Chicago in 1958. She graduated from Pepperdine University and the University of Denver. Miscik served for twenty-five years in the U.S. intelligence community, including as director for intelligence programs at the National Security Council from 1995 to 1996. She became the CIA's first female deputy director for intelligence from 2002 to 2005. On retirement from CIA, she was named the global head of sovereign risk at Lehman Brothers. She was cohead of the Obama transition team for the intelligence community in 2008. She is currently president and vice chair of Kissinger Associates, an international consulting firm based in New York. She also serves on the boards of the Council on Foreign Relations, the American Ditchley Foundation, and In-Q-Tel, a unique collaborative venture between the U.S. intelligence community and the private sector in Silicon Valley.[156] Given her career in the U.S. intelligence community, Miscik was a very strong candidate for appointment to the board.

Thomas Hinman Moorer—Member 1981–1985

Thomas Hinman Moorer was born in Mount Willing, Alabama, on February 9, 1912. He attended the U.S. Naval Academy, where he graduated in 1933, and was commissioned as an ensign. He also graduated from the Naval War College with an advanced degree in 1953. During his forty-one-year naval career, Moorer attained the rank of admiral at the age of forty-five and served as the chief of naval operations from 1967 to 1970 and as the chairman of the Joint Chiefs of Staff under President Nixon from 1970 until his retirement in 1974.[157] After retiring from the military, Moorer became the director of Blount, Inc., and shortly before being named to the PFIAB he joined the Washington Advisory Board of Hill and Knowlton. Moorer was a reasonable appointment given his high-level military experience.

John Lewis Morrison—Member 2005–2010

John Lewis Morrison was born in Minneapolis, Minnesota, on April 6, 1945. He completed his B.A. degree in 1967 at Yale University and continued at Harvard University to earn an M.B.A. in 1971. While at Yale, Morrison was an all-star athlete and scholar and later competed as a member of the U.S. Olympic hockey team in 1972.[158] On completing his M.B.A., Morrison entered private industry. Highlights of his career include serving as executive vice chair of Pillsbury and chair of U.S. Consumer Foods. Since 1989, Morrison has been the executive vice president, consumer food group chair, and then managing director of Goldner, Hawn, Johnson and Morrison—a private equity investment firm.[159] Morrison appears to have been largely a political appointment.

Franklin David Murphy—Member 1969–1972

Franklin David Murphy was born in Kansas City, Missouri, on January 29, 1916.[160] He graduated from the University of Kansas in 1936 and received his medical degree from the University of Pennsylvania in 1941. After serving in the army during World War II, Murphy returned to the University of Kansas as a member of the faculty. He eventually became dean of the medical school and then chancellor of the university. In 1960, he left Kansas and joined the University of California, Los Angeles (UCLA), guiding the university through the turbulent years of the Vietnam War and greatly improving its academic reputation and facilities. In 1968, Murphy left UCLA to become chair of the Times Mirror Company, the parent company of the *Los Angeles Times* and many other prominent newspapers.[161] Murphy died on June 16, 1994.[162] Given his academic and business experience, Murphy was a reasonable appointment to the board.

Robert Daniel Murphy—Member 1961–1972, Intelligence Oversight Board Chair 1976–1977

Robert Daniel Murphy born in Milwaukee, Wisconsin, on October 28, 1894, and attended Marquette University. In 1920, Murphy received a law degree from George Washington University, and in 1928 he received an LL.M., also from George Washington University. After graduating from law school, Murphy joined the State Department. When Germany occupied France, Murphy was assigned to the U.S. embassy in Paris and later served at the U.S. Mission in Vichy. Murphy played a key role in deceiving the Germans as to U.S. invasion plans for North Africa and was there in 1942 when Allied forces landed. Murphy subsequently served on General Eisenhower's staff in Europe from 1942 until the end of the war. During the Berlin Blockade of 1948, Murphy served as political adviser to Gen. Lucius Clay, who was in charge of the U.S. Zone in occupied Germany. Murphy was appointed ambassador to Japan in 1952, where he helped negotiate the Korean War armistice agreement.[163] In 1953, Murphy was named assistant secretary to the deputy undersecretary for political affairs, and in 1955 the deputy undersecretary for political affairs. Murphy was designated a career ambassador in 1956. During the Lebanon crisis of 1958, Murphy was sent to the region as a personal representative of President Eisenhower. In 1959, Murphy was named undersecretary of state, the top position for a career officer, before retiring in 1960.[164] After retirement, Murphy became chair of the board of Corning Glass. Murphy died on January 9, 1978.[165] Murphy was a very strong candidate for board membership given his military service and government experience.

Peter O'Donnell Jr.—Member 1981–1985

Peter O'Donnell Jr., who was perhaps the least well-known appointee to the PFIAB, completed a B.S. in mathematics at the University of the South and an M.B.A. at the University of Pennsylvania's Wharton Graduate School.[166] O'Donnell founded the O'Donnell Foundation in 1957, where he serves as chair, president, and CEO. The foundation focuses on improving science and engineering education.[167] O'Donnell admitted that the CIA had used his family's foundation as a secret funding conduit.[168] In addition to his philanthropy, O'Donnell was also active in the Republican Party. He was one of three Texas businessmen who raised money for the Virginia Republican gubernatorial candidate J. Marshall Coleman in 1981. He served as chair of the Texas State Republican Committee, and he was the national chair of the Goldwater Draft Committee (also known as the "Suite 3505 Committee").[169] He contributed over $140,000 to George W. Bush's two gubernatorial campaigns. In spite of his brush with the intelligence community, O'Donnell appears to have been largely a political appointee.

Frank Pace Jr.—Member 1961–1972

Frank Pace Jr. was born in Little Rock, Arkansas, on July 5, 1912, and finished high school at the age of fourteen. At the urging of his mother, Pace attended preparatory school before enrolling at Princeton University. After Princeton, Pace attended Harvard Law School, graduating in 1936, and returned to Little Rock to serve as an assistant district attorney. Pace then accepted the position of general counsel for the Revenue Department of the state of Arkansas. With the outbreak of World War II, Pace joined the U.S. Army Air Corps and was commissioned a second lieutenant in 1942. Pace resigned as a major in 1946 and returned to Washington, DC, to serve on the staff of Attorney General Tom Clark. In 1948, he became assistant director of the Bureau of the Budget. President Truman selected Pace to become the director of the Bureau of the Budget in 1949 at the age of thirty-six. Pace enjoyed a reputation as an efficient and effective administrator and was well thought of by President Truman. In April 1950, the thirty-seven-year-old Pace was selected to succeed Gordon Gray as secretary of the army. Pace resigned as secretary of the army in January 1953, after Eisenhower won the presidency.[170] After retirement, Pace became the chair of the board of General Dynamics at forty-nine years of age.[171] He also served as chair of the board for the Corporation of Public Broadcasting and president of the International Executive Service Corps. Pace died on January 8, 1988.[172] Given his military and high-level government service, Pace was a reasonable appointment to the board.

Marie-Elisabeth Lucienne Paté-Cornell—Member 2001–2010

Marie-Elisabeth Lucienne Paté-Cornell was born in Dakar, Senegal, on August 17, 1948.[173] She completed her B.S. in mathematics in Marseilles, France, in 1968. She stayed in France to complete an M.S. in mathematics and computer science in 1970 and an engineering degree in 1971 from the Institut Polytechnique de Grenoble. The next year, Paté-Cornell enrolled at Stanford University, where she completed an M.S. in operations research in 1972 (her second M.S.) and her Ph.D. in engineering-economics systems in 1978.[174] Paté-Cornell remained in academe, teaching at the Massachusetts Institute of Technology and Stanford, and is currently a professor in and the chair of the Department of Management Science and Engineering at Stanford. In addition, Paté-Cornell is a senior fellow at the Stanford Institute for International Studies. Paté-Cornell also serves on a number of directorship and advisory boards, including the advisory council of NASA's Jet Propulsion Laboratory, board of trustees of the Aerospace Corporation, chair of the board of advisers of the Naval Postgraduate School, the Army Science Board, the NASA Advisory Council, and the Air Force Scientific Advisory Board. Most recently, Paté-Cornell served as a consultant to the

Columbia Accident Investigation Board. Paté-Cornell was a strong candidate for board membership given her academic credentials and defense-related advisory board service.

Henry Ross Perot—Member 1981–1985

Henry Ross Perot was born in Texarkana, Texas, on June 27, 1930. He graduated from the U.S. Naval Academy in 1953 and was commissioned soon after. After serving four years in the navy, Perot joined IBM as a data-processing-system salesperson.[175] In the late 1960s, Perot became involved in the Nixon administration's effort to improve the treatment of American prisoners of war in Vietnam. In 1979, the Iranian government seized two of his Electronic Data Systems (EDS) employees, and Perot organized a rescue mission made up of EDS employees and led by a former U.S. special forces colonel. The mission was successful only after pro-Ayatollah demonstrators stormed the jail where the employees were kept, freeing all prisoners.[176] Despite his direct experience with covert action, Perot was largely a political appointment to the board.

William Perry—Member 1990–1993

William Perry was born in Vandergrift, Pennsylvania, on October 11, 1927. Beginning in 1947, Perry served in the U.S. military during the occupation of Japan and remained in the reserves until 1955.[177] On returning to the United States, Perry enrolled at Stanford University, earning his bachelor's degree in mathematics in 1949 and his master's degree in 1950. On graduation, Perry returned to Pennsylvania to teach math at Pennsylvania State University and to work as a senior mathematician at the HRB-Singer Corporation. In 1954, Perry became the director of the electronic defense laboratories at GTE-Sylvania, where he remained until 1964. Perry graduated from Pennsylvania State University with a doctorate in mathematics in 1957.[178] In 1964, Perry left GTE-Sylvania and cofounded ESL, an electronics firm based in California. From 1966 until 1977, he also acted as a technical consultant to the Department of Defense. In 1977, he was appointed the undersecretary of defense for Research and Engineering, where he remained until 1981. After Reagan's inauguration, Perry left government to become the managing director of Hambrecht and Quist, an investment banking firm. In 1985, Perry founded Technologies, Strategies, and Alliances (TSA) near Washington, DC, and served as the company's first chair.[179] While chair of TSA, Perry also served as a trustee for the Carnegie Endowment for International Peace, as a member of the Defense Science Board and the Carnegie Commission on Science, Technology, and Government, and as cochair of the Aspen Strategy Group of the Aspen Institute of Humanistic Studies.[180] He served on the board until President Clinton's election. Under Clinton,

Perry would serve as deputy secretary of defense (1993–94) and later secretary of defense (1994–97). Perry was a very strong candidate for appointment to the board given his academic credentials and extensive high-level government experience.

Harold William Pote—Member 1993–1996

Harold William Pote was born in Philadelphia on September 18, 1946.[181] Pote received his B.A. from Princeton University in 1968 and his M.B.A. from Harvard University in 1972. After graduation, Pote joined the faculty of La Salle College as an assistant professor—a position he held intermittently until 1979. In 1974, Pote became the director of investor relations for Fidelcor and Fidelity Bank in Philadelphia. From 1984 to 1988, Pote served as Fidelcor's chair of the board and CEO for Fidelity Bank, briefly serving as president and CEO of Fidelcor. After leaving Fidelcor in 1988, Pote spent five years as the CEO for the Special Situation Fund in New York City. In 1993, Pote became a partner in the private investing firm the Beacon Group (which was later acquired by J. P. Morgan). In 2000, Pote was named the head of regional banking for J. P. Morgan Chase. Pote ended his time there as the vice chair of retail financial services in 2004. In 2004, Pote was named the president, CEO, and trustee of the real estate investment firm American Financial Realty Trust (AFR). Pote became the president and chief executive of AFR in late 2006 and held those positions until his sudden death on June 27, 2007.[182] Pote appears to have been largely a political appointee.

Lois Dickson Rice—Member 1993–2001

Lois Dickson Rice was born in Portland, Maine, on February 28, 1933. She graduated Phi Beta Kappa and magna cum laude from Radcliffe College in 1954. After completing her education, Rice became the director of counseling services for the National Scholarship Service and Fund for Negro Students in New York City until 1959. From 1959 to 1981, Rice worked with the College Board in New York and Washington, DC, serving as vice president beginning in 1973.[183] Between 1963 and 1964, Rice also worked as a program officer for the Ford Foundation. In 1981, Rice began working for the Control Data Corporation and eventually became the senior vice president of government and public affairs. In 1991, Rice was named the Miriam K. Carliner Scholar in the guest scholars program at the Brookings Institute. Rice also serves as a professional consultant to government and private customers in the areas of business and education partnerships, higher education finance, and equality of opportunity in higher education.[184] To be sure, Rice had some generic public policy experience, but she nonetheless appears to have been largely a political appointee.

Charles S. Robb—Member 2005–2009

Charles S. Robb was born in Phoenix, Arizona, on June 26, 1939. In 1961, Robb received his B.A. degree from the University of Wisconsin and in 1973 completed his J.D. at the University of Virginia. Robb served on active duty in the Marine Corps from 1961 to 1973 and in the Marine Corps reserves until 1991.[185] Robb worked in legal affairs in both public and private sectors in civilian life. In 1982, he embarked on a career in politics, serving as Virginia's lieutenant governor and governor between 1978 and 1986 and as U.S. senator from 1988 to 2001. While on Capitol Hill, Robb was a member of the Armed Services Committee, the Senate Select Committee on Intelligence, the Foreign Relations Committee, the Democratic Policy Committee, the Democratic Technology and Communications Committee, the subcommittee on readiness, and the subcommittee on sea power. On leaving the Senate in 2001, Robb joined the faculty at George Mason University as a distinguished professor of law and public policy.[186] Robb has also served on a number of high-level government advisory bodies, including the secretary of state's Arms Control and Nonproliferation Advisory Board, the FBI Director's Advisory Board, and the National Intelligence Council's Strategic Analysis Advisory Board and, most recently, cochaired the Commission on the Intelligence Capabilities of the U.S. regarding Weapons of Mass Destruction and was a member of the 2006 Iraq Study Group.[187] Robb was a strong candidate for the board given his experience in Congress and on many intelligence-oriented advisory boards.

Nelson Aldrich Rockefeller—Member 1969–1974

Nelson Aldrich Rockefeller was born in Bar Harbor, Maine, on July 8, 1908. The son of the industrial magnate and philanthropist John D. Rockefeller, Nelson graduated from Dartmouth College in 1930. After college, he worked in several Rockefeller family businesses. Though he remained loyal to his father's Republican roots, Rockefeller's bipartisan activities in government included serving as the director of the Office of Inter-American Affairs from 1940 to 1944, assistant secretary of state for Latin American Affairs from 1944 to 1945 under President Roosevelt, chair of the Advisory Board on International Development under President Truman, and undersecretary of health, education, and welfare under President Eisenhower. Rockefeller also served as special assistant to the president for foreign affairs from 1954 to 1955 and chair of the President's Advisory Committee on Government Organization.[188] In the 1950s, Rockefeller chaired the relatively secret "Forty Committee," a group of high-ranking government officials that oversaw the CIA's clandestine activities. He served four terms as governor of New York from 1959 to 1973. Though Rockefeller failed in his quest for the presidential nomination in 1960, 1964, and 1968, he used his influence in 1960 to moderate the Republican platform, even summoning then vice president Nixon to his New York penthouse in what Barry Goldwater called "The Munich of the Republican Party."[189] Rockefeller died on January 27, 1979.[190] Rockefeller was a reasonable candidate for the board given his extensive government experience in foreign affairs and in intelligence-related positions.

Joe M. Rodgers—Member 1981–1985

Joe M. Rodgers was born in Bay Minette, Alabama, on November 12, 1933. He received his bachelor's degree from the University of Alabama in 1956 before joining the U.S. Coast Guard, serving for two years as a lieutenant. In 1959, Rodgers entered the construction industry with Burgess, Inc., as chief engineer before moving to Dixie Concrete Pipe Company in 1963. In 1966, he started Rodgers Construction in Nashville, Tennessee.[191] He sold his company (though it retained the Rodgers name) and managed then governor Reagan's unsuccessful campaign in Tennessee before becoming the finance chair of the Republican Party in 1978. Rodgers was named U.S. ambassador to France in 1985.[192] He died on February 2, 2009. Rodgers appears to have been largely a political appointee.

Eugene Victor Debs Rostow—Member 1983–1985

Eugene Victor Debs Rostow, brother of former national security adviser Walt Whitman Rostow, was born in Brooklyn, New York, on August 25, 1913. He received both his bachelor's and his law degrees from Yale University in 1933 and 1937, respectively, before pursuing postgraduate work at King's College, Cambridge University. After receiving his LL.B., Rostow practiced law in New York City for several years before becoming a professor at Yale. During World War II, Rostow worked for the State Department on the Lend Lease program before also serving as assistant executive secretary of the Economic Commission of Europe.[193] In 1955, Rostow became the dean of the Yale Law School, a post he held until 1966, when President Johnson appointed him as undersecretary of state for political affairs. Breaking with the Nixon administration's détente policy with the Soviet Union in 1976, he became the chair of the Committee on the Present Danger. In 1981, President Reagan appointed him to head the Arms Control and Disarmament Agency.[194] He died on November 26, 2002. Rostow was a reasonable appointment to the board given his previous State Department and ACDA service.

Warren Bruce Rudman—Member 1993–1995, Vice Chair 1995–1998, Acting Chair 1995–1996, Chair 1997–2001

Warren Bruce Rudman was born in Boston on May 18, 1930. He attended Valley Forge Military School in Wayne, Pennsylvania, where he graduated in 1948. Rudman went on to receive his B.A. from Syracuse University in 1952 and on graduation served for two years in the U.S. Army. After earning an LL.B. from Boston College in 1960, Rudman practiced law in his hometown of Nashua, New Hampshire.[195] After ten years practicing law, New Hampshire governor Walter Petersen appointed Rudman as his special gubernatorial counsel. This position led to Rudman's election as New Hampshire state attorney general, a position he held until 1976. Rudman left public service in 1976 to join the law firm Sheehan, Phinney, Bass, and Green in Manchester, New Hampshire.[196] Rudman's senatorial career began in December 1980, when the New Hampshire governor appointed him to fill the congressional vacancy caused by the resignation of Senator John A. Durkin. After serving two terms, Rudman decided not to run for reelection in 1992.[197] Not long after Rudman returned to private law practice in Washington, DC, Clinton selected him to serve on his PFIAB. Rudman was tapped as vice chair of the PFIAB in 1995 under Chair Thomas Foley. Between the untimely death of Les Aspin and Foley's appointment, Rudman served as the acting chair of the PFIAB, the first person to serve as PFIAB chair from the opposite political party as the White House.[198] Because Rudman's committee service in congress did not include service on armed services, foreign affairs, or intelligence committees, he appears to have been largely a political appointee.

Edward L. Ryerson—Member 1956–1961

Edward L. Ryerson was born in Chicago on December 3, 1886. He received his Ph.B. from Yale in 1908 as well as an honorary M.A. (1932) and an LL.D. (1962). He also attended the Massachusetts Institute of Technology in 1909. He was chair of Inland Steel but additionally served as director of Northern Trust, Quaker Oats, Illinois Bell Telephone, International Harvester, American Brake Shoe, New York Life Insurance, and the Atchison, Topeka, and Santa Fe Railway. He was part of the delegation of U.S. steel and iron ore mining representatives to the Soviet Union in 1958 as well as a lecturer for Fulbright exchange programs in Australia. Ryerson served on the board of many foundations and received numerous medals and awards. He died August 2, 1971.[199] Despite his distinguished business career, Ryerson appears to have been largely a political appointee.

Harrison Hagan Schmitt—Member 1983–1985

Harrison Hagan Schmitt was born in Santa Rita, New Mexico, on July 3, 1935. He received his bachelor's degree in science from the California Institute of Technology in 1957 and studied at the University of Oslo for one year afterward. Returning to the United States, Schmitt received his Ph.D. in geology from Harvard University in 1964. After graduation, Schmitt joined the U.S. Geological Survey for one year before moving to NASA in 1965, where he would eventually serve as the lunar module pilot on Apollo 17.[200] After returning from space, Schmitt was named among the first Sherman Fairchild Distinguished Scholars at the California Institute of Technology in 1973. A year later, Schmitt was appointed NASA assistant administrator for energy programs, a post in which he oversaw NASA assistance to other agencies working on energy-related projects. In 1975, Schmitt retired from NASA to run successfully for the U.S. Senate. During his six years as a New Mexico senator, Schmitt served on the Commerce, Science, and Transportation Committee, on the Banking, Housing and Urban Affairs Committee, and on the Ethics Committee as the ranking Republican.[201] Schmitt was a reasonable appointment to the board given his NASA experience and the increasingly important role of space in intelligence affairs.

Bernard Schriever—Member 1985–1990

Bernard Schriever was born in Bremen, Germany, on September 14, 1910. His family came to the United States in 1917 and lived in New Braunfels, Texas. After naturalization around 1923, Schriever graduated with a bachelor's degree in architectural engineering from Texas A&M University in 1931. As an undergraduate ROTC cadet, Schriever received a commission in the Army Air Flying School and flew airmail missions before earning a master's degree from Stanford University in aeronautical engineering in 1942.[202] Though Schriever held many leadership posts in the military, he is best known for his role in the birth of the U.S. intercontinental ballistic missile program in the 1950s as head of the Air Force Air Research and Development Command's Western Development Division. In 1961, Schriever attained the rank of general and commanded the Air Force Systems Command. He retired in 1966 after thirty-five years in the air force. After leaving the military, Schriever consulted and served on advisory panels for corporate and government clients.[203] He died on June 20, 2005. Given his military background, Schriever was a strong candidate for the board.

Lt. Gen. Brent Scowcroft—Chair 2001–2005

Brent Scowcroft was born in Ogden, Utah, on March 19, 1925. He graduated from the U.S. Military Academy at West Point in 1947 and then earned an M.A. in 1953 and a Ph.D. in international relations in 1967, both from Columbia University. His military career included a number of domestic and international posts, including stints at diplomatic missions, military educational institutes, and the Pentagon. In 1970, he was named special assistant to the director of the Joint Staff.[204] Scowcroft was posted to the White House in 1972 as a military assistant to the president and a year later was reassigned as the deputy assistant to the president for national security affairs. After two years at this post, Scowcroft retired from military service in 1975. On his retirement, Scowcroft was named the national security adviser, serving until 1977. In 1982, Scowcroft became vice chair of Kissinger Associates, an international consulting firm, and remained at that position until his reappointment as national security adviser under President George H. W. Bush. With Bush's departure from office in 1993, Scowcroft left the White House to become the president of the Forum for International Policy. Scowcroft also participated in the President's Commission on Defense Management and the President's Special Review Board on the Iran/Contra Affair.[205] In 1994, Scowcroft founded the Scowcroft Group, an international business advisory firm, and he remains the firm's president. Scowcroft was an ideal candidate for board membership given his academic credentials, military service, and high-level government experience.

Paul Seabury—Member 1981–1985

Paul Seabury was born in Hempstead, New York, on May 6, 1923. He received his bachelor's degree in government from Swarthmore College in 1946 and his doctorate from Columbia University in 1953. After graduating, Seabury joined the faculty at the University of California, Berkeley. He held positions as full professor, assistant dean, faculty chair of the College of Letters and Sciences, and provost of the University of California, Santa Cruz. In addition to his academic career, Seabury was active in government and politics. During the 1960s, he was a consultant to the State Department, and in 1967 President Johnson appointed him to the Board of Foreign Scholarships.[206] He was also a member of the Americans for Democratic Action but resigned in 1968 to protest the organization's endorsement of Eugene McCarthy for president. In the 1970s, Seabury worked as a foreign policy consultant to the Democratic National Committee and as a director of Freedom House and the League for Industrial Democracy. He was also a member of the Committee on the Present Danger and Social Democrats, USA.[207] He died on October 17, 1990. Seabury was a reasonable candidate for the board, primarily in light of his academic background in defense and international relations.

George Shultz—Member 1974–1976

George Shultz was born in New York, New York, on December 13, 1920, and graduated from Princeton in 1942 with a degree in economics. After college, Shultz joined the Marines and served until 1945.[208] Shultz earned a doctorate in industrial economics from the Massachusetts Institute of Technology (MIT) in 1949, where he also taught until 1957. Shultz then left MIT to take a position teaching at the University of Chicago graduate school, where he became dean in 1962. Before joining the Nixon administration, Shultz worked as a fellow at the Center for Advanced Study in the Behavioral Sciences at Stanford University. Under President Nixon, Shultz served as secretary of labor from 1969 to 1970, then as the director of the

Office of Management and Budget (OMB) from 1970 to 1972. In 1972, Shultz left OMB to become secretary of the Treasury, replacing John Connally, and remained there until 1974, when he became executive vice president of the Bechtel Corporation. He also served as the chair of the Council of Economic Advisers, negotiating several trade agreements with the Soviets in 1973 and representing the United States at the Tokyo Round of the General Agreement on Tariffs and Trade.[209] Given his academic credentials and high-level government experience, Schultz was a strong candidate for board membership.

Stanley S. Shuman—Member 1995–2001

Stanley S. Shuman was born in Cambridge, Massachusetts, on June 22, 1935. Shuman completed his academic career at Harvard University, earning his B.A. in 1956, his J.D. in 1959, and his M.B.A. in 1961. After completing his M.B.A., Shuman began working with the New York City–based Allen and Company, an investment and banking firm, where he served as executive vice president, managing director, and member of the executive committee.[210] Shuman also served on the board of directors for the News Corporation from 1982 to 2005 as well as on the boards of the News American Holdings, Sesac, and Six Flags.[211] Shuman's history as a longtime Democrat with major contributions to the Democratic national convention made his appointment to the board controversial.[212] Shuman appears to have been largely a political appointee.

Admiral John H. Sides, USN (Ret.)—Member 1965–1968

John H. Sides was born in Roslyn, Washington, on April 22, 1904. Sides graduated from the U.S. Naval Academy at Annapolis in 1925. In 1931, Sides attended postgraduate training in naval ordnance at Annapolis and then at the University of Michigan, where he earned an M.S. degree in 1934. Sides served in the Ammunition Section of the Navy's Bureau of Ordnance from June 1937 to July 1939. During World War II, he served at the Ammunition and Explosives Section, Research and Development Division of the Bureau of Ordnance.[213] After graduating from the National War College in May 1948, Sides was assigned as deputy to the assistant chief of naval operations for guided missiles. Admiral Sides was associated with the navy's guided missile programs throughout much of his career. After a couple of subsequent postings, Sides was selected to become the director of the Guided Missile Division, Office of the Chief of Naval Operations, in February 1952. In 1956, he assumed the position of deputy to the special assistant to the secretary of defense for guided missiles at the Pentagon. A year later, he became the director of the Weapons Systems Evaluation Group, Office of the Secretary of Defense. Admiral Sides's final billet in the navy was as commander in chief, U.S. Pacific Fleet, where he served from

August 1960 until his retirement in October 1963.[214] On retirement, Admiral Sides served as a senior military adviser to Lockheed Aircraft. Sides died on April 3, 1978.[215] In light of his military background, Sides was a reasonable candidate for board membership.

Robert Forman Six—Member 1981–1985

Robert Forman Six was born in Stockton, California, on June 25, 1907. He was educated in Stockton's public school system but never attended college. Instead, he focused on flying, earning his pilot's license at the age of twenty-two aboard an OX-5 Alexander Eagle Rock biplane. With family money, he was able to acquire a 40 percent share in a new airline called Varney Speed Lines in 1936. Though the carrier had only one route, from Pueblo, Colorado, to El Paso, Texas, Six saw an opportunity in the fledgling company. In 1937, he changed its name to Continental Airlines and began aggressively expanding into new territory. The company grew under his leadership to become one of the biggest air carriers in the United States and made air travel accessible and affordable to the mass public.[216] He died on October 6, 1986. Six appears to have been exclusively a political appointee.

William French Smith—Member 1985–1990

William French Smith was born in Wilton, New Hampshire, on August 26, 1917. He received his B.A. from the University of California, Los Angeles, in 1939 and his law degree from Harvard in 1942. From 1942 until 1946, Smith served as a lieutenant in the U.S. Naval Reserves.[217] After leaving the armed forces, Smith joined the law firm Gibson, Dunn, and Crutcher in Los Angeles, where he rose to the rank of partner during his thirty-five-year tenure. After being one of the major backers of Reagan's bid for the governorship of California in 1966, Smith was appointed by Reagan to the Board of Regents of the University of California, a move that would lead to Smith's participation in Reagan's informal group of advisers later known as the "Kitchen Cabinet."[218] In addition to his time in the private sector, Smith served as a member of the U.S. Advisory Commission on International, Educational, and Cultural Affairs, president of the Los Angeles World Affairs Council, and a member of the Los Angeles Committee on Foreign Relations. He was also a member of the advisory council of the Harvard University School of Government and the Advisory Board of the Center for Strategic and International Studies. He also served as chair of the California delegation to the Republican national convention in 1968 and the vice chair in 1972 and 1976.[219] Smith died on October 29, 1990. He appears to have been largely a political appointee to the board.

Maurice Sonnenberg—Member 1992–2000

Maurice Sonnenberg completed his B.S. at the School of Foreign Service at Georgetown University and his M.S. in international law at New York University. Though his professional expertise was in foreign trade and restructuring businesses for foreign operations and markets, Sonnenberg also served in both the Air National Guard and the Air Force Reserve. Sonnenberg's career spanned the gamut of government service, and his posts included cochair of the National Commission for the Review of the Research and Development Programs of the U.S. Intelligence Community, vice chair of the National Commission on Terrorism, and a member of the U.S. Commission on Reducing and Protecting Government Secrecy. Sonnenberg advised President George H. W. Bush and his administration on such diverse issues as the Brady Bill and the North American Free Trade Agreement. He also served as a member of the U.S. observer team for Central American elections held during the administrations of former presidents George H. W. Bush and Bill Clinton. He held an appointment to the President's Export Council, advised the U.S. Commission on the Status of Puerto Rico in industrial and economic issues, and participated in the Economic Commission for Europe. Sonnenberg recently joined the international investment firm Bear Stearns as a senior international adviser focusing on Latin American and European political and professional affairs.[220] Sonnenberg, given his extensive government experience, including in the intelligence community, was a strong candidate for the board.

John Harrison Streicker—Member 2001–2005

John Harrison Streicker graduated from Princeton in 1964 and earned his J.D. at Yale Law School in 1967. Streicker has worked in the private sector all his life and is currently chair of the board of Sentinel Real Estate—a New York City–based real estate asset manager and one of the largest holders of apartment properties in the United States. Streicker is also the former chair of the Community 5 Board—a New York City municipal advisory group.[221] Streiker appears to have been exclusively a political appointee.

Gen. Maxwell D. Taylor—Member 1961, 1965–1969, Chair 1969–1970

Maxwell D. Taylor was born in Keystesville, Missouri, on August 26, 1901. Taylor attended the U.S. Military Academy at West Point, graduating fourth in his class in 1922. On graduation, Taylor was commissioned a second lieutenant in the Corps of Engineers. In 1926, Taylor transferred to the Field Artillery branch. In 1927, Taylor was sent to France to study French, after which he was posted to West Point as an instructor of French and an assistant professor of Spanish. In 1932, he attended the Command and General Staff

College at Fort Leavenworth, Kansas. Taylor was then sent to the American embassy in Tokyo, Japan, where he studied Japanese. He also served a short stint as an assistant military attaché in Peking, China. After completing his tour in Asia, Taylor returned to the United States and entered the Army War College, graduating in June 1940. In 1942, Taylor participated in the development of the army's first airborne divisions. Assigned to the Eighty-second Airborne Division, Taylor took part in the Italian Campaign in 1943. In 1944, Taylor became the commanding general of the 101st Division and participated in campaigns in the Ardennes.[222] In 1945, Taylor was selected to serve as the superintendent of the U.S. Military Academy. After a tour as deputy chief of staff for operations and administration of the army, Taylor assumed command of the Eighth U.S. Army in Korea in February 1953. In June 1955, Taylor became the chief of staff of the army, a position he held until his retirement in June 1959.[223] Taylor's objections to the Eisenhower administration's "Massive Retaliation" doctrine led him to resign as chief of staff in 1959. In 1961, President Kennedy recalled Taylor to active duty to serve as military representative of the president with a joint appointment to the PFIAB.[224] Kennedy subsequently appointed Taylor as the chairman of the Joint Chiefs of Staff, a position he held from 1962 to 1964. In 1964, Taylor was nominated and confirmed to be the U.S. ambassador to South Vietnam. Taylor returned from South Vietnam in 1965. That same year, he was reappointed to the PFIAB and accepted another part-time role as a special consultant to President Johnson on Vietnam policy, in violation of Executive Order 10938, which prohibited PFIAB members from serving in government. In 1966, Taylor became the president of the Institute for Defense Analysis—a federally funded research and development center—a position he held concurrently with his duties as a PFIAB member and special consultant to the president.[225] President Johnson selected Taylor to replace Clark Clifford as chair of the PFIAB in February 1968, a position he held until January 1969, when Johnson left office. He died on April 19, 1987. Given his extensive military experience and service at high levels in the White House, Taylor was a very strong candidate for membership on the board, though his simultaneous service on the board and in the Kennedy and Johnson administrations did establish a troubling precedent.

Edward Teller—1971–1977

Edward Teller was born in Budapest, Hungary, on January 15, 1908. A mathematical prodigy, Teller left Hungary in the wake of World War I and pursued his university studies in Germany, where he received his doctorate in physics from the University of Leipzig in 1930. He began work in the United States as a professor at George Washington University, where he remained until 1941. Soon after, he joined the Manhattan Project at Los Alamos, New Mexico, and was indispensable to the American effort to develop the atomic bomb. When the war ended, Teller returned to teaching, this time at the University of Chicago. In 1954, he became associate director of Lawrence Livermore Laboratory and director in 1958. One of the foremost experts in the atomic energy field, Dr. Teller was the recipient of the Albert Einstein Award, the Enrico Fermi Award, the National Medal of Science, and the Presidential Medal of Freedom.[226] Teller died on September 9, 2003. Teller's academic credentials and intimate knowledge of nuclear weapons made him an ideal candidate for the board.

John Goodwin Tower—Member 1987–1990, Chair 1990–1991

John Goodwin Tower was born in Houston, Texas, on September 29, 1925. During World War II, he served in the U.S. Navy in the Pacific theater for three years. He graduated in 1948 from Southwestern University and then received his master's degree in political science from Southern Methodist University (SMU) in 1953. He also attended the London School of Economics for a year after graduating from SMU. Tower was on the faculty at Midwestern State University in Wichita Falls, Texas, from 1951 until 1960, when he made a successful bid for the U.S. Senate seat vacated by Lyndon Johnson.[227] While in the Senate, Tower served as chair of the Committee on Armed Services and of the Republican Policy Committee. He was also a member of the Budget Committee and the Committee on Banking, Housing, and Urban Affairs. Tower was active in Republican politics for several decades, serving as a delegate to the Republican national convention seven times and as chair in 1980. In 1985, after Tower left the Senate, President Reagan appointed him as a delegate to the Negotiations on Nuclear and Space Arms in Geneva. Later, Tower chaired the Iran-Contra Commission.[228] The commission's report was critical of many officials and castigated the president and his closest advisers for their lack of control of the National Security Council. Tower died in an airplane crash on April 5, 1991. Because he had some national security and intelligence experience in Congress, Tower was a reasonable candidate for appointment to the board.

Caspar Willard Weinberger—Member 1988–1990

Caspar Willard Weinberger was born in San Francisco on August 18, 1917. He received his bachelor's and law degrees from Harvard in 1938 and 1941, respectively. After leaving school, Weinberger joined the army and served with the Forty-first Infantry Division and on the intelligence staff of Gen. Douglas MacArthur. When the Japanese surrendered, Weinberger returned to law, working as a clerk for a federal judge and then joining Heller, Ehrman, White, and McAuliffe in San Francisco. After only a few years, Weinberger decided to enter politics and won a seat in the California assembly.[229] In 1970, President Nixon appointed him chair of the Federal Trade Commission. Weinberger soon moved to the Office of Management and Budget (OMB) as deputy director under George Shultz. When Shultz replaced John Connally as secretary of the Treasury in May 1972, Weinberger became director of the OMB. Weinberger moved six months later to be the secretary of health, education, and welfare. Weinberger left government in 1975 to become special counsel to the Bechtel Corporation. In 1980, he returned as an economic adviser to president-elect Reagan. Behind only Robert McNamara, Weinberger was the second-longest-serving secretary of defense with nearly seven years at the helm of the Department of Defense.[230] Weinberger died on March 28, 2006. Given Weinberger's extensive experience in government, particular as secretary of defense, he was a strong candidate for board membership.

Seymour Weiss—Member 1981–1985

Seymour Weiss was born in Chicago on May 15, 1925. After a stint in the U.S. Naval Reserves, he received his B.A. from the University of Pennsylvania in 1945 and his master's degree in international relations four years later from the University of Chicago. After graduating, he worked for the Bureau of the Budget until 1952, when he took a position with the Mutual Security Agency (MSA) as the director of military assistance coordination. After the MSA was abolished in 1955 as part of a national security restructuring plan, Weiss joined the Department of State as a foreign service officer. From 1960 to 1967, Weiss was the director of the State Department's Office of Political and Military Affairs. Later, he was the director of the Office of Strategic Research and Intelligence and a senior member of the secretary of state's planning and coordination staff. He later served as the deputy director of the policy planning staff and then the director of the Department of Political and Military Affairs in 1973. After a lengthy term in Washington, Weiss ended his State Department career as ambassador to the Bahamas from 1974 to 1976.[231] In late 1976, Weiss served on the advisory panel of the controversial Team B project in alternative intelligence assessment.[232] He died on September 23, 1992. Given his foreign affairs and intelligence background, Weiss was a strong candidate for board membership.

Thomas E. Wheeler—Member 2011–present

Thomas Wheeler received his undergraduate degree in 1971 from Ohio University and an M.B.A. in 1985 from Baldwin Wallace College. A career businessman, Wheeler founded a number of telecommunications companies before becoming CEO of the Cellular Telecommunications and Internet Association. He is currently managing director of Core Capital Partners, an investment company. Aside from his business expertise in telecommunications, Wheeler has no significant professional qualification for board membership and, thus, appears to be largely a political appointee.[233]

Albert Dewell Wheelon—Member 1983–1988

Albert Dewell "Bud" Wheelon was born in Moline, Illinois, on January 18, 1929. He received his B.A. from Stanford University and his doctorate in physics from the Massachusetts Institute of Technology in 1952.[234] After graduation, Wheelon began his career in national defense by joining Douglas Aircraft and then Ramo-Woolridge (started by two former Hughes Aerospace employees and the predecessor to TRW) in 1953. Wheelon remained at Ramo-Woolridge until joining the CIA in 1962. At the CIA, Wheelon served as the first director of science and technology and oversaw the Corona satellite program, which succeeded the U-2 as the primary intelligence-gathering platform for the United States. He also supervised the development of the SR-71 reconnaissance plane.[235] Wheelon left the board in 1988, about the same time as he retired from Hughes Aircraft. His extensive defense industry and intelligence community background made Wheelon an ideal candidate for the board.

Edward Bennett Williams—Member 1976–1977, 1981–1985

Edward Bennett Williams was born in Hartford, Connecticut, on May 31, 1920. He received an A.B. from the College of the Holy Cross in 1941 and graduated with an LL.B. from Georgetown University in 1945. He became a high-profile trial lawyer by defending many well-known clients, "from the teamsters' leader James R. Hoffa to Senator Joseph McCarthy." Williams later became a senior partner of the law firm Williams, Connolly, and Califano in Washington, DC, president and director of the Washington Redskins, and general counsel for Georgetown University. Williams died on August 13, 1988.[236] Williams appears to have been largely a political appointee.

James Quinn Wilson—Member 1985–1990

James Quinn Wilson was born in Denver, Colorado, on May 27, 1931. He received his B.A. from the University of the Redlands in 1952 and his doctorate from the University of Chicago in 1959. He joined the faculty of Harvard University in 1961 and eventually became the Henry Lee Shattuck Professor of Government. During his time at Harvard, he also served as the director of the Massachusetts Institute of Technology–Harvard University Joint Center for Urban Studies, becoming one of the most respected experts on crime in the country. In 1985, he moved to the University of California, Los Angeles, as the James Collins Professor of Management and Public Policy.[237] Because of his expertise in the area of crime, Wilson served on numerous governmental commissions and panels. He died on March 1, 2012. In light of his broad and distinguished academic career focusing on a wide range of public policy issues, Wilson was a strong candidate for board membership.

Peter Barton Wilson—Member 2001–2005

Peter Barton Wilson was born in Lake Forest, Illinois, on August 23, 1933. Wilson attended Yale and earned a B.A. in English literature in 1955. He later completed his J.D. at the University of California, Berkeley, in 1962. After working in the private sector, Wilson represented Sacramento in the California state legislature from 1966 to 1971.[238] Wilson went on to become mayor of San Diego, a U.S. senator, and, most recently, governor of California from 1991 until 1998. While in the U.S. Senate, he was a member of the Armed Service Committee and a noted proponent of strengthening national defense.[239] Since he retired from public service, Wilson has worked in the private sector, most recently as a principal in the Bingham Consulting Group and counsel to Bingham McCutchen in 2002.[240] Given his service on the Senate Armed Services Committee, Wilson was a plausible candidate for the board.

Albert James Wohlstetter—Member 1985–1990

Albert James Wohlstetter was born in New York, New York, on December 19, 1913. He attended Columbia University, earning both his bachelor's and his master's degrees before joining the War Production Board during World War II. After a stint in the private sector, Wohlstetter joined the Rand Corporation as a consultant and then a senior staff member. He stayed at Rand for fourteen years and briefly worked as a visiting professor at the University of California, Los Angeles, and the University of California, Berkeley, before moving to the University of Chicago. After sixteen years as a professor in Chicago, Wohlstetter left to become the director of research at PAN Heuristics in 1979.[241] He died on January 10, 1997. As one of America's leading "defense intellectuals," with long service at Rand and solid academic credentials, Wohlstetter was a strong candidate for the board.

Philip David Zelikow—Member 2001–2003

Philip David Zelikow was born in New York, New York, on September 21, 1954. Zelikow received a B.A. in history and political science from the University of the Redlands in 1977, a J.D. from the University of Houston in 1981, and a master's and a doctorate from the Fletcher School of Law and Diplomacy at Tufts University in 1984 and 1995, respectively. After passing the state bar in 1979, Zelikow worked as an attorney in both the public and the private sectors.[242] In 1984, he left private practice to work as a professor at the Naval Post Graduate School and joined the Department of State as a Foreign Service officer. In 1989, Zelikow was named the director for European security at the National Security Council. Zelikow was the executive director of the National Commission on Terrorist Attacks upon the United States (the 9/11 Commission).[243] Most recently, Zelikow served as the counselor of the U.S. Department of State—the special adviser and consultant to the secretary of state—from February 2005 to December 2006. Zelikow alternated between government service and academe, working at the John F. Kennedy School at Harvard before taking his current position as the White Burkett Miller Professor of History at the University of Virginia and the director of the University of Virginia's Miller Center for Public Affairs. Given his academic background and long record of government experience, Zelikow was a strong candidate for board membership.

Elmo Russell Zumwalt Jr.—Member 1996–2000

Elmo Russell Zumwalt Jr. was born in San Francisco on November 29, 1920. In 1942, he earned his bachelor's with distinction from the U.S. Naval Academy. Zumwalt later earned advanced degrees from the Naval War College in 1953 and the National War College in 1962. Commissioned as an ensign in the U.S. Navy in 1942, Zumwalt rose through the ranks and became the youngest officer to reach the rank of admiral in July 1970 at the age of forty-nine. He ended his career as the chief of Naval operations, retiring in 1974. In 1976, Zumwalt mounted an unsuccessful bid for a Democratic senatorial seat in Virginia. After leaving public service, Zumwalt spent some time as the president of the American Medical Building Corporation in Wisconsin. He died on January 2, 2000.[244] In view of his long navy career, Zumwalt was a reasonable candidate for board membership.

EXECUTIVE STAFF MEMBERS

Russell A. Ash—PFIAB and/or National Security Council Staff ca. 1954–1975

Russell Ash had prior professional experience with the FBI, but little else is known about his background or his direct experience working on intelligence issues. He joined the National Security Council (NSC) staff in 1954 and was responsible for personnel security and internal security coordination for the NSC. In 1956, the board was added to his portfolio. Wheaton Byers reported that Ash served mostly as a personal assistant to Chair Anderson and that he did not play a very active role in the actual activities of the board. Ash often traveled with Anderson whenever Anderson took an overseas trip on behalf of the board.[245] In January 1963, he conducted a review of some records of the NSC 5412/2 group on behalf of the PFIAB, and he occasionally gave the PFIAB status reports on the implementation of their prior recommendations.[246]

Jane E. Baker—Research and Administrative Officer ca. 1999[247]

Carol Blair—Administrative Officer ca. 2005[248]

Gerard P. Burke—Executive Secretary 1970–1973

Gerard Burke earned his bachelor's degree from the College of the Holy Cross and his J.D. from Georgetown University Law School. He served for five years on active duty in the U.S. Navy before joining the National Security Agency (NSA), serving as special assistant to the director of the NSA prior to his appointment as PFIAB executive secretary. After leaving the board's staff, Burke went into the private sector, establishing the Parvus Group, Information Security International, and Jericho Ltd., all companies that specialize in corporate security matters. He also worked for other companies during this period, including Reliance National and ACE USA Aerospace.[249]

Robert L. Butterworth—Staff Member 1984–1988

Robert Butterworth earned his bachelor's degree from the University of Washington and his Ph.D. from the University of California, Berkeley. He came to government from academe, having been a tenured associate professor at Pennsylvania State University. He started his government career as a staff member of the Senate Select Committee on Intelligence and after his PFIAB service worked at the Department of Defense. In 1991, he left government service and founded Aries Analytics, a corporate consulting company.[250]

Wheaton Byers—Staff 1970–1973, Executive Secretary 1973–1977

Wheaton Byers was born in Pennsylvania on December 14, 1925. Byers joined the navy in 1944 after graduating from high school and served as a quartermaster in the Pacific theater. After leaving the navy, he attended Williams College in Williamstown, Massachusetts, where he received a degree in economics in 1950. After graduation, Byers became an operations officer with the CIA. He had several overseas assignments, including The Hague, Belgrade, and Berlin. When the resignation of J. Patrick Coyne left an opening on the staff of the PFIAB in 1970, the board requested a CIA employee, and Director of Central Intelligence Richard Helms himself sent Byers to serve as the special assistant to the executive secretary. Byers served in that capacity for three years before serving as executive secretary until 1977.[251]

Brig. Gen. John F. Cassidy—Staff Director ca. 1956[252]

J. Patrick Coyne—Staff Director ca. 1959, Executive Secretary ca. 1970[253]

J. Patrick Coyne began a career in the intelligence field around 1940, although specific details about his educational background and earlier work experience are unknown. Later in his career he served as an assistant director of the FBI and later joined the staff of the National Security Council (NSC). In 1948, he was appointed by Truman as a GS-15 adviser to the NSC to work on intelligence issues. He retained this position during the Eisenhower administration as a GS-17. In May 1959, he was appointed to be the staff director for the PBCFIA as a GS-18. By 1964, he had served in "various intelligence capacities" for the Truman, Eisenhower, Kennedy, and Johnson administrations.[254]

Randy Wayne Deitering—Assistant Director 1987–1989, Deputy Executive Director 1989–1995, Acting Executive Director 1995–1998, Executive Director 1998–2003

Randy Wayne Deitering was born in Allen County, Indiana, on February 24, 1949. Deitering graduated with honors from Southern Connecticut State University with a B.S. in political science in 1971.[255] After completing his master's degree in the comparative politics of Russia and Eastern Europe at New York University in 1973, Deitering joined the Department of the Air Force as an intelligence analyst, where he worked on Soviet-bloc political and military affairs for three years before moving to the CIA in 1978. At the CIA, Deitering served as a branch chief and as a senior analyst and on the staff of the DCI. In 1987, Deitering left the CIA to join the PFIAB staff as an assistant director. In 1989, Deitering was named the deputy executive director of the PFIAB, a position he held until 1995, when he was named the PFIAB's acting executive director. In 1998, Deitering was named executive director, where he served until his retirement in 2003.[256] After retirement from the PFIAB, Deitering became the CIA's officer-in-residence at the University of South Carolina, where he taught courses in national security in 2003 and 2004.[257]

Capt. Fred R. Demech Jr.—Deputy Executive Director 1981–1983, Executive Director 1983–1984, 1988–1989

Fred R. Demech Jr. was born in Taylor, Pennsylvania, on June 1, 1940. Demech attended Wilkes College, where he received his BA in 1961, and graduated from the Naval War College. After graduating from Wilkes, Demech joined the U.S. Navy as a cryptologist and rose through the ranks to captain, during which time he served as the executive assistant to three senior flag officers, as research and technical officer on two ships, and as executive officer at several shore stations. In 1981, Demech became deputy executive director for the PFIAB before being promoted to executive director in 1983. In 1984, Demech left his post at the PFIAB as he was transferred to direct a signals intelligence site in Scotland.[258] In 1988, Demech returned to the PFIAB as executive director, where he served until 1989. He died on March 11, 2011.

Joan Avalyn Dempsey—Executive Director 2003–2005

Joan Avalyn Dempsey received a B.A. from Southern Arkansas University and a master of public administration degree from the University of Arkansas in 1983.[259] Dempsey served in the U.S. Navy as a cryptology technician and in 1983 entered federal service in the Office of Naval Intelligence.[260] She has worked in a number of intelligence positions during her long career, including deputy assistant secretary of defense for intelligence, chief of staff to Director of Central Intelligence (DCI) George Tenet, and the first-ever deputy DCI for community management in October 1997.[261] After leaving public service, Dempsey was hired as a vice president at Booz, Allen, and Hamilton in 2005.[262]

Randall M. Fort—Staff Member, Assistant Director, and Deputy Executive Director, 1982–1987

Randall Fort was born in Richmond, Indiana, on July 4, 1956. He earned a B.A. at George Washington University in 1978. He did further study of Japanese at the University of Cincinnati and Ohio State University before taking a Henry Luce Scholarship to work for a member of the Japanese Diet in 1980–1981. His government service began in 1976 when he worked for Congressman Bill Gradison of Ohio on both his campaign and his congressional staff. After his PFIAB service, Fort served in intelligence-related positions in the Departments of State and the Treasury. Fort spent the years from 1993 through 2006 in the private sector at TRW and Goldman Sachs. From 2006 through 2009, he served as assistant secretary of state for intelligence and research.[263]

Frank W. Fountain—Assistant Director, Chief Counsel, ca. 1999[264]

Margie M. Kinney—Secretary 1962–1965[265]

Harold R. Lawrence—Deputy Staff Director ca. 1956[266]

Brendan G. Melley—Assistant Director 1998–2001[267]

Brendan G. Melley graduated from Providence College and completed the postgraduate intelligence program at the Defense Intelligence Agency (DIA). After several years of active duty in the U.S. Army, ultimately serving as a collection manager for combatant commands at the DIA, Melley spent the mid-1990s working for the director of the DIA as a professional staffer for the Commission on the Roles and Capabilities of the U.S. Intelligence Community and as a senior consultant to Booz, Allen, and Hamilton. In 2001, Melley served under Senators George Mitchell and Warren Rudman on the Sharm el-Sheikh Fact Finding Committee that produced the "Mitchell

Plan." From late 2001 until 2005, Melley was the director for counter-proliferation, proliferation strategy, and homeland defense and director for intelligence programs for the National Security Council (NSC). After leaving public service, Melley became an associate vice president at the Cohen Group, a global business consulting firm.[268]

Mark F. Moynihan—Member ca. 1999[269]

Mark F. Moynihan is a career CIA officer. At the end of the Clinton administration, Moynihan returned to the CIA. He is a proponent of collaboration between scientific and intelligence communities and in 2001 authored an article in *Physics Today* arguing that academic scientists play an essential role in helping the intelligence community exploit technology for national security.[270]

Sammie L. Newman—Secretary ca. 1959[271]

Lionel Olmer—Special Assistant to the Executive Secretary 1973–1977, Executive Secretary 1977[272]

Lionel Olmer was born in New Haven, Connecticut, on November 11, 1934. He graduated from the University of Connecticut in 1956 and earned a J.D. from the American University in 1963. He joined the U.S. Navy and became a specialist in cryptology and tactical intelligence. He also did a tour on the staff of the chief of naval operations. On retirement from government in 1977, he worked for four years for Motorola and was on the board of directors of the International Rescue Committee, serving as chair of the committee's Washington advisory group. He was nominated to be undersecretary of the treasury in 1981.[273]

Stefanie R. Osburn—Executive Director ca. 2005

Stefanie R. Osburn received her B.A. from the Georgia Southern University. Osburn then spent the next twenty years with the CIA. Prior to her appointment as the PFIAB's executive director, Osburn served as first the chief of staff for the deputy director of central intelligence for community management and then, after the creation of the director of national intelligence, as the chief of staff for the deputy director of national intelligence for management.

Homer Pointer—General Counsel ca. 2009

Homer Pointer received his J.D. from the University of Texas in 1973 and a master of laws from George Washington University in 1984. He served as a U.S. Navy Judge Advocate General officer, including with the U.S. Central Command. He is a member of the Texas bar.[274]

Roosevelt A. Roy—Administrative Officer ca. 1999[275]

Gary Schmitt—Executive Director 1984–1988

Gary Schmitt earned his B.A. from the University of Dallas and his doctorate from the University of Chicago in 1980. Schmitt was also a member of the faculty of the University of Virginia from 1977 to 1979. In 1981, Schmitt joined the staff of the Senate Select Committee on Intelligence, where he stayed until 1984. From 1982 to 1984, Schmitt was also the minority staff director of the committee.[276] Schmitt is now resident scholar and director of advanced strategic studies at the American Enterprise Institute.[277]

Nina Stewart—Assistant Executive Director 1987–1989, Executive Director 1989–1991

Originally from Dallas, Nina Stewart received her B.A. from Abilene Christian University and studied law at George Washington University. She began her career as a police officer and detective in Dallas and transferred into federal service as a diplomatic security officer. She rose through the ranks to become special assistant to the assistant secretary of state for diplomatic security before moving to the PFIAB in 1987 as assistant executive director. Under President Bush, Stewart served as executive director of the PFIAB until October 1, 1991, when she resigned to take a position as the deputy assistant secretary of defense for counterintelligence.[278]

Lieutenant General Charles Norman Wood—Executive Director 1981–1983

Charles Norman Wood was born in Dallas, Texas, on March 7, 1938. After graduating from the University of Texas at Austin in 1960, Wood joined the U.S. Air Force as a pilot. During his military career, Wood served two tours in Vietnam as a reconnaissance plane pilot and then multiple tours on intelligence staffs. After leaving Southeast Asia, Wood returned to school and received his master's degree in public administration from Auburn University in 1974. He graduated from the National War College in 1979. Before being appointed as executive secretary of the PFIAB, Wood was assistant deputy chief of staff at U.S. Strategic Air Command headquarters in Omaha, Nebraska.[279] In late 1983, Wood was promoted to the rank of brigadier general and left his position at the PFIAB. Wood retired from the air force in 1992 with the rank of lieutenant general.

Eugene F. Yeates—Executive Director 1992–1995

Eugene F. Yeates spent the bulk of his career at the National Security Agency (NSA), ultimately serving there as the chief of the Office of Policy. On October 14, 1992, Yeates was designated as executive director of the PFIAB by President George H. W. Bush.[280] After serving on the PFIAB for three years, Yeates left to take a private-sector position at the Science Applications International Corporation (SAIC). In 1996, Yeates was interviewed by the Commission on the Roles and Capabilities of the U.S. Intelligence Community (better known as the Aspin-Brown Commission) concerning his role as former PFIAB executive director and position as senior vice president at SAIC.[281] Yeates achieved some notoriety after he testified in support of an in-camera affidavit the NSA filed in response to the Citizens against Unidentified Flying Objects Secrecy effort to secure NSA documents in 1980.[282]

Notes

The following abbreviations have been used throughout the notes:

AB JFK = Appointment Books of President John F. Kennedy
ALIC = Archives Library Information Catalog
ARRB = Assassination Records Review Board
AS = Alphabetical Subseries
BC = Board of Consultants
BC-FIA = Board of Consultants [on Foreign Intelligence Activities]
CPP = Carter Presidential Papers
CREST = CIA Records Search Tool
CSTB = Computer Science and Telecommunications Board
DA = Departments and Agencies
DCI = Director of Central Intelligence
DDEL = Dwight D. Eisenhower Presidential Library, Abilene, KS
DDI = Deputy Director of Intelligence
DD/P = Deputy Director (Plans)
DSC = Department of Special Collections, HGARC
Eisenhower Records = Eisenhower, Dwight D.: Records as President
EO = Executive Order
FG = File Group
FIAB = Foreign Intelligence Advisory Board
FRUS, 1964–1968, vol. 10 = *Foreign Relations of the United States, 1964–1968*, vol. 10, *National Security Policy* (Washington, DC: U.S. Government Printing Office, 2001)
FRUS, 1964–1968, vol. 32 = *Foreign Relations of the United States, 1964–1968*, vol. 32, *Dominican Republic; Cuba; Haiti; Guyana* (Washington, DC: U.S. Government Printing Office, 2005)
FRUS, 1964–1968, vol. 33 = *Foreign Relations of the United States, 1964–1968*, vol. 33, *Organization and Management of Foreign Policy; United Nations* (Washington, DC: U.S. Government Printing Office, 2001)
FRUS, 1969–1976, vol. 2 = *Foreign Relations of the United States, 1969–1976*, vol. 2, *Organization and Management of U.S. Foreign Policy, 1969–1972* (Washington, DC: U.S. Government Printing Office, 2006)
FRUS, 1969–1976, vol. 6 = *Foreign Relations of the United States, 1969–1976*, vol. 6, *Vietnam, January 1969–July 1970* (Washington, DC: U.S. Government Printing Office, 2005)
GRFL = Gerald R. Ford Library, Ann Arbor, MI
GHWBPL-TR = George H. W. Bush Presidential Library Textual Records
HGARC = Howard Gottlieb Archival Research Center, Boston University
IASC = Institute Archives and Special Collections, MIT Libraries, Cambridge, MA
IOB = Intelligence Oversight Board

IOBSF = Intelligence Oversight Board Subject File
JCL = Jimmy Carter Library and Museum, Atlanta, GA
JCS = Joint Chiefs of Staff
JFKL = John F. Kennedy Presidential Library, Boston
LBJPL = Lyndon B. Johnson Presidential Library, Austin, TX
LCP = Leo Cherne Papers
HGARC = Howard Gottlieb Archival Research Center, Boston University
MC = Manuscript Container
NARA = National Archives and Records Administration, College Park, MD
NARA 2 = National Archives and Records Administration Location 2, College Park, MD
NF = Name Files
NIE = national intelligence estimate
NIO = national intelligence officer
NNSA = National Nuclear Security Administration
NRC = National Research Council
NSC = National Security Council
NSCF = NSC Files
NSCIF = NSC Institutional Files
NSF = National Security Files
ODM = Office of Defense Mobilization
OF = Office Files
OFB = Official File Book
OFJM = Office Files of John Macy
OMB = Office of Management and Budget
OSANSA = Office of the Special Assistant for National Security Affairs
OSS = Office of the Staff Secretary
OWHPS = Office of the White House Press Secretary
PBCFIA = President's Board of Consultants on Foreign Intelligence Activities
PFIAB = President's Foreign Intelligence Advisory Board
POF = President's Office Files
PJK = Papers of James Killian
PPF = President's Personal File
PPJFK = Papers of President John F. Kennedy
SAS = Special Assistant Series
SF = Subject Files
SS = Subject Series
USIA = U.S. Information Agency
WHCF = White House Central Files
WHO = White House Office
WHSF = White House Special Files
WHSP2 = White House Study Project No. 2

The following interviews have been cited in short form (e.g., "Interview with Source A") throughout the notes:

Interview with Byers = Telephone Interview with Wheaton Byers, former PFIAB executive secretary, May 8, 2006
Interview with Crowe = "Interview with William J. Crowe Jr.," June 8, 1998, *The*

Foreign Affairs Oral History Collection of the Association for Diplomatic Studies and Training, 3, at http://memory.loc.gov/cgi-bin/query/D?mfdip:1:./temp/~ammem_1YQr::

Interview with Gates = Interview with Robert M. Gates, former DCI, April 12, 2006, College Station, TX

Interview with Schmitt = Interview with Gary Schmitt, former PFIAB executive secretary, May 30, 2006

Interview with Source A, a former PFIAB member, May 3, 2006

Interview with Source B, a former cabinet official, April 17, 2007

Interview with Source E, a former PFIAB staffer, May 31, 2006

Interview with Source F, a former PFIAB member, June 13, 2006

Interview with Source G, August 15, 2006

Interview with Source H, a former senior administration official, June 1, 2006

Interview with Source I, June 13, 2006

Interview with Source L, May 3, 2006

Interview with Source M, January 8, 2007

Interview with Source P, a former White House official, April 18, 2006

Interview with Source Q, May 25, 2007

Interview with Source R, a former PFIAB staffer, May 25, 2006

Interview with Source S, June 1, 2006

Interview with Source T, a former senior official, January 9, 2007

Interview with Source U, January 8, 2007

Interview with Source XX, April 9, 2008

INTRODUCTION

1. Anne Armstrong, "Bridging the Gap: Intelligence and Policy," *Washington Quarterly* 12, no. 1 (Winter 1989): 23.

2. On the limits of outside advisory boards, see Thomas E. Cronin and Stanford D. Greenberg, *The Presidential Advisory System* (New York: Harper & Row, 1968), 8–9; and Morton H. Halperin, "The Gaither Committee and the Policy Process," *World Politics* 13, no. 3 (April 1961): 373. For firsthand, insider accounts of two recent such boards, see Loch K. Johnson, *The Threat on the Horizon: An Inside Account of America's Search for Security After the Cold War* (New York: Oxford University Press, 2011); and Ernest R. May, "When Government Writes History: A Memoir of the 9/11 Commission," *New Republic,* May 23, 2005, 30–35.

3. H. Andrew Boerstling and Richard A. Best, *Intelligence Oversight in the White House: The President's Foreign Intelligence Advisory Board and the Intelligence Oversight Board,* Congressional Research Service Report 96-619F (Washington, DC: Library of Congress, 1996); *The President's Foreign Intelligence Advisory Board: An Historical and Contemporary Analysis (1955–1975),* Congressional Research Service Report 75-225F (Washington, DC: Library of Congress, 1975); and Hale Foundation, *The President's Foreign Intelligence Advisory Board (PFIAB)* (Washington, DC: Hale Foundation, 1981).

4. See, e.g., Jeffery Richelson, *The U.S. Intelligence Community* (Cambridge, MA: Ballinger, 1985), 287, 307.

5. Anne Karalakas, "History of the Central Intelligence Agency," in *The Central Intelligence Agency: History and Documents,* ed. William M. Leary (Birmingham: University of Alabama Press, 1984), 74. This view dovetails with the general view

that such bodies are irrelevant. For a summary of the literature on the subject, see Thomas R. Wolanin, *Presidential Advisory Commissions: Truman to Nixon* (Madison: University of Wisconsin Press, 1975), 11.

6. Peter Moffat, "Interview with Howard Meyers," Association for Diplomatic Studies and Training Foreign Affairs Oral History Project, March 31, 2000, at http://memory.loc.gov/cgi-bin/query/r?ammem/mfdip:@field(DOCID+mfdip2004mey03).

7. Quoted in Halperin, "The Gaither Committee and the Policy Process," 379.

8. "Report of the Advisory Committee on Historical Diplomatic Documentation, January 1–December 31, 2001," at http://www.fas.org/sgp/advisory/state/hac01.html.

9. Leo Cherne, memorandum, "A PFIAB Valedictory," September 21, 1988, LCP, DSC, HGARC; and Leo Cherne, memorandum for the record, August 3, 1983, PFIAB (July–December 1983), LCP, DSC, HGARC.

10. Warren Rudman (former PFIAB chair) to Roman Popadiuk, March 8, 2006 (in the author's possession).

11. See, most recently, James Taranto, "Cynical, Not Criminal," *Wall Street Journal,* June 4, 2010.

12. President's Foreign Intelligence Advisory Board: A Special Investigative Panel, *Science at Its Best, Security at Its Worst: A Report on Security Problems at the U.S. Department of Energy* (Washington, DC: U.S. Government Printing Office, 1999). The report is also available, as of October 17, 2007, at http://www.fas.org/sgp/library/pfiab/index.html.

13. Warren Rudman, "Perspectives on National Security in the Twenty-First Century," Seminar on Intelligence, Command, and Control at Harvard University (Boston), April 22, 2002.

14. Anne L. Armstrong to Leo Cherne, Washington, DC, September 20, 1984, PFIAB-Misc. 01/01/84–11/31/85, LCP, DSC, HGARC; Seymour Weiss to Anne Armstrong, Bethesda, MD, September 27, 1984, PFIAB-Misc. 01/01/84–11/31/85, LCP, DSC, HGARC; Leo Cherne to Anne Armstrong, New York, NY, October 10, 1984, PFIAB-Misc. 01/01/84–11/31/85, LCP, DSC, HGARC; and Robert F. Six to Anne L. Armstrong, Los Angeles, CA, October 22, 1984, PFIAB-Misc. 01/01/84–11/31/85, LCP, DSC, HGARC.

15. These criteria come from Wolanin, *Presidential Advisory Commissions,* 130–31. Johnson (*The Threat on the Horizon,* 366) also suggests that such boards "have a multiplicity of functions," including "symbolic reassurance," generating policy-relevant information, public education, and providing a "'cooling off' period" during crises.

16. Aspin-Brown Commission, "The Need for Policy Guidance," in *Intelligence and National Security: The Secret World of Spies, An Anthology,* ed. Loch K. Johnson and James J. Wirtz, 2nd ed. (New York: Oxford University Press, 2008), 258.

17. Anne L. Armstrong to Leo Cherne, Washington, DC, September 20, 1984, PFIAB-Misc. 01/01/84–11/31/85, LCP, DSC, HGARC; Seymour Weiss to Anne Armstrong, Bethesda, MD, September 27, 1984, PFIAB-Misc. 01/01/84–11/31/85, LCP, DSC, HGARC; Leo Cherne to Anne Armstrong, New York, NY, October 10, 1984, PFIAB-Misc. 01/01/84–11/31/85, LCP, DSC, HGARC; and Robert F. Six to Anne L. Armstrong, Los Angeles, CA, October 22, 1984, PFIAB-Misc. 01/01/84–11/31/85, LCP, DSC, HGARC.

18. Wolanin, *Presidential Advisory Commissions,* 5.

19. Robert Jervis employs the "stepchild" metaphor in his "Intelligence and

Foreign Policy: A Review Essay," *International Security* 11, no. 3 (Winter 1986–97): 143. Important exceptions to this include Richard K. Betts, *Surprise Attack* (Washington, DC: Brookings, 1982); Ernest May, *Knowing One's Enemies: Intelligence Assessment Before the Two World Wars* (Princeton, NJ: Princeton University Press, 1985); and, most recently, Amy B. Zegart, *Flawed by Design: The Evolution of the CIA, JCS, and NSC* (Stanford, CA: Stanford University Press, 1999).

20. There is an extensive literature on presidential style. For a summary, see Norman C. Thomas and Joseph A. Pika, *The Politics of the Presidency*, 4th ed. (Washington, DC: Congressional Quarterly Press, 1996). Two important applications of this argument to national security policy include I. M. Destler, "National Security Advice to U.S. Presidents: Some Lessons from Thirty Years," *World Politics* 29, no. 2 (January 1977): 143–76; and Thomas Preston, *The President and His Inner Circle: Leadership Style and the Advisory Process in Foreign Affairs* (New York: Columbia University Press, 2001).

21. Zegart, *Flawed by Design*, 77.

22. Wolanin, *Presidential Advisory Commissions*, 5; Kraft as cited in Destler, "National Security Advice to U.S. Presidents," 144–45.

1. DWIGHT D. EISENHOWER

1. Anne Karalakas, "History of the Central Intelligence Agency," in *The Central Intelligence Agency: History and Documents*, ed. William M. Leary (Birmingham: University of Alabama Press, 1984), 19.

2. Jeffrey T. Richelson, *The Wizards of Langley: Inside the CIA's Directorate of Science and Technology* (Cambridge, MA: Westview, 2002), 13; and Donald E. Welzenbach, "Science and Technology: Origins of a Directorate," *Studies in Intelligence*, 1953, at http://www.faqs.org/cia/docs/126/0000253110/SCIENCE-AND-TECHNOLOGY:-ORIGINS-OF-A-DIRECTORATE.html.

3. William E. Pemberton, "Truman and the Hoover Commission," *Whistlestop: The Official Newsletter of the Harry S. Truman Library Institute* 19, no. 3 (1991), at http://www.trumanlibrary.org.

4. Welzenbach, "Science and Technology," 17.

5. Michael Warner and J. Kenneth McDonald, *U.S. Intelligence Community Reform Studies since 1947* (Washington, DC: Center for the Study of Intelligence, 2005), 15–17.

6. Quoted in ibid.

7. David M. Barrett, *The CIA and Congress: The Untold Story from Truman to Kennedy* (Lawrence: University Press of Kansas, 2005), 225.

8. Barrett, *The CIA and Congress*, 233.

9. Karalakas, "History of the Central Intelligence Agency," 64–66.

10. Morton H. Halperin, "The Gaither Committee and the Policy Process," *World Politics* 13, no. 3 (April 1961): 360.

11. Karalakas, "History of the Central Intelligence Agency," 30–31.

12. Allen W. Dulles, DCI, to President Dwight D. Eisenhower, Washington, DC, November 15, 1955, BC-FIA (1), SS, AS, WHO, OSS: Records, 1952–61, DDEL.

13. Ibid.

14. Ibid.

15. Ibid.

16. Ibid.

17. Welzenbach, "Science and Technology," 17.

18. Col. A. J. Goodpaster, U.S. Army Staff Secretary, Memorandum for Record, November 16, 1955, BC-FIA (1), SS, AS, WHO, OSS: Records, 1952–61, DDEL.

19. Goodpaster to Dulles, December 13, 1955, BC-FIA (2), SS, AS, WHO, OSS: Records, 1952–61, DDEL.

20. Goodpaster, Memorandum for Record, November 22, 1955, BC-FIA (1), SS, AS, WHO, OSS: Records, 1952–61, DDEL.

21. Ibid.

22. Goodpaster, Memorandum for Record, December 7, 1955, BC-FIA (2), SS, AS, WHO, OSS: Records, 1952–61, DDEL.

23. Dulles to Governor Sherman Adams, Assistant to the President, Washington, DC, November 30, 1955, BC-FIA (1), SS, AS, WHO, OSS: Records, 1952–61, DDEL.

24. Attachment to ibid.

25. Dulles to Adams, Washington, DC, December 7, 1955, PBCFIA, OF 309, OFB 2 of 2, Eisenhower Records, WHCF, 1953–61, DDEL.

26. Ibid.

27. Goodpaster to Adams, Washington, DC, December 21, 1955, BC-FIA (2), SS, AS, WHO, OSS: Records, 1952–61, DDEL.

28. Ibid.

29. Press Release on BC-FIA, January 13, 1956, BC-FIA (2), SS, AS, WHO, OSS: Records, 1952–61, DDEL; Goodpaster to Adams, n.d., BC (2), Subject, Alphabetical, Records, 1952–61, DDEL; and draft letter to Gen. James H. Doolittle, Washington, DC, n.d., BC-FIA (1), SS, AS, WHO, OSS: Records, 1952–61, DDEL. (Note: The draft status of the letter was determined by handwritten notes signifying as such, complete with handwritten concurrence from Dulles.)

30. Eisenhower to Joseph P. Kennedy, January 11, 1956, PBCFIA, OF 309, OFB 2 of 2, Eisenhower Records, WHCF, 1953–61, DDEL.

31. Security Clearance for Members of the Board of Consultants, February 1, 1956, BC-FIA (3), SS, AS, WHO, OSS: Records, 1952–61, DDEL.

32. Dulles to Adams, December 7, 1955, PBCFIA, OF 309, OFB 2 of 2, Eisenhower Records, WHCF, 1953–61, DDEL.

33. Edward L. Ryerson to Eisenhower, Chicago, IL, January 17, 1956, PBCFIA, OF 309, OFB 2 of 2, Eisenhower Records, WHCF, 1953–61, DDEL.

34. Goodpaster, Memorandum for Record, December 7, 1955, BC (2), Subject, Alphabetical, Records, 1952–61, DDEL; Dulles to Eisenhower, Washington, DC, January 14, 1956, PBCFIA, OF 309, OFB 2 of 2, Eisenhower Records, WHCF, 1953–61, DDEL.

35. Eisenhower to Dr. James Killian, Conolly, Lt. Gen. Doolittle, Benjamin Fairless, Gen. John E. Hull, Joseph Kennedy, Robert A. Lovett, and Ryerson, January 11, 1956, PBCFIA, OF 309, OFB 2 of 2, Eisenhower Records, WHCF, 1953–61, DDEL.

36. Ibid.

37. Killian to Sherman, January 16, 1956, PBCFIA, OF 309, OFB 2 of 2, Eisenhower Records, WHCF, 1953–61, DDEL.

38. Eisenhower to Doolittle, Fairless, Hull, Lovett, and Ryerson, n.d., PBCFIA, OF 309, OFB 2 of 2, Eisenhower Records, WHCF, 1953–61, DDEL.

39. Goodpaster, Memorandum of Conference with the President, December 20, 1956, PBCFIA, First Report to the President [December 1956–August 1956] (1), NSC, SS, WHO, OSANSA: Records, 1952–61, DDEL.

40. Immediate Release by James C. Hagerty, Press Secretary to the President, January 13, 1956, PBCFIA, OF 309, OFB 2 of 2, Eisenhower Records, WHCF, 1953–61, DDEL.

41. Immediate Release (including attached EO 10656) by Hagerty, February 6, 1956, PBCFIA, OF 309, OFB 2 of 2, Eisenhower Records, WHCF, 1953–61, DDEL.

42. Joseph Kennedy to Eisenhower, July 18, 1956, PBCFIA, OF 309, OFB 2 of 2, Eisenhower Records, WHCF, 1953–61, DDEL.

43. Joseph Kennedy to Adams, July 18, 1956, PBCFIA, OF 309, OFB 2 of 2, Eisenhower Records, WHCF, 1953–61, DDEL.

44. Ibid.

45. Tim Weiner, *Legacy of Ashes: The History of the CIA* (New York: Doubleday, 2007), 165.

46. J. Patrick Coyne to President John F. Kennedy, Tab 2: List of Members and Former Members of PBCFIA, Washington, DC, May 14, 1961, FIAB Briefing Material 5/61, POF, DA, PPJFK, JFKL.

47. Minnich, Typewritten Note, n.d., PBCFIA, OF 309, OFB 2 of 2, Eisenhower Records, WHCF, 1953–61, DDEL.

48. Coyne to President Kennedy, Tab 2, May 14, 1961, FIAB Briefing Material 5/61, POF, DA, PPJFK, JFKL.

49. Killian, PBCFIA Chair, to Adams, Washington, DC, June 14, 1957, PBCFIA, OF 309, OFB 2 of 2, Eisenhower Records, WHCF, 1953–61, DDEL.

50. Killian to Adams, Washington, DC, May 20, 1957, PBCFIA, OF 309, OFB 2 of 2, Eisenhower Records, WHCF, 1953–61, DDEL.

51. Robert Gray to Adams, Washington, DC, May 28, 1957, PBCFIA, OF 309, OFB 2 of 2, Eisenhower Records, WHCF, 1953–61, DDEL.

52. Killian to Adams, June 14, 1957, PBCFIA, OF 309, OFB 2 of 2, Eisenhower Records, WHCF, 1953–61, DDEL; Brig. Gen. John F. Cassidy, PBCFIA Staff Director, to Goodpaster, Handwritten Memorandum, Washington, DC, June 14, 1957, BC-FIA (4), SS, AS, WHO, OSS: Records, 1952–61, DDEL.

53. Killian to Adams, Washington, DC, July 17, 1957, PBCFIA, OF 309, OFB 2 of 2, Eisenhower Records, WHCF, 1953–61, DDEL.

54. Robert Gray, Assistant to the President, to Governor Colgate Darden, Washington, DC, July 19, 1957, PBCFIA, OF 309, OFB 2 of 2, Eisenhower Records, WHCF, 1953–61, DDEL; and Coyne to President Kennedy, Tab 2, May 14, 1961, FIAB Briefing Material 5/61, POF, DA, PPJFK, JFKL.

55. Eisenhower to Killian, Special Assistant to the President, and Hull, February 28, 1958, PBCFIA, OF 309, OFB 2 of 2, Eisenhower Records, WHCF, 1953–61, DDEL; and Eisenhower to Killian, January 15, 1960, PBCFIA, OF 309, OFB 2 of 2, Eisenhower Records, WHCF, 1953–61, DDEL.

56. Killian to Hull, PBCFIA Chair, Washington, DC, October 30, 1959, PBCFIA, OF 309, OFB 2 of 2, Eisenhower Records, WHCF, 1953–61, DDEL.

57. Hull to Goodpaster, Washington, DC, November 30, 1959, PBCFIA, OF 309, OFB 2 of 2, Eisenhower Records, WHCF, 1953–61, DDEL.

58. Coyne to President Kennedy, Tab 2, May 14, 1961, FIAB Briefing Material 5/61, POF, DA, PPJFK, JFKL.

59. Fairless to Hull, Washington, DC, December 31, 1959, PBCFIA, OF 309, OFB 2 of 2, Eisenhower Records, WHCF, 1953–61, DDEL.

60. Eisenhower to Hull, Ryerson, Darden, Doolittle, Lovett, Conolly, and Baker, PBCFIA Members, Washington, DC, January 7, 1961, PBCFIA, OF 309, OFB 2 of 2, Eisenhower Records, WHCF, 1953–61, DDEL.

61. Cassidy to E. Frederic Morrow, Washington, DC, May 15, 1956, BC-FIA (3), SS, AS, WHO, OSS: Records, 1952–61, DDEL.

62. Harold L. Lawrence, PBCFIA Deputy Staff Director, to Bernard M. Shanley, Secretary to the President, Washington, DC, December 18, 1956, PBCFIA, OF 309, OFB 2 of 2, Eisenhower Records, WHCF, 1953–61, DDEL.

63. The PBCFIA (Contact List), Room 297, Executive Office Building, July 28, 1959, PBCFIA, OF 309, OFB 2 of 2, Eisenhower Records, WHCF, 1953–61, DDEL; and Goodpaster to Bob Hampton, Washington, DC, November 30, 1959, PBCFIA, OF 309, OFB 2 of 2, Eisenhower Records, WHCF, 1953–61, DDEL.

64. PBCFIA (Contact List), July 28, 1959, PBCFIA, OF 309, OFB 2 of 2, Eisenhower Records, WHCF, 1953–61, DDEL.

65. Coyne to President Kennedy, Tab 2, May 14, 1961, FIAB Briefing Material 5/61, POF, DA, PPJFK, JFKL.

66. Goodpaster to Jerry Morgan, Washington, DC, December 28, 1956, BC-FIA (4), SS, AS, WHO, OSS: Records, 1952–61, DDEL; and Killian to Goodpaster, February 7, 1958, BC-FIA (5), SS, AS, WHO, OSS: Records, 1952–61, DDEL.

67. Eisenhower to Killian, Conolly, Doolittle, Fairless, Hull, Joseph Kennedy, Lovett, and Ryerson, January 11, 1956, PBCFIA, OF 309, OFB 2 of 2, Eisenhower Records, WHCF, 1953–61, DDEL.

68. Coyne to President Kennedy, Tab 2, May 14, 1961, FIAB Briefing Material 5/61, POF, DA, PPJFK, JFKL.

69. Goodpaster, Memorandum of Conference with the President, December 20, 1956, PBCFIA, First Report to the President (1), NSC, SS, WHO, OSANSA: Records, 1952–61, DDEL.

70. Release by Hagerty (including attached EO 10656), February 6, 1956, PBCFIA, OF 309, OFB 2 of 2, Eisenhower Records, WHCF, 1953–61, DDEL; Daily Appointment Cards, December 20, 1956, October 24, 1957, December 16, 1958, February 2, 1960, and January 5, 1961, Eisenhower Records, Daily Appointments, 1953–61, DDEL.

71. Ryerson to Eisenhower, January 17, 1956, PBCFIA, OF 309, OFB 2 of 2, Eisenhower Records, WHCF, 1953–61, DDEL.

72. Daily Appointment Card, December 20, 1956, Eisenhower Records, Daily Appointments, 1953–61, DDEL; Goodpaster, Memorandum of Conference with the President, December 20, 1956, PBCFIA, First Report to the President (1), NSC, SS, WHO, OSANSA: Records, 1952–61, DDEL.

73. Daily Appointment Card, October 24, 1957, Eisenhower Records, Daily Appointments, 1953–61, DDEL; Goodpaster, U.S. Army, Memorandum of Conference with the President, October 28, 1957, October '57 Staff Notes (1), Dwight David Eisenhower Diary Series, Eisenhower, Dwight D.: Papers as President of the United States, 1953–61 [Ann Whitman File], DDEL.

74. Daily Appointment Card, December 16, 1958, Eisenhower Records, Daily Appointments, 1953–61, DDEL.

75. Daily Appointment Card, February 2, 1960, Eisenhower Records, Daily Appointments, 1953–61, DDEL.

76. Daily Appointment Card, January 5, 1961, Eisenhower Records, Daily Appointments, 1953–61, DDEL.

77. Eisenhower to Killian, Conolly, Doolittle, Fairless, Hull, Joseph Kennedy, Lovett, and Ryerson, January 11, 1956, PBCFIA, OF 309, OFB 2 of 2, Eisenhower Records, WHCF, 1953–61, DDEL.

78. Ibid.

79. Killian, PBCFIA Chair, to Eisenhower, Washington, DC, May 14, 1956, PBCFIA, OF 309, OFB 2 of 2, Eisenhower Records, WHCF, 1953–61, DDEL.

80. Killian to Eisenhower, May 14, 1956, PBCFIA, OF 309, OFB 2 of 2, Eisenhower Records, WHCF, 1953–61, DDEL.

81. Adams to Killian, May 15, 1956, PBCFIA, OF 309, OFB 2 of 2, Eisenhower Records, WHCF, 1953–61, DDEL.

82. Ibid.

83. Coyne to President Kennedy, Tab 2, May 14, 1961, FIAB Briefing Material 5/61, POF, DA, PPJFK, JFKL.

84. Cassidy to Morrow, May 15, 1956, BC (3), Subject, Alphabetical, Records, 1952–61, DDEL.

85. Ibid.

86. Darden to Gen. Wilton B. Persons, Assistant to the President, September 6, 1960, PBCFIA, OF 309, OFB 2 of 2, Eisenhower Records, WHCF, 1953–61, DDEL.

87. Darden to Persons, September 6, 1960, PBCFIA, OF 309, OFB 2 of 2, Eisenhower Records, WHCF, 1953–61, DDEL; Gwen to Stephens, Washington, DC, September 16, 1960, PBCFIA, OF 309, OFB 2 of 2, Eisenhower Records, WHCF, 1953–61, DDEL.

88. Killian, PBCFIA Chair, to Eisenhower, Washington, DC, December 20, 1956, PBCFIA, First Report to the President (1), NSC, SS, WHO, OSANSA: Records, 1952–61, DDEL; and Goodpaster, U.S. Army, Memorandum of Conference with the President, January 19, 1957, BC-FIA (4), SS, AS, WHO, OSS: Records, 1952–61, DDEL.

89. Goodpaster, Memorandum of Conference with the President, January 19, 1957, BC (4), Subject, Alphabetical, Records, 1952–61, DDEL.

90. Killian, PBCFIA Chair, to Adams, Washington, DC, May 12, 1956, PBCFIA, OF 309, OFB 2 of 2, Eisenhower Records, WHCF, 1953–61, DDEL.

91. Goodpaster, Memorandum of Conference with the President, December 20, 1956, PBCFIA, First Report to the President (1), NSC, SS, WHO, OSANSA: Records, 1952–61, DDEL.

92. James S. Lay, NSC Executive Secretary, to DCI, October 28, 1957, PBCFIA, Second Report to the President [October 1957–July 1958] (2), NSC, SS, WHO, OSANSA: Records, 1952–61, DDEL.

93. Dulles to Members of the U.S. Communications Intelligence Board and the Intelligence Advisory Committee, Washington, DC, March 25, 1958, PBCFIA, Second Report to the President (2), NSC, SS, WHO, OSANSA: Records, 1952–61, DDEL.

94. Killian to Eisenhower, December 20, 1956, PBCFIA, First Report to the President (1), NSC, SS, WHO, OSANSA: Records, 1952–61, DDEL.

95. Goodpaster, Memorandum of Conference with the President, January 19, 1957, BC (4), Subject, Alphabetical, Records, 1952–61, DDEL.

96. The Joint Study Group Report on Foreign Intelligence Activities of the United States Government, December 15, 1960, Papers Received since January 10, 1961 (3), Papers Received since January 10, 1961 Series, WHO, OSANSA: Record, 1952–61, DDEL.

97. Coyne to President Kennedy, Tab 2, May 14, 1961, FIAB Briefing Material 5/61, POF, DA, PPJFK, JFKL.

98. Ibid.

99. Coyne to President Kennedy, Tab 3: Summary of Recommendations Submitted to the President by the PBCFIA, Washington, DC, May 14, 1961, FIAB Briefing Material 5/61, POF, DA, PPJFK, JFKL.

100. Dulles to the NSC Executive Secretary, Memorandum (with attached CIA

comments on PBCFIA recommendations), Washington, DC, January 25, 1957, PB-CFIA, First Report to the President [December 1956–August 1958] (2), NSC, SS, WHO, OSANSA: Records, 1952–61, DDEL.

101. S. Everett Gleason, Acting NSC Executive Secretary, to NSC Statutory Members and the DCI, Memorandum (with enclosed memorandum from President Eisenhower), Washington, DC, August 5, 1957, PBCFIA, First Report to the President [December 1956–August 1958] (10), NSC, SS, WHO, OSANSA: Records, 1952–61, DDEL.

102. Summary of Recommendations Submitted to the President by the PBCFIA, November 25, 1959, BC-FIA (6), SS, AS, WHO, OSS: Records, 1952–61, DDEL.

103. Lay to the DCI and Secretary of Defense, Washington, DC, January 29, 1957, PBCFIA, First Report to the President [December 1956–August 1958] (3), NSC, SS, WHO, OSANSA: Records, 1952–61, DDEL.

104. Ibid.

105. Lay to the Secretary of Defense and DCI, Washington, DC, May 23, 1957, PBCFIA, First Report to the President (1), NSC, SS, WHO, OSANSA: Records, 1952–61, DDEL.

106. Ibid.

107. Ibid.

108. Summary of Recommendations, November 25, 1959, BC (6), Subject, Alphabetical, Records, 1952–61, DDEL.

109. Lay to the DCI and Secretary of Defense, Washington, DC, January 29, 1957, PBCFIA, First Report to the President [December 1956–August 1958] (4), NSC, SS, WHO, OSANSA: Records, 1952–61, DDEL.

110. Dulles to the NSC Executive Secretary, Memorandum (with attached CIA comments on PBCFIA recommendations), Washington, DC, January 25, 1957, PBCFIA, First Report to the President (2), NSC, SS, WHO, OSANSA: Records, 1952–61, DDEL.

111. Lay to the DCI and Secretary of Defense, January 29, 1957, PBCFIA, First Report to the President (4), NSC, SS, WHO, OSANSA: Records, 1952–61, DDEL

112. Lay to the DCI and the JCS Chair, Washington, DC, May 23, 1957, PBCFIA, First Report to the President (1), NSC, SS, WHO, OSANSA: Records, 1952–61, DDEL.

113. Lay to the DCI and JCS Chair, Washington, DC, February 13, 1958, PBCFIA, First Report to the President (4), NSC, SS, WHO, OSANSA: Records, 1952–61, DDEL.

114. Lay to the DCI and JCS Chair, Washington, DC, September 29, 1959, PBCFIA, First Report to the President [December 1956–August 1958] (5), NSC, SS, WHO, OSANSA: Records, 1952–61, DDEL.

115. Summary of Recommendations, November 25, 1959, BC (6), Subject, Alphabetical, Records, 1952–61, DDEL.

116. Lay to the DCI, Washington, DC, January 29, 1957, PBCFIA, First Report to the President [December 1956–August 1958] (6), NSC, SS, WHO, OSANSA: Records, 1952–61, DDEL.

117. Dulles, Memorandum for the President, Washington, DC, April 30, 1957, at http://www.foia.cia.gov/.

118. Lay to the DCI, January 29, 1957, PBCFIA, First Report to the President (6), NSC, SS, WHO, OSANSA: Records, 1952–61, DDEL.

119. Lay to the DCI, Memorandum Regarding Recommendation 4, Washington,

DC, May 23, 1957, PBCFIA, First Report to the President (1), NSC, SS, WHO, OSANSA: Records, 1952–61, DDEL.

120. Summary of Recommendations, November 25, 1959, BC (6), Subject, Alphabetical, Records, 1952–61, DDEL.

121. Excerpt in Coyne to McGeorge Bundy, May 1961, 1–2, FIAB Briefing Material 5/61, POF, DA, PPJFK, JFKL. This document is a digest of board activities in the area of covert action from its inception until the Kennedy administration took office.

122. Dulles to the NSC Executive Secretary, Memorandum (with attached CIA comments on PBCFIA recommendations), January 25, 1957, PBCFIA, First Report to the President (2), NSC, SS, WHO, OSANSA: Records, 1952–61, DDEL.

123. Daniel Lawler and Carolyn Yee, ed., "Note on U.S. Covert Actions," in *FRUS, 1964–1968,* vol. 32.

124. Robert Cutler, Special Assistant to the President, to the DCI, Memorandum (with attached Recommendation No. 5), Washington, DC, March 4, 1957, PBCFIA, First Report to the President [December 1956–August 1958] (7), NSC, SS, WHO, OSANSA: Records, 1952–61, DDEL.

125. Coyne to Bundy, May 1961, 11, FIAB Briefing Material 5/61, POF, DA, PPJFK, JFKL.

126. Ibid., 12.

127. Ibid., 13.

128. Ibid., 15.

129. Summary of Recommendations, November 25, 1959, BC (6), Subject, Alphabetical, Records, 1952–61, DDEL.

130. Coyne to Bundy, May 1961, 4, FIAB Briefing Material 5/61, POF, DA, PPJFK, JFKL.

131. Dulles to the NSC Executive Secretary, Memorandum (with attached CIA comments on PBCFIA recommendations), January 25, 1957, PBCFIA, First Report to the President (2), NSC, SS, WHO, OSANSA: Records, 1952–61, DDEL.

132. Lay to the Director of the USIA and DCI, Washington, DC, May 23, 1957, PBCFIA, First Report to the President (1), NSC, SS, WHO, OSANSA: Records, 1952–61, DDEL.

133. Summary of Recommendations, November 25, 1959, BC (6), Subject, Alphabetical, Records, 1952–61, DDEL.

134. Dulles to the NSC Executive Secretary, Memorandum (with attached CIA comments on PBCFIA recommendations), January 25, 1957, PBCFIA, First Report to the President (2), NSC, SS, WHO, OSANSA: Records, 1952–61, DDEL.

135. Lay to the Secretary of Defense and DCI, Washington, DC, January 29, 1957, PBCFIA, First Report to the President [December 1956–August 1958] (8), NSC, SS, WHO, OSANSA: Records, 1952–61, DDEL.

136. Lay to the Secretary of Defense and DCI, May 23, 1957, PBCFIA, First Report to the President (1), NSC, SS, WHO, OSANSA: Records, 1952–61, DDEL.

137. Lay to the Secretary of Defense and DCI, January 29, 1957, PBCFIA, First Report to the President (8), NSC, SS, WHO, OSANSA: Records, 1952–61, DDEL; Typewritten Memorandum (unsigned), February 10, 1958, Baker Panel (ODM Science Advisory Committee) [May 1957–July 1958], SAS, SS, WHO, OSANSA: Records, 1952–61, DDEL; Typewritten Memorandum (unsigned), February 6, 1958, Baker Panel (ODM Science Advisory Committee) [May 1957–July 1958], SAS, SS, WHO, OSANSA: Records, 1952–61, DDEL; and Summary of Recommendations, November 25, 1959, BC (6), Subject, Alphabetical, Records, 1952–61, DDEL.

138. Dulles to the NSC Executive Secretary, Memorandum (with attached CIA comments on PBCFIA recommendations), January 25, 1957, PBCFIA, First Report to the President (2), NSC, SS, WHO, OSANSA: Records, 1952–61, DDEL.

139. Lay to the Secretary of Defense and DCI, January 29, 1957, PBCFIA, First Report to the President (8), NSC, SS, WHO, OSANSA: Records, 1952–61, DDEL.

140. Ibid.

141. Dulles to NSC Executive Secretary, April 26, 1957, in http://www.foia.cia.gov/.

142. Lay to the Secretary of Defense and Director, ODM, Washington, DC, May 23, 1957, PBCFIA, First Report to the President (1), NSC, SS, WHO, OSANSA: Records, 1952–61, DDEL.

143. Lay to the Secretary of Defense and DCI, Washington, DC, January 29, 1957, PBCFIA, First Report to the President (8), NSC, SS, WHO, OSANSA: Records 1952–61, DDEL; Typewritten Memorandum (unsigned), February 10, 1958, Baker Panel (ODM Science Advisory Committee) [May 1957–July 1958], SAS, SS, WHO, OSANSA: Records, 1952–61, DDEL; Typewritten Memorandum (unsigned), February 6, 1958, Baker Panel (ODM Science Advisory Committee) [May 1957–July 1958], SAS, SS, WHO, OSANSA: Records, 1952–61, DDEL; and Summary of Recommendations Submitted to the President by the PBCFIA, November 25, 1959, BC-FIA (6), SS, AS, WHO, OSS: Records, 1952–61, DDEL.

144. "News Release: Eisenhower Library Releases Formerly Secret Documents," February 2, 2006, DDEL, available through Media Department.

145. Typewritten Memorandum (unsigned), the "Baker Report" "Scientific Judgments on Foreign Communications Intelligence," February 5, 1958, Baker Panel (ODM Science Advisory Committee) [May 1957–July 1958], SAS, SS, WHO, OSANSA: Records, 1952–61, DDEL. For a more recent discussion, see "William O. Baker's Odyssey," *Chemical and Engineering News,* November 25, 1996, 27–28.

146. Lay to the Secretary of Defense, DCI, and Special Assistant to the President for Science and Technology, Washington, DC, February 10, 1958, PBCFIA, First Report to the President (8), NSC, SS, WHO, OSANSA: Records, 1952–61, DDEL.

147. Summary of Recommendations, November 25, 1959, BC (6), Subject, Alphabetical, Records, 1952–61, DDEL.

148. Dulles to the NSC Executive Secretary, Memorandum (with attached CIA comments on PBCFIA recommendations), January 25, 1957, PBCFIA, First Report to the President (2), NSC, SS, WHO, OSANSA: Records, 1952–61, DDEL; and Lay to the Secretary of Defense, Washington, DC, January 29, 1957, PBCFIA, First Report to the President [December 1956–August 1958] (9), NSC, SS, WHO, OSANSA: Records, 1952–61, DDEL.

149. Lay to the Secretary of Defense, Washington, DC, May 23, 1957, PBCFIA, First Report to the President (1), NSC, SS, WHO, OSANSA: Records, 1952–61, DDEL.

150. Lay to the DCI, Washington, DC, January 29, 1957, PBCFIA, First Report to the President (9), NSC, SS, WHO, OSANSA: Records, 1952–61, DDEL.

151. Ibid.; Dulles to the NSC Executive Secretary, Memorandum (with attached CIA comments on PBCFIA recommendations), January 25, 1957, PBCFIA, First Report to the President (2), NSC, SS, WHO, OSANSA: Records, 1952–61, DDEL.

152. Lay to the DCI, January 29, 1957, PBCFIA, First Report to the President (9), NSC, SS, WHO, OSANSA: Records, 1952–61, DDEL.

153. Lay to the DCI, Memorandum regarding Recommendation No. 9,

Washington, DC, May 23, 1957, PBCFIA, First Report to the President (1), NSC, SS, WHO, OSANSA: Records, 1952–61, DDEL.

154. Summary of Recommendations, November 25, 1959, BC (6), Subject, Alphabetical, Records, 1952–61, DDEL.

155. Dulles to the NSC Executive Secretary, Memorandum (with attached CIA comments on PBCFIA recommendations), January 25, 1957, PBCFIA, First Report to the President (2), NSC, SS, WHO, OSANSA: Records, 1952–61, DDEL.

156. Lay to the DCI, January 29, 1957, PBCFIA, First Report to the President (9), NSC, SS, WHO, OSANSA: Records, 1952–61, DDEL.

157. Lay to the DCI, Memorandum regarding Recommendation No. 10, Washington, DC, May 23, 1957, PBCFIA, First Report to the President (1), NSC, SS, WHO, OSANSA: Records, 1952–61, DDEL.

158. Gleason to NSC Statutory Members and the DCI, Memorandum (with enclosed memorandum from President Eisenhower), August 5, 1957, PBCFIA, First Report to the President (10), NSC, SS, WHO, OSANSA: Records, 1952–61, DDEL.

159. Summary of Recommendations, November 25, 1959, BC (6), Subject, Alphabetical, Records, 1952–61, DDEL.

160. Richelson, *The Wizards of Langley,* 23.

161. Summary of Recommendations, November 25, 1959, BC (6), Subject, Alphabetical, Records, 1952–61, DDEL.

162. Lay to the DCI, Washington, DC, October 28, 1957, PBCFIA, Second Report to the President (2), NSC, SS, WHO, OSANSA: Records, 1952–61, DDEL.

163. Lay to the DCI, Washington, DC, March 14, 1958, PBCFIA, Second Report to the President (2), NSC, SS, WHO, OSANSA: Records, 1952–61, DDEL.

164. Summary of Recommendations, November 25, 1959, BC (6), Subject, Alphabetical, Records, 1952–61, DDEL.

165. Lay to the DCI, October 28, 1957, PBCFIA, Second Report to the President (2), NSC, SS, WHO, OSANSA: Records, 1952–61, DDEL.

166. Summary of Recommendations, November 25, 1959, BC (6), Subject, Alphabetical, Records, 1952–61, DDEL.

167. Ibid.

168. Gordon Gray to the DCI, Memorandum (with enclosed Third Report of PBCFIA), Washington, DC, December 24, 1958, PBCFIA, Third Report to the President [October 1958–November 1959] (1), NSC, SS, WHO, OSANSA: Records, 1952–61, DDEL.

169. Summary of Recommendations, November 25, 1959, BC (6), Subject, Alphabetical, Records, 1952–61, DDEL.

170. Gordon Gray to the DCI, Memorandum (with enclosed Third Report of PBCFIA), December 24, 1958, PBCFIA, Third Report to the President (1), NSC, SS, WHO, OSANSA: Records, 1952–61, DDEL.

171. Summary of Recommendations, November 25, 1959, BC (6), Subject, Alphabetical, Records, 1952–61, DDEL.

172. Weiner, *Legacy of Ashes,* 133–35, 154.

173. Coyne to Bundy, May 1961, 10, FIAB Briefing Material 5/61, POF, DA, PPJFK, JFKL.

174. Ibid., 15–16. See also Weiner, *Legacy of Ashes,* caption after 334.

175. Coyne to Bundy, May 1961, 18, FIAB Briefing Material 5/61, POF, DA, PPJFK, JFKL.

176. Ibid., 19.

177. Gordon Gray to the DCI, Memorandum (with enclosed Third Report of PBCFIA), December 24, 1958, PBCFIA, Third Report to the President (1), NSC, SS, WHO, OSANSA: Records, 1952–61, DDEL; and Lay to the DCI, December 29, 1959, PBCFIA, Third Report to the President (1), NSC, SS, WHO, OSANSA: Records, 1952–61, DDEL.

178. Dulles to NSC Executive Secretary, February 16, 1959, at http://www.foia.cia.gov; Lay to the DCI, March 3, 1959, PBCFIA, Third Report to the President (1), NSC, SS, WHO, OSANSA: Records, 1952–61, DDEL.

179. Lay to the PBCFIA Chair, November 5, 1959, PBCFIA, Third Report to the President (1), NSC, SS, WHO, OSANSA: Records, 1952–61, DDEL.

180. Summary of Recommendations, November 25, 1959, BC (6), Subject, Alphabetical, Records, 1952–61, DDEL.

181. Gordon Gray to the DCI, Memorandum (with enclosed Third Report of PBCFIA), December 24, 1958, PBCFIA, Third Report to the President (1), NSC, SS, WHO, OSANSA: Records, 1952–61, DDEL.

182. Summary of Recommendations, November 25, 1959, BC (6), Subject, Alphabetical, Records, 1952–61, DDEL.

183. Lay to the Under Secretary of State, Deputy Secretary of Defense, Special Assistant to the President for National Security Affairs, and DCI, December 29, 1958, PBCFIA, Third Report to the President [October 1958–November 1959] (2), NSC, SS, WHO, OSANSA: Records, 1952–61, DDEL.

184. Coyne to Bundy, May 1961, 27, FIAB Briefing Material 5/61, POF, DA, PPJFK, JFKL.

185. Summary of Recommendations, November 25, 1959, BC (6), Subject, Alphabetical, Records, 1952–61, DDEL.

186. Gordon Gray to the DCI, Memorandum (with enclosed Third Report of PBCFIA), December 24, 1958, PBCFIA, Third Report to the President (1), NSC, SS, WHO, OSANSA: Records, 1952–61, DDEL.

187. Coyne to President Kennedy, Tab 3, May 14, 1961, FIAB Briefing Material 5/61, POF, DA, PPJFK, JFKL.

188. Gordon Gray to the DCI, Memorandum (with enclosed Third Report of PBCFIA), December 24, 1958, PBCFIA, Third Report to the President (1), NSC, SS, WHO, OSANSA: Records, 1952–61, DDEL; and Summary of Recommendations, November 25, 1959, BC (6), Subject, Alphabetical, Records, 1952–61, DDEL.

189. Gordon Gray to the DCI, Memorandum (with enclosed Third Report of PBCFIA), December 24, 1958, PBCFIA, Third Report to the President (1), NSC, SS, WHO, OSANSA: Records, 1952–61, DDEL.

190. Summary of Recommendations, November 25, 1959, BC (6), Subject, Alphabetical, Records, 1952–61, DDEL.

191. Gordon Gray to the DCI, Memorandum (with enclosed Third Report of PBCFIA), December 24, 1958, PBCFIA, Third Report to the President (1), NSC, SS, WHO, OSANSA: Records, 1952–61, DDEL.

192. Coyne, NSC Representative on Internal Security, Memorandum (Special Meeting following 393rd NSC Meeting), January 19, 1959, PBCFIA, Third Report to the President (2), NSC, SS, WHO, OSANSA: Records, 1952–61, DDEL.

193. Summary of Recommendations, November 25, 1959, BC (6), Subject, Alphabetical, Records, 1952–61, DDEL.

194. Lay to Gen. Graves P. Erskine, Assistant to the Secretary of Defense (Special

Operations), March 9, 1960, PBCFIA, Fourth Report to the President [January 1959–March 1960], NSC, SS, WHO, OSANSA: Records, 1952–61, DDEL.

195. Coyne to President Kennedy, Tab 3, May 14, 1961, FIAB Briefing Material 5/61, POF, DA, PPJFK, JFKL.

196. Lay to the DCI, March 10, 1960, PBCFIA, Fifth Report to the President [December 1959–July 1960] (1), NSC, SS, WHO, OSANSA: Records, 1952–61, DDEL.

197. Coyne to President Kennedy, Tab 3, May 14, 1961, FIAB Briefing Material 5/61, POF, DA, PPJFK, JFKL.

198. Dulles to NSC Executive Secretary, March 1, 1960, at http://www.foia.cia.gov.

199. Lay to the DCI, March 9, 1960, PBCFIA, Fifth Report to the President (1), NSC, SS, WHO, OSANSA: Records, 1952–61, DDEL.

200. Coyne to President Kennedy, Tab 3, May 14, 1961, FIAB Briefing Material 5/61, POF, DA, PPJFK, JFKL.

201. Lay to the Secretary of Defense and DCI, January 26, 1960, PBCFIA, Fifth Report to the President [December 1959–July 1960] (2), NSC, SS, WHO, OSANSA: Records, 1952–61, DDEL.

202. Lay to the PBCFIA Chair, March 24, 1960, PBCFIA, Fifth Report to the President (2), NSC, SS, WHO, OSANSA: Records, 1952–61, DDEL.

203. Marion W. Boggs, Acting Executive Secretary, to the Secretary of Defense and DCI, July 29, 1960, PBCFIA, Fifth Report to the President (2), NSC, SS, WHO, OSANSA: Records, 1952–61, DDEL.

204. Coyne to President Kennedy, Tab 3, May 14, 1961, FIAB Briefing Material 5/61, POF, DA, PPJFK, JFKL.

205. Coyne, PBCFIA Staff Director, to Goodpaster, Washington, DC, December 14, 1959, BC-FIA (6), SS, AS, WHO, OSS: Records, 1952–61, DDEL.

206. Coyne to President Kennedy, Tab 3, May 14, 1961, FIAB Briefing Material 5/61, POF, DA, PPJFK, JFKL.

207. Lay to the DCI, January 26, 1960, PBCFIA, Fifth Report to the President (2), NSC, SS, WHO, OSANSA: Records, 1952–61, DDEL.

208. Memorandum for Gordon Gray and Lay (with handwritten note "Approved by the President 4/6/60"), April 1, 1960, PBCFIA, Fifth Report to the President (2), NSC, SS, WHO, OSANSA: Records, 1952–61, DDEL.

209. Coyne to President Kennedy, Tab 3, May 14, 1961, FIAB Briefing Material 5/61, POF, DA, PPJFK, JFKL.

210. Lay to the DCI, June 8, 1960, PBCFIA, Sixth Report to the President [May 1960–January 1961] (2), NSC, SS, WHO, OSANSA: Records, 1952–61, DDEL; and Boggs to the Secretary of Defense, August 5, 1960, PBCFIA, Sixth Report to the President (2), NSC, SS, WHO, OSANSA: Records, 1952–61, DDEL.

211. Richelson, *The Wizards of Langley*, 30.

212. Coyne to President Kennedy, Tab 3, May 14, 1961, FIAB Briefing Material 5/61, POF, DA, PPJFK, JFKL.

213. Lay to the Secretary of Defense, June 8, 1960, PBCFIA, Sixth Report to the President (2), NSC, SS, WHO, OSANSA: Records, 1952–61, DDEL.

214. Lay to the Secretary of Defense, August 24, 1960, PBCFIA, Sixth Report to the President (2), NSC, SS, WHO, OSANSA: Records, 1952–61, DDEL.

215. Goodpaster to Gordon Gray, July 20, 1960, PBCFIA, Sixth Report to the President (2), NSC, SS, WHO, OSANSA: Records, 1952–61, DDEL; and Lay to the Secretary of State and DCI, June 8, 1960, PBCFIA, Sixth Report to the President (2), NSC, SS, WHO, OSANSA: Records, 1952–61, DDEL.

216. Lay to the Secretary of State and DCI, June 8, 1960, PBCFIA, Sixth Report to the President (2), NSC, SS, WHO, OSANSA: Records, 1952–61, DDEL.

217. Coyne to President Kennedy, Tab 3, May 14, 1961, FIAB Briefing Material 5/61, POF, DA, PPJFK, JFKL.

218. Lay to the DCI, June 8, 1960, PBCFIA, Sixth Report to the President (2), NSC, SS, WHO, OSANSA: Records, 1952–61, DDEL.

219. Lay to the DCI, August 22, 1960, PBCFIA, Sixth Report to the President (2), NSC, SS, WHO, OSANSA: Records, 1952–61, DDEL.

220. Dulles to Gordon Gray, January 9, 1961, at http://www.foi.cia.gov.

221. Coyne to President Kennedy, Tab 3, May 14, 1961, FIAB Briefing Material 5/61, POF, DA, PPJFK, JFKL.

222. Boggs to the DCI, October 31, 1960, PBCFIA, Seventh Report to the President [October 1960–January 1961], NSC, SS, WHO, OSANSA: Records, 1952–61, DDEL.

223. Coyne to President Kennedy, Tab 3, May 14, 1961, FIAB Briefing Material 5/61, POF, DA, PPJFK, JFKL.

224. Boggs to the DCI, October 31, 1960, PBCFIA, Seventh Report to the President , NSC, SS, WHO, OSANSA: Records, 1952–61, DDEL.

225. Dulles to the Executive Secretary, NSC, January 5, 1961, PBCFIA, Seventh Report to the President , NSC, SS, WHO, OSANSA: Records, 1952–61, DDEL.

226. Brief for Discussion with the President, December 23, 1960, PBCFIA, Seventh Report to the President, NSC, SS, WHO, OSANSA: Records, 1952–61, DDEL.

227. Gordon Gray, Special Assistant to the President, to the Secretary of Defense, November 2, 1960, PBCFIA, Seventh Report to the President, NSC, SS, WHO, OSANSA: Records, 1952–61, DDEL.

228. Gordon Gray to the Secretary of Defense and JCS Chair, December 30, 1960, PBCFIA, Seventh Report to the President, NSC, SS, WHO, OSANSA: Records, 1952–61, DDEL.

229. Hull to Eisenhower, October 4, 1960, PBCFIA, Seventh Report to the President, NSC, SS, WHO, OSANSA: Records, 1952–61, DDEL.

230. Gordon Gray to the Secretary of Defense, November 2, 1960, PBCFIA, Seventh Report to the President, NSC, SS, WHO, OSANSA: Records, 1952–61, DDEL; and Gordon Gray to Hull, December 5, 1960, PBCFIA, Seventh Report to the President, NSC, SS, WHO, OSANSA: Records, 1952–61, DDEL.

231. Gordon Gray to Hull, December 5, 1960, PBCFIA, Seventh Report to the President, NSC, SS, WHO, OSANSA: Records, 1952–61, DDEL.

232. Eisenhower to the Attorney General, December 7, 1960, BC-FIA (7), SS, AS, WHO, OSS: Records, 1952–61, DDEL.

233. Coyne to President Kennedy, Tab 3, May 14, 1961, FIAB Briefing Material 5/61, POF, DA, PPJFK, JFKL.

234. Boggs to the Secretary of Defense, October 31, 1960, PBCFIA, Seventh Report to the President, NSC, SS, WHO, OSANSA: Records, 1952–61, DDEL.

235. Lay to PBCFIA Chair, December 29, 1960, PBCFIA, Seventh Report to the President, NSC, SS, WHO, OSANSA: Records, 1952–61, DDEL.

236. Coyne to Bundy, May 1961, 30, FIAB Briefing Material 5/61, POF, DA, PPJFK, JFKL.

237. All are from Coyne to President Kennedy, Tab 3, May 14, 1961, FIAB Briefing Material 5/61, POF, DA, PPJFK, JFKL.

238. Coyne to Bundy, May 1961, 30–31, FIAB Briefing Material 5/61, POF, DA, PPJFK, JFKL.
239. Ibid., 31.
240. The Joint Study Group Report on Foreign Intelligence Activities of the United States Government, December 15, 1960, Papers Received since January 10, 1961 (3), Papers Received since January 10, 1961 Series, WHO, OSANSA: Record, 1952–61, DDEL.
241. Ibid.
242. Ibid.
243. Welzenbach, "Science and Technology," 20–21.
244. Killian quoted in Welzenbach, "Science and Technology," 21.
245. Ibid., 15–16.
246. Douglas F. Garthoff, *Directors of Central Intelligence as Leaders of the Intelligence Community, 1946–2005* (Washington, DC: Center for the Study of Intelligence, 2005), 32–33.
247. Ibid., 34.
248. Ibid., 32–33.
249. Summary of Recommendations, November 25, 1959, BC (6), Subject, Alphabetical, Records, 1952–61, DDEL.
250. Garthoff, *Directors of Central Intelligence*, 34–35.
251. Ibid., 35.
252. Release by Hagerty, January 13, 1956, PBCFIA, OF 309, OFB 2 of 2, Eisenhower Records, WHCF, 1953–61, DDEL.

2. JOHN F. KENNEDY

1. John S. Chwat, *The President's Foreign Intelligence Advisory Board: An Historical and Contemporary Analysis (1955–1975),* Congressional Research Service Report 75-225F (Washington, DC: Library of Congress, 1975), 7.
2. Clark Clifford with Richard Holbrooke, *Counsel to the President: A Memoir* (New York: Random House, 1991), 351.
3. For further details on Joseph P. Kennedy's "uncomfortable" and short tenure on the Eisenhower board, see James Killian, *The Education of a College President* (Cambridge, MA: MIT Press, 1985), 329.
4. H. Andrew Boerstling and Richard A. Best, *Intelligence Oversight in the White House: The President's Foreign Intelligence Advisory Board and the Intelligence Oversight Board,* Congressional Research Service Report 96-619F (Washington, DC: Library of Congress, 1996), 2.
5. The Hale Foundation, *The President's Foreign Intelligence Advisory Board (PFIAB)* (Washington, DC: Hale Foundation, 1981), 4; and Clifford, *Counsel to the President,* 351.
6. Jack Raymond, "U.S. May Abandon a Top Policy Unit; Kennedy Reported Planning to End Coordinating Board of the Security Council," *New York Times,* February 10, 1961, 7.
7. Memorandum, PFIAB, Washington, DC, December 1, 1963, Minutes of Meeting of January 30, 1964, PFIAB, ARRB, Record 206-10001-10002, NARA.
8. McGeorge Bundy to James R. Killian, Chair, Washington, DC, February 27, 1961, PJK, MC 423, Box 36, Folder 4/8, IASC.

9. Bundy to Killian, Western Union Telegram, Washington, DC, March 14, 1961, PJK, MC 423, Box 36, Folder 4/8, IASC.

10. Ibid.

11. Bundy to Killian, April 10, 1961, PJK, MC 423, Box 36, Folder 4/8, IASC.

12. Ibid.

13. Ibid.

14. Killian, *The Education of a College President,* 337.

15. Bundy to Killian, April 10, 1961, PJK, MC 423, Box 36, Folder 4/8, IASC.

16. Clifford, *Counsel to the President,* 353.

17. On the Bay of Pigs, see Peter Wyden, *Bay of Pigs* (New York: Jonathan Cape, 1979). The definitive account of the Guatemala operation is Richard Immerman, *The CIA in Guatemala* (Austin: University of Texas Press, 1983).

18. Quoted in Clifford, *Counsel to the President,* 350.

19. Killian, *The Education of a College President,* 337.

20. Arthur M. Schlesinger, *A Thousand Days: John F. Kennedy in the White House* (Cambridge, MA: Riverside, 1965), 296.

21. Ibid.

22. Clifford, *Counsel to the President,* 351.

23. Theodore C. Sorensen, *Kennedy* (New York: Harper & Row, 1965), 630.

24. Arthur B. Focke, General Counsel, to Robert F. Kennedy, Attorney General, Washington, DC, April 27, 1961, FG 732 PFIAB, WHCF, SF, JFKL.

25. Robert Kennedy, Attorney General, to President John Kennedy, Washington, DC, April 27, 1961, FG 732 PFIAB, WHCF, SF, JFKL.

26. J. Patrick Coyne to Bundy, Washington, DC, April 28, 1961, FG 732 PFIAB, WHCF, SF, JFKL.

27. Immediate Release, Office of the White House Press Secretary, Washington, DC, May 4, 1961, FG 732 PFIAB, WHCF, SF, JFKL.

28. Ibid.

29. Tim Weiner, *Legacy of Ashes: The History of the CIA* (New York: Doubleday 2007), 177–79.

30. Anne Karalakas, "History of the Central Intelligence Agency," in *The Central Intelligence Agency: History and Documents,* ed. William M. Leary (Birmingham: University of Alabama Press, 1984), 76.

31. Immediate Release, May 4, 1961, FG 732 PFIAB, WHCF, SF, JFKL.

32. The draft press release and the letter to potential PFIAB members are attached to Nicholas deB. Katzenbach, Assistant Attorney General, to the Attorney General, April 27, 1961, FG 732 PFIAB, WHCF, SF, JFKL. The handwritten comments are found between the draft press releases and letters to potential PFIAB members attached to ibid.

33. Laurence Burd, "Kennedy Sets Up Review of Intelligence; Appoints Advisors to Improve System," *Chicago Daily Tribune,* May 5, 1961, 1-5.

34. Immediate Release, May 4, 1961, FG 732 PFIAB, WHCF, SF, JFKL.

35. Immediate Release, Office of the White House Press Secretary, May 16, 1961, FIAB, 1960–1961, POF, DA, PPJFK, JFKL.

36. Immediate Release, Office of the White House Press Secretary, July 17, 1961, FG 732 PFIAB, WHCF, SF, JFKL.

37. Killian, *The Education of a College President,* 174.

38. James Killian, *Sputnik, Scientists and Eisenhower: A Memoir of the First*

Special Assistant to the President for Science and Technology (Cambridge, MA: MIT Press, 1977), 94.

39. Killian, *The Education of a College President,* 330.

40. Bundy to Killian, April 10, 1961, PJK, MC 423, Box 36, Folder 4/8, IASC.

41. Ibid.

42. Coyne to Bundy, April 28, 1961, FG 732 PFIAB, WHCF, SF, JFKL.

43. Carroll Kilpatrick, "Gen. Taylor Made Aide to Kennedy; Former Staff Chief Will Be Advisor on Military Affairs," *Washington Post,* June 27, 1961, A1; and Joseph Loftus, "Taylor Named Kennedy Adviser in Military and Intelligence Field; Former Army Chief Recalled—Berlin Problem Will Be One of First Tackled," *New York Times,* June 27, 1961, 13.

44. Tom Wicker, "Pace Is Appointed Kennedy Adviser; To Join Intelligence Board—2 Americas' Aides Sworn," *New York Times,* July 18, 1961, 12.

45. "Pace Named to Aid Kennedy on Intelligence," *Los Angeles Times,* July 18, 1961, 4.

46. Clifford, *Counsel to the President,* 351–52.

47. William L. Langer, *In and Out of the Ivory Tower* (New York: Neale Watson Academic, 1977), 222.

48. Quoted in Clifford, *Counsel to the President,* 350.

49. Memorandum for the File, Washington, DC, February 4, 1964, Minutes of Meeting of January 30, 1964, PFIAB, ARRB, Record 206-10001-10002, NARA.

50. Monday, May 15, 1961 (Daily Schedule), Palm Beach, FL, AB JFK (January 21, 1961–December 31, 1961), JFKL.

51. Memorandum, PFIAB, December 1, 1963, Minutes of the Meeting of January 30, 1964, Record 206-10001-10002, PFIAB, ARRB, NARA, 3.

52. Memorandum for the File, Washington, DC, November 9, 1962, PFIAB, Meeting of the Board, November 9, 1962, Record 206-10001-10010, PFIAB, ARRB, NARA; and J. R. Killian Jr. to McGeorge Bundy, Washington, DC, October 13, 1962, FG 732 PFIAB, WHCF, SF, JFKL.

53. Memorandum for the File, Washington, DC, January 25–26, 1963, PFIAB, Meeting of the Board, January 25–26, 1963, PFIAB, ARRB, Record 206-10001-10011, NARA.

54. Roger Hilsman, Handwritten Notes, January 25, 1963, Roger Hilsman Papers, Subjects, Intelligence, FIAB, JFKL.

55. PFIAB, Agenda for Meetings, Washington, DC, January 25–26, 1963, PFIAB, Meeting of the Board, January 25–26, 1963, PFIAB, ARRB, Record 206-10001-10011, NARA.

56. Chwat, *The President's Foreign Intelligence Advisory Board,* 9.

57. Laurence Burd, "Kennedy Goes on 2D Cruise; Maps Parleys," *Chicago Daily Tribune,* July 3, 1961, 1-3.

58. Alvin Shuster, "CIA Circulates Account of Itself; But 20-Page Handout Tells Little New about Agency," *New York Times,* July 9, 1961, 38.

59. PFIAB Agenda for Meetings, Washington, DC, December 27–28, 1962, PFIAB, Meeting of the Board, December 27–28, 1962, PFIAB, ARRB, Record 206-10001-10008, NARA; and Agenda for the Meeting, Washington, DC, April 23, 1963, PFIAB, Meeting of the Board, April 23, 1963, PFIAB, ARRB, Record 206-10001-10005, NARA.

60. Agenda, December 27–28, 1962, PFIAB, Meeting of the Board, December 27–28, 1962, PFIAB, ARRB, Record 206-10001-10008, NARA; and Agenda for

Meetings, Washington, DC, June 25–26, 1963, PFIAB, Meeting of the Board, June 25–26, 1963, PFIAB, ARRB, Record 206-10001-10004, NARA.

61. Order from President Kennedy, n.d., FG 732 PFIAB, WHCF, SF, JFKL.

62. Coyne to President Kennedy, Tab 6: Coyne, Memorandum to the PFIAB Entitled "Future Undertakings of the Board," Washington, DC, May 14, 1961, FIAB Briefing Material 5/61, POF, DA, PPJFK, JFKL.

63. Ibid.

64. Ibid.

65. Excerpts from Minutes of PFIAB, Meeting with Respect to Covert Actions Matters, Washington, DC, n.d., 10, Consideration of Covert Action Matters by President Kennedy's Foreign Intelligence Advisory Board, PFIAB, ARRB, Record 206-10001-10017, NARA.

66. Robert Kennedy, Attorney General, to James R. Killian, PFIAB Chair, Washington, DC, n.d., FIAB, 1960–1961, POF, DA, PPJFK, JFKL.

67. Coyne to President Kennedy, Washington, DC, July 14, 1961, FIAB, 1960–1961, POF, DA, PPJFK, JFKL.

68. Excerpts from Minutes with Respect to Covert Actions Matters, n.d., 8, Covert Action Matters, PFIAB, ARRB, Record 206-10001-10017, NARA.

69. Agenda for Meetings, Washington, DC, December 27–28, 1962, PFIAB, Meeting of the Board, December 27–28, 1962, PFIAB, ARRB, Record 206-10001-10006, NARA; Agenda for Meetings, Washington, DC, March 8–9, 1963, PFIAB, Meeting of the Board, March 8–9, 1963 (the board met with the president on March 9, 1963), PFIAB, ARRB, Record 206-10001-10012, NARA; Agenda for Meeting, Washington DC, April 23, 1963, PFIAB, Meeting of the Board, April 23, 1963, PFIAB, ARRB, Record 206-10001-10005, NARA; and Agenda for Meetings, Washington DC, April 2–3, 1964, PFIAB, Meeting of the Board, April 3–4, 1963, PFIAB, ARRB, Record 206-10001-10006, NARA.

70. Coyne to the PFIAB, Washington, DC, January 25, 1963, PFIAB, Meeting of the Board, January 25–26, 1963, PFIAB, ARRB, Record 206-10001-10011, NARA.

71. Clifford, *Counsel to the President,* 354.

72. Ibid.

73. Ibid., 354–55.

74. Excerpts from Minutes with Respect to Covert Actions Matters, n.d., 11–12, 14–15, Covert Action Matters, PFIAB, ARRB, Record 206-10001-10017, NARA.

75. Clifford, *Counsel to the President,* 355.

76. Douglas F. Garthoff, *Directors of Central Intelligence as Leaders of the Intelligence Community, 1946–2005* (Washington, DC: Center for the Study of Intelligence, 2005), 41–42, 46–47.

77. Bundy to President Kennedy, March 25, 1963, Memos to the President, 3/63–4/63, NSF, McGeorge Bundy Correspondence, PPJFK, JFKL.

78. Ibid.

79. Ibid.

80. "Clifford Named to Killian Post; Kennedy Appoints Him to Foreign Intelligence Body Assesses Activities," *New York Times,* April 24, 1963, 11.

81. "Cloudy Intelligence," *New York Times,* April 29, 1963, 29.

82. J. R. Killian Jr., "Clark Clifford Endorsed," *New York Times,* May 12, 1963, Week in Review, E10; and Clifford, *Counsel to the President,* 359.

83. Coyne, Memorandum for the Board, September 11, 1963, Meeting of the PFIAB on September 12–13, 1963, PFIAB, ARRB, Record 206-10001-10001, NARA.

84. Agenda for Meeting of the Board's Cuban Panel, December 6, 1962, PFIAB, Agenda for Meetings of December 6, 1962 of the Board's Cuban Panel, PFIAB, ARRB, Record 206-10001-10009, NARA.

85. Agenda for Meetings, September 12–13, 1963, Meeting on September 12–13, 1963, PFIAB, ARRB, Record 206-10001-10001, NARA.

86. Excerpts from Minutes with Respect to Covert Actions Matters, n.d., 19, Covert Action Matters, PFIAB, ARRB, Record 206-10001-10017, NARA.

87. Agenda for Meetings, Washington, DC, June 25–26, 1963, PFIAB, Meeting of the Board, June 25–26, 1963, PFIAB, ARRB, Record 206-10001-10004, NARA.

88. Agenda for Meetings, April 2–3, 1964, Minutes of Board Meeting of April 2–3, 1964, PFIAB, ARRB, Record 206-10001-10006, NARA.

89. Agenda for Meetings, Washington, DC, November 21–22, 1963, PFIAB, Agenda for Meeting of November 21–22, 1963, PFIAB, ARRB, Record 206-10001-10003, NARA.

90. Coyne, Memorandum for the Board, September 11, 1963, Meeting on September 12–13, 1963, PFIAB, ARRB, Record 206-10001-10001, NARA.

91. Agenda for Board's Cuban Panel, December 6, 1962, Meetings of December 6, 1962 of the Board's Cuban Panel, PFIAB, ARRB, Record 206-10001-10009, NARA.

92. Memorandum for the File, Washington, DC, June 28, 1963, Meeting of the President's Foreign Intelligence Advisory Board on June 25–26, 1963, PFIAB, ARRB, Record 206-10001-10004, NARA.

93. Coyne to Members of the PFIAB, Washington, DC, August 25, 1961, PJK, MC 423, Box 36, Folder 3/8, IASC.

94. Summary of Recommendations Submitted to the President by the PFIAB, May 1961–November 22, 1963, December 1, 1963, Minutes of Meeting of January 30, 1964, PFIAB, ARRB, Record 206-10001-10002, NARA.

95. Excerpts from Minutes with Respect to Covert Actions Matters, n.d., 8, Covert Action Matters, PFIAB, ARRB, Record 206-10001-10017, NARA.

96. Summary of Recommendations, May 1961–November 22, 1963, December 1, 1963, 19, Minutes, January 30, 1964, PFIAB, ARRB, Record 206-10001-10002, NARA.

97. Memorandum for the File, Regarding Conversation with John McCone, August 21, 1962, Gordon Gray—PFIAB, General Correspondence, Name, Gordon Gray Papers, DDEL.

98. Gray to Wheaton B. Byers, December 10, 1974, Gordon Gray—PFIAB, General Correspondence, Name, Gordon Gray Papers, DDEL.

99. Ibid.

100. Ibid.

101. Coyne to President Kennedy, Tab 6, May 14, 1961, Board Briefing Material 5/61, POF, DA, PPJFK, JFKL.

102. Ibid.

103. Ibid.

104. Ibid. See also Tab 3: Summary of Recommendations Submitted to the President by the President's Board of Consultants on Foreign Intelligence Activities, attached to ibid.

105. Text is quoted in full as it appears in Summary of Recommendations, May 1961–November 22, 1963, December 1, 1963, Minutes, January 30, 1964, PFIAB, ARRB, Record 206-10001-10002, NARA.

106. This recommendation is quoted exactly as it appears in Summary of

Recommendations, May 1961–November 22, 1963, December 1, 1963, Minutes, January 30, 1964, PFIAB, ARRB, Record 206-10001-10002, NARA. However, the original quotation contains a typographical error—the Joint Study Group on Foreign Intelligence submitted its report and forty-three recommendations on December 15, 1960, not December 15, 1961.

107. The recommendations of October 17 do not appear in consecutive order in the archival material. Each recommendation here is numbered as it is in Summary of Recommendations, May 1961–November 22, 1963, December 1, 1963, Minutes, January 30, 1964, PFIAB, ARRB, Record 206-10001-10002, NARA.

108. Coyne to President Kennedy (PFIAB "Memorandum of Conclusions and Recommendations Approved by the Board at Its Meeting of July 18, 1961" enclosed), Washington, DC, July 19, 1961, FIAB, 1960–1961, POF, DA, PPJFK, JFKL.

109. Ibid.

110. Summary of Recommendations, May 1961–November 22, 1963, December 1, 1963, 1, Minutes, January 30, 1964, PFIAB, ARRB, Record 206-10001-10002, NARA.

111. Nicholas deB. Katzenbach, Assistant Attorney General, to the Attorney General, n.d., FIAB, 1960–1961, POF, DA, PPJFK, JFKL. While this memo is undated, it was likely issued soon after receipt of a July 12, 1961, memorandum from PFIAB Chair Killian seeking the Department of Justice's legal opinion on this issue.

112. Summary of Recommendations, May 1961–November 22, 1963, December 1, 1963, 27, Minutes, January 30, 1964, PFIAB, ARRB, Record 206-10001-10002, NARA.

113. Jeffrey Richelson, ed., *Science, Technology, and the CIA: A National Security Archive Electronic Briefing Book,* September 10, 2001, at http://www.gwu.edu/~nsarchiv/NSAEBB/NSAEBB54.

114. Clifford, *Counsel to the President,* 379.

115. Summary of Recommendations, May 1961–November 22, 1963, December 1, 1963, 1, Minutes, January 30, 1964, PFIAB, ARRB, Record 206-10001-10002, NARA.

116. Coyne to President Kennedy (PFIAB "Memorandum of Conclusions and Recommendations" enclosed), July 19, 1961, FIAB, 1960–1961, POF, DA, PPJFK, JFKL.

117. Summary of Recommendations, May 1961–November 22, 1963, December 1, 1963, 1, Minutes, January 30, 1964, PFIAB, ARRB, Record 206-10001-10002, NARA.

118. Ibid.

119. The dates of these meetings are May 15, May 26, June 7, June 30–July 2, July 18, October 16–17, and December 9, 1961; January 19–20, March 23–24, May 11–12, June 25–26, September 28, November 9, December 6–7, and December 27–28, 1962; and January 25–26, March 8–9, April 23, June 25–26, September 12–13, and November 21–22, 1963. Excerpts from Minutes with Respect to Covert Actions Matters, n.d., 8, Covert Action Matters, PFIAB, ARRB, Record 206-10001-10017, NARA.

120. Summary of Recommendations, May 1961–November 22, 1963, December 1, 1963, 2–3, Minutes, January 30, 1964, PFIAB, ARRB, Record 206-10001-10002, NARA.

121. Ibid.

122. Ibid., 3–4.

123. Ibid.

124. Ibid.

125. Ibid., 5–6.

126. Ibid.

127. President Kennedy to DCI Dulles, November 29, 1961, FG 11-2 CIA, 1-1-61–4-30-62, Executive, WHCF, SF, PPJFK, JFKL.

128. Summary of Recommendations, May 1961–November 22, 1963, December 1, 1963, 5, Minutes, January 30, 1964, PFIAB, ARRB, Record 206-10001-10002, NARA.

129. Killian, *The Education of a College President*, 338.

130. Chalmers M. Roberts, "McCone Selection Criticized by Some," *Washington Post*, October 23, 1961, A10.

131. Killian, *The Education of a College President*, 338.

132. Text is quoted in full as it appears in Summary of Recommendations, May 1961–November 22, 1963, December 1, 1963, 9, Minutes, January 30, 1964, PFIAB, ARRB, Record 206-10001-10002, NARA.

133. Ibid., 19.

134. Ibid., 9.

135. Ibid.

136. Ibid.

137. Ibid., 10–11.

138. Ibid.

139. Ibid., 15–16.

140. Ibid.

141. Ibid., 8.

142. Ibid.

143. Garthoff, *Directors of Central Intelligence*, 47–48.

144. Summary of Recommendations, May 1961–November 22, 1963, December 1, 1963, 8–9, Minutes, January 30, 1964, PFIAB, ARRB, Record 206-10001-10002, NARA.

145. Jeffrey T. Richelson, *The Wizards of Langley: Inside the CIA's Directorate of Science and Technology* (Cambridge, MA: Westview, 2002), 162.

146. Ibid., 40–41; and Donald E. Welzenbach, "Science and Technology: Origins of a Directorate," *Studies in Intelligence* 30, no. 2 (Summer 1986): 22–24, at http://www.foia.cia.gov/docs/DOC0000253110/DOC_000253110.pdf.

147. Welzenbach, "Science and Technology," 23.

148. Quoted in ibid., 25.

149. Ibid., 26.

150. President Kennedy to Killian, August 8, 1962, FG 11-2, 5-1-62–8-16-62, Executive, WHCF, SF, PPJFK, JFKL.

151. Hanson W. Baldwin, "Soviet Missiles Protected in 'Hardened' Position; Soviet's Missiles Are Protected with 'Hardened' Emplacements," *New York Times*, July 26, 1962, 1.

152. *The Presidential Recordings: John F. Kennedy: The Great Crises*, vol. 1, *July 30–August 1962*, ed. Timothy Naftali (New York: W. W. Norton, 2001), 186.

153. Ibid., 187–88.

154. Ibid., 188.

155. Ibid., 189.

156. Ibid.

157. Ibid., 195. This preceded the more well-known CELOTEX surveillance

operations against journalists suspected of receiving leaks in the early 1970s revealed in the "Family Jewels" memorandum for DCI James Schlesinger of May 16, 1973, available at http://www.gwu.edu/~nsarchiv/NSAEBB/NSAEBB222/family_jewels_full_ocr.pdf.

158. Summary of Recommendations, May 1961–November 22, 1963, December 1, 1963, 18, Minutes, January 30, 1964, PFIAB, ARRB, Record 206-10001-10002, NARA.

159. President Kennedy to Killian, August 8, 1962, FG 11-2, 5-1-62–8-16-62, Executive, WHCF, SF, PPJFK, JFKL.

160. Ibid.

161. Summary of Recommendations, May 1961–November 22, 1963, December 1, 1963, 9, Minutes, January 30, 1964, PFIAB, ARRB, Record 206-10001-10002, NARA.

162. Coyne, Memorandum for the Members, Washington, DC, November 20, 1963, PFIAB, Agenda for Meeting of November 21–22, 1963, PFIAB, ARRB, Record 206-10001-10003, NARA.

163. Summary of Recommendations, May 1961–November 22, 1963, December 1, 1963, 19–21, Minutes, January 30, 1964, PFIAB, ARRB, Record 206-10001-10002, NARA.

164. Ibid.

165. Attachment to Memorandum to Bundy, December 27, 1963, FIAB vol. 1, NSF, Intelligence File, LBJPL.

166. Summary of Recommendations, May 1961–November 22, 1963, December 1, 1963, 19, Minutes, January 30, 1964, PFIAB, ARRB, Record 206-10001-10002, NARA.

167. Ibid., 20–22.

168. Clifford, *Counsel to the President,* 356.

169. Ibid.

170. Ibid., 357.

171. Ibid., 356.

172. Memorandum for the File, Washington, DC, November 9, 1962, PFIAB, Meeting of the Board, November 9, 1962, PFIAB, ARRB, Record 206-10001-10010, NARA.

173. Clifford, *Counsel to the President,* 357–58.

174. William A. Tidwell, Memorandum for the Record, "Instructions Concerning the Handling of Certain Information Concerning Cuba," September 1, 1962, in *CIA Documents on the Cuban Missile Crisis, 1962,* ed. Mary S. McAuliffe (Washington, DC: CIA, October 1992), 33.

175. Killian, Memorandum to the President, February 4, 1963, in ibid., 365.

176. The "policy failure case" is made in Max Holland, "The 'Photo Gap' That Delayed Discovery of Missiles in Cuba," *Studies in Intelligence* 49, no. 4 (2005): 15–30, and "The Politics of Post Mortems," *Washington Decoded,* February 11, 2009, at http://www.washingtondecoded.com/site/2009/02/the-politics-of-postmortems.html; Dino A. Brugioni, *Eyeball to Eyeball: The Inside Story of the Cuban Missile Crisis* (New York: Random House, 1991), 133–40; and Kenneth Michael Absher, *Mind-Sets and Missiles: A First Hand Account of the Cuban Missile Crisis* (Carlisle, PA: U.S. Army War College, August 2009), 36–38.

177. Special National Intelligence Estimate No. 85-3-62, "The Military Build-up in Cuba," September 19, 1962, in McAuliffe, ed., *CIA Documents on the Cuban Missile Crisis,* 93.

178. Memorandum for the File, Washington, DC, December 6–7, 1962, 1, PFI-AB, Agenda for Meetings of December 6, 1962 of the Board's Cuban Panel, PFIAB, ARRB, Record 206-10001-10009, NARA.

179. Ibid., 15.

180. "Interview with William McAfee," September 9, 1997, Foreign Affairs Oral History Collection of the Association for Diplomatic Studies and Training, at http://memory.loc.gov/cgi-bin/query/S?ammem/mfdipbib:@field(AUTHOR+@od1(McAfee,+William)).

181. DCI to the PFIAB, Report to the PFIAB on Intelligence Community Activities relating to the Cuban Arms Build-Up (April 14 through October 14, 1962), n.d., Cuba, Subjects, Guidelines for Executive or Public Testimony, Report to President's FIAB on International Community, NSF, Countries, PPJFK, JFKL.

182. Clifford, *Counsel to the President,* 358.

183. Discussed in Roberta Wohlstetter, "Cuba and Pearl Harbor: Hindsight and Foresight," Rand Memorandum RM-4328-ISA (Santa Monica, CA: Rand, April 1965), 26.

184. Clifford, *Counsel to the President,* 357.

185. Ibid., 358.

186. Agenda for Meetings, December 27–28, 1962, PFIAB, Agenda for Meetings of December 27–28, 1962, PFIAB, ARRB, Record 206-10001-10008, NARA.

187. Clifford, *Counsel to the President,* 358.

188. Ibid., 355.

189. Ibid.

190. Kennedy quoted in Holland, "The 'Photo Gap,'" 30.

191. Killian, Memorandum, in McAuliffe, ed., *CIA Documents on the Cuban Missile Crisis,* 367.

192. Ibid., 369.

193. James R. Killian Jr., Memorandum for President Kennedy, February 4, 1963, in McAuliffe, ed., *CIA Documents on the Cuban Missile Crisis,* 363.

194. John McCone, Director, to President Kennedy, Washington, DC, February 28, 1963, Killian, James R 2/4–3/7/63, POF, Special Correspondence, PPJFK, JFKL; and "Conclusions," in McAuliffe, ed., *CIA Documents on the Cuban Missile Crisis,* 376.

195. "Conclusions," in ibid., 373, 375.

196. Killian, Memorandum, in ibid., 367.

197. Memorandum for the File, Washington, DC, January 25–26, 1963, 1–2, PFIAB, Agenda for Meeting of January 25–26, 1963, PFIAB, ARRB, Record 206-10001-10011, NARA.

198. Memorandum for the File, Washington, DC, March 11, 1963, PFIAB, Meeting of the Board, March 8–9, 1963 (the Board met with the President on March 9, 1963), PFIAB, ARRB, Record 206-10001-10012, NARA.

199. John McCone, Director, to President Kennedy, Washington, DC, February 28, 1963, Killian, James R 2/4–3/7/63, POF, Special Correspondence, PPJFK, JFKL.

200. Ibid.

201. Bundy to Evelyn Lincoln, Washington, DC, March 7, 1963, Killian, James R 2/4–3/7/63, POF, Special Correspondence, PPJFK, JFKL.

202. Memorandum for the File, March 11, 1963, 1, PFIAB, Meeting of the Board, March 8–9, 1963 (the Board met with the President on March 9, 1963), PFIAB, ARRB, Record 206-10001-10012, NARA.

203. March 9, 1963 (Daily Schedule), AB JFK (January 1, 1963–November 21, 1963), JFKL.

204. Killian, Memorandum, in McAuliffe, ed., *CIA Documents on the Cuban Missile Crisis*, 367.

205. Ibid., 363.

206. Ibid., 366.

207. Ibid.

208. Ibid., 367.

209. Ibid., 369–70.

210. Memorandum, Miscellaneous Week End Reading, February 2, 1963, Memos to the President, 1/21/63–2/28/63, NSF, McGeorge Bundy Correspondence, PPJFK, JFKL.

211. Memo, Miscellaneous, Memos, 1/21/63–2/28/63, NSF, McGeorge Bundy Correspondence, PPJFK, JFKL.

212. Summary of Recommendations, May 1961–November 22, 1963, December 1, 1963, 23–24, Minutes, January 30, 1964, PFIAB, ARRB, Record 206-10001-10002, NARA.

213. Ibid.

214. Bundy to President Kennedy, January 20, 1963, Memos to the President, 1/1/63–1/20/63, NSF, McGeorge Bundy Correspondence, PPJFK, JFKL.

215. Ibid.

216. Ibid.

217. Summary of Recommendations, May 1961–November 22, 1963, December 1, 1963, 27–28, Minutes, January 30, 1964, PFIAB, ARRB, Record 206-10001-10002, NARA.

218. Coyne, Memorandum for the Members, November 20, 1963, Agenda for Meeting of November 21–22, 1963, PFIAB, ARRB, Record 206-10001-10003, NARA.

219. Memorandum for the File, Washington, DC, November 21–22, 1963, 1, PFIAB, Agenda for Meeting of November 21–22, 1963, PFIAB, ARRB, Record 206-10001-10003, NARA.

220. Ibid.

221. Ibid., 54.

222. Ibid., 55.

223. Ibid.

224. These statistics, used by PFIAB chair Clifford to brief President Johnson on the board's activities under President Kennedy, are from Memorandum for the File, February 4, 1964, 6, Minutes, January 30, 1964, PFIAB, ARRB, Record 206-10001-10002, NARA. Clifford also cites these exact numbers in his memoirs (see Clifford, *Counsel to the President*, 351).

225. Memorandum for the File, February 4, 1964, 6, Minutes, January 30, 1964, PFIAB, ARRB, Record 206-10001-10002, NARA.

226. Clifford, *Counsel to the President*, 351.

227. Bundy to President Kennedy, Handwritten Memo, n.d., Killian, James R. 2/4–3/7/63, POF, Special Correspondence, PPJFK, JFKL.

228. "William O. Baker's Odyssey," *Chemical and Engineering News*, November 25, 1996, 29.

3. LYNDON B. JOHNSON

1. Clark Clifford, *Counsel to the President: A Memoir* (New York: Random House, 1991), 378.

2. J. H. Doolittle to President Lyndon B. Johnson, Washington, DC, August 10, 1964, FG-732/A, EX FG 731 (6/10/64–), LBJPL.

3. Immediate Release, OWHPS, August 10, 1965, PFIAB, OFJM, LBJPL.

4. We could find no direct evidence for why Augustus Long declined the appointment, but, given the death of his first wife in 1963 and remarriage in 1964, combined with his continuing business obligation to Texaco, it is likely that his decision was the result of both personal and professional considerations. See Patrick McGeehan, "Augustus C. Long, 97, Chief of Texaco in 50s and 60s," *New York Times,* November 21, 2001.

5. Immediate Release, OWHPS, Austin, TX, February 23, 1968, PFIAB (Box 41), NSF, Subject File, LBJPL; and Clifford, *Counsel to the President,* 489.

6. Clifford, *Counsel to the President,* 351–52.

7. Ibid., 352.

8. Edward L. Sherman to John W. Macy Jr., Washington, DC, June 10, 1965, PFIAB, OFJM, LBJPL.

9. John J. McCloy to John T. Connor, Secretary of Commerce, New York, NY, May 6, 1965, PFIAB, OFJM, LBJPL.

10. Handwritten Note to the File (entitled "Board of Foreign Intelligence"), n.d. (handwritten "6-21"), PFIAB, OFJM, LBJPL.

11. Macy to John Clinton, July 12, 1965, PFIAB, OFJM, LBJPL.

12. Macy to President Johnson, Washington, DC, July 21, 1965, PFIAB, OFJM, LBJPL.

13. Clifford to President Johnson, Washington, DC, September 16, 1965, PFIAB (Box 41), NSF, Subject File, LBJPL.

14. Long to Clifford, PFIAB Chair, September 15, 1965, PFIAB (Box 41), NSF, Subject File, LBJPL.

15. Bundy to President Johnson, Washington, DC, September 17, 1965, PFIAB (Box 41), NSF, Subject File, LBJPL.

16. Bundy to Long, New York, NY, October 30, 1965, PFIAB (Box 41), NSF, Subject File, LBJPL.

17. Ibid.

18. Bundy to Bill Moyers, Washington, DC, November 6, 1965, PFIAB (Box 41), NSF, Subject File, LBJPL.

19. Joe Laitin to Moyers, Washington, DC, November 11, 1965, PFIAB (Box 41), NSF, Subject File, LBJPL.

20. J. Patrick Coyne to Terry Scanlon, Washington, DC, March 2, 1966, PFIAB, OFJM, LBJPL.

21. Ibid.

22. Macy to Jack Valenti, Washington, DC, March 2, 1966, PFIAB, OFJM, LBJPL.

23. Senator Mike Monroney (unsigned) to President Johnson, February 16, 1968, PFIAB, OFJM, LBJPL; JWM, Memorandum for Mr. Cox, United States Civil Service Commission, February 13, 1968, PFIAB, OFJM, LBJPL.

24. Macy to Robert Cox, Washington, DC, February 23, 1968, PFIAB, OFJM, LBJPL.

25. Clinton P. Anderson to President Johnson, Washington, DC, February 28, 1968, PFIAB, OFJM, LBJPL.

26. Bob Faiss to Jim Jones, October 29, 1968, FG-732 PFIB, EX FG 731 (6/10/64–), LBJPL.

27. Maxwell D. Taylor, PFIAB Chair, to President Johnson, Washington, DC, November 25, 1968, FIAB Vol. 2 [1 of 4], NSF, Intelligence File, LBJPL.

28. Clifford, *Counsel to the President,* 353.

29. Agenda for Meeting, Washington, DC, January 30, 1964, Minutes, January 30, 1964, PFIAB, ARRB, Record 206-10001-10002, NARA.

30. Clifford, PFIAB Chair, to John A. McCone, DCI (with attached "Subjects Suggested by Board Members for Discussion by the Director of Central Intelligence at the Board Meeting for January 30, 1964"), Washington, DC, January 16, 1964, Minutes, January 30, 1964, PFIAB, ARRB, Record 206-10001-10002, NARA.

31. Memorandum for the File, Washington, DC, January 30, 1964, 5–7, Minutes, January 30, 1964, PFIAB, ARRB, Record 206-10001-10002, NARA.

32. Ibid., 9–10.

33. Agenda for Meeting, Washington, DC, June 4, 1964, Minutes of the Board, Meeting of June 4, 1964, PFIAB, ARRB, Record 206-10001-10013, NARA.

34. Memorandum for the File, Washington, DC, June 17, 1964, 1, Minutes of the Board, Meeting of June 4, 1964, PFIAB, ARRB, Record 206-10001-10013, NARA.

35. Ibid., 3.

36. Ibid., 4.

37. Ibid., 10–13.

38. Ibid., 15–16.

39. Memorandum for the File, Washington, DC, June 5, 1964, 1, Covert Action Panel Meeting 5/6/64 (discussion with Secretary, Special Group, et al.), PFIAB, ARRB, Record 206-10001-10014, NARA.

40. Ibid., 2–4.

41. Memorandum for the File, Washington, DC, August 6–7, 1964, Minutes of the Board, Meeting of August 6 and 7, 1964, PFIAB, ARRB, Record 206-10001-10007, NARA.

42. Agenda for Meetings, Washington, DC, August 6–7, 1964, Minutes of the Board, Meeting of August 6 and 7, 1964, PFIAB, ARRB, Record 206-10001-10007, NARA.

43. Ibid.

44. Agenda for Meetings, Washington, DC, October 1–2, 1964, 1–2, Minutes of the Board, Meeting of October 1 and 2, 1964, PFIAB, ARRB, Record 206-10001-10000, NARA.

45. Ibid., 3.

46. Memorandum for the File, Washington, DC, April 5, 1965, 1, Minutes of the Board, Meeting of October 1 and 2, 1964, PFIAB, ARRB, Record 206-10001-10000, NARA.

47. Ibid.

48. Memorandum for the File, Washington, DC, April 5, 1965, 2, Minutes of the Board, Meeting of October 1 and 2, 1964, PFIAB, ARRB, Record 206-10001-10000, NARA.

49. Ibid., 5–6.

50. Ibid., 28.

51. Ibid., 29.

52. John A. Bross to the DCI, September 15, 1965, CIA-RDP-80B01676R000500010061, CREST, ALIC, NARA.

53. PFIAB, Meeting Agenda, Washington, DC, November 22, 1965, PFIAB (Box 41), NSF, Subject File, LBJPL.

54. Bross to the DCI, January 20, 1966, CIA-RDP80B0167R0005000100076-5, CREST, ALIC, NARA.

55. W. F. Raborn to Clifford, January 29, 1966, CIA-RDP-80B01676R000500010074–1, CREST, ALIC, NARA.

56. Memorandum to the DD/P (unsigned), DDI, Deputy Director for Support, Deputy Director for Science and Technology, May 23, 1966, CIA-RDP-80B0167R000500010101–6, CREST, ALIC, NARA.

57. Bross, Memorandum for the Record, August 1, 1966, CIA-RDP-80B0167R000500010086–4, CREST, ALIC, NARA.

58. Bross, Memorandum for the Record, October 4, 1966, CIA-RDP-80B01676R000500010070–1, CREST, ALIC, NARA.

59. Walt Rostow to President Johnson, Cable Message, December 5, 1966, PFIAB (Box 41), NSF, Subject File, LBJPL.

60. Clifford to Rostow, February 2, 1967, Memorandum, PFIAB (Box 41), NSF, Subject File, LBJPL.

61. Taylor, PFIAB Chair to Helms, DCI, Washington, DC, September 25, 1968, CIA-RDPB00529R000200110005–6, CREST, ALIC, NARA.

62. Taylor to Helms, September 25, 1968, RDPB00529R000200110005–6, CREST, ALIC, NARA.

63. Bross, Memorandum for the Record, February 8, 1968, CIA-RDP-71B00529R000200110022–7, CREST, ALIC, NARA.

64. Taylor to President Johnson, Washington DC, February 23, 1968, PFIAB (Box 41), NSF, Subject File, LBJPL.

65. Lt. Gen. Marshall S. Carter to Maxwell Taylor, PFIAB Chair, Fort George G. Meade, MD, April 10, 1968, FIAB Vol. 2 [1 of 4], NSF, Intelligence File, LBJPL.

66. Bross, Memorandum for the Record, April 16, 1968, CIA-RDP-71B00529R000200110021–8, CREST; ALIC, NARA.

67. Bross, Memorandum for the Record, August 12, 1968, CIA-RDP-71B00529R000200110011-9, CREST, ALIC, NARA.

68. Taylor, PFIAB Chair, to Rostow, Washington, DC, April 18, 1968, FIAB Vol. 2 [1 of 4], NSF, Intelligence File, LBJPL.

69. "218. Letter from the Chairman of the PFIAB (Taylor) to Secretary of Defense Clifford," in FRUS, 1964–1968, vol. 10, at http://www.state.gov/historicaldocuments/frus/1964-68v10/d218.

70. Coyne to PFIAB Members, Washington, DC, June 1, 1964, Minutes of the Board, Meeting of June 4, 1964, PFIAB, ARRB, Record 206-10001-10013, NARA.

71. Bundy to Chair, U.S. Intelligence Advisory Board, Washington, DC, May 14 1964, FIAB Vol. 2 [4 of 4], NSF, Intelligence File, LBJPL.

72. Memorandum for the File, Washington, DC, June 5, 1964, Covert Action Panel Meeting 5/6/64 (discussion with Secretary, Special Group, et al.), PFIAB, ARRB, Record 206-10001-10014, NARA.

73. Taylor, PFIAB Chair, to Secretary of State Dean Rusk, Washington, DC, May 3, 1968, PFIAB (Box 41), NSF, Subject File, LBJPL.

74. Taylor to Rusk, May 3, 1968, PFIAB (Box 41), NSF, Subject File, LBJPL.

75. Bross, Memorandum for the Record, October 28, 1966, CIA-RDP-71B00528R0020010090-9, CREST, ALIC, NARA.

76. "222. Report Submitted," in *FRUS, 1964–1968*, vol. 10, at http://www.state.gov/historicaldocuments/frus/1964-68v10/d222.

77. Clifford to the Secretary of State, the DCI, and the Director, DIA, Washington DC, October 12, 1965, PFIAB (Box 41), NSF, Subject File, LBJPL.

78. Tim Weiner, *Legacy of Ashes: The History of the CIA* (New York: Doubleday 2007), 263.

79. Clifford, PFIAB Chair to President Johnson, Washington DC, October 4, 1964, FIAB Vol. 2 [3 of 4], NSF, Intelligence File, LBJPL.

80. "222. Report Submitted," in *FRUS, 1964–1968*, vol. 10, at http://www.state.gov/historicaldocuments/frus/1964-68v10/d222.

81. Ibid.

82. Bundy to the Attorney General, Secretary of State, Secretary of Defense, and Chair of the USIB, February 8, 1964, FIAB Vol. 1 [2 of 2], NSF, Intelligence File, LBJPL.

83. The following are contained in Marshall S. Carter, Acting DCI, to Special Assistant for National Security Affairs, "Measures for Strengthening the Counterintelligence Posture of the United States," March 10, 1964, FIAB Vol. 2 [2 of 4], NSF, Intelligence File, LBJPL.

84. Cyrus Vance, Deputy Secretary of Defense, to Bundy, Special Assistant to the President for National Security Affairs, Washington, DC, March 10, 1964, FIAB Vol. 1 [1 of 2], NSF, Intelligence File, LBJPL.

85. Ibid.

86. Ibid.

87. Bundy to the Secretary of State, Secretary of Defense, and Attorney General, Washington, DC, April 24, 1964, FIAB Vol. 1 [1 of 2], NSF, Intelligence File, LBJPL.

88. Acting Secretary of State George Ball to Bundy, "Measures for Strengthening the Counterintelligence Posture of the United States," May 9, 1964, FIAB Vol. 2 [2 of 4], NSF, Intelligence File, LBJPL.

89. Marshall S. Carter, Acting DCI, to Special Assistant for National Security Affairs, "Measures for Strengthening the Counterintelligence Posture of the United States," March 10, 1964, FIAB Vol. 2 [2 of 4], NSF, Intelligence File, LBJPL.

90. Howard J. Osborn to the Deputy Director for Support, July 30, 1965, CIA-RDP83B00823R000400110012–9, CREST, ALIC, NARA.

91. Coyne to Rostow, Washington, DC, January 31, 1967, 1, FIAB Vol. 2 [2 of 4], NSF, Intelligence File, LBJPL.

92. Ibid., 2.

93. Bundy to the Secretary of Defense and the DCI, April 10, 1964, FIAB Vol. 1 [1 of 2], NSF, Intelligence File, LBJPL.

94. Bundy to the Secretary of Defense and the PFIAB Chair, June 26, 1964, FIAB Vol. 2 [3 of 4], NSF, Intelligence File, LBJPL.

95. Memorandum (unsigned) to Bundy, Special Assistant to the President for National Security Affairs, Washington, DC, March 20, 1964, FIAB Vol. 1 [1 of 2], NSF, Intelligence File, LBJPL.

96. Coyne to Bundy, Washington, DC, July 15, 1965, FIAB (Box 41), NSF, Subject File, LBJPL.

97. Written submissions to PFIAB since January 1, 1965, n.d., FIAB (Box 41) NSF, Subject File, LBJPL.

98. Coyne to Bundy, Washington, DC, January 7, 1966, FIAB (Box 41), NSF, Subject File, LBJPL.

99. Coyne to Bundy, Washington, DC, May 9, 1964, 1, FIAB Vol. 2 [4 of 4], NSF, Intelligence File, LBJPL.

100. Ibid., 2.

101. Ibid., 3.

102. Coyne to Dr. Marvin Gentile, Deputy Assistant Secretary for Security, Department of State, May 13, 1964, FIAB Vol. 2 [4 of 4], NSF, Intelligence File, LBJPL.

103. Clifford, PFIAB Chair, to President Johnson, Memorandum with Attached PFIAB Report, Washington, DC, May 2, 1964, 2, FIAB Vol. 2 [4 of 4], NSF, Intelligence File, LBJPL.

104. Jeffrey T. Richelson, *The Wizards of Langley: Inside the CIA's Directorate of Science and Technology* (Cambridge, MA: Westview, 2002), 112–24.

105. The following guidelines are contained in Clifford to President Johnson, May 2, 1964, 7–10, FBIA Vol. 2 [4 of 4], NSF, Intelligence File, LBJPL.

106. "206. Memorandum from Director of Central Intelligence McCone to the President's Special Assistant for National Security Affairs (Bundy)," in *FRUS, 1964–1968*, vol. 33, at http://www.state.gov/historicaldocuments/frus/1964-68v33/d206.

107. "205. Memorandum from the Deputy Secretary of Defense Vance to the President's Special Assistant for National Security Affairs (Bundy)," in ibid., at http://www.state.gov/historicaldocuments/frus/1964-68v33/d205.

108. Jeffrey T. Richelson, "Civilians, Spies, and Blue Suits: The Bureaucratic War for Control of Overhead Reconnaissance, 1961–1965," National Security Archive Monograph, January 2003, 47, at http://www.gwu.edu/~nsarchiv/monograph/nro/.

109. Ibid., 52.

110. Ibid.

111. Clifford, PFIAB Chair, to President Johnson, Washington DC, October 4, 1964, FIAB Vol. 2 [3 of 4], NSF, Intelligence File, LBJPL.

112. Ibid.

113. Ibid.

114. Ibid.

115. Clifford to President Johnson, Washington, DC, November 1, 1965, Clifford, Clark M. 1/1/1965–12/31/1966, WHCF, Name File, LBJPL.

116. Bundy to the Secretary of State, Secretary of Defense, and DCI, Washington, DC, January 4, 1966, FIAB Vol. 2 [3 of 4], NSF, Intelligence File, LBJPL.

117. Bundy to the Secretary of State, Secretary of Defense, and DCI, January 4, 1966, FIAB Vol. 2 [3 of 4], NSF, Intelligence File, LBJPL.

118. Coyne, PFIAB Executive Secretary, to Rostow, Washington, DC, March 2, 1967, FIAB Vol. 2 [1 of 4], NSF, Intelligence File, LBJPL.

119. Clifford, *Counsel to the President*, 427.

120. Rostow to the President, November 7, 1967, NSF, Files of Walt W. Rostow, Box 3, McNamara, Robert S.—SEA [Southeast Asia] Top Secret/Sensitive.

121. Clifford, PFIAB Chair, Memorandum, n.d., McNamara, Robert S.—SEA Top Secret/Sensitive; Files of Walt W. Rostow, Box 3; NSF; LBJPL, 1.

122. Ibid., 2.

123. Ibid., 3.

124. Rostow to the Secretary of State, Secretary of Defense, and DCI, Washington, DC, September 28, 1966, FIAB (Box 41), NSF, Subject File, LBJPL.

125. Rostow to the Secretary of State, Secretary of Defense, and DCI, Washington, DC, June 9, 1966, FIAB Vol. 2 [2 of 4], NSF, Intelligence File, LBJPL.

126. Clifford, PFIAB Chair, to President Johnson, Washington, DC, May 20, 1966, FIAB Vol. 2 [2 of 4], NSF, Intelligence File, LBJPL.

127. Clifford to President Johnson, "U.S. Shootdown of Chinese Communist (Chicom) MIG 17 on May 12, 1966," Washington, DC, June 3, 1966, FIAB Vol. 2 [2 of 4], NSF, Intelligence File, LBJPL.

128. Ibid.

129. Ibid.

130. Ibid.

131. Rostow to President Johnson, Washington, DC, June 7, 1966, FIAB Vol. 2 [2 of 4], NSF, Intelligence File, LBJPL.

132. Rostow to McNamara (Dear Bob), June 11, 1966, FIAB Vol. 2 [2 of 4], NSF, Intelligence File, LBJPL.

133. Taylor, PFIAB Chair, to President Johnson, Washington, DC, June 7, 1968, 1, FIAB Vol. 2 [1 of 4], NSF, Intelligence File, LBJPL.

134. Ibid., 1–2.

135. Ibid., 2.

136. Ibid.

137. Ibid.

138. Ibid., 2–3.

139. Ibid., 3.

140. Ibid.

141. Ibid., 3–4.

142. Ibid., 4.

143. Ibid., 5.

144. Bromley Smith to the DCI, Washington DC, July 29, 1968, FIAB Vol. 2 [1 of 4], NSF, Intelligence File, LBJPL.

145. Ibid.

146. Carter to Taylor, Fort George G. Meade, Maryland, April 10, 1968, PFIAB Vol. 2 [1 of 4], NSF, Intelligence File, LBJPL.

147. Taylor, PFIAB Chair, to Rostow, Washington, DC, April 19, 1968, FIAB Vol. 2 [1 of 4], NSF, Intelligence File, LBJPL.

148. Taylor, PFIAB Chair, to Rostow, Washington, DC, June 10, 1968, FIAB Vol. 2 [1 of 4], NSF, Intelligence File, LBJPL.

149. Rostow to Clifford, Secretary of Defense, June 11, 1968, FIAB Vol. 2 [1 of 4], NSF, Intelligence File, LBJPL.

150. Ibid.

151. Taylor, PFIAB Chair, to President Johnson, Washington, DC, August 2, 1968, 1, PFIAB (Box 41), NSF, Subject File, LBJPL.

152. Ibid., 3.

153. Ibid.

154. "268. Memorandum from the Chairman of the PFIAB (Clifford) to President Johnson," in *FRUS, 1964–1968,* vol. 33, at http://www.state.gov/historicaldocuments/frus/1964-68v33/d268.

155. Ibid.

156. Ibid.

157. Ibid.

158. All these recommendations are contained in ibid.

159. Bundy to the Secretary of State, September 8, 1965, FIAB Vol. 2 [3 of 4], NSF, Intelligence File, LBJPL.

160. Ibid.

161. President Johnson to the DCI, Washington, DC, September 24, 1965, FIAB Vol. 2 [3 of 4], NSF, Intelligence File, LBJPL.

162. Clifford, PFIAB Chair, to Rostow, Washington, DC, August 3, 1966, FIAB Vol. 2 [2 of 4], NSF, Intelligence File, LBJPL.

163. Ibid., 2.

164. Ibid., 5.

165. Rostow to the Director, DIA, Washington, DC, August 4, 1966, FIAB Vol. 2 [2 of 4], NSF, Intelligence File, LBJPL.

166. Rostow to the Secretary of State, Washington, DC, August 4, 1966, FIAB Vol. 2 [2 of 4], NSF, Intelligence File, LBJPL.

167. Rostow to the Secretary of State, August 4, 1966, FIAB Vol. 2 [3 of 4], NSF, Intelligence File, LBJPL.

168. Itinerary: Dr. William L. Langer and Mr. A. Russell Ash, n.d., FIAB (Box 41), NSF, Subject File, LBJPL.

169. Rostow to the Secretary of State, Washington, DC, November 18, 1966, FIAB Vol. 2 [2 of 4], NSF, Intelligence File, LBJPL.

170. Clifford, PFIAB Chair, to Rostow, Washington, DC, August 2, 1966, 1, FIAB Vol. 2 [2 of 4], NSF, Intelligence File, LBJPL.

171. Ibid., 2.

172. Rostow to the Secretary of State, November 18, 1966, FIAB Vol. 2 [2 of 4], NSF, Intelligence File, LBJPL.

173. "211. Memorandum from the Chairman of the PFIAB (Taylor) to President Johnson," in *FRUS, 1964–1968*, vol. 10, at http://www.state.gov/ historicaldocuments/frus/1964-68v10/d211.

174. "214. Telegram from the President's Special Assistant (Rostow) to President Johnson in Texas," in ibid., at http://www.state.gov/historicaldocuments/ frus/1964-68v10/d214.

175. Rostow note to President Johnson, August 26, 1968, FIAB Vol. 2 [2 of 4], NSF, Intelligence File, LBJPL.

176. "215. Letter from Secretary of Defense Clifford to Chairman of the PFIAB (Taylor)," in *FRUS, 1964–1968,* vol. 10, at http://www.state.gov/historicaldocuments/ frus/1964-68v10/d215.

177. "216. Letter from the Chairman of the PFIAB (Taylor) to Secretary of Defense Clifford," in ibid., at http://www.state.gov/historicaldocuments/frus/1964-68v10/d216.

178. "218. Letter from the Chairman of the PFIAB (Taylor) to Secretary of Defense Clifford," in ibid., at http://www.state.gov/historicaldocuments/frus/1964-68v10/ d218.

179. Bross, Memorandum for the Record, January 16, 1968, CIA-RDP-71B00529R000200010070–5, CREST, ALIC, NARA.

180. Richelson, *The Wizards of Langley,* 145–46.

181. For a detailed discussion of the differences between OXCART and the SR-71, see Carl Duckett, Deputy Director for Science and Technology, to DCI, "PFIAB Discussion of OXCART Phase-Out," October 13, 1967, FIAB Vol. 2 [2 of 4], NSF, Intelligence File, LBJPL.

182. PFIAB Submission for June 30, 1968, OXCART, June 30, 1968, CIA-RD-P3302415A000400400013–8, CREST, ALIC, NARA.

183. Taylor to President Johnson, November 25, 1968, 6, FIAB Vol. 2 [1 of 4], NSF, Intelligence File, LBJPL.

184. Ibid., 6–7.
185. Ibid., 11.
186. Ibid.
187. Ibid.
188. Ibid., 12.
189. Richelson, *The Wizards of Langley,* 167–69.
190. Coyne to Bundy, "Scientific and Technical Efforts in the Foreign Intelligence Field (CIA)," July 20, 1965, 6, FIAB Vol. 2 [2 of 4], NSF, Intelligence File, LBJPL.
191. Ibid., 11.
192. Vance to Bundy, June 6, 1984, FIAB Vol. 2, NSF, Intelligence File, LBJPL.
193. Taylor to President Johnson, November 25, 1968, 12, FIAB Vol. 2 [1 of 4], NSF, Intelligence File, LBJPL.
194. Ibid.
195. Ibid.
196. Ibid., 13.
197. Ibid.
198. Ibid.
199. Ibid.
200. Ibid. The "303 Committee" succeeded the 5412/2 Special Group as the overseeing body for covert operations. It is so named for National Security Action Memorandum 303.
201. Ibid., 14.
202. Ibid.
203. Ibid.
204. Ibid.

4. RICHARD M. NIXON

1. "180. Memorandum from [name not declassified] of the Central Intelligence Agency (CIA) to the President's Assistant for National Security Affairs–Designate (Kissinger)," in *FRUS, 1969–1976,* vol. 2, p. 368.
2. "188. Executive Order 11460," in ibid., 383 n. 1.
3. "186. Editorial Note," in ibid., 376–77.
4. Tom Jones, Records Office, Memorandum for the Record (with attachment EO 11460), Washington, DC, March 20, 1969, FG 208, PFIAB, Folder 1, WHCF, SF, NARA 2.
5. President Richard M. Nixon to the Secretary of State, Secretary of Defense, DCI, and PFIAB Chair, March 24, 1969, FG 208, PFIAB, Folder 1, WHCF, SF, NARA 2.
6. Jones, Memorandum for the Record (with attachment EO 11460), March 20, 1969, FG 208, PFIAB, Folder 1, WHCF, SF, NARA 2.
7. Nixon to Bob Haldeman and John Erlichmann, January 7, 1969, FG 208, PFIAB, Folder 1, WHCF, SF, NARA 2.
8. Nixon, EO, March 8, 1972, FG 208, PFIAB, Folder 2, WHCF, SF, NARA 2.
9. Interview with Byers.
10. Immediate Release, OWHPS, March 20, 1969, FG 208, PFIAB, Folder 1, WHCF, SF, NARA 2.
11. William L. Langer to Nixon, January 20, 1969, FG 208, PFIAB, Folder 7, WHCF, SF, NARA 2; and Adm. John Sides to Nixon, January 20, 1969, FG 208, PFIAB, Folder 7, WHCF, SF, NARA 2.

12. Maxwell D. Taylor to Nixon, Washington, DC, April 9, 1970, FG 208, PFIAB, Folder 7, WHCF, SF, NARA 2.

13. John S. Chwat, *The President's Foreign Intelligence Advisory Board: An Historical and Contemporary Analysis (1955–1975)*, Congressional Research Service Report 75-225F (Washington, DC: Library of Congress, 1975).

14. Al Haig to Ron Ziegler, Washington, DC, August 2, 1972, FG 208, PFIAB, Folder 8, WHCF, SF, NARA 2.

15. Interview with Byers.

16. Ibid.

17. Ibid.

18. Ibid.

19. Ibid.

20. *Who's Who in America*, vol. 8, *1982–1985* (Wilmette, IL: Marquis Who's Who, 1985), s.v. "Clark, Mark Wayne."

21. Peter Flanigan to Henry Kissinger, Washington, DC, May 22, 1969, FG 208, PFIAB, Folder 1, WHCF, SF, NARA 2.

22. Flanigan to John Mitchell, August 11, 1969, FG 208, PFIAB, Folder 1, WHCF, SF, NARA 2.

23. Bob Houdek to Dwight Chapin, Washington, DC, April 12, 1969, FG 208, PFIAB, Folder 1, WHCF, SF, NARA 2.

24. Schedule Proposal, Washington, DC, January 31, 1972, FG 208, PFIAB, Folder 2, WHCF, SF, NARA 2.

25. Chwat, *The President's Foreign Intelligence Advisory Board.*

26. Memorandum for the Record, October 11, 1973, CIA-RDP-84B00506R000100040085-8, CREST, ALIC, NARA.

27. Interview with Source L.

28. Ibid.

29. Interview with Byers.

30. Memorandum for DCI, December 3, 1971, CIA-RDP91M00696R000300110022-8, CREST, ALIC, NARA.

31. Memorandum for the Record, October 22, 1971, CIA-RDP-80B01086A000800090001-5, CREST, ALIC, NARA.

32. Memorandum for the Record, October 11, 1973, CIA-RDP-84B00506R000100040085-8, CREST, ALIC, NARA; Memorandum for the Record, October 22, 1971, CIA-RDP80B01086A000800090001-5, CREST, ALIC, NARA.

33. Robert W. Galvin to George W. Anderson Jr., Chicago, IL, August 6, 1974, Wheaton Byers Papers (in the authors' possession).

34. Interview with Byers.

35. Interview with Source L.

36. E. H. Knoche, Director, Strategic Research, to the DCI, November 20, 1973, CIA-DP91M00696R000300110023-7, CREST, ALIC, NARA.

37. Memorandum for DCI, Deputy DCI, Executive Director–Comptroller, DDI, DD/P, Deputy Director for Science and Technology, September 28, 1972, CIA-RD-P75B00514R0002002000002-1, CREST, ALIC, NARA.

38. Memorandum, Draft Report to the PFIAB and the Agency History for FY 1972, June 19, 1972, CIA-RDP84–00780R004900020015-3, CREST, ALIC, NARA.

39. Intelligence Community Staff Summary, 1974, CIA-RDP-80M01082A000900200011-3, CREST, ALIC, NARA.

40. Interview with Source L.

41. Ibid.

42. William J. Hopkins to Larry Higby, May 7, 1969, FG 208, PFIAB, Folder 1, WHCF, SF, NARA 2.

43. Lt. Gen. Vernon A. Walters, Deputy DCI, to USN Admiral (Ret.) Anderson, PFIAB Chair, Washington, DC, March 1, 1973, Staff Secretary, PFIAB, Box 190, WHSF, Staff and Office Files, NARA 2.

44. President Nixon, April 9, 1969, FG 208, PFIAB, Folder 1, WHCF, SF, NARA 2.

45. Clare Boothe Luce to Kissinger, May 4, 1970, Clare Boothe Luce, Box 824, NSCF, NF, NARA 2.

46. Rose Mary Woods to Nixon, August 6, 1973, Luce, Clare Booth, Folder 15, PPF, Name, SF 1969–1974, WHCF, NARA 2.

47. Robert M. Behr to Kissinger, April 3, 1970, John S. Foster, Box 841, NSCF, NF, NARA 2.

48. Jeanne W. Davis to Kissinger, November 20, 1970, FG 208, PFIAB, Folder 1, WHCF, SF, NARA 2.

49. Interview with Source L.

50. "191. Memorandum from [name not declassified] of the CIA to DCI Helms," in *FRUS, 1969–1976*, vol. 2, p. 388.

51. "210. Editorial Note," in ibid., 446.

52. "344. Record of Meeting," in *FRUS, 1969–1976*, vol. 6, p. 1122.

53. Ibid.

54. Ibid., 1124.

55. "224. Editorial Note," in *FRUS, 1969–1976*, vol. 2, p. 482. See also "220. Memorandum from DCI Helms to the President's Assistant for National Security Affairs (Kissinger)," in ibid., 476–78.

56. "234. Memorandum from Wayne Smith and Andrew Marshall of the NSC Staff to the President's Assistant for National Security Affairs (Kissinger)," in ibid., 389, 523 n. 2.

57. "273. Memorandum from Nixon to His Assistant (Haldeman)," in ibid., 389, 620–21.

58. "191. Memorandum from [name not declassified] of the CIA to DCI Helms," in ibid., 389.

59. For discussion of this debate, see Anne Hessing Cahn, *Killing Détente: The Right Attacks the CIA* (University Park: Pennsylvania State University Press, 1998), 50–69.

60. DCI William Colby to President Nixon, May 18, 1974, CIA-RD-P80R01720R0000900080030-8, CREST, ALIC, NARA.

61. Anderson, PFIAB Chair, to Nixon, Washington, DC, October 20, 1972, 1969–1974, Folder 14, PPF, Name, SF, WHCF, NARA 2.

62. DCI Colby to Nixon, May 18, 1974, 2, CIA-RDP80R01720R0000900080030-8, CREST, ALIC, NARA.

63. Ibid., 3.

64. Ibid.

65. George A. Carver Jr., February 8, 1974, CIA-RD080R01720R000900100024-2, CREST, ALIC, NARA.

66. Memorandum for Director of Naval Intelligence, February 8, 1974, CIA-RDP80M01048A000800150016-3, CREST, ALIC, NARA.

67. Memorandum for the Director, August 2, 1972, CIA-RDP-75B00514R000200200003-0, CREST, ALIC, NARA.
68. Colby to Edward Teller, Washington, DC, April 16, 1974, CIA-RDP80R01720R000900090020-8, CREST, ALIC, NARA.
69. "198. Memorandum from the President's Assistant for National Security Affairs (Kissinger) to Nixon," in *FRUS, 1969–1976*, vol. 2, p. 409.
70. Quoted in Cahn, *Killing Détente*, 112.
71. "194. Memorandum of Conversation," in *FRUS, 1969–1976*, vol. 2, p. 404.
72. Attachment: Study Prepared by the Staffs of the OMB and the National Security Council, in ibid., 504.
73. Anderson to Colby, Washington, DC, November 8, 1973, CIA-RDP91M00696R000300110023-7, CREST, ALIC, NARA.
74. "200. Memorandum from the President's Assistant for National Security Affairs (Kissinger) to President Nixon," in *FRUS, 1969–1976*, vol. 2, pp. 412–13.
75. Taylor, PFIAB Chair, to Kissinger, Washington, DC, September 8, 1969, PFIAB, Box H-282, Folder 1, NSCIF, NARA 2.
76. Interview with Byers.
77. Charles C. Joyce Jr. to Kissinger, Intelligence Information Handling, Washington, DC, December 11, 1969, PFIAB Box H-283, Folder 1, NSCIF, NARA 2.
78. "204. Memorandum from the Consultant to the NSC (Joyce) to the President's Assistant for National Security Affairs (Kissinger)," in *FRUS, 1969–1976*, vol. 2, pp. 420–23. For Haig's comments, see ibid., 423 n. 6.
79. Memorandum for the Deputy DCI, March 31, 1970, CIA-RDP72-00310R000100350002-7, CREST, ALIC, NARA.
80. Joyce to Kissinger, Tab A: Memorandum for the President, Washington, DC, December 11, 1969, PFIAB, Box H-282, Folder 1, NSCIF, NARA 2.
81. Report of Project ASPIN, July 1970, CIA-RDP78-04723A000400050002-6, CREST, ALIC, NARA.
82. Executive Committee Morning Meeting Notes—30 July 1969, CIA-RDP73-00027R000100110003-6, CREST, ALIC, NARA.
83. COINS (Community Online Intelligence System), n.d., CIA-RDP-79M00097A000300010026-1, CREST, ALIC, NARA.
84. Ibid.
85. Anderson to Colby, Washington, DC, September 25, 1973, CIA-RDP-80B01495R000100120014-6; CREST, ALIC, NARA.
86. Ibid.
87. Edward L. Allen, Memorandum for the Record, June 8, 1970, CIA-RDP-80B01439R000500110006-1, CREST, ALIC, NARA.
88. External Reviews of the Intelligence Community, n.d., 23, CIA-RDP-87B01034R000700230001-3, CREST, ALIC, NARA.
89. Ibid.
90. Note for the Director, March 22, 1972, CIA-RDP80B01439R000500100016-1, CREST, ALIC, NARA.
91. Memorandum for National Intelligence Officer for Economics, May 31, 1974, CIA-RDP80M01082A000600130009-7, CREST, ALIC, NARA.
92. Ibid.
93. Ibid.
94. External Reviews of the Intelligence Community, n.d., 27, CIA-RDP-87B01034R000700230001-3, CREST, ALIC, NARA.

95. Interview with Byers.

96. "211. Memorandum from the Director of the Program Analysis Staff, NSC (Lynn) to the President's Assistant for National Security Affairs (Kissinger)," in *FRUS, 1969–1976*, vol. 2, pp. 448–52.

97. "229. Memorandum from the President's Deputy Assistant for National Security Affairs (Haig) to the President's Assistant for National Security Affairs (Kissinger)," in ibid., 491.

98. "212. Memorandum from the Director of the Program Analysis Staff, NSC (Smith) to the President's Assistant for National Security Affairs (Kissinger)," in ibid., 452.

99. "213. Editorial Note," in ibid., 455.

100. "218. Memorandum from the President's Deputy Assistant for National Security Affairs (Haig) to the President's Assistant for National Security Affairs (Kissinger)," in ibid., 472–73.

101. Ibid., 473, 474–75.

102. Attachment—Memorandum from the President's Assistant for National Security Affairs (Kissinger) and the Director of Management and Budget (Schultz) to Nixon, in *FRUS, 1969–1976*, vol. 2, pp. 493–94.

103. Attachment—Study Prepared by the Staffs of the Office of Management and Budget and the National Security Council, in ibid., 494.

104. Ibid., 497.

105. "230. Memorandum from Assistant Director, OMB (Schlesinger) to the Director (Schultz)," in *FRUS, 1969–1976*, vol. 2, p. 513.

106. Ibid., 523 n. 3.

107. "Document #32: President's Foreign Intelligence Advisory Board, Memorandum for President's File, Subject: President's Foreign Intelligence Advisory Board Meeting with the President, June 4, 1971, June 4, 1971. Top Secret, 8 pp.," in *Science, Technology and the CIA: A National Security Archive Electronic Briefing Book*, ed. Jeffrey T. Richelson, September 10, 2001, at http://www.gwu.edu/~nsarchiv/NSAEBB/NSAEBB54/.

108. Franklin Lincoln to Nixon, New York, NY, June 8, 1971, CIA-RDP-80B01086A000800080009-8, CREST, ALIC, NARA; and Kissinger to Lincoln, Washington, DC, July 12, 1971, FG 208, PFIAB, Folder 2, WHCF, SF, NARA 2.

109. "Document #32," in Richelson, ed., *Science, Technology and the CIA*.

110. "233. Memorandum from Thomas Latimer of the National Security Council Staff to the President's Deputy Assistant for National Security Affairs (Haig)," in *FRUS, 1969–1976*, vol. 2, pp. 520–21.

111. "Document #32," in Richelson, ed., *Science, Technology and the CIA*.

112. "236. Memorandum from the President's Deputy Assistant for National Security Affairs (Haig) to the President's Assistant for National Security Affairs (Kissinger)," in *FRUS, 1969–1976*, vol. 2, pp. 528–29.

113. "235. Memorandum from the Director of the Policy Analysis Staff, National Security Council (Smith) to the President's Assistant for National Security Affairs (Kissinger)," in ibid., 525.

114. "238. Memorandum from the President's Deputy Assistant for National Security Affairs (Haig) to the President's Assistant for National Security Affairs (Kissinger)," in ibid., 533–34; and "242. Memorandum by the President," in ibid., 540–43.

115. "244. Editorial Note," in ibid., 547–48.

116. Interview with Byers.

117. "Document #32," in Richelson, ed., *Science, Technology and the CIA.*
118. "274. Memorandum from Nixon to the PFIAB Chair (Anderson)," in *FRUS, 1969–1976*, vol. 2, pp. 621–22.
119. Anderson to Nixon, Washington, DC, October 20, 1972, Anderson, George, Folder 14, PPF, Name, SF 1969–1974 [A], WHCF, NARA 2.
120. Note to DCI Colby (with attachment entitled "PFIAB Talking Paper: Human Source Collection"), July 12, 1974, CIA-RDP80M01082A000900190003-4, CREST, ALIC, NARA.
121. External Reviews of the Intelligence Community, n.d., 26, CIA-RDP-87B01034R000700230001-3, CREST, ALIC, NARA.
122. Interview with Byers.
123. Memorandum for the Executive Secretary, PFIAB, August 1, 1974, CIA-RDP80M01082A000900190003-4, CREST, ALIC, NARA.
124. "179. Memorandum from DCI Helms to President-Elect Nixon," in *FRUS, 1969–1976*, vol. 2, pp. 363–64.
125. Interview with Byers.
126. Jeffrey T. Richelson, *The Wizards of Langley: Inside the CIA's Directorate of Science and Technology* (Cambridge, MA: Westview, 2002), 172.
127. Anderson to Nixon, December 7, 1973, Wheaton Byers Papers (in the authors' possession).
128. Meeting with the PFIAB, February 8, 1974, PFIAB 1971–74, Confidential Files, SF, WHCF, NARA 2.
129. Anderson to Nixon, December 7, 1973, Wheaton Byers Papers (in the authors' possession).
130. "The Energy Problem," 1973, Wheaton Byers Papers (in the authors' possession).
131. Interview with Source L.
132. Talking Paper: The China Intelligence Effort, June 3, 1970, CIA-RDP-73B00148A000200030018-9, CREST, ALIC, NARA.
133. ONE Memorandum on the Problem of a Sino-Soviet War, February 11, 1971, CIA-RDP79R00967A001500010006-9, CREST, ALIC, NARA.
134. Memorandum for General Counsel, July 16, 1971, CIA-RDP-80R01720R000200160036-0, CREST, ALIC, NARA.
135. Bud Krogh to Erlichman, Washington DC, February 4, 1972, FG 208, PFIAB, Folder 1, WHCF, SF, NARA 2.
136. Anderson to Nixon, May 19, 1972, FG 208, PFIAB, Folder 2, WHCF, SF, NARA 2.
137. USN Adm. (Ret.) Anderson, PFIAB Chair, to Nixon, Washington, DC, May 19, 1972, FG 208, PFIAB, Folder 2, WHCF, SF, NARA 2.
138. Anderson to Nixon, October 11, 1972, FG 208, PFIAB, Folder 2, WHCF, SF, NARA 2.
139. Memorandum for DCI, November 20, 1973, CIA-RDP91M00696R000300110023-7, CREST, ALIC, NARA.
140. Executive Secretary's Note, October 2, 1973, Wheaton Byers Papers (in the authors' possession).
141. *Final Report of the Select Committee to Study Governmental Operations with Respect to Intelligence Activities*, bk. 1, *Foreign and Military Intelligence* (commonly referred to as the Church Committee Report), Report No. 94-755, Senate, 94th Cong., 2nd sess., April 23, 1976, 64, at http://www.aarchlibrary.org/pulbi/reports/book1/pdf/churchB1_4_President.pdf.

142. Kissinger to Nixon, Washington, DC, September 2, 1969, Nelson Rockefeller, Box 831, NSCF, NF, NARA 2.

143. Ibid.

144. Ibid.

145. Ibid.

146. Kissinger to Nixon, Washington, DC, July 14, 1970, FG 208, PFIAB, Folder 1, WHCF, SF, NARA 2.

147. "Morning Meeting Action Item," July 14, 1970, CIA RD-P80R01720R000600070018-6, CREST, ALIC, NARA.

148. Memorandum for DCI, August 30, 1971, CIA-RDP-80B01086A000800080006-1, CREST, ALIC, NARA.

149. Memorandum to NIOs for SEA [Southeast Asia], USSR, CF [Conventional Forces], and WE [Western Europe], June 5, 1974, CIA-RDP91M00696R000300110018-3, CREST, ALIC, NARA.

150. Anderson, PFIAB Chair, to Kissinger, Washington, DC, October 11, 1972, FG 208, PFIAB, Folder 2, WHCF, SF, NARA 2.

151. Deputy DCI Briefing for PFIAB Meeting of October 9, 1970, October 7, 1970, CIA-RDP79T00827A002200050005–4, CREST, ALIC, NARA.

152. Interview with Source L.

153. "Interview with David E. Mark," Association for Diplomatic Studies and Training Foreign Affairs Oral History Project, July 28, 1989, at http://memory.loc.gov/cgi-bin/query/r?ammem/mfdip:@field(DOCID+mfdip2004mar02).

154. Kissinger to Nixon, Washington, DC, April 14, 1971, Robert Murphy, Box 828, NSCF, NF, NARA 2.

155. "Document #32," in Richelson, ed., *Science, Technology and the CIA.*

156. Anderson to Nixon, Washington, DC, September 6, 1973, FG 208, PFIAB, Folder 3, WHCF, SF, NARA 2.

157. Harold H. Saunders and Samuel M. Hoskinson to General Haig, December 12, 1972, John Connally, Box 81, NSCF, NF, NARA 2.

158. "218. Memorandum from the President's Deputy Assistant for National Security Affairs (Haig) to the President's Assistant for National Security Affairs (Kissinger)," in *FRUS, 1969–1976*, vol. 2, p. 475.

159. "219. Editorial Note," in ibid., 475–76.

160. "230. Memorandum from Assistant Director, OMB (Schlesinger) to the Director (Schultz)," in ibid., 516.

161. "290. Transcript of a Memorandum to the President's Assistant (Haldeman) Dictated by President Nixon," in ibid., 658.

162. Richard Helms, *A Look over My Shoulder: A Life in the Central Intelligence Agency* (New York: Random House, 2003), 382, 393, 395.

163. Arthur M. Schlesinger Jr., *The Imperial Presidency* (Boston: Houghton Mifflin, 1973).

164. For a careful empirical study that marks the 1970s as the high point in the institutionalization of the presidency, see Lyn Ragsdale and John J. Theis III, "The Institutionalization of the American Presidency, 1924–92," *American Journal of Political Science* 41, no. 4 (October 1997): 1280–1318.

5. GERALD R. FORD/JIMMY CARTER

1. Christopher Andrew, *For the President's Eyes Only: Secret Intelligence and the American Presidency from Washington to Bush* (New York: Harper Collins, 1995), 422.

2. Ibid., 397.

3. Loch K. Johnson, "Accountability and America's Secret Foreign Policy: Keeping an Eye on the Central Intelligence Agency," *Foreign Policy Analysis* 1, no. 1 (2005): 102–3.

4. Marvin C. Ott, "Partisanship and the Decline of Intelligence Oversight," *International Journal of Intelligence and Counter-Intelligence* 16, no. 1 (Spring 2003): 73–74. See also Amy Zegart, *Flawed by Design: The Evolution of the CIA, the JCS, and NSC* (Palo Alto, CA: Stanford University Press, 1999), 22–36.

5. Ott, "Partisanship and the Decline of Intelligence Oversight," 74.

6. Johnson, "Accountability and America's Secret Foreign Policy," 104.

7. Ibid.

8. Ott, "Partisanship and the Decline of Intelligence Oversight," 74–75.

9. Johnson, "Accountability and America's Secret Foreign Policy," 105.

10. Richard A. Best Jr., *Proposals for Intelligence Reorganization, 1949–2004,* Congressional Research Service Report RL32500 (Washington, DC: Library of Congress, 2004), 17.

11. Ibid.

12. Although the Pike Committee's recommendations were eventually published on February 11, 1976, immediate publication of its final report was not authorized by the House, and a version was published in the *Village Voice*. See Gerald K. Haines, "Looking for a Rogue Elephant: The Pike Committee Investigations and the CIA," *The Pike Committee Investigations and the CIA,* May 8, 2007, at https://www.cia.gov/library/center-for-the-study-of-intelligence/kent-csi/v0142n05/pdf/v42i5a07p.htm.

13. Best, *Proposals for Intelligence Reorganization,* 17.

14. "Appendix A: The Evolution of the U.S. Intelligence Community—an Historical Overview," in *Preparing for the 21st Century: An Appraisal of U.S. Intelligence* (Washington, DC: U.S. Government Printing Office, 1996), at http://www.gpoaccess.gov/int022.pdf.

15. Hale Foundation, *The President's Foreign Intelligence Advisory Board (PFIAB)* (Washington, DC: Hale Foundation, 1981), 20.

16. Commission on CIA Activities within the United States, *Report to the President* (commonly referred to as the Rockefeller Commission Report), June 1975, 81–82, at http://www.history-matters.com/archive/church/rockcomm/pdf/RockComm_Chap7_External.pdf.

17. Hale Foundation, *The President's Foreign Intelligence Advisory Board,* 20.

18. Ibid., 14.

19. W. E. Colby to Lt. Gen. Brent Scowcroft, Deputy Assistant to the President for National Security Affairs, Washington, DC, September 3, 1976, CIA-RDP84-00780R006600060008-8, CREST, ALIC, NARA.

20. Colby to Scowcroft, Washington, DC, September 3, 1975, CIA-RDP84-00780R006600060008-8, CREST, ALIC, NARA.

21. John O. Marsh Jr. to Phil Buchen, Colby, Henry Kissinger, Ed Levi, Jim Lynn, Don Rumsfeld, Jim Schlesinger, Washington, DC, September 30, 1975, CIA-RDP80M01066A000800250006-3, CREST, ALIC, NARA.

22. DCI Colby to Marsh, Counselor to the President, Washington, DC, October 3, 1975, CIA-RDP77M00144R000500020016-1, CREST, ALIC, NARA.

23. Marsh to Buchen, Colby, Kissinger, Levi, Lynn, Rumsfeld, Schlesinger, Washington, DC, October 16, 1975, CIA-RDP80M01066A00800250004-5, CREST, ALIC, NARA.

24. Lt. Gen. Samuel V. Wilson to the DCI, October 29, 1975, CIA-RDP-80M01066A000800250001-8, CREST, ALIC, NARA.

25. John S. Chwat, *The President's Foreign Intelligence Advisory Board: An Historical and Contemporary Analysis (1955–1975),* Congressional Research Service Report 75-225F (Washington, DC: Library of Congress, 1975), 12.

26. Anderson, PFIAB Chair, to President Gerald R. Ford, Washington, DC, September 24, 1975, EO 11905 (1), PFIAB, SF, LCP, Box 2, GRFL.

27. Ibid.

28. Ibid.

29. Ibid.

30. Ford to the U.S. Congress, OWHPS, Washington, DC, February 18, 1976, EO 11905 (1), PFIAB, SF, LCP, Box 2, GRFL.

31. EO, OWHPS, Washington, DC, February 18, 1976, EO 11905 (1), PFIAB, SF, LCP, Box 2, GRFL.

32. Ibid. Sitting on the CFI are the DCI (as chair), the deputy secretary of defense for intelligence, and the deputy assistant to the president for national security affairs, according to EO 11905.

33. Statement by the President, OWHPS, Washington, DC, February 18, 1976, EO 11905 (3), PFIAB, SF, LCP, Box 2, GRFL.

34. EO, February 18, 1976, EO 11905 (1), PFIAB, LCP, Box 2, GRFL.

35. Fact Sheet: The President's Actions concerning the Foreign Intelligence Community, OWHPS, Washington, DC, February 18, 1976, EO 11905 (3), PFIAB, SF, LCP, Box 2, GRFL.

36. Byers, Executive Secretary, PFIAB, to WHPS, Washington, DC, March 3, 1976, PFIAB—Membership Expansion (New Board), PFIAB, SF, LCP, Box 6, GRFL.

37. Ibid.

38. Quoted in Hale Foundation, *The President's Foreign Intelligence Advisory Board,* 20.

39. Ibid., 13.

40. Ibid.

41. *Final Report of the Select Committee to Study Governmental Operations with Respect to Intelligence Activities,* bk. 1, *Foreign and Military Intelligence* (commonly referred to as the Church Committee Report), Report No. 94-755, Senate, 94th Cong., 2nd sess., April 23, 1976, 63–64, at http://www.aarclibrary.org/publib/church/reports/book1/pdf/ChurchB1_4_President.pdf.

42. Loch K. Johnson, "Governing in the Absence of Angels: On the Practice of Intelligence Accountability in the United States," in *Who's Watching the Spies? Establishing Intelligence Service Accountability,* ed. Hans Borin, Lock K. Johnson, and Ian Leigh (Washington, DC: Potomac, 2005), 57–78. This paper was originally prepared for the workshop "Making Intelligence Accountable," held September 19–20, 2003, in Oslo, Norway, sponsored by the Geneva Centre for Democratic Control of Armed Forces (Switzerland), the Intelligence Oversight Committee of the Norwegian Parliament and the Human Rights Centre, and the Department of Law of the University of Durham (United Kingdom).

43. Cherne to [former] President Ford, New York, June 20, 1977, 3, PFIAB Termination (2), PFIAB, SF, LCP, Box 6, GRFL.

44. Ibid.

45. Although he was not requested to do so by the president, Connally resigned

in 1975 while under federal indictment for bribery charges. He was acquitted and returned to serve on the PFIAB in March when President Ford expanded the board.

46. Rockefeller resigned from the board when he became vice president under Ford.

47. Interview with Byers; and Interview with Source A.

48. Anderson, PFIAB Chair, to Rumsfeld, Assistant to the White House, Washington, DC, November 5, 1974, PFIAB 1974, Staff Secretary James E. Connor, 1974–77, GRFL.

49. Ibid.

50. Interview with Source A.

51. Douglas P. Bennett to Ford, Washington, DC, February 11, 1976, Cherne, Leo—PFIAB Chair—Appointment, PFIAB, SF, LCP, Box 2, GRFL.

52. Interview with Source P.

53. David J. Wimer to Ford, Washington, DC, September 25, 1974, PFIAB 1974, Staff Secretary Connor, 1974–77, GRFL; Samuel A. Schulhof to Ford, Washington, DC, October 24, 1974, PFIAB 1974, Staff Secretary Connor, 1974–77, GRFL; Bennett to Richard Cheney, Washington, DC, February 16, 1976, PFIAB 1976, Staff Secretary Connor, 1974–77, GRFL; Connor to Bennett, Washington, DC, November 25, 1975, PFIAB 1976, Staff Secretary Connor, 1974–77, GRFL; Bennett to Ford, Washington, DC, September 26, 1975, PFIAB 1975, Staff Secretary Connor, 1974–77, GRFL; Bennett to Ford, Washington, DC, July 16, 1975, PFIAB 1975, Staff Secretary Connor, 1974–77, GRFL; and Byers, Executive Secretary, PFIAB, to Robert D. Linder, Chief Executive Clerk, Washington, DC, August 11, 1976, FG 208, PFIAB, 03/11/76–01/20/1977, SF, WHCF, GRFL.

54. Name List, Tab D—Possible Candidates for Membership, n.d., PFIAB—Membership Expansion (New Board), PFIAB, SF, LCP, Box 6, GRFL; PFIAB, Member's Attendance at Board Meetings since 1 August 1973, n.d., Intelligence—PFIAB, Richard Cheney Files, 1974–77, GRFL.

55. Bennett to Ford, September 26, 1975, PFIAB 1975, Staff Secretary Connor, 1974–77, GRFL; Bennett to Ford, July 16, 1975, PFIAB 1975, Staff Secretary Connor, 1974–77, GRFL; Bennett to Ford, Washington, DC, n.d., PFIAB 1975, Staff Secretary Connor, 1974–77, GRF; and Bennett to Ford, Washington, DC, October 20, 1975, PFIAB 1975, Staff Secretary Connor, 1974–77, GRFL.

56. President Jimmy Carter to Byers, PFIAB Executive Secretary, February 25, 1977, FG 241/A, 1/20/77–1/20/81, Box FG-202, JCL; and Interview with Byers.

57. Cherne, PFIAB Chair, to the Assistant to the President for National Security Affairs and the DCI, Washington, DC, March 1, 1977, PFIAB 1-12/77 [CF, O/A 714], Staff Offices, Counsel, Lipshutz, CPP, WHCF, JCL.

58. Byers to Members of the PFIAB, Washington, DC, December 18, 1975, PFIAB—Membership Expansion (New Board), PFIAB, SF, LCP, Box 6, GRFL.

59. Draft National Security Decision Memorandum to the Secretary of Defense, Deputy Secretary of State, and DCI, August 15, 1975, PFIAB/NIEs (5), NSC Staff Convenience Files—Program Analysis Staff, Office of the Assistant to the President for National Security Affairs, Kissinger and Scowcroft: Files, (1972) 1974–77, GRFL.

60. Interview with Byers; and Interview with Source A.

61. Thomas J. English to Mary Louise Odom, Washington, DC, November 8, 1976, PFIAB Budget, PFIAB, SF, LCP, Box 4, GRFL.

62. Byers, Executive Secretary, PFIAB, to Leslie C. Arrends, Washington, DC, March 11, 1976, PFIAB—Membership Expansion (New Board), PFIAB, SF, LCP, Box 6, GRFL.

63. Interview with Source A.

64. Interview with Byers; and Interview with Source A.

65. [Name redacted] to [name redacted], February 19, 1975, CIA-RDP-80B01622R000100040034-8, CREST, ALIC, NARA.

66. Interview with Source P.

67. Agenda, Economic Intelligence (1), PFIAB, SF, LCP, Box 2, GRFL.

68. Ibid.

69. [Name redacted] to the DCI, November 12, 1974, CIA-RDP91M00696R000300110007-5, CREST, ALIC, NARA.

70. Memorandum for the Record, December 5, 1974, CIA-RDP-85T00875R002000010037-5, CREST, ALIC, NARA.

71. [Name redacted] to the DCI, November 12, 1974, 2, CIA-RDP91M00696R000300110007-5, CREST, ALIC, NARA.

72. Ibid., 3.

73. Ibid.

74. Schedule Proposal from Anderson, PFIAB Chair, June 10, 1975, FG 208, PFIAB 08/09/74–12/31/75, SF, WHCF, GRFL.

75. Lt. Gen. Samuel V. Wilson, Deputy to the DCI for the Intelligence Community, to the DCI, January 23, 1975, CIA-RDP91M00696r000300110006-6, CREST, ALIC, NARA.

76. Lt. Gen. Wilson, Deputy to the DCI for the Intelligence Community, to the DCI, January 24, 1975, 1, CIA-RDP91M00696R000300110005-7, CREST, ALIC, NARA.

77. Ibid., 2.

78. Ibid.

79. [Name redacted] to the DCI, May 21, 1975, CIA-RDP-80B01495R001000240022-4, CREST, ALIC, NARA.

80. [Name redacted] to Addressee, November 28, 1975, CIA-RDP-80M01133A001100090012-5, CREST, ALIC, NARA.

81. [Name redacted] to General Counsel, Legislative Counsel, March 24, 1976, CIA-RDP78M0266R000800120013-4, CREST, ALIC, NARA.

82. [Name redacted] to Carey, June 4, 1976, CIA-RDP78M02660R000800110007-2, CREST, ALIC, NARA, 3.

83. Chair's Guide to the October 7–8, 1976 PFIAB Meetings, PFIAB Meetings, PFIAB, SF, LCP, Box 6, GRFL.

84. Ibid.

85. Draft Agenda for December 1976 Meeting, PFIAB Meetings, PFIAB, SF, LCP, Box 6, GRFL.

86. Ibid.

87. Warren S. Rustand, Appointments Secretary to the President, to Cherne, March 7, 1975, FG 208, PFIAB 08/09/74–12/31/75, SF, WHCF, GRFL.

88. Ibid.

89. Cherne to William Casey, Washington, DC, April 28, 1975, Cherne, Leo—Europe Trip (2), PFIAB, SF, LCP, Box 1, GRFL.

90. Nancy Gemmel to Rustand, February 14, 1975, FG 208, PFIAB 08/09/74–12/31/75, SF, WHCF, GRFL; Gemmel to Rustand, February 28, 1975, FG 208, PFIAB 08/09/74–12/31/75, SF, WHCF, GRFL; Rustand, Appointments Secretary to the President, to Teller, June 27, 1975, FG 208, PFIAB 08/09/74–12/31/75, SF, WHCF, GRFL.

91. Interview with Byers; and Interview with Source A.

92. Cherne to (former) President Ford, June 20, 1977, 3, PFIAB Termination (2), PFIAB, SF, LCP, Box 6, GRFL.

93. PFIAB Briefings, August 1, 1973, PFIAB Meetings, PFIAB, SF, LCP, Box 6, GRFL.

94. Interview with Byers.

95. Anne Hessing Cahn, *Killing Détente: The Right Attacks the CIA* (University Park: Pennsylvania State University Press, 1998), 106–7.

96. Helmut Sonnenfeldt to the Secretary of State, Washington, DC, July 22, 1975, PFIAB/NIEs (5), NSC Staff Convenience Files—Program Analysis Staff, Office of the Assistant to the President for National Security Affairs, Kissinger and Scowcroft: Files, (1972) 1974–77, GRFL.

97. An Alternative NIE, June 18, 1975, PFIAB/NIEs (5), NSC Staff Convenience Files—Program Analysis Staff, Office of the Assistant to the President for National Security Affairs, Kissinger and Scowcroft: Files, (1972) 1974–77, GRFL.

98. Ibid.

99. Anderson, PFIAB Chair to President Ford, Washington, DC, August 8, 1975, PFIAB/NIEs (5), NSC Staff Convenience Files—Program Analysis Staff, Office of the Assistant to the President for National Security Affairs, Kissinger and Scowcroft: Files, (1972) 1974–77, GRFL.

100. Ibid.

101. Ibid.

102. Ibid.

103. Ibid.

104. Ibid.

105. Draft National Security Decision Memorandum, August 15, 1975, PFIAB/NIEs (5), NSC Staff Convenience Files—Program Analysis Staff, Office of the Assistant to the President for National Security Affairs, Kissinger and Scowcroft: Files, (1972) 1974–77, GRFL.

106. Jan Lodel and Richard Ober to Secretary Kissinger, September 4, 1975, PFIAB/NIEs (5), NSC Staff Convenience Files—Program Analysis Staff, Office of the Assistant to the President for National Security Affairs, Kissinger and Scowcroft: Files, (1972) 1974–77, GRFL.

107. Colby quoted in Cahn, *Killing Détente*, 118–19.

108. Carver quoted in ibid., 131.

109. Tim Weiner, *Legacy of Ashes: The History of the CIA* (New York: Doubleday, 2007), 351–52.

110. Cahn, *Killing Détente*, 128, 139, 160–61.

111. Ibid., 126–27.

112. Richard T. Boverie to Scowcroft, June 21, 1976, PFIAB/NIEs (5), NSC Staff Convenience Files—Program Analysis Staff, Office of the Assistant to the President for National Security Affairs, Kissinger and Scowcroft: Files, (1972) 1974–77, GRFL.

113. Cahn, *Killing Détente*, 5.

114. Interview with Gates.

115. Anne Hessing Cahn and John Prados, "Team B: The Trillion-Dollar Experiment," *Bulletin of the Atomic Scientists* 49, no. 3 (1993): 22–31.

116. Interview with Gates.

117. Interview with Source P.

118. Andrew F. Smith, *Rescuing the World: The Life and Times of Leo Cherne*

(New York: State University of New York Press, 2002), 163; and Cahn and Prados, "Team B."

119. Cahn and Prados, "Team B."

120. "Minutes, National Security Council Meeting, January 13, 1977," NSC Meeting Minutes, GRFL, November 28, 2001, at http://www.fordlibrarymuseum.gov/library/document/nscmin/770113.pdf.

121. Cahn, *Killing Détente,* 176–77.

122. Bush quoted in ibid., 161.

123. Ibid., 188–89.

124. Cahn and Prados, "Team B."

125. Ibid.; and "Minutes, National Security Council Meeting (Thursday, January 13, 1977)," NSC Meeting Minutes, GRFL.

126. *The National Intelligence Estimates A-B Team Episode concerning Soviet Strategic Capability and Objectives,* Report of the Senate Select Committee on Intelligence, Subcommittee on Collection, Production, and Quality (Washington, DC, February 16, 1978), Soviet Union, PFIAB, SF, LCP, Box 7, GRFL.

127. Cahn, *Killing Détente,* 179.

128. Michael J. Deutch to Leo Cherne, Executive Director of the Research Institute of America, Washington, DC, May 10, 1976, Terrorism, PFIAB, SF, LCP, Box 7, GRFL.

129. David L. Milbank, *CIA Report on International and Transnational Terrorism: Diagnosis and Prognosis,* May 1976, Terrorism, PFIAB, SF, LCP, Box 7, GRFL.

130. Ibid.

131. Ibid.

132. Interview with Byers.

133. Smith, *Rescuing the World,* 161.

134. Cherne, Executive Director of the Research Institute of America, to W. D. Eberle, Executive Director of the Council on International Economic Policy, New York, NY, November 7, 1974, Economic Intelligence (2), PFIAB, SF, LCP, Box 2, GRFL.

135. Smith, *Rescuing the World,* 163.

136. Transcript, September 1974, Oral Report to PFIAB, Economic Intelligence (2), PFIAB, SF, LCP, Box 2, GRFL.

137. Cherne, PFIAB Chair, to Secretary William E. Simon, Washington, DC, June 4, 1976, CIA-RDP79M00467A0031000030015-9, CREST, ALIC, NARA, 3.

138. William E. Simon to DCI Bush, Washington, DC, June 15, 1976, 1, CIA-RDP-79M00467A0031000030015-9, CREST, ALIC, NARA; and DCI Bush to Secretary Simon, Washington, DC, June 29, 1976, 1, CIA-RDP79M00467A0031000030015-9, CREST, ALIC, NARA.

139. Interview with Byers.

140. Ibid.

141. Interview with Source A.

142. Interview with Byers.

143. Byers, Memorandum for the Members (with attached paper on the Counterintelligence Problem in the United States), Washington, DC, May 8, 1975, Rockefeller Commission, PFIAB, SF, LCP, Box 6, GRFL.

144. [Name redacted] to Gen. Vernon Walters, E. H. Knoche, June 2, 1976, 2, CIA-RDP80M01048A001100140042-1, CREST, ALIC, NARA.

145. Ibid.

146. Ibid., 3.

147. National Foreign Counterintelligence Policy, Activity, and Production, CIA-RDP80M00165A000500340004-9, CREST, ALIC, NARA.

148. PFIAB Meetings, PFIAB, SF, LCP, Box 6, GRFL; Cherne to the President, December 3, 1976, PFIAB Meetings, PRIAB, SF, LCP, Box 6, GRFL.

149. Lionel Olmer, Memorandum for the Members, Washington, DC, August 26, 1976, PFIAB Meetings, PFIAB, SF, LCP, Box 6, GRFL.

150. Teller to All PFIAB Members, Livermore, CA, September 5, 1976, Teller, Edward, PFIAB, SF, LCP, Box 7, GRFL.

151. Ibid.

152. Casey to All PFIAB Members, October 6, 1976, Wheaton Byers Papers (in the authors' possession).

153. Olmer, Memorandum for the Members, August 26, 1976, PFIAB Meetings, PFIAB, SF, LCP, Box 6, GRFL.

154. Deputy DCI Knoche to Cherne, PFIAB Chair, Washington, DC, January 3, 1977, CIA-RDP80M00165A002300050015-9, CREST, ALIC, NARA.

155. Ibid.

156. William Wells, Deputy Director of Operations, to the Deputy DCI, January 5, 1977, CIA-RDP80M00165A002300050014-0, CREST, ALIC, NARA.

157. Ibid.

158. [Name redacted] to [name redacted], Washington, DC, December 17, 1976, CIA-RDP91M00696R000200070006-2, CREST, ALIC, NARA.

159. Memorandum, PFIAB, Washington, DC, July 21, 1976, PFIAB Meetings, PFIAB, SF, LCP, Box 6, GRFL.

160. "Takes Two to Tap" (transcript of Brooke Gladstone interviewing Morton Halperin), *On the Media (from NPR),* February 17, 2006, at http://www.onthemedia .org/2006/feb/17/takes-two-to-tap.

161. Memorandum, PFIAB, July 21, 1976, PFIAB Meetings, PFIAB, SF, LCP, Box 6, GRFL.

162. Interview with Source A.

163. President Ford to the Attorney General, July 22, 1976, Marsh, John O., Jr., PFIAB, SF, LCP, Box 3, GRFL.

164. John Pike and Steven Aftergood, "Project Jennifer Hughes *Glomar Explorer,*" *Federation of American Scientists Intelligence Resource Program,* September 14, 2000, at http://www.fas.org/irp/program/collect/jennifer.htm.

165. Ibid.

166. Interview with Byers; and Interview with Source A.

167. Robert J. Lipshutz, Counsel to the President, to the Archivist of the United States, Washington, DC, August 15, 1977, Intelligence Oversight Board [CF, O/A 375], Staff Offices, Hugh A. Carter, CPP, WHCF, JCL.

168. "Headline: Espionage/Shadrin: *NBC Evening News for Monday,* October 28, 1985," Television News Archive, Vanderbilt University, at http://tvnews.vanderbilt .edu/program.pl?ID=540463.

169. Interview with Source A.

170. Interview with Byers.

171. "U.S. Investigating Loss of Notebook Containing National Security Data: Record of Talks Abroad by a Ford Intelligence Aide Reportedly Found Their Way to Ex-Convict," *New York Times,* September 16, 1976.

172. Ibid. The *Los Angeles Times* sent Casey to Hong Kong after he persuaded it that he could meet there with Patty Hearst. Laurence Stern, "The Intelligence Advisor and 'the Green Book Affair,'" *Washington Post,* September 16, 1976.

173. Robert Dietrich, "Tribune's Alert on CIA Data Ignored," *San Diego Evening Tribune,* April 14, 1976.

174. Ibid.

175. Statement by Cherne to the Intelligence Oversight Board at a Meeting Chaired by Ambassador Robert Murphy and Attended by Stephen Ailes and Cherne, May 4, 1976, Green Book—Patty Hearst Affair (1), PFIAB, SF, LCP, Box 3, GRFL.

176. Cherne, Speech Notes for PFIAB Dinner, 1976, PFIAB Dinner Speeches, PFIAB, SF, LCP, Box 4, GRFL, 4.

177. Ibid., 6.

178. Ibid., 9.

179. Ibid., 10.

180. Ibid., 10–11.

181. Cherne to Former President Ford, New York, NY, June 20, 1977, PFIAB—Termination (2), PFIAB, SF, LCP, Box 6, GRFL.

182. Ibid.

183. DCI Bush to Cherne, PFIAB Chair, Washington, DC, January 17, 1977, PFIAB—Termination (1), PFIAB, SF, LCP, Box 6, GRFL.

184. Lodal quoted in Cahn, *Killing Détente,* 105.

185. H. Andrew Boerstling and Richard A. Best Jr., *Intelligence Oversight in the White House: The President's Foreign Intelligence Advisory Board and the Intelligence Oversight Board,* Congressional Research Service Report 96-619F (Washington, DC: Library of Congress, 1996), 3.

186. Smith, *Rescuing the World,* 166.

187. Statement by the President, OWHPS, Washington, DC, May 5, 1977, Intelligence Oversight Board: Board Members and Staff, 4/1977–6/1977 [CF, O/A 711], Staff Offices, Counsel, Lipshutz, CPP, WHCF, JCL.

188. White House Study Project, Report No. 2, December 23, 1976, III-3, WHSP2 (1), PFIAB, SF, LCP, Box 8, GRFL.

189. Ibid., XVII-22.

190. Ibid., III-3.

191. Ibid., XVII-14.

192. Ibid., n.p.

193. Stansfield Turner, *Burn Before Reading: Presidents, CIA Directors, and Secret Intelligence* (New York: Hyperion, 2005), 158.

194. Ibid., 193.

195. Ibid.

196. Douglas F. Garthoff, *Directors of Central Intelligence as the Leaders of the U.S. Intelligence Community, 1946–2005* (Washington, DC: U.S. Government Printing Office, 2005), 132.

197. Interview with Gates.

198. Interview with Byers.

199. The Vice President and the DCI to President Carter, Washington, DC, April 14, 1977, Intelligence Overview Notebook I, c6/1977 [CF, O/A 716], Staff Offices, Counsel, Lipshutz, CPP, WHCF, JCL.

200. Ibid.

201. The Vice President to President Carter, Washington, DC, April 25, 1977,

Intelligence Oversight Board: Miscellaneous Closed, 3/1977–12/1977 [CF, O/A 711], Staff Offices, Counsel, Lipshutz, CPP, WHCF, JCL.

202. Robert Lipshutz to Robert Linder, Washington, DC, April 29, 1977, Intelligence Oversight Board: Miscellaneous Closed, 3/1977–12/1977 [CF, O/A 711], Staff Offices, Counsel, Lipshutz, CPP, WHCF, JCL.

203. William M. Nichols, General Counsel, OMB, to Robert Linder, Washington, DC, May 2, 1977, Intelligence Oversight Board: Miscellaneous Closed, 3/1977–12/1977 [CF, O/A 711], Staff Offices, Counsel, Lipshutz, CPP, WHCF, JCL.

204. Cherne, PFIAB Chair, Memorandum for Members, Washington, DC, February 19, 1877, PFIAB—Termination (1), PFIAB, SF, LCP, Box 6, GRFL.

205. Ibid.

206. Cherne, PFIAB Chair, to Senator Claiborne Pell, Washington, DC, May 3, 1977, PFIAB—Termination (2), PFIAB, SF, LCP, Box 6, GRFL.

207. President Carter to Cherne, Washington, DC, May 4, 1977, FG 241/A 01/20/77–01/20/81, Box FG-202, JCL.

208. Zbigniew Brzezinski, Memorandum—Meeting with Tip O'Neill and House Leaders, Washington, DC, May 12, 1977, Document No. NLC-7-30-2-4-5, JCL, 4.

209. Cherne, PFIAB Chair, Memorandum for Members, Washington, DC, February 19, 1877, PFIAB—Termination (1), PFIAB, SF, LCP, Box 6, GRFL.

210. Interview with Byers.

211. "The Hostage Crisis in Iran," *Jimmy Carter Library and Museum*, February 9, 2006, at http://www.jimmycarterlibrary.org/documents/hostages.phtml; and William J. Daugherty, "A First Tour Like No Other," *Studies in Intelligence* 41, no. 5 (Spring 1998): 31, 40, 41.

212. Don Gregg to Brzezinski, March 5, 1980, Document No. NLC-7-29-6-18-8, JCL.

213. Ibid.

214. Paul B. Henze to Brzezinski, Cherne, and PFIAB, March 6, 1980, Document No. NCL-7-29-6-19-7, JCL.

215. Otto Kreisher, "Desert One," *Air Force Magazine Online* 82, no. 1 (January 1999), at http://www.airforce-magazine.com/MagazineArchive/Pages/1999/January%201999/0199desertone.aspx.

216. David M. Abshire, "For a Presidential Advisory Board," *New York Times*, May 3, 1980, 23.

217. Gregg to Brzezinski, May 15, 1980, Document No. NLC-7-29-6-17-9, JCL.

218. Ibid.

219. Smith, *Rescuing the World*, 166.

220. Gregg to Brzezinski, May 15, 1980, Document No. NLC-7-29-6-17-9, JCL.

221. Gregg to Brzezinski, March 5, 1980, Document No. NLC-7-29-6-18-8, JCL.

6. RONALD W. REAGAN

1. John T. Woolley and Gerhard Peters, "Executive Order 12331: President's Foreign Intelligence Advisory Board," *The American Presidency Project*, October 20, 1981, at http://www.presidency.ucsb.edu/ws/index.php?pid=43157&st=12331 &st1=#axzz1b5DfqZum.

2. Bill Roeder, "Reviving a Presidential Panel," *Newsweek*, November 24, 1980, Periscope Section, 37.

3. Interview with Source E.

4. Hale Foundation, *The President's Foreign Intelligence Advisory Board (PFIAB)* (Washington, DC: Hale Foundation, 1981), 23.

5. Ibid., 25.

6. Ibid., 24.

7. Richard V. Allen, Assistant to the President for National Security Affairs, to Leo Cherne, New York, NY, April 21, 1981, PFIAB, January–June 1981, LCP, DSC, HGARC.

8. Interview with Source A.

9. Woolley and Peters, "Executive Order 12331."

10. Randy Fort to Anne Armstrong, Washington, DC, April 1, 1983, PFIAB, General—January–June 1983, LCP, DSC, HGARC.

11. Interview with Source A; and Interview with Source B.

12. Interview with Source A.

13. Cherne to Adm. Daniel J. Murphy, Chief of Staff in the Office of the Vice President, New York, NY, May 25, 1984, PFIAB, Misc.—January 1, 1984 to November 31, 1985, LCP, DSC, HGARC. For more details on Kissinger's Central America report, see Henry Kissinger, *Report of the National Bipartisan Commission on Central America* (Washington, DC: U.S. Government Printing Office, 1984).

14. Cherne to Murphy, May 25, 1984, PFIAB, Misc.—January 1, 1984 to November 31, 1985, LCP, DSC, HGARC.

15. John T. Woolley and Gerhard Peters, "Executive Order 12624—Increasing the Number of Members of the President's Foreign Intelligence Advisory Board," *The American Presidency Project,* January 8, 1988, at http://www.presidency.ucsb.edu/ws/index.php?pid=34943.

16. *Marquis Who's Who on the Web,* 2006, s.v. Howard Henry Baker Jr., at http://www.marquiswhoswho.com/.

17. Armstrong, PFIAB Chair, to Cherne, Washington, DC, September 20, 1984, PFIAB, Misc.—January 1, 1984 to November 31, 1985, LCP, DSC, HGARC. See also the "For Official Use Only" summary of PFIAB responses to the above memo in the same folder.

18. Martin Anderson, *Revolution: The Reagan Legacy* (Stanford, CA: Hoover Institution Press, 1990), 364–68.

19. Evan Thomas, *The Man to See: Edward Bennett Williams, Ultimate Insider; Legendary Trial Lawyer* (New York: Simon & Schuster, 1991), 468.

20. Ibid., 468.

21. Interview with Source A.

22. Interview with Schmitt.

23. Peter T. Kilborn, "Reagan Drops 11 in Foreign Policy Advisory Group," *New York Times,* November 5, 1985, A15.

24. Interview with Gates.

25. Kilborn, "Reagan Drops 11 in Foreign Policy Advisory Group."

26. Interview with Source A; and Interview with Source E.

27. John T. Woolley and Gerhard Peters, "Executive Order 12537—President's Foreign Intelligence Advisory Board," *The American Presidency Project,* October 28, 1985, at http://www.presidency.ucsb.edu/ws/index.php?pid=37979.

28. Interview with Schmitt.

29. Interview with Source E.

30. PFIAB Consultants for FY 1985, PFIAB, Misc.—January 1, 1984 to November 31, 1985, LCP, DSC, HGARC.

31. Interview with Source R.

32. Col. C. Norman Wood, Executive Director, to PFIAB Board Members

(Agenda for SAC/JSTPS Tour on September 15, 1983 attached), Washington, DC, August 15, 1983, PFIAB, July–December 1983, LCP, DSC, HGARC.

33. Tentative Agenda for PFIAB Meeting, July 10–11, 1985, PFIAB, Misc.—January 1, 1984 to November 31, 1985, LCP, DSC, HGARC.

34. Armstrong to PFIAB Board Members, Washington, DC, January 18, 1985, PFIAB, Misc.—January 1, 1984 to November 31, 1985, LCP, DSC, HGARC.

35. Interview with Source A. Kenneth Michael Absher, a former CIA station chief, reports that understanding the DCI was a constant challenge.

36. Interview with Source E.

37. Armstrong to Board Members, January 18, 1985, PFIAB, Misc.—January 1, 1984 to November 31, 1985, LCP, DSC, HGARC.

38. Interview with Source E.

39. Interview with Schmitt.

40. Cherne to Vice President George H. W. Bush, Washington, DC, June 28, 1984, PFIAB, Misc.—January 1, 1984 to November 31, 1985, LCP, DSC, HGARC.

41. Comments from Board Members on Organization and Operations, Telecon, November 4, 1983, PFIAB, July–December 1983, LCP, DSC, HGARC.

42. Interview with Source E.

43. Ibid.

44. Ibid.

45. Interview with Schmitt; and Interview with Source E.

46. Interview with Source E.

47. Interview with Schmitt.

48. Armstrong to Board Members, January 18, 1985, PFIAB, Misc.—January 1, 1984 to November 31, 1985, LCP, DSC, HGARC.

49. Anderson, *Revolution,* 354.

50. "American Embassy Moscow—Brief History," U.S. Department of State: Embassy of the United States, Moscow, Russia, at http://moscow.usembassy.gov/about_the_embassy.html.

51. Stephen Engelberg, "Reagan Was Told in '85 of Problem in Moscow Embassy," *New York Times,* April 3, 1987, A1.

52. Elaine Sciolino, "U.S. Urged to Raze Moscow Chancery," *New York Times,* June 23, 1988, A1.

53. Engelberg, "Reagan Was Told in '85 of Problem in Moscow Embassy."

54. Interview with Source B.

55. Sciolino, "U.S. Urged to Raze Moscow Chancery."

56. Stephen Engelberg, "Washington Talk: Intelligence Security; Whither Moscow Embassy Scandal?" *New York Times,* December 9, 1987, B6.

57. "American Embassy Moscow—Brief History."

58. Quoted in Thomas, *The Man to See,* 467.

59. Ted Agres, "Embassy in Moscow 'Riddled with KGB,'" *Washington Times,* March 27, 1985, A1, A8; CIA-RDP96-00788R001900650007-5, CREST, ALIC, NARA.

60. Engelberg, "Reagan Was Told in '85 of Problem in Moscow Embassy."

61. Herbert Romerstein and Stanislav Levchenko, *The KGB against the "Main Enemy": How the Soviet Intelligence Service Operates against the United States* (Lanham, MD: Lexington, 1989), 282–83, 285, 291–95.

62. Ibid., 294–95, 285–86.

63. Robert M. Gates, *From The Shadows: The Ultimate Insider's Story of*

Five Presidents and How They Won the Cold War (New York: Simon & Schuster, 1997), 365.

64. William Safire, "Bush Is Ready to Sink Intelligence Advisory Group," *St. Petersburg Times,* February 17, 1989.

65. Patrick E. Tyler, "CIA Moscow Informant Vanishes; Source Says Disappearance May Be Related to Howard Case," *Washington Post,* October 6, 1985, A3.

66. Engelberg, "Washington Talk: Intelligence Security; Whither Moscow Embassy Scandal?"

67. Tim Wiener, *Legacy of Ashes: The History of the CIA* (New York: Doubleday, 2007), 416.

68. Ibid., 363–64.

69. Romerstein and Levchenko, *The KGB against the "Main Enemy,"* 283; and Gates, *From the Shadows,* 362.

70. Louise Branson, "Yurchenko Tells New Details of 'Escape,'" *United Press International,* November 14, 1985.

71. John Mintz, "FBI Chief Doubts Defection of Yurchenko Was Staged; Soviet Gave Valuable Data, Webster Says," *Washington Post,* December 2, 1985, A1.

72. Safire, "Bush Is Ready to Sink Intelligence Advisory Group."

73. Interview with Schmitt.

74. Patrick E. Tyler, "Ex-Defector Yurchenko Reappears in Moscow," *Washington Post,* April 13, 1983, A29.

75. Gates, *From the Shadows,* 362.

76. D. Moore, "Another Defector Slams CIA," *Telegraph,* November 18, 1985.

77. Engelberg, "Washington Talk: Resettling of Defectors: A Job between Agencies," *New York Times,* August 2, 1989, B6.

78. Interview with Source R.

79. Interview with Schmitt.

80. Lou Cannon, "Justice Probe Fails to Disclose Source of Leaks on Mideast," *Washington Post,* December 16, 1983.

81. Thomas, *The Man to See,* 467.

82. Philip Taubman, "Analyst Said to Have Quit CIA in Dispute," *New York Times,* September 28, 1984, A1.

83. Cannon, "Justice Probe Fails to Disclose Source of Leaks on Mideast."

84. David Hoffman, "President Said to Be Unaware of Sweep of Polygraph Order; Directive Surprised Many Senior Aides," *Washington Post,* December 24, 1985, A1.

85. Ernst Volkman, *Espionage: The Greatest Spy Operations of the 20th Century* (New York: Wiley, 1996), 21.

86. Cherne to Anderson, Washington, DC, April 5, 1983, PFIAB, 8. Strategic Materials 1981–, LCP, DSC, HGARC.

87. Cherne to Members of the PFIAB Economic Intelligence Panel, Washington, DC, April 4, 1983, 1, PFIAB, 8. Strategic Materials 1981–, LCP, DSC, HGARC.

88. Ibid., 2–6.

89. Cherne to Alan Greenspan, Washington, DC, April 8, 1983, PFIAB, 8. Strategic Materials 1981–, LCP, DSC, HGARC.

90. Cherne, PFIAB Vice Chair, to Donald Regan, Secretary of the Treasury, Washington, DC, April 19, 1983, PFIAB Banking, LCP, DSC, HGARC.

91. Interview with Source E.

92. Interview with Schmitt.

93. Interview with Source R.

94. Interview with Source E.

95. Michael Levi, "Strategic Arms Reduction Treaty (START I) Chronology," *The Federation of American Scientists: Weapons of Mass Destruction,* at http:// www.fas.org/nuke/control/start1/chron.htm.

96. William Safire, "ESSAY; Preserve Your PFIAB," *New York Times,* February 16, 1989, A35.

97. "War Games: Soviets, Fearing Western Attack, Prepared for Worst in '83," *CNN Perspective Series: Cold War, Episode 22: STAR WARS,* at http://peteara.ro/ id-480109-cold-war-star-wars-1981-1988-22-24.

98. Interview with Schmitt.

99. "War Games," *CNN.*

100. Interview with Source E.

101. Ibid.

102. "Intelligence Community Improved and Pulling Together Dr. Albert Wheelon of PFIAB Tells AFIO Audience," *Periscope* 10, no. 3 (Summer 1985): 2.

103. Jeffrey Richelson, *The Wizards of Langley: Inside the CIA's Directorate of Science and Technology* (New York: Basic Books, 2002), 234–36.

104. Interview with Source E.

105. Seymour Weiss to Armstrong and Cherne, Washington, DC, September 19, 1985, PFIAB, Misc.—January 1, 1984 to November 31, 1985, LCP, DSC, HGARC.

106. Thomas, *The Man to See,* 466.

107. Gates, *From the Shadows,* 355–56.

108. Interview with Source E.

109. PFIAB Bimonthly Meeting Agenda, May 12, 1983, PFIAB, General—January–June 1983, LCP, DSC, HGARC.

110. Interview with Source E.

111. PFIAB Agenda, November 10, 1983, PFIAB, July–December 1983, LCP, DSC, HGARC.

112. Interview with Source E.

113. Interview with Schmitt.

114. Personal Recollections of Kenneth M. Absher, former CIA Clandestine Officer and Station Chief. For further discussion on this subject, see Duane R. Clarridge, *A Spy for All Seasons* (New York: Scribner, 1997), 252–59.

115. Interview with Schmitt.

116. Interview with Source E.

117. Interview with Source A; and Interview with Source E.

118. Interview with Source E.

119. Interview with Schmitt.

120. Interview with Source A.

121. Interview with Schmitt.

122. President's Intelligence Oversight Board, White House, Washington, DC, October 18, 1984, PFIAB, Misc.–January 1, 1984 to November 31, 1985, LCP, DSC, HGARC.

123. Bob Woodward, "Contra War Secretly Run by Three NSC Officials; Benefactors Donated Millions to Pay for Operation," *Washington Post,* February 27, 1987, A1.

124. Timothy S. Robinson, *National Law Journal News Service—PR Newswire,* March 31, 1987.

125. Interview with Source E.

126. Interview with Schmitt.

127. Comments from Board Members on Organization and Operations, Telecon, November 4, 1983, LCP, DSC, HGARC.

7. GEORGE H. W. BUSH

1. William Safire, "Preserve Your Piffiab," *New York Times,* February 16, 1989, Late City Final Edition, sec. A.

2. William Safire, "Bush Is Ready to Sink Intelligence Advisory Group," *St. Petersburg Times,* February 17, 1989, City Edition.

3. Interview with Source B.

4. Jeff Gerth and Sarah Bartlett, "Kissinger and Friends and Revolving Doors," *New York Times,* April 30, 1989, Late City Final Edition, sec. 1.

5. Ibid.

6. Ibid.

7. Jeff Gerth, "Foreign Policy; Rightist Conservatives Keep Eye on Kissinger," *New York Times,* January 24, 1989, Late City Final Edition, sec. B.

8. "Kissinger Is Target of Senate Action," *Saint Louis Post-Dispatch,* May 24, 1989, Three Star Edition.

9. Bill Gertz, "Congress to Consider Bills to Curb Intelligence Groups," *Washington Times,* September 15, 1989, Final Edition.

10. Martin Walker, "Kissinger in Firing Line over China Connections: Congress Revives Two Bills to Smoke Out Influence of Former Secretary of State," *London Guardian,* December 19, 1989.

11. Henry A. Kissinger to President George H. W. Bush, January 22, 1990, GHWBPL-TR, Box 199, FG 006-14, 001986-169264.

12. Interview with Source R.

13. Interview with Source F.

14. Michael Wines, "Bush Scraps Intelligence Board, Appointing a New Panel of 6," *New York Times,* July 17, 1990, Late Edition—Final, sec. A.

15. Interview with Gates.

16. Interview with Source R.

17. Michael Wines, "Bush Scraps Intelligence Board, Appointing a New Panel of 6."

18. Inman became the target of *New York Times* columnist William Safire, who opposed the nomination in a column accusing him of dishonesty and tax fraud. Inman charged Safire and Senator Robert Dole with "McCarthyism" when he withdrew his name from consideration. Judy Keen and Steve Komarow, "Inman Out; Claims Plot by Critics," *USA Today,* January 14, 1994; and William Safire, "Essay: Cold Comfort Level," *New York Times,* December 23, 1993, Late Edition-Final, sec. A.

19. "Excerpts from the Senate's Debates on the Nomination of Tower," *New York Times,* March 3, 1989, Late City Final Edition, sec. A.

20. Elaine Sciolino, "Washington at Work; A Year After Rejection in Senate, Tower Replays Loss of Coveted Job," *New York Times,* April 5, 1990, Late Edition—Final, sec. A.

21. Interview with Gates.

22. James Thompson to President George H. W. Bush, May 15, 1990, GHWBPL-TR, Box 199, FG006-14, 001986-169264.

23. *Marquis Who's Who on the Web,* s.v. "James Thompson," at http://search .marquiswhoswho.com/executable/SearchResults.aspx?db=E.

24. Senator Arlen Specter to President George H. W. Bush, April 19, 1990, GHWBPL-TR, Box 199, FG006-14, 171662-348577.

25. Résumé of John E. Sheehan, GHWBPL-TR, Box 199, FG006-14, 171662-348577.

26. Ibid.

27. Representative William McCollum to President George H. W. Bush, March 2, 1990, GHWBPL-TR, Box 199, FG006-14, 001986-169264.

28. Ibid.

29. Ibid.

30. "Attorney General Bill McCollum," at http://en.wikipedia.org/wiki/Bill_McCollum.

31. "Checklist of White House Press Releases," *Weekly Compilation of Presidential Documents* 28, no. 42 (October 1992): 1969.

32. Michael Wines, "Bush to Streamline Advisory Panel on Intelligence," *New York Times*, March 12, 1990, Late Edition—Final, sec. A.

33. Interview with Source R; and Interview with Source P.

34. Interview with Source R.

35. Ibid.

36. Michael Wines, "Bush to Streamline Advisory Panel on Intelligence."

37. William Safire, "Intelligence Fiasco at the CIA," *St. Petersburg Times,* April 28, 1990, City Edition, sec. A.

38. Ibid.

39. Interview with Source R.

40. Interview with Source P; and Interview with Source F.

41. Interview with Gates.

42. Interview with Source F.

43. Michael Wines, "The Iraqi Invasion; U.S. Says Bush Was Surprised by the Iraqi Strike," *New York Times,* August 5, 1990, Late Edition-Final, sec. 1.

44. Tim Weiner, *Legacy of Ashes: The History of the CIA* (New York: Doubleday, 2007), 426. In his memoirs, Colin Powell asserts that, on August 1, Gen. Norman Schwarzkopf informed then secretary of defense Dick Cheney that he thought that "they're [Iraq] going to attack." Colin Powell, *My American Journey* (New York: Random House), 461.

45. Weiner, *Legacy of Ashes,* 427.

46. William Safire, "Panel Needs to Assess U.S. Failures in Iraq," *St. Louis Post-Dispatch,* July 7, 1991, Five Star Edition.

47. Ibid. Colin Powell gives a different account of the issue of the seven hundred modern Iraqi tanks in his memoirs. According to him, Schwarzkopf was well aware that "the gate was still slightly open" and that "some Republican Guard Units and T-72 tanks could slip away." This information was given to the president himself but did not provoke any serious debate about the decision to end the war. Nor did Powell mention any reports of an impending military coup against Saddam. Instead, he argued that the decision to end the war was based entirely on the simple fact that the United States achieved all military objectives. See Powell, *My American Journey,* 523.

48. R. Jeffrey Smith, "Congress to Investigate U.S. Intelligence on Iraq; Hearings Will Review Apparent Shortcomings," *Washington Post,* March 18, 1991.

49. Interview with Source F.

50. Interview with Source B.

51. Ibid.

52. Interview with Source R.

53. Interview with Gates.

54. Jeffrey Richelson, *The Wizards of Langley: Inside the CIA's Directorate of Science and Technology* (New York: Basic, 2002), 250.

55. Interview with Gates.

56. Ibid.

57. Interview with Source F.

58. Ibid.

59. Heather Tyrell, "Iraqi Troops Could Be 'Sitting Ducks' for Air Strike," *Press Association*, December 4, 1990, Home News sec.

60. Interview with Source F.

61. Ibid.

62. Interview with Source F.

63. Bobby Inman and Russ Bruemmer, "Innuendo Is No Basis for Rejection," *Los Angeles Times*, August 5, 1991.

64. Bill Gertz, "Probe of Bloch 'Cover-up' Sought," *Washington Post*, August 7, 1989, Final Edition.

65. Douglas Garthoff, *Directors of Central Intelligence as Leaders of the U.S. Intelligence Community, 1946–2005* (Washington, DC: CIA Center for the Study of Intelligence, 2005), 196.

66. "National Security Review 29," Federation of American Scientists Intelligence Resource Program, at http://www.fas.org/irp/offdocs/nsr/nsr29.pdf.

67. Ibid.

68. Ibid.

69. Garthoff, *Directors of Central Intelligence as Leaders of the U.S. Intelligence Community*, 196.

70. "National Security Directive 67," GHWBPL-TA, at http://bushlibrary.tamu.edu/research/pdfs/nsd/nsd67.pdf.

71. Garthoff, *Directors of Central Intelligence as Leaders of the U.S. Intelligence Community*, 202.

72. "National Security Directive 67," GHWBPL-TA.

73. Garthoff, *Directors of Central Intelligence as Leaders of the U.S. Intelligence Community*, 196.

74. "Executive Order 12334," December 4, 1981, National Archives: The Federal Register, at http://www.archives.gov/federal-register/codification/executive-order/12334.html.

75. "Executive Order 12701," February 14, 1990, American Presidency Project: George Bush Document Archive, at http://www.presidency.ucsb.edu/ws/index.php?pid=59352.

76. "Illinois Governor Named to Intelligence Post," *Washington Times*, February 27, 1990, sec. A.

8. WILLIAM J. CLINTON

1. John T. Woolley and Gerhard Peters, "Executive Order 12863: President's Foreign Intelligence Advisory Board," *The American Presidency Project*, September 13, 1993, at http://www.presidency.ucsb.edu/ws/index.php?pid=59355.

2. Douglas Jehl, "Elite Intelligence Panel Is Refilled, in Usual Way," *New York Times*, April 25, 1993, 28A.

3. Walter Pincus, "White House Labors to Redefine Role of Intelligence Community; With Cold War's End, Budget Cuts Force Changes at Major Agencies," *Washington Post,* June 13, 1994, 8A.

4. Warren Rudman, "Perspectives on National Security in the Twenty-First Century," *Seminar on Intelligence, Command, and Control,* Program on Information Resources Policy at the Center for Information Policy Research at Harvard University, April 22, 2002, at http://pirp.harvard.edu/pubs_pdf/rudman/rudman-i02-1.pdf.

5. Cynthia M. Nolan, "Internal Forms of Intelligence Oversight" (paper presented at the annual meeting of the International Studies Association, Dan Diego, March 22, 2006), 12, at http://convention2.allacademic.com/one/isa/isa06/ index.php.

6. Jehl, "Elite Intelligence Panel Is Refilled"; and "Biography: Vernon E. Jordan, Jr.," *Akin, Gump, Strauss, Hauer, & Feld LLP,* 2007, at http://www.akingump.com/vjordan/.

7. Rudman, "Perspectives on National Security."

8. Special Investigative Panel, PFIAB, "Science at Its Best, Security at Its Worst: A Report on Security Problems at the U.S. Department of Energy" (June 1999), at http://www.fas.org/sgp/library/pfiab/index.html.

9. The Mitchell Plan was a comprehensive set of recommendations offered to President George W. Bush for ending the escalating Israeli-Palestinian conflict. It called for the United States to back measures by both the leadership and the people of Israel and Palestine to end the violence and reaffirm commitments to previous agreements and accords; work to rebuild confidence by identifying, condemning, and discouraging violent incitement in all forms; and resume negotiations aimed at security cooperation and trust-building efforts. For further details, see "Sharm el-Sheikh Fact-Finding Committee: The Mitchell Plan; April 30, 2001," *Avalon Project at Yale Law School,* 1996–2007, at http://avalon.law.yale.edu/subject_menus/mideast.asp.

10. "Brendan Melley: Associate Vice President," *The Cohen Group,* 2006, at http://www.cohengroup.net/about/teammember.cfm?id=26.

11. Mark F. Moynihan, "The Scientific Community and Intelligence Collection: Academic Scientists Continue to Play a Vital Role in Helping the Intelligence Community Exploit Technology for National Security," *Physics Today* 53 (December 2000): 51–56, at http://link.aip.org/getpdf/servlet/GetPDFServlet?filetype=pdf&id=PHTOAD000053000012000051000001&bypassSSO=1.

12. Special Investigative Panel, PFIAB, "Science at Its Best."

13. Interview with Source H.

14. Jehl, "Elite Intelligence Panel Is Refilled."

15. Rudman, "Perspectives on National Security."

16. Interview with Source H.

17. Ibid.

18. Loch Johnson, "The Aspin-Brown Intelligence Inquiry," *Studies in Intelligence* 48, no. 3 (2004), https://www.cia.gov/library/center-for-the-study-of-intelligence/csi-publications/csi-studies/studies/vo148n03/article01.html.

19. Interview with Crowe, 3.

20. Nolan, "Internal Forms of Intelligence Oversight."

21. Rudman, "Perspectives on National Security."

22. Interview with Source H.

23. Douglas Garthoff, *Directors of Central Intelligence as Leaders of the U.S. Intelligence Community, 1946–2005* (Washington, DC: CIA Center for the Study of Intelligence, 2005), 273.

24. Rudman, "Perspectives on National Security."

25. Ibid.

26. Ibid.

27. Interview with Crowe, 2.

28. John Prados, "No Reform Here: A Blue-Ribbon Panel Proved Once Again That 'Intelligence Reform' Is Something of an Oxymoron," *Bulletin of Atomic Sciences* 55, no. 9 (September 1, 1996): 56.

29. Loch K. Johnson, *The Threat on the Horizon: An Inside Account of America's Search for Security After the Cold War* (New York: Oxford University Press, 2011), 22–24.

30. Johnson, "The Aspin-Brown Intelligence Inquiry."

31. "Members Appointed by Congress," *Intelligence Reform, 1990s: Commission on Roles and Capabilities of the U.S. Intelligence Community, President's 2 February 1995 Statement*, 1998–2007, at http://intellit.org/reform_folder/reform90s_folder/reform90scommem.html.

32. Prados, "No Reform Here," 56.

33. Johnson, "The Aspin-Brown Intelligence Inquiry."

34. L. Britt Snider, "Commentary: A Different Angle on the Aspin-Brown Commission," *Studies in Intelligence: Journal of the American Intelligence Professional* 49, no. 1 (2005), at https://www.cia.gov/library/center-for-the-study-of-intelligence/csi-publications/csi-studies/studies/v0149n01/html_files/different_angle_11.htm.

35. Johnson, "The Aspin-Brown Intelligence Inquiry."

36. Snider, "A Different Angle on the Aspin-Brown Commission."

37. "Executive Summary," *GPO Access: Preparing for the 21st Century: An Appraisal of U.S. Intelligence*, August 28, 2000, at http://www.gpoaccess.gov/int/int003.pdf.

38. "Preface," *GPO Access: Preparing for the 21st Century: An Appraisal of U.S. Intelligence*, August 28, 2000, at http://www.gpoaccess.gov/int/int002.pdf.

39. "Statement by the Press Secretary: Presidential Announcement on Intelligence Community Reforms," *Intelligence Reform, Materials from the 1990s: Commission on Roles and Capabilities of the U.S. Intelligence Community, President's 23 April 1996 Statement*, 1998–2007, at http://intellit.org/reform_folder/reform90s_folder/reform90scompres.html.

40. Johnson, *The Threat on the Horizon*, 366, 369.

41. Interview with Source H.

42. IOB, *Report on the Guatemala Review*, Center for International Policy, at http://www.ciponline.org/iob.htm.

43. Anthony S. Harrington, IOB Chair, to Anthony Lake, Assistant to the President for National Security Affairs, April 7, 1995, Federation of American Scientists Intelligence Resource Program, 1999, at http://www.fas.org/irp/news/1995/950410m.htm.

44. IOB, *Report on the Guatemala Review*.

45. Harrington to Lake, April 7, 1995, Federation of American Scientists Intelligence Resource Program.

46. Ibid.

47. IOB, *Report on the Guatemala Review*.

48. Ibid.

49. Ibid.

50. Ibid.

51. Ibid.
52. Ibid.
53. Ibid.
54. Ibid.
55. Ibid.
56. The IOB refrained from making specific conclusions on the Ortiz case, which, at the time, was still under Department of Justice investigation.
57. IOB, *Report on the Guatemala Review.*
58. Ibid.
59. Office of the White House Press Secretary, Lyon, France, June 28, 1996, *ibiblio—the Public's Library and Digital Archive,* at http://www.ibiblio.org/pub/archives/whitehouse-papers/1996/Jun/1996-06-28-Press-Secretary-on-Intelligence-Oversight-Report.
60. Harrington to Lake, April 7, 1995, Federation of American Scientists Intelligence Resource Program.
61. Office of the White House Press Secretary, Lyon, France, June 28, 1996, *ibiblio—the Public's Library and Digital Archive.*
62. For further detail, see "Wen Ho Lee and Los Alamos," *WashingtonPost.com,* 2002–2005, at http://www.washingtonpost.com/wp-dyn/nation/specials/nationalsecurity/chineseespionage/index.html.
63. Special Investigative Panel, PFIAB, "Science at its Best," iv; and Rudman, "Perspectives on National Security."
64. Special Investigative Panel, PFIAB, "Science at its Best," abstract.
65. Ibid., "Panel Members, PFIAB Staff, and PFIAB Adjunct Staff."
66. Ibid., iv.
67. Ibid.
68. Ibid., i.
69. Ibid., iii.
70. Ibid., ii.
71. Ibid., iii.
72. Ibid., iv.
73. Ibid., 2.
74. Ibid., 5.
75. Ibid., 6.
76. Ibid., 7.
77. Ibid., 11.
78. Ibid., 3–4.
79. Ibid., 6.
80. Ibid., 10.
81. Ibid., 12.
82. Ibid., 4.
83. Ibid., 5.
84. Ibid., 8.
85. Ibid., 11.
86. Ibid., 1.
87. Ibid., 5.
88. Ibid., 8.
89. Ibid., 13–14.
90. Ibid., 22.

91. Ibid., 24.
92. Ibid., 20.
93. Ibid., 13.
94. Ibid., 18.
95. Ibid., 19.
96. Ibid., 16.
97. Ibid., 21.
98. Ibid., 29.
99. Ibid., 30.
100. Ibid., 40.
101. Ibid., 41.
102. Ibid., 36–37.
103. Ibid., 35, 37–38.
104. Ibid., 38.
105. Ibid., 39.
106. Ibid., 44.
107. Ibid., 45.
108. Ibid., 43.
109. Ibid., 46.
110. Ibid., 47.
111. Ibid., 47–49.
112. Ibid., 54.
113. Ibid., 55.
114. Office of the White House Press Secretary, June 15, 1999, Federation of American Scientists Intelligence Resource Program, 1999, at http://www.fas.org/irp/news/1999/06/990615-prc-wh1.htm.
115. "President's Advisory Board Validates Republican Approach: Kyl-Domenici-Murkowski Amendment Improves Security and Accountability at U.S. Nuclear Labs," United States Senate Republican Policy Committee, June 21, 1999, at http://www.senate.gov/~rpc/releases/1999/fr062199.htm.
116. "Amendments Submitted: Foreign Operations, Export Financing, and Related Programs Appropriations Act, 2001-Kyl (and Domenici) Amendment No. 3558," Federation of American Scientists: Program on Government Secrecy, June 21, 2000, at http://www.fas.org/sgp/congress/2000/kyl.html.
117. Floyd Spence, Chair of the House Armed Services Committee, "Reforming the Department of Energy: Safeguarding America's Nuclear Secrets," *National Security Report: Background and Perspective on Important Nuclear Security and Defense Policy Issues* 3, no. 3 (September 1999), 3, at http://www.dtic.mil/cgi-bin/GetTRDoc?Location=U28doc=GetTRDoc.pdf&AD=377468.
118. Ibid., 4.
119. Ibid., 3.
120. Ibid., 3–4.
121. Ibid., 4.
122. "NNSA Homepage," *National Nuclear Security Administration,* at http://www.nnsa.doe.gov/index.htm.
123. Richard W. Mies, Adm. USN (Ret.), to Ambassador Linton Brooks, NNSA Administrator, May 2, 2005, National Nuclear Security Administration: Reading Room, at http://www.hsdl.org/?view&did-459130.
124. Ibid.

125. Vernon Loeb, "Panel Criticizes CIA's Investigation of Deutch," *Washington Post,* May 6, 2000, A9.

126. "PFIAB Documents Released by Clinton," Secrecy News from the Federation of American Scientists Project on Government Secrecy, March 19, 2001, at http://www.fas.org/sgp/news/secrecy/2001/03/031901.html.

127. Ibid.

128. Ibid.

129. Ernest Volkman, *Espionage: The Greatest Spy Operations of the 20th Century* (New York: Wiley, 1996), 16.

130. Ibid., 17.

131. Ibid., 22–25.

132. Interview with Source F; and Interview with Source R.

133. Interview with Source H.

134. Rudman, "Perspectives on National Security." Board interest in this predated Rudman. See Interview with Crowe, 3.

135. Ibid.

136. "Assistant Secretary for Infrastructure Protection, Robert P. Liscouski," *The CIP Report (Hosted by the National Center for Technology and Law School at the George Mason University School of Law)* 1, no. 11 (May 2003), at http://cipp.gmu/archive/cip_report_May2003_HomalandSecurity.pdf.

137. Jeffrey Richelson, *The Wizards of Langley: Inside the CIA's Directorate of Science and Technology* (New York: Basic, 2002), 285.

138. Interview with Source H.

139. Ibid.

140. Interview with Source F.

141. Ibid.

142. Ibid.

9. GEORGE W. BUSH

1. Andrew Zajac, "Intelligence Watchdog Slow to Bite: Critics Contend Bush Marginalized Panel by Failing to Fill Posts Until 2 Years into Term," *Chicago Tribune,* April 3, 2006.

2. Ibid. See also James Risen and Todd S. Purdum, "A Nation Challenged: The Politics of Intelligence; Inquiries into Failures of Intelligence Community Are Put Off Until Next Year," *New York Times,* November 23, 2001, B5.

3. Risen and Purdum, "A Nation Challenged."

4. Warren Rudman, "Perspectives on National Security in the Twenty-First Century," *Seminar on Intelligence, Command, and Control,* Program on Information Resources Policy at the Center for Information Policy Research at Harvard University, April 22, 2002, at http://pirp.harvard.edu/pubs_pdf/rudman/rudman-i02-1.pdf.

5. Risen and Purdum, "A Nation Challenged."

6. Richard Wolffe and Holly Bailey, "Oval: Look Who's Joined Bush's Intel Panel; Bush May Be Besieged by Charges of Cronyism, but They Don't Seem to Have Affected His Picks for a Panel Assessing Intelligence Matters; Plus, Alito, the Talkie," Newsweek: Web Exclusive Commentary, November 2, 2005 at http://www.msnbc.msn.com/id/9900921/site/newsweek/print/1/displaymode/1098/.

7. Robert Bryce, "Top-Secret Cronies," Salon.com, November 17, 2005, at http://dir.salon.com/story/news/feature/2005/11/17/pfiab/.

8. John T. Woolley and Gerhard Peters, "Executive Order 13301: Increasing

the Number of Members on the Intelligence Oversight Board," The American Presidency Project, May 14, 2003, at http://www.presidency.ucsb.edu/ws/index.php?pid=61396&st=13301&st1=.

9. John T. Woolley and Gerhard Peters, "Executive Order 13376: Amendments to Executive Order 12863, Relating to the President's Foreign Intelligence Advisory Board," The American Presidency Project, April 13, 2005, at http://www.presidency.ucsb.edu/ws/index.php?pid=61469&st=13301&st1=.

10. John Solomon, "In Intelligence World, a Mute Watchdog," *Washington Post,* July 15, 2007, A1, A3; and Charlie Savage, "President Weakens Espionage Oversight," *Boston Globe,* March 14, 2008.

11. Walter Pincus, "President Gets to Fill Ranks of New Intelligence Superstructure; Reform Legislation Is Set to Be Signed into Law on Friday," *Washington Post,* December 16, 2004, A35.

12. Jonathan Weisman, "Bush Adviser Helped Law Firm Land Job Lobbying for CNOOC," *Washington Post,* July 12, 2005, D1.

13. Immediate Release, Office of the White House Press Secretary, October 27, 2005, The White House, at http://www.fas.org/irp/news/2005/10/wh102705.html.

14. Immediate Release, Office of the White House Press Secretary, December 19, 2005, The White House, at http://www.presidency.ucsb.edu/ws/index.php?pid=82312&st=Robb&st1=.

15. Immediate Release, Office of the White House Press Secretary, September 5, 2006, The White House, at http://www.presidency.ucsb.edu/ws/index.php?pid=82679&st=bovin&st1=.

16. Wolffe and Bailey, "Oval: Look Who's Joined Bush's Intel Panel."

17. Interview with Source G.

18. Wolffe and Bailey, "Oval: Look Who's Joined Bush's Intel Panel."

19. Interview with Source XX.

20. Interview with Source G.

21. Ibid.

22. Al Kamen, "In the Loop: Zero de Mayo," *Washington Post,* May 2, 2003, A29.

23. Interview with Source Q.

24. Interview with Source U.

25. Ibid.

26. Interview with Source G.

27. Interview with Source XX.

28. Interview with Source I.

29. "Sharm el-Sheikh Fact-Finding Committee Report," U.S. Department of State, April 30, 2001, at http://domino.un.org/unispal.nsf/0/6e61d52eaacb860285256d2800734e9a?OpenDocument.

30. Interview with Source U.

31. "NSPD-5: Review of U.S. Intelligence," Federation of American Scientists Intelligence Resource Program, October 3, 1997, at http://www.fas.org/irp/offdocs/nspd/nspd-5.htm.

32. Vernon Loeb, "Two Panels Begin Reviewing Technologies and Reorganization," *Washington Post,* July 3, 2001.

33. Walter Pincus, "Intelligence Shakeup Would Boost CIA; Panel Urges Transfer of NSA, Satellites, Imagery from Pentagon," *Washington Post,* November 8, 2001, A01.

34. For discussion, see Walter Pincus, "Rumsfeld Cast Doubt on Intelligence Reform; Changes Suggested by Presidential Panel," *Washington Post,* April 9, 2002, A17; Spencer Ackerman, "Small Change," *New Republic,* December 13, 2004, 12; and follow-up discussion with Source P, April 22, 2009.

35. Loch K. Johnson, "Assessing an Earlier Panel on Intelligence: The Aspin-Brown Intelligence Inquiry; Behind Closed Doors of a Blue Ribbon Commission," *Studies in Intelligence: Journal of the American Intelligence Professional* 48, no. 3 (2004), at https://www.cia.gov/library/center-for-the-study-of-intelligence/csi-publications/csi-studies/studies/vol48n03/article01.html.

36. Katherine Shrader, "New Spy Chief Inherits a Work in Progress and a Report Card That's Still Out," *Associated Press,* January 8, 2007.

37. Interview with Source M.

38. "Reviewing the Intelligence on Iraq," *New York Times,* May 26, 2003, A14.

39. Interview with Source I.

40. Walter Pincus, "White House Faulted on Uranium Claim; Intelligence Warnings Disregarded, President's Advisory Board Says," *Washington Post,* December 24, 2003, A1.

41. "White House Ignored CIA Warnings about Iraq Uranium Story, Report Says," *Associated Press,* December 24, 2003.

42. Interview with Source M.

43. Interview with Source Q.

44. Ibid.

45. Interview with Source U.

46. Terry Frieden, "Watchdog Says FBI Violated Surveillance Rules," CNN.com—Law Center, October 25, 2005, at http://www.lexisnexis.com.proxy.library.nd.edu/us/lnacademic/results/docview/docview.do?docLinkInd=true&risb=21_T9479048872&format=GNBFI&sort=BOOLEAN&startDocNo=451&resultsUrlKey=29_T9479048875&cisb=22_T9479048874&treeMax=true&treeWidth=0&csi=266325&docNo=458.

47. Solomon, "In Intelligence World, a Mute Watchdog."

48. Zajac, "Intelligence Watchdog Slow to Bite."

49. Interview with Source XX. See also Richard Sisk, "Behind the Goss Toss; W's 'Alarmed' Panel Sealed Top Spy's Fate," *New York Daily News,* May 7, 2006, 2.

50. Jeff Stein, "Goss' Management Missteps Made Him a Rare White House Casualty," *Congressional Quarterly,* May 7, 2006, at http://jeffstein.info/2005/05/gross-mismangement-missteps-made-him-rare-07.html.

51. Mark Mazzetti, Scott Shane, and Elisabeth Bumiller, "Exit of Spy Chief Viewed as Move to Revamp CIA," *New York Times,* May 7, 2006, 1.

52. Interview with Source M.

53. "About the Iraq Study Group," *United States Institute of Peace,* at http://www.usip.org/programs/initiatives/iraq-study-group.

54. Interview with Source Q.

55. Interview with Source S.

56. Interview with Source Q.

57. Interview with Source Q.

58. Interview with Source U.

59. Interview with Source Q.

60. Zajac, "Intelligence Watchdog Slow to Bite."

61. Peter Baker and Walter Pincus, "Bush Signs Intelligence Reform Bill; President

Now Must Find Experienced Hand to Guide 15 Agencies," *Washington Post,* December 18, 2004, A1.

62. Interview with Source Q.
63. Pincus, "President Gets to Fill Ranks of New Intelligence Superstructure."
64. Interview with Source U.
65. Interview with Source I.
66. Interview with Source G.
67. Interview with Source Q.
68. Interview with Source U.
69. Interview with Source Q.
70. Interview with Source U.
71. Interview with Source S.
72. Ibid.

CONCLUSION

1. "President Obama Signs Executive Order to Amend Executive Order 13462," White House, Washington, DC, October 29, 2009, at http://www.whitehouse.gov/the-press-office/president-obama-signs-executive-order-amend-executive-order-13462.

2. "Remarks by the President Before Meeting with the President's Intelligence Advisory Board Co-Chairmen and Senior Leadership of the Intelligence Community," White House, Washington, DC, October 28, 2009, at http://www.whitehouse.gov/the-press-office/remarks-president-meeting-with-presidents-intelligence-advisory-board-co-chairmen-a.

3. "Press Briefing by Press Secretary Robert Gibbs, 5/21/10," White House, at http://www.whitehouse.gov/the-press-office/press-briefing-press-secretary-robert-gibbs-52110.

4. Josh Gerstein, "Panel Found 'Distracted' DNI," *Politico,* June 2, 2010, at http://www.politico.com/news/stories/0610/38061.html.

5. Walter Pincus and Anne E. Kornblut, "President Rethinking His Pick for Director of National Intelligence," *Washington Post,* May 27, 2010, A6.

6. David Ignatius, "Obama Seeks to Reshape Intel Operations with Choice of Clapper," *Washington Post,* June 9, 2010, A21.

7. Siobhan Gorman, "Move to Enhance Spy Chief's Clout," *Wall Street Journal,* May 22, 2010.

8. "Interview with Representative Mike Rogers," *Defense News,* February 14, 2011, at http://www.defensenews.com/story.pip?i-5699303.

9. Michael D. Shear, "Sestak: Bill Clinton Offered Him Job to Quit Race," *Washington Post,* May 28, 2010; and James Taranto, "Cynical, Not Criminal," *Wall Street Journal,* June 4, 2010.

10. Marc Ambinder, "The Night Beat," Atlantic.com, June 1, 2010 at http://www.theatlantic.com/politics/archive/2010/06/the-night-beat-what-israeli-intelligence-thought-they-knew-about-the-ships/57544/.

11. Two of the most widely cited examples of this literature are James David Barber, *The Presidential Character: Predicting Performance in the White House* (New York: Pearson, 2009); and Alexander George and Eric Stein, "Presidential Management Styles and Models," in *Presidential Personality and Performance,* ed. Alexander L. George and Juliette George (Boulder, CO: Westview, 1998). Applications of the theory to foreign policy and national security affairs include Thomas Preston, *The President and His Inner Circle: Leadership Style in Foreign Affairs* (New York: Columbia University Press, 2001); and I. M. Destler, "National Security

Advice to U.S. Presidents: Some Lessons from Thirty Years," *World Politics* 24, no. 2 (January 1977): 143–76. Finally, for an application of this approach to the study of the PFIAB, see Cynthia M. Nolan, "The PFIAB Personality: Studying the Presidents and Their Foreign Intelligence Boards" (paper presented at the International Studies Association convention, New York, February 2009).

12. See George and Stein, "Presidential Management Styles and Models," 199–280; and Barber, *The Presidential Character.* For a very helpful summary chart, see Nolan, "The PFIAB Personality," app. B, 38.

13. Lyn Ragsdale and John J. Theis III, "The Institutionalization of the American Presidency, 1924–92," *American Journal of Political Science* 41, no. 4 (October 1997): 1280–1318. For a classic discussion of institutionalization, see Samuel P. Huntington, *Political Order in Changing Societies* (New Haven, CT: Yale University Press, 1966), 1–92.

14. Destler, "National Security Advice to U.S. Presidents," 144–45.

15. Ragsdale and Theis, "The Institutionalization of the American Presidency," 1302. This finding follows Arthur Schlesinger Jr., *The Imperial Presidency* (Boston: Houghton Mifflin, 1973).

16. Ragsdale and Theis, "The Institutionalization of the American Presidency," 1283.

BIOGRAPHICAL SKETCHES OF PFIAB MEMBERS

1. "David M. Abshire," Richard Lounsbery Foundation, 2007, at http://rlounsbery.org/officers_board/bios/Abishire.html.

2. Intelligence Oversight Board, Stephen Ailes, Tab D—Biographical Data—Board and Staff, n.d., Intelligence Oversight Board—History, IOBSF, LCP, Box 9, GRFL.

3. "Lew Allen Jr.," Marquis Who's Who on the Web, at http://marquiswhoswho.com.

4. "Lew Allen Jr." U.S. Air Force online, at http://www.af.mil/information/bios/bio.asp?bioID=4508.

5. "George Whelan Anderson Jr., Admiral, United States Navy," Arlington National Cemetery Website, December 8, 2006, at http://www.arlingtoncemetery.net/gwanders.htm.

6. "Martin Carl Anderson," Marquis Who's Who on the Web, 2006, at http://www.marquiswhoswho.com.

7. "Cresencio S. Arcos, Jr.," Marquis Who's Who on the Web, 2006, at http://www.marquiswhoswho.com.

8. "Cresencio (Cris) Arcos: Government Affairs Counselor," Kirkpatrick & Lockhart Preston Gates Ellis, LLP: Professionals, at http://en.wikipedia.org/wiki/Cresencio_S._Arcos,_Jr.

9. "Arends, Leslie Cornelius (1895–1985)," Biographical Directory of the United States Congress, at http://bioguide.congress.gov/scripts/biodisplay.pl?index=A000216.

10. "Armstrong, Anne Legendre," Marquis Who's Who on the Web, 2006, at http://www.marquiswhoswho.com.

11. Jay Horning, "Armstrong Cut a Path Other Women Followed in Politics: Newsmakers Revisited," *St. Petersburg Times,* November 1, 1987, 25A.

12. Martin Anderson, *Revolution: The Reagan Legacy* (Palo Alto, CA: Hoover Institution Press, 1990), 360.

13. Evan Thomas, *The Man to See: Edward Bennett Williams, Ultimate Insider; Legendary Trial Lawyer* (New York: Simon & Schuster, 1991), 467.

14. Joseph E. Persico, *Casey: The Lives and Secrets of William J. Casey: From the OSS to the CIA* (New York: Viking Penguin, 1990), 305.

15. Anderson, *Revolution: The Reagan Legacy,* 360.

16. Interview with Source T.

17. "Les Aspin, January 21, 1993–February 3, 1994, 18th Secretary of Defense, Clinton Administration," Defenselink-Histories of the Secretaries of Defense, at http://www.defenselink.mil/specials/secdef_histories/bios/aspin.htm.

18. Ibid.

19. "Zoë Baird," Marquis Who's Who on the Web, 2006, at http://www.marquiswhoswho.com.

20. Jill Smolowe, "TIME Capsule: The Embattled Nomination of Zoe Baird," *Time.com,* February 1, 1993, at http://www.time.com/time/magazine/article/0,9171,977610,00.html.

21. "Zoe Baird," Markle Foundation: Who We Are, Board of Directors, 2004, at http://www.markle.org/about_markle/who_we_are/management/zoe_baird.php.

22. "Howard Henry Baker, Jr.," *Marquis Who's Who* on the Web, 2006, at http://www.marquiswhoswho.com.

23. Steven V. Roberts, "Baker Called Calm but Too Cautious," *New York Times,* June 20, 1988, B7.

24. Martin Tolchin, "The White House Crisis: Man in the News; The Great Conciliator: Howard Henry Baker, Jr.," *New York Times,* February 28, 1987, Section 1, 7.

25. Michael Noll, "William Oliver Baker: A Biography and Tribute," Dr. William Oliver Baker, 2006, at http://www.williamobaker.org.

26. "James Love Barksdale," Marquis Who's Who on the Web, 2006, at http://www.marquiswhoswho.com.

27. "James L. Barksdale," TimeWarner-Management-Board of Directors, April 4, 2006, at http://www.timewarner.com/corp/management/board_directors/bio/barksdale_james.html.

28. "James L. Barksdale: President and CEO, Barksdale Management Corporation," America's Promise Alliance: Board Member Biography, at http://search.intelius.com/James-Barksdale-RRn3h1g.

29. "Robert Hilliard Barrow," Marquis Who's Who on the Web, 2006, at http://www.marquiswhoswho.com.

30. "General Robert H. Barrow—Deceased, 27th Commandant of the Marine Corps," at https://slsp.manpower.usmc.mil/gosa/biographies/rptBiography.asp?PERSON_ID=414&PERSON_TYPE=General.

31. "Robert Hilliard Barrow," Marquis Who's Who on the Web, 2006, at http://www.marquiswhoswho.com.

32. Member Ratings Chart, 1984, Loose Documents, LCP, Box 72, DSC, HGARC.

33. "Bloch, Richard L," *Who's Who in America, 1982–1983,* 42nd ed. (Wilmette, IL: Marquis Who's Who, 1982), 301.

34. "White House Coffee Guest List: October 13, 1995," WashingtonPost.com, at http://www.washingtonpost.com/wp-srv/politics/special/campfin/coffees/101395.htm; and "Executive Profile: Richard L. Bloch," BusinessWeek, 2000–2007, at http://investing.businessweek.com/businessweek/research/stocks/private/person.asp?personId=559632&privcapId=1856842&previousCapId=261524&previousTitle=City%20National%20Corp.

35. Campaign donations made by Bloch to various Democratic nominees and to the Democratic National Committee were found in archival searches of the Huffington Post's site at http://www.fundrace.org and the nonpartisan Web site at http://www.campaignmoney.com; and Bill Gertz, "DNC Donors Put On Spy Panel; Signals Access to Intelligence Can Be Bought," *Washington Times,* March 10, 1997, A1.

36. "Alfred S. Bloomingdale," Marquis Who's Who on the Web, 2006, at http://www.marquiswhoswho.com.

37. David W. Dunlap, "Alfred Bloomingdale, Diner's Club Developer, Dies," *New York Times,* August 24, 1982, B10.

38. "Major Donors to Reagan's Fund," *New York Times,* March 21, 1981, 9.

39. "Boren, David Lyle (1941–)," Biographical Directory of the United States Congress, at http://bioguide.congress.gov/scripts/biodisplay.pl?index=b000639.

40. "Frank Borman," Marquis Who's Who on the Web, 2006, at http://www.marquiswhoswho.com.

41. Fred Howard, "Frank Borman: Born to Fly," *Washington Post,* October 2, 1988, X5.

42. "Denis A. Bovin Joins BISYS(R) Board of Directors," PRNewswire, June 27, 2001, at http://www.prnewswire.com/news-releases/denis-a-bovin-joins-bisysr-board-of-directors-72340677.html.

43. "William Ralph Brody," at http://www.salk.edu/about/brody.html.

44. *Who's Who In America,* vol. 7, *1977–1981* (Chicago: Marquis Who's Who, 1981), s.v. Bruce, David K. E.; "Bruce, David Kirkpatrick Este," The Political Graveyard: A Database of Historic Cemeteries, at http://politicalgraveyard.com/bio/bruce.html; and "David K. E. Bruce," Notable Names Database, at http://www.nndb.com/people/115/000057941.

45. "John Shelby Bryan," Brazoria County Historical Museum, at http://www.bchm.org/gene/d0000/g0001756.html.

46. Millicom, "Corporate History," at http://www.millicom.com/about/about.cfm.

47. Kevin Gray, "The Summer of Her Discontent," *New York Magazine,* September 13, 1999.

48. "Zbigniew Brzezinski," Marquis Who's Who on the Web, 2006, at http://www.marquiswhoswho.com.

49. Ibid.

50. Douglass Martin, "W. Glenn Campbell, Shaper of Hoover Center, Dies at 77," *New York Times,* November 28, 2001, D11.

51. "In Memoriam: W. Glenn Campbell," Hoover Institution Newsletter [online], Winter 2002, at http://media.hoover.org/documents/newsletter_2002winter.pdf.

52. Member Ratings Chart, 1984, Loose Documents, LCP, DSC, HGARC.

53. "President Obama Announces Members of President's Intelligence Advisory Board," The White House, December 23, 2009, at http://www.whitehouse.gov/the-press-office/president-obama-announces-members-presidents-intelligence-advisory-board.

54. G. J. A. O'Toole and Ann Z. Caracristi, *The Encyclopedia of American Intelligence and Espionage: From the Revolutionary War to the Present* (New York: Facts on File, 1988), 88.

55. CSTB, NRC, "Cryptography's Role in Securing the Information Society," app. A, "Contributors to the NRC Project on National Cryptography Policy," at http://www.nap.edu/openbook.php?record_id=5131&page=341.

56. "Ann Caracristi," National Security Agency: Central Security Service, at http://www.nsa.gov/about/cryptologic_heritage/women/honorees/caracristi.shtml.

57. CSTB, NRC, "Cryptography's Role in Securing the Information Society," app. A.

58. *Who Was Who in America,* vol. 9, *1986–1989* (Wilmette, IL: Marquis Who's Who, 1989), s.v. Casey, William Joseph.

59. Intelligence Oversight Board, Leo Cherne, Tab D—Biographical Data—Board and Staff, n.d., Intelligence Oversight Board—History, IOBSF, LCP, Box 9, GRFL.

60. *Who Was Who in America,* vol. 13, *1998–2000* (Wilmette, IL: Marquis Who's Who, 2000), s.v. Clifford, Clark McAdams.

61. *Who Was Who in America,* vol. 11, *1993–1996* (Wilmette, IL: Marquis Who's Who, 1996), s.v. Connally, John Bowden.

62. *Who's Who in America,* vol. 4, *1961–1968* (Chicago: Marquis Who's Who, 1968), s.v. Conolly, Richard L.; and Arlington National Cemetery, "Richard Lansing Conolly," Arlington National Cemetery Web site, at http://www.arlingtoncemetery.net/rlconolly.htm.

63. Bruce Anderson, "An Admiral at the Court of St. James's: From Submarine Captain to the Highest Levels of the Pentagon to U.S. Ambassador, William Crowe Has Been Both a Centrist and a Contrarian," *Stanford Magazine,* at http://www.stanfordalumni.org/news/magazine/1997/sepoct/articles/crowe.html.

64. "William James Crowe, Jr.," Marquis Who's Who on the Web, 2006, at http://www.marquiswhoswho.com.

65. Anderson, "An Admiral at the Court of St. James's."

66. "Arthur B. Culvahouse, Jr.," O'Melveny & Myers LLP: Lawyers, 2000–2008, at http://www.omm.com/arthurbculvahousejr.

67. *Who's Who in America,* vol. 7, *1977–1981* (Chicago: Marquis Who's Who, 1981), s.v. Darden, Colgate Whitehead, Jr.; Biographical Directory of the United States Congress, "Darden, Colgate Whitehead, Jr.," U.S. Congress, http://bioguide.congress.gov/scripts/biodisplay.pl?index=D000050; and The Political Graveyard: A Database of Historic Cemeteries, "Darden, Colgate Whitehead, Jr.," at http://politicalgraveyard.com/bio/danielson-darke.html.

68. "Robert Addison Day, Jr.," Marquis Who's Who on the Web, 2006, at http://www.marquiswhoswho.com.

69. "Pioneer Profiles: George W. Bush's $100,000 Club—Robert Addison Day, Jr.," Texans for Public Justice—The Pioneers: George W. Bush's $100,000 Club, July 2000, at http://www.tpj.org/pioneers/robert_day.html.

70. "John Mark Deutch," Marquis Who's Who on the Web, at http://www.marquiswhoswho.com.

71. "John M. Deutch," George H. W. Bush Presidential Library Textual Records, Box 199, FG006-14, 171662-348577. While at MIT, Deutch urged Secretary of Defense Dick Cheney to lift the ban on gays in college ROTC programs; see "MIT Provost Urges Military to Lift Ban on Gays in ROTC," *Washington Times,* April 19, 1990.

72. "John M. Deutch Biography," Massachusetts Institute of Technology Online, at http://web.mit.edu/chemistry/deutch/biography.html.

73. Ibid. Soon after retiring as director of central intelligence, Deutch would find himself at the center of a firestorm of controversy when classified material was found on an unclassified, government-owned home computer connected to a modem. The attorney general declined to prosecute him, and President Clinton pardoned him

on his last day in office. "Central Intelligence Agency Inspector General Report of Investigation: Improper Handling of Classified Material by John M. Deutch," Federation of American Scientists Online, at http://www.fas.org/irp/cia/product/ig_deutch.html.

74. "William O. DeWitt, Jr.," Marquis Who's Who on the Web, 2006, at http://www.marquiswhoswho.com.

75. "The Bill DeWitt File," Cincinnati.com: The Enquirer, October 10, 2003, at http://www.enquirer.com/editions/2003/10/10/loc_ohdewitt10bio.html; and "Bush Donor Profile: William O. DeWitt, Jr.," Texans for Public Justice, February 18, 2004, at http://www.tpj.org/docs/pioneers/pioneers_view.jsp?id=26.

76. Who's Who in America, vol. 11, 1993–1996 (Wilmette, IL: Marquis Who's Who, 1996), s.v. Doolittle, James H.

77. "Sidney D. Drell, 2000," The Enrico Fermi Award: 2000's Laureates, at http://science.energy.gov/fermi/award-laureates/2000s/drell/.

78. "Sidney D. Drell, Senior Fellow," The Hoover Institution, 2007, at http://www.hoover.org/bios/drell.html.

79. JASON is an informal group founded by Drell in 1960 that consists of academic scientists from all disciplines and assists the U.S. government on matters involving science and technology.

80. "Sidney D. Drell, Deputy Director Emeritus," Stanford Linear Accelerator Center: Director's Office, August 1, 2007, at http://www-group.slac.stanford.edu/do/people/drell.html.

81. "Thomas F. Eagleton," Marquis Who's Who on the Web, 2006, at http://www.marquiswhoswho.com.

82. "Eagleton, Thomas Francis (1929–2007)," Biographical Directory of the United States Congress: 1774–Present, at http://bioguide.congress.gov/scripts/biodisplay.pl?index=E000004.

83. Adam Clymer, "Thomas F. Eagleton, 77, a Running Mate for 18 Days, Dies," New York Times, March 5, 2007, B7; and Larry J. Sabato, "Thomas Eagleton's Mental Health—1972," Washington Post: Special Report: Clinton Accused, 1998, at http://www.washingtonpost.com/wp-srv/politics/special/clinton/frenzy/eagleton.htm.

84. "James O. Ellis, Jr.," NNDB, 2008, at http://www.nndb.com/people/808/000128424.

85. "Biography—James O. Ellis, Jr.," Lockheed Martin, 2008, at http://www.lockheedmartin.com/investor/corporate_governance/boardofdirectors/bio-ellis.html.

86. "James O. Ellis, Jr.," Marquis Who's Who on the Web, 2006, at http://www.marquiswhoswho.com.

87. "Donald Louis Evans," Marquis Who's Who on the Web, 2006, at http://www.marquiswhoswho.com.

88. "Bush Donor Profile: Donald L. Evans," Texans for Public Justice, May 10, 2004, at http://www.tpj.org/docs/pioneers/pioneers_view.jsp?id=576.

89. "Martin C. Faga," NNDB, 2008, at http://www.nndb.com/people/137/000168630.

90. "Mr. Martin C. Faga," Mitre Corporation: About Us: Board of Trustees, November 3, 2006, at http://www.mitre.org/about/bot/faga.html.

91. Ibid.

92. Who's Who in America, vol. 4, 1961–1968 (Chicago: Marquis Who's Who, 1968), s.v. Fairless, Benjamin F.; and Fairless to Hull, December 31, 1959, President's Board of Consultants, OF 309, Book 2 of 2, WHCF, 1953–61, DDEL; and

"Benjamin F. Fairless," Horatio Alger Association of Distinguished Americans, at http://www.horatioalger.com/members/member_info.cfm?memberid=fai58.

93. "Curriculum Vita of Martin S. Feldstein," National Bureau of Economics Research, at http://www.nber.org/feldstein/cv.html.

94. "Martin Feldstein," Harvard University: Belfer Center for Science and International Affairs—Experts, at http://belfercenter.ksg.harvard.edu/experts/825/martin_feldstein.html.

95. "Thomas Stephen Foley," Marquis Who's Who on the Web, 2006, at http://www.marquiswhoswho.com.

96. "Thomas S. Foley," The Trilateral Commission, October 2007, at http://www.trilateral.org/membship/bios/tf.htm.

97. "Ambassador Thomas Foley," International Council Member Experience, Belfer Center for Science and International Affairs at the John F. Kennedy School of Government, Harvard University, at http://belfercenter.ksg.harvard.edu/experts/314/ambassador_thomas_foley.html.

98. "Stephen Friedman," Marquis Who's Who on the Web, 2006, at http://www.marquiswhoswho.com.

99. "Stephen Friedman," Welcome to the White House: Current PFIAB Members, at http://clinton4.nara.gov/WH/EOP/pfiab/boardmembers.html#friedman.

100. "Robert W. Galvin," Harvard Business School, Leadership: 20th Century Great American Business Leaders, 2004, at http://www.hbs.edu/leadership/database/leaders/292/.

101. Independent Institute, "Robert W. Galvin," at http://www.independent.org/aboutus/person_detail.asp?id=874.

102. *Who's Who in America,* vol. 8, *1982–1985* (Chicago: Marquis Who's Who, 1985), s.v. Gray, Gordon; and William Gardner Bell, "Secretaries of War & Secretaries of the Army: Portraits and Biographical Sketches–Gordon Gray," Army Center for Military History, 2001, at http://www.army.mil/cmh-pg/books/Sw-SA/Gray.htm.

103. "Alan Greenspan," Marquis Who's Who on the Web, 2006, at http://www.marquiswhoswho.com.

104. Dan Seligman, "Outfront: I Remember Alan," Forbes.com, January 30, 2006, at http://www.forbes.com/home/free_forbes/2006/0130/052.html.

105. "Greenspan to End 18-Year Tenure," ABC News—Money, January 30, 2005, at http://abcnews.go.com/Business/story?id=1244855&page=1.

106. "Hagel, Charles Timothy (Chuck) (1946–)," Biographical Directory of the United States Congress, at http://bioguide.congress.gov/scripts/biodisplay.pl?index=h001028.

107. "James Hamilton: Partner," Bingham McCutchen LLP, 2007, at http://www.bingham.com/Lawyer.aspx?LawyerID=716.

108. "Lee Herbert Hamilton," Marquis Who's Who on the Web, 2006, at http://www.marquiswhoswho.com.

109. "Lee H. Hamilton," Woodrow Wilson International Center for Scholars: About the Wilson Center, April 26, 2007, at http://www.wilsoncenter.org/staff/lee-hamilton.

110. Ibid.

111. "Anthony S. Harrington," Marquis Who's Who on the Web, 2006, at http://www.marquiswhoswho.com.

112. Ibid.

113. "Robert J. Hermann, ANSI HSSP Special Advisor," Homeland Security

Standards Panel, ANSI Standards Activities, January 2003, at http://www.ansi.org/standards_activities/standards_boards_panels/hssp/hermann.aspx?menuid=3.

114. "Robert Jay Hermann," Marquis Who's Who on the Web, 2006, at http://www.marquiswhoswho.com.

115. *Who's Who in America*, vol. 6, *1974–1976* (Chicago: Marquis Who's Who, 1976), s.v. Hull, John Edwin; and Arlington National Cemetery, "John Edwin Hull," Arlington National Cemetery Website, http://www.arlingtoncemetery.net/jehull.htm.

116. "Ray L. Hunt," NNDB, 2008, at http://www.nndb.com/people/521/000055356/.

117. "Ray Lee Hunt," Marquis Who's Who on the Web, 2006, at http://www.marquiswhoswho.com.

118. Hunt was named a "Minor League Pioneer" in 2000 because his pledge of $100,000 in campaign funds was not confirmed. "Bush Donor Profile: Ray Lee Hunt," Texans for Public Justice, December 5, 2003, at http://www.tpj.org/docs/pioneers/pioneers_view.jsp?id=618.

119. "William George Hyland," Marquis Who's Who on the Web, at http://www.marquiswhoswho.com.

120. "Mr. William G. Hyland," Strategic Studies Institute of the U.S. Army War College online, at http://www.strategicstudiesinstitute.army.mil/pubs/people.cfm?q=407.

121. "Bobby Ray Inman," Marquis Who's Who on the Web, at http://www.marquiswhoswho.com.

122. Ibid.

123. "Washington Dateline," Associated Press, March 12, 1990, Monday PM cycle.

124. "Leon Jaworski," Marquis Who's Who on the Web, 2006, at http://www.marquiswhoswho.com.

125. John T. Woolley and Gerhard Peters, "Ronald Reagan: Appointment of 19 Members of the President's Foreign Intelligence Advisory Board, and Designation of the Chairman and Vice Chairman," The American Presidency Project, October 20, 1981, at http://www.presidency.ucsb.edu/ws/print.php?pid=43158.

126. For a more detailed account, see Robert B. Boettcher, *Gifts of Deceit: Sun Myong Moon, Tongsun Park, and the Korea Scandal* (New York: Holt, Rinehart & Winston, 1980).

127. "David Elmer Jeremiah," Marquis Who's Who on the Web, 2006, at http://www.marquiswhoswho.com.

128. Ibid.

129. "Admiral David E. Jeremiah, USN Ret.," ManTech International Corporation: Board of Directors, 2007, at http://www.mantech.com/about/board.asp.

130. CIA, "Jeremiah News Conference," June 2, 1998, at https://www.cia.gov/news-information/press-releases-statements/press-release-archive-1998/jeremiah.html.

131. "President Obama Announces Members of President's Intelligence Advisory Board."

132. "Arnold Lee Kanter," Marquis Who's Who on the Web, 2006, at http://www.marquiswhoswho.com.

133. Ibid.

134. John T. Woolley and Gerhard Peters, "Appointment of Arnold Kanter as Special Assistant to the President for National Security Affairs," American

Presidency Project [online], June 5, 1989, at http://www.presidency.ucsb.edu/ws/index.php?pid=17109.

135. "The Scowcroft Group Regrets to Announce the Death of Our Friend and Colleague, Arnold Kanter," at http://www.scowcroft.com/html/announcements/Arnie%20Kanter.pdf.

136. *Who's Who in America,* vol. 5, *1969–1973* (Chicago: Marquis Who's Who, 1973), s.v. Kennedy, Joseph Patrick; Notable Names Database, "Joseph P. Kennedy," Notable Names Database, at http://www.nndb.com/people/317/000024245/.

137. *Who's Who in America,* vol. 9, *1985–1989* (Wilmette, IL: Marquis Who's Who, 1989), s.v. Killian, James Rhyne, Jr.; and J. Patrick Coyne to the PFIAB, Washington, DC, May 15, 1961, Foreign Intelligence Advisory Board Briefing Material 5/61, President's Office Files, Departments and Agencies, Papers of President Kennedy, JFKL.

138. "Jeanne Kirkpatrick," Right Web Profile, International Relations Center, December 12, 2006, at http://rightweb.irc-online.org/profile/1250.

139. The Nobel Foundation, "Henry Kissinger: The Nobel Peace Prize 1973, Biography," Nobel Prize, 1973, at http://nobelprize.org/nobel_prizes/peace/laureates/1973/kissinger-bio.html.

140. "Henry Alfred Kissinger," Marquis Who's Who on the Web, 2006, at http://www.marquiswhoswho.com.

141. Interview with Source E.

142. "President Obama Announces Members of President's Intelligence Advisory Board."

143. *Who's Who in America,* vol. 10, *1989–1993* (Wilmette, IL: Marquis Who's Who, 1993), s.v. Land, Edwin H.; and James Killian, *The Education of a College President* (Cambridge, MA: MIT Press, 1985), 174.

144. "James Calhoun Langdon, Jr.," Marquis Who's Who on the Web, 2006, at http://www.marquiswhoswho.com; and "Biography: James C. Langdon, Jr., Partner," Akin Gump Strauss Hauer & Feld LLP-Attorneys at Law, 2008, at http://www.akingump.com/jlangdon.

145. "Bush Donor Profile: James (& Sandy) C. Langdon Jr.," Texans for Public Justice, December 5, 2003, at http://www.tpj.org/docs/pioneers/pioneers_view.jsp?id=126.

146. *Who's Who in America,* vol. 7, *1977–1981* (Wilmette, IL: Marquis Who's Who, 1981), s.v. Langer, William L.

147. William Gardner Bell, "Commanding Generals and Chiefs of Staff (1775–2005): Portraits & Biographical Sketches of the United States Army's Senior Officer–Lyman Louis Lemnitzer," Army Center for Military History, at http://www.army.mil/cmh-pg/books/cg&csa/Lemnitzer-LL.htm.

148. "Alfred Lerner," Marquis Who's Who on the Web, 2006, at http://www.marquiswhoswho.com; and "Alfred Lerner," UDaily: Archive (University of Delaware), December 12, 2002, at http://www.udel.edu/PR/UDaily/01-02/lerner121202.html.

149. *Who's Who in America,* vol. 11, *1993–1996* (Wilmette, IL: Marquis Who's Who, 1996), s.v. Lincoln, Franklin Benjamin.

150. Interview with Byers.

151. Suggestions for Possible Panel of Twelve Consultants to the NSC (with attached Biographical Sketches), Meetings with the President—1958 (3), Special Assistant Series, Presidential Subseries, WHO, Office of the Special Assistant for

National Security Affairs: Records, 1953–61, DDEL; *Who's Who in America,* vol. 9, *1985–1989* (Wilmette, IL: Marquis Who's Who, 1989), s.v. Lovett, Robert Abercrombie; "Robert A. Lovett," U.S. Department of Defense, at http://www .defenselink.mil/specials/secdef_histories/bios/lovett.htm; and "Robert A. Lovett," Notable Names Database, at http://www.nndb.com/people/046/000057872/.

152. *Who's Who in America,* vol. 9, *1985–1989* (Wilmette, IL: Marquis Who's Who, 1989), s.v. Luce, Clare Boothe.

153. PFIAB, Washington, DC, n.d., PFIAB, Box H-282, Folder 4, NSC Institutional Files, NARA 2.

154. "Gordon Coppard Luce," Marquis Who's Who on the Web, 2006, at http://www.marquiswhoswho.com; and http://bios.marquiswhoswho.com/ gordon_coppard_luce/retired_savings_bank_executive/5197318.

155. "President Obama Announces Members of President's Intelligence Advisory Board."

156. Ibid.

157. "Thomas Hinman Moorer," Marquis Who's Who on the Web, 2006, at http://www.marquiswhoswho.com.

158. "John Lewis Morrison," Marquis Who's Who on the Web, 2006, at http:// www.marquiswhoswho.com.

159. "John L. Morrison (Jack)," Goldner Hawn, 2006, at http://www.ghjm.com/ jmorrison.html.

160. *Who's Who in America,* vol. 11, *1993–1996* (Wilmette, IL: Marquis Who's Who, 1996), s.v. Murphy, Franklin David.

161. "Franklin Murphy, 1960–1968," UCLA Past Leaders, 2007, at http://www .pastleaders.ucla.edu/murphy.html.

162. *Who Was Who in America,* vol. 11, *1993–1996* (Wilmette, IL: Marquis Who's Who, 1996), s.v. Murphy, Franklin David.

163. Martin Weil, "Robert D. Murphy, Diplomat, Advisor to Presidents, Dies," *Washington Post,* January 11, 1978, Metro, C9.

164. Ibid.

165. *Who Was Who in America,* vol. 7, *1977–1981* (Wilmette, IL: Marquis Who's Who, 1981), s.v. Murphy, Robert Daniel.

166. "Peter O'Donnell, Jr., Chairman, O'Donnell Foundation," National Math and Science Initiative, 2007, at http://nationalmathandscience.org/about-us/ former-board-member/peter-odonnell-jr.

167. "Four Receive Honorary Degrees at SMU Commencement," Southern Methodist University, May 19, 2008, at http://www.smu.edu/newsinfo/stories/ commencement2008-honoraries.asp.

168. "VII. The Bush Profiteers: 100 Donors Who Enjoy Hands-Off, Handout Government: 5. Peter O'Donnell, Jr. (Dallas): $141,000," Texans for Public Justice—The Governor's Gusher: The Sources of George W. Bush's $41 Million Texas War Chest, 2000, at http://info.tpj.org/reports/gusher/profiteers.html.

169. Donald P. Baker, "Texans to Help Coleman Fund," *Washington Post,* September 3, 1981, B7; and Jay D. Hartz, "The Impact of the Draft Goldwater Committee on the Republican Party," Ashbrook Center for Public Affairs at Ashland University (from Continuity: A Journal of History), 2000, at http://www.ashbrook .org/articles/hartz-draftgoldwater.html.

170. Keith D. McFarland, "Biography of Frank Pace Jr.," reprinted with permission from Stanley Sandler, ed., *The Korean War: An Encyclopedia* (New York:

Garland Publishing, 1995), at http://www.state.nj.us/military/korea/biographies/pace.html.

171. "Pace Named to Aid Kennedy on Intelligence," *Los Angeles Times,* July 18, 1961, 4.

172. William Gardner Bell, "Secretaries of War & Secretaries of the Army: Portraits and Biographical Sketches—Frank Pace Jr.," Army Center for Military History, May 22, 2001, at http://www.army.mil/cmh-pg/books/Sw-SA/Pace.htm.

173. "Marie-Elisabeth Lucienne Pate-Cornell," Marquis Who's Who on the Web, 2006, at http://www.marquiswhoswho.com.

174. "Elisabeth Pate-Cornell: Burt and Deedee McMurty Professor and Chair, Biography," Stanford University: Department of Management Science and Engineering, at http://www.stanford.edu/dept/MSandE/people/faculty/mep/index.html.

175. "Henry Ross Perot," Marquis Who's Who on the Web, 2006, at http://www.marquiswhoswho.com.

176. "H. Ross Perot," Famous Texans, at http://www.famoustexans.com/rossperot.htm.

177. "Perry, William J.," The Hoover Institution online, http://www.hoover.org/fellows/9689.

178. "William James Perry," Marquis Who's Who on the Web, at http://search.marquiswhoswho.com.

179. Ibid.

180. "William J. Perry," George H. W. Bush Presidential Library Textual Records, Box 199, FG006-14, 171662-348577.

181. "Harold William Pote," Marquis Who's Who on the Web, 2006, at http://www.marquiswhoswho.com.

182. "In Memoriam: Harold ("Hal") W. Pote," American Financial Realty Trust, at http://www.encyclopedia.com/doc/1G1-165752195.html.

183. "Lois D. Rice," Marquis Who's Who on the Web, 2006, at http://www.marquiswhoswho.com.

184. "Lois Dickson Rice," Brookings Institute: Experts, 2007, at http://www.brookings.edu/experts/r/ricel.aspx.

185. "Mr. Charles S. Robb," Mitre Corporation: About Us: Board of Trustees, November 3, 2006, at http://www.mitre.org/about/bot/robb.html.

186. "Chuck Robb (Charles Spittal)," Marquis Who's Who on the Web, 2006, at http://www.marquiswhoswho.com.

187. "Mr. Charles S. Robb," Mitre Corporation: About Us: Board of Trustees, November 3, 2006, at http://www.mitre.org/about/bot/robb.html.

188. "Rockefeller, Nelson Aldrich (1908–1979)," Biographic Directory of the United States Congress, 1774–Present, at http://bioguide.congress.gov/scripts/biodisplay.pl?index=R000363.

189. Mark O. Hatfield, with the Senate Historical Office, "Nelson A. Rockefeller (1974–1977)," reprinted with permission from *Vice Presidents of the United States, 1789–1993* (Washington: U.S. Government Printing Office, 1997), 505–12, United States Senate Online, at http://www.senate.gov/artandhistory/history/resources/pdf/nelson_rockefeller.pdf.

190. *Who Was Who in America,* vol. 7, *1977–1981* (Wilmette, IL: Marquis Who's Who, 1981), s.v. Rockefeller, Nelson Aldrich.

191. "Joe M. Rodgers," Marquis Who's Who on the Web, 2006, at http://www.marquiswhoswho.com.

192. James F. Clarity and Warren Weaver Jr., "Briefing; Mr. Ambassador," *New York Times,* September 14, 1985, 8.

193. "Eugene Victor Rostow," Marquis Who's Who on the Web, 2006, at http://www.marquiswhoswho.com.

194. Harold Hongju Koh, "In Memoriam: Dean Eugene V. Rostow," *Yale Law Review,* Summer 2003, 16–17, at http://www.law.yale.edu/ylr/pdfs/v50-2/Rostow.pdf.

195. "Rudman, Warren Bruce (1930–)," Biographical Directory of the United States Congress: 1774—Present, at http://bioguide.congress.gov/scripts/biodisplay.pl?index=R000497.

196. "Warren Bruce Rudman," Marquis Who's Who on the Web, 2006, at http://www.marquiswhoswho.com.

197. "Rudman, Warren Bruce (1930–)," Biographical Directory of the United States Congress: 1774–Present, at http://bioguide.congress.gov/scripts/biodisplay.pl?index=R000497.

198. Warren Rudman, "Perspectives on National Security in the Twenty-First Century," Seminar on Intelligence, Command, and Control, April 22, 2002, at http://pirp.harvard.edu/pubs_pdf/rudman/rudman-i02-1.pdf.

199. Dulles to Adams (Attached Biographical Sketch of Ryerson), November 30, 1955, Board of Consultants (1), Subject, Alphabetical, Records, 1952–61, DDEL; and *Who's Who in America,* vol. 5, *1969–1973* (Chicago: Marquis Who's Who, 1973), s.v. Ryerson, Edward Larned.

200. "Harrison Hagan Schmitt," Marquis Who's Who on the Web, 2006, at http://www.marquiswhoswho.com.

201. "Biographical Data: Harrison H. Schmitt," Lyndon B. Johnson Space Center, National Aeronautics and Space Administration, at http://www.jsc.nasa.gov/Bios/htmlbios/schmitt-hh.html.

202. "Bernard Adolph Schriever," Marquis Who's Who on the Web, 2006, at http://www.marquiswhoswho.com.

203. Louie Estrada, "Bernard Schriever Dies: General Led Missile Development," *Washington Post,* June 23, 2005, B07.

204. "Lieutenant General Brent Scowcroft," Air Force Link–Official Website of the United States Air Force, at http://www.af.mil/information/bios/bio.asp?bioID=7095.

205. "Brent Scowcroft," Marquis Who's Who on the Web, 2006, at http://www.marquiswhoswho.com.

206. Alfonso A. Narvaez, "Paul Seabury, 67, U.S. Authority on Foreign Policy and Educator," *New York Times,* October 19, 1990, A28.

207. Stephen Schwartz, "Berkeley Professor Paul Seabury, 67," *San Francisco Chronicle,* October 18, 1990, B7.

208. *Who's Who in America,* vol. 15, *2002–2004* (Wilmette, IL: Marquis Who's Who, 2004), s.v. Shultz, George Pratt.

209. "George P. Shultz," Hoover Institution, 2007, at http://www.hoover.org/bios/shultz.html.

210. "Stanley S. Shuman," Welcome to the White House: Current PFIAB Members, at http://clinton4.nara.gov/WH/EOP/pfiab/boardmembers.html#shuman.

211. "Stanley S. Shuman," Marquis Who's Who on the Web, 2006, at http://www.marquiswhoswho.com.

212. Gertz, "DNC Donors Put on Spy Panel."

213. Transcript of Naval Service (biography attached), Adm. John Harold Sides, U.S. Navy, June 21, 1963, Sides, Admiral J. H., USN (Ret.), OFJM, LBJL.

214. Ibid.

215. Barbara Campbell, "Adm. John Sides Dies; Led Fleet in Pacific," *New York Times,* April 6, 1978, B10.

216. "Robert Six," Wikipedia, at http://en.wikipedia.org/wiki/Robert_Six.

217. "William French Smith," Marquis Who's Who on the Web, 2006, at http://www.marquiswhoswho.com.

218. "William French Smith (1981–1985): Attorney General," American President: An Online Resource, Ronald Wilson Reagan (1911–2004), hosted by the Miller Center of Public Affairs at the University of Virginia, 2007, at http://www.millercenter.virginia.edu/academic/americanpresident/reagan/essays/cabinet/666.

219. John T. Woolley and Gerhard Peters, "Ronald Reagan: Appointment of William French Smith as a Member of the President's Foreign Intelligence Advisory Board," American Presidency Project, February 28, 1985, at http://www.presidency.ucsb.edu/ws/print.php?pid=38264.

220. Pranay Gupte, "Maurice Sonnenberg: A Concerned Optimist," *New York Sun,* March 23, 2005.

221. "Streicker Gift to Build New Washington Road Bridge: John H. Streicker '64 Helps Create a New Campus Connection," Giving to Princeton: News & Events, 2008, at http://giving.princeton.edu/news/archive/streickerbridge.xml; and Ava McAlpin, "Campus Planning: Alum Donates Campus Bridge," DailyPrincetonian.com, December 11, 2006, at http://www.dailyprincetonian.com/archives/2006/12/11/news/16943.shtml.

222. Immediate Release, OWHPS, June 26, 1961, 2, Taylor, Maxwell D. (Gen.) Mo., OFJM, LBJL.

223. Ibid., 3–4.

224. Ibid.

225. Rosemary McBride to George Christian, Biography of Gen. Maxwell Davenport Taylor, USA (Ret.), February 23, 1968, FG-732/A, EX FG 731, June 10, 1964, LBJL.

226. "Father of the H-Bomb Dies," BBC News Online, September 10, 2003, at http://news.bbc.co.uk/2/hi/americas/3095692.stm.

227. "Tower, John Goodwin (1925–1991)," Biographic Directory of the United States Congress, 1774–Present, at http://bioguide.congress.gov/scripts/biodisplay.pl?index=T000322.

228. "John Goodwin Tower," Marquis Who's Who on the Web, 2006, at http://www.marquiswhoswho.com.

229. "Caspar Willard Weinberger," Marquis Who's Who on the Web, 2006, at http://www.marquiswhoswho.com.

230. David Stout and Maria Newman, "Caspar W. Weinberger, Who Served 3 Republican Presidents, Is Dead at 88," *New York Times,* March 29, 2006, A21.

231. "Seymour Weiss," Marquis Who's Who on the Web, 2006, at http://www.marquiswhoswho.com.

232. *Team B, Intelligence Community Experiment in Competitive Analysis: Soviet Strategic Objectives: An Alternative View: Report of Team "B"* (Washington, DC: U.S. Government Printing Office, 1976).

233. White House, "President Obama Announces More Key Administration Posts," April 27, 2011 at http://www.whitehouse.gov/the-press-office/2011/04/27/president-obama-announces-more-key-administration-posts.

234. "Albert Dewell Wheelon," Marquis Who's Who on the Web, 2006, at http://www.marquiswhoswho.com.

235. "Corona: The First Reconnaissance Satellites, Dr. Albert Wheelon," Kavli Institute for Theoretical Physics at the University of California, Santa Barbara, October 15, 2003, at http://online.kitp.ucsb.edu/online/colloq/wheelon1.

236. "Edward Bennett Williams: 1920–1988," Georgetown Law Library, at http://www.ll.georgetown.edu/about/bio_ebwilliams.cfm.

237. "James Quinn Wilson," Marquis Who's Who on the Web, 2006, at http://www.marquiswhoswho.com.

238. "Pete Wilson," Marquis Who's Who on the Web, 2006, at http://www.marquiswhoswho.com.

239. "Pete Wilson, Distinguished Visiting Fellow," The Hoover Institution, 2007, at http://www.hoover.org/bios/2811421.html.

240. "Pete Wilson," Bingham McCutchen LLP, 2007, at http://www.bingham.com/Lawyer.aspx?LawyerID=485.

241. "Albert James Wohlstetter," Marquis Who's Who on the Web, 2006, at http://www.marquiswhoswho.com.

242. "Philip David Zelikow," Marquis Who's Who on the Web, 2006, at http://www.marquiswhoswho.com.

243. "Philip D. Zelikow," Harvard University: Belfer Center for Science and International Affairs–Experts, at http://belfercenter.ksg.harvard.edu/experts/948/philip_d_zelikow.html.

244. "Admiral Elmo Russell Zumwalt, Jr., USN," Department of the Navy–Naval Historical Center, July 3, 2006, at http://www.history.navy.mil/faqs/faq93-1.htm.

245. Interview with Byers. See also "National Security File, Name File," n.d., at http://www.brookings.edu/projects/archive/nsc/~/media/Files/Projects/nsc/staff/sources/Johnson_Library_Data.pdf.

246. Memorandum for the File, Cuba (Review on 1/10/63 of Records 0f the Special NSC 5412/2 Group), Washington, DC, January 11, 1963, PFIAB Agenda for Meeting of January 25–26, 1963, PFIAB, ARRB, Record 206-10001-10011, NARA.

247. Special Investigative Panel, PFIAB, "Science at its Best, Security at its Worst: A Report on Security Problems at the U.S. Department of Energy," June 1999.

248. Richard Wolffe and Holly Bailey, "Oval: Look Who's Joined Bush's Intel Panel; Bush May Be Besieged by Charges of Cronyism, but They Don't Seem to Have Affected His Picks for a Panel Assessing Intelligence Matters; Plus, Alito, the Talkie," Newsweek: Web Exclusive Commentary, November 2, 2005, at http://www.msnbc.msn.com/id/9900921/site/newsweek/print/1/displaymode/1098/.

249. Veritas Intelligence, "Gerard P. Burke, Chairman, Board of Advisors," 2008, at http://www.veritasintelligence.com/burke.html; and "ACE Aerospace Names Gerard P. Burke, Jr. Vice President of Satellite Unit," Philadelphia, May 8, 2000, at http://www.thefreelibrary.com/ACE+Limited+Reports+Second+Quarter+Earnings.-a063778254.

250. Interview with Source R; "Our Contributors," Aerospace Power Journal (Fall 2001): 127, at http://www.airpower.au.af.mil/airchronicles/apj/apj01/fal01/bios.pdf; and "Dr. Robert L. Butterworth," n.d., at http://www.ndu.edu/inss/symposia/jointops99/butterworth.html.

251. Wheaton Bradish Byers, Resume, Bethesda, MD, February 1976, Byers, Wheaton, LCP, GRFPL.

252. Brig. Gen. John F. Cassidy, PBCFIA Staff Director, to E. Frederic Morrow, Washington, DC, May 15, 1956, Board of Consultants [on Foreign Intelligence Activities] (3), Subject Series, Alphabetical Subseries, WHO, Office of the Staff Secretary: Records, 1952–61, DDEL.

253. PBCFIA (Contact List), Room 297, Executive Office Building, July 28, 1959, PBCFIA, OF 309, Official File Book 2 of 2, Eisenhower, Dwight D.: Records as President, WHCF, 1953–61, DDEL; A. J. Goodpaster to Bob Hampton, Washington, DC, November 30, 1959, PBCFIA, OF 309, Official File Book 2 of 2, Eisenhower, Dwight D.: Records as President, WHCF, 1953–61, DDEL.

254. Memorandum for the file, Washington, DC, February 4, 1964, Minutes of Meeting of January 30, 1964, PFIAB, ARRB, Record 206-10001-10002, NARA; Handwritten Memorandum (with attachment on J. Patrick Coyne), James R. Killian, Washington, DC, (ca.) December 26–28, 1962, Papers of James Killian, MC 423, Box 36, Folder 2/8, IASC.

255. "Randy W. Deitering," Marquis Who's Who on the Web, 2006, at http://www.marquiswhoswho.com.

256. Immediate Release, "President Clinton Names Randy W. Deitering as the Executive Director of the President's Foreign Intelligence Advisory Board," Office of the White House Press Secretary, December 2, 1998.

257. "The World Comes to the Classroom in the Department of Government and International Studies," GINT Exchange, June 2003.

258. "Fred R. Demech, Jr.: Director of Operations, Superiority," Northrop Grumman Missions Systems—Biography, received via facsimile on May 12, 2006.

259. Department of Political Science, From the Tower (Fall 2006): 6, at http://www.uark.edu/depts/plscinfo/News/Files/Newsletter2006.pdf.

260. "Joan Avalyn Dempsey," United States Geospatial Intelligence Foundation: About: Board, at http://usgif.org/about/board/23-joan-avalyn-dempsey.

261. Immediate Release, Office of the White House Press Secretary, October 2, 1997; Federation of American Scientists Intelligence Resource Program, October 3, 1997, at http://fas.org/irp/news/1997/97100303_tpo.html.

262. "Joan Avalyn Dempsey," United States Geospatial Intelligence Foundation: About: Board, at http://usgif.org/about/board/23-joan-avalyn-dempsey.

263. U.S. Department of State, "Biography—Randall M. Fort," January 21, 2009, http://www.state.gov/outofdate/bios/72993.htm.

264. PFIAB, "Science at Its Best, Security at Its Worst."

265. "Margie M. Kinney, Former 'Weather Lady' for WMAR," Baltimoresun.com, January 23, 2011, at http://articles.baltimoresun.com/2011-01-23/iphone/md-ob-iphone-margie-kinney-20110123_1_small-radio-stations-weather-wmar.

266. Harold L. Lawrence, PBCFIA Deputy Staff Director, to Bernard M. Shanley, Secretary to the President, Washington, DC, December 18, 1956, PBCFIA, OF 309, Official File Book 2 of 2, Eisenhower, Dwight D.: Records as President, WHCF, 1953–61, DDEL.

267. PFIAB, "Science at Its Best, Security at Its Worst."

268. "Brendan Melley: Associate Vice President," The Cohen Group, 2006, at http://www.cohengroup.net/news/archives/news020905.cfm.

269. PFIAB, "Science at Its Best, Security at Its Worst."

270. Mark F. Moynihan, "The Scientific Community and Intelligence Collection: Academic Scientists Continue to Play a Vital Role in Helping the Intelligence

Community Exploit Technology for National Security," Physics Today Online, 2001, at http://scitation.aip.org/getabs/servlet/GetabsServlet?prog=normal&id=P HTOAD000053000012000051000001&idtype=cvips&gifs=yes&bypassSSO=1.

271. PBCFIA (Contact List) July 28, 1959, President's Board of Consultants, OF 309, Book 2 of 2, WHCF, 1953–61, DDEL.

272. Cherne, PFIAB Chair, to the Assistant to the President for National Security Affairs and the DCI, Washington, DC, March 1, 1977, PFIAB 1-12/77 [CF, O/A 714], Staff Offices, Counsel, Lipshutz, Carter Presidential Papers, WHCF, JCL.

273. Interview with Byers; and Ronald Reagan, "Nomination of Lionel H. Olmer to Be an Under Secretary of Commerce," February 12, 1981, at http://www .presidency.ucsb.edu/ws/index.php?pid=43398; and Ronald Reagan, "Nomination of Lionel H. Olmer to be an Under Secretary of Commerce for International Trade," February 12, 1981, at http://www.presidency.ucsb.edu/ws/index.php?pid=43398.

274. Steven Keeva, "Lawyers in the War Room," *American Bar Association Journal,* December 1991, 52–59; and "Homer Pointer, III," at http://lawyers.justia.com/ lawyer/homer-pointer-iii-268499.

275. PFIAB, "Science at Its Best, Security at Its Worst."

276. "Gary J. Schmitt," American Enterprise Institute for Public Policy Research: Scholars & Fellows, 2005, at http://www.aei.org/scholar/gary-j-schmitt/.

277. American Enterprise Institute for Public Policy Research, "Gary Schmitt," at http://www.aei.org/scholar/103.

278. Nina Stewart to President George H. W. Bush, September 16, 1991, George H. W. Bush Presidential Library Textual Records, Box 199, FG006-14, 171662-348577; President George H. W. Bush to Nina Stewart, November 13, 1991, George H. W. Bush Presidential Library Textual Records, Box 199, FG006-14, 171662-348577.

279. "Lieutenant General C. Norman Wood," Air Force Link Biographies, May 1990, at http://www.af.mil/information/bios/bio.asp?bioID=7644.

280. "Appendix C—Checklist of White House Press Releases," The George H. W. Bush Presidential Library and Museum, 2007, at http://bushlibrary.tamu.edu/ research/public_papers.php?id=5148&year=&month=.

281. "Appendix D: List of Interviewees," GPO Access: Commission on the Roles and Capabilities of the United States Intelligence Community, August 28, 2000, at http://www.gpoaccess.gov/int/int025.pdf.

282. "On the Secrecy of NSA Records on UFOs (Redacted), In-Camera Affidavit of Eugene F. Yeates, *Citizens against UFO Secrecy v. NSA,* October 9, 1980," Federation of American Scientists: National Security Agency, 2007, at http://www .fas.org/irp/nsa/yeates-ufo.pdf.

Index

www.ingramcontent.com/pod-product-compliance
Lightning Source LLC
Chambersburg PA
CBHW020340100426
42812CB00029B/3194/J